THE CAMBRIDGE
ANCIENT HISTORY

VOLUME SIX

THE
CAMBRIDGE
ANCIENT HISTORY

EDITED BY

J. B. BURY, M.A., F.B.A.
S. A. COOK, Litt.D.
F. E. ADCOCK, M.A.

VOLUME VI

MACEDON

401—301 B.C.

CAMBRIDGE UNIVERSITY PRESS

Published by the Syndics of the Cambridge University Press
Bentley House, 200 Euston Road, London NW1 2DB
American Branch: 32 East 57th Street, New York, N.Y.10022

ISBN: 0 521 04488 X

First edition 1927
Reprinted with corrections 1933 1953
Reprinted 1964 1969 1975

Printed in Great Britain
at the University Printing House, Cambridge
(Euan Phillips, University Printer)

PREFACE

VOLUME Five was named Athens, for it described the period in which the Greek states moved in the orbit of that city. The Persian Empire, weakened and inert, receded into the background and, for sixty years, could exert no real influence on the course of history. But, as the power of Athens waned, the subtlety of the satrap Tissaphernes and the energy of the young Prince Cyrus found scope, and with the fall of the Athenian Empire Persia re-enters the scene as a chief actor. The first chapter of the volume gives a sketch of what little is known of Persian history after Plataea and Mycale, followed by an account of the enterprise of Cyrus, the famous march of the Ten Thousand and the vicissitudes of the Persian monarchy which, for the two succeeding generations, had an intermittent but not unimportant effect on Greek affairs. By an irony of history the very policy which helped to keep the Greek states divided and weak prepared the way for the rise of Macedon, the power destined to overthrow the once-vigorous empire which had absorbed the ancient kingdoms of the East. It is for this reason that the present volume, entitled Macedon, begins with a chapter dedicated to Persia.

In Greece itself there remained the older Great Powers, Sparta, Athens, Thebes, but none of these three had the will and the power to assert a lasting hegemony in Greece or to promote a unity which would have forestalled the achievement of Macedon. We trace, first, the ascendancy of Sparta which did not go unchallenged in Greece, and maintained a precarious existence while Sparta became an ally instead of an opponent of Persia. We then see Athens conjure up a League which appeared to some to be the ghost of her Empire, a League which had an insufficient *raison d'être* in the reaction against Spartan repression. A more substantial, though equally shortlived, product of the same reaction was the rise of Thebes to freedom and then to hegemony. A single battle broke the military prestige of Sparta and with it her political domination. Thebes assisted in the Peloponnese a movement towards federation, but was not strong enough or enterprising enough to carry the movement farther, and the death of Epaminondas, her greatest statesman, at Mantinea left the field

open for the advance of the rival of voluntary federation, the
military monarchy.

Such a monarchy had been foreshadowed in the rule of
Dionysius the tyrant of Syracuse, but his power did not long
survive him, and, while it lasted, it was used to support the policy
of Sparta. The death of Dionysius and the death of Epaminondas
end the first period covered by this volume. We have now seen
the failure of Greece to achieve unity for itself or to cast off political ideals which had outlived their practical usefulness.

At this point we turn to Egypt and to Palestine, the two regions
of the East which had a significance apart from Persia. On the
one hand, we witness the end of the oldest national culture in the
world as Egypt waits for a conqueror to bring to her a new
civilization, that of Greece. On the other, amid the political
obscurity of the Jews, events of far-reaching importance can
be traced, culminating in the establishment of the Judaism in
which Christianity was to find its birth. In this century, the
century of Alexander the Great, the ancient world is turning
from the old order towards the new.

We now enter upon the central epoch of the volume, the rise
of Macedon, an event due primarily to the genius of Philip but
prepared for and made possible by the bankruptcy of Greek
statecraft exhibited in the preceding chapters. In little more than
twenty years Macedon became strong enough to impose unity
upon the Greeks and to lead the West to the conquest of the
East. The city-state with its insistence on particularism surrendered the lead to the military monarchy. The orators of Athens
had used their powers either, as Isocrates, in advocating union
or, as Demosthenes, in striving to inspire with new life the ideal
of the city-state. A Macedonian now carried out the aspirations
of the one and defeated the efforts of the other. In Sicily, as by
contrast, we see the Corinthian Timoleon achieve, by force of
sincerity and resolution, a brief local triumph of the ideals
of the free city-state. But here, too, time only waited for an
Agathocles.

During the period under review Athens had not the power to
create such masterpieces of the imagination as the plays of
Aeschylus, Sophocles, and Euripides. Her literary gifts now
served either politics or philosophy, and it is in the speculative
philosophy of the Athenian schools that the Greece of the Fourth
Century made her greatest contribution to the thought of the
world. We halt here to survey this intellectual activity, and then

reach the third and final epoch, the career of Alexander and the immediate destiny of the heritage of power which he left behind him.

It fell to Alexander to reverse completely the dream of Darius the Great and Xerxes, which was to bring the free cities of Greece under the Persian yoke. The immediate consequences of Alexander's career of conquest may be said to be the union of East and West, but what he accomplished was a much greater thing than this: he imposed Hellenic civilization on the world. Alexander transcended the political ideas of the Greeks, that is to say he reached convictions which lay beyond the vision of contemporary Greeks. But he never entirely grew out of the political ideas, either practical or speculative, in which he had been brought up. At this point, therefore, there follows a review of the political ideas of fourth-century Hellas. The volume closes with a survey of the achievements of Greek art and architecture—sculpture moving towards a new realism, architecture 'stiffening into academic rigour.'

Volume VII, which will, it is hoped, appear in 1928, will open with a sketch of the ideas of the new age and with the political setting of the Mediterranean world into which the Roman Republic was to enter, a late comer. The story of its rise, which demands a continuous treatment, has therefore been reserved to that volume, in which will be described the growth of Rome, until, with the defeat of Hannibal, she takes her place as the most powerful state in the ancient world. Until this moment comes, the political instincts of Roman statecraft had not assumed significance outside the city and the circle of her immediate neighbours.

In the present volume the story of Persia (Chapter I) and the great events of the age of Alexander (Chapters XII–XV) are from the pen of Mr W. W. Tarn. Chapters II–IV, the Ascendancy of Sparta, the New Athenian League and Thebes are by Dr M. Cary. In Chapter V Professor Bury writes on Dionysius I and Dr H. R. Hall in Chapter VI resumes and completes the history of Ancient Egypt. Similarly in the following chapter Dr S. A. Cook carries on the history of the political and religious development of Palestine and of her immediate neighbours. The career of Philip is narrated in two chapters (VIII and IX) by Mr A. W. Pickard-Cambridge. In Chapter X Mr Hackforth continues the history of Sicily from the death of the tyrant Dionysius to the death of the liberator Timoleon. In Chapter XI Mr Cornford

writes of the Athenian Philosophical Schools, and in Chapter XVI
Dr E. Barker discusses Greek Political Thought and Theory in
the Fourth Century. These two Chapters complement each other,
for it was not easy for the Greeks to separate political from metaphysical speculation. In Chapter XVII Professor Beazley resumes
the survey of Greek Art and Mr D. S. Robertson that of Greek
Architecture.

A second volume of plates, illustrating this and the preceding
volume, is being prepared by Mr Seltman, to whom the editors
are indebted for his assistance and advice particularly on points of
numismatics.

The bibliographies in this volume, as in the preceding, are of
necessity selective and, as a general rule, works are not mentioned
which have been absorbed into the common stock of opinion on
the various topics. But it appeared to the editors that an especial
need would be met by the full and systematized bibliographies on
Alexander and his successors which have been prepared by Mr
Tarn.

The editors have to thank the contributors for their co-operation,
which goes beyond the writing of their several chapters. Dr Hall
desires to thank Mr H. M. Last, who read his chapter in manu-
script. Mr Tarn would acknowledge his obligation to Dr G. F. Hill
and Mr Sidney Smith for valuable help. Mr Robertson has again
to thank Mr Gow for his assistance. Professor Bury wishes to
thank Messrs Macmillan for the permission to quote at length
a passage from his *History of Greece*. Dr Cook desires to express
his thanks to the Rev. W. A. L. Elmslie and the Rev. F. S. Marsh
for criticisms and suggestions.

Acknowledgements are due to Messrs Philip and Son for
Maps 1 and 2, to Messrs Baedeker for Map 4, to Messrs Macmillan for Maps 5, 6, and 7, to Mr Tarn for his preparation of
Maps 1 and 8, and to Dr Cary for Map 3. The sheet containing
plans of temples which will be found at the end of Chapter XVII
has been arranged by Mr Robertson, and acknowledgements are
due to the Librairie Orientaliste Paul Geuthner, Paris, and
Monsieur C. Dugas for No. 1, to Messrs Walter de Gruyter and
Co., Berlin and Leipzig, for No. 2, to the Preussische Akademie
der Wissenschaften and Dr T. Wiegand for No. 3, and to the
Council of the Society for the Promotion of Hellenic Studies for
No. 4.

Mr G. V. Carey, late Fellow of Clare College, has made the
General Index and Index of Passages, and the editors would

acknowledge his valuable help in the difficult task of preserving the uniformity which is appropriate to a work of this kind.

This, as former volumes, owes much to the care and skill of the Staff of the University Press, to whom the editors would express their gratitude.

The design on the cover is the head of Alexander from a coin of Lysimachus in the possession of Mr Seltman.

J. B. B.
S. A. C.
F. E. A.

March 1927

TABLE OF CONTENTS

CHAPTER I

PERSIA, FROM XERXES TO ALEXANDER

By W. W. TARN, M.A.

Sometime scholar of Trinity College, Cambridge

CHAPTER II

THE ASCENDANCY OF SPARTA

By M. CARY, D.Litt.

Reader in Ancient History in the University of London

CHAPTER III

THE SECOND ATHENIAN LEAGUE

By M. Cary

CHAPTER IV

THEBES

By M. Cary

CONTENTS

CHAPTER V

DIONYSIUS OF SYRACUSE

BY J. B. BURY, M.A., F.B.A.

Fellow of King's College and Regius Professor of Modern History
in the University of Cambridge

CONTENTS

CHAPTER VI

EGYPT TO THE COMING OF ALEXANDER

By H. R. Hall, D.Litt., F.B.A., F.S.A.
Keeper of Egyptian and Assyrian Antiquities, British Museum

CHAPTER VII

THE INAUGURATION OF JUDAISM

By Stanley A. Cook, Litt.D.
Fellow of Gonville and Caius College, Cambridge,
University Lecturer in Oriental Languages

CONTENTS

CONTENTS

CHAPTER IX

MACEDONIAN SUPREMACY IN GREECE

By A. W. Pickard-Cambridge

CHAPTER X

SICILY, 367 TO 330 B.C.

By R. Hackforth, M.A.
Fellow of Sidney Sussex College, Cambridge,
and University Lecturer in Classics

CONTENTS

CHAPTER XI

THE ATHENIAN PHILOSOPHICAL SCHOOLS

BY F. M. CORNFORD, M.A.

Fellow of Trinity College, Cambridge, and University Lecturer in Classics

CHAPTER XII

ALEXANDER: THE CONQUEST OF PERSIA

By W. W. Tarn

CHAPTER XIII

ALEXANDER: THE CONQUEST OF THE FAR EAST

By W. W. Tarn

CHAPTER XIV

GREECE: 335 TO 321 B.C.

BY W. W. TARN

CHAPTER XV

THE HERITAGE OF ALEXANDER

By W. W. Tarn

CHAPTER XVI

GREEK POLITICAL THOUGHT AND THEORY
IN THE FOURTH CENTURY

By Ernest Barker, M.A., D.Litt., LL.D.

Principal of King's College, London; late Fellow
of New College, Oxford

CHAPTER XVII

GREEK ART AND ARCHITECTURE

By J. D. Beazley, M.A., Lincoln and Merton Professor of Classical Archaeology and
Art in the University of Oxford and D. S. Robertson, M.A., Fellow of Trinity
College, Cambridge, and University Lecturer in Classics[1]

[1] Sections i–ii (Art) are by Professor Beazley, Sections iii–vi (Architecture) are by
Mr Robertson.

BIBLIOGRAPHIES

CONTENTS

LIST OF MAPS, TABLES, PLANS, ETC.

CONTENTS

LIST OF MAPS, TABLES, PLANS, ETC.

CHAPTER I

PERSIA, FROM XERXES TO ALEXANDER

I. XERXES AND HIS SUCCESSORS

SALAMIS and Plataea settled that Persia should not expand into Europe (vol. IV, chs. IX and X). Her European conquests could no longer be held; in 479 she lost Sestos and the Hellespont, in 478 Byzantium and the Bosporus; with the fall of Eïon soon afterwards Thrace and Macedonia recovered their independence. Doriscus and some forts in the Gallipoli peninsula remained, but were lost after the Eurymedon. During the rest of the century Persia's foreign policy turns on two questions: are the Greek cities of the Aegean seaboard to be in her sphere or in that of Athens, and can she continue to hold Egypt? These two questions are treated elsewhere (vol. V, chs. II and III), and this chapter deals only with Persia's internal history.

Xerxes' return to Sardes after Salamis was not a flight, but was due to a fresh revolt of Babylon, where one Shamash-erba had assumed the crown, with the full royal title of 'King of Babylon and King of the Lands'; from Sardes Xerxes could keep touch both with Babylon and Mardonius. Babylon's final revolt was easily suppressed, and Xerxes now deprived the city of her exceptional position in the empire and made Babylonia an ordinary satrapy. He ordered the destruction of Marduk's great temple, E-sagila, which Alexander found in ruins, and removed from it the statue of Marduk, thus rendering meaningless the accession ceremony of taking the hands of Bel; he razed Babylon's remaining fortifications, abolished various native customs, and bestowed upon Persians the estates of many prominent Babylonians. The name of

Note. For Cyrus and the Ten Thousand Xenophon's *Anabasis* furnishes a good contemporary narrative. Apart from this episode, the only continuous source for Persian history, after Herodotus ends, is Diodorus XI–XVII, though parts are also covered by the fragments of Ctesias, Plutarch's Life of Artaxerxes II, Nepos' Life of Datames, and Justin; the information is generally poor. The writings of Isocrates, the speeches of Demosthenes, and various other material given in the Bibliography, afford some help; but little comes from inscriptions, though the long record in Lycian from Xanthos (see p. 3, n. 1), could it be read, might be invaluable, as the proper names suggest. Diodorus' dating is often confused, and the chronology of the reigns depends primarily on Babylonian king-lists and dated contracts.

Babylon was dropped from the royal title, and henceforth Xerxes and his successors call themselves only 'King of the Lands'; and Aramaic gradually replaces Babylonian as the language of official intercourse west of Babylonia. About the same time Xerxes' brother Masistes, satrap of Bactria, also failed in an attempt to revolt; the empire was far too strong as yet for isolated local movements to succeed. Xerxes built himself a new palace at Persepolis, which was never completed; otherwise he seemingly spent the rest of his reign in idleness and sensuality at Susa, a period which supplies the background for the book of Esther (p. 168), until, some time before April 464, in the 21st year of his reign, he was murdered by a courtier, Artabanus. He may not have been a personal coward, but he had few merits; he was vainglorious and weak, licentious and cruel, and even his pride was not of the kind which illumines misfortune. His murder represented a definite movement against his house. Artabanus also murdered his eldest son Darius, with the alleged help of his third son Artaxerxes (Artakhshatra), to whom he represented that Darius had murdered Xerxes. Artabanus must have had much support, for he reigned seven months, was recognized in Egypt, and defeated Xerxes' second son Hystaspes. But Artaxerxes outwitted him; he bided his time, allowed Artabanus to remove those who stood between him and the throne, and then turned on the usurper and defeated and killed him.

Artaxerxes I, called Long-Hand—whether from a physical peculiarity or political capacity is uncertain,—dated his reign as from Xerxes' death. It opened with the revolt of Inarōs in Egypt (see p. 138). Though the revolt was ultimately suppressed, Artaxerxes nevertheless made concessions which left Inaros' son Thannyras and one Psammetichus in possession of subordinate princedoms, and after Amyrtaeus' death (p. 140) his son Pausiris was also permitted to retain his father's principality. These concessions may be evidence of political wisdom on Artaxerxes' part rather than of weakness, for the destruction of the Athenian expedition in aid of Inaros had been a notable victory; certainly when during his reign Herodotus visited Egypt he found it quiet and well-ordered. Artaxerxes also showed a tolerant wisdom in his dealings with the Jews (see below, p. 168). In the West however he suffered a definite setback, and at the so-called Peace of Callias in 449–8 Persia definitely abandoned the Aegean and the cities on its seaboard (see vol. v, p. 87 *sq.*, p. 470 *sq.*). In domestic affairs, he was not strong enough to resist his mother Amestris, Xerxes' widow (who had already exhibited her cruelty during Xerxes' life

in her mutilation of a supposed rival), and though Inaros had
submitted under definite covenants, Artaxerxes surrendered him
to Amestris' importunity and a horrible death; it was the beginning of the palace rule of women which for two generations was to
weaken Persia. The immediate result was the revolt of Artaxerxes'
friend Megabyxus, the conqueror of Egypt, who had guaranteed
to Inaros his life. The obscure story which has survived shows
Megabyxus as alternately in revolt and in favour, as exiled and
restored, his changes of fortune depending upon the intrigues of
Amestris and Artaxerxes' wife Amytis; the political reasons behind
the story are lost. Artaxerxes died in spring 424, after reigning
40 years. What can be descried of his character is an energy in
youth that afterwards died out, some political wisdom, and a vein
of weakness. But he seems to have been a better ruler than his
father or his son.

The usual struggle for the throne followed his death. His sole
legitimate son succeeded him as Xerxes II, but was promptly
murdered by his half-brother Sogdianus, who reigned some months
and was then defeated by another half-brother, Ochus, and
thrown into a slow furnace, a punishment which now becomes
usual. The Babylonian chronology did not recognize Xerxes II
and Sogdianus as kings, and seemingly added the duration of their
reigns to that of Artaxerxes. Ochus took the crown very early in
423 as Darius II; Greeks nicknamed him *Nothos*, 'the bastard.'
He did not lack courage, but was otherwise a worthless character,
dominated by his half-sister and wife Parysatis, a monster of
cruelty. Her government provoked a series of blind revolts.
First the King's brother Arsites rose and was overthrown and put
to death; in this war, if tradition be true, both sides for the first time
used Greek mercenaries. Then Pissuthnes of Lydia rose, and was
defeated by Hydarnes' son Tissaphernes[1], a man who was to play
a large part in Persian history; in 413 he received the Lydian
satrapy as a reward, but did not reduce Pissuthnes' son Amorges till
412 (vol. v, p. 314). A brief outbreak in Media in 410 was followed
by Terituchmes' conspiracy. Darius' eldest son Arsaces had
married Tissaphernes' sister Statira, and his daughter Amestris
Tissaphernes' brother Terituchmes; and Terituchmes formed a
wide-reaching plot to overthrow Darius. He was betrayed and
killed, and Parysatis in her vengeance almost exterminated
Hydarnes' house; Arsaces' prayers indeed saved Statira, but

---

[1] Kalinka, *Tituli Lyciae* no. 44, c. l. 11: cizzaprñna widrñnah; see Bugge
in Benndorf's *Festschrift*, p. 233. This relationship explains Tissaphernes'
history.

Parysatis poisoned her many years later. Tissaphernes she could not reach; but in 407, taking advantage of his failure to prevent the temporary revival of Athens' power, she persuaded Darius to appoint her favourite younger son Cyrus satrap of Lydia, Phrygia, and Cappadocia, with the supreme command in Asia Minor. Tissaphernes thus lost Lydia and was restricted to Caria and the Ionian cities, and Parysatis' actions naturally made him the irreconcilable enemy both of herself and Cyrus. The weakness of Darius' rule did not affect the efficiency of his satraps, as Pharnabazus, Tissaphernes, and Cyrus all showed in their dealings with Greece; but it undoubtedly encouraged Egypt to revolt (p. 143).

In 405 Darius contracted an illness which raised the question of the succession. Of his thirteen children by Parysatis many were dead; Arsaces, the eldest son, naturally expected the crown, but Parysatis hoped to secure it for Cyrus. The story, however, that Cyrus had a good claim according to the precedent set by Darius I in Xerxes' case, because he had been born after his father became king and Arsaces before, cannot be true; otherwise Cyrus could not have been over sixteen when in 407 he was sent to the coast as commander-in-chief, and this seems impossible. Darius in his illness sent for his two sons, and Cyrus came with Tissaphernes, who pretended to be his friend; but on Darius' death, some time before April 404, Arsaces secured the succession, and Tissaphernes at once denounced Cyrus to him as plotting his murder. Whether it was true cannot be said; Cyrus was imprisoned, but Parysatis saved his life and procured his return to his satrapy, where, enraged and humiliated, he prepared to enforce his pretensions in arms. Arsaces took the name of Artaxerxes II; he was nicknamed Mnemon (Abiātaka), from his excellent memory.

II. THE ENTERPRISE OF CYRUS

Cyrus is the one sympathetic figure among the later Achaemenids, though it is difficult to disentangle the real man from Xenophon's eulogies, not only in the *Anabasis* but also in the *Cyropaedia* (if it be true that Xenophon's portrait of the elder Cyrus partly represents what he believed the younger Cyrus would have become). Cyrus obviously possessed ambition and courage, great energy, and the power of attracting men's devotion; he was generous in giving, more generous in promising; and beyond any other Persian he seems to have understood Greeks and been understood by them. But his unprovoked murder of his cousins, and his barbarous mutilation of all offenders, attest his inherited

cruelty; and his defects of judgment were serious. He failed
throughout to understand that Tissaphernes was his real danger,
and his knowledge that Greek hoplites could defeat Persian
infantry blinded him to the fact that Persia's strength did not lie
in infantry; his expedition had failed before it started, for, with all
Cappadocia at his disposal, he set out to conquer the empire with
some 2600 horse.

His first aim was to collect a Greek force without alarming
Artaxerxes. All the Ionian cities except Miletus had revolted to
him from Tissaphernes, and the siege of Miletus gave him a
pretext for enrolling mercenaries; he subsidized a Spartan exile,
Clearchus, to raise troops and employ them in Thrace till required;
and his Greek friends Aristippus of Larissa, Sophaenetus of
Stymphalus, Socrates of Achaea, and Gorgias' pupil Proxenus of
Boeotia, also recruited men, who were engaged to attack either
Tissaphernes or Pisidia. There was hardly as yet a regular class of
mercenaries in Greece, and the men were largely adventurous
spirits who hoped to make money, and included some rough
characters. Xenophon, a young Athenian and pupil of Socrates,
came simply as Proxenus' friend, without military rank; he liked
war, and his admiration for Sparta perhaps made continued
residence in Athens uncomfortable. Sophaenetus wrote the first
story of the expedition, and Xenophon probably wrote his own
account, the *Anabasis*, largely because he thought Sophaenetus
had overlooked his merits; he published it under the assumed
name of Themistogenes. He must have kept a diary, but on the
retreat it was sometimes scantily posted up, and though he gives
each day's distance in parasangs (said to be Persian for 'mile-
stones'[1]), these are not accurate measurements; along the Royal
Road from Sardes to Thapsacus the distances were known, but
after Thapsacus his parasangs can only represent some rough
system of time-measurement[2]; even to Persians the parasang, like
the modern *farsang*, varied in different districts with the nature of
the ground. As, in addition, he wrote many years after the events
he records, some mistakes are inevitable; but the real weakness in
his vivid narrative is that there is only his own word for the part
he himself played.

Early in 401 B.C. Cyrus collected most of his army at Sardes, and
announced that he meant to chastise the Pisidians; but Tissaphernes guessed his real objective, and with 500 horse rode hard
to Susa to warn the King. About March Cyrus started; at Colossae

---

[1] A. Hoffmann-Kutschke, *Phil.* LXVI, 1907, p. 189.
[2] The credit for first detecting this is due to Layard.

Menon of Larissa, another pupil of Gorgias, joined him, bringing Aristippus' men, and Clearchus joined at Celaenae, completing his force, which included (besides Asiatics) 9600 Greek hoplites and 2300 Greek and Thracian peltasts and light-armed; they brought a long train of carts and many women, both free hetaerae and slave girls. Clearchus, who commanded, was a stern disciplinarian, not popular, but trusted in battle. As Cyrus approached Iconium, Syennesis IV of Cilicia, Persia's vassal, found himself in a dilemma; he wanted to be on the winning side, but did not know which side it would be; so he sent his wife Epyaxa to Cyrus with a large sum of money, which enabled him to pay the Greeks, and reinsured himself by sending his eldest son to Artaxerxes. From Iconium Cyrus went by Tyana in Cappadocia toward the Cilician Gates, the impregnable pass over the Taurus through which a camel could not go without unloading till Ibrahim blasted the modern road. He had saved Syennesis' face by sending Menon with Epyaxa into Cilicia by Laranda, which officially turned the Gates; Syennesis duly withdrew his men, and Cyrus passed through, but Menon lost 100 men plundering, and the Greeks in anger sacked Tarsus. They now suspected that their objective was Artaxerxes, and mutinied; but Clearchus handled them very well, and Cyrus promised extra pay and assured them that he was only marching against Abrocomas, satrap of Syria.

At Issus Cyrus was joined by his fleet, commanded by the Egyptian Tamōs, father of his friend Glōs, and also by a Spartan squadron; Sparta had not officially declared war on Artaxerxes, but she had encouraged Clearchus and was unofficially supporting Cyrus. The fleet brought him 700 hoplites under the Spartan Cheirisophus, while 400 Greeks deserted to him from Abrocomas. Cyrus had brought up the fleet in order to turn the 'pillar of Jonah,' the pass between Issus and Myriandrus, if Abrocomas held it, but Abrocomas, who was possibly playing a double game, was not there; the pass was open, as were the Syrian Gates beyond Myriandrus, and Cyrus reached the Euphrates at Thapsacus without incident. There he announced that he was marching against Artaxerxes, and overcame the hesitation of the Greeks by higher pay and still higher promises. Abrocomas had hurried to Thapsacus before him and after crossing had burnt all the boats, but the river was exceptionally low, and Cyrus' men waded across; it was taken as a sign of divine favour that the Euphrates had done obeisance to the future king, a curious parallel to the sea's obeisance to Alexander at Mount Climax (see p. 364). They now turned down the Euphrates and marched southward along the east bank; the country was chiefly desert, the later civilization along the river being largely a creation of the Seleucids, and the sportsman in Xenophon found much to interest him: the wild asses, which could only be taken by driving; the ostriches, which no one could get near; and the bustards, which could be ridden down, like wild turkeys on the Pampas. Early in September they reached Babylonia, and perceived that an army was retiring before them. They passed a great trench, with a narrow passage left between it and the Euphrates—whether it was a canal or (as Xenophon thought) a fortification seems very doubtful—and the next day came somewhat unexpectedly upon Artaxerxes' army near the village of Cunaxa, some 45 miles north of Babylon; possibly the mound Kunish south of Felluja.

III. THE BATTLE OF CUNAXA

Artaxerxes had deferred battle as long as possible, for he was expecting his brother from Susa and Abrocomas from Phoenicia; but both came too late (Abrocomas having presumably taken the regular Tigris route), and he had to stand to cover Babylon without them. He had only three satraps with him, Tissaphernes, Arbaces of Media, and Gobryas of Babylon, and probably something over 30,000 men; the infantry were poorly armed, but he had at least 6000 horse, perhaps more, most of them probably Persians and Medes. It was an army collected in a hurry, and far from representative of Persia's strength; and though it depended for victory entirely on its cavalry, the absence of the satraps of Eastern Iran, Armenia, and Syria (Cappadocia being controlled by Cyrus) shows that none of the cavalry which was to form the powerful wings at Gaugamela was present. The scythed chariots, as the battle shows, were few and inefficient; Xenophon's 200 is a stereotyped figure which recurs at Gaugamela, and an extant work which passed as Xenophon's shows how the Persians had neglected this arm. Xenophon says that Cyrus had 10,400 Greek hoplites and 2500 Greek and Thracian peltasts and light-armed, figures which presuppose that not a man had fallen out on the march from Celaenae; as the men were numbered, Xenophon must have omitted some reinforcements. Cyrus also had about as many native infantry, but only some 2600 horse, 600 of whom were his bodyguard, heavily-armed swordsmen; in all perhaps somewhere about 28,000 men. Xenophon's statement that Cyrus had 100,000 Asiatic troops and Artaxerxes 900,000 is of interest, as it shows that to an educated Athenian a figure like 100,000 had no meaning[1]. Both armies were drawn up in similar order, and the battle shows there was little difference in length between the two lines. Artaxerxes' infantry were in line on either wing, and in the centre between them were Tissaphernes with a strong cavalry force and Artaxerxes with the 1000 horse of the guard; the other two satraps with their cavalry were on the flanks. The Greek hoplites under Clearchus, less a strong camp-guard, formed Cyrus' right wing, the Asiatics under his friend Ariaeus his left; between them were Cyrus and his bodyguard; the peltasts and 1000 horse covered Clearchus' right flank and rested on the Euphrates, the remaining 1000 horse covered Ariaeus' left.

Xenophon's account of the battle of Cunaxa is unsatisfactory; he saw little of it, and was misled both by a report he heard that Tissaphernes was on the left and by his own absurd figures, which brought Artaxerxes himself outside Cyrus' left; and his story is inconsistent with the certain fact that Cunaxa left Tissaphernes the man of the hour and that to him Artaxerxes ascribed his victory. Fortunately traces remain of a more understanding account, probably that of Sophaenetus, which explain this[2]. As Cyrus knew that a Persian king always took the centre, his dispositions were so obviously wrong that some later writer invented a story that he had ordered Clearchus to occupy the centre and Clearchus had refused. What Cyrus did do when he saw his mistake—Xenophon heard the order given—was to order Clearchus to incline to the left, to bring the Greeks opposite Artaxerxes; but Clearchus, who saw that the Greeks would in any case be threatened on their left flank by the strong Persian cavalry of the centre, refused to expose his right flank also by withdrawing it from the river. One cannot blame him; Cyrus had put him on the right, and Alexander's diagonal advance at Gaugamela shows that Cyrus' manœuvre would have been impossible unless the flanks had been as well guarded as Alexander's were. The battle opened with the Greeks charging and easily routing the infantry of Artaxerxes' left, while the cavalry on the Persian left charged through the peltasts along the river. Neither attack produced any result; the Persians rode straight on instead of taking Clearchus in rear, and Clearchus threw away the one chance of the day by going straight on, though he was on Artaxerxes' flank. As Ariaeus with Cyrus' left was held,

[1] On Persian armies generally see p. 360 *sq.*, p. 367.

[2] The reference is to Diodorus' (*i.e.* Ephorus') third source, independent both of Xenophon (if he used Xenophon at all) and of Ctesias; it gives the correct arrangement of the Persian army Beloch suggests Sophaenetus, and no alternative is apparent.

Clearchus' advance opened a gap in the line, and Tissaphernes decided the battle by throwing his cavalry into the gap, followed by Artaxerxes and the guard, threatening alike Clearchus' rear and Ariaeus' inner flank; it was the manœuvre which the Persians nearly brought off at Gaugamela and Antigonus I did bring off at Paraetacene. Cyrus, hopelessly deficient in cavalry, had nothing with which to meet them but his bodyguard; with these he charged, in a gallant attempt to retrieve as a soldier the battle he had lost as a general. He cut his way through to Artaxerxes and slightly wounded him, but was then overborne and killed; his left wing, outflanked and with nothing more to fight for, fled; and Artaxerxes' crown was secure, while Clearchus was still uselessly pursuing the defeated infantry. The Greeks returned to find the battle over; the Persian horse, with no need to charge unbroken hoplites, watched them till dark, retreating when they advanced, and at nightfall the Greeks returned to their camp, while 340 Thracians deserted. Cyrus' death was a good thing for Greece; for the weapon subsequently furnished to Persia by the King's Peace (p. 58) might, in his energetic hands, have transformed Greek history.

IV. THE RETREAT OF THE TEN THOUSAND
TO TRAPEZUS[1]

A formal demand for the unconditional surrender of the Greeks was made next day and refused. The Persians took some days to decide how to deal with them. A century later they would naturally have entered Artaxerxes' service; but seemingly he regarded them as Cyrus' friends and hated them accordingly. They were so slow to grasp the real position that they offered Ariaeus the crown, which of course he declined; Cyrus' friends were only thinking of how to make their peace with Artaxerxes. They could count on Parysatis' help, and presumably Parysatis and Tissaphernes, who had the support of his sister the queen Statira, were struggling for the control of the weak King; the result was ultimately a compromise. Cilicia became a satrapy, but otherwise Cyrus' Asiatic friends were pardoned; later on Ariaeus became satrap of Phrygia (now definitely severed from the Hellespontine satrapy), Mithridates of Cappadocia, and Glos Artaxerxes' admiral. This was as far as Parysatis' influence reached. The King could not deny his debt to Tissaphernes; he gave him Cyrus' satrapies, the

[1] See map to illustrate the route of the Ten Thousand, facing p. 1.

command in Asia Minor, and full power to deal with the Greeks. It was not Tissaphernes' aim to destroy them; he had not nearly enough cavalry in any case, and the canals made it impossible to wear down the Greeks as the Parthians were later to wear down the Romans at Carrhae. His fear was that they might establish themselves permanently in some strong position among the canals and give much trouble, and his first object was to get them out of Babylonia by any means. The Greeks on their side knew that they could not cross the Mesopotamian desert again without supplies; they occupied some villages, but, fortunately for themselves, did not accept a treacherous proposal by Ariaeus to guide them home; and when after two days Artaxerxes offered them a truce, Clearchus, who had learnt that he could not fight successfully without cavalry, gladly accepted. Tissaphernes came and went, sympathizing with their desire to go home, till the struggle at court was decided; then he pledged himself to secure their safe return, and they swore to do no harm. He led them south-east into Babylonia, making for the bridge of boats over the Tigris at Sittace on the Babylon-Susa road; on their way they passed the 'Median wall' near Babylon, the rampart some $17\frac{1}{2}$ miles long which Nebuchadrezzar had built from Opis (subsequently a village of Seleuceia)[1] to Sippara to guard Babylon, at the point where the Tigris and Euphrates most nearly approach each other. After crossing the Tigris Tissaphernes turned north, and took them straight up the river past Opis, and so without incident to the greater Zab, its principal tributary. This section of Xenophon's narrative is in disorder; he misplaces Opis—he may have transferred the name to another town—and never mentions the lesser Zab.

At the Zab the suspicion which had been growing between the two armies came to a head, and Clearchus sought to remove it by a conference with Tissaphernes; among other things he offered him the services of the Greeks to put down the revolt in Egypt. Tissaphernes disclaimed any idea of treachery, and invited Clearchus and his officers to dinner; Clearchus went with Proxenus, Menon, Socrates, Agias, and 20 company commanders; all were seized and sent to Artaxerxes and all were put to death except Menon, who according to report died later under torture.

---

[1] Eratosthenes (Strabo, II, 80) gives the distance from Opis to Euphrates as some 200 stades, which may mean either 19 or 25 miles. This figure, conjoined with Nebuchadrezzar's 5 kas-pu for his wall, renders impossible the traditional location of Opis at the Adhem-mouth [as in Maps 1 and 5 in vol. III].

Xenophon has much ill to say of Menon, and Ctesias, Artaxerxes' Greek physician, makes him responsible for Clearchus' death; but Plato had a different idea of Menon, and the accusations may only mean that, while Xenophon and Ctesias admired Clearchus, Menon notoriously did not[1]. Tissaphernes' treachery was possibly due to personal hatred of Clearchus, the friend of Cyrus and Parysatis, and to the belief that without leaders the Greeks would be helpless, and must either surrender or be destroyed by the Carduchi; but possibly he was merely obeying Artaxerxes' orders.

The Greeks were at first stunned by Clearchus' arrest; but they decided to go on, and chose new generals, Xenophon, who says he played a leading part in the decision, receiving Proxenus' command, while Cheirisophus as a Spartan took the lead, important steps being settled in general conference. To move more easily, they burnt their carts and tents, which must have meant that the women had to go on foot; if the march of the Ten Thousand was a feat, the march of the women was a marvel. The horses, however, they used as pack-animals; one man brought away 3000 gold darics, another some valuable carpets. They advanced in hollow square up the Tigris past the ruins of 'Larisa' (Calah) and 'Mespila' (Nineveh), Cheirisophus leading and Xenophon commanding the rearguard, while Tissaphernes followed, worrying them with cavalry and slingers to keep them moving; they improvised a few horse and slingers as a reply. Thus amid frequent skirmishes they reached Jezireh, where the modern road crosses the Tigris and the hills of Kurdistan come down to the river. A Rhodian offered to take them across the river native fashion on skins stuffed with grass, but a strong body of cavalry on the farther bank rendered this impossible; they had not the catapults which enabled Alexander thus to cross the Jaxartes in face of cavalry. So they struck into the hills of Kurdistan, which Persia had never conquered; and Tissaphernes left them.

The aim of the Greeks was, roughly, to reach 'Paphlagonia,' *i.e.* Sinope or one of her colonies, and they believed that to do this they must sooner or later cross the arrow-swift Tigris: and prisoners had told them that beyond Kurdistan lay Armenia, where they could cross the Tigris near its source and go anywhere they chose. They followed the regular route through Kurdistan, but began with a battle, for the route ran uphill through a pass which was held in force by the Carduchian archers. They caught two natives, and by killing one induced the other to speak; he

[1] Xenophon, *Anab.* II, 5, 28 and 6, 21 *sq.*; Ctesias, fr. 91 ed. Gilmore; Plato, *Meno* (the general picture). See Bruhn in Fr. Leo's Χάριτες, p. 1.

showed them another though difficult path which turned the pass, and after a severe fight and considerable loss they got through. They took seven days to traverse Kurdistan, fighting perpetually, and Xenophon had to neglect his diary; and when they reached the Centrites, the Armenian boundary, they found Artaxerxes' son-in-law Orontes, satrap of 'Eastern Armenia' (*i.e.* Darius' eighteenth satrapy), holding the farther bank. Some foragers however found a ford higher up, and by skilful strategy the army got across, out-manœuvring Orontes, whose men gave little trouble; but the Carduchi swarmed down on them as they were crossing, and afforded Xenophon the opportunity of a brilliant little rearguard action. They crossed the Bitlis river, which they thought was the Tigris, went by Bitlis to Mush, crossed the Teleboas (Murad su) into 'Western Armenia' (the thirteenth satrapy, Armenia proper), met its satrap Tiribazus, and made an agreement with him that neither side should harm the other.

Henceforth their route is uncertain; Xenophon does not say what they knew, or if they were aiming at a particular point or going blindly northward; probabilities alone can be indicated. From Mush they probably bore westward to the Gunek river; on their way they honoured their agreement by burning some houses, and when a deserter reported that Tiribazus, who had followed them, meant to ambush them, they sent out a force which surprised and plundered his almost empty camp. Their one thought now was to escape quickly from his neighbourhood lest he should occupy the passes ahead. It had begun to snow; but apparently they left the road and went north across the hills for three days with local guides till they struck the western Euphrates, which they crossed somewhere westward of Erzerum. They were now not far from Gymnias and the road to Trapezus, and had taken a good line; but whether this was due to luck or judgment is unfortunately unknown. But the snow was increasing every day; it prevented them striking into the hills north of the Euphrates, and they turned and went slowly eastward along the river for two days, with the bitter wind in their faces[1]. On the third day the gale became a blizzard; the snow deepened rapidly, and they spent a terrible night in the open; they were suffering from hunger, frost-bite, and snow blindness, and many men and animals died. Next day Cheirisophus pushed on with the main body, while Xenophon had a hard task to round up and bring in the sick and stragglers; but after great difficulties all were collected and safely housed in a group of prosperous underground villages on the Erzerum

[1] Boreas to Xenophon includes the east wind: *Anab.* v, 7, 7.

plateau, where they rested and feasted; the headman of Xenophon's village told them that to the north lay the Chalybes, and that he knew the road.

After a week's rest they started with the headman as guide; but before leaving someone carried off his son, and Xenophon took 17 horses which he was rearing for Artaxerxes, exposing the man to the King's vengeance. Naturally therefore he led them astray, and guided them, not north to the Chalybes, but east to the upper Araxes. On the third day Cheirisophus saw something was wrong, and struck the man, who escaped; Xenophon and Cheirisophus quarrelled over this, and Xenophon's slurred account of these unhappy days suggests that they were not a memory he cared to dwell on. They were now completely lost; but, finding that the Araxes was locally called Phasis, they thought it was the river of Colchis and that by following it they would reach the Black Sea. They followed it eastward for seven days before discovering their mistake; they retraced their steps for two days and then turned north towards the country of the independent Taochi, one of the fixed points of their route; they successfully turned the tribesmen who were guarding the ascent, and reached the plain of Kars. Here they found it hard to get food, for the Taochi had brought their cattle into the fortified villages; one village gave them a desperate fight, and when taken the women first slew their children and then themselves; even Xenophon seems to feel that all was not quite right. How far north they went is uncertain, but ultimately they fought their way through the mountains of the warlike Chalybes and reached the Harpasus river; and eight days easy marching along the river brought them to the native town of Gymnias, to which they had been so close seven weeks before when the snow turned them. From Gymnias a road ran to Trapezus; but the guide they got diverged from the road in order to attack a hostile tribe. It was here, when crossing a mountain called Theches (unidentified), that Xenophon heard a great commotion in the van and galloped forward, thinking it was the enemy; but the men were cheering and pointing to the distant Euxine, and crying 'Thalatta, thalatta'—'The sea, the sea.' A few days later they were at Trapezus.

V. THE TEN THOUSAND: FROM TRAPEZUS TO PERGAMUM

From the Taochi to Trapezus they had come through tribes which had never been subject to Persia, and west of Trapezus the one-time Persian rule had vanished; the north of Asia Minor was an impossible country to hold from the southward, as Alexander's successors found. Darius' nineteenth satrapy, which had extended from the Macrones west of Trapezus to Paphlagonia, no longer existed; while beyond it Corylas, the native king of Paphlagonia, was Persia's vassal in name only, and Bithynia was completely independent. The sea and the coastal trade were controlled by the Greek cities of Sinope and Heraclea, Sinope having a chain of tributary colonies—Cotyora, Cerasus, Trapezus—stretching eastward; the once independent Amisus apparently belonged to Corylas. None of these cities, not even Sinope, was a match for this great body of armed men which had suddenly issued from the mountains. Trapezus was friendly, but could not supply shipping to take them home by sea, as they hoped. She did her best; they camped on her territory and she sent out food; she gave Cheirisophus a ship, and he went off to Byzantium to the Spartan admiral Anaxibius in the hope of getting transports; and when the army, on Xenophon's proposal, decided to collect ships for themselves by piracy, she lent them two warships. A Lacedaemonian, Dexippus, and an Athenian were put in command. Dexippus promptly deserted and took his ship to Byzantium; but the Athenian, more conscientious in wrong-doing, brought in all the merchantmen he could catch. Food however ran short, and Trapezus, fearing they would raid her subject villages, directed their arms against a hostile tribe, the Drilae, at whose hands they nearly met with disaster. Lack of supplies then compelled them to move on; they put the women and baggage on ship-board and themselves marched to Cerasus; their numbers were now reduced to 8600, which implies a loss of nearly 4000 fighting men since leaving Cunaxa, a loss chiefly inflicted by lighter-armed tribesmen.

At Cerasus they began to get out of hand. Danger had held them together on the march to Trapezus; with that pressure removed, their voluntary discipline vanished, and each section claimed to act for itself. The native villages of Cerasus' territory were friendly, and sent food; nevertheless one company attacked a village and was cut to pieces. The village sent ambassadors to the army, and Xenophon accepted the good offices of the magistrates of Cerasus; but the army murdered the ambassadors, nearly stoned a magistrate, and created such a panic that the towns-people fled to their ships or into the sea. How Xenophon got the army away is not recorded, but later he did persuade them to hold an enquiry, and three officers were fined; he may have felt a certain satisfaction in recording that Sophaenetus was one (p. 5). From this time Xenophon becomes more and more the one force making for order among these turbulent men; as an Athenian he really was more civilized than the majority, though the ascendancy he acquired was due to his own character.

After leaving Cerasus they entered the land of the Mossy-noeci, 'tower-dwellers,' who are described as most uncivilized: they tattooed themselves and talked to themselves out loud, and prized their children in proportion to their breadth. Their clans were ruled by kings who lived each at the top of a wooden tower seven stories high, whence he administered justice; he was never allowed to come out—a well-known and widespread form of taboo. They had a supreme king in a tower which the Greeks called Metropolis, and had conquered some iron-working Chalybes, who acted as their blacksmiths. The Greeks found a civil war going on; they allied themselves with the nearer clans, took the Metropolis for them, and burnt the unhappy god-king alive in his tower. Thence they went through the Tibareni to Cotyora; but Cotyora had heard of their doings at Cerasus and closed her gates, and some envoys from Sinope threatened, if Cotyora's lands were touched, to call in Corylas and his Paphlago-nians; Xenophon in reply suggested that the Greeks might help Corylas to take Sinope, whereon the envoys became less truculent and friendship was established. But Xenophon was so impressed by what he heard of the difficulty of crossing the rivers Iris and Halys that he thought it would be better if the army settled somewhere and founded a city, obviously with himself as 'founder,' and a design was attributed to him of turning back and seizing Phasis; the troops nearly stoned him when they heard of it, but he talked them back into good humour. Meanwhile some of the leaders had discovered some wealthy merchants from Sinope and Heraclea, and by threats extorted a promise of sufficient trans-ports and a large sum of money. With Corylas they made a treaty, and entertained his envoys with an exhibition of their different national dances, ending up with a slave-girl with a little shield who danced the Pyrrhic dance very prettily. The ships came, but not the money, and there was more trouble before they finally went on board and sailed to Sinope; there Cheirisophus rejoined with the news that Anaxibius would engage and pay them when they reached the Straits.

Their pre-occupation now was to get booty to take home, and, as they thought they might do better under a single leader, they offered Xenophon the command, and on his prudent refusal elected Cheirisophus. They then sailed to Heraclea—hardly as yet the powerful state of a century later—and proposed, against Cheirisophus' wishes, to hold the city to ransom; Heraclea manned her walls, Cheirisophus' brief command ended, and the army broke up into three fractions. One tried to raid the Bithynians, and was cut up and surrounded and only saved—so Xenophon suggests—by the Bithynians guessing that he was coming to the rescue. The three fractions reunited at Calpe on the Bithynian coast, where Cheirisophus died. Meanwhile Pharnabazus, satrap of Hellespontine Phrygia, had come to the support of the Bithynians, hoping by their aid to prevent the Greeks entering his satrapy, and when part of the Greeks next went out to plunder they unexpectedly met his cavalry, who slew 500 of them; there was great alarm in the camp at Calpe, and they stood to arms all night. But Xenophon understood that attack may be the best defence; he led out the army next day, and for perhaps the first time in Greek history employed reserves, stationing three companies behind the line with orders to reinforce threatened points; they were not true reserves, as they were not under the general's hand, but nothing of the sort was seen again till Gaugamela. There was however no real battle; the light-armed Bithynians drove in Xenophon's peltasts, but were not going to face the spear-line, and Pharnabazus confined himself to covering his allies' retreat, while the Greeks made little attempt to pursue, 'for,' says Xenophon, 'the cavalry made them afraid'; few lives were lost, and Xenophon's reserves never got a chance. The Greeks returned to Calpe, and again Xenophon seems to have thought of founding a city; but nothing came of it.

They now came in touch with the power of Sparta. They hoped that Cleander, the Spartan harmost (governor) of Byzantium, would come for them with a fleet; he came with only two triremes and Dexippus, the man who had deserted from Trapezus, and walked straight into a dispute about some captured cattle. There was the usual riot; the army tried to stone Dexippus, and Cleander himself had to run. He was furious at having shown fear, and threatened to have the army outlawed from every Greek city; and for the first time Xenophon was afraid, for he knew that Cleander had power to carry out his threat. He prevailed on the two men implicated to surrender themselves, and Cleander behaved very well; having satisfied his honour by securing the culprits, he forgave and released them, and promised the army a welcome at Byzantium. The army went on to Chrysopolis near Chalcedon; thence, at Pharnabazus' request, Anaxibius brought them across to Byzantium, where Xenophon proposed to leave them and remain. Anaxibius told the men they would get their promised pay outside the city; they quitted it accordingly, whereon he shut the gates and left them outside without money or food. When they perceived the trick they burst a gate and forced their way in again; Anaxibius fled to his ships, and there was universal panic, for the men were thoroughly angry and Byzantium lay at their mercy. But Xenophon, who was still there, went to them, persuaded them to pile arms and listen to him, and then talked them round into leaving the city quietly without doing any damage; it was far the greatest thing he ever did.

They left Byzantium and camped near Perinthus, where many deserted, and the supersession of Cleander and Anaxibius led to Xenophon joining them once more; but Cleander's successor was hostile, and even sold their sick whom Cleander had humanely housed in Byzantium; and Xenophon and the 6000 who remained, left destitute and without prospects in a Thracian midwinter, took service with Seuthes, a dispossessed Thracian prince living by brigandage. They spent the winter sacking villages for Seuthes from the Aegean to the Euxine, and he cheated them of their pay; but by spring (399) the position had altered again; Sparta had declared war on Tissaphernes and sent Thibron to Asia, and two of Thibron's officers came to Thrace and engaged Xenophon's force (see below, p. 38 *sq.*). He took them across to Lampsacus and led them to Pergamum, then held by his friend Gongylus, one of a group of Greek dynasts ruling petty principalities in Aeolis; and on Gongylus' advice Xenophon, who was penniless, turned freebooter himself, attacked the stronghold of a wealthy Persian landowner, and after a preliminary repulse captured the man and all his property, securing booty enough to set him up for life.

Here the story of the Ten Thousand really ends, those who remained—under 6000—being merged in Thibron's army; they had left Cunaxa over 12,000 strong, and (allowing liberally for desertions at Perinthus) must have had at least 5000 casualties before reaching Byzantium. Whether Xenophon stayed with them is uncertain, but apparently his own city had no use for his considerable military talent; he subsequently joined Agesilaus, served under him in Asia, and fought for Sparta against Athens'

friend Thebes at Coronea (394), for which Athens formally
exiled him. Sparta, however, gave him an estate at Scillus in Elis,
then under her control, where he lived for some twenty years,
hunting on the mountains and writing many of the books which
have made him famous; the *Anabasis* itself *may* be later, between
370 and 367. He lost his estate after Leuctra (371); but the
political position then enabled Athens to recall Sparta's friend,
and to Athens he returned, though possibly he died at Corinth.
It is tempting to apply to him Juvenal's most famous lines: he
performed a march without precedent across savage mountains;
his reward has been to become a textbook for schoolboys.

Cyrus' expedition has often been regarded as a prelude to
Alexander's, a view which Arrian emphasized when he took
Xenophon's title, *Anabasis*, for his own book, and outdid the list
of superlatives applied by Xenophon to Cyrus with his own more
eloquent list in eulogy of Alexander. Cyrus to Xenophon was as
much the king by natural right as Alexander to Aristotle: the
forces of nature do homage to both. But the prelude must not be
taken to mean too much. The march of the Ten Thousand, though
a great feat of courage and endurance, was unfortunately useful to
Isocrates' propaganda against Persia; and Isocrates, to prove his
contention that Persians were cowards (one figures Alexander
smiling over the *Panegyricus*), drew a picture which has coloured
much of literature since—a picture of 6000 men, the scum of
Greece, defeating the whole strength of Asia, till Artaxerxes in
despair betook himself to treachery, preferring to face the gods
rather than the Greeks, and even so failed, and the 6000 returned
home in greater security than many a friendly embassy. It is
barely even the conventional half-truth. Cyrus marched almost
the whole time through friendly territory or desert; he was defeated
by an army quite unrepresentative of Persia's strength; only
about half of the Greeks got back to Byzantium; and Xenophon,
very honestly, records their fear of the cavalry of a single satrap.
As the Greeks on their retreat were never attacked in earnest by
any Persian army, that retreat no more proved Persia helpless
than the destruction of the great Athenian expedition to the Delta
had proved her invincible. Cyrus made men feel that Persia had
become *accessible*; but her real weakness, the fact that her land-
system could not produce infantry capable of facing Greek hoplites,
had long been known. From the military point of view, the
position as between Greek infantry and Persian cavalry in Asia
was, at best, indecisive; and the one lesson taught by Cyrus' expedition was that no one need hope to conquer Persia without a

cavalry force very different from any which Greece had yet envisaged. That was the lesson which Alexander was to apply.

VI. THE GREAT KING AND THE SATRAPS

The internal history of Persia from 401 to 335 B.C. is the story of a struggle between the central government and its outlying provinces. The position at the end of the struggle was, that Darius' conquests east of the Hindu Kush and the provinces along the south coast of the Black Sea were permanently lost, though when and how the Indian districts secured independence is unknown; but Egypt, independent until 343, was re-conquered, the western seaboard, after many vicissitudes, was re-incorporated in the empire, and the separatist tendencies of the western satraps were for the time overcome. Though Darius' empire was not fully restored, the tradition of Persia's weakness only partially accords with the facts; and if she passed through a period of confusion, so did Greece. The quarrels in Greece and Agesilaus' abortive expedition, which are described elsewhere (pp. 40 *sqq.*), convinced the Achaemenid kings, unfortunately for themselves, that no real danger could threaten from the West; and throughout the period their pre-occupation is with Egypt, which consistently supported every revolt against them. Meanwhile a great change was proceeding in Greece; perpetual wars, the large number of exiles, and the absence of any outlet by colonization for the surplus population, had enormously increased the class of Greeks ready to serve as mercenaries; these tended to form a world by themselves, and Persia came to depend too much upon them.

After Cunaxa Tissaphernes began attacking the Greek cities, with the result that in spring 399 Sparta declared war on him (p. 38). The successive Spartan commanders, Thibron and Dercyllidas, freed some Aeolian towns; but the war dragged on till Conon returned from Cyprus to Tissaphernes' enemy Pharnabazus, and the two secured Artaxerxes' consent to attack Sparta seriously by sea. Then (396) Sparta sent Agesilaus to Asia. In successive campaigns he overran Lydia, defeated Tissaphernes before Sardes, penetrated inland to Paphlagonia, and wasted Pharnabazus' satrapy. He had no plans beyond plunder, and only met the coastal satraps; but he brought about Tissaphernes' fall and death, Artaxerxes surrendering the man who had saved his throne to Parysatis, who thus annihilated Hydarnes' line (p. 3) and avenged Cyrus. Pharnabazus, however, by lavish subsidies, raised a Greek league against Sparta; in 394 Agesilaus was

recalled, and in the same year Conon and Pharnabazus defeated the
Spartan fleet off Cnidus, and restored the Long Walls at Athens
(see below, pp. 43 *sqq.*). In 389 Conon's friend Evagoras of Salamis,
who had hellenized his city, revolted with support from Athens
and Achoris of Egypt, and mastered Cyprus. Meanwhile Sparta
had come to realize that she could not maintain her position
without Persian support; after much intriguing her envoy
Antalcidas secured this, and in 386 Athens was compelled to
accept the shameful 'King's Peace,' dictated to the Greek states
by the King. The Asiatic Greek cities, and Cyprus, were abandoned
to Persia; the provision that all other Greek cities should be independent, and that any who did not accept the peace would be
compelled by Persia to do so, made Persia the arbiter of Greece,
with the right of perpetual interference. It was the greatest
success in the West which Persia ever achieved.

With Sparta firmly bound to Persia, Artaxerxes was free to
attack Egypt; but this obscure war (385–3) brought him no
success, while Egypt's ally Evagoras raised Phoenicia against him.
Thereon he changed his plans, and in 381, after great preparations, attacked Evagoras. Evagoras' fleet was defeated by the
Persian admiral Glos off Citium, and he was shut up in Salamis.
Achoris deserted him, but he succeeded in playing off the Persian
commanders Tiribazus and Orontes against each other; Orontes
gave him good terms (380) and he kept his kingdom as Persia's
vassal. Artaxerxes then collected an army to attack Egypt, now
ruled by Nectanebo I, the Egyptian Nakhtenēbef, and gave the
command to the Carian Datames, satrap of Cappadocia, who had
just conquered Paphlagonia and Sinope[1], and again carried Persian
arms to the Black Sea. Datames, however, was first diverted to the
reconquest of Cataonia and then removed; he had been too successful to please the jealous king. Pharnabazus succeeded him
and in 374 invaded Egypt; but he quarrelled with the leader of
his mercenaries, the Athenian Iphicrates, and the expedition
failed. In 367, thanks to Pelopidas, Persia abandoned Sparta
for Thebes, henceforth her most consistent friend in Greece.

Datames had fled to Cappadocia, and defied all efforts to subdue
him; he was practically independent, with his capital at Sinope,
whence he controlled the coastal trade. His success brought on
the Satraps' Revolt. About 366 Ariobarzanes of Hellespontine
Phrygia rose, followed by Orontes, who was hereditary satrap of
Armenia; Mausolus, the native dynast and satrap of Caria, now

---

[1] Extant coins of Sinope bear the name of Datames. See Volume of
Plates ii, 4, *f.*

a separate satrapy, secretly favoured them. Many Greek cities, and most of the coast peoples from Syria to Lydia, also revolted; and when Autophradates of Lydia, at first loyal, had to join, Persia seemed cut off from the sea. Orontes, who was of royal blood, had the supreme command; as he coined gold, he was possibly aiming at the throne. Finally Tachos of Egypt, Nectanebo's successor, supported the rebels, and as Persia stood with Thebes, Athens and Sparta aided Tachos[1]; Agesilaus took command of his army, and the Athenian Chabrias of his fleet. Chabrias showed him how to raise money by holding the priestly colleges to ransom, and he prepared to invade Syria. But the satraps were united by no principle and distrusted each other, and treachery served Artaxerxes where the sword had failed; Orontes came over, and received Mysia and the coast as a reward; Datames was assassinated, and Ariobarzanes betrayed and crucified; in 359 a revolt in Egypt replaced Tachos by his son Nectanebo II (the Egyptian Nakht-horeḥbe). Autophradates and Mausolus made their peace and kept their satrapies; Phoenicia and the coast peoples must have made their peace also, but Paphlagonia, Northern Cappadocia, and Pontus were definitely lost. The Greek towns suffered in the war, and some fell into the hands of tyrants.

By 360 or 359 the revolt was over; and between December 359 and March 358 Artaxerxes died in peace, at an advanced age. Greek writers call him mild and magnanimous; his acts reveal him as sensual and weak, cruel and faithless. He sacrificed the enemies of Cyrus to his mother, the friends to his wife; to succeed in his service was more fatal than to fail, as Tissaphernes and Datames found. He left Persia weaker; for the recent troubles had not really been liquidated. He built the great throne-room at Susa; and his reign has a certain religious significance, for he introduced Asiatic polytheism into Zoroastrianism, raising temples to the nature-goddess Anaitis in the chief cities of his empire and establishing the Sacaean festival (see vol. iv, pp. 192, 211).

VII. ARTAXERXES III AND THE RECONQUEST OF EGYPT

His son Artaxerxes III (Ochus), who succeeded him after putting his numerous brothers to death, was cruel enough; but he possessed energy and a policy, and was efficient up to a point. The source of the late troubles was the right which the satraps had

[1] The British Museum possesses a unique gold coin with Athenian types and the name of Tachos. See Volume of Plates ii, 4, h.

long arrogated of waging private war; he dealt firmly with this, and in 356 ordered them to disband their private armies. Most obeyed, and again became subordinates. Two only refused: Artabazus, who had succeeded Ariobarzanes in Hellespontine Phrygia, and Orontes. Artabazus had relations with Egypt as brother-in-law of the Rhodian Mentor, who commanded Necta-nebo's mercenaries; Athens too at first supported him, but was frightened off when Ochus sent an ultimatum. Then in 353 he obtained help from Thebes; but after some preliminary success he was beaten and fled with Mentor's brother Memnon to Philip of Macedonia. Why Thebes changed sides is obscure. Whether Orontes remained in arms is uncertain; in any case, Ochus thought that his rear was now sufficiently secure for him to attack Egypt. He invaded Egypt (probably in 351, but the date is very uncertain) by the dangerous sea-road along the great Serbonian bog, lost part of his army, and had to return; his failure was the signal for renewed risings. The Athenian commanders at the Hellespont offered Orontes help[1]; most of Cyprus, led by Salamis, revolted, together with part of Phoenicia, where Ochus had been mad enough to ill-treat the Sidonians; Tennes (Tabnit) of Sidon allied himself with Nectanebo, who sent him Mentor and 4000 mercenaries. Ochus again secured the friendship of Thebes by a subsidy for the Sacred War (see p. 227), and possibly that of Philip of Macedonia, and somehow isolated Orontes, who apparently lost Mysia but managed to retire to Armenia. Cyprus was ultimately reduced by Idrieus, Mausolus' successor in Caria, aided by the Athenian Phocion with 8000 mercenaries, and one Pnytagoras installed at Salamis; but the satraps detailed to reduce Sidon were defeated, and Ochus took command himself. Apparently in 347 he diverted Sidon's traffic to Ake[2]; but Sidon itself he did not take till 345, the captives for his harem reaching Babylon in October[3]. The tradition says that Tennes, having won over Mentor, finally betrayed the city, but the people fired it and destroyed it and themselves. Sidon, however, if damaged, was soon restored; but, except for Tyre (which gained by Sidon's overthrow), Phoenicia remained disaffected at heart, as did much of Cyprus, hampering Persia at sea. Mentor and his mercenaries entered the Great King's service.

---

[1] It is not certain whether Orontes was in open revolt at this time; see below, p. 228.

[2] This depends on Newell's discovery of an era of Ake dated 347.

[3] S. Smith, *Babylonian Historical Texts*, 1924, p. 149. See, however, below, p. 153.

In 343 Ochus, his rear secure at last, again prepared to attack Egypt, and sent envoys to Greece for assistance. Thebes, in return for his subsidy, gave him 1000 men, Argos 3000, and the Asiatic Greeks 6000. Athens refused aid, but promised friendship, provided he did not attack Greek cities; that is, she undertook not to help the Egyptians. Ochus invaded Egypt that winter. Nectanebo held the river line (the Pelusiac arm of the Nile) with a strong force of Greek mercenaries; but Ochus had the sense to give his Greek generals a free hand, while Nectanebo did not. Mentor sowed distrust between Greeks and Egyptians; Nectanebo abandoned the river line before it was really forced, and retired to Memphis; and Ochus mastered the country, but outraged Egyptian sentiment by violating temples and killing the Apis calf. Nectanebo vanished into Ethiopia, to reappear in Egyptian romance as the father of Alexander, the avenger of Egypt on the Persians (p. 155).

The conquest of Egypt made Mentor and his fellow-general Bagoas the Chiliarch, who worked together, the most important forces in Persia; the Chiliarch, commander of the Guard, had now really become Grand Vizier. Mentor was appointed general on the coast and proceeded to reduce various petty dynasts in Asia Minor; late in 342 he captured and sent to Ochus Hermeias, tyrant of Atarneus and Assos, the friend of Aristotle, who married his niece and had lived at his court till 344, when he went to Mitylene. Hermeias had relations with Philip; and Aristotle's nephew Callisthenes, in his panegyric on Hermeias, said that he refused to reveal Philip's plans to Ochus, and was executed, showing great constancy. Certainly Aristotle wrote an ode in his honour and dedicated his statue at Delphi. But very different accounts of Hermeias were also current (for, like Callisthenes himself later, he became a battleground for opposing interests), and it may be doubted if Ochus thought much about Philip's plans, or regarded Macedonia in a different light from the various Greek states; for, though he helped to prevent Philip taking Perinthus in 340, he refused Athens' request for a subsidy for the war against Philip, and let Athens and Thebes fall unsupported at Chaeronea, a terrible blunder. Whatever his grievance against Athens for her refusal of help in 343, Thebes was his friend, and since 342 he had had the power to intervene, had he desired (p. 250 sq.).

Mentor had procured the recall of Artabazus and Memnon; he died before 338, and Memnon took over his mercenaries, but not his extensive powers. In the summer of that year Bagoas poisoned

Ochus and made his son Arses king. Ochus had had great success, but he was no statesman; he left his successors to face Macedonia with Phoenicia disaffected and Athens and Thebes crushed. In 336 Bagoas poisoned Arses, and set up as king a collateral, Darius III Codomannus, who promptly poisoned Bagoas, the best thing he did.

Nothing had happened in the 65 years since Cunaxa to show that Persia was too weak to resist a serious invasion, especially if anything should arouse Iranian national sentiment. It was however a noteworthy phenomenon that some of the coastal dynasts, like Mausolus the Carian and Hermeias the Paphlagonian, had perhaps begun to foreshadow Hellenism, *i.e.* the extension of Greek culture to Asiatics. Hermeias established a coterie of philosophers at Assos, and in the 'companions' who shared his power some have traced the influence of philosophic ideas, though others consider them his partners in business. Mausolus certainly adopted Greek elements; he enlarged Halicarnassus by a synoecism of neighbouring towns in Hellenic fashion, and the Mausoleum, the tomb built for him by his widow Artemisia, was a great Greek work of art. But these were externals; in spirit the satrap Mausolus remained an Asiatic, and did not always know how to conciliate the Greeks under his rule. The strongest link between Greece and Persia was forged by the mercenaries; this outer Hellenic fringe caused many in Greece to regard Persia as their champion against Macedonia, and probably even contributed elements to the literary tradition about Alexander.

CHAPTER II

THE ASCENDANCY OF SPARTA

I. LYSANDER'S SETTLEMENT

THE end of the Peloponnesian War is one of the most clearly defined turning-points in Greek History. No previous Greek war, as Thucydides pointed out, drew in such large measure upon the resources of Greece, and none had a more decisive issue. These facts, however, are hardly sufficient to establish the common opinion that the Peloponnesian War was the culminating catastrophe of Greek History, the 'suicide of Greece,' and that the later chapters of that history are but the record of a prolonged death-agony. The damage inflicted upon Greece by the War was by no means irreparable. Its wastage in life and wealth was hardly proportionate to its extent and duration. Except before Syracuse and in the concluding naval actions, the fighting was mostly desultory and resulted in no heavy slaughter. On land the destruction of crops and even the despoiling of plantations inflicted no loss which a few years' cultivation could not repair. On sea the ships of Athens and her allies, in whose hands the trade of Greece was mostly gathered, had carried on with little interruption. Again, and this is the most vital point, the effect of the War upon the mental life of the Greeks was not permanently ruinous. No doubt the strain and exasperation of a long-protracted conflict left its mark: in the fourth century the Greek people lacked that youthful buoyancy which inspired it after the 'great deliverance' of the Persian Wars. But as yet its capacity for sustained effort and constructive imagination was little impaired, as the history of Greek art, literature and science, no less than of politics and strategy, declares. In fine, the fourth century was not an age of senile decay, but of mature and active manhood.

Note. The continuous ancient sources of the narrative in this and the following two chapters are Xenophon, *Hellenica*, III–VII and Diodorus, XIV–XVI. The fragments of the *Hellenica Oxyrhynchia* and of Ctesias' *Persica*, the speeches of Lysias and Andocides, and the writings of Isocrates supply contemporary evidence. Of the secondary sources Plutarch (*Lives of Lysander, Pelopidas*, etc.) is the most important after Diodorus.

For the other literary sources and for the archaeological evidence see the Bibliography.

The destruction of the Athenian Empire at the peace of 404 B.C. was a political event of the first magnitude. At first sight it might appear an irreparable disaster, for that Empire represented the first resolute attempt to solve the key problem of Greek politics, the assembling of the scattered Greek communities into a United States of Greece. But the seeds of decay had been planted in the Athenian state-system when the Athenians on their own confession degraded a free confederacy of allies into a 'tyranny' whose sanction lay in sheer force. The Peloponnesian War merely hastened its dissolution, but did not cause it. Nay more, the disappearance of the Athenian Empire left a clear site for a new and better structure; and Sparta, upon whom the political reconstruction of Greece devolved, possessed several important qualifications for that task. Although the Spartans fell as far below the general average of Greek culture as the Athenians surpassed it, their military prowess and the reputation which they enjoyed for stability of character were more important assets in a political leader than sheer brilliancy of intellect. After the Peloponnesian War their prestige stood higher than that of the Athenians at the zenith of their fortunes: indeed, as Xenophon said, 'a Spartan could now do as he liked in any Greek town.' Last but not least, Sparta had in her Peloponnesian League a ready-made pattern for the production of a general Hellenic League which should be at once comprehensive and liberal.

It may be objected that no Greek federation could be permanent, because the passion for local autonomy overrode the sense of Greek nationality, and that Sparta of all states could least afford to disregard this sentiment, since she had represented the Peloponnesian War as a crusade against 'tyranny.' True enough, in the fifth century Greek jealousy for local autonomy had grown more powerful. But Greek national consciousness had also been quickened, for the remembrance of a common victory over Persia, and the universal comradeship of the Olympic games, then at the zenith of their popularity, had stimulated the sense of Greek solidarity. In the fourth century local dialects and alphabets were being replaced by a common language and script; the theatre and the schools of Athens were standardizing Greek thought; and above the babel of ephemeral politicians who proclaimed that Greeks were made to destroy each other, the voice could be heard of those who preached national union as the true goal of Greek politics. Moreover the meaning of the word 'autonomy' requires definition. So long as a Greek state was unfettered in its internal administration and had a voice in the framing of any foreign policy for which it might have to fight, it retained its 'autonomy,' as that term was commonly understood. Thus autonomy was perfectly compatible with membership of a federal state, and Sparta could quite well proceed to form such a state without violating any of her pledges.

But would Sparta grasp her chance? During the Persian Wars she had led the Greeks like one who has greatness thrust upon him, and at the earliest moment she had bolted from her responsibilities as a national leader. Her outlook was by her own tradition almost confined to the Peloponnese. In 404 B.C., however, tradition counted for nothing in the shaping of Spartan policy. The government of the ephors, the guardians of Spartan tradition, had been virtually suspended, and all real power was vested for the time being in the hands of the war-winner Lysander. His victory at Aegospotami, no less complete and profitable than Octavian's 'crowning mercy' at Actium, gave him an authority like that which Octavian used to remodel the policy of Rome. The future of Sparta and Greece alike lay in Lysander's hands: his was an opportunity such as had never come to Themistocles or Pericles.

The architect of the New Greece was not without qualifications for his task. He had more than the usual Spartan capacity for leadership, for he was conspicuously free from love of wealth, the Spartans' besetting sin, and unlike most of his fellow-citizens he could 'slip on a fox hide where a lion's skin did not avail.' He also had a talent for organization which had been one of the decisive factors in the Peloponnesian War, and, in theory at least, he knew that a people accustomed to freedom must be led, not driven. To such a man it should have been possible to grasp the essentials of a lasting political settlement, and to devise the means of carrying it into effect. But Lysander's good qualities were nullified by his consuming passion, a love of power which blinded him to morality and even to reason. Among a people which had acquired more than the elements of political decency he professed that 'dice served to cheat boys, and oaths to cheat men.' Though all Greek history proclaimed that despotism was not a stable form of government, he cast himself for the rôle of a despot.

The methods by which Lysander proceeded to establish his personal ascendancy over Greece are illustrated by his dealings with Miletus in 405 B.C. In this town he instigated a bloody oligarchic uprising and installed a government which in the nature of things could only maintain itself by sheer force. Immediately after the capitulation of Athens he led his victorious fleet to Samos, and having reduced this one remaining Athenian ally he expelled the entire population and handed over the island to a party of oligarchic refugees, at whose head he set up a 'decarchy' or Government of Ten (summer 404). Later in the year he made a tour of the Aegean Sea with a fresh squadron which was nominally commanded by his brother Libys but in reality stood under his own orders. The primary purpose of this expedition seems to have been to confirm the surrender of the states which had deserted Athens after Aegospotami, and to acquire a palpable proof of this surrender in the shape of war-contributions. But the principal use which Lysander made of his authority was to create more decarchies. It was probably during this tour that the decarchic system of government was made general throughout the Aegean area. In all the cities visited by him he placed despotic power in the hands of a few men drawn from his own adherents. In many instances these revolutions were attended with further violence—at Thasos, Lysander massacred his opponents wholesale after decoying them with a false offer of amnesty—in every case they left the city at the mercy of blind fanatics or mere adventurers, the scum that bubbles up in the cauldron of civil war. Indeed the more worthless the decarchies, the better they suited Lysander, for the less they could rely on the support of the governed, the more they depended on him. As a further precaution Lysander confirmed and probably extended the system of garrisoning the Aegean cities with mercenary forces under Spartan 'harmosts' or governors, whose maintenance became a charge upon the victims of this supervision. By these means he at once gratified many influential Spartans who coveted lucrative posts overseas, and provided a prop for the authority of the decarchs.

In the pursuit of his personal ambition Lysander threw away an opportunity of constructive statesmanship such as is not often repeated in a nation's history. The best that can be said of his settlement is that it was too bad to last. As we shall see presently, his prestige at home did not endure long, and after his fall some of his worst measures were rescinded. Yet the Spartan empire never recovered from the bad start which Lysander gave it. The example of arbitrary interference in the affairs of the dependent states created a precedent which had a fatal attraction for Lysander's successors, and for the duration of Sparta's ascendancy the idea of an equitable Greek federation was lost out of sight.

II. SPARTAN HOME AFFAIRS

Before we trace the consequences of Lysander's settlement in the Aegean area, it will be well to pass under review the domestic crises of Sparta after the Peloponnesian War, and her relations with the states of the Greek mainland.

One unforeseen result of the War was a sudden glut of precious metals in Sparta. The spoils of victory which Lysander and his agents brought home are credibly reported to have amounted to some 2000 talents. The tribute imposed upon the Athenians and their former allies is estimated to have exceeded 1000 talents, and although this total is probably exaggerated we need not doubt that Sparta exacted from her dependents more than she spent upon them. To these public revenues should be added the money which Spartan officials diverted into their own pockets, no inconsiderable sum, if these officials acted up to the usual Spartan reputation for rapacity. This accumulation of money, it is true, was strictly speaking illegal, for an ancient statute roundly forbade Spartan citizens to possess gold or silver. But in an imperial state which had to maintain mercenary forces and equip men-of-war such a statute was plainly obsolete, and although the ephors made a rule that precious metal must still not be gathered in private hands, this ordinance was only enforced in isolated cases. The makers of the ordinance were readily bribed to turn a blind eye on smugglers, and ere long the possession of gold at Sparta became a matter for open boasting.

This influx of treasure, it may safely be said, brought no good to its owners. The Spartans did not devote it to productive purposes, but were content to remain dependent on their Helot population for subsistence. Neither did they use it for the relief of their own war-victims, the so-called 'Hypomeiones' or 'Inferiors.' These were mostly citizens who had been prevented by military service from supervising the cultivation of their land lots and had therefore fallen in arrears in their contribution to their 'phiditia' or messes. By an inexorable law these defaulters, while still liable to non-combatant duties at the discretion of the ephors, lost the Spartan franchise and its social privileges. The Inferiors constituted a peculiar danger, in that they had the ability, which the Helots lacked, to organize rebellion. In 398 B.C. a conspiracy for a general uprising of Inferiors, Helots and Perioeci was actually planned by a disfranchised citizen named Cinadon. This plot, it is true, was easily suppressed, for its author began by talking unguardedly and ended by betraying his accomplices. But since nothing was done to remove its causes, the discontent of the Inferiors remained a latent peril to the state.

On the other hand, there is little evidence of positive harm accruing from Sparta's enrichment. The accumulation of money consequent upon the Peloponnesian War must not be confused with the concentration of landed wealth which Aristotle noted as a characteristic of Sparta in his own day, and it is the latter, not the former process, that caused the eventual rapid decline in Sparta's citizen population. Again, though we need not doubt that those who broke the laws by acquiring gold and silver further contravened them by spending it on what would have seemed to Lycurgus culpable luxury, we must admit that the discipline and endurance of the Spartan home levy was not impaired thereby. In their last losing battles the Spartans displayed the same steady valour as at Thermopylae or Plataea.

Another consequence of Sparta's aggrandizement was a severe strain upon her man-power. It is not known whether the wastage of the Peloponnesian War had caused a serious absolute decrease in Sparta's population. But after 404 B.C. the enlargement of her responsibilities created fresh calls upon her human resources. For her overseas garrisons, it is true, she employed mercenaries drawn from other Greek districts, but the governors and their staffs were mostly Spartan citizens, and as overseas service was highly popular the numbers of the staff were probably none too small. Thus Sparta's foreign-service drafts depleted her effectives at home. Hence the Spartan home levies were increasingly diluted with Perioeci. During the Peloponnesian War the normal proportion of Perioeci to Spartans in a field company was three to two; in 390 B.C. it was two to one. As a means of increasing their effective man-power, and at the same time of palliating the perpetual discontentment of the serf population, the ephors had, during the Peloponnesian War, granted personal freedom to Helots who volunteered for military service. But this policy was not carried beyond the experimental stage. Enfranchisement on a large scale, by depleting the stock of serf labour which was reckoned indispensable to the cultivation of the land, would have undermined the economic basis of Spartan society. Rather than stint their land the Spartans resolved to eke out their military resources with increased drafts of Perioeci. It must be admitted that this makeshift was remarkably successful. The Perioeci, being incorporated in the same platoons and squads as the Spartans, acquired a sufficient measure of Spartan discipline, and their loyalty stood the test of several hard-fought battles.

The chief source of danger to Sparta's internal stability lay in the revolutionary ambitions of Lysander, which became a menace to the victors no less than to the vanquished. After the reduction of Samos the Spartan generalissimo accepted divine worship from his clients in that city and surrounded himself with a bevy of court-poets. On the monument erected by him at Delphi out of the spoils of Aegospotami his figure was exhibited in the forefront amid a company of gods, while his vice-admirals stood huddled along the back wall. Lysander's arrogance bore an ominous resemblance to the demeanour of Pausanias after his victories in the Persian Wars and heralded a fresh attack upon the Spartan constitution.

The trial of strength between the war-winner and the home authorities began in the autumn of 404 B.C., when a new board of ephors assumed office. This board proved less complaisant to Lysander than its predecessors. It rebuffed him by breaking up a colony of his former naval officers which he had established on his own authority at Sestos, and it clearly proved its intention of disarming him by taking the final settlement of Athenian affairs out of his hands and transferring it to his enemy, King Pausanias (see vol. v, p. 371). The policy of the ephors was confirmed by the Council of Elders, who acquitted Pausanias of a charge of treason preferred against him by Lysander's friends after the king's return from Athens, and it was continued in 403–2 B.C. by the magistrates of that year. In the autumn of 403 B.C. or the spring of 402 B.C. Lysander was permitted to make a fresh tour of inspection among the overseas dependencies, but he acquired a new enemy in the person of the Persian satrap Pharnabazus, whose territory he plundered in the vain belief that his victim would not dare to ask for redress. Pharnabazus however lodged a complaint at Sparta, and the ephors, who at this stage had good reason not to incur an open breach with Persia, recalled Lysander and several of his harmosts. Lysander obeyed the summons. Unlike the war-winners who overturned the Roman Republic, he could not settle his quarrel with the home authorities by a sudden military *coup*. The ephorate possessed what the Roman Senate lacked, a home levy whom no foreign-service *soldatesca* could overawe.

But although Lysander had been disarmed for the time being, he did not finally abandon his hope of a revolution. The dictator-ship which he had lost might yet be recovered and set on a perma-nent basis if only he could secure for himself the succession to the aged king Agis; the usurpation of absolute power which King Cleomenes accomplished in the third century would not lie beyond the means of King Lysander in the fourth. Accordingly he conceived a plan of making the Spartan kingship elective instead of hereditary, and under pretence of a pilgrimage he visited the sanctuary of Zeus Ammon, and also sounded the oracles of Delphi and Dodona, so as to obtain, *more Lycurgeo*, religious sanction for his constitutional schemes (see vol. III, p. 562, n. 2). But the priests could tell the difference between a Lycurgus and a Lysander, and, true to their usual practice, they refused to abet political intrigue. Thus Lysander's plan broke down at the outset, for nothing short of a divine sanction could have commended his revolutionary proposals to the Spartan folk-moot.

For a while Lysander was reduced to a waiting rôle. But in 399 B.C. a new opportunity offered. In that year the long expected death of King Agis brought about a disputed succession. The claims of the heir-apparent Leotychidas were contested by Agis' half-brother Agesilaus on the ground that Leotychidas was not a son of Agis but of the Athenian Alcibiades (vol. v, p. 314). Into this fray Lysander threw himself with all his vigour, hoping that Agesilaus, who had hitherto made no display of his talents and ambitions, would permit the king-maker to exercise the royal power on his behalf. The eventual success of Agesilaus was no doubt due in part to Lysander, who explained away a warning from Delphi against a 'lame reign' as referring not to his client's physical deformity but to the halting pedigree of Leotychidas. But Agesilaus also owed his election to other causes such as his personal geniality, which had won him many friends, and, in any case, he was not prepared to repay Lysander by becoming his puppet. As we shall see presently (p. 41), the new king took an early opportunity of declaring his independence, and Lysander henceforth resigned himself to his reduction to the rank of an ordinary citizen.

There was a saying in Sparta that 'Greece could not have endured two Lysanders.' This is an understatement of the case. Had Lysander realized his ambitions, he would have exercised a despotism in Greece as ruthless as that which Dionysius wielded in Sicily, yet without the justification of a great national emergency which made Dionysius a deliverer no less than an oppressor (see below, chap. v). Greece and Sparta alike would have found a single Lysander beyond the limits of their endurance.

The reaction of Sparta's foreign conquests upon her domestic affairs was on the whole singularly small. Her conservatism made her all but impervious to those influences which transformed Rome after the Punic and Macedonian Wars.

III. SPARTA'S DEPENDENTS IN THE GREEK HOMELAND

In the Peloponnese the authority of Sparta, which had been seriously impaired by her early failures in the War, was not wholly restored by her later successes, for the people of Elis took little or no part in the last campaigns against Athens, and in defiance of Sparta's ruling (see vol. v, p. 255) they retained possession of the borderland of Triphylia. At the close of the War the Spartans took no immediate steps against the Eleans, but in 401 B.C. they ordered them to surrender not only Lepreum but all their other dependencies, and in the ensuing year they sent King Agis at the head of a large allied force to coerce them. The Eleans offered a long but purely passive resistance behind the walls of their fortified towns. Agis' columns, being thus left free to ravage the countryside, did their work so thoroughly and so persistently that in 399 B.C. the Eleans sued for peace. The terms of the previous year's ultimatum were now enforced upon them. Of the dependent communities which were detached from them Triphylia and the villages of the Lower Alpheus valley received their independence, the hill-country on the Arcadian border was made over to the nearest Arcadian communities.

While the Spartans thus repaid the Eleans in full for their insubordination, they offered no return for the loyalty of their remaining allies. Considering that their armies, and still more so their fleets, had been indispensable instruments of Sparta's victory over Athens, the loyal Peloponnesians were morally, if not legally, entitled to a share of the war-booty, and had they gone further and claimed a voice in the government of Sparta's new empire overseas, they would scarcely have exceeded their equitable rights. Yet the Spartans appropriated all the fruits of victory to themselves and sent their confederates home empty-handed. This shabby treatment of course did not make the Peloponnesians any the more zealous in fulfilling their treaty obligations, and in their operations against the democrats at the Piraeus (see vol. v, p. 371), and against the Eleans, the Spartans lacked their usual contingent from Corinth. As we shall see presently, the Corinthians did not stop short at this species of passive resistance. On the other hand, there is no good evidence that at this stage the Spartans introduced harmosts and decarchies into the Peloponnese. Moreover, however much Sparta's allies might nurse their grievances, they could not readily forget that it was to her that they owed the '*pax Peloponnesiaca*' which was their economic mainstay, and in

Sparta's new empire those veterans of the war who wished to make a profession of soldiering could find plenty of employment. The discontent in the Peloponnese would probably not have passed beyond the smouldering stage, had not other fires broken out close by.

Among the neighbouring states the one which contained most inflammable material was Athens. The misrule of the Thirty Tyrants could not but leave many bitter memories here. After the restoration of the democracy several agents of the Thirty had to stand a trial, and we may fairly assume that many victims of the Thirty would have liked to wreak their vengeance on Sparta for installing and abetting these oppressors. The soreness of feeling which the misrule of the Thirty engendered is forcibly illustrated in the forensic speeches which the orator Lysias, himself a victim of their cupidity, directed against one surviving member of them, and against one of their agents. The deadly calm of Lysias' tone betrays a deep-seated resentment, and the irrelevant vindictiveness with which he blackens the memory of Theramenes shows that his anger was indiscriminate as well as profound.

Furthermore, the lost empire of Athens could not be readily forgotten by the proletariat who had found their livelihood in the navy and the administrative services, and by the evicted landowners from the cleruchies. Indeed the hope of restoring the spacious days of Pericles lived on in Athens for another half century and at times became the determinant factor in Athenian politics. Nevertheless in the early years of the restored democracy the desire for *revanche* was firmly repressed, and the yoke of Sparta was borne with unfaltering acquiescence.

This submissive policy was imposed upon Athens by a new political party which from the fourth century onwards acquired an ever-increasing preponderance. Under stress of the sufferings inflicted by the Peloponnesian War the more solid elements of the Athenian population who subsisted on agriculture and industry began to draw together in opposition to those who lived on the perquisites of empire. After the restoration of 403 B.C. these 'moderates' made a better economic recovery than the 'imperialists' whose vocation was now gone. In 401 B.C. their numbers were increased by the break-up of the separatist settlement at Eleusis (vol. v, p. 375) and the repatriation of the moderate section among the *émigrés*. Under the leadership of some old associates of Theramenes who had acquired prestige by sharing in Thrasybulus' forlorn hope, the new party seized and for several years maintained the initiative in shaping Athenian policy. Under their influence the Athenian people abode strictly by the settlement of 403 B.C. The amnesty to political offenders was made secure by a new law which required the law-courts to stay all proceedings against defendants who could show that the amnesty covered their case; and not a single clear instance of the amnesty being broken is on record. To avoid opening up old wounds Anytus, one of the 'moderate' leaders, renounced his just claims to properties which had been confiscated under the Thirty, and Thrasybulus himself waived his rights in the same way. For fear of further complications the 'moderates' even defeated an equitable proposal by Thrasybulus that the Athenian franchise should be conferred *en bloc* upon those foreigners who had flocked to his standard, and only allowed certain selected categories of metics to receive citizenship. The obligations imposed upon Athens by Sparta were likewise observed with religious care. In spite of financial difficulties which drove the Athenians to issue plated coins[1] and even to pronounce unjust sentences of confiscation on well-to-do defendants in the courts, the debts contracted at Sparta by the Thirty were honoured by their successors and gradually repaid, and Athenian contingents were sent to serve under Spartan orders in Elis and Asia Minor. From Athens the Spartans at first had nothing to fear.

The conciliatory attitude of Athens towards Sparta stood in marked contrast to the provocative policy of Thebes. This city owed to the Lacedaemonians its restoration to the headship of the Boeotian League, and while it rendered good service to Sparta during the Peloponnesian War it had fully repaid itself for its exertions by systematically looting the occupied areas of Attica. But when the Thebans claimed their share of the spoils of the maritime war, they were met with a point-blank refusal, despite the fact that they were not dependents of Sparta but free and equal allies. In return for this rebuff they both refused assistance to Sparta in her campaign against Elis and furnished assistance to the exiles whom the Thirty had banished from Athens, and Sparta had endeavoured to outlaw from all Greece (vol. v, p. 369). A further cause of offence was provided by Spartan activities in Thessaly (see p. 36) where Thebes had hopes of establishing her own influence. A few years later, when the Spartan king Agesilaus made an unauthorized but inoffensive landing on the Boeotian coast, the Theban government drove him off with threats of open force. Thus were laid the seeds of a long and bitter quarrel, which presently broke out into open war. But the anti-Spartan party in

---

[1] For these coins see the Volume of Plates ii, 4, *e.*

Thebes had to reckon with a strong minority who desired to restore good relations with Sparta, and until they had won allies outside of Boeotia they were in no position to try a fall with their former allies.

Of the remaining Greek states Thessaly alone requires notice here. This district had scarcely been touched by the turmoil of the Peloponnesian War, but ever since the decay of its federal institutions it had been distracted by the conflicting ambitions of its principal landlords, whose wealth enabled them to arm their tenants or to hire professional troops. In 404 B.C. Lycophron, the chief noble of Pherae, engaged and heavily defeated the armies of Larissa and other Thessalian towns; but he was presently held in check by Aristippus, who had established a quasi-despotic ascendancy in Larissa and provided himself with a strong mercenary corps. These internal dissensions made Thessaly a prey to foreign intervention. The Macedonian king Archelaus, who had successfully begun the task of modernizing his country and organizing it for foreign conquest, entered Thessaly on the invitation of some exiles from Larissa and made himself master of that town (c. 400 B.C.). This encroachment on Greek soil by a prince who was an ostentatious patron of Greek culture, yet was regarded by most Greeks as a barbarian, made some impression beyond the borders of Thessaly. A leading Greek rhetorician, Thrasymachus of Chalcedon, issued an appeal on behalf of Larissa, whose gist is probably contained in an extant rhetorical exercise of the second century A.D. The appeal was not without effect, for the Spartans, to whom it was principally directed, actually sent a force which occupied the frontier fortress of Heraclea and installed a garrison at Pharsalus (399 B.C.). These operations, we may assume, were but the opening moves in a war of liberation against the usurper Archelaus. But in the selfsame year the death of Archelaus, which threw Macedonia into a state of prolonged confusion, automatically set Larissa free. The Spartans thereupon turned their attention from Thessaly in order to pursue with more energy another war of Hellenic deliverance, of which we shall speak presently. For the time being Thessaly was left to its own devices, and Medius, the successor of Aristippus at Larissa, resumed an indecisive war with Lycophron.

This survey of Greek affairs has shown that Sparta missed her chance of establishing a permanent Hellenic peace and prepared for fresh inter-Hellenic conflicts by estranging some of her chief allies. Yet her authority was not immediately threatened with any active rebellion. Like the Athenian empire at the outset of the

Peloponnesian War, the Spartan empire at the beginning of the fourth century was too strong to be overthrown without foreign intervention. The first successful attack upon the Spartan empire originated not in Greece but in Persia.

IV. SPARTA'S RELATIONS WITH PERSIA

Of all the legacies which the Peloponnesian War bestowed upon Sparta none was more embarrassing than the debt which she had contracted with Persia in accepting subsidies from that power. By the terms of her pact she was bound to hand over to Persia 'all the land in Asia which belonged to the King,' *i.e.* all the Greek cities of Asia Minor whom Sparta had but lately delivered from the yoke of Athens. At the end of the War Sparta stood in an awkward dilemma. By honouring her contract she would dishonour herself in the eyes of Greece. If she went back on her promise, she would furnish Persia with a *casus belli*, and although she might clear herself morally by offering to refund the subsidies, it was by no means certain whether Persia would forego her legal rights and accept an equitable compromise. Still less certain were the prospects of success in a Persian war. True enough, Persia was not as strong as she was big. Under a succession of weak kings, and none of them weaker than the reigning sovereign, Artaxerxes II, she was beginning to dissolve into her component satrapies, whose rulers were often disloyal both to the King and to each other; and her military machine was woefully out of date. Given the loyal support of her dependents new and old, Sparta need not have feared a trial of strength with Persia, and a victorious Persian war would have been as good a cement for her empire as it had been for the Delian League. But could Sparta make sure that her home front would not fail her? In view of the course which events actually took, she was entitled to have misgivings on this point.

The course which Sparta actually adopted was a series of tacks between the opposite policies of compliance and defiance. In 404 B.C., contrary to her compact, she concluded peace with Athens without consulting Persia. On the Hellespontine seaboard, whose satrap Pharnabazus as yet commanded little influence, she kept the Greek towns in her own possession. On the other hand she ceded the Ionian towns to prince Cyrus, whom she could not decently or safely offend. In 401 B.C., when Cyrus rebelled against his brother, she gave him every facility to recruit Greek mercenaries and thus incidentally to rid Greece of unemployed soldiers; yet realizing that Cyrus might fail, or that if he succeeded he might become as dangerous to Greece as his name-sake, the founder of the Persian empire, she gave him no overt support. After Cyrus' death the ephors at first appeared anxious to put themselves right with Artaxerxes. In 400 B.C. they forbade the remnant of Cyrus' Greek auxiliaries to settle down in Pharnabazus' satrapy and bundled them away into the backwoods of Thrace. But before the year was out they changed their course and definitely broke with Persia.

The reason for this sudden reversal of policy is to be found in the action of the satrap Tissaphernes, who had been reduced during Cyrus' governorship to the Carian province, but after Cyrus' death resumed control of Lydia. In 404 B.C. Tissaphernes had seized Miletus, the chief Greek town on the Carian coast, and thrown a garrison into it. In 400 B.C. he proceeded against the towns of Cyrus' former province, which had profited by Cyrus' rebellion to slip out of Persian control, and laid siege to Cyme. The threatened Greek cities appealed to Sparta, and not in vain. It may be that Cyrus' Anabasis and the retreat of the Ten Thousand were beginning to alter Sparta's ideas of Persian power. In any case, she had little reason to give anything away to Tissaphernes, for this satrap, unlike Cyrus, had never properly kept his part of the bargain with Sparta in the payment of subsidies; and though Sparta might at a pinch have made an amicable cession of Greek territory to Persia, she could not decently connive at its forcible conquest.

In the autumn of 400 B.C. the ephors dispatched an expeditionary force of some 5000 men, mostly Peloponnesians, to Ephesus. On their arrival they discovered that Tissaphernes had withdrawn from Cyme. But their commander Thibron, not to be denied, carried the war into enemy country. After a preliminary foray into the Maeander valley, where the Persian horse soon headed him off, he reinforced himself with the 6000 Greek survivors of Cyrus' Anabasis, who now passed out of Thrace into Spartan service, and in the summer of 399 B.C. opened a new attack in the hilly hinterland of Cyme. In this broken country the Persian cavalry was unable to molest his advance, and its impotence encouraged several local dynasts of Greek origin, and chief among them the lords of the castle of Pergamum, to make common cause with him. On the other hand Thibron made little headway against strongholds which offered resistance. In spite of the contributions which he had imposed upon his allies he ran short of funds; and not having realized enough booty to pay his large forces he weakly gave them licence to plunder the Greek towns where they were quartered. The ephors hereupon, while approving Thibron's policy of attack, recalled him to Sparta and entrusted the execution of his plans to a former officer of Lysander named Dercyllidas.

The new commander was content at first to carry on Thibron's campaign; but, thanks to the better discipline which he maintained and to the mutinous disposition of the Greek mercenaries employed by the local dynasts, he met with prompt success. In a whirlwind campaign of eight days he carried the whole coastline of the Troad and the Scamander valley, and in the castle of Scepsis he seized enough treasure to maintain his 8000 soldiers for a year. At the end of the season the satrap of the Hellespontine region Pharnabazus, who had evidently been caught unprepared, concluded a truce with Dercyllidas, and in the spring of 398 B.C. he extended it over the whole of that year. This left Dercyllidas free to undertake a minor but urgent task in the Gallipoli peninsula, where the scattered Greek population was unable to protect its highly cultivated lands from the inroads of plundering Thracians. These inroads Dercyllidas checked for a while by repairing the fortifications on the Bulair isthmus.

So far the Greeks had hardly crossed swords with Tissaphernes, who had, as was his wont, left Pharnabazus in the lurch. Yet until Tissaphernes had been forced to come to an agreement the Greek cities could enjoy no security. In 397 B.C. therefore the ephors ordered Dercyllidas to attack Tissaphernes in his Carian province and sent a small naval squadron to co-operate with him. But this double assault was never carried out, for Tissaphernes, who had summoned Pharnabazus to his aid and received his loyal support, was strong enough to threaten a counter-attack upon the Ionian seaboard. Dercyllidas, who had advanced from Ephesus across the Maeander, was caught up on his retreat along the river valley by the Persian field force, and a panic which seized his Asiatic recruits nearly involved the whole Greek army in disaster. But the Peloponnesians and Cyrus' old troops held firm, and Tissaphernes, who had seen Greek hoplites carrying all before them at Cunaxa, called off his attack.

The campaign of 397 having thus ended in a deadlock, the rival captains arranged an armistice until the ensuing year and threw out feelers to ascertain the terms of a definitive peace. At this stage it is likely that the Spartans would have accepted any settlement that safeguarded the liberties of the Asiatic Greeks. But the Persian commanders made an unreasonable stipulation that the Spartans should withdraw all their troops without offering guarantees as to their own movements. Their object in parleying was probably nothing more than to gain time while a new Persian armament was being prepared in another quarter.

V. THE PERSIAN THALASSOCRACY

In the previous winter Pharnabazus had paid a visit to the Persian court in order to urge upon the King the need of a naval counter-stroke against the Greeks. So successful was his suit that he obtained a commission to raise a fleet, and a sum of 500 talents. With this fund he betook himself to Cyprus, which he had selected for his naval base (spring 397 B.C.). This island, a standing battle-ground between Greeks and Phoenicians, had since 410 B.C. been almost wholly absorbed into the dominion of a Greek captain of fortune named Evagoras. Having wrested the city of Salamis from the Phoenicians by a daring *coup de main* and installed himself as king of that town, Evagoras had attracted to his service adventurers from all parts of Greece, and with their help he had made such systematic conquests, that by 399 B.C. the Greeks had come to call him 'king of Cyprus.' Having made these conquests without any commission from his overlord the Persian king, he further compromised himself by neglecting to pay his tribute. But in 398 B.C. he showed a sudden desire to put himself right with Persia and sent up the sums due from him. The reason for this change of policy may be found in the influence exerted upon him by his most distinguished guest, the former Athenian admiral Conon, who was scheming to use Evagoras for the furtherance of his own plans, the avenging of Aegospotami and the restitution of the Athenian empire. Evagoras, who had a sentimental affection for Athens as the focus of Greek culture, and had more than once rendered the Athenians political aid, fell in so far with Conon's proposals that he allowed him to send a petition to Artaxerxes reinforcing Pharnabazus' plea. It was no doubt in view of this petition, which was presented at court on Conon's behalf by the King's Greek house-surgeon Ctesias, that Pharnabazus resolved to use Evagoras and Conon as his principal coadjutors in the naval war. On his arrival at Salamis he presented Conon with an admiral's commission from Artaxerxes and left him in charge of the naval preparations. In the summer of 397 B.C., as we have seen, Pharnabazus was back on the western front, where he joined hands with Tissaphernes against Dercyllidas. The truce which the satrap subsequently arranged with Dercyllidas was no doubt intended to let Pharnabazus' naval policy mature.

When news of Persia's naval effort reached Sparta, the ephors, realizing that the war was taking a critical turn, convened a congress of their allies, the first since 404 B.C. The congress resolved on energetic counter-preparations and agreed to raise a fresh expeditionary force of 8000 men for service under the new king Agesilaus (winter 397–6). The decision of the congress was mainly due to Lysander, who at this time still believed that he could use Agesilaus for his own purposes and counted on restoring his dominion in the Aegean area through the king's agency. In the spring of 396 B.C. Lysander went out to Asia as chief of staff to Agesilaus. He immediately set to work to secure appointments of all sorts for his nominees. But the king readily divined Lysander's purpose and lost no time in asserting his authority. Although Agesilaus had hitherto neither solicited nor received any high command, he was determined to make the most of his present opportunity. Indeed he fancied himself a second Agamemnon leading forth the Greeks in a new Trojan War, and it was in hopes of repeating Agamemnon's farewell sacrifices at Aulis that he made a preliminary excursion to Boeotia, with results which we have already noticed (p. 35). He therefore refused to let Lysander exercise any patronage and presently dispensed with his services altogether.

In the campaigns of 396 B.C. and 395 B.C. Agesilaus revealed unsuspected powers of generalship, and he was well served by his army, whom he infected with his own enthusiasm. At the expiry of the armistice in the summer of 396 B.C., he hoodwinked Tissaphernes by a pretended attack on Caria, and, having thus only Pharnabazus left to deal with, made a bold advance into Phrygia, where he plundered freely until a defeat inflicted upon his horsemen by the superior Persian cavalry compelled him to retreat. Having reinforced his mounted contingent, Agesilaus resumed the attack in the spring of 395 B.C. This time he played the double bluff on Tissaphernes by proclaiming his intention to attack Sardes and keeping to it. Advancing from Ephesus by way of Smyrna he arrived close to Sardes before Tissaphernes, who had guessed that the real attack would fall on Caria, could overtake him. Before the Persian infantry could come up he decoyed the horse into an ambuscade and put it out of action for that season. Having thus won a free road Agesilaus made a promenade up the Hermus and Cogamis valleys and back along the Maeander. This expedition finally rid the Greeks of Tissaphernes, who was now discredited at the Persian court and put to death at the instance of the mother of his former rival Cyrus. His successor, the vizier

Tithraustes, showed even less fight; by offering a six months' truce and a *danegeld* of 30 talents he treacherously persuaded Agesilaus to transfer his attention to Pharnabazus. Agesilaus, being thus left free to attack Phrygia, now undertook a truly ambitious invasion. Advancing up the Caïcus he gained the Phrygian plateau and came out on the Sangarius valley at Gordium. From here he struck back along the river to the Sea of Marmora, establishing his winter quarters within Pharnabazus' grounds by Dascylium.

This foray, the last which Agesilaus made on Asian soil, fell short of complete success, in that the Spartan king failed to carry any fortified centre, and therefore could not establish a secure line of communications. Nevertheless he had accomplished a march of some 500 miles without serious hindrance from Pharnabazus, and he had won over the hill-tribes as far east as Paphlagonia for a systematic attack upon Pharnabazus' province in 394 B.C. It is even reported that Agesilaus now dreamt of lopping all Asia Minor from the Persian empire. Not that Agesilaus was in any position to anticipate Alexander's conquests. His cavalry was weak, his siege-train non-existent, and his tactical ability did not match his undoubted powers as a strategist. From end to end the Spartan campaigns in Asia were mere predatory raids, and as the war went on it became increasingly clear that the invaders could not force a decision. Yet these campaigns fully attained their primary object of protecting the Greek towns; they demonstrated afresh the invincibility of the Greek hoplite; and they brought together the Spartans and their allies in a common enterprise. The reason for their discontinuance after 395 B.C. is to be found not in their own lack of success, but in Persia's effective counter-attacks on other fronts.

In 396 B.C. the Persian naval offensive was opened by Conon at the head of an advance squadron of 40 ships, mostly manned by Greek rowers. This flotilla was all but destroyed on its first venture, for the hitherto lethargic Spartan admiral, sallying forth from his base at Rhodes, drove it into the Carian port of Caunus and put it under blockade. The intervention of Tissaphernes and Pharnabazus, who were at this time guaranteed by armistice against an attack from Agesilaus, saved Conon from disaster, for on their approach the Spartan admiral raised the blockade. A further reinforcement of 40 ships which Conon now received enabled him to draw closer to Rhodes, where the mere news of his approach precipitated a democratic revolution and defection from Sparta. The offerings which King Artaxerxes dedicated to Athena at Lindus in memory of this event no more than repaid a just debt, for the example of rebellion set by Rhodes eventually changed the whole face of the war.

In its immediate strategic effects, however, the revolt of Rhodes was of little consequence, for Conon was unable to follow up his success. Owing to the remissness of Artaxerxes in providing funds for the payment of his fleet, the crews became mutinous and could scarcely be prevented from disbanding. It was fortunate for Conon that in 395 B.C. no counter-attack was attempted by the Spartan admiral, who was content to wait on some decisive move by Agesilaus on land. After a year's inaction Conon at length paid personal visits to Tithraustes and to the Persian king (late 395). From both of these sources he drew fresh supplies of money, and from the King he also obtained a commission for Pharna-bazus to assume the nominal supreme command by sea. In 394 B.C. Pharnabazus and Conon resumed naval operations. To secure better co-operation between the Spartan army and fleet, the ephors had left the choice of an admiral for this year in the hands of Agesilaus, who gave the command to his brother-in-law Peisander, a man who made up in resolution for what he lacked in experience. The new Spartan commander at first showed no more fight than his predecessors. A change on the home front, which we shall describe presently, had compelled Agesilaus to abandon his projected campaign in the interior of Asia Minor and to with-draw the greater part of his forces into Europe. While this retreat was in progress, Peisander was content to cover his brother-in-law's movements. But after Agesilaus' departure he offered battle near Cnidus, and with 85 ships of his own engaged the Persian fleet, now augmented to some 100 sail (August 394). On the centenary of Lade history repeated itself. While Peisander's Peloponnesian crews gave a good account of themselves, the con-tingents drawn from the insular and Asiatic Greeks broke into a general flight, Peisander himself fell fighting, and the whole of his fleet was sunk or scattered. At one stroke the Persian navy became undisputed master of the Aegean Sea.

How are we to account for the poor spirit displayed by a Greek squadron fighting on behalf of Greek liberty against an enemy over whom the Greeks had held a moral ascendancy since Salamis? In the first place, the Persian navy was largely manned by Greek crews and led by a Greek admiral. Secondly, Sparta's insular and Asiatic dependents had come to the conclusion that the price paid by them for Spartan protection was too high. The débâcle at Cnidus completed the proof of what the revolt at Rhodes had already indicated, that in the Aegean area Sparta had come to be viewed as an oppressor rather than a defender.

Thus in the catastrophe of Cnidus we recognize the fruits of Lysander's policy of government by harmosts and decarchies. Though little is recorded of the actual performance of these rulers, such evidence as we have plainly shows that they generally followed the example of the Thirty Tyrants at Athens. True enough, after Lysander's fall in 402 B.C. the ephors allowed the dependent cities to revert to their previous form of government, and it is not unlikely that they diminished the overseas garrisons. But this arrangement was overturned by Agesilaus, who restored the system of Lysander in all its essential features. In following out this policy the Spartan king did not act at Lysander's dictation, neither did he have recourse to Lysander's sanguinary methods. But he copied Lysander's example in setting up narrow oligarchies drawn from his personal adherents. At first sight it may seem strange that Agesilaus should have repeated Lysander's mistakes. Jealous as he was of the authority which attached by right to the kingly office, he did not share Lysander's aspirations to a political dictatorship. But the king was a convinced believer in oligarchic methods of government, and though herein he acted from sentiment rather than cool calculation, he shared Lysander's excessive zeal on behalf of his personal followers. We may probably acquit Agesilaus' oligarchies of the gross excesses which marked the rule of Lysander's decarchies, but we cannot be surprised at their unpopularity, for they exercised an essentially arbitrary rule in communities which were accustomed to a democratic or at any rate a responsible form of government.

The same discontents which caused the loss of Sparta's fleet at Cnidus brought about the collapse of Sparta's overseas empire after that defeat. The appearance of Conon's victorious squadron in Aegean waters was the signal for a general rebellion against Sparta's authority, and only at a few isolated points, where sufficient garrisons had been left by Agesilaus before his departure, was Sparta's supremacy maintained. In one campaign Sparta lost the fruits of her victory over Athens and was reduced once more to the rank of a continental power.

VI. THE CORINTHIAN WAR

But the loss of her naval empire is not a full measure of the damage which Persia inflicted upon Sparta. The naval attack which obtained its decision at Cnidus was supplemented by a political offensive whose success was equally complete. In 396 B.C. Pharnabazus was encouraged by the anti-Spartan insurrection at Rhodes to try the effect of propaganda behind the Spartan fighting line. For this purpose he dispatched a Rhodian named Timocrates—presumably one of the revolutionary leaders—on a diplomatic mission to Greece. Among the states which Timocrates visited, Thebes and Corinth were already estranged from Sparta; and Argos, as usual, was ready to take part where a coalition against Sparta was in the making. At Athens the first news of naval preparations in Cyprus had roused the dormant hopes of a new empire. While Thrasybulus joined hands with the moderates in maintaining a correct attitude towards Sparta, the imperialists, led by Cephalus and Epicrates, sent unofficial messages to Susa and smuggled out men and material to Conon. In these four cities Timocrates secured the ascendancy of a party which desired an open breach with Sparta. As an earnest of Persian support the Rhodian brought with him a liberal supply of gold. The institution of payment for attendance at the Athenian Assembly may be regarded as a result of Timocrates' bounty; and it is not unlikely that personal bribery played its part in mobilizing opinion against Sparta. But we need not doubt that the promise of Persian co-operation by sea and of further rebellions among Sparta's overseas dependents were the main inducements to Sparta's enemies in Greece Proper to risk an open conflict.

The 'Corinthian War,' as this conflict came to be called, was precipitated in summer 395 B.C. by the action of Thebes in taking sides in a fortuitous frontier quarrel between the Phocians and Western Locrians, and invading the land of Phocis. Though there is no convincing evidence that this quarrel was originally fomented by the Thebans, it is clear that they overran Phocis with the deliberate intention of forcing war upon Sparta, for when the ephors in answer to an appeal from the Phocians offered to arbitrate the dispute in a council of their allies, the Thebans refused to negotiate.

In view of their commitments in Asia, the Spartans had good reason to avoid a fresh war at home; but once the war was fastened upon them they took prompt measures to carry it into the enemy country. While King Pausanias assembled the Peloponnesian army, Lysander was commissioned to raise a force of Phocians and other Central Greeks and enter Boeotia by the Cephisus valley. These rapid strokes took the Thebans unawares, for Pausanias crossed Mt Cithaeron without opposition, and Lysander was allowed to carry Orchomenus by friendly overtures and to penetrate into Boeotia as far as Haliartus. At this point Lysander planned to join forces with Pausanias, but his message was intercepted and Pausanias' march thereby delayed. Nevertheless Lysander attempted a *coup de main* upon Haliartus, only to find himself trapped between the defenders of the town and a Theban field force which hurried up to the spot. The Spartan general himself was killed and his army routed in this surprise, but had Pausanias come at once to the rescue the defeat might yet have been retrieved. The Spartan king, however, gave the Thebans time to receive reinforcements from Athens, their nearest ally, and rather than risk an engagement with an enemy who had now grown superior in numbers and morale he agreed to evacuate Boeotia under a convention.

On his return to Sparta Pausanias was put on trial and only escaped death by timely flight. The chagrin of the Spartans at the failure of the Boeotian campaign need cause no wonder, for the entire political situation was thereby altered. The quadruple alliance between Thebes, Athens, Corinth and Argos, which had been thrown out of gear by Sparta's quick initiative, was now put into working order, and a congress was convened at Corinth for the joint prosecution of the war. The first measure of the congress was to invite Sparta's remaining allies to rebellion. In the Peloponnese the appeal failed in its main purpose, but it deterred the Spartans from ordering any fresh levies for the best part of a year. In Central and Northern Greece, where Sparta's arm could no longer reach, not only the neighbours of Thebes, such as the Locrians and Euboeans, but the more distant peoples such as the Acarnanians, the Chalcidians and most of the Thessalians, joined the coalition.

In the spring of 394 B.C., while Sparta stood inactive, the new coalition assumed the offensive. A joint expedition of Boeotians and Argives co-operated with Medius of Larissa in expelling the Spartan garrison from Pharsalus, and on its way home took by surprise the fortress of Heraclea; another composite army under the Theban Ismenias drove the Phocians out of the field. These preliminary successes encouraged the coalition to force a decision by invading Laconia. At midsummer the full confederate force mustered at Corinth. Had this army advanced forthwith, it might have prevented the concentration of the enemy forces and so reduced Sparta to desperate straits. But the allies wasted time discussing tactical details, and this delay enabled the Spartans to push forward to the Isthmus, collecting their allies as they went. The decisive action of the campaign was therefore fought, not in

Laconia, but on the plain between Sicyon and Corinth; and instead of the Spartans facing hopeless odds they brought up a force of 20–25,000 men which roughly equalled that of the enemy. The battle of Nemea was a typical encounter of the pre-scientific age of Greek warfare. As the armies moved up into action the opposing lines edged away to the right, so that each right wing eventually overlapped and enfiladed the adversary's left. At one end of the field the Argives and Corinthians overbore Sparta's allies; at the other the Spartans outfought the Athenians, who broke away in disorder, despite the efforts of Thrasybulus to rally them. Thus far the battle remained drawn; but the Spartans checked their pursuit in Cromwellian fashion and caught in the flank three successive enemy divisions as these returned separately to their base, inflicting heavy losses upon each. The action of Nemea was in so far decisive as it deterred the confederates from ever attempting another offensive on a large scale.

From henceforth the Spartans maintained the initiative in the land operations of the war. But they were prevented from exploiting their advantage by the extensive fortifications of the Isthmus, behind which the beaten enemy forces soon rallied. In addition to its own ring wall Corinth had a pair of 'Long Walls' to connect it with Lechaeum on the Corinthian Gulf, and a chain of forts to guard the defiles in the mountainous tract between the city and its eastern port of Cenchreae. Before attacking this position the Spartans decided to await the result of a new invasion of Boeotia which befel some two or three weeks after Nemea.

In the spring of 394 B.C. the ephors, believing that all available men were required for home defence, recalled Agesilaus from Asia. The Spartan king, however loth to abandon his crusade against Persia, obeyed the home government's summons with prompt loyalty. Leaving only a few garrisons in Asia he made a rapid march home through Macedonia and Thessaly with the greater part of his forces. In Thessaly the horsemen of the cities allied to Thebes hovered round his column but dared not engage him at close quarters. Thus Agesilaus arrived unscathed in Central Greece, where he received reinforcements from Phocis and Orchomenus and a division which came from the Peloponnese across the Corinthian Gulf. Advancing with this combined force into Boeotia he was brought to battle in the gap of Coronea by a general levy of the coalition states. In this encounter, as at Nemea, each right wing routed its opponents; the victorious Spartans thereupon turned inward to cut off the winners on the other flank; but the Theban division thus intercepted rallied and despite heavy casualties cut its way clear through the Spartan obstruction. In effect, Coronea was a Theban victory, for it definitely stayed Agesilaus' advance. Having left a small force to protect Orchomenus and Phocis and disbanded the veterans of his Asiatic campaigns, the Spartan king led back the rest of his force to the Peloponnese by way of the Corinthian Gulf.

The failure of Agesilaus' Boeotian campaign left the Spartans no effective point of attack except at Corinth, which was the keystone of the enemy coalition. A tedious war of positions ensued round this city. At first the Spartans tried the effect of systematically ravaging the Corinthian territory. By 393 B.C. the Corinthian landowners began to agitate for peace. But the Corinthian war-party met this clamour by instituting a massacre among its opponents and calling in a garrison from Argos. For the rest of the war Corinth remained under Argive control: nominally it was even absorbed into the Argive state and stood to Argos as Acharnae or Marathon stood to Athens. Some Corinthian dissentients nevertheless contrived to admit a Spartan force within the Long Walls. Having gained a foothold within the Corinthian lines, the Spartans not only defeated a determined attempt by a large confederate force to dislodge them, but made a clear gap through the Long Walls, and captured the ports of Lechaeum on the western, of Sidus and Crommyon on the eastern seaboards of Corinth.

The blockade thus established round Corinth was relieved in 392 B.C. by the Athenians, who realized that if Corinth fell the way would lie open for a Spartan invasion of Attica. Lechaeum and the Long Walls were recaptured by the Athenian hoplite levy, and the Long Walls were repaired by an Athenian labour corps. The pressure upon Corinth was further eased by an Athenian flying column which penetrated the Peloponnese as far as Arcadia. The leader of this column was a soldier of fortune named Iphicrates, who may be regarded as the prototype of the fourth-century *condottieri*. His soldiers, professionals like himself, constituted the first of those light corps which henceforth played a substantial part in Greek military history. While they dispensed with the expensive equipment of the hoplite, these 'peltasts' were drilled with no less care than the heavy troops and under favourable circumstances could defeat them in a set combat. Iphicrates' corps at once established an ascendancy over Sparta's allies, and its forays must have seriously hampered Sparta's operations against Corinth.

The campaigns of 393–2 B.C. on the Greek mainland thus ended in a stalemate. We must now follow the course of the naval war from the battle of Cnidus. In 394 B.C. the victorious Persian fleet sailed up the east Aegean coast, expelling the Spartan garrisons as it went. In 393 B.C. it made a prolonged cruise in European waters. After a preliminary descent on the coast of Laconia and on Cythera, where an Athenian governor was left in charge, Pharnabazus and Conon repaired to the Isthmus and contracted a formal treaty of alliance between Persia and the enemies of Sparta in Greece. Having made a parting gift of money to his new allies, Pharnabazus sailed home. But Conon obtained permission from his colleague to take a strong detachment to Athens and to employ the crews and the remainder of Pharnabazus' funds in reconstructing the Long Walls. The repair of these fortifications had been commenced in 394 B.C. with the help of Thebes and other allies, but owing to lack of funds and labour the work had proceeded but slowly. With Conon's assistance the Long Walls were practically completed in 393 B.C., though they did not receive the finishing touches until 391 B.C. It is not unlikely that the sudden emission of gold coins from the mint of Thebes at this period was an effect of the Persian subsidies[1].

VII. A NEW PACT BETWEEN SPARTA AND PERSIA

The visit of Conon to Athens had a far-reaching effect on the war. After the restoration of the Long Walls the Athenians were free to take a lesser interest in the politics of the mainland and to devote themselves again to maritime expansion. The impulse to this renewal of the old imperial policy was given by Conon himself, who stayed on in Athens after the departure of his fleet and resumed active Athenian citizenship. Though he failed in an attempt to negotiate a treaty with the Syracusan despot Dionysius, Conon succeeded in contracting alliances with several of the Aegean cities recently liberated by him. These states, having forfeited the protection of Sparta, had now to consider whether they could stand alone. True enough, they had little to fear from Pharnabazus, who had promised to respect the autonomy of the towns set free by him and Conon, and not to impose garrisons upon them. But though Pharnabazus might be trusted, there was little likelihood of other Persian governors keeping their hands off. In view of these risks the Aegean cities began to cast about for fresh alliances. One short-lived League, in which Rhodes, Cnidus,

---

[1] See the Volume of Plates ii, 4, *j*.

Iasus, Samos, Ephesus and Byzantium were associated, has come to our notice through its coins[1]. The common type of these pieces, Heracles strangling the snakes, was evidently borrowed from Thebes, which had recently adopted it for the Boeotian coins as a symbol of liberty. But the general tendency among the Aegean states was to seek a *rapprochement* with Athens. In 393 B.C., or shortly after, Rhodes, Cos, Cnidus, Carpathus, Eretria are known to have made fresh alliances with Athens, and the same probably holds true of Ephesus, Chios, Erythrae, Mitylene and some other towns. At the same time the Athenians resumed possession of Lemnos, Imbros and Scyros, and by 390 B.C. they had recovered the sacred island of Delos.

This gathering of the fruits of Persia's victory by Athens afforded Sparta an opportunity of creating a rift between Persia and her Greek allies. In pursuit of this war-aim, the ephors decided to write off their overseas possessions, which in any case appeared irrecoverable, and to execute another *volte-face* in their Persian policy. At the end of 393 B.C. a Spartan envoy named Antalcidas visited Tiribazus, the new satrap of Lydia, and protested that Sparta, not Athens, was his friend. In proof thereof he declared that Sparta was now prepared to cede all the Greek cities of Asia to Persia and stipulated nothing beyond the enjoyment of their autonomy for the other states of Greece, whereas Athens was plainly reviving the anti-Persian imperialism of Cimon's age. With these arguments Antalcidas carried his point against the pleas of a counter-embassy from Athens, Thebes, Corinth and Argos. In proof of his conversion Tiribazus at once supplied the Spartan with money for the equipment of a new fleet and arrested Conon, the head of the Athenian mission, as a deserter from the Persian navy.

Tiribazus' reversal of policy was supported by the logic of facts, and it was eventually confirmed by the Persian court. But when the Lydian satrap went to Susa to obtain a royal warrant for his procedure he found that the King was little disposed to transfer his affections at such short notice. Far from sanctioning Tiribazus' change of front, Artaxerxes detained him at court and sent an officer named Struthas, with Ionia for his province, to resume active co-operation with Athens (end of 392). Meantime Conon escaped from prison and returned to his patron Evagoras, but, before he could render further aid to the Athenians, he fell sick and died.

Stung by the rejection of their advances, the ephors prepared

1 See the Volume of Plates ii, 4, *k* to *p*.

to resume active warfare with Persia, and at the same time opened
negotiations with their enemies in Greece. In the winter of 392–
1 B.C. they summoned a peace congress to Sparta and proposed
a general settlement on the basis of 'autonomy for all.' Under
this convenient formula, which was henceforth impressed into
service wherever diplomatists met to settle the map of Greece,
Sparta offered to let Athens complete her fortifications, rebuild
her fleet and retain her new connections with the Aegean states;
from Argos she required the liberation of Corinth and from Thebes
a guarantee not to coerce Orchomenus. The Thebans, who had
come to consider that the war was a luxury beyond their means,
assented to these conditions; the Argives refused on behalf of
themselves and Corinth. At Athens the case for acceptance was
put in a still extant speech by the envoy Andocides, who had no
difficulty in showing that Sparta was offering a good bargain.
But his arguments were met with the familiar cries, 'we want
back our cleruchies,' and 'the democracy is in danger.' Andocides and his colleagues were sent into exile for their pains; the
terms which they brought from Sparta were rejected.

Had the Assembly voted for peace, Argos must certainly have
given way, and a settlement more equitable than that of 386 B.C.
would have been the result. As it was, Athens dragged Thebes
back into the war, and hostilities were resumed in 391 B.C. along
the whole front. At first the fighting went in favour of Sparta.
King Agesilaus once more pierced the Long Walls of Corinth,
while his brother Teleutias with a Spartan fleet recaptured
Lechaeum. In 390 B.C. the king passed through the gap in the
Long Walls to the eastern side of the Isthmus and wrested from
the Argives the stewardship of the Isthmian festival then in process of celebration. After dealing this *coup de théâtre* he returned
to the Corinthian Gulf and carried the posts of Peiraeum and
Oenoe in the extreme north of the Corinthian territory. By these
captures he deprived Corinth of its remaining pasture-grounds
and severed its communications with Boeotia.

Corinth was now in greater danger than ever; but once more
the Athenians came to the rescue. Shortly after the fall of Peiraeum the corps of Iphicrates caught a company of 600 Spartans
marching to Lechaeum without the usual flank-guard of cavalry.
Choosing their own range and rallying promptly from each
counter-attack, the peltasts had the hoplites at their mercy; under
the fire of their javelins the Spartan company broke into pieces
and was all but destroyed. Though this encounter was no true
measure of the relative merits of weight and speed in battle, yet

by its moral effect it profoundly influenced the course of the war.
A separate peace overture which the Boeotians had been making
to King Agesilaus was hastily withdrawn. On the other hand, the
prestige of the Spartan fighting forces was so much lowered that
they could scarcely maintain discipline among Sparta's auxiliaries.

After the battle of Lechaeum Iphicrates followed up his success by recapturing the posts of Oenoe, Sidus and Crommyon.
The blockade of Corinth was thus once more broken. But Iphicrates' exploits did not lure Athens or her allies into more
ambitious ventures. Once Corinth had been made safe, they
remained content to hold their ground. On the other hand, the
Spartans were henceforth reduced to making mere demonstra-
tions. In 389 B.C. and 388 B.C. Agesilaus made two successful
forays into Acarnania. By these expeditions he confirmed the
loyalty of the Achaeans, whose outlying possessions on the north
coast of the Gulf were now restored to them, and made the Acarnanians purchase peace at the price of their independence; but he
derived no strategic advantage from them. In 387 B.C. Agesipolis,
the successor of King Pausanias, invaded Argolis but occupied no
permanent posts there.

The only other land operation that requires notice was an
expedition which the Spartans directed against Struthas in 391 B.C.
Its commander Thibron was even more unfortunate than in
399 B.C. Having recovered possession of Ephesus for a base, he
made plundering incursions into the Maeander valley, but was
presently killed with a great part of his force in a surprise attack
by Struthas' horse. This was Sparta's last Anabasis into Asia.

The issue of the Corinthian War was thus left to be fought out
on sea. While Artaxerxes was practising his usual economies by
laying up his ships, Athens in misplaced reliance on him had
dispensed with a fleet of her own. This gave the Spartans a new
opportunity. With Tiribazus' subsidies they had built a fresh
squadron which eventually totalled 27 sail. In 390 B.C. this
flotilla recaptured Samos and Cnidus and made preparations for
the reconquest of Rhodes. But here its achievements came to an
end. In 389 B.C. a new Athenian fleet of 40 sail appeared under
Thrasybulus. In this last campaign of his the hero of Phyle made
no direct attack upon the Spartans. His chief preoccupation was
to raise funds for the upkeep of his squadron. To this end he re-
imposed the customs duties of the Delian Confederacy on the
cities which had again allied with Athens, and plundered the
territories of the rest. The penury of Thrasybulus, and the
methods by which he relieved it, epitomize the decline and fall of

the revived Athenian Empire. They were fatal to Thrasybulus himself, who was killed during a piratical raid on Aspendus in southern Asia Minor, and to his treasurer Ergocles, whom the Athenians subsequently executed on a charge of extortion and embezzlement. Nevertheless Thrasybulus achieved some important successes. In the northern Aegean he enrolled Thasos as an ally. By winning over Byzantium and Chalcedon and securing the friendship of the Thracian chieftains on either side of the Gallipoli peninsula, he restored the free use of the Black Sea route to Athens. With the help of the Mityleneans he conquered all the minor towns of Lesbos. In addition, the mere presence of his fleet prevented fresh conquests by the Spartan squadron.

In 388–7 B.C. the centre of operations shifted to the Dardanelles, where Dercyllidas had retained the key positions of Sestos and Abydos for Sparta. Here again the Athenians got the upper hand, for under Iphicrates' leadership they penned up Dercyllidas' successor in Abydos.

But the decision in the naval war was imposed not by Athens but by Persia, and Persia's final stroke was delivered in aid of Sparta against Athens. The reason for Persia's ultimate rally to the side of Sparta is to be found in a new turn of events on Cyprus, where King Evagoras resumed his attack upon the communities, both Greek and Phoenician, which had not yet submitted to him, and thus roused the suspicions of his Persian overlord. In defence of the threatened cities Artaxerxes mobilized a fresh army under the new Lydian satrap Autophradates, and a fleet under a native dynast named Hecatomnus who had succeeded Tissaphernes in the satrapy of Caria. Evagoras in turn invoked the aid of the Athenians, and they with greater chivalry than discretion sent two small squadrons to his support (389 and 387 B.C.). The warning which Antalcidas had given to Tiribazus about the dangers of a revived Athenian Empire thus came true. In 388 B.C. moreover the same envoy was sent by the ephors to Susa to drive home his point. Artaxerxes now required no further convincing. To give effect to his new friendship with Sparta he recalled Pharnabazus from Phrygia and reinstated Tiribazus in Lydia.

In 387 B.C. Tiribazus had a small squadron ready to co-operate with the Spartans. In the same year Dionysius of Syracuse, who had in past years received support from Sparta (p. 131), sent 20 ships in answer to an appeal for assistance. Antalcidas, taking charge of the combined squadrons of Sparta, Persia and Syracuse, 80 sail in all, was now able to deal a decisive blow. With

this overwhelming force he entered the Dardanelles and cut off
the Athenian fleet.

The way to a general peace was thus laid open, for the Athenians, who had previously been the chief obstacle to a settlement,
now became most eager for it. The new empire for whose sake
they had prolonged the war had proved a burden rather than a
benefit. Besides the contributions levied upon the allies, the
upkeep of their navy had entailed a property-tax and increased
customs duties upon themselves. Athenian commerce had suffered at the hands of a flotilla established by the Spartans at Aegina,
and the Piraeus itself had been raided by this force (387). Thus
the policy of naval expansion, which the landowners of Attica had
steadily opposed, fell into temporary disfavour with the urban
population of Athens and Piraeus. A contemporary comedy of
Aristophanes, the *Plutus*, shows that the old spirit of adventure,
to which he had formerly given expression in his *Birds*, was for
the time being dead: the dominant issue for the Athenians was
now to make ends meet. At the news of Antalcidas' successes the
price of corn rose sharply and completed the disillusionment of
the imperialists.

Towards the end of 387 B.C. Tiribazus summoned delegates
from all the belligerents to Sardes to receive conditions of peace;
and the delegates came. The terms proved to be the same as
Antalcidas had suggested in 393 B.C.: all the Asiatic mainland
and the island of Cyprus to be the King's; Lemnos, Imbros and
Scyros to remain Athenian dependencies, as of old; all other Greek
states, great and small, to receive autonomy.

When the delegates referred this *paix octroyée* to their respective
states, there was some demur on the part of the Argives, who
wanted to keep Corinth in their own pocket, and of the Thebans,
who apprehended that in the name of autonomy they would have
to dissolve the Boeotian League. But Athens gave these
recalcitrants no support, and the mere mobilization of a general
Peloponnesian levy by King Agesilaus sufficed to disarm their
opposition. Early in 386 B.C. the peace was everywhere accepted
and carried into effect: the Athenians dissolved their alliances in the
Aegean area, the Argives withdrew from Corinth, and the Thebans conceded full independence to the other Boeotian cities.
Thus the Corinthian War was concluded by a settlement which
was sometimes styled the 'Peace of Antalcidas,' but was commonly
known by the more appropriate name of the 'King's Peace.'

CHAPTER III

THE SECOND ATHENIAN LEAGUE

I. GENERAL CONDITION OF GREECE IN 386 B.C.

OF the diplomatic settlements in Greek History none has been more severely censured than the 'King's Peace.' Six years after its conclusion the Athenian pamphleteer Isocrates indicted it in his most famous treatise, the *Panegyricus*, as a national disgrace; and the general verdict of historians has found a true bill on this count. The procedure by which a Persian satrap communicated his king's sovereign pleasure to the Greek belligerents was in itself a humiliation, and the actual terms of the peace were even more dishonouring. In ceding the cities of the Asia Minor seaboard to Persia the Greeks alienated one of the finest portions of their heritage. These cities had not only maintained a close intercourse with their homeland, but had in a large measure imparted their culture to it: by any test they constituted an integral part of the Greek nation. Moreover the state to which the Greeks forfeited this prize was a power whose civilization had been arrested while Greek culture advanced by leaps and bounds. In the art of war more particularly Persia had been completely outdistanced by the Greeks. Her horsemen were still formidable; but no Persian army or fleet would dare to match itself against the Greeks in set battle. Greek admirals in command of Greek crews had obtained for Persia her recent naval victories; Greek mercenaries had formed the backbone of Cyrus' insurrectionary force, and henceforward loyal and disloyal satraps competed for the services of Greek auxiliaries. That a state which was as dependent on its Greek soldiers as the decadent Roman Empire was on its Germans should nevertheless dictate political terms to the Greek people was a strange paradox and a scathing commentary on Hellenic statesmanship.

For this condition of things, as Isocrates rightly emphasized, the blame fell chiefly upon Sparta. It was Sparta that set the example of bargaining away Greek assets in order to enlist foreign allies against a Greek adversary, that suggested and enforced the conditions of the King's Peace. But Sparta's adversaries were thickly tarred with the same brush. The war of which the King's Peace was the outcome was largely of their making; it sprang from trivial discontents or selfish desires of aggrandizement; and it stabbed Sparta in the back at the very moment when she had established a new front against Persia in defence of national Greek interests.

But however the blame should be apportioned, it must not be supposed that the guilty parties took Isocrates' advice and repented. Nay rather they contracted a habit of invoking Persia as a party to their quarrels, and it was more by good luck than by good management that Persia was prevented from exploiting these quarrels any further. In the fourth century the crime of 'medism' became respectable in Greece, and it remained in honour so long as the Mede remained to medize with.

Again, however rigorously we may condemn the betrayal of Asiatic Greece to Persia, we must acknowledge that for the Greek homeland the King's Peace afforded quite a tolerable settlement. The principle of 'autonomy for all' was in theory an ideal ruling for the composure of Greek disputes, and the practical interpretation which Sparta put upon it gave little ground for discontent. True enough, the ephors relaxed the rule in their own favour when they imposed tribute upon some of the Aegean islands which remained attached to them, and they overstrained it in dissolving the Boeotian League. By the constitution of this league Boeotia was divided into eleven electoral districts, each of which supplied an equal quota of money or soldiers for federal purposes, and an equal number of representatives to the federal court, council and executive. Of these constituencies no less than four were made up out of Theban territory; the federal congress was held in Thebes; and the other cities had to find the subsistence-money for their deputies. It therefore appears probable that the Thebans usually had a working majority at the congress. But in view of the superior size and central position of Thebes this arrangement did not constitute an unfair advantage. It is significant too that, except for a monopoly of coinage, Thebes conceded to the other cities their fair share of executive functions. Moreover, though the federal authorities probably had full control of Boeotian foreign policy, they do not appear to have unduly restricted local self-government. In breaking up the Boeotian League, therefore, the Spartans did Greek autonomy no service, and a disservice to Greek unity. On the other hand, they were fully justified in asserting the independence of Corinth against Argos, and in preventing Athens from converting her maritime allies into tributaries.

In any case, the King's Peace provided the belligerent Greeks with a *modus vivendi*, and this for the time being was the one thing needful. The Corinthian War, treading on the heels of a yet greater conflict, had aggravated the unsettlement of Greece and threatened to afflict it with a chronic unrest. The most characteristic symptom of the ensuing period was the growth of the habit of professional soldiering among the Greeks. This habit was an almost unmitigated evil. It withdrew from productive enterprise the most vigorous and resourceful young men and disseminated the desire of living not by work but by plunder. On the high seas piracy again became rife; within the cities the struggle for political power grew fiercer as this power was more and more perverted to the economic exploitation of party victories. In the more orderly states the conflict assumed the comparatively harmless form of a scramble for state doles and pay; in the unruly ones contending parties made play with the almost meaningless catchwords of 'oligarchy' and 'democracy' in order to expropriate each other. While the citizens thus gambled for their livelihood, honest industry was relegated to metics or slaves. To the states which employed them the mercenaries were a ruinous source of expense. Hence the beneficent expenditure on public buildings which characterized the sixth and fifth centuries became more rare in the fourth. Outside the great national sanctuaries such as Olympia, Delphi and Epidaurus, where money for new construction was still forthcoming, the temple of Athena Alea at Tegea is the only notable piece of architecture in Greece in the early fourth century (see below, chap. XVII). To raise the necessary revenues, not only had direct imposts and 'liturgies' to be increased, but harmful underhand taxes such as the sale of monopolies and depreciation of coinage (by the reduction of standards) became increasingly common, and rich men were liable to have their property confiscated with or without legal pretext.

Yet Greece had economic opportunities in plenty. Her industry, though lacking the fillip of fresh technical inventions, remained supreme in the artistic excellence of its products. Agricultural methods were being improved by pioneers who substituted for the conventional biennial fallow a three-year shift with a restorative course of leguminous plants or artificial grasses. At Athens, if not elsewhere in Greece, commerce was being stimulated by bankers who attracted the increasing stocks of gold and silver and out of these deposits advanced capital for shipping enterprise. These improvements in method moreover were accompanied by increased openings for trade. In the Greek lands a growing

refinement of taste created a demand for more costly food, housing
and furniture. Abroad the decline of the Etruscan market was
compensated by the growth of commerce with Carthage and the
revival of the Black Sea trade. Consequently for those who retained old habits of industry the fourth century was a period of
economic stability or even prosperity. The small landowners, so
far as is known, held their own, except perhaps round a few towns
like Athens where enriched manufacturers or traders seeking to
invest their gains in real estate bought them up. The small captains of industry were notoriously prosperous; and the large
traders and manufacturers, though exposed to graver risks, often
realized handsome profits. Few Greek communities, if any, had
a happier fourth-century history than the small town of Megara,
which eschewed political flutters and attended strictly to business.

Economic recovery thus lay within reach of Greece. But first
of all the country required a respite from predatory politics.

In narrating the sequel to the King's Peace we shall first consider its effects on Persia and her new subjects. From Persia's
standpoint the peace was a godsend. The example of rebellion
which Evagoras had recently set in Cyprus showed ominous signs
of spreading. To say nothing of the naval assistance provided
by Athens (see above, p. 53), Hecatomnus the Carian satrap had
secretly supplied Evagoras with money, and King Achoris, who had
recently consolidated the rebel authority in Egypt, entered into
overt alliance with him. So long as his attention was riveted on the
war in the Aegean, King Artaxerxes appeared unable to cope with
these insurrections; but on conclusion of the King's Peace he at
once set about to reduce the rebel chiefs. In 385 an army of
unknown composition was conducted by Tithraustes and Pharnabazus against Achoris. After a three years' campaign, the scene
of which was apparently laid in Palestine, the Persian force retired
beaten. Its defeat was followed by the secession of the native
ruler of Cilicia and of the city of Tyre. The revolt of Tyre was of
special importance in that it strengthened Evagoras' naval position
and united two natural adversaries, Greeks and Phoenicians, in
a common rebellion. But in the meantime the satrap Tiribazus
had been raising an army and fleet among his new Greek subjects
on the Aegean coast. In 382 this force was sent to recover Cyprus.
In its first campaign it displayed poor discipline and effected
nothing. But in 381 Greek fought it out with Greek in a naval
battle off Citium in which Evagoras was decisively beaten. Dissensions which broke out among the Persian commanders prevented them from exploiting their victory to the full. In the

ensuing year Tiribazus' successor Orontes was content to make a truce with Evagoras which confirmed him in his kingship at Salamis, and the attack upon Achoris was apparently not renewed. Nevertheless the rebel coalition was effectively broken. Evagoras was henceforth content to retain the sovereignty of Salamis, and after his death in 374 his son Nicocles abode by the settlement of 380.

The foregoing account shows that the Asiatic Greeks were made at once to feel the full weight of Persian domination. The Greek levies, if Isocrates is to be believed, were treated by their new masters with barbaric severity. To the blood-tax which Persia exacted so promptly money imposts were added, and in the citadels of some towns Persian garrisons were stationed. Yet burdens hardly less grievous had been imposed upon the Greek cities by Sparta; indeed in the long run the Persian yoke probably proved the lighter. Though the satraps of Lydia and Phrygia did not follow the example of the Carian ruler Hecatomnus and his son Mausolus, who set up their court in the Greek city of Halicarnassus and attracted Greek artists and men of letters to their residence, yet they found it worth while to conciliate subjects whose economic and military aptitudes were a source of strength to themselves. Whether the Greek towns under Persian rule experienced any general revival of material welfare cannot be ascertained; but the local prosperity of Cyzicus is strikingly attested by its copious issues of electrum coins[1], which circulated through Greece in competition with the Persian darics. In any case, for better or worse, the Asiatic Greeks were united to Persia by what appeared to be a permanent tie. For their own part they made no attempt at rebellion, and until the coming of the Macedonians none of their European compatriots stirred a finger to obtain their release.

II SPARTA'S POLICY OF PRECAUTIONS

While the first clause of the King's Peace effectively secured the permanent subjugation of the Asiatic Greeks, the second clause failed from the outset to guarantee universal autonomy for the remainder: indeed the very power which had imposed this clause set the example of violating it. By this disregard of her own rulings Sparta plunged Greece into a series of fresh crises and fired the train which exploded her own supremacy. Her inconsistency appears all the stranger, in that the settlement of

[1] See H. v. Fritze, *Die Elektronprägung von Kyzikos*, Nomisma vii (1912).

386 B.C. completely confirmed her authority in Greece. While Argos resumed its policy of self-isolation, Corinth rejoined the Peloponnesian League. The Boeotian cities, not excluding Thebes, entered into conventions with Sparta which bound them to send contingents when asked for; and the states of Euboea followed suit. So surely was Sparta's ascendancy restored that shortly after 386 B.C. she was able to group her dependents in the Peloponnese and Central Greece into a number of administrative provinces, upon each of which an equal quota of military liabilities was imposed.

Why then did Sparta not respect her own settlement? Because she let herself be perverted by the personal prejudices of Agesilaus. The undoubted ability displayed by this king in the recent war had invested him with an authority which he made all the more lasting and effective for exercising it through strictly constitutional channels and with due respect to the prerogatives of the ephors. In matters of imperial policy Agesilaus remained for many years an adviser whose counsel was equal to law. Unfortunately for Sparta, he had taken no warning from the collapse of Sparta's overseas empire, but persisted in the discredited policy of interfering with the constitutions of the dependent states and of imposing 'safe' governments upon them.

Of pretexts for the accomplishment of his purpose Agesilaus found no lack. The party spirit in Greek cities which had been raised to fever pitch by the Peloponnesian War was again inflamed by the Corinthian War. In the Peloponnese more particularly the warfare of factions continued after the general peace had been signed. By way of gaining a party advantage certain groups labelled themselves friends of Sparta, accused their adversaries of disloyalty to Sparta, and ended by inviting Spartan interference. Of the details of these quarrels and of Sparta's interventions little is recorded; but we may gather from certain known instances how little regard Sparta paid to the autonomy of her dependents in regulating their affairs.

In the autumn of 385 the ephors sent a point-blank request to the Arcadian city of Mantinea to demolish its fortifications, and proceeded to enforce their demand by laying siege to the town. King Agesipolis, who commanded this punitive expedition, took advantage of a spate in the river Ophis to dam up the waters to flood level and by their sudden release to carry away the upper courses of the ring-wall which were built of unburnt brick. Having thus reduced the Mantineans he cantoned them out among the four or five villages out of which the city had been

originally compacted, and upon this aggregate of scattered settlements he imposed an oligarchic government. In defence of these
measures it may be urged that Mantinea had been seriously
disaffected during the recent war; and Xenophon may be right in
asserting that its former inhabitants benefited by residing nearer
to their plots of land 'and being rid of the troublesome demagogues.' But Sparta's precautions for its future loyalty were a
manifest infringement of Mantinea's autonomy.

In 383 Sparta began a series of coercive measures against
Phlius, a town which was of some strategic importance, in that it
commanded one of the subsidiary roads to the Isthmus, and had,
like Mantinea, come under suspicion of disloyalty. A pretext for
intervention was furnished by some political exiles who appealed
to Sparta for reinstatement. The Phliasian government readmitted
the exiles on Sparta's demand, but failed to satisfy their claims to
restitution of confiscated property, and thus drove them to renew
their solicitations in Sparta. In the autumn of 381 Agesilaus, who
had friends among the appellants, obtained authority to conduct
an expedition against Phlius. After the rejection of his ultimatum,
which called upon the Phliasians to admit a Spartan garrison into
their citadel, he invested the town. By a notable effort of endurance
the besieged held out for twenty months, but in the spring of 379
they were starved into surrender. A committee drawn in equal
numbers from the townspeople and the exiles was appointed by
Agesilaus to draft a new constitution and 'to determine who
should live and who should die.' We need not doubt that actually
the émigrés had it all their own way in constitution-making and in
dealing out life and death.

In 382 the Spartans involved themselves and their allies in a
more serious war on the northern confines of Greece, where the
cities of Chalcidice under the leadership of Olynthus had established a powerful confederation. This League, which probably had
its origin at the time of the Peloponnesian War and was primarily
directed against Athens, was carried on after the fall of the
Athenian Empire as a means of resisting the occasional forays of
plundering Thracians and the more systematic encroachments of
Macedonia, whose enterprising king Archelaus (413–399) had
constructed two great instruments of conquest, a regular army
and military roads, and lost no opportunity of using them. A
period of usurpations and disputed successions, which set in after
Archelaus' death and again reduced Macedon to a mere aggregate of baronies, gave the Chalcidians an opportunity of defending
their seaboard by invading the hinterland. Taking advantage of

the domestic difficulties of King Amyntas III (*c.* 393–369 B.C.), they not only extorted commercial concessions but acquired a piece of borderland from him; and when Amyntas repented of his bargain and sought to recover the borderland they retaliated by taking his capital Pella and a further wide strip of Macedonian territory. By 382 B.C. the Chalcidians had also entered into negotiations with the tribes of western Thrace with a view to possessing the gold mines of Mt Pangaeus, and they were on the point of contracting alliances with Athens and Thebes. These remarkable successes made it appear certain that the League could eventually draw in all the Greeks on the Macedonian coast; and although some important cities such as Amphipolis and Mende do not appear to have joined it, yet even those communities which resisted absorption admitted that their aversion to the League would wear off sooner or later. But the League would not be kept waiting. It prepared to annex the outstanding towns by compulsion only to find that the recalcitrants had superior force on their side. Two of the threatened cities, Acanthus and Apollonia, had appealed to Sparta and secured her assistance.

It need hardly be pointed out that the Acanthian envoy who described the League as a danger to Sparta's supremacy in Greece was exaggerating. On general grounds of policy, therefore, Sparta had little interest in checking the League's growth. The question whether she had any legal right to coerce the League is not so easy to determine. So far as is known, the League put no restraint upon the local liberties of its constituent members, except that it controlled their foreign and military policy, and that it compelled them to grant to each other full freedom of intercourse and inter-marriage. The League as such therefore did not violate the right of any Greek city to be autonomous. On the other hand, the forcible incorporation of Acanthus and Apollonia into the League constituted a manifest breach of the principle of autonomy. But unless the League was a signatory of the King's Peace—a point on which we have no information—it is not clear whether Sparta had any *locus standi* in the case.

Before taking action on the appeal of Acanthus and Apollonia the Spartans referred their suit to a congress of allies. From their allies they got more support for a war policy than might have been expected. Therefore, without waiting to try the effect of a friendly remonstrance upon the Chalcidians, they dispatched an advance force to garrison the threatened towns and in its wake sent a general Peloponnesian levy under Agesilaus' brother Teleutias (summer 382). Begun in a hurry, the Chalcidian War ended at leisure. With the help of King Amyntas and of a vassal prince from the Macedonian uplands named Derdas, whose horsemen outfought the excellent Chalcidian cavalry, Teleutias beat the federal army out of the field, and in 381 he was able to invest Olynthus. But the besiegers had to spend two years before Olynthus, and during the siege they lost two of their commanders. In summer 381 Teleutias was killed in a sortie; some twelve months later his successor, King Agesipolis, died of fever. In 379 the Olynthians were at last starved into surrender. Their League was dissolved, and its individual members were enrolled as dependent allies of Sparta.

Unlike the expeditions against Mantinea and Phlius, the Chalcidian War could be justified on better grounds than mere military precaution. The disruption of the League, though in itself no more defensible than the dissolution of the Boeotian federation, was of no lasting consequence, for a few years later the Chalcidians affederated themselves again. In the conduct of the war the Spartans showed unusual consideration for their allies. Besides consulting them on the expediency of making war, they gave them the opportunity of commuting their military liabilities for a money payment which was used to hire mercenary substitutes. But the effort required to win the war placed a considerable strain upon the Spartan alliance. Moreover the opening moves of the war gave rise to an incident which finally discredited Sparta as a champion of Greek liberties.

In summer 382 a section of the advance force proceeding to Chalcidice happened to halt near Thebes on its way through Central Greece. Its commander Phoebidas was approached by one of the 'polemarchs' or chief magistrates of Thebes named Leontiades, who offered to deliver the city into Sparta's hands. Phoebidas, who was anxious to win a reputation *quand même*, fell in with this proposal. By collusion with Leontiades he stole into Thebes during the siesta hour and made his way unnoticed to the citadel, which at that season was in sole possession of the worshippers at a special women's festival. Thus Phoebidas won Thebes *ambulando*. But the crucial question remained whether the Spartan government would uphold his action. First impressions at Sparta were hostile to Phoebidas, if only because he had exceeded his orders. But Leontiades, who would have had to pay dear for his treason if Thebes had recovered freedom to punish him, went in person to Sparta to scare the ephors with stories of Theban disloyalty; and Agesilaus, whose constitutional fondness for 'acts of precaution' was reinforced in this case by an unsleeping grudge against the captured city, cunningly suggested that the acid test was whether Phoebidas had not brought gain to Sparta. Eventually the ephors decided to maintain a permanent garrison at Thebes. According to a story of doubtful value Phoebidas himself was put on trial and heavily fined. If so, the fine was probably never collected; in any case, his work was not disowned.

In extenuation of Sparta's policy it might be urged that the anti-Spartan party at Thebes was still on even terms with Sparta's adherents, and that their leader Ismenias, so far from lending a hand against the Chalcidians, was negotiating a treaty with them. But assuming that Thebes had evil intentions, we cannot admit that she had the power to give effect to them, as in 395 B.C. In 382 she had no support from her former partners in the Corinthian War, and she had lost control over the other Boeotian towns, all of whom had advertized their independence by the issue of separate municipal coinages[1]. Under such conditions Thebes was no more formidable than Mantinea or Phlius. On the other hand, Sparta proceeded to aggravate her breach of faith by the execution of Ismenias at the orders of a court composed of three Spartans and one delegate from each allied city. Not only was this assize absolutely illegal, but the prisoner's alleged offence, the receipt of money from Persia, was one which Sparta least of all Greek powers could afford to reprobate.

Whatever strategical advantages accrued to Sparta from her occupation of Thebes were more than counterbalanced by the moral detriment which she thereby suffered. Not only judicious critics such as Isocrates but avowed partisans like Xenophon denounced Sparta's treachery. It is doubtful whether any other single act of Sparta went so far to lower her prestige. Conversely the Thebans were not crippled by Sparta's sudden blow but stimulated to an effort of self-deliverance which changed the whole political map of Greece.

III. THE RISE OF THEBES

At first sight indeed Sparta's authority appeared to have been greatly strengthened by her new conquest. Following up their success, the Spartans threw a garrison into Thespiae on some pretext or other, and invited the former inhabitants of Plataea, who had long been domiciled in Attica with a modified Athenian franchise, to resume possession of their city. The territories of

[1] For coins of this period of Thespiae, Plataea, and Orchomenus, see Volume of Plates ii, 6, *a*, *b*, *c*.

Mycalessus and Pharae were also detached from Thebes and constituted into independent states; and it was probably also in 382 that the narrow oligarchies which we find shortly after in possession of all the Boeotian towns were installed. In Thebes a force of no less than 1500 men was maintained, and Leontiades kept constant guard against counter-revolutions. Not content with the death of Ismenias and the self-banishment of some 300 of Ismenias' adherents, Leontiades imprisoned some 150 more of his adversaries and procured the assassination of Androcleides, his principal surviving opponent, who had sought safety in Athens. On the other hand, he apparently did not deem it necessary to introduce sweeping constitutional changes, and he seems to have abstained from wanton insults and spoliations.

Nevertheless a government which had sold Thebes' independence and called in a foreign garrison could never be popular; neither could it disarm all its outlaws as it had disarmed Androcleides. At Athens a number of refugees who had eluded Leontiades' bravoes eventually formed a conspiracy under the leadership of two prominent exiles, Melon and Pelopidas. The plotters were fortunate enough to find accomplices in Thebes, one of whom, a certain Phillidas, was secretary to the polemarchs and stood in their confidence. In December 379 seven refugees from Athens slipped into Thebes disguised as country folk. Having changed their costume at the house of an accomplice they made their next public appearance as choice examples of female beauty. Under this seductive semblance they were introduced by Phillidas to a wine-party in the house of the polemarch Archias, to which Leontiades' principal followers had been invited. According to a story which looks like a later piece of embroidery Archias had received warning of danger from two separate quarters, but had allowed Phillidas to reassure him and agreed to leave over 'business till to-morrow.' In any case he and his friends were as drunk as they were surprised and went down without a struggle. Leontiades, who was subsequently cornered by some of the conspirators in his own house, made a good fight for his life but was eventually brought down by Pelopidas.

The liberators, having thus destroyed the Theban government at one blow, immediately constituted themselves into a provisional administration. Their first act was to call their fellow-citizens to arms for an attack upon the Spartan garrison in the citadel. Had this force acted promptly, it should at this stage have found little difficulty in scattering and disarming the insurgents. But its commander lost his nerve completely. First of all, he gave the Thebans time to muster their forces and to head off the reinforcements which he had summoned from Thespiae, and allowed a corps of Athenian sympathizers who had been waiting on the Boeotian frontier to make their way to Thebes. On the next day, finding himself invested by the joint Theban and Athenian forces, he agreed to evacuate his post without waiting for the relief expedition which presently arrived from the Peloponnese. Small wonder that the Spartan Council of Elders condemned him and his principal lieutenant to death.

The departure of the Spartan garrison left the Theban liberators free to consummate their revolution by giving their city its first democratic constitution. But it remained to be seen whether the young Theban democracy could hold its own against Sparta in a set war. At the first news of rebellion the ephors had sent out King Cleombrotus, brother of the late Agesipolis, with a flying column. This force was deflected by the presence of an Athenian division on the main road to Thebes via Eleutherae, and had to pick its way along the difficult pass from Megara to Plataea. Nevertheless Cleombrotus drove off the defenders of the defile with heavy loss and descended into the Theban plain. Here he learnt that the city had been made proof against a *coup de main*, and being ill equipped for a midwinter campaign, he returned home without further fighting. But on his retreat he strengthened the garrison at Thespiae and made preparations for a more serious invasion in spring. So little confidence had the Thebans in their power to resist single-handed the full enemy levy that they made an offer of submission to Sparta.

We do not know whether the ephors gave any consideration to this proposal. In any case, before the negotiations could proceed far the whole face of the war was changed by another unrehearsed incident, a worthy pendant to the seizure of Thebes in 382. The hero of this new adventure was the commander of the garrison at Thespiae, who was not satisfied with the waiting rôle assigned to him but aspired to emulate the exploits of Phoebidas. This officer—his name was Sphodrias—shrewdly suspected that the ephors would like to see an end of the armed neutrality of Athens, which at times had played over into open partnership with Thebes. He rightly imagined that by seizing the Piraeus he would put Athens at Sparta's mercy; and he opportunely remembered that the Athenians had never troubled to complete the rebuilding of the Piraeus gates. He therefore planned a night attack upon the harbour of Athens; but he made his calculations with incredible carelessness. The distance from Thespiae to the

Piraeus was some 45 miles; from Plataea, which was probably the starting-point of his march, it was fully thirty miles; his route lay across Mt Cithaeron, which was almost certainly snow-bound at that season. Yet he reckoned to accomplish his journey between sunset and sunrise. It is no matter for surprise that Sphodrias was still some ten miles short of his goal when daybreak compelled him to turn back. But he had advanced far enough to betray his purpose, and to remove all doubts on his attitude he plundered the Attic countryside on his retreat.

Sphodrias' raid befel at a moment when public opinion at Athens wavered between the alternative policies of neutrality and active co-operation with Thebes. By way of requiting the services once rendered by Thebes to Thrasybulus and the other victims of the Thirty Tyrants, the Athenians had gone so far as to shelter the Theban refugees from Leontiades' persecution in spite of protests by Sparta; they had turned a blind eye on two of their strategi who led a volunteer force to assist in the expulsion of the Spartans from Thebes; and they had closed their frontiers to Cleombrotus on his winter expedition into Boeotia. But a strong current of opinion ran in favour of continued peace with Sparta. To say nothing of the neighbourly jealousy that had long subsisted between them and Thebes, the Athenians, as we shall presently see, had themselves done well out of the peace of the last few years and for the moment were in no mood for warlike adventures. When it became evident that Sparta intended to prosecute the spring campaign with energy, they made an almost panicky attempt to whitewash themselves by putting on trial and condemning to death the two strategi at whose escapade they previously had connived. When three Spartan envoys who happened to be in Athens at the time of Sphodrias' raid—no doubt in connection with the trial of the strategi—pledged their government to give full satisfaction for Sphodrias' aggression, they promptly calmed the Athenians' first outburst of anger. Had these promises been redeemed, there is little doubt that Athens would have taken no further action.

In dealing with the similar case of Phoebidas in 382 the ephors had had their hands tied by their obligations to Leontiades; in Sphodrias' case they were free to let justice take its course. When Sphodrias was summoned before the Elders, he felt so sure of condemnation that he defaulted at the trial. Nevertheless he was acquitted. His personal friends made a great effort and won over King Agesilaus, who once more, as in Phoebidas' case, used his authority to condone a subordinate's breach of discipline.

5-2

The result of the trial provoked severe comment in Sparta itself. To the Greeks in general it suggested that Sphodrias had all along been hand in glove with the ephors. Of collusion between Sphodrias and other parties there was indeed no evidence. Nay rather we may at once reject the story that Sphodrias was acting under Spartan orders, and the rival contemporary tradition that he had been bribed by some Theban intriguers who banked on his failure. For the Spartans to lay odds on Sphodrias or the Thebans to lay odds against him would have been a particularly foolish gamble, for Thebes could not afford to make a present of Athens to Sparta, and Sparta did a very bad piece of business by driving Athens into the arms of Thebes. Yet we cannot be surprised that Sparta's good faith was called into question. At Athens the acquittal of Sphodrias brought about a quick revulsion of feeling: without further hesitation the Assembly made alliance with Thebes.

The coalition between Athens and Thebes was put to the test in the summer of 378, when Agesilaus invaded Boeotia with a Peloponnesian levy of some 20,000 men. Although Agesilaus had incurred temporary discredit by his provocative foreign policy, and in recognition of that fact had left over the command of the previous winter expedition to his colleague Cleombrotus, the ephors wisely entrusted to him the leadership in the larger summer campaign. By an unsuspected compact with a stray mercenary corps Agesilaus forestalled his adversaries in occupying the Cithaeron passes and thus reached his advanced base at Thespiae without a struggle. On entering Theban territory he was brought up short by a line of trenches and palisades. This novel defence was the work of an Athenian named Chabrias, who had been sent to assist the Thebans with a strong force of peltasts. Like his countryman Iphicrates, Chabrias was a professional *condottiere*. In recent years he had taken service with the rebel kings of Cyprus and Egypt, and though the Athenians presently recalled him at the instance of their old friend Pharnabazus, he had gained some experience of field-fortifications in the Nile delta. The use of field-works, however, was never fully appreciated by the Greeks, who shirked the fatigue of throwing them up; and their first experiment with such defences was a failure. Agesilaus slipped through a negligently guarded sector of the fortifications and proceeded to ravage the Theban plain systematically, while the defenders, who dared not face the Spartans in a field battle, took shelter behind their city walls. But like the Athenians who sacrificed their crops in 431 B.C., the Thebans won the campaign by resolute inactivity. Unable either to outfight or to outstarve his enemy, Agesilaus retired from Boeotia without obtaining his decision.

In 377 B.C. the land campaign took a precisely similar course. By arrangement with the Spartan governor of Thespiae Agesilaus again secured the Cithaeron passes before the Thebans were ready for him. By turning the field defences he once more gained access to the Theban plain. But he failed, as before, to induce the enemy to fight for their crops, and his Peloponnesian allies displayed such insubordination that he beat an early retreat.

The two successive invasions of Boeotia had been so far effective that in 377 the shortage of food in Thebes became serious. But in the ensuing autumn or winter an opportune assault upon Histiaea, the last remaining possession of Sparta in Euboea, gave the Thebans naval communication with Thessaly and enabled them to revictual themselves from that quarter.

In the season of 376 the Thebans' power of endurance was not tried so severely. In the spring the Spartans sent out their usual expeditionary force. But as Agesilaus had fallen ill the command devolved upon Cleombrotus. This king, though not lacking in strategic skill, had no heart in a vendetta against Thebes. By misfortune or design he failed to carry the Cithaeron barrier and fell back without having molested the Thebans. Henceforth the Spartans made no further attempt to invade Boeotia by the Isthmus route, and although they considered a plan for turning the Cithaeron defences by transporting their forces across the Corinthian Gulf, they were deterred from their purpose by the preponderant naval forces of Athens.

No sooner were the Thebans rid of the Spartan field forces than they assumed the initiative in Boeotia and proceeded to recover the neighbouring towns. Of their operations in 376 and 375 hardly anything is known, but the story of one significant episode in these campaigns has come down to us. A Theban corps having made an unsuccessful attack on Orchomenus during the temporary absence of its Spartan garrison fell in by accident with the Spartan force on its return, and thus was committed to a fight with an army of twice its own strength (375 B.C.). Nothing daunted, its commander Pelopidas charged home and cut his way through with great slaughter. Although the total numbers engaged were small, this battle of Tegyra greatly enhanced Theban prestige. The instrument of Thebes' victory was a newly formed division of 300 regular troops known as the 'Sacred Band,' who were subsisted at public expense and acquired a Spartan proficiency in arms. These troops had originally been distributed over the entire Theban battle front, but at Tegyra they were collected into a separate company. In view of its performance in this battle the Sacred Band was henceforth regularly used as the spear-head of the Theban column of attack.

The effect of Thebes' military successes was enhanced by a political reaction against the oligarchies installed by Sparta in the minor Boeotian towns. Consequently by 374 B.C. the Thebans had recovered by force or by amicable surrender all the Boeotian cities except Orchomenus, Thespiae and Plataea. The reconquered cities probably followed the example of Thebes in setting up democracies, and at some time between 374 and 371 they were incorporated in a new Boeotian League. In the new federation a popular assembly supplanted, or more probably supplemented, the former federal Council, and the number of federal constituencies was reduced from eleven to seven, of which Thebes appropriated three. In other respects the constitution of the new League appears to have followed that of its predecessor; the Thebans again reserved the right of issuing coins to themselves, but they do not seem to have claimed any novel prerogative. But in actual practice their ascendancy over the other towns and their power of shaping the League's foreign policy were more complete than ever.

IV. THE NEW ATHENIAN THALASSOCRACY

The defection of Boeotia, following upon the revolt of Thebes, did not complete the tale of Sparta's losses in the warfare of the 'seventies. While her authority on land was being undermined, the last remains of her naval power were being annihilated, and the ascendancy among the maritime states of Greece was being definitely restored to Athens.

It may appear strange that the Athenians should once more have revived ambitions of supremacy in Greece which the double defeat of the Peloponnesian and Corinthian Wars had seemingly dispelled for ever. But, as we have already seen in the preceding chapter, the memories of the fifth century could not be readily effaced in Athenian minds; on the other hand, as the fourth century wore on, the traces of the havoc wrought by the recent wars were gradually obliterated.

The economic condition of Athens, though less brilliant than in the Periclean age, compared well with that of her neighbours. The land of Attica stood once more under intensive cultivation, and although some of the richer citizens appear to have given less personal attention to their estates, others devoted their capital to the systematic improvement of the soil. At the Laurium mines operations on a large scale were not resumed until the second half of the fourth century. On the other hand, the quarries of Pentelicus benefited by the growing demand for Attic marble. The ceramic industries of Athens gradually lost their markets in Etruria and South Italy, but found compensation in an increased traffic with southern Russia. The revival of the Athenian carrying trade was even more complete. In western waters the growth of Syracusan empire no doubt acted as a check upon Athenian commerce, but in the eastern seas the Attic merchantmen fully recovered their former position. Indications are not lacking of increased intercourse between Athens and Phoenicia, and of the resumption of active trade on the north Aegean coast. But these gains were of little significance compared with the expansion of Athenian trade along the northern coast of the Black Sea. In this district a dynasty of native rulers known as the 'Spartocidae' had towards the end of the fifth century united the Greek cities on either side of the Kertsch straits and the adjacent hinterland into one extensive realm which presently became one of the chief centres of wheat production in the Greek world. In the reign of Satyrus I (433–389 B.C.) the Athenians were granted exemption from the usual export duties at the ports of the Crimea, and under Leucon (389–349) their privilege was confirmed. An important traffic in grain thus grew up between Theodosia, the chief exporting centre, and the Piraeus. Of the wheat cargoes which came to the Piraeus Attic law allowed one third to be re-exported, and we need not doubt that Athenian skippers took advantage of this permission to ply a general trade in corn with the importing cities of the Aegean area. To such an extent did the maritime commerce of Athens revive that by 370 B.C. the city had the reputation of deriving most of its livelihood from the sea.

The increased demand for money which followed upon this revival of commerce gave in its turn a fresh impetus to the business of banking. Money-lenders became deposit bankers, and out of their growing loan-funds made large advances to merchants. As an example of this new development we may mention the bank of a metic named Pasion. The working capital of this financier was no longer wholly made up out of his private means, but a considerable portion was derived from sums paid in to him by one set of customers and lent out by him to another set. In the dealings of this firm the transition from money-lending to banking in the proper sense of that term is apparent. Another

innovation which we may probably attribute to the Athenian
money-dealers of this period is the system of making payments
between bank customers by mere book-entries without cash
transfers. This improvement in the technique of banking was a
natural outcome of the rigid system of accountancy in Athenian
public finance, which must have provided the necessary habits of
accuracy in book-keeping. The flow of capital towards enterprise which was created by these new methods was of especial
benefit to the Athenian shipping trade; and at a time when Athens
had lost her imperial revenues and her monopoly of coinage in
the Aegean area, she nevertheless became, because of her banks,
the principal money market of Greece.

While Athens was regaining her economic pre-eminence she
also acquired an enviable immunity from those domestic dis-
turbances which elsewhere in Greece were becoming endemic.
The rule of the Thirty Tyrants had done this much good, that all
Athenians high and low had acquired a healthy horror of revolution, and rich as well as poor loyally accepted the existing democratic constitution. Hence in the fourth century Athens enjoyed
a higher measure of political stability than in the fifth.

Last but not least, the intellectual and artistic achievements of
Athens had hardly if at all declined from the level of the Periclean
age, and the prestige accruing to her from them was actually
growing. The Acropolis had become a show-place like Olympia
or Delphi; the Attic drama was reproduced on every Greek stage;
Attic literature was exported in book form all over the Greek
world; and the Attic dialect was becoming the universal language of educated Greece. Pericles' boast that Athens was the
school of Greece was coming true, and this in an age when, in
Isocrates' words, the name of 'Greek' was becoming a mark of
culture rather than of race.

In 380 B.C. the claims of Athens to the hegemony of Greece
were formulated and made known to the entire Greek world in
one of Isocrates' masterpieces, the *Panegyricus*. In this treatise
the Athenian pamphleteer denounced the results of the King's
Peace and indicated a new confederation under Athenian leadership as the remedy for Greece's political ills. But before the
publication of this treatise the Athenians had already taken the
first steps towards realizing his programme. The ink was hardly
dry on the King's Peace before they commenced to resume those
alliances which the Peace had forced them to abandon. In 386
or 385 they made a treaty with Hebryzelmis, king of the Odrysian
Thracians on the Gallipoli peninsula. About the same time they

came to a new understanding with Chios, and within the next few years made fresh pacts with Mitylene, Byzantium and Rhodes.

Early in 377 the Athenians took advantage of the bad impression caused by Sparta's recent abuses of power to pass a decree inviting all neighbouring states, both Greek and barbarian, excepting only the subjects of Persia, to form a league of mutual defence, with the special object of preventing fresh inroads on Greek autonomy by Sparta. The executive power of the league was to be vested in Athens; but its policy was to be framed by concurrent discussion in two co-ordinate congresses. The one branch of this bipartite parliament was to consist of the Athenian Council and Assembly, the other was to be a synod of representatives from all the other states of the league, also sitting in Athens, but containing no Athenian members. The autonomy of Athens' allies was to be scrupulously respected. Elaborate precautions were devised against the establishment of Athenian cleruchies on allied soil, and measures were even taken to expropriate such few Athenians as owned land in allied territory. It is probable that a federal court was also set up, though the point is under dispute.

The constitution of the new league suffered from two serious deficiencies. No regulations were drawn up for the delicate task of assessing the military and financial liabilities of its members; and no machinery was provided for removing a deadlock between the two branches of congress. In actual practice both these omissions, and especially the lack of a proper system of assessment, were to prove detrimental to the league's efficiency. Nevertheless the project was one of the most statesmanlike schemes put forward by Greek constitution-makers. The self-denying spirit in which the Athenians debarred themselves from acquiring any unfair advantage over their allies offers a striking proof that they had taken to heart their previous failures as rulers of an empire. As a bond of union between the Greek states the Second Athenian Confederacy, as the league is usually styled, had the peculiar merit of making full allowance for the Greek cities' love of autonomy; and at a time when the rival Spartan Confederacy was about to break up it offered not a mere paper scheme but a practical instrument of government.

In actual fact the success of the Athenian manifesto fell far short of its deserts. The existing allies of Athens, Chios, Byzantium, Mitylene, Rhodes, Methymna and Thebes enrolled themselves as original members of the Confederacy. In summer 377 the greater part of Euboea came in, and some scattered cities in the northern Aegean were drawn in by a recruiting flotilla under Chabrias, thus bringing the total to fifteen members. But for the present most of the Aegean states held aloof, and Sparta's allies on the mainland resisted the solicitations of an Athenian mission which vainly coaxed them to throw off a well-tried if not wholly happy allegiance.

In spite of these disappointments, the Athenians prepared for a vigorous prosecution of the war against Sparta. Realizing that frequent calls would be made upon their purses they remodelled their machinery for levying property-taxes. In order to distribute their incidence more evenly they made a general assessment of their total wealth, both real and personal. The declared total of 6000 talents (£1,400,000) appears impossibly small as tried by modern standards, and it probably fell considerably short of the real total; yet it is roughly in keeping with other estimates of the wealth of Greek states. As a further means of equalizing the burden the Athenians apportioned all their tax-payers into 100 'Symmories' or groups of approximately equal aggregate wealth, each of which contributed an equal quota of the sum required from year to year and made its own arrangements for assessing its corporate liability upon its individual members.

The failure of the Spartan offensive against Boeotia made it unnecessary for the Athenians to raise large forces for the land war: only in 378 does any considerable Athenian army appear to have taken the field. But from 376 onwards they were called upon to make a considerable naval effort. Unable to force a decision against Thebes, the Spartans in 376 undertook a naval campaign against Athens. A Peloponnesian fleet of 65 sail established bases on Aegina and the nearest of the Cyclades and held up the Athenian corn ships off Euboea. The Athenians, no less resolute, raised by dint of hard taxation and conscription a squadron of 83 sail. With this armada their admiral Chabrias set free the corn ships and by an attack upon Naxos, the principal ally of Sparta among the Cyclades, forced the Peloponnesians to fight. In the battle of Naxos the Athenians gained a victory which might have been as complete as that of Aegospotami, had not Chabrias called off the pursuit in order to rescue the crews of his damaged vessels. Even so his success was decisive: for the next 54 years the Athenians remained masters of the Aegean. As a result of their victory they at once gathered in numerous fresh recruits to their new confederacy. In 376–5 most of the Cyclades renewed their alliance with Athens, and about this time the sanctuary of Delos, which had temporarily fallen into Athenian hands in 390 and again in 377, was definitely brought back under Athenian control. In 375 Chabrias made a prolonged cruise in the northern Aegean, in the course of which he enlisted the reconstituted Chalcidian League and a string of other states extending as far as Lesbos and the Sea of Marmora. It was probably also due to Chabrias that King Amyntas made a treaty with the Athenians and gave them facilities for importing the valuable ship-timber of Macedonia. In the same year another Athenian fleet under Conon's son Timotheus sailed round Peloponnesus at the request of the Thebans and deterred a Peloponnesian army from attacking Boeotia by way of the Corinthian Gulf. The same squadron also defeated a new Peloponnesian fleet of 55 sail off the Acarnanian coast and obtained several new recruits for the Athenian Confederacy in north-western Greece, chief among them being the Acarnanians, Alcetas king of the Molossi, and the island of Corcyra, where a democratic faction had invoked Athenian assistance against the preponderant oligarchy.

In the campaigns of 376–5 the Athenians swept the seas as they never had done since the early years of the Peloponnesian War, and they reared their Confederacy from a puny childhood to a vigorous youth. But the price which they paid for these successes was almost prohibitive. In spite of the contributions which their most recent allies had paid on entering the league, the expenses of their fleet more than absorbed their available funds. By 376 Athenian finances had got into such disorder that a special commissioner named Androtion was appointed to reorganize them. It was probably on his recommendation that the Athenians imposed upon the three richest members of each Symmory the duty of paying in advance its entire yearly quota of property-tax, and conferred upon them the right of subsequently recovering from the other members of the Symmory. While the burden of the war thus grew heavier, the reasons for waging it became less compelling. So far as their own safety was concerned the Athenians had nothing further to fear from Sparta, and as the conflict wore on they felt less and less inclined to fight the battles of Thebes. Although the Thebans had contributed a few ships to the Athenian fleet they had given their allies no financial support and thus created the impression that they were not pulling their weight.

V. JASON OF PHERAE

In 374 accordingly the Athenians made peace overtures and found the Spartans willing. No further effort on Sparta's part appeared likely to retrieve her failures on land and sea, and but recently her impotence had been brought home to her by an embassy from her last remaining ally in northern Greece, whose appeal for help she was constrained to refuse. This appeal came from Polydamas the ruler of Pharsalus, a city which, like most of Thessaly, had shown hostility to Sparta during the Corinthian War, but had since resumed friendly relations. The adversary against whom Polydamas invoked assistance was Jason, the successor of Lycophron at Pherae, who had revived Lycophron's plan of extending his dominion over all Thessaly. Having recruited a large mercenary corps out of his great personal fortune Jason had in the course of the 'seventies reduced the other Thessalian cities, which apparently made no attempt to combine against him, and in 374 Pharsalus alone remained free. Although Polydamas received a tempting offer of an amicable settlement with Jason, he resolved to make a fight for his independence, and acting on a hint which Jason had generously, or with a cunning prescience of its uselessness, presented to him, he went to Sparta in person to press his suit. To say nothing of their obligations to Polydamas, it was manifestly in the interest of the Spartans to check the further growth of Jason's power. In contrast with his predecessor, Jason had given overt if intermittent support to Sparta's enemies: he had attacked the Spartan post at Histiaea, and in 374 he entered into a short-lived alliance with Athens. Nevertheless the Spartans ruefully left Polydamas to shift for himself. Such few troops as they could raise for distant service they were obliged at this juncture to send to Orchomenus and Phocis, which were being urgently menaced with a Theban offensive.

The negotiations between Athens and Sparta led to a prompt conclusion of peace (midsummer 374). While reasserting *pro forma* the autonomy of all Greeks, the Athenians recognized Sparta's ascendancy in the Peloponnese and the Spartans acknowledged the Athenian Confederacy. It is not known what consideration, if any, was given to the status of the Boeotian League as reconstructed by Thebes; but it is probable that the Thebans signed the peace as members of the Athenian Confederacy, and in any case the Spartans withdrew their remaining garrisons from Boeotia, thus acquiescing *de facto* in Thebes' recent conquests.

The peace of 374 was hailed with great satisfaction at Athens, and to commemorate the event Cephisodotus, the kinsman of Praxiteles, was commissioned to make statues of Mother Peace and Infant Plenty[1]. This monument, however, was the only durable result of the negotiations, for the peace died in the hour of its birth. On returning from his cruise in the Ionian Sea Timotheus landed some democratic exiles from Zacynthus on that island, and the Athenians endorsed his action so far as to admit the 'Zacynthian demos' as an independent community into their Confederacy. The Spartans, on the other hand, used this breach of the treaty as a pretext for the immediate resumption of hostilities. The reason for this sudden change of front may be found in a promise of assistance from Sparta's old ally Dionysius, who was free for the moment to divert his attention from Sicilian to Greek politics[2]. In concert with Dionysius the Spartans decided to acquire Corcyra as the chief link of communication between Greece and Sicily. An advance squadron sent out on the chance of carrying the island by surprise failed in its purpose; but in the spring of 373 a squadron drawn from all Sparta's maritime allies drove the Corcyraeans off the seas and with the help of a strong landing force put Corcyra town under blockade. To this attack the Athenians replied by fresh levies of soldiers and ships. With the help of Jason and of King Alcetas of the Molossi they at once sent a small peltast force over land to the relief of Corcyra. But their naval preparations were delayed month after month by lack of funds. As their admiral Timotheus shrank from offending Athens' allies by forcibly impressing men and money, he could only obtain skeleton crews for his fleet. While he lay to, or made futile recruiting cruises in the Aegean, the besieging force all but starved out the Corcyraeans. But the Spartan commander lost his prize over some petty pecuniary quests. By embezzling the pay of his mercenaries he so impaired their discipline that they let themselves be thoroughly routed in an eleventh-hour sortie by the defenders. Thus Corcyra gained a breathing-space until the arrival of the relief squadron. Towards the end of summer the Athenians replaced Timotheus by Iphicrates, who showed less scruple in impressing crews and presently made for Corcyra with 70 sail. The mere news of his approach sufficed to send the Peloponnesian force scuttling homewards, and a small Syracusan squadron which had been sent out to join hands with them fell instead into Iphicrates' grasp. In the following year Iphicrates

---

[1] See below, p. 539.
[2] See below, p. 132.

remained in the western sea and gained some fresh allies. But though he was less delicate than Timotheus in exacting contributions from the allies he eventually sank into the same state of indigence as his predecessor. Once more the Athenians were reminded that a successful naval campaign could be as ruinous as a disastrous one.

A change in the temper of the Athenians had already set in towards the end of 373, when Timotheus was put on trial but acquitted. Their ardour was further damped by the prospect of an open breach with Thebes. Although the Thebans had contributed some ships to Timotheus' fleet, they almost came to blows with Athens over the Boeotian border towns recently evacuated by Sparta. While the Athenians snatched Oropus, the Thebans pounced upon Plataea and for a second time destroyed the buildings and expelled the inhabitants (373), and shortly after they turned the Thespians adrift in similar fashion. The Plataeans flocked back to Athens, where their grievances were ventilated by Isocrates in a pamphlet which censured the Thebans with outspoken severity.

At the same time the Athenians suffered a disappointment in their failure to secure an alliance with Jason. Such an alliance appeared all the more desirable since the return of Polydamas from his futile errand to Sparta and the consequent surrender of Pharsalus to the tyrant of Pherae. The whole of Thessaly now acknowledged Jason's authority, and its reunion under one chief was signalized by the revival of the obsolete title of 'tagus,' or federal commander, in Jason's favour. But the more reason the Athenians had to covet the friendship of Jason, the less was this ambitious ruler disposed to subserve Athenian interests. Rumour declared that he intended to challenge the naval supremacy of Athens, and conflicts with Athens were foreboded by his intervention in Macedonia, where King Amyntas became his ally and was thus withdrawn from the Athenian sphere of influence.

The peace movement in Athens found a powerful advocate in Callistratus, a politician who by virtue of his oratory had established over the Assembly an ascendancy similar to that of Pericles or Demosthenes. As late as 373 B.C. Callistratus had stood for a vigorous war policy, but he had since realized that Athenian finances would not bear the strain of further fighting.

While Athenian policy was thus gravitating towards peace, the Spartans had sent Antalcidas on a fresh mission to the Persian court, and the Persian king, who at this time was projecting a new campaign against Egypt and wished to see the Greek soldiers demobilized in order that he might attract them to his own service, dispatched an envoy to Sparta to mediate a general peace (spring 371).

In summer 371 a peace congress was convened at Sparta. The Athenian delegates, headed by Callistratus, discussed the issues that lay between them and the Spartans with statesmanlike frankness and soon came to an understanding with them. Under cover of the consecrated formula of 'autonomy for all,' they not only, as in 374, secured recognition for the Athenian Confederacy, but induced the Spartans to withdraw their garrisons from their remaining dependencies. On these terms the treaty was actually signed by all parties and confirmed by oath. But on the day after its conclusion the Theban delegate Epaminondas asked for permission to substitute 'Boeotians' for 'Thebans' on the document.

Why did Epaminondas call for this belated amendment? The most probable explanation is that during the negotiations he had assumed that the precedent established by the peace discussions of 374 would hold good and Thebes' claim to sign for Boeotia would be accepted as a matter of course, but that he had misgivings when he found that on behalf of the Athenian Confederacy not only Athens but the allies of Athens all and single were taking the oath, thus implying that each delegate could only bind his own particular city. But whatever his motive, Epaminondas' request was a perfectly reasonable one, for he was entitled to assume that the substance of his claim to sign on behalf of all Boeotia had already been conceded, and that the alteration which he proposed was a mere affair of drafting. Nevertheless King Agesilaus refused on Sparta's behalf to make any change in the treaty. This pedantic adherence to the strict letter of the treaty was a piece of sharp practice in which the personal animus of Agesilaus against Thebes is only too apparent. But the Spartan ephors and the Athenian delegates must bear part of the blame, for either of these could have brought him to reason had they cared to do so. Nevertheless Epaminondas had little cause for complaint: the history of the next three weeks was to show that Agesilaus had really played into his hands.

CHAPTER IV

THEBES

I. THE BATTLE OF LEUCTRA

WHEN the peace congress of 371 B.C. broke up the Theban
delegates went home in utter despondency. Not only did
Thebes now appear in the light of a peace-breaker, but she had no
allies left that she could count on. Her hold upon the other
Boeotian towns was precarious; her friendship with Jason was of
problematic value; her relations with Athens had been further
compromised by the recent peace negotiations. On the other hand,
the Spartans assured themselves that they would shortly settle
accounts with Thebes on their own terms. Under the pretext of
enforcing the peace upon the recalcitrant Thebans they could now
resume their invasion of Boeotia, and in the next campaign they
knew that Athens would maintain at least an attitude of friendly
neutrality. In confident expectation of a complete victory they
spoke of settling the Boeotian question once for all by treating
Thebes as they had previously dealt with Mantinea. The very
existence of Thebes as a city was now at stake.

Such was the eagerness of the Spartans to follow up their
advantage that they did not wait to observe the formalities of the
recent peace convention, which stipulated that they must first
obtain the free consent of their allies before they mobilized them
in execution of the peace terms. Without further consultations
they ordered King Cleombrotus, who was again stationed in Phocis
with a composite force of Peloponnesians and Central Greeks, to
ascertain whether the Thebans were still acting in contravention
of the peace by retaining their hold on the other Boeotian cities,
and if so, to invade their territory forthwith.

The Spartan king, finding that the Boeotian League had not
wound itself up, and that a federal Boeotian force was ready to
receive him in the defile of Coronea, advanced by a coast track
which had been left unguarded, and scored a preliminary success
by capturing the naval arsenal at Creusis and twelve Theban men-
of-war. From this point he turned inland and reached the edge
of the Theban plain at Leuctra. Here he found himself confronted by the Boeotian levy, which had the advantage of operating
on inner lines and was thus able to retrieve its initial strategic
defeat (July–August 371).

The Boeotian generals were at first divided in their opinions as to the wisdom of accepting battle, but eventually decided to fight. Their forces were, if anything, fewer, and the contingents of some of the Boeotian towns were of doubtful loyalty. On the other hand, if they declined battle there was a danger that the Boeotian League might dissolve of its own accord, and that the people of Thebes would cry out for peace rather than submit to another invasion and loss of further harvests. Moreover, since the victory of Tegyra, the Theban commanders had reason to believe that Theban troops could win battles even against considerable odds, and two of their representatives on the board of Boeotarchs, Pelopidas and Epaminondas, strongly favoured a fighting policy, for they not only grasped the necessity of waging a battle but saw the means of winning it.

The field of Leuctra, on which the Boeotians accepted Cleombrotus' challenge, was a level and unimpeded plain of some 1000 yards in width, extending between two low ridges on which the opposing armies lay encamped: an ideal battle-ground for hoplite forces. Cleombrotus' army was arrayed in the usual fashion, with the Spartan contingent standing twelve deep on the right wing. On the Boeotian side the Theban division was drawn up in an unusually deep formation of fifty ranks and took station opposite the Spartan forces, so that the best troops on either side might engage at once without having to hunt each other across the battle-field. This disposition was probably due to Epaminondas, a comparatively untried general but an accomplished battle-thinker.

The action opened with a cavalry duel. The Spartans, who had done nothing to remedy the defects revealed in their horse by the Asiatic and Chalcidic campaigns, had only an improvised troop to oppose to the well mounted and well trained Theban horsemen, and were flung back by these upon their own infantry. The Spartan line had scarcely been reformed before the Theban infantry, with the Sacred Band at its head and the victorious cavalry acting as a flank guard, broke in upon it. For a while the Spartan foot held firm, but the cumulative pressure of the deep Theban column eventually carried it off its feet. By this encounter the battle was won and lost along the whole front. As soon as the Spartans gave ground, their allies in the centre and left wing fell back without waiting for the Boeotian centre and right to follow up the onset of the Thebans.

The action of Leuctra was not a big battle even according to Greek standards. The total number of troops actually engaged

probably did not exceed 10,000, and the duration of the combat
must have been brief. In spite of its heavy casualties, which included King Cleombrotus and 400 out of the 700 Spartan citizens
on the field, the defeated army made an orderly retreat, and the
Theban pursuit stopped short under the steep bluffs on which the
Spartan camp was perched. Yet Leuctra opened a new chapter
in military history, because of the novelty of Epaminondas'
tactics. This novelty did not consist in the deepening of the Theban
column so as to form a phalanx or 'roller': such formations had
been used by the Thebans in several previous actions, though no
doubt the earlier phalanxes did not move with such precision as
the *corps d'élite* which Pelopidas and his colleagues had trained.
Neither can the disposition of the Boeotian line *en échelon* be
regarded as an important innovation, though such an oblique
alignment might serve to correct the tendency of Greek battle
fronts to slew round against the clock. More importance attaches
to the close co-operation between foot and horse which subsequently became a characteristic of Macedonian battle-tactics.
But the originality of Epaminondas' tactics lay chiefly in the
choice of his point of attack: he had discovered the master principle that the quickest and most economical way of winning a
military decision is to defeat the enemy not at his weakest but at
his strongest point.

Judged by its immediate political results, Leuctra had no
particular importance, but viewed in the light of its ultimate consequences, it forms a landmark in political no less than in military
history. At Sparta government and people alike bore up under
the shock of unexpected disaster with perfect calm. The last
available troops were mobilized under Agesilaus' son Archidamus
and in face of this display of firmness Sparta's allies made no
premature move. In central and northern Greece the Thebans
were disappointed in their hope of setting a snowball rolling. The
Athenians made no attempt to conceal their chagrin at Thebes'
victory and treated the messenger of 'good news' with ostentatious
rudeness. The attitude of Jason, though far more loyal, was
hardly more helpful. The Thessalian ruler lost no time in coming
to the help of the Thebans: though it is not clear whether he was
already on the march before the battle of Leuctra, he certainly
made a rapid journey through the hostile Phocian country and
arrived in the Theban camp shortly after the combat. The Thebans
at once invited him to join them in the attack upon the Spartan
camp before Archidamus should have come up. But Jason declined the offer. Whether he was secretly jealous of the Thebans'

triumph, or whether, as seems more likely, the reinforcements which he brought with him were not sufficiently numerous to carry the strong Spartan position, he tamely advised his allies to evict their enemy by diplomacy rather than by force of arms. Having negotiated a truce which allowed the Spartans to evacuate Boeotia without further molestation, Jason concluded that the campaign was at an end and withdrew as suddenly as he had come.

On his return to Thessaly Jason dismantled the fortress of Heraclea, thus indicating that he intended to keep open the passage between northern and central Greece. In the ensuing year he made great preparations for a visit to Delphi, where he proposed to preside over the Pythian festival due to be held in September 370, and in anticipation of resistance to his progress by the Phocians he called out a federal Thessalian levy. While we may safely reject the alarmist rumour that his real purpose was to plunder the Delphic temple treasures, we must accept the general Greek tradition that he had some ulterior object in view. According to Isocrates Jason had in mind a crusade against Persia. It is possible that he intended to make a formal announcement to this effect and to invite the co-operation of the other Greek states at the Pythian festival. Failing this, we may conjecture that he proposed to reconstitute the Delphic Amphictyony as an instrument of Thessalian ascendancy in Central Greece (see above, vol. IV, p. 59). But whatever his precise purpose at Delphi, it is evident that Jason regarded his dominion in Thessaly as a base for the conquest of a wider world, and in view of his untiring energy and great diplomatic ability he might well have anticipated Philip of Macedon in constructing a United States of Greece, had his life been spared. But before he set out from Pherae he was struck dead by some conspirators whose motives have never come to light.

While Athens held aloof and Jason fought for his own hand, it appeared that Thebes had won a barren triumph at Leuctra. Yet the effects of her victory presently showed through. Archidamus, who had fallen in with the remnants of Cleombrotus' army in the Megarid, made no attempt to retrieve the campaign but retired to Corinth and disbanded his force. After his departure the Thebans obtained a free hand in Central Greece and proceeded to recover their supremacy in that region. Orchomenus, which had asserted its independence since 395, rejoined the Boeotian League, only to repent of its submission a few years later and suffer destruction for its infidelity (364). The Locrians and Aetolians also resumed their alliance with Thebes, and even the Phocians came to terms (371–70).

II. THEBAN ASCENDANCY IN NORTHERN GREECE

The death of Jason, who must have acted as a check on Thebes'
expansion had his programme at Delphi been carried out, gave
the Thebans an opportunity of embracing all Central Greece
under their protectorate. The small states of the Spercheus valley
transferred their allegiance from Pherae to them, and the fortress
of Nicaea, which subsequently served the Thebans as the key to
Thermopylae, may have been founded by them on this occasion.
At the same time the Euboeans in the east and the Acarnanians
in the west deserted the Athenian Confederacy and threw in their
lot with Thebes. To consolidate their recent gains the Thebans
created a new confederation of Central Greek states. This League
was ostensibly designed for common defence, but in actual fact
it served as an instrument for fresh Theban conquests.

The ascendancy acquired by Thebes in Central Greece was
reflected in the history of Delphi in the ensuing years. The
Thebans did not, as it seems, take any great part in the reconstruction of the temple of Apollo, which had been severely
damaged towards the end of the 'seventies by an earthquake, or
more probably by the flooding of a subterranean stream. But
they set up a special treasure-house to contain the trophies of
Leuctra; and they exerted their power on the Amphictyonic
Council by inducing that body to impose a belated fine on Sparta
for the illegal seizure of Thebes in 382, and to banish from
Delphi a faction of local residents who had manifested sympathy
with Athens (363 B.C.).

Shortly after the formation of the Central Greek Confederacy
the Thebans began to carry their arms beyond the limits of
Central Greece. In Thessaly Theban intervention was presently
invited by the political chaos into which Jason's death plunged
that country. At Pherae the dominion of Jason's family was so
well consolidated that it withstood an epidemic of sudden deaths
within its ranks. Of Jason's brothers, Polyphron slew Polydorus
(370), and was in turn slain by a third brother or a nephew named
Alexander (369). The last usurper established himself firmly in
Jason's stead and even went as far as to issue coins bearing his
own name[1]. But while Jason's successors retained Pherae, they
lost the other Thessalian towns, and the title of 'tagus' which each
in turn assumed carried no legal authority and no effective power.
In their unavailing attempts to retain or recover the rest of
Thessaly the rulers of Pherae displayed such ruthlessness that

[1] See Volume of Plates ii, 6, *e*.

they drove the other cities to call in foreign aid against them. Polyphron had recourse to wholesale banishments at Larissa and put to death Polydamas, whose willing submission to Jason had made Pharsalus safe for the rulers of Pherae; but his record of frightfulness was quite eclipsed by Alexander, whose lust of cruelty appears to have bordered on insanity. In 368 the Aleuadae of Larissa, who had thrown open the gates of Thessaly to Archelaus of Macedon some thirty years previously, once more invoked Macedonian aid against the power of Pherae. The Macedonian king Alexander II (369–8), who had but recently succeeded his father Amyntas, at once came to the rescue and occupied both Larissa and Crannon with a military force; but like Archelaus before him he kept these towns for himself as prizes of war. Once more the parts of Thessaly and Macedon were reversed, the suzerainty of Jason being replaced by a Macedonian domination. Alexander's usurpation did not raise up another Thrasymachus to proclaim a Greek crusade against a 'barbarian' invader (p. 36), but the Thessalian cities which lay between the millstones of Macedon and Pherae looked about in their turn for assistance from abroad. In 399 B.C. they had applied to Sparta; they now asked for Theban intervention.

At the time when this appeal was made (summer 369), the Thebans were already committed to other foreign adventures, but they raised a small expeditionary force and entrusted it to Pelopidas, who henceforth made Thessalian affairs his special province. In his first Thessalian campaign Pelopidas evidently considered that Macedon, not Pherae, was the point of danger, for his first care was to safeguard the country against Macedonian encroachments. Having wrested Crannon and Larissa from King Alexander, he tendered his good offices in a dispute which had arisen between the Macedonian monarch and one of his chief barons, Ptolemy of Alorus, and thus disarmed the king's hostility. So little did Pelopidas fear Alexander of Pherae at this stage that he endeavoured to procure for him the legal authority of a 'tagus' by amicable arrangement with the other Thessalians, and when Alexander refused to guarantee the rights of the other cities he made no attempt to coerce him but left the issue in suspense.

In the ensuing year (368) the Macedonian settlement of Pelopidas was overthrown by Ptolemy, who murdered King Alexander and established himself as regent on behalf of Alexander's brother Perdiccas. But Ptolemy in turn was beset by a fresh pretender and found himself compelled to accept a new settlement at the hands of Pelopidas, despite the fact that the

Theban envoy had been sent out without an army at his back.
The Macedonian regent renounced all claims on Thessaly and
gave hostages for his future behaviour. Among these hostages was
the late king's younger brother Philip, who subsequently proved
that Thebes had been a school as well as a prison house to him.

Pelopidas' second Macedonian settlement outlived the ensuing
vicissitudes of the Macedonian dynasty: not till Philip became
king did Thebes or Thessaly have anything further to fear from
Macedon. The success of his negotiations emboldened Pelopidas
on his return to seek an interview with Alexander of Pherae, in
the hope that this ruler would now see reason. But Alexander
repaid Pelopidas' trustfulness by taking him prisoner. This
treacherous act meant war for Thebes. But the despot of Pherae
had previously assured himself of support from Athens, and with
the help of an Athenian auxiliary corps he waged a successful
guerilla war against a large force which the Thebans sent to
retrieve Pelopidas. Cut off from all supplies, the invading army
had to beat a retreat which would probably have ended in disaster,
had the soldiers not deposed their generals and thrust the command upon Epaminondas, who was serving at that time in the
ranks. Epaminondas led his comrades safely home. In the
following year he received official command of a fresh relief force
which compelled Alexander to surrender Pelopidas and renounce
his recent conquest of Pharsalus (spring 367). But neither
Epaminondas nor Pelopidas at this time attempted a general
Thessalian settlement.

In the following years Alexander was left free to resume his
conquests in eastern and southern Thessaly, but the wholesale
terrorism which he practised upon the vanquished encouraged the
remaining cities to prolong their resistance. In 364 Alexander's
enemies again turned to Thebes for succour. The Thebans
resolved to interfere in force; but an untimely eclipse of the sun
(13 July 364) gave them an excuse for backing out. Pelopidas,
the appointed leader of the expedition, nevertheless marched out
with a skeleton force of 300 mounted volunteers, which he reinforced as best he could with Thessalian levies. With this
scratch army he attacked Alexander on the ridge of Cynoscephalae, and despite the far superior numbers of Alexander, who
had recently recruited a powerful infantry corps, hurled his
opponent off the crest. During the pursuit the Theban general
threw away his life in a rash attempt to slay Alexander with his
own hand, but his Theban horsemen completed the rout of Alexander's forces. A second Theban army which was dispatched

shortly after (autumn 364) to avenge Pelopidas' death found nothing to do but to receive Alexander's surrender. The would-be 'tagus' of Thessaly was restricted to the possession of his native Pherae and became a subject-ally of Thebes in company with the Achaeans and Magnesian borderers who had previously been under his yoke. The other Thessalian cities were grouped into four cantons recalling the 'tetrades' of early Thessalian history; but for purposes of foreign policy they were combined into a single confederation under an official carrying the new name of 'archon.' This confederation no doubt was intended to owe allegiance to Thebes no less than Alexander. But while Alexander duly performed his obligations and even made war upon his former Athenian allies, the Thessalian Confederacy presently leagued itself with Athens against Alexander (361). Thus Thebes fell short of acquiring complete control over Thessaly, and her interest in Thessalian affairs, which had never been more than spasmodic, did not long survive Pelopidas.

III. THE DISRUPTION OF THE PELOPONNESIAN LEAGUE

The same desultory and therefore ineffective policy was adopted by the Thebans in their dealings with the Peloponnese. In this district the withdrawal of Sparta's 'harmosts' and garrisons by the terms of the peace of 371 gave promise of better relations between Sparta and her allies. The *pax Peloponnesiaca* was further confirmed by a new compact which the signatories of the peace (with the insignificant exception of Elis) made after the battle of Leuctra, pledging themselves to support the settlement of 371 against all comers. This compact constituted a great triumph for Athens, at whose instance it had been formed, for she now stood at the head of a mainland league. To the Greeks in general it offered a basis for a wider settlement, for given a reasonably free hand in Boeotia and Central Greece, the Thebans could hardly have refused to honour it.

But the memory of Sparta's past oppressions could not be obliterated in an instant, and the arbitrary manner in which she had rushed her allies into the campaign of Leuctra could only serve to revive it. The spell of Sparta's military prestige, which had been for centuries the chief safeguard of the Peloponnesian peace, was broken once for all by the disaster of Leuctra. At the news of that battle, the Peloponnese was thrown into a ferment which broke all bonds of past tradition and of diplomatic obligations.

At Corinth and Sicyon, where the interests of industry and commerce apparently acted as a restraining force, the conservative parties repelled all attacks upon the constitution and maintained friendly relations with Sparta. But the agrarian communities of the Central Peloponnese were swept along in a general political upheaval. At Argos, where demagogues had raised the cry of 'treason,' the masses perpetrated wholesale executions of oligarchic suspects and finished in the best style of the French Revolution by rending their own champions. The Eleans proceeded to the reconquest of the subject districts lost in 399 B.C. and at once recovered the lower Alpheus valley.

But the most momentous revolution took place in Arcadia, which now for the first and last time became the centre of Peloponnesian politics. As might have been expected, the villages into which Sparta had dissected Mantinea again coalesced into a city (spring 370): the stone foundations of the new ring wall, which was strengthened with towers and overlapping curtains at each gate, are still visible. But a far greater scheme of reconstruction was initiated by the anti-Spartan party at Tegea, which proposed the gathering of the several Arcadian communities into a new confederation. In Tegea itself the federalists only carried their point by sheer force, but elsewhere they met with general support, and only Orchomenus and Heraea stood out. The Arcadian federation was composed of a general assembly (the 'Ten Thousand'), to which all Arcadian freemen had access, and of a council to which each constituent community sent its quota of delegates. A standing federal army of 5000 men was subsequently recruited among the numerous Arcadian soldiers of fortune who had hitherto taken service under foreign banners, and was placed under the command of the 'strategus,' the chief federal official. To pay these mercenaries a special federal coinage was struck[1]. No permanent federal capital appears to have been chosen at the outset.

The formation of the Arcadian League out of a far-flung group of communities whom geography and history alike had sundered was a considerable achievement, and had the League's government been wiser it might have taken Sparta's place as the stabilizer of the Peloponnese. But from the first the League proved a storm-centre. Hardly had it been established than it tried to coerce Orchomenus and Heraea into membership (autumn 370). This action, which constituted a clear breach of the recent compact with Athens, caused the Spartans in turn to violate the agreement by taking the field against Arcadia without consulting their allies.

[1] See Volume of Plates ii, 6, f.

The Athenian league of peace thus died a sudden death, and in its stead a war coalition was formed. In reply to Sparta's aggression the Arcadians entered into compacts with Argos and Elis, both of whom had old accounts to settle with Sparta. From Athens, whose pacific efforts they had just nullified, they received a rebuff. But their overtures to Thebes, which the Eleans backed up with a loan of money, brought a new and formidable ally into the field.

At Thebes the victory of Leuctra, by removing the menace of foreign invasion, had opened the door to party strife. The small proprietors who had no doubt suffered most under invasion now desired to 'rest and be thankful.' But to Pelopidas and Epaminondas Leuctra was the beginning rather than the end. They took it for granted that their victory must be followed up, and they did not stop to think whether Thebes commanded the requisite prestige or force to become an empire-maker as well as an empire-breaker. In 370 their personal ascendancy, though declining, was still strong enough to secure acceptance of the Arcadians' suit, and they were presently sent out with a force which contained contingents from all Central Greece and from Thessaly. The mere arrival of this army in Arcadia caused King Agesilaus, who had been operating not without success against Mantinea, to evacuate the country (autumn 370). Orchomenus and Heraea now joined the League, and the primary object of Thebes' expedition was fulfilled. But the Arcadians and other peoples of the Central Peloponnese, who considered that the present opportunity for territorial aggrandizement and for plundering the virgin lands of Laconia was too good to be lost, clamoured for an advance into enemy country, and they drew their allies into a new midwinter campaign.

The task which Epaminondas, the allies' commander-in-chief, had undertaken was none of the easiest. Besides the difficulty of co-ordinating the movements of some 50,000 men advancing through unfamiliar mountain country on winter roads which were probably snow-bound, he was beset with endless wranglings among the officers of his ill-assorted coalition. Nevertheless his march upon Sparta was executed with admirable precision. The Arcadians, Central Greeks and Argives moved by three converging routes to Caryae, and proceeded thence along the Oenus valley to Sellasia, where the Elean contingent fell in. The united force then slipped past Sparta and gained the right bank of the Eurotas below the city. As the invaders passed through Laconia considerable bodies of Helots and even of Perioeci joined them, and inside Sparta, disaffected citizens, presumably of the inferior class, hatched more than one conspiracy. Considering that Sparta was not fortified, we cannot doubt that Epaminondas could have forced his way in. But the price of entrance was higher than he cared to pay. Under the leadership of Agesilaus, whose long experience and sound nerve never showed to better advantage, the Spartans had prepared a hot reception for the invaders. The enemies within the gates had been detected and summarily suppressed; by a timely promise of emancipation numerous loyal Helots had been induced to take up arms; and before Epaminondas could press home his attack a strong corps from the Isthmus states slipped through the invading army and threw itself into the city. Moreover, as Sparta's defences grew stronger, Epaminondas' effectives steadily dwindled, for nothing could prevent the Arcadians from straggling for plunder. Unable to lure his adversary into the open, and unwilling to acquire Sparta at a prohibitive cost, Epaminondas eventually withdrew his forces and after a rapid raid on the Laconian shipyards at Gytheum retired to Arcadia. Thus Sparta weathered the sudden crisis and postponed by some 150 years the day of capitulation to an invader.

Nevertheless the campaign of 370–69 left a lasting mark upon Peloponnesian history. Before returning home Epaminondas paid a visit to Mt Ithome, the natural citadel of Messenia, and there laid the foundations of a new city of Messene which was to be at once the stronghold and the capital of a new Messenian state. In addition to the revolted Helots and Perioeci of Messenia and Laconia, Epaminondas invited all Messenian refugees abroad to become citizens of the new commonwealth. For the construction of the town and its ring wall Epaminondas engaged the best craftsmen of Greece: from the proceeds of the rich booty of Laconia he could afford to defray a heavy builders' bill. The fortifications of Messene, which enclosed a wide enceinte, were erected in finely wrought ashlar: their remains furnish one of the best extant specimens of Greek military architecture[1]. So impregnable was this fastness that the Spartans apparently made no attempt to attack it: with the exception of a few places on the south coast, Messenia was now definitely freed from Spartan domination. Thus the Spartans lost at one blow almost one half of their territory and more than half of their serfs. Dearth of land and labour henceforth reduced their population more effectively than the wastage of war, and the economic basis of their military supremacy was shattered.

[1] See Volume of Plates ii, 12, *a*.

Although Epaminondas had crowded all the incidents of his campaign into a space of a few months, his return home was now long overdue. A further reason for a speedy retreat was imposed upon him by the appearance of a hostile force under Iphicrates in Arcadia. Unable at first to take a new alignment in the chaos of Peloponnesian politics, the Athenians had finally decided that they must establish a front against Theban imperialism. In response to an appeal for aid from Sparta they dispatched their full citizen levy to intercept the Theban retreat (spring 369). This force, it is true, consisted mainly of recruits whom Iphicrates dared not pit against Epaminondas' veterans, and it did not even contest the Isthmus passage against the Thebans. But it served at any rate to speed the parting guests, and it prevented them from leaving garrisons to hold open for them the gates of the Peloponnese.

On their return to Thebes Epaminondas and Pelopidas were greeted with an impeachment for exceeding the terms of their commission, which probably had limited them to defensive action on behalf of Elis and Arcadia. The trial, which was presumably held before the federal court of Boeotia, ended in an acquittal and the reinstatement of both generals.

In summer 369 B.C. Pelopidas, as we have seen (p. 85), entered upon a new field of conquest in Thessaly. At the same time Epaminondas was sent to conduct a second campaign in the Peloponnese, where Sparta's enemies, unable to combine effectively among each other, and threatened by the new alliance between Sparta and Athens, had again applied to Thebes for assistance. Despite their fresh commitments in Thessaly, the Thebans sent a confederate force of Central Greeks under Epaminondas to restore contact with the Central Peloponnesians. In anticipation of this move the Athenians had re-occupied the Isthmus lines and had strengthened their garrison with a Spartan division which had been brought across by sea. Thus Epaminondas encountered at the outset a line of defences which in the Corinthian War had proved almost impregnable. But by a surprise attack on the western sector, where the garrison displayed a negligence unusual among Spartan troops, Epaminondas easily carried the position. Once through the Isthmus lines he speedily joined hands with the Arcadians, Argives and Eleans and with their assistance carried the harbour towns of Sicyon and Pellene, thus securing a naval line of communication with the Peloponnese.

It was probably during this visit to the Peloponnese that Epaminondas founded a second city destined to fulfil, like Messene, the

double function of a fortress and a political capital. At the head
of the Alpheus valley, on the thoroughfare from Laconia to
western Arcadia and Elis, he marked out a site for a *Megale Polis*
or 'Great City,' which was to serve as a place of assembly for the
Arcadian federation and a frontier barrier against Spartan reprisals. The area of this site, which exceeded even that of Messene,
was divided by the river Helisson into two separate portions. The
southern sector was the meeting-place of the federal congress, and
in addition to temporary accommodation for participants in the
assembly it probably contained the permanent quarters of the
standing federal army. Excavations conducted by British scholars
in 1890–1 have shown that the theatre, where the Assembly met,
and the Thersilion or Council Hall, were planned on a most
generous scale, suggesting that the founders of Megalopolis (as
the city was usually called) were sanguine of obtaining good
attendances at the congress. The northern sector was probably
set apart as the permanent dwelling-place of the population from
some twenty neighbouring villages which was induced or coerced
to migrate into the city. As Megalopolis received a double share
of representation on the federal council, we may assume that its
permanent population was intended to grow far beyond that of
the other Arcadian communities.

The foundation of Megalopolis completed the overthrow of
Sparta's old ascendancy in the Peloponnese, for it provided the last
link in the fortress chain extending from Argos through Tegea
or Mantinea to Messene, by which Sparta henceforth was hemmed
in securely. But the same act also undermined the new ascendancy
of Thebes. Secure in the possession of their new fortress capital,
the Arcadians no longer felt the need of a Theban protectorate
and indeed began to resent it as a bar to their own claim to
supremacy in the Peloponnese.

IV THE DIPLOMATIC FAILURES OF THEBES

The full effects of Epaminondas' second campaign in the Peloponnese declared themselves in the following year. At the end
of 369 B.C. the Thebans expressed their disappointment at the
negative result of the summer's operations by not re-electing
Epaminondas and by suspending their operations in the Peloponnese. On the other hand, the Arcadians, whose new standing army
was available for field service in all seasons, began single-handed
a new war of conquest. Led by Lycomedes of Mantinea, who had
been the first to proclaim the defiant doctrine, '*Arcadia farà da
se*,' they made distant forays to the Messenian seaboard and

seized the border lands of Lasion and Triphylia in defiance of the Eleans. The conquest and annexation of these latter territories, soon led to recriminations between the Eleans and their aggressors, and the erection of an Arcadian war monument at Delphi, in which a figure of 'Triphylus' was exhibited among Arcadia's ancestral heroes, was an additional insult to the injured people.

But Arcadia's war fever was no true index of the general state of feeling in Greece. The other belligerents had mostly come to realize that they could hardly hope to secure fresh gains or to retrieve past losses. This war weariness, moreover, did not escape the notice of certain bystanders who wished to demobilize the belligerents in order to attract to their own service the mercenary troops thus set free. Among these interested brokers of peace was Dionysius of Syracuse, who had demonstrated his loyalty to his old Spartan allies by sending them a small corps of Gaulish and Spanish mercenaries to assist in the campaign of 369, yet was more anxious to bargain than to fight for them. His peace manifestos met with a prompt response among the Athenians, who conferred Attic franchise upon him (June 368) and awarded the first prize at the Lenaea of 367 to a play from his pen (p. 132 *sq.*); but it is not certain whether his envoys actually contributed to bringing the parties together. Another peace offensive was opened by Philiscus of Abydos, an emissary of the Persian satrap Ariobarzanes, who was charged with the recruitment of a Greek 'foreign legion' and engaged in peace conversations as a means towards this end. Thanks to Philiscus' good offices a peace congress was held at Delphi which appears to have been attended by all the Greek belligerents (early 368). But a good opportunity for a general settlement was thrown away by the Spartans, who claimed the restitution of Messenia and even, if tradition is to be believed, raised anew their obsolete objections to the Boeotian League.

The firm attitude adopted by Sparta at the congress was probably due to the expectation of further help from Dionysius, who actually sent a fresh contingent to the Peloponnese in the spring of 368, besides contracting a formal alliance with Athens[1]. With the assistance of Dionysius' corps the Spartans resumed the offensive in the campaign of 367 and advanced close upon Megalopolis. This expedition nearly ended in disaster, for the Argives and Messenians came to the rescue of the Arcadians, and the Spartans found their retreat cut off. But their commander

---

[1] *I.G.*[2] ii, 1, 105, probably passed in March 367 B.C. See p. 132 *sq.*

Archidamus kept his nerve; by a bold and unexpected charge he not only cleared his path with little loss to himself but inflicted heavy casualties upon his adversaries. The news of this 'Tearless Battle' broke down that stoic Spartan reserve which had stood proof against all recent disasters; in spite of its name, the victory was celebrated at Sparta with hysterical sobbings. Nevertheless the campaign of 367 left everything as before. The death of Dionysius, which occurred in the course of the year, deprived Sparta of a powerful if not very effective ally, and apart from one small contingent which he supplied in 365, his son Dionysius II rendered no further assistance.

In the winter of 367–6 B.C. the scene of war was transferred to the Great King's palace at Susa, where delegates of the Greek belligerents fought a vigorous diplomatic campaign for Persia's support. The ball was set rolling by the Spartans, who sent Antalcidas to renew his ill-famed but profitable compact of 386 B.C. To counteract Antalcidas' influence the Thebans dispatched Pelopidas, shortly after his release from custody at Pherae. The Athenians and Thebes' Peloponnesian allies followed suit. The honours of the day went to Pelopidas, who made a favourable personal impression and had an easy case to plead, in view of Thebes' past record of medism. As spoils of victory Pelopidas brought home a royal rescript ordaining that the Spartans should renounce Messenia and the Athenians should lay up their warships.

The first impression which this declaration made among Thebes' adversaries was so painful that the Athenians put to death one of their envoys and Antalcidas anticipated execution by committing suicide. The Thebans resolved to take advantage of this consternation by bluffing their opponents into an immediate acceptance of Persia's terms. Having summoned a general congress at Thebes, they invited the delegates to swear to the peace there and then (early in 366). But this manœuvre failed completely. On further reflection the Greek belligerents had realized that the Persian king was in no position to enforce his recommendations, as he had been in 386 B.C. At the congress Lycomedes, the Arcadian deputy, took his usual independent line and flatly denied Thebes' right to dictate a settlement. By this action he killed the congress, and a subsequent attempt by the Thebans to salvage their peace by separate bargainings with their adversaries met with no better fate.

In the meantime the Thebans overreached themselves in another political deal which nullified the results of a successful military campaign. After a year's deliberate abstention from Peloponnesian affairs they had undertaken a third campaign in the Peloponnese at the instigation of Epaminondas, who had recovered his influence after his recent successes in Thessaly (summer 367). Epaminondas' objective was the coastline of Achaea, the possession of which would go a long way to convert the Corinthian Gulf into a Theban lake. His personal prestige sufficed, as usual, to rally the wavering loyalty of the central Peloponnesians. The decisive stroke in the campaign was dealt by the Argives, who cleared a passage through the Isthmus lines by a rear attack upon the Spartan and Athenian garrisons. Once inside the Peloponnese, Epaminondas had an easy task. With the reinforcements which presently poured in from all his Peloponnesian allies he gathered so strong a force that the Achaean league submitted to him without a combat and was enrolled as ally of Thebes[1]. But in the year following upon the Theban expedition a political blunder converted its victory into a defeat. Epaminondas, who was a loyal but not a fanatic democrat, had consistently ignored the harsh law by which the Thebans had ordered all captured Boeotian refugees to be put to death, and in Achaea he had refused to overthrow the existing oligarchies on the abstract ground that such governments normally sympathized with Sparta. But the Theban democracy, with doctrinaire zeal, cancelled his capitulations and sent 'harmosts' to Achaea to effect democratic revolutions. This high-handed policy, which recalled the worst days of Spartan imperialism, was all the more foolish, as Thebes could spare no troops to garrison Achaea. A counter-revolution by the oligarchic exiles presently swept the new democracies away, and the restored oligarchs played up to the part which Thebes had imposed upon them by making alliance with Sparta. For this failure it was but a meagre compensation that the Thebans recovered the border town of Oropus from the Athenians (summer 366) and defeated an attempt by a turncoat demagogue named Euphron to expel their garrison from Sicyon.

A further diplomatic defeat was inflicted upon Thebes towards the end of 366 by the conclusion of an alliance between Athens and Arcadia. This compact was the work of Thebes' old antagonist Lycomedes, who rightly calculated that the Athenians would resume their broken relations with Arcadia in order to separate her from Thebes. It was not concluded without protest

---

[1] There is a federal Achaean coinage issued probably at this period. See Volume of Plates ii, 6, *g*, and W. Wroth, *Num. Chron.* 1902, pp. 324 *sqq.*

from the Thebans, who sent Epaminondas to the federal Arcadian congress to measure his eloquence against that of the Athenian Callistratus. But Lycomedes carried the day, and, though he died shortly after, he lived long enough to secure the ratification of the alliance at Athens.

It now remained to be seen whether the Athenians would resume the part of arbitrators in the Peloponnese which they had played for a brief moment after Leuctra. The Arcadian treaty was a handsome testimonial to a power which appeared to be alone able to offer alliances on a basis of genuine autonomy. But the Athenians promptly belied their reputation by a piece of sharp practice that recalled the exploits of Phoebidas and Sphodrias. The better to secure the Isthmus lines against fresh surprises, they resolved to appropriate Corinth as the Argives had done in the Corinthian War, but instead of taking over the city by agreement they attempted to carry it by a *coup de main*. But with an artlessness that did little credit to their knavery they allowed their project to be mentioned quite openly in the Assembly. The Corinthians of course got wind of the plot. Politely but firmly they refused admittance at Cenchreae to an Athenian fleet which presently arrived 'to assist Corinth against her secret enemies,' and ushered the existing Athenian garrison out of the Isthmus lines.

But the Corinthians had only steered clear of Charybdis to run foul of Scylla. Having taken over the entire Isthmus defences, they confided this service to a citizen named Timophanes, who promptly betrayed his trust by making himself tyrant. Fortunately the mercenary corps which was the instrument of Timophanes' power played false in turn to its master, for they allowed him to be assassinated by a few patriots under the leadership of the tyrant's brother Timoleon. The Corinthians thus recovered their liberty, but after their double surprise they decided to contract out of a war which was degenerating into mere brigandage and opened negotiations with Thebes. Though pressed to transfer themselves to the Theban side and thus to obtain revenge against Athens, they refused to turn their arms against their former allies, and before breaking away from their old confederates they endeavoured to obtain the inclusion of Sparta in the peace. The Spartans rejected the good offices of Corinth rather than abandon their claim to Messenia. Indeed the war for the possession of this land was henceforth waged with pen no less than sword. A famous rhetorician Alcidamas of Elaea supported Messenia's independence on a principle which only Euripides had dared to enunciate before him, that 'freedom was the birthright of all mankind.' On the other side Isocrates entered the lists with a pamphlet which urged the Spartans to evacuate their city for the time being and to entrench themselves on some Laconian Mt Ithome rather than give away their heritage. Thus Sparta stood aloof from the peace. But the Corinthians signed it with a clear conscience. At the same time too they secured a settlement for the minor states of Argolis such as Epidaurus, and for the little fortress of Phlius, which had hitherto stood valiantly by Sparta in spite of the incessant attacks from Argos, Arcadia and Sicyon (winter 366–5).

V. THE FAILURE OF ARCADIAN IMPERIALISM

The war-weariness to which Corinth succumbed gave promise that the fighting would flicker out on each successive battle-front. But the fires had been damped down without being extinguished, and the spluttering of a few live embers presently caused them to flare up again. In 365, after several years of quiescence, the Eleans determined to enforce a clause in the Persian rescript of 367–6 which awarded to them the debatable lands on the Arcadian border. The Arcadians retaliated vigorously, and with the help of a contingent from Athens, which had recognized the *casus foederis*, beat the Eleans out of the field and invaded their territory. Though they failed to take the capital they permanently occupied Olympia and Pylos, thus securing access to the plains of the Alpheus and Peneus, and systematically harried the Elean lowlands. The Eleans now cast about for allies and successively enlisted the Achaeans and the Spartans. The Achaeans threw a garrison into the city of Elis, and a Spartan force under Archidamus made a sudden foray into Arcadian territory and fortified a position at Cromnus which threatened Megalopolis (late in 365 or early in 364). The Arcadians in turn invoked their allies. The Athenians, who had stipulated that they should not serve against Sparta, held back; but the Argives and Messenians came to the rescue, and the Thebans, who had also received a call, seized the opportunity of reasserting their influence and sent a small contingent. This coalition only kept the field long enough to reduce Cromnus and take prisoner its garrison, but by this success they set the Arcadians free to round upon the Eleans, who had meanwhile done nothing to assist the hard-pressed Spartans at Cromnus (spring 364). Reinforced by an Argive and Athenian corps, the Arcadians strengthened their defences at Olympia; and they induced the people of the surrounding region of Pisatis to set themselves up as a 'Panama Republic,' and to assume the custody of the Olympian sanctuary and of the quadrennial games that fell due in midsummer 364. The new stewards of the course attracted sufficient competitors to make up the usual events, and although an Elean force interrupted proceedings by an unexpected attack upon the sacred enclosure, this intrusion was repelled, and the games were concluded under Pisatan auspices.

The Eleans had now been fought to a standstill; and as the Spartans made no further move after their mishap at Cromnus, the Arcadians held their conquests unmolested. Their seizure of the Olympic sanctuary does not appear to have made any deep impression upon Greece; moreover, their claim that Pisatis had formerly been an independent state and was the original trustee of the holy places was probably quite well founded. But the dominion which the Arcadians exercised in Olympia through their Pisatan men-of-straw exposed them to a dangerous temptation. The regular army which had been the instrument of their recent conquests was an expensive luxury. It is probable that from the outset it lived largely on plunder; in 364 B.C. it repaid itself for the conquest of Olympia by raiding the sacred treasures. It is true that the raid ostensibly took the form of a loan, and that the gold coins issued out of its proceeds bore the name of Pisa[1], not of Arcadia; but these subterfuges probably deceived nobody.

Considering that compulsory loans from temples were not an uncommon expedient in Greek statecraft, we must admit that the Arcadians strained rather than broke Greek conventions. Yet the gold obols of Pisa presently burnt holes in their pockets. Their religious scruples, moreover, prompted the further question whether on broad grounds of policy a standing mercenary army was desirable at all. Being largely of Arcadian nationality, this force had a large vote in the federal synod, and as its professional interests lay in the direction of warfare and plunder without end, it naturally favoured a more adventurous policy than the more substantial and settled population desired. Eventually the Mantineans protested in the federal congress against the use of the sacred moneys, and after a sharp tussle with the federal authorities, who vainly endeavoured to stifle the protests by prosecuting their authors for treason, they won over a majority of the Assembly. Taking the bull by the horns, the Assembly went so far as to abolish the payment of the federal forces and to replace the mercenaries with an unpaid 'white guard.' At the same time it offered peace to the Eleans, who abandoned their claims to Lasion

[1] For specimens of these gold coins see Volume of Plates ii, 6, *d.*

and Triphylia in consideration of receiving back Olympia and their other recent losses. It is not known whether compensation was offered for the abstracted temple treasures. The terms were accepted, and a feud which had become one of the chief menaces to the peace of the Peloponnese was thus ended (winter 363–2).

But the settlement of the Elean question revived a problem which had become the crux of Peloponnesian politics, whether Peloponnesian disputes should be submitted to the arbitration of Thebes. Before the completion of the negotiations with Elis some members of the Arcadian executive appealed to Thebes for intervention against the Arcadian assembly. The Thebans, who had participated in the campaign for the recovery of Cromnus, had at least a formal right of complaint for having been ignored in the peace discussions, and they decided to exercise their right in a forcible manner. In concert with the Arcadian malcontents they sent a small force to purge Arcadia as they had purged Achaea in 366. The commander of this force appeared at the ceremony of swearing to the Elean peace, which the Arcadian executive had by collusion convened to Tegea (where feeling presumably ran strongest against the peace party), and having reassured the delegates by taking the oath in his own person he arrested as many of them as he could lay hands on. But the Mantinean representatives, who were the birds best worth bagging, had already flown. The fugitives at once called the rest of Arcadia to arms, and the Theban maladroit was glad to ransom himself by surrendering his captives.

VI. THE BATTLE OF MANTINEA

This fiasco left the Thebans no option but to renounce their interests in Arcadia or to reassert their authority by a crushing display of force. Epaminondas, as usual, was all for drastic measures, and urged that it would be treason for Thebes to desert her own partisans in the Peloponnese. After their recent successful intervention in Thessaly the Thebans were in the mood for one more Peloponnesian adventure. They resolved to coerce the Arcadian independents and made preparations for a great military effort, in which all the Central Greeks and Thessalians were required to participate.

The Theban mobilization had the immediate effect of splitting up the Arcadian federation and dividing the Peloponnese into two hostile camps. While the northern portion of Arcadia stood firm by Mantinea, the southern section, including Tegea and Megalopolis, threw in its lot with Thebes. The Argives and Messenians also held firm to the Theban alliance. But the Mantineans gained the support of their new Elean friends and of Thebes' old enemies Achaea and Sparta. Of the Isthmus states Sicyon adhered to Thebes, while Corinth and Megara remained neutral. On the other hand, Athens promised support to Mantinea. Thus almost the entire Greek homeland was drawn into one or other of two closely matched coalitions (spring 362).

In the ensuing campaign the first problem for both parties was to concentrate their scattered contingents. Epaminondas, who was first in the field with his Central Greek and Thessalian levy, passed unchecked through the Isthmus and then halted at Nemea in order to intercept the Athenian forces. But the Athenians outwitted their enemy by using the sea route to Laconia and proceeding thence to Arcadia, and while the Thebans were wasting time on a false trail his opponents effected a general concentration at Mantinea. Nevertheless Epaminondas kept the initiative in his hands. Having joined forces with his Peloponnesian allies at Tegea he made a sudden night march upon Sparta, the capture of which would have been of little strategic but of high moral value. At this moment Sparta was practically defenceless. Part of the Spartan forces had already reached Mantinea[1]; the main army under Agesilaus had only just started out from Sparta, but as Tegea barred the direct road to Mantinea, it was proceeding by a more circuitous route through Pellene and Asea, and thus stood but little chance of falling in with Epaminondas. But a deserter brought news to Agesilaus just in time for him to double back to Sparta; and Epaminondas, who probably had only a flying column with him, made no serious attempt to break into the strongly defended town but presently fell back upon Tegea. From this point he immediately sent forward his Theban and Thessalian horsemen towards Mantinea in order to seize the Mantinean harvest, then in process of being cut. As the main army had meantime moved off to the rescue of Sparta by the Asea route, the Mantinean territory should have fallen an easy prey to the invaders. But an Athenian cavalry troop, which had just arrived at Mantinea after several days of forced marching, sallied out and by a vigorous charge routed the marauders, who were perhaps just as jaded as their attackers. In this action the historian Xenophon lost a son, but with that self-suppression which characterizes more than one part of his *Hellenica* he left it to others to commemorate this incident.

After this second check Epaminondas took no further ad-

_____
[1] See map facing p. 102.

vantage of his position at Tegea, which allowed him to operate on inner lines, but permitted the enemy to concentrate in full force at Mantinea. The mischances of his campaign and shortage of supplies determined him to force a decision in a pitched battle. Though in numbers he was scarcely if at all superior to his opponents, each side probably numbering some 25,000 men, yet by his personal ascendancy he had created a fine fighting spirit through all his force, and his Boeotian contingent, which was now drilled uniformly on the Theban model, was capable of winning a battle single-handed.

The level upland valley in which Mantinea and Tegea were situated is narrowed in the middle like an hour-glass by two spurs projecting from the adjacent longitudinal ranges. Between these spurs Epaminondas' opponents had taken up a position in defence of Mantinea which could only be carried by a frontal attack. As at Leuctra, Epaminondas decided to stake everything on an overwhelming thrust against the enemy's key position. Instead of dressing his whole front by the left, he again, as at Leuctra, kept his centre and right wing lagging in successive *échelons*. As a further means of deferring the action on his right flank he posted a detachment on the rising ground at the edge of the battlefield, so as to take in flank any sudden advance by the enemy's left wing. On his own left wing he drew up his entire Boeotian infantry corps in a deep ramming formation, and on its flank a similar wedge of cavalry interspersed with quick-footed javelin-men. To put his adversaries off their guard he changed direction during his advance and turned in under a mountain spur on his left. Here he made the deception complete by halting his men and making them ground arms. So successful was this ruse that the enemy concluded that he had called off his attack and was going to pitch camp, and under this impression relinquished their battle order. When their formation was thoroughly broken up, Epaminondas right-turned again into line of battle and made a surprise onset.

Of the details of this combat we have no trustworthy account. It is clear, however, that Epaminondas achieved his primary purpose, for the Boeotian columns pierced the Spartan and Mantinean fronts facing them and thereby unhinged the entire enemy line. A sweeping victory now lay in Epaminondas' grasp, but before he could drive home his success the Theban general was struck with a mortal wound. To such an extent was Epaminondas the brain of his army that the moment it lost his guidance it became paralysed. The Boeotian horse and foot suspended their pursuit, and the light-armed men blundered aimlessly across to the enemy's left wing, where the Athenians made short work of them. The centre and right wing of Epaminondas' force paused before it became seriously engaged. Thus the loss of one man converted a decisive victory into an unprofitable draw.

In the history of ancient warfare Epaminondas is an outstanding figure. In his methodical exploitation of Greek shock tactics, in his handling of multiple columns on the march, and in the personal magnetism by which he bound men of diverse cities and political interests into his service, he will bear comparison with the great Macedonian captains who followed him and indeed may be called his pupils. As a politician Epaminondas deserves full credit for his freedom from that rancorous spirit of party which obsessed most politicians of his age and bore off like a harpy the infant Theban democracy. On the other hand, he does not rank as a great Panhellenic patriot: indeed we may ascribe even to Agesilaus a clearer appreciation of the need for Panhellenic solidarity. His political vision does not appear to have extended beyond an ill-defined suzerainty of Thebes over Greece, or to have envisaged any better instrument of control than haphazard military intervention. His political achievements therefore were mainly negative. In liberating the Helots of Messenia and in saving the Boeotian League from disruption Epaminondas performed tasks of sound constructive statesmanship; in destroying the supremacy of Sparta in the Peloponnese he also destroyed the *pax Peloponnesiaca* which had been the most consistent stabilizing force in Greek politics, and failed to supply any passable substitute. In urging on Thebes to an imperial policy he was blind to her deficiencies in man-power and mobilizable wealth, in political experience and in prestige; and he failed to realize that the military supremacy of his city which was so essentially his handiwork was by that very token a wasting asset, contingent upon his own life.

It is said that Epaminondas' parting advice to his countrymen was to make a speedy peace. The Thebans, who had never given a consistent support to Epaminondas' policy of adventures and therefore hardly required his prompting, at once convened a new congress. At this meeting the only serious difficulty that arose was over Messenia: rather than recognize its independence, the Spartans stood out of the settlement. But such was the general war-weariness that the other belligerents abandoned all outstanding claims and guaranteed each other's possessions by a general defensive alliance.

MAP 5

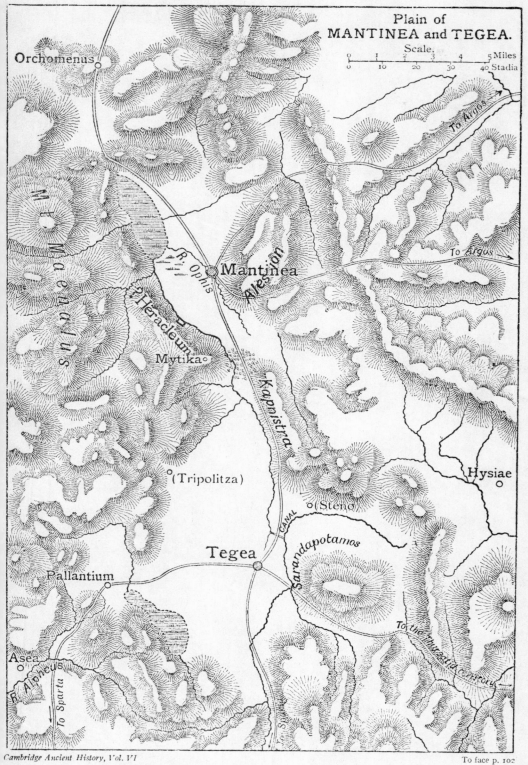

Plain of
MANTINEA and TEGEA.

Scale.

Orchomenus

To Argos

To Argos

Mt Maenalus

R. Ophis

Mantinea
Alesion

?Heracleum

Mytika

Kapnistra

(Tripolitza)

Hysiae

(Steno)

CANAL

Sarandapotamos

Tegea

Pallantium

To the Thyreatid territory

Asea

R. Alpheus

To Sparta

VII. THE DECLINE OF THE ATHENIAN NAVAL LEAGUE

This compact marks a distinct advance towards the formation of a Greek League of Cities, in that its signatories not only renounced mutual aggression but recognized the need of active mutual support, and instead of giving the peace of Greece in trust to a single imperial state made its defence a general obligation upon the Greek powers. The general treaty, moreover, was re-inforced by a specific convention drawn up shortly after (second half of 362 or first half of 361) by Athens, Achaea, Phlius and the reconstructed Arcadian League with the same object in view. Yet such alliances remained mere expressions of a pious opinion failing some provision for the regular interchange of opinion among their members, and the prompt execution of common resolutions. Greece had to wait twenty-four years longer until a statesman of real constructive ability provided her with a federal machinery that was at once equitable and efficient (p. 266 *sq.*).

In the absence of any effective scheme of co-operation among the land powers of the Greek world, the revived maritime league of Athens remained for the moment the only centre of union which might serve as the nucleus of a general Greek Confederacy. This league, as we have seen (chap. iii), failed to attract the states of the Greek mainland. The Thebans, who had been enrolled among its original members, did not remain in it for long, and in seceding from it they detached the Acarnanians, Euboeans and Chalcidians (371 b.c.). But most of the maritime allies adhered to Athens and took part in the various peace congresses between 374 and 362 b.c. In securing the freedom of the seas the Athenian Confederacy accomplished work of manifest value, and if the Athenians had remained true to its original principle of mutual defence, it might well have lived on and even experienced a new growth.

But the Athenians had not learnt sufficiently the lesson of their past failures, and the naval ascendancy which they had recovered in the warfare of the 'seventies was again perverted from purposes of defence to be an instrument of oppression. The first symptom of a relapse into former errors may be discerned in the renewed interest which the Athenians displayed in their long-lost colony of Amphipolis. In the convention with the Peloponnesian states drawn up after the battle of Leuctra they had stipulated for a free hand in dealing with the city, and in 369 their general Iphicrates was sent out with a squadron to recapture it, but failed in his mission.

But the real starting-point in their career of acquisitive imperialism was 366 B.C. In that year Callistratus, who had consistently advocated a policy of defensive alliances on a basis
of strict autonomy, was accused of treason consequent upon the
loss of Oropus. By a brilliant display of oratory he secured
his acquittal; but he lost his political ascendancy, and a few
years later he succumbed to a charge of 'having advised the
demos ill,' and went into exile[1]. He was supplanted in the
public favour by Timotheus. This soldier of fortune, undis-
mayed by the fiasco of his campaign in 373, still pressed for
a policy of naval adventure. In 366 he was entrusted with a
powerful armament and a roving commission in Aegean waters.
The Athenian general had been enjoined to treat Persia with
respect, but he saw little reason for keeping to his instructions.

The Persian empire, having recovered from one epidemic of
rebellions in the 'eighties, was passing through a second and
even more dangerous crisis in the 'sixties. In Egypt the native
prince Nectanebo I (378–361) maintained his independence
against all comers: in 374 he repelled an invasion by a large
composite force of Persian levies and Greek mercenaries
under Pharnabazus and Iphicrates. A few years later (c. 366) a
fresh insurrection in Phoenicia and Cilicia deprived the King of
the best part of his war fleet. But the most serious rebellion broke
out in Asia Minor, whose governors, long accustomed to passive
disloyalty, now became openly mutinous. In Cappadocia a
capable native satrap named Datames was goaded by a palace
intrigue into open insurrection. His example was followed to
east and west by the governor of Armenia and by Ariobarzanes
the successor of Pharnabazus, whose efforts to recruit a mercenary
force in Greece we have already noticed. In Caria Hecatomnus'
son Mausolus played the same double game as his father had
practised in the Cyprian war; and Autophradates the satrap of
Lydia was eventually constrained by his rebel neighbours to make
common cause with them (367–6). For a while all Asia Minor
was lost to the King. But in the long run the Persian governors
proved yet more disloyal to each other than to their overlord.
Several of the lesser mutineers deserted back to Artaxerxes, and
after the deaths of the ringleaders, Datames and Ariobarzanes
(c. 360), the King's authority was re-established (p. 20 sq.).

[1] The exile of Callistratus is to be set not later than the autumn of
361 B.C., see P.W. s.v. Kallistratos. After some years of exile he returned
to Athens as a suppliant, but the death sentence passed on him *in absentia*
was put into effect.

'Persia's difficulty is my opportunity' was the motto of more than one Greek soldier of fortune. In 366 the Spartan king Agesilaus, profiting by the lull in the war at home, entered into Ariobarzanes' pay as a recruiting officer and diplomatic agent. After the campaign of Mantinea the aged king again turned *condottiere* and fought his last battles in the employ of the rebel princes of Egypt (p. 150 *sq.*).

While Agesilaus was earning subsidies for Sparta, Timotheus was acquiring territory for Athens. After a ten months siege (366–5) Samos capitulated to him, and in return for services unspecified Ariobarzanes made over to him the important station of Sestos on the Hellespont (365). In the following years (364–3) Timotheus was sent to the Macedonian coast, where Iphicrates had wasted four years in futile endeavours to recover Amphipolis. The new commander did no better against this fortress, but with the help of the Macedonian king Perdiccas, who had recently murdered the regent Ptolemy and now was eager to buy the recognition of Athens, he wrested Torone, Potidaea, Pydna, Methone, and several other cities from the Chalcidian League.

In 364 Timotheus' campaigns suffered a brief interruption through the sudden appearance of an unsuspected enemy fleet. In this year the Thebans, having left the Peloponnese to work out its own perdition, had won a free hand for enterprise in a new field. At the instigation of Epaminondas, who rightly perceived that Athens was now his chief adversary, and that the quickest means of checkmating her would be to demolish her naval supremacy, they annexed the Locrian harbour of Larymna and there built an armada of 100 warships. This fleet, by far the greatest that ever sailed under a Boeotian flag, so took the Athenians by surprise that they for the moment let the trident drop from their hands. Under Epaminondas' pennant the Boeotian interlopers sailed unopposed to the Propontis and won over Byzantium from Athens. After this rapid success they returned home, apparently without attempting to procure other defections, although the islands of Naxos and Ceos declared for them; and the new turn which Peloponnesian politics took in the ensuing years precluded them from undertaking a second cruise. By her failure to follow up her first naval success Thebes probably lost nothing in the long run: although she could supply ships and men, she lacked the funds which were indispensable for sustained naval operations.

In 362 the Athenians received another unexpected blow from their former ally Alexander of Pherae, now a vassal of Thebes.

Not only did Alexander's flotilla make successful tip-and-run raids among the Cyclades, but it inflicted some loss upon its Athenian pursuers before it slipped back into its port at Pagasae. But this foray, like that of Epaminondas, was more annoying than dangerous.

After these diversions the Athenians were able to resume operations in the region of the Hellespont. In this quarter the Thracian king Cotys (383–60), who was not content like his predecessors Medocus and Hebryzelmis to leave his seaboard in foreign hands, offered persistent opposition to the seizure of new stations by Athens. But after his death the greater part of the Gallipoli peninsula passed into Athenian hands.

This acquisition, together with the recapture of Euboea in 357, marks the limit of Athens' naval expansion in the fourth century. Judged by the map, Athenian imperialism might appear to have been justified once more. In reality, however, the grasping policy of Timotheus killed the Second Athenian Confederacy as surely as Pericles' and Cleon's overbearing attitude had killed the First. For a second time the Athenian protectorate played over into a tyranny. It was perhaps but a small matter when Athens punished rebellions on the islands of Ceos and Naxos by limiting their jurisdiction (363–2). The establishment of cleruchies at Samos (365) and Potidaea (361), though undeniably contrary to the spirit of the Second Confederacy, did not infringe its letter, as these two acquisitions were not formally enrolled in the League. But the financial consequences of the new imperialism were utterly ruinous. Athenian war expenditure, which had already been swollen by the cost of the mercenaries on garrison duty at the Isthmus, was further inflated by the upkeep of a fleet whose gradual increase to a total of over 250 ships is recorded in a series of contemporary navy-lists which have been preserved on inscriptions. The yearly contributions of the allies, amounting at most to 350 talents, together with the proceeds of the Athenian property tax, proved woefully inadequate to cover the military outlay. The straits to which lack of funds had reduced Timotheus in 373 became a normal experience of each successive admiral. The more considerate commanders, such as Timotheus himself, had recourse to the private generosity of their ships' captains, or paid their debts in token money issued for eventual redemption in silver out of the spoils of war. The more reckless ones black-mailed the allied cities and plundered the merchant shipping of the Aegean. By the end of the 'sixties the Second Athenian Confederacy was irredeemably bankrupt; from being an instrument of security to the Aegean communities it was degenerating into an Algerian pirate organization.

Thus the history of the decade after Leuctra marks the final failure of city-state imperialism on land and sea. This failure, coupled with the constant recrudescence of faction fighting within the several cities, the general unsettlement and the partial impoverishment which followed upon the political unrest, might lead the reader to infer, as some of the most keen-sighted of Greek contemporaries did in fact conclude, that the decline and fall of Greece had now definitely set in. But *quand Dieu efface il se prépare à écrire*. The ensuing chapters will show that Greece was on the eve of a great political reconstruction.

CHAPTER V

DIONYSIUS OF SYRACUSE

I. CARTHAGINIAN INVASIONS. 409–406 B.C.

THE victory of Syracuse over Athens (vol. v, chap. x) did
not lead immediately, as might have been expected, to an
assertion of her dominion over all the Greek communities of
Sicily. But her victory led, as in the case of Athens after the
Persian War, to a distinct development of democracy. The absence
of Hermocrates on naval work in the cause of Sparta and of the
Peloponnesians removed the gravest obstacle to the plans of the
democratic party (vol. v, p. 312 *sq.*). After the triumphant defeat
of the Athenian expedition the elated Syracusans decided to take
an active part in destroying the Athenian Empire altogether,
whereby they would repay the debt they owed their Peloponnesian
allies for the decisive assistance they had sent to Sicily. Accordingly Syracusan and other Siceliote forces sailed to the coasts of
Asia Minor to reinforce the Spartan armies which were now
acting with Persian help against the cities which belonged to the
Athenian Empire. The statesman Hermocrates, who had been
the most effective leader of the Syracusans in resisting the Athenians, was the most conspicuous of the generals commanding these
Sicilian contingents, which seem to have made a very good impression by their gallantry and good behaviour. In the meantime in
Syracuse itself party warfare had broken out and, in the absence
of Hermocrates, one of his political opponents named Diocles
had gained preponderant influence in the Assembly, and had
induced it to pass a decree of banishment against Hermocrates
and the other absent generals (compare above vol. v, p. 346).
Diocles, the chief opponent of Hermocrates, made changes and
adopted ideas which seem to have been inspired by Athenian
practice. The transfer of power from the military and other civil
authorities was especially important, and the magistrates, who

Note. The source for the continuous narrative of events in this Chapter
is Diodorus Siculus (XIII–XV), who derived his information from the works
of the Syracusan Philistus, and also from the works of Ephorus and Timaeus.
His chronology is very unsatisfactory and he has omitted much; he can
be supplemented here and there by Xenophon and other writers (see the
Bibliography).

No official documents of the Syracusan state during this period are extant were now appointed by lot, were restricted in their control of the Assembly.

This democratized state had now to face the danger of a new Carthaginian invasion. The fact that Carthage, since her repulse at Himera in 480 B.C. (vol. IV, pp. 379 *sqq.*), had been quiescent in Sicily we may perhaps partly attribute to troubles with the native Africans, but now she thought that the weakening of the Sicilian communities by the war with Athens offered a good opportunity for her to strengthen her hold on the island. The frontier dispute between Selinus and Segesta, which had now been resumed, afforded her a welcome pretext when Segesta appealed to her for help.

Mercenaries were enlisted in Spain and troops raised in Libya until the army exceeded 100,000 men, well provided with all the resources of Punic siege-craft. The transports, 1500 in number, were covered by a battle-fleet of 60 warships. In 409 B.C. all was ready, and the suffete Hannibal was appointed commander. The obsession of vengeance for his grandfather, Hamilcar, who fell in the great disaster at Himera made him eagerly accept the duty. He crossed to the neighbourhood of Motya and, joining forces with his Sicilian allies, marched to Selinus which was taken, sacked and destroyed, despite a brave resistance. Hannibal, having performed the duty which he had been sent by the state to perform, then turned his thoughts to his personal plans of vengeance. He marched to Himera and besieged it, but before his troops could force an entrance, help came from Syracuse, under the command of Diocles. Hannibal was forced to resort to stratagem, and declared that his plan was to march upon Syracuse. Anxious to return to protect his native town, Diocles persuaded the Himeraeans to abandon their city. Half the inhabitants were put on a squadron of 25 triremes which had just appeared, and sailed for Messana, while the remainder were to hold out until the ships returned. Meanwhile Hannibal pressed the siege with redoubled vigour. When the returning ships were in sight of the doomed city, the Spanish troops of Hannibal broke through the walls and massacred the inhabitants. Himera perished utterly. The solemn rites of torture and death were held on the spot where Hamilcar had died[1]. Leaving troops to support the allies of Carthage, Hannibal returned to Carthage, content with revenge and his success at Selinus.

[1] The increase of Punic influence is illustrated by the cessation of coinage of Segesta and a change in that of Panormus which had hitherto been purely Hellenic. We now find on the coins of Panormus the enigmatic Punic legend ZIZ: see the Volume of Plates ii, 6, *h*.

But at this very moment there returned to Sicily the Syracusan Hermocrates to trouble the peace both of Carthage and of his own city. He had with him a small fleet and army procured by the parting gifts of his friend Pharnabazus the satrap. Failing to secure admission to Syracuse, he resolved to distinguish himself by warfare against the national enemy. He made Selinus his base and ravaged the territories first of Motya and then of Panormus. Phoenician Sicily was no longer inviolate. These successes invited a reaction in his favour, which he sought to increase by sending back to Syracuse the bones of the citizens which Diocles had left unburied before the walls of Himera. The solemn procession marked the contrast between his achievement and the failure of his democratic rival. Diocles was exiled, but the Syracusans refused to vote the recall of Hermocrates. For, not without reason, they suspected that he was determined to be the master of Syracuse. Thereupon Hermocrates sought to force an entry, but his friends failed him, and he fell in the agora near the gate of Achradina.

The Syracusans who had not wished to gain a tyrant at the price of Carthaginian enmity sought to disown the activities of Hermocrates in Western Sicily, but the Carthaginians, at once encouraged and infuriated, decided to send another great expedition and subdue Greek Sicily once for all. Before we follow the fortunes of this army we may pause to notice how the destroyed city of Himera lived again in the new town of Thermae founded near its site. Though intended to be purely Carthaginian and Libyan, the Greeks who migrated to this settlement on the hill of the hot springs soon made it practically a Greek city[1]. Its inhabitants were generally known as Himeraeans. It is the modern Termini.

While embassies had gone to and fro between Syracuse and Carthage, the recruiting agents of Carthage had hired mercenaries in Spain, the Balearic islands, and Italy. These with contingents from the African allies and dependencies made up an armament which even exceeded the Grand Army of 409. Hannibal was again in command, with his younger kinsman Himilco as his chief lieutenant. His first task was not easy, the safe passage of his transports to Sicily in the face of the Syracusan fleet. This he achieved by exposing a squadron to defeat near Mt Eryx while the remainder of his ships crossed in safety to the south-west of the island (406 B.C.). His first objective was Acragas. She had for many years enjoyed a prosperous neutrality in the Sicilian wars, and had become famous for her luxury. A characteristic regula-

[1] On the Punic coins of this city, at first without inscriptions, presently appears the legend ΘΕΡΜΙΤΑΝ. See Volume of Plates ii, 6, *i*.

tion existed that the guards in the watch-towers should have only the scant comfort of a mattress, two pillows and a quilt. But the city was strong by nature and art, and the Greeks of eastern Sicily and southern Italy promised to send a relieving army. With a Spartan, Dexippus, as commander and with a stiffening of Campanian mercenaries, the Acragantines resolved to resist. The Carthaginians fortified their main camp on the right bank of the river Hypsas and assailed the western wall of the city. To help their assaults they began to construct a huge causeway. For this purpose stones were taken in the necropolis and notably from the tomb of Theron, until a thunderbolt falling on the tomb, and a pestilence, to which Hannibal himself fell a victim, aroused the superstitions of the soldiers. But Himilco was as adroit as his kinsman. The tombs were left untouched, a boy was sacrificed to Moloch, and the causeway was completed.

With the approach of the relieving army of the Greeks came the crisis of the siege. The Syracusan commander Daphnaeus, at the head of 30,000 foot and 5000 horse crossed the river Himeras and defeated the forces posted to block his way. But the treachery or the incompetence of the generals within the city allowed these troops to escape, and the strong camp to the west of the city saved the Carthaginian army. The superior Syracusan cavalry cut off supplies until the Carthaginians were in great straits. But Himilco contrived to capture a convoy bringing food by sea from Syracuse to Acragas and, in a moment, the situation was reversed. The Campanian mercenaries in the city proved disloyal as food became scarce. Dexippus was suspected of being responsible for the further misfortune of the desertion of the Italiote and Sicilian allies, and the men of Acragas were left alone to defend their city as best they could. They came to the amazing resolve to abandon it and marched out at night unmolested. Himilco entered the city and sacked it; the great temple of Zeus was doomed by the victor to remain unfinished. By this time winter had set in, and the general made Acragas his winter quarters hoping to refound it as a Carthaginian city.

II. RISE OF DIONYSIUS. 405 B.C.

Sicily was now in great peril; it looked as if the whole island might be enslaved by the Carthaginian invader. For the fall of Acragas the Syracusan generals were widely blamed; whether incompetent or corrupt they were not the men to deal with a great crisis. But a deliverer arose, a friend of Hermocrates who had been left for dead in the last fight in the agora, who realized that this

was a good opportunity to destroy the already weakened democracy of Syracuse. His name was Dionysius, and he made a
speech in the Assembly so violent that he had to be fined, but he
would not be silenced and carried his point, through the generosity
of his friend Philistus, the historian, who promised to pay each
fine as it was imposed. New generals were appointed of whom
Dionysius was one. This was his first step to supreme power;
he then worked against his colleagues spreading suspicions of
their loyalty. He was elected sole general with unlimited powers
—*strategos autocrator* (p. 116). This was the second step towards
tyranny. His next move was to march the Syracusan army to
Leontini. The day after his arrival there, a rumour was spread
abroad that he had been compelled to seek sanctuary in the
Acropolis on account of an attempt on his life, and the citizens
of Syracuse gave him a bodyguard of 600 soldiers. Dionysius
thus attained the supreme power. He did not attempt to change
the constitution; the Assembly still met[1].

Dionysius was one of those Greek politicians of the same order
as Peisistratus and Themistocles, who had been prefigured in
early Greek legend by Odysseus, the man of crafty counsels;
never at a loss to find a way out of difficulties, far-seeing and
extraordinarily astute, gaining his ends by tortuous paths. He
was to become the most remarkable statesman in the Greek
world of his day, and having secured the firm mastery of Syracuse
he was to rule nearly the whole of Sicily and ultimately he was to
create an Empire northwards into Italy, wielding a power not
only such as no Sicilian potentate had ever wielded before, but so
large and formidable that Greeks compared his position in Western
Europe with that of the Persian King in the East.

The real reason of the rise of Dionysius to power was the
crying need of a competent general to oppose Carthage, but at
this time, although he was destined to live to be the defender of
Hellenic Sicily, he did not fulfil the hopes of the Syracusans. In
command of a large army and fleet he proceeded to Gela, which
Himilco was besieging. One of the first incidents of the siege
was the plunder of the precinct of Apollo outside the walls. The
famous statue of the god was sent to Tyre, the mother city of
Carthage. As at Acragas, the Carthaginians had a strongly fortified camp which the relieving army hoped to take by a simul-
taneous assault from several sides. Dionysius and his mercenaries
failed to carry out their part, the Italiote and Siceliote forces were

[1] He induced the Assembly to double the pay of the army, Diodorus
XIII, 95.

defeated separately and the attack was a complete failure. The Geloans had defended their city stoutly; their fate was now debated in a private council. It was decided that the people should abandon their city immediately, and Dionysius on his march to Syracuse also persuaded the people of Camarina to leave their homes, and a piteous train of fugitives from both towns took the road to Syracuse. The south coast of Sicily was lost and the Carthaginian army might be expected on the heels of the fugitives. This extraordinary end to the campaign aroused suspicion that Dionysius was in league with the Carthaginians. The Italiote allies marched home and the Syracusan horsemen determined to overthrow the tyrant. They attacked his house and ill-treated his wife. Dionysius hurried to the city, which he entered by burning the gate of Achradina, and forced the rebels to fly to Aetna. There can be little question that in abandoning the defence of Gela and Camarina, Dionysius was deliberately playing into the hand of Himilco, and the treaty which he made with this general clearly shows his desire to conciliate Carthage. On the other hand the Carthaginian army had been weakened by sickness and Himilco may well have shrunk from undertaking the most arduous siege of all, that of Syracuse itself.

The stipulations of the peace between Syracuse and Carthage now arranged by Dionysius and Himilco were as follows: Carthage was to keep Acragas, Selinus and Thermae and the Elymian and Sican towns were to remain her subjects. Gela and Camarina were to be tributary and unwalled cities. The Sicels were to be free, and Messana and Leontini were recognized as independent commonwealths. The Carthaginians were to guarantee the rule of Dionysius over Syracuse and the integrity of Syracusan territory.

It will be observed that in this treaty Carthage and Syracuse disposed of the whole island. The clause respecting Leontini was an exception to the general principles of the treaty and was evidently intended to cause future embarrassment to Syracuse. Dionysius cannot well have approved of this, but we must remember that the treaty was almost dictated by the victor. No mention was made of Catana or Naxos, ancient enemies of Syracuse, evidently an offset to the independence of Leontini. The clause about the Sicels is noteworthy, and we shall subsequently see its significance. Thus the Carthaginian invasion ended in the complete establishment of Dionysius as tyrant of Syracuse; he had not the least intention of observing the terms of the treaty, but he had gained Carthaginian recognition.

Syracuse under Dionysius was a military state, and as lord of Syracuse, he was primarily and above all a war-lord. The fleet of Syracuse was rapidly increased, and the forests of Italy and Aetna were felled to build new warships, some of them with four and five banks of oars. The Carthaginians had used against the Greeks all the devices of oriental siege-craft. Dionysius replied by the yet more effective inventions of his engineers, above all, great catapults which could batter the walls of towns from a range of some two or three hundred yards. But more fruitful than these material inventions was Dionysius' scientific study of the co-ordination of all arms, cavalry, heavy-armed infantry and light-armed troops on the field of battle. The outworn formulas of Greek warfare were cast aside, and with the campaigns of Diony-sius, as with those of Napoleon, we enter on a new phase in the art of war. The boldness of Brasidas, the strategical talents of Cimon had performed wonders in the older style of warfare. Dionysius, even though he may have lacked their natural gifts, surpasses them as the first great scientific soldier, the forerunner of Epaminondas and the great Macedonians.

Dionysius' skill in fortification was first applied to his own security, and the Island (Ortygia) which was the Acropolis of Syracuse, became an impregnable fortress. It was completely cut off from the city by a wall, and this conversion of the Island into a separate fortified quarter was somewhat as if William III of England had seated himself in the Tower of London and, ejecting all the inhabitants from their abodes, had turned the City of London into barracks. It was impossible to enter the Island from Achradina except through five successive gates, and the ends of the Island were protected by two castles. In the lesser harbour new docks were built and it became the chief naval arsenal. A mole admitting only one ship at a time further secured the safety of the Syracusan navy. No citizens were allowed to dwell on the Island who were not definitely supporters and trusted friends of the tyrant, who was surrounded here by his foreign mercenaries.

We may here pause a moment to consider the qualities of character that helped to establish the long reign of this singular man. The antecedents of Dionysius are unknown to us; he was what we may call a *novus homo*, that is, he was a political upstart; all we know of him is that his father's name was Hermocrates, and he was the son-in-law of Hermocrates the statesman; thus he probably began life as a political opportunist, having no attach-ments to any particular party, no sentiments or traditions to move him in any special direction. He seems to have been entirely free from superstition, as he did not scruple to plunder temples: for example, he stripped off the golden garment of Zeus in the temple at Syracuse observing that such a robe was no use to the god, being too hot in summer and too cold in winter[1]. He had no reverence or feeling for historical tradition. He was largely indifferent to public opinion, although he could make use of it when it suited him for his own purposes, and he took little account of Greek customs and conventions. He was a bigamist; contrary to the universal usage of the Greeks he married two wives, Doris of Locri and Aristomache of Syracuse, and lived happily with them both at the same time. His methods were utterly unscrupulous, but he was not a vulgar tyrant. He allowed nothing to stand in the way of his gaining his political ends, and consequently he was often cruel and oppressive, but he did not indulge in cruelty for its own sake. He was not a man of luxurious tastes or habits; orgies and debaucheries, such as we hear of in other tyrants, were not the order of the day in his palace. At first, Syracusan citizens had not very much to fear from his covetousness for their private property, nor had they to dread outrages upon the honour of their families. We can in fact impute little blame to his private life, although we know little of it. These merits were probably the secret of his being able to preserve his tyranny safely. He showed his freedom from sentiment towards the past most conspicuously, perhaps, by his treatment of Naxos, which we shall presently narrate (p. 119). All Sicilians reverenced this city as the oldest Greek colony in the island, older than Syracuse itself. We cannot imagine any other Greek potentate in Sicily venturing to destroy the place and hand over the site to the Sicels. Free from the sentiments and prejudices common to nearly all Greek politicians, Dionysius looked upon the world in a detached manner, unlike most Hellenic statesmen. He approached every problem which presented itself in a temper of what we may perhaps call political realism. As examples of this attitude of mind may be mentioned his rich rewards to his friends and servants and his enfranchisement of slaves, out of whom he formed a class of New Citizens. But there was no lack of people in Syracuse who clearly saw that their constitutional tradition had been broken and who felt no loyalty to a tyrant surrounded by foreign mercenaries.

One of the first acts of Dionysius after the Carthaginians had gone was to attack Herbessus, a Sicel town on the borders of Syracusan and Leontine territory, probably to be identified with

---

[1] Aelian, *V.H.* 1, 20.

Pantalica. The citizens in the army were mutinously inclined and, having slain one of their officers, broke into open revolt. Dionysius fled back to Syracuse and took refuge in his own fortress. The rebellious citizens joined with exiled knights at Aetna and sent pressing messages to Messana and Rhegium for help, and they responded by sending eighty triremes (403 B.C.). Dionysius was so hard pressed by the besiegers that he called a council of his staunchest supporters, and how desperate these deemed the situation is shown by a famous remark of one Heloris, 'Tyranny is a fair winding-sheet.' Though most of his friends urged him to flee, Dionysius made up his mind to leave the city openly. He asked the besiegers to let him leave Syracuse and he was given five triremes. He succeeded in obtaining the help of some Campanian mercenaries who had been in the service of Carthage, and with them occupied the hills of Epipolae. In a quarter of the city for the first time called Neapolis Dionysius routed the insurgents, but this victory was followed by a policy of leniency and returning rebels were accepted again as citizens. The occupation of the Sican town of Entella by the Campanians was a notable result of this episode. By exterminating the men and marrying the women the Campanians made the first Italian settlement in Sicily.

During the rule of Dionysius the outward forms of a Commonwealth at Syracuse had been continued and Dionysius governed the State as a constitutional Magistrate of the Commonwealth. He was elected, so far as we know, every year by the Assembly as *strategos autocrator*, or Supreme General without colleagues. This title lent itself extremely well to masking the position of tyrant. It regularized as it were the absolute military powers which he held and, just as at Athens under the tyranny of Peisistratus the forms of the Solonian constitution were still practised, and the Solonian magistrates still appointed, though of no political importance, so the ordinary affairs of Syracuse seem to have been conducted according to the old constitutional practices, though always at the discretion of the tyrant[1]; just as Gelon and the Deinomenidae had in old days wielded their authority under the same title of *strategos autocrator*. Although there was only one Strategos there was a *nauarch* or commander of the fleet, who may have been appointed formally every year by the Assembly, but was actually chosen by Dionysius; in fact Leptines, the tyrant's brother, held this post continuously until he fell into disgrace and was succeeded by another brother of the tyrant.

[1] See Diodorus XIII, 94.

The Phrourarchs, or Wardens of Forts, about whose appointment we have no clear evidence, were completely subservient to Dionysius. Philistus the historian was at one time Phrourarch of Syracuse.

III. DIONYSIUS AND THE SICELS. 403 B.C.

Both Syracuse and Carthage had come to see that the power of the Sicel cities was seriously to be reckoned with, and this was shown in a stipulation of the recent treaty with Carthage. The Sicel communities were mainly in the east and north-east of the island, in regions neighbouring to Syracusan territory. While Himilco would naturally regard them as a counterpoise to Syracuse, an active Syracusan government would naturally seek to bring them under its control. Dionysius showed a firm grasp of the situation by his promptness in opening a campaign against the Sicel cities and we have seen him in his first enterprise at Herbessus, cut short by events which recalled him suddenly to Syracuse. This campaign against the Sicels was his first breach of the treaty with Carthage, which he had never intended to observe. When he had left Syracuse tranquil he next appears at Enna. In this hellenized city there was an ambitious citizen with the Greek name of Aeimnestus who was bent on seizing supreme power. He was a tool ready for Dionysius at whose instigation he made himself tyrant, but having gained the power he refused to admit Dionysius inside the gates. The tyrant of Syracuse now turned to the people of Enna and incited them to resist the tyranny he had himself helped to make. When the people were in the Agora clamouring for freedom, Dionysius, accompanied by a few light-armed troops, had climbed up a steep unguarded path and appeared in dramatic fashion on the scene. He seized the tyrant and handed him over to the citizens to punish. He left the city immediately without drawing any advantage for himself out of the situation. It is said that his motive was to gain the confidence of other Sicel towns. He next proceeded against Herbita, of which the ruler was Archonides, son or grandson of Archonides the coadjutor of Ducetius forty years before (vol. v, p. 161). But he was unable to take the city, and made peace with the Herbitaeans. This peace, we are expressly told, was made with the people of Herbita, not with their ruler. The result was a breach between Archonides and his people, for we find him founding the new city of Halaesa on the north coast to the west of Cale Acte, and settling there a mixed crowd of mercenaries as well as some of the Herbitaeans who were loyal to their prince.

This city was distinguished from other places of the same name by being called Archonidean Halaesa[1].

Archonides was probably the most representative Sicel of this time, and at Herbita were probably best preserved the traditions of the old Sicel confederation which Ducetius, helped by the first Archonides, had founded.

Some years later we find Dionysius in possession of a title which would be more appropriate to Archonides—the title 'Ruler of Sicily' (Ἄρχων τῆς Σικελίας). This is the title by which he is described ten years later in a decree of the Athenians[2]. We have no direct evidence that he used it of himself, yet when we find it used of him officially by the Athenian Chancery we can hardly fail to infer that it was the style he himself used in his dealings with foreign Powers. When in the course of his lifetime Dionysius had come to be the master of the greater part of the island, the term 'Ruler of Sicily' might seem to express very aptly his position in the Western world, a position going much beyond that of a Lord of Syracuse and representing almost the whole of non-Punic Sicily; but the puzzle remains how did Dionysius come to acquire this title, which, when one comes to think of it, is almost as strange as if we should find a powerful Spartan king (say Agesilaus) describing himself or being described by others as Archon of the Peloponnese. Some further explanation seems wanted. It is the conjecture of the present writer that this title was borne by Archonides and that it was conferred on Dionysius by the Herbitaeans either on this occasion or in a later year (395 B.C.) when it is recorded that Dionysius made a treaty with Herbita[3]. He could thus assume the rôle of successor of Ducetius and claim to be a protector and leader of all the Sicel communities,—dynast of the Sicels, to use the phrase which Diodorus (XII, 8) used of Ducetius. In the states of the mother-country few people understood the difference between Sicels and Siceliotes and it would there be generally taken for granted that Dionysius was the lord of the whole island, and not merely General of Syracuse[4].

[1] Archonides probably settled at and ruled Halaesa himself, but we hear nothing more of him.

[2] *I.G.*[2] II, 1, 18 (394–3 B.C.); also *ib.* 103, 105 of the years 369–8 and 368–7.   [3] Diodorus XIV, 78, 7.

[4] A connection between the Sicels and the title Archon of Sicily had already been suspected by A. J. Evans but he leaves its nature vague (see Freeman's *Hist. of Sicily*, vol. IV, Supp. 1, p. 212); to explain how Dionysius could adopt the title, an hypothesis of the kind suggested in the text seems imperatively required.

The Greek cities were next attacked by the tyrant, Aetna was captured, and the refugees and malcontents who were its inhabitants were dispersed. In fear Catana and Leontini had formed an alliance[1], but no attack was necessary upon Catana, for traitors within her gates, as was also the case at Naxos, admitted Dionysius in return for gold. The fate of these two cities was terrible. Their inhabitants were driven from their homes, and Catana was handed over to Campanian mercenaries, and from being a Greek city became the second Italian town in Sicily. The fate of Naxos was worse; it was utterly destroyed, its name hardly kept alive by a handful of settlers and its territory handed over to the Sicels. The 'Archon of Sicily' thus restored to the Sicels the place where the Greeks had founded their first colony more than three centuries before (vol. III, p. 672). This event was no integral part of the policy of Dionysius; his chief motive in this campaign was to recover Leontini, and the unusual severity which the tyrant showed towards Catana and Naxos was clearly designed for this end. To reduce Leontini by arms would have proved a long and difficult task. When the Syracusan army approached the walls, the Leontines gladly accepted the offer to become Syracusan citizens and forsook their city.

This act was a definite breach of the stipulation in the treaty with Carthage that Leontini was to be independent. Dionysius knew that his campaign would rouse deep resentment and was determined to be well prepared for the coming struggle. He proceeded to make Syracuse impregnable, and remembering lessons that had been taught him by the Athenian siege, he designed a plan for the fortification of the heights of Epipolae. At Euryalus Dionysius built his great castle with its underground chambers and galleries, the ruins of which are perhaps the most striking monument of Syracuse[2]. Walls to join this outpost to the city were built with amazing swiftness by 60,000 freedmen supervised by Dionysius himself. Three miles of wall were built in twenty days and the fortification, when complete, made Syracuse the strongest of all Greek cities[3].

[1] This alliance is attested by a coin (hemidrachm) of Leontini and Catana. Obverse: head of Apollo wreathed with bay; bay leaf and berry [legend: ΛΕΟΝ (τινων)]. Reverse: bull (river Simaethus); fish below [legend: ΚΑΤΑΝΑΙΟΝ], see Evans, *Num. Chron.* xvi, 1896, pp. 128 *sqq.* and the Volume of Plates ii, 6, *k.*   [2] See the Volume of Plates ii, 12, *b.*

[3] Diodorus XIV, 18, only describes the building of one wall, that on the north, but the southern wall was its necessary complement and must have been completed before the Carthaginian siege of Syracuse.

IV. FIRST WAR WITH CARTHAGE. 398–392 B.C.

The object of Dionysius in his first war with Carthage was not only to deliver Greek cities from Phoenician rule but to conquer Phoenician Sicily itself. The tributary towns of Gela and Camarina and the subject towns of Acragas and Thermae, and the Elymian town Eryx received him as a friend. As soon as the news came that the Syracusan army was approaching, the Greeks of the subject cities massacred the Carthaginians with great cruelty. 'At the head of a host which for a Greek army seems immense—80,000 foot, it is said, and more than 3000 horse—Dionysius advanced to test his new siege-engines on the walls of Motya. This city, which now for the first and for the last time becomes the centre of a memorable episode in history, was like the original Syracuse, an island town; but, though it was joined to the mainland by a causeway, the town did not, like Syracuse, spread to the mainland. It was surrounded entirely by a wall, of which traces still remain; and the bay in which it lay was protected on the sea side by a long spit of land. The men of Motya were determined to withstand the invader to the uttermost, and the first measure they took was to insulate themselves completely by breaking down the causeway which bound them to the mainland. Thus they hoped that Dionysius would have to trust entirely to his ships to conduct the siege, and that he would be unable to make use of his artillery. But they knew not the enterprise of Dionysius nor the excellence of his engineer department. The tyrant was determined to assault the city from solid ground, and to bring his terrible engines close to the walls. He set the crews of his ships to the work of building a mole far greater than the causeway which the Motyans had destroyed; the ships themselves, which he did not destine to play any part in the business of the siege, he drew up on the northern coast of the bay. The mole of Dionysius at Motya forestalls a more famous mole which we shall hereafter see erected by a greater than Dionysius at another Phoenician island town, older and more illustrious than Motya (p. 374).

While the mole was being built, Dionysius made expeditions in the neighbourhood. He won over the Sicans from their Carthaginian allegiance, and he laid siege to Elymian Segesta and Campanian Entella. Both these cities repelled his attacks, and leaving them under blockade he returned to Motya when the solid bridge was completed. In the meantime, Carthage was preparing an effort to rescue the menaced city. She tried to cause a diversion by sending a few galleys to Syracuse, and some damage was caused to ships that were lying in the Great Harbour. But Dionysius was not to be diverted from his enterprise; he had doubtless foreseen such an attempt to lure him away, and knew that there was no real danger. Himilco, the Carthaginian admiral, seeing that Dionysius was immovable, sailed with a large force to Motya and entered the bay, with the purpose of destroying the Syracusan fleet, which was drawn up on the shore. Dionysius seems to have been taken by surprise. For whatever reason, he made no attempt to launch his galleys; he merely placed archers and slingers on those ships which would be first attacked. But he brought his army round to the peninsula which forms the western side of the bay, and on the shores of this strip of land he placed his new engines. The catapults hurled deadly volleys of stones upon Himilco's ships, and the novelty of these crushing missiles, which they were quite unprepared to meet, utterly disconcerted the Punic sailors, and the Carthaginians retreated. Then Dionysius, who was no less ready to treat earth as water than to turn sea into land, laid wooden rollers across the neck of land which formed the northern side of the bay, and hauled his whole fleet into the open sea. But Himilco did not tarry to give him battle there; he went back to Carthage, and the men of Motya were left unaided to abide their fate.

As the site of the island city required a special road of approach so its architecture demanded a special device of assault. Since the space in the city was limited, its wealthy inhabitants had to seek dwelling-room by raising high towers into the air; and to attack these towers Dionysius constructed siege towers of corresponding height, with six storeys, which he moved up near the walls on wheels. These wooden *belfries*, as they were called in the Middle Ages, were not a new invention, but they had never perhaps been built to such a height before, and it is not till the Macedonian age, which Dionysius in so many ways foreshadows, that they came into common use. It was a strange sight to see the battle waged in mid-air. The defenders of the stone towers had one advantage; they were able to damage some of the wooden towers of the enemy by lighted brands and pitch. But the arrangements of Dionysius were so well ordered that this device wrought little effect; and the Phoenicians could not stand on the wall which was swept by his catapults, while the rams battered it below. Presently a breach was made, and the struggle began in earnest. The Motyans had no thought of surrender; dauntless to the end they defended their streets and houses inch by inch. Missiles rained on the heads of the Greeks who thronged through, and each of the lofty houses had to be besieged like a miniature town. The wooden towers were wheeled within the walls; from the topmost storeys bridges were flung across to the upper storeys of the houses, and in the face of the desperate inhabitants the Greek soldiers rushed across these dizzy ways, often to be flung down into the street below. At night the combat ceased; both besiegers and besieged rested. The issue was indeed certain; for however bravely the Motyans might fight, they were far outnumbered. But day after day the fighting went on in the same way, and Motya was not taken. The losses on the Greek side were great, and Dionysius became impatient. Accordingly he planned a night assault, which the Motyans did not look for, and this was successful. By means of ladders a small band entered the part of the town which was still defended, and then admitted the rest of the army through a gate. There was a short and sharp struggle[1],' and the Greeks were victorious.

The doom of the Motyans was what might have been expected. It was the answer of the Sicilian Greeks to the slaughter inflicted by Hannibal upon the men of Himera. The victorious soldiers massacred every human being in the streets of Motya without regard to age or sex. At last Dionysius was able to stay this useless slaughter of victims who would have fetched a price in the slave-market by issuing an order that any of the conquered who survived should be spared if they sought refuge in certain shrines. The soldiers then concentrated their attention upon booty. Those of the enemy who thus escaped death were sold as slaves, but there was one class of his foes for whom a harsher doom was reserved; these were the Greek mercenary soldiers in the Carthaginian service. In helping and serving the barbarian against the Greek cities of Sicily they had proved themselves renegades to Hellas; and Dionysius decided, doubtless with the general approval of his army, to treat them with exceptional rigour and make an example of them which might deter others from doing as they had done. He doomed them to the lingering death of crucifixion, a torture which it was quite unusual for Greeks to inflict upon their prisoners, an act worthy of a Punic not of a Greek commander. Dionysius was not usually or instinctively cruel, and in this instance he must have had reasons for considering cruelty politic, but in any case he stood far below the level of the standards of humanity which governed the conduct of Alexander the Great. Having

[1] Diodorus XIV, 47–53. This paraphrase is quoted, with the permission of Messrs Macmillan, from Bury's *History of Greece*, pp. 648–51.

left a Sicel garrison in the conquered city, Dionysius returned to Syracuse for the winter, but in the spring he returned to western Sicily, to proceed against Segesta, which was still holding out (397 B.C.).

Carthage awakened to see her Sicilian dominion in grave peril and again Himilco commanded an expedition to retrieve the disaster. His forces were perhaps almost equal to those of Dionysius, but though he succeeded in landing the larger part of his army at Panormus, some of his transports were sunk by the Syracusan admiral Leptines, brother of the tyrant. The events that followed are difficult to explain and make us pause to consider the actions of Dionysius as a military commander. We do not find him fighting pitched battles; diplomacy played a large part even in his siege-warfare. Eryx fell by treason to the enemy, and Himilco captured Motya, which had been taken the year before by Dionysius in what was perhaps his most brilliant military exploit. The Carthaginian army marched without any attempt being made to intercept it, and yet a check to the progress of Himilco would have effectually gained the object Dionysius had set out to attain, namely the capture of Segesta. Thus in his second campaign the tyrant lost everything he had won in his first. Himilco did not trouble to rebuild Motya, but founded a new city hard by which was destined to continue the history of Motya. This city of Lilybaeum (Marsala) was protected by the sea on two sides and on the other two by walls with deep ditches, and it was for many centuries the great naval station of Carthage in Sicily far more famous than Motya.

Himilco's eyes were now fixed upon Syracuse, whither Dionysius had retired ravaging the country through which he believed that the Carthaginians must march. But Himilco, using his fleet to protect him and furnish supplies, advanced along the north coast towards Messana, intending thus to control the Straits and intercept possible help from Italy or Hellas. The inhabitants of Messana fled to the surrounding hills leaving the city empty; the Carthaginian general destroyed it so completely that its site could hardly be identified. We have seen how Dionysius gave the lands of Naxos to the Sicels, but we have no evidence that he had gained their friendship. Himilco now made a bid for that friendship, and so these, the most ancient inhabitants of the island, were wooed by the Carthaginian and the Greek general alike.

Dionysius now sought to cover Syracuse by holding a strong position some sixteen miles north of the city. Thence, on the news that an eruption of Aetna had forced Himilco to march

inland and so become separated from his fleet, he advanced north
to Catana with fleet and army, hoping to prevent the junction of
the enemy forces. But the plan miscarried. The Syracusan fleet
though slightly inferior in numbers—180 as against 200 ships—
was partly of quadriremes and quinqueremes, the Dreadnoughts
of Greek naval warfare. But the tyrant's brother Leptines who
commanded made the mistake of dividing his forces and was
utterly defeated with the loss of half his fleet. The Syracusan
army, which had remained the passive spectator of the disaster,
fell back on Syracuse. It was a dangerous moment for Greek
civilization and urgent messages were sent to Sparta, to Corinth,
and to Italy, begging for help. The Carthaginian fleet sailed in
triumph into the Great Harbour, while Himilco's army encamped
on the banks of the river Anapus, and the unfortunate Syracusans
trembled with fear and anger at the sacrilegious acts of their
enemies. Himilco and his guards were quartered within the
precincts of the temple of Zeus, and the sanctuaries of Demeter
and Kore on the south-west of Achradina were despoiled.
Himilco immediately proceeded, according to the practice of
Carthaginian warfare, to protect his army and fleet. This he did
by building three strong forts, one at Plemmyrium, one at Dascon
and the third near his own camp. By this time the winter had set
in and put an end to active operations[1]. While Dionysius awaited
the arrival of his allies, the Syracusans had quite different ideas
as to what they were to do when this help arrived. They were
angry with their tyrant, who instead of bringing them victory had
accepted defeat, and they determined to overthrow him with the
help of the Peloponnesians. But the latter, above all the Spartan
admiral Pharax, declared plainly that the object of their expedition
was to help Dionysius. Alarmed at this outburst of disaffection
in the city, Dionysius endeavoured to win the Syracusans back to
their allegiance. In the meantime a plague broke out in the
Carthaginian army encamped in the unwholesome swamps of
the Anapus, and gave an opportunity for Dionysius to show his
skill in attack. He gave orders to his fleet under Leptines and
Pharax to attack off Dascon. Syracusan horsemen and mercenary
foot-soldiers were sent to assail the camp on the west side at night,
but it had been secretly arranged that the cavalry should desert
the mercenaries during the battle and ride round to the east.
But this was only a feint; the real attack was on the east with the
help of ships sent across the bay, and at Polichna the assault was
led by Dionysius himself. The attack was entirely successful,

---

[1] On the chronology see Beloch, *Griech. Geschichte* III², 2, pp. 369 *sqq.*

the mercenaries were slaughtered, both forts captured and the victorious Syracusan army rushed to the shore and burnt the Carthaginian fleet. The completeness of this victory stands in striking contrast with the fiasco at Gela nine years before.

The Greeks wished to exterminate if possible their Punic enemy, but this was not the policy of Dionysius. Feeling that it was not entirely in his interest as tyrant of Syracuse to obliterate the Carthaginian power in Sicily, he made a secret agreement with Himilco. It is said that he accepted a bribe of 300 talents: such a charge was certain to be made and it may be true, for Dionysius was the last man to refuse payment for doing what he wished to do. The agreement was that the Carthaginian citizens in the enemy's army should make their escape by night, while Dionysius called off his troops from their attack on the enemy's camp. Himilco had forty triremes still seaworthy and held Plemmyrium, which controlled the exit from the Great Harbour. During the respite from attacks by land he embarked his citizen-troops and sailed off. The Corinthian allies of Syracuse heard the sound of the ships leaving the harbour; but the tyrant purposely delayed his preparations, and no more than the rearguard of the Punic fleet was sunk by the Corinthians, who anticipated the orders to attack which never came. The Sicels who had fought on the side of Carthage scattered to their homes. The remainder of Himilco's troops, abandoned and in despair, were slain or enslaved, except the Iberian mercenaries, who stood to their arms stoutly until Dionysius took them into his service. Himilco returned to Carthage vanquished, his career ended and only disgrace before him, but there was no treaty between Carthage and Syracuse.

The positions of the two foes were now reversed, the Greek cause in Sicily had triumphed (396 B.C.) and the larger part of the island was under the lordship of Dionysius. Only the original part of the western corner remained to Carthage[1]. Perhaps no

[1] Freeman has made the Carthaginian wars of Dionysius a sort of frame for the chronology of his reign. He distinguishes four Punic Wars, incorrectly in the view of the present writer. He ends his 'first Punic war' at this point. There was a cessation of hostilities for four years, but the two enemy states remained in a state of war until 392 B.C., when active hostilities again broke out. Then the peace was made which terminated the first war with Carthage. We should therefore only count three Punic Wars. The *de facto* abandonment by Carthage of territory east of the Phoenician corner of the island must have been expressly admitted in the treaty of 392 B.C., though such a clause is not mentioned by our only ancient authority, Diodorus XIV, 96. See E. Meyer, *Gesch. d. Altertums* V, p. 121 *sq.* and Beloch, *op. cit.* III², 2, p. 187 *sq.*

more favourable moment had ever come for attempting completely
to destroy Phoenician rule in Sicily than immediately after the
great defeat of Himilco's expedition. Carthage was embarrassed
by a revolt of her subjects in Africa and any Greek leader who
had at heart the cause of Helias against the Semite barbarian
would hardly have failed to press home his victory. But Dionysius
made no attempt to drive the Phoenicians out of the island, so he
cannot be described as a single-minded champion of Hellas.
We must recognize that it was a fixed principle in the policy
of Dionysius not to press the Carthaginians too hard and that
he never aimed at making Sicily a Greek island. He seemed
to have considered it more expedient for Syracuse and himself to
suffer the Phoenicians as neighbours, hoping by their menace to
protect his own despotic rule.

During the next few years (395–92 B.C.) Dionysius was more
preoccupied with establishing his authority over the Sicel towns,
which, it will be remembered, had been his first concern after the
first invasion of Himilco (p. 115 *sq.*). He captured Enna, for there
were traitors in the city and one of the weapons in the wars of
Dionysius was bribery. The same instrument of war gained him
Cephaloedium. Morgantina also submitted and treaties were
made with Herbita and the tyrants of Centuripa and Agyrium.
Dionysius also made an alliance with Assorus and made peace
with Herbessus. But of all the Sicel towns it was perhaps most important to reduce the new stronghold which Himilco had encouraged his allies to found at Tauromenium, which threatened any
Syracusan army on its way to the north. Dionysius resolved to
attack it in winter, but was unsuccessful in his rather dramatic
attempt to take the citadels, nearly losing his life in a precipitous
descent down the cliffs after his repulse. We may remark that,
as in this case, when some difficult and dangerous adventure was
to be carried through, Dionysius never shrank from leading his
soldiers in person[1].

But the Carthaginians were to reappear on the scene (392 B.C.).
The cause of the new hostilities is obscure. We know that Dionysius gained possession of Solus, the most easterly of the three
ancient Phoenician colonies, through treachery, but we have no
record that a special attempt against it was made by the tyrant.
Mago was commander of the forces and garrisons in the Carthaginian possessions in Sicily. It may have been the occupation of
Solus, together with the blow which Tauromenium had dealt to

[1] As Archon of Sicily Dionysius had now under his dominion either as
allies or subjects all the Sicel communities except Tauromenium.

the prestige of the tyrant, that caused him to march against Messana, which had been recently rebuilt as a Syracusan colony. He was met by Dionysius with superior forces and was decisively defeated in a pitched battle. He then sailed for Carthage to obtain reinforcements, while Dionysius marched against Rhegium. The city was hard pressed, but the news that a new Carthaginian army had landed forced the tyrant to make an armistice, while he turned to face Mago a second time. The war that followed was waged in the centre of the island among the hills of the Sicels whom Mago attempted to win over, but Dionysius was vigorously supported by his friend Agyris, the tyrant of Agyrium. This campaign, of which we have few details, ended in Mago suing for peace, perhaps driven to do so by the successful intercepting of his supplies by Agyris and his men, who had the great advantage of knowing the hill-country well. In the treaty that followed, the Sicels were acknowledged to be under Dionysius and there was a special clause giving him Tauromenium. The inhabitants of this town were thus dishonourably abandoned by Carthage who had settled them there. Dionysius lost no time in taking possession of the stronghold. He drove the Sicels out and re-peopled it with mercenaries.

V. THE ITALIAN WARS OF DIONYSIUS AND HIS LATER WARS WITH CARTHAGE

We have already seen that Dionysius, by his attack on Rhegium, had recognized the close connection between the north-east corner of Sicily and the south-east corner of Italy. The Straits of Messina were too narrow to bound his policy or his ambitions. But the control of the straits was his first concern. No sooner had Himilco left Sicily (396) than Dionysius had undertaken the rebuilding of Messana, which the Carthaginian had razed to the ground (p. 123). He re-peopled it with settlers from the Italian cities of Locri and Medma, and to these he would have added Messenians whom the Spartans had driven out of Greece after the power of their Athenian protectors was broken. But the Spartans were unwilling to see the national spirit of the Messenians thus encouraged, and Dionysius, who had every reason not to offend his allies, settled the Messenian refugees in a new city which he built some thirty miles due west of Messana on the north coast. It was a hill-city called Tyndaris (of which ruins still remain) and it soon became very prosperous. The exiles of Catana and Naxos (p. 119) now proved useful to Rhegium, whose people saw in the foundation of Tyndaris a menace to themselves. They founded as a counter-stroke the town of Mylae on the peninsula of that name, but it was captured almost at once by the Messenians with the help of Syracusan mercenaries.

Now that peace was made with Carthage, Dionysius was in a position to carry out his designs against the Greek cities of Southern Italy. He made Locri, which was always very friendly to him, the base of his operations. He attacked Rhegium by land and sea (390 B.C.)[1], but the attack failed, as Rhegium called in the help of the confederation of the Italiote cities which had been formed primarily to resist the growing power of the Lucanians. Dionysius escaped with difficulty, and with more logic than phil-hellenism allied himself with the barbarian Lucanians so that they might together make war on the Italiote cities. In the following year the Lucanians invaded the territory of Thurii and, when the Thurians retorted in kind, inflicted upon them a crushing defeat. Seeing ships coasting along, the escaped Italiotes swam out to them for refuge. It was the Syracusan fleet under Leptines, who, in place of completing the victory, arranged an armistice between the Lucanians and the Italiotes. On hearing of this, Dionysius naturally deprived his brother of his command for ex-ceeding his instructions, and replaced him by another brother, Thearidas (389 B.C.).

Probably in the same summer Dionysius marched against Caulonia, the neighbour of Locri, and laid siege to the town. He had to face a relieving army of 25,000 foot and 2000 horse which had concentrated at Croton under the command of a Syracusan exile, Heloris. Dionysius, whose own forces were equal to those of the enemy, decided to meet them in open battle. He surprised the enemy's vanguard at dawn near the river Elleporus; Heloris was slain and the main body was defeated as it came up in haste and disorder. With politic clemency Dionysius released his prisoners, not even demanding ransom, although a very con-siderable sum was lost by this forbearance. The cities of the Italiote league voted golden crowns to the tyrant and withdrew their support from his enemies. Caulonia and Hipponium con-tinued at war, but first one and then the other were taken and destroyed. The inhabitants were transplanted to Syracuse where they became citizens and their territory was given to Locri. Rhegium bought an armistice by the surrender of its fleet and the payment of an indemnity of 300 talents. But Dionysius had not yet finished with Rhegium.

To hold for himself the Italian side of the Straits of Messina

[1] See for the date E. Meyer, *op. cit.* v, p. 129.

had become to Dionysius a vital interest. In the next year
(388 B.C.) he picked a quarrel with the Rhegines and, after holding
out for nearly a year, Phyton their brave general was forced to
capitulate. Those of the inhabitants who could pay a mina as
ransom were freed, the remainder were sold into slavery. Phyton
was flogged before the army and drowned with his kinsfolk.
The cruelty which Dionysius, contrary to his usual policy, exercised against the Rhegines and their general was due to a long
cherished hatred which was explained in antiquity by the following
story. It is said that he asked for a wife to be chosen from among
the noble maidens of Rhegium, but they contemptuously refused
and added the insult of offering him the hangman's daughter.
They had turned Dionysius into a hangman at their own cost.
The Straits of Messina were now firmly held for Syracuse. Croton,
the leading Italiote city, was taken eight years later (379 B.C.), on
which occasion he plundered the temple of Hera on the promontory of Lacinium and carried off a famous dress of the goddess
which he later sold to the Carthaginians for 120 talents. The
Italian power of the tyrant was firmly established.

In close connection with the designs of Dionysius for extending
his dominions into Italy were his schemes for controlling the
Adriatic, but of these schemes we have the most fragmentary
records. He seems to have formed a conception of a Northern
Empire for which the Adriatic sea was in some ways what the
Pontic sea was for the Athenian Empire. It was bordered by
barbarous inhabitants and touched large rivers and unexplored
lands. It was the ambition of Dionysius to make his influence
supreme in the Adriatic and make it a source of revenue by
collecting dues from all ships sailing the Gulf. He wished Syracuse to take the place of Corinth and Corcyra, in whose hands
Adriatic enterprise, so far as it went, had chiefly lain. But on the
eastern side it went little north of Epidamnus and Apollonia.
The great work of Dionysius was to found Issa (Lissa) and
Pharos on neighbouring islands; Syracusan colonists were planted
on the island of Issa, and Pharos is said to have been a Parian
colony under the auspices of Dionysius. On the Italian coast
opposite to these islands Syracusan exiles founded Ancona and
thus formed a commercial station that proved useful to the plans
of the tyrant. There are inscriptions from Issa and Pharos dating
from a time soon after their foundation[1]. The Syracusan origin

---

[1] For instance there is a stone recording an agreement between Issa and
the inhabitants of Black Corcyra (Curzola), Ditt. *Syll.*³ 141. The date of
this stone seems to be about 385 B.C.

of Issa is illustrated in an interesting manner by its early coinage, which is Sicilian in character[1]. That Dionysius had a keen eye for strategic positions is shown by the subsequent history of Issa as one of the most important naval stations in the Adriatic Gulf. He does not seem to have penetrated far into the Illyrian hinterland, but he had designs on Epirus and made an alliance with Alcetas of Molossia. Dionysius did great service to Greek merchants by suppressing the brigandage of the Illyrian pirates who infested these waters.

The power of Dionysius reached its high-water mark and the frontiers of his dominions their farthest limit about the year 385 B.C. By his conquests in Italy he had acquired nearly the whole of Magna Graecia. With his ally Locri he controlled continuous territory from the Straits of Messina as far north as the river Crathis and his dominion extended round the Tarentine Gulf including Thurii, Heraclea, Metapontum and Tarentum to the heel of Italy where the tribes of Iapygia and the Messapians were his dependent allies[2]. He also secured footholds in Apulia and thus had some control of the coast between Iapygia and Picenum. On the west side, outside Greek territory, the Lucanians were allied to him. South of the Lucanian frontier he planned to build a wall twenty miles long across the narrow Isthmus from Scylletium (Squillace) to the western sea, but this wall was never built[3]. The power of Dionysius over the towns on the east side extended to the convenient ports of Brundisium (Brindisi) and Hydrus (Otranto) which may be said to have enabled him to control the entry into the Adriatic. Brundisium would be for centuries the most convenient place of embarkation from Italy for Epirote ports, to reach North Greece, Macedonia and Thrace.

Nothing shows more strikingly the extent of the prestige of Dionysius, than the fact that in the year of his conquest of Rhegium, which was the same year in which the Gauls captured Rome, an embassy was sent to him by the victorious barbarians offering him an alliance (387 B.C.)[4]. We do not know whether anything definite was contemplated by this alliance, but the Cisalpine Gauls, who were at this moment the strongest military power in Italy, might be of great service to Dionysius in prosecuting his plans on the western coast of the Adriatic from Ancona to the Po and Venetia. These barbarians furnished a new

---

[1] See the Volume of Plates ii, 6, *j.*
[2] See map 6 and Evans in Freeman's *Hist. of Sicily*, vol. IV, p. 218.
[3] Strabo VI, 261. Pliny, *N.H.* III, 95.
[4] Justin XX, 5.

source of supply of mercenaries; we find Dionysius employing Gaulish troops in his later years.

The tyrant was however soon engaged in a new war (*Second War with Carthage* 383 B.C.) the result of which deprived him of some of his gains. He had only just won Croton and the surrounding land when in the west of the island he lost territory. His alliances with some of the dependent cities of his old Punic foe doubtless caused friction. Little is known of the war, but Dionysius won a battle in which Mago was killed and Carthage proposed peace. The tyrant declined to make peace except on the condition that Carthage should evacuate Sicily entirely. A truce was made which gave Carthage time to prepare for a new contest. Mago's son arrived with a large army; a great battle was fought at Cronium, perhaps in 378 B.C.[1], in which Dionysius was defeated with enormous slaughter and his brother Leptines was slain. The position was thus entirely reversed, and in the treaty which was now concluded the tyrant had to pay 1000 talents and the frontier between Carthage and Syracuse was fixed by the river Halycus, instead of the river Mazarus as it had hitherto been.

Ten years later there broke out the *Third War with Carthage* (c. 368 B.C.). The moment was opportune, for once again pestilence was raging in Africa and many of the subjects of Carthage were in revolt. Dionysius led a new expedition into the west of Sicily —30,000 foot, 3000 horse, 300 triremes. He won back Selinus and Campanian Entella. He also captured Eryx and occupied its harbour Drepanum (Trapani) which served as his naval base for besieging Lilybaeum. His first brilliant military success against Carthage thirty years before had been the siege of Motya. The siege of Motya's successor Lilybaeum was his last military operation against the Punic foe, but it was not to be a success. He was obliged to raise the siege and then the Carthaginians surprised and seized his fleet in the haven of Drepanum.

VI. RELATIONS OF DIONYSIUS WITH EASTERN GREECE

Throughout his reign Dionysius was the ally of Sparta. He was helped by Sparta to establish his tyranny at the very outset, and both states found the alliance to be to their mutual advantage.

---

[1] Beloch, *op. cit.* III², 2, p. 376, dates this battle to 375 B.C. adducing Diodorus xv, 46, 2. Diodorus xv, 15–17 narrates the whole of the war under the year 383–2. How long it lasted cannot be determined with certainty.

After the fall of Athens Sparta departed from her old well-known tradition of opposing tyrannies, and in exercising her own tyrannical hegemony she had no objection to coming to terms with tyrants. We do not know in what year the formal alliance was concluded, but at some stage Lysander himself doubtless did much to cement the friendship, since we know that he visited Syracuse. He must have been deeply impressed by the magnificent fortifications of the vast city, the largest he had seen, and not less by the great naval armaments of Dionysius. The Greek world had been watching with interest the growth of the military power of the tyrant of Syracuse as shown in his war with Carthage. The Athenian Assembly passed a decree in honour of Dionysius and of his brothers Leptines and Thearidas, and of his brother-in-law Polyxenus[1]. The power of the tyrant of Syracuse aided Sparta to impose the King's Peace upon the Greek States and in 387–6 he sent to their aid twenty triremes which appeared at Abydos (p. 53). The knowledge that his resources were behind Sparta may have induced some of the unwilling Greek States to accept the Peace. At the preceding Olympic festival (388 B.C.) Dionysius had arranged to play an important part, he sent a magnificent embassy, his chariots were to compete in the races and some of his poems were to be recited. But the Hellenic spirit had been aroused by the speech of Lysias, and the envoys from Syracuse were not allowed to sacrifice and their tents were attacked. The Athenian orator denounced the tyrant and expressed his amazement that Sparta overlooked and tolerated the injuries which he inflicted on Greeks both in Sicily and in Italy. Lysias spoke bitterly, for he himself had Syracusan ancestors and his father had been a citizen of Thurii[2]. The chariots of Syracuse were allowed to compete but won no prize, and the crowd refused to hear the poems of Dionysius.

Fourteen years later Dionysius at least promised help to Sparta (p. 77); in 369 B.C. he sent troops to Corinth to help in the campaign against the Thebans (p. 93); the last time we hear of him helping his ally Sparta was in the spring of 367 B.C., on the occasion of a minor victory of Archidamus over the Arcadians known as 'the tearless battle' (see above, p. 94). Shortly before this (368 B.C.) we find the Athenians passing a decree in honour of Dionysius and his sons (*I.G.*[2] II, I, 103), and in the following year, 367 B.C., an alliance was made between

[1] *I.G.*[2] II, I, 18 (394–3 B.C.).

[2] Isocrates (*Panegyricus*, 380 B.C.) agrees with the views of Lysias but does not express himself so vehemently.

Athens and the tyrant[1]. This was the last year of the life of Dionysius.

VII. DEATH OF DIONYSIUS. 367 B.C.

In the days of Dionysius Syracuse was not a centre of attraction for famous poets such as those who came to the court of Hiero, and heralded abroad his virtues and magnificence and the fame of his exploits, but still the court of Dionysius had some literary pretensions. The tyrant himself was interested in the new dithyrambic poetry then coming into vogue and known to us by the *Persians* of Timotheus of Miletus which was discovered in recent years[2]. Another proficient in this style of poetry was Philoxenus of Cythera who came to Syracuse to reside at the court. Dionysius also wrote tragedies which gained second and third prizes in the Athenian theatre, but he was always longing and hoping for a first prize. At home he gained little sympathy with his poetical efforts; the fact is his 'bad poems' were almost proverbial. But Dionysius was inordinately sensitive as to their merits. Philoxenus obstinately refused to praise them, and it is said that the tyrant sent him to languish in the stone quarries. So the story runs, with the amusing sequel that when received again at court Philoxenus, being pressed for his opinion on a new poem of the tyrant, answered by beckoning to an officer with the words 'back to the quarries.' His ready wit gained him forgiveness.

Exceptions to the dearth of distinguished visitors in Syracuse were two famous pupils of Socrates, Aristippus the Cyrenaic and Plato. The dealing of Dionysius with Plato was not to his honour. It is not certain why Plato undertook a journey to western Greece (389–8 B.C.), but he did not miss the opportunity of seeing a tyrant's court from within. We do not know what passed between them, but Dionysius was not attracted by the philosopher, who most certainly would not have flattered him. So he packed him on board a Spartan vessel which conveyed him to Aegina, where a Spartan fleet was stationed at the time. There he was sold in the slave-market, but was ransomed by a friend from Cyrene for 20 minae (p. 315). There was, however, one in the court circle of whom Syracuse had more reason to be proud than of any of the distinguished strangers who visited her. This was a son of her own,

[1] *I.G.*[2] II, 1, 105. Beloch's inference, *op. cit.* III[2], 2, p. 201, from this inscription that the title Archon of Sicily was hereditary is not here accepted.

[2] *Timotheos, Die Perser*, ed. U. von Wilamowitz-Moellendorff. 1903.

the historian Philistus, who as a writer of military history seems
not unworthy to have been a contemporary of Thucydides. He
was one of the richest men in Syracuse, and he had shown his
great faith in the ultimate success of Dionysius as we have seen
(above, p. 112). He had been one of the most intimate and trusted
counsellors of Dionysius and had married his niece[1], daughter
of Leptines, but in the end he quarrelled with his master and
lived in banishment till the tyrant's death. He seems to have
spent his exile somewhere on the coast of the Adriatic and there
is some evidence which connects him with Hadria. During his
exile he composed a history of the reign of Dionysius in which
we are told that he omitted the worst deeds of the tyrant and
flattered him, hoping to be recalled. In the next reign he was able
to return to Syracuse and he became admiral of the fleet.

In the same year that Dionysius had to face the failure of his
military operations at Lilybaeum and the loss of his fleet, he was
surprised and consoled by the news from Athens that his tragedy
The Ransom of Hector had been awarded a first prize at the
Lenaean festival. It has of course been suggested that the Athenian judges were influenced by political considerations, in view of
the fact that an alliance with the tyrant was being negotiated at
the time. But however poor the drama of Dionysius may have
been, it is difficult to believe that it would have been awarded the
prize at Athens if he had not some mastery of technique and could
not write correct verses. Overjoyed at this long delayed triumph
he celebrated his victory with an unwonted intemperance. He
was stricken down by a fever and his death is attributed to the
effects of a soporific.

VIII. ESTIMATE OF DIONYSIUS

One of the most prominent features in the age of Dionysius
was the growth of the employment of mercenaries throughout the
Greek world and neighbouring states. By no one was this practice
so consistently and extensively adopted as by the tyrant of Syracuse.
Both his own power and the strength of his city depended on
foreign troops. We cannot even guess at the amount of the budget
of Dionysius, but it is clear that one of the largest and most
constant item of expense was the maintenance of his mercenary
forces—Italians (Campanians), Iberians, Gauls, and soldiers from
the Peloponnese. The extensive fortifications of Syracuse must
have been a severe drain on the resources of the city, and also

[1] Plutarch, *Dion* 11, states that it was this marriage, contracted without
the permission of Dionysius, which caused the exile of Philistus.

the maintenance of the navy. To meet these expenses the citizens of Syracuse were heavily taxed, and in some cases the levy amounted to confiscation. In five years' time a citizen's whole capital could be paid away in taxes[1]. A cattle tax was imposed that made the owners prefer to slaughter their beasts rather than pay it[2]. The tyrant levied exceptionally heavy war-taxes, and he made himself guardian of all orphans. Much money was gained from the spoils of war such as the military success at Motya, the sale of conquered peoples as slaves, in other cases their ransoms; and the sacrilegious plunder of temples became a constant source of income to Dionysius. He made an attack on the Etruscans which had the plunder of the rich temple at Agylla as its real object, out of which he gained 1500 talents. He even planned an attack on the Temple at Delphi aided by Illyrians, but this scheme was prevented from being realized by the Spartans. Besides these violent expedients for raising money Dionysius also resorted to methods almost as disreputable, amongst which, it is alleged, was the depreciation of the Syracusan coinage. We are told that on one occasion he placed a mark on coins making them count as double their proper value.

Under the rule of Dionysius Syracuse far exceeded the natural bounds of a Greek city-state; indeed the policy of the tyrant encouraged her growth, until Syracuse was probably the most populous city in the Hellenic world, and may be compared with the Antioch and Alexandria of a later age. His statecraft went beyond the parochial bounds of neighbouring hatreds and friendships. Syracuse became more than the leading city of Sicily; she became a continental power, and not only established colonies on the mainland to which her island geographically belonged, but made herself felt in lands beyond the Adriatic. This empire, though retaining old constitutional forms, was really a military monarchy. The ruler and his army were the state; the policy of the ruler was personal, the sentiments of the army were professional. With Dionysius came in, as has been said, innovations in the arts of war which were to have a profound influence on the history of the Macedonian monarchies of which his rule was the forerunner. Some of his military operations, for instance the siege of Motya, remind us of those of Alexander. He also, like the Spartan Lysander, anticipated the custom of deification.

[1] Aristotle, *Pol.* VIII (v), 11, p. 1313 b.
[2] [Aristotle] *Oecon.* II, 20. E. Meyer, *op. cit.* v, p. 105, does not accept this literally.

Apart from his significance for the future, Dionysius owes his prominence in history to the fact that in spite of his occasionally vacillating policy, he was a remarkably successful champion of Europe against the Semite. At long intervals Carthage produced talented generals and displayed her ambition, and in the last decade of the fifth century and the first decade of the fourth the revived ambition of Carthage was served by men of marked capacity. This dangerous conjunction Dionysius faced with success. Although it was left for the Romans finally to win Sicily for Europe and expel the Carthaginians completely, still Dionysius had in fact almost achieved this. But though the tyrant saved the Greeks in saving himself, he was not interested in the development of Hellenic civilization. We see him destroying Hellenic cities and founding Italian communities in their place. Where policy demanded it, he did not scruple to ally himself with Lucanians and Gauls against the Greek cities of Italy. Little as Dionysius can have foreseen it, his Italian policy marks an early stage in the reaction which was to end in the Italian conquest of Sicily more than a century later.

Dionysius stands out as the ablest and most important Greek statesman between Pericles of Athens and Philip of Macedon. By the originality of his ideas and the daring of his schemes he stands apart from all the rulers of his time and was the pioneer of a new age in which the conditions of the world would be transformed. So far as we know, he asked for little advice and help in his more important acts and we hear seldom of his official counsellors. We may suspect that he often asked and took the advice of Philistus, but there is no reason for thinking that this friend guided his policy or originated any of the plans by which he amazed or dismayed his contemporaries. As an unconstitutional monarch he was able to accomplish much which would have been impossible for a statesman in a constitutionally governed Greek state; but, for his tyranny, his reputation suffered. He was execrated in Sicily and Italy; and in old Greece he was considered by public opinion to be a scourge of the Greek world and even after his death his claims to greatness were never, or never fully, realized.

CHAPTER VI

EGYPT TO THE COMING OF ALEXANDER

I. THE ACHAEMENID RULE

THE re-establishment of Persian authority in Egypt described in vol. III, chap. XIV, probably meant a more intensive control of the country; and for the first time we hear of Persian officials even in subordinate positions, such as the desert-guard Atyuhi son of Artames, who inscribed his name on the rocks of the Wadi Hamamat, the much used caravan route from Koptos to Kuseir on the Red Sea. Military commanders were always Persians, and so apparently were the chief judges[1]. There is little doubt that a host of Persian tax-gatherers, many of them probably Egyptians, but many also Syrians, Babylonians, and Persians, now descended upon the country, and extorted as much from it as they could to fill the coffers of the Great King at Susa. The obstinacy with which the Persians continued to exert their authority over Egypt whenever they could down to the fall of the Achaemenian empire was no doubt due to its value as a milch-cow. The country had become enormously rich, as wealth went then, under the Saïtes, and continued to be so under the Persians, in spite of repeated invasions, massacres and oppression. The large number of demotic contracts and other (including Aramaic) documents of the reign of Darius show what a volume of internal trade and other business then existed, but they cease for the time after the revolt of Khababesha and the imposition of the hard yoke of Xerxes. In the second half of the fifth century Aramaic contracts rather than demotic are found, often bearing Jewish, Syrian or even Babylonian names, which show that a crowd of small oriental traders had followed the Persians and their tax-gatherers into Egypt. The Persians were always friendly to the Jews, as they had been since the days of Cyrus. No doubt the Jewish trade when not mere bazaar-chaffering[2] was chiefly connected with the East. As a consequence

Note. For the ancient sources of this chapter see the Bibliography.

[1] As 'Damidāta and his colleagues' in a conveyance-papyrus of 465 B.C. (Cowley, *Aramaic Papyri of the Fifth Century*, p. 17). The assessors may have been Egyptians, though *ibid.* p. 51 Bhāgafrāña (Megaphernes) the chief judge has apparently a Persian assessor, Nepheyan, and a Babylonian, Mannuki.

[2] The Jews were the *bakkāl*-keepers of the time, as the Greeks were under the Romans and are now.

of the long war with Athens and her allies, trade with Greece must almost have ceased, and Naucratis been hard hit. But we cannot doubt the great extent of the foreign trade by land and sea with Arabia, Syria, Phoenicia, Ionia, and Greece, chiefly conducted by foreign caravaneers and shipmen, of which we have indications, as in the time of Amasis. The bilingual Stele of Hor, inscribed in Egyptian and Aramaic, in the Berlin Museum, dated in Xerxes' fourth year, is a relic of some Syro-Egyptian merchant, probably: and the Minaean stele already mentioned (vol. III, p. 310) testifies to trade with southern Arabia. By this time the Arab tribe of the Nabataeans (who had occupied Edom after the Babylonish captivity of the Jews a century before had enabled the Edomites to move westward into the Negeb of Judaea) were established at Petra, where they controlled the two crossing trade-routes from the Gulf of Akaba to Syria and from Egypt to Babylonia.

Xerxes made no attempt to popularize himself with his Egyptian subjects as his father did; no monuments bear his name, and his Egyptian inscription as 'Khshayarsha, Pharaoh the Great' (sic) on the well-known trilingually inscribed alabaster vases found at Halicarnassus and elsewhere, hardly looks as if it had been devised by an Egyptian at all. Later on the priests of Buto refer to him plainly as 'that scoundrel Xerxes' (see vol. III, p. 315).

No Egyptian fought at the Eurymedon (467 or 466 B.C.), when Cimon attacked the Persians nearer home, and freed temporarily the last Greek cities that had been tributary to the Great King, who now died (465) at the hands of Artabanus, and was eventually succeeded by his son Artakhshastra or Artaxerxes. The death of Xerxes was the signal for another revolt in the Delta, under a certain Ienharoū, the Inarōs of the Greeks, son of Psammetichus, 'king of the Libyans,' no doubt a scion of the Saïte royal house. The Persian tax-gatherers and receivers were expelled, and Achaemenes the viceroy with them; while the remnant of his troops was driven into Memphis. As always, the commanding strategic position of Memphis, with its vice-like grip on the throat of Egypt, cutting off the Delta, then as now the most populous part of Egypt, from the Upper Country, prevented the South from giving any aid to Inaros. He seemed unable to make any further headway, and the Persians were probably gathering strength, Achaemenes having returned with an army, when a *deus ex machinâ* appeared in the shape of the Athenian generals who were now with two hundred galleys carrying on Cimon's war off the coast of Cyprus. This fleet was able and ready to aid any enemy of the Persians and at the same time restore the trade of Athens and her confederates with Egypt, which had probably suffered much from Persian hostility (see vol. v, pp. 77 *sqq.*). The appearance on the Nile of the triremes and the hoplites of their inveterate little enemy Athens can hardly have been of good cheer to the Persian leaders. Achaemenes probably fought badly, and he was killed and his army defeated by the Egyptians at Papremis, where Herodotus, years later, saw the skulls and bones of the combatants still covering the ground. The remnant fled to Memphis, where they surrendered to the Athenian fleet, which had now appeared on the scene. The body of Achaemenes was sent to Artaxerxes as an intimation of his defeat, but troubles at home prevented the King from moving at once.

'The Athenians remained in Egypt,' says Thucydides (1, 109 *sq.*), 'and they experienced varied fortunes of war. At first they were masters of the country. So the King (Artaxerxes) sent a Persian named Megabazus to Sparta with money, in order that he might persuade the Peloponnesians to invade Attica and so draw the Athenians away from Egypt. But when he had no success in his mission, and the money was being spent in vain, Megabazus was recalled to Asia with what was left of it, and the King sent Megabyxus son of Zopyrus with a great army to Egypt. When he arrived he defeated the Egyptians and their allies, and expelled the Greeks from Memphis, finally shutting them up in the island of Prosopis. There he besieged them for a year and six months, until in the end, having drained the canal and diverted its waters elsewhere, their ships were left high and dry, most of the island was joined to the surrounding land, and crossing with his foot-soldiers he captured it. Thus then the cause of the Greeks in Egypt was lost, after six years of war. A few of them, out of so many, managed to escape through Libya to Cyrene, but the majority perished. Egypt again passed into the possession of the King, with the exception of Amyrtaeus, the king in the fens, whom the Persians could not catch on account of the great extent of the fens: also the fenmen are the most warlike of the Egyptians. Inaros the king of the Libyans, who had caused all this trouble in Egypt, was betrayed and captured, and impaled[1]. Fifty triremes, which had been sent by the Athenians and their allies to relieve the forces already

---

[1] He was not actually crucified (or impaled) till five years later, owing to a breach of the treaty of surrender to Megabyxus, which had guaranteed him his life. This flouting of his honour by the King probably led to the rebellion of Megabyxus in Syria (450) which is to be connected with Cimon's renewed attack on Cyprus (Wells, *J.H.S.* xxvii, 1907, pp. 37 *sqq.*).

in Egypt, sailed into the Mendesian mouth of the Nile in ignorance of what had happened. But they were attacked both by land and sea, and the greater part destroyed by the Phoenician fleet, a few ships only escaping. Thus ended the great Egyptian expedition of the Athenians and their allies' (455–4 B.C.).

Inaros is called a Libyan by Thucydides on account of the Libyan origin of his family and the position of his fief; he was no doubt a Saïte. According to Herodotus (III, 15) Thannyras his son was permitted by Artaxerxes to succeed to his father's princedom, as also was Pausiris, son of Amyrtaeus, to that of his father. Inaros and Amyrtaeus were apparently forgotten by Manetho, in spite of the vogue of Inaros in legend as a popular hero (vol. III, p. 290), and not included in his dynastic list; possibly Amyrtaeus was confused by him or his copyists with the other king of the same name a little later (p. 144). In 449 Amyrtaeus was still king 'in the fens' and sent to Cimon, now besieging Citium in Cyprus, for help. The sixty ships he sent returned after Cimon's death, and Amyrtaeus was probably killed by the Persians or died soon after. There are no monuments of either king; they had no time for any.

Artaxerxes I never visited Egypt himself and erected no monuments there. For us his reign there is (or rather those of his satraps are) interesting only as the period of the visit of Herodotus, which is to be dated most probably at some time between the years 448, when peace was made with Persia, and 445, when he was at Athens before his visit to Thurii, where he took part in the colonization in 443 B.C. (see vol. v, p. 417). Before 448 a man of such strong Athenian sympathies as Herodotus would hardly be able to visit a part of the Persian Empire[1]. Egypt was then at profound peace, but it was a peace of exhaustion and sullen resignation. The death of Cimon, followed by the fruitless victory off the Cyprian Salamis, the reconciliation of the revolted satrap of Syria, Megabyxus, with his master, and the so-called Peace of Callias (448) signified the end of Athenian efforts against Persia and in aid of Egypt: the Persian power now had a respite, which was confirmed by the Peloponnesian War.

The Egyptians simply waited. The Persian kings had not fulfilled the promise of Darius or even of Cambyses: they came not to Egypt, which knew nothing of her self-styled pharaohs, and would not be reconciled to rulers far away in Asia. It was not till the Ptolemies ruled in and from Egypt as Egyptian kings that the nation was more or less reconciled to a foreign dynasty. But

[1] Jacoby, s.v. Herodotus: Pauly-Wissowa, Suppl. (1913).

Herodotus did not know what was at the back of the Egyptian mind; he saw only the surface prosperity of the country, which however was certainly less than it had been in the days of Amasis, to which he refers (vol. III, pp. 306 *sqq.*). It is in some ways a pity that he was not there at a more interesting period, but he gives an extraordinarily vivid description of the land and people as it was in the middle of the fifth century. Everything was going on as it always had; the festivals and services of the gods were celebrated openly and without fear of interruption (the Persians never interfered with the religion of their subjects), commerce and manufactures flourished in spite of heavy imposts often unjustly enforced or increased. The land stood open to foreign travellers, who could inspect the temples and all the 'sights' of the country without difficulty or apparently the risk of fanatical objections. 'But for the bleaching bones of the fallen in the fight that had taken place, nothing in Egypt seems to have recalled the struggles of a few years before.'[1] The recuperative power of the Egyptians after disaster has always been extraordinary. It has been pointed out[2] that the struggles of Persian and Egyptian were practically confined to the Delta and the neighbourhood of Memphis, so that naturally no sign of devastation would be visible to the traveller in Upper Egypt. But then as now the Delta was the really important portion of Egypt, and was visited in detail by Herodotus; had many signs of ruin and depopulation been visible there he would assuredly have mentioned them.

His description of the religious observances and the life of the people generally has always been of fascinating interest from his own day (when the Greeks, as at a much later period Heliodorus in his *Aethiopica* says, were always eager to hear queer tales about Egypt) to ours. It is the more interesting because but for the alteration of religion it might almost have been written to-day. Egypt was much the same then as she had been two thousand years before and as she is now. His vivid picture of the festival at Bubastis is repeated now in little by the describer of any great *mōlid* or festival of a Moslem saint. The tourist and his dragoman existed then as they do now: Herodotus himself was a tourist and was often the victim of his ignorant and pretentious dragoman, the type that still flourishes to-day. But at the same time Herodotus picked up a good deal of perfectly good information, and there is no reason to doubt that he actually conversed with and derived historical knowledge from priests. They may not have been and probably were not of the highest rank in the hierarchy, but

[1] Wiedemann, *Äg. Gesch.* p. 691.   [2] Wiedemann, *loc. cit.*

Herodotus after all was an educated Greek gentleman of means and leisure, and would not forgather with priests of any but the educated type, of historical and antiquarian tastes, though he may not have met many. Hence his history does not depend exclusively on Greek information and imagination, and the stories of ignorant dragomans. He derived it largely from the Egyptians themselves and the testimony of his own eyes (II, 147). It certainly is by no means so useless as it has been made out to be. It is true that he makes the Saïtes immediately succeed the pyramid-builders, but we can see that for this (which was possibly his own idea, τῆς ἐμῆς ὄψιος) he had a reason, as to an outside observer the Saïte type of art would seem remarkably like that of the pyramid-time[1]. We have no notion who his blind king 'Anysis' was, except that his name undoubtedly represents the Libyan princes of Ma at Heracleopolis (Hanes), but we see that his history of the Saïtes is quite good history, and his tales of Rhampsinitus (Ramses III) are interesting examples of folk-tales about kings who lived in the popular memory[2]. His inaccuracies, major or minor, do not matter now that we have the actual records to study, and are more than atoned for by the interest of the general narrative; so that in spite of detraction, which we now see to be unnecessary, Herodotus's description of Egypt will always remain one of the greatest of our classics.

The Thirty Years Peace, which was concluded between Athens and Sparta in 445, lasted less than half its intended duration, being followed by the outbreak of the Peloponnesian War in 431. But both states were at peace with Persia, and it mattered little to the Egyptians whether Athens or Sparta were at peace or war with each other if they were both at peace with the Great King. In 445–4 a great gift of corn from Egypt reached the Piraeus, sent, it was said, by a 'king' named Psammetichus, in response to a request from Athens. Peace with both Persia and Sparta enabled the Athenians to import corn from Egypt without difficulty. The

---

[1] Möller (Äg. Zeitschrift 1920, p. 7), thinks that Herodotus confused the name of Menkaurē' the Pyramid-builder with that of Uohkerē' or Bocchoris, who was also called Bochorinis (from his other name Boknranef), so that Herodotus calls Menkaurē' Mykerinos. Thus confusing Menkaurē' with Bocchoris, he naturally placed the Pyramid-builders immediately before the Saïtes. But the explanation of the present writer seems simpler.

[2] One notices that he perpetuates an error characteristically Saïte, which calls the king 'Ramses Si-Nit,' 'son of Neith,' the goddess of Saïs. Ramses III of course had nothing to do with Neith, and called himself Ḥiḳon (' Prince of Heliopolis ').

'king' was some Saïte dynast (possibly Thannyras or his successor, who may well have been called Psammetichus).

In the midst of the Peloponnesian War Artaxerxes of the Long Hand died (424), and its continuance kept Egypt impotently still till the end of the century, throughout the undistinguished reigns of his successors, who left no record in Egypt with the exception of Darius Nothus (and he but a slight one). From his reign (407 B.C.) dates the important Aramaic papyrus found at Aswān (Syene) which contains the complaint of the priests of the local Jewish colony at Yēb (Elephantine) to Begvahi or Bagohi (Bagoas) the Persian governor of Judah, and the sons of Sanballat, against Waidrang (or perhaps better Vidarnag; ? Hydarnes) the Persian general at Syene, for having allowed the Egyptian priests of Khnum to destroy and pillage the temple of Yahu and his contemplar goddesses, Ashima and Anath, at Yēb (p. 180). This Jewish colony is first mentioned under Darius I in 494 B.C. It was founded as a military colony under the XXVIth Dynasty, when as we have seen (vol. III, p. 293 sq.) Jewish mercenaries were often hired and stationed in Egypt. Later it became a regular settlement, the men of which were organized in *degels* or detachments, each under a Persian commander. Its members owned lands and held slaves. It was remarkable for its possession of a fully-equipped temple for sacrifice instead of the orthodox synagogue, and for its polytheism[1].

The fall of Athens after Aegospotami and the destruction of her Long Walls by the Peloponnesians 'to the sound of flutes' (for Sparta's allies indeed thought 'that that day was to be the beginning of freedom for Hellas') in 404 gave to Sparta the hegemony of Greece. And it was not long before the new leader of the Hellenes found herself at loggerheads with the old enemy Persia, and the chance of Egypt, which had revolted in 404 after the death of Darius Nothus and had preserved a precarious independence during those years owing to the quarrel of Artaxerxes and Cyrus, came again. For after the defeat of Cyrus at Cunaxa Persia and Sparta made war upon each other. But when it appeared

---

[1] See for the latest literature and conclusions Cowley, *Aramaic Papyri of the Fifth Century B.C.*, pp. viii *sqq.* Under the Persians a Persian always commanded the colony on the military side, which however had probably already become of less importance than its civil side as a large element of the population of Yēb. In the time of Xerxes (465) a Persian named Warizath commanded. Among the troops in garrison at Syene we find such names as Dargman son of Harshin, a Khorazmian (Persian from Khwarezm), Hosea son of Petekhnum (Egyptianized Jew), Meshullam son of Hosea (Jew), Sinkashid son of Nabusumiskun (Babylonian): an interesting example of the mixture of races subject to the Great King.

that the thalassocracy of Sparta had only been destroyed to re-habilitate that of Athens, the old enemy of Persia, there was reaction. Conon the Athenian admiral of the Great King was disgraced, and Persia moved steadily towards the inevitable re-conciliation with Sparta which would set free the King's fleets and armies to re-assert his authority in Egypt.

II. THE LAST NATIVE MONARCHY

The leader of the revolt in 404, Amyrtaeus II (Amonirdisu), probably a grandson of the older Amyrtaeus, had made himself king. He is recorded by Manetho as having reigned six years (XXVIIIth Dynasty). The Demotic Chronicle (see p. 145) com-memorates him as 'the first after the Medes.' His royalty was but precarious till Sparta went to war, and only survived on account of the preoccupation of Artaxerxes with the treason of his brother Cyrus. After Cunaxa and shortly before his assassination the Greek general of the Ten Thousand, Clearchus, offered the satrap Tissaphernes the services of his men to put down the Egyptian revolt (p. 10).

Next year, in 400, the Egyptian Tamōs, whom Cyrus had made ruler of Ionia, fled to Egypt before the coming of Tissaphernes, and was there murdered with his family by another 'king Psam-metichus,' who may be another local Saïte, but was more probably Amyrtaeus[1], who no doubt hoped in this way to ingratiate himself with the victorious Artaxerxes. But his action was not in accordance with the feeling of the time, which, evidently, was strongly anti-Persian. In 398 probably, when Sparta was at full war with Persia, and the coast was clear, an Egyptian leader of soldiery, Naif'aurud, gave the signal for a revolt that immediately was successful. He was apparently the prince of Bindid (or Mendes, as the Greeks called it), in the Delta. The Greeks called him Nepherites (Manetho) or Nephereus (Diodorus). Amyrtaeus was no doubt killed. No monuments of him exist[2] and we have only one contemporary reference to his reign, in one of the papyri

---

[1] 'Psammetichus' seems to have been regarded almost as a generic name for Egyptian kings, and at any rate it was the most probable name to write down if the real one was unknown or had been forgotten.

[2] The relics ascribed to him by Wiedemann, *Äg. Gesch.* p. 694, belong to Rudamon, of the XXIIIrd Dynasty (vol. III, p. 265), whose name was formerly considered to be the original of Amyrtaeus (as 'Amonrud'), which is really Amonirdisu as we know from the Demotic Chronicle. It was pronounced something like 'Amordaiso.'

from Elephantine[1]. Nepherites was crowned king, and was the first of Manetho's XXIXth Dynasty.

In 396 a great armament of 300 ships was assembled in the ports of Phoenicia, in all probability in preparation for an attempt to recover Egypt for the Great King, though it was to be expected that Conon the Athenian admiral and his friend Evagoras the Cypriote king would endeavour to divert the armada to the Aegean in order to challenge the new thalassocracy of Sparta. The Spartans at any rate thought this probable themselves. In this year they opened negotiations with Nepherites for an alliance with Egypt, whose complete independence of Persia was now generally realized. Nepherites eagerly seized the chance of securing Greek succours in case of Persian attack, and on his part is said to have offered Sparta wood for building 100 triremes and 500,000 bushels of corn. The latter is a possible offer, but where in Egypt he was to find wood good enough to build a single trireme with, much less a hundred, is not apparent. It is to be noted however that he could offer no actual ships and would not offer any men. When the corn-ships reached Rhodes they were captured by Conon, and Sparta never got them.

About four years later Nepherites was succeeded by Muthes, who is unknown to the monuments, and he by Psammouthis or Pše(re)mut, who is said to have been an impious person, but nevertheless has left inscriptions in a temple or two, in spite of his reign having lasted, like that of his predecessor, hardly more than a year. Psammouthis was followed on the throne by his enemy the foreign (?) prince Hakori, whom the Greeks called Achoris (390). According to a tradition in the strange Ptolemaic jumble of prophecies, which are found in the so-called 'Demotic Chronicle' at Paris, Hakori was not really the rightful heir, any more than Psammouthis whom he probably killed or Muthes whom we know nothing about, since Naif'aurud had left a young son who afterwards reigned as Nakhtenēbef. But Hakori justified his reign by his acts; 'he was allowed to fulfil the time of his rule as prince, because he had been generous to the temples'[2].

---

[1] Cowley, *loc. cit.* pp. 129 *sqq.*; dated in the fifth year of 'Amortais the king,' 400–399 B.C.

[2] The new arrangement of these kings given above is the result of a discovery made by M. Daressy in the inscriptions of a chapel built by Psammouthis at Karnak and completed by Hakori, from which it is evident that Muthes and Psammouthis preceded Hakori instead of succeeding him, as used to be thought (*Annales du Service*, xviii, 1919, p. 37 ff.). This agrees with the indication of the Paris 'Demotic Chronicle.' Werner Schur (*Zur*

Evagoras, who since the battle of Cnidus (where he fought in person) and the partial rehabilitation of his Athenian friends, had become suspect at Susa as too philhellenic in sympathy and harbouring designs against Persia, had apparently given no active help to his suzerain. Instead, he had made himself master of the other Greek and Phoenician towns in Cyprus (p. 20). Now (in 389), emboldened by the Persian inaction, he determined to revolt against Artaxerxes, and so forestall the enmity of the King, who was bent on the ruin of so powerful a vassal. Hakori naturally hastened to support him. This alliance of Evagoras with Egypt determined the Persians to listen to the peace-overtures of Sparta, who was weary of the unsuccessful campaign in Asia, and had opened negotiations through her admiral Antalcidas and the satrap Tiribazus. These two were so certain that the Great King also was disposed towards peace that in 388 they joined their fleets against the fleets of Athens, which was now as suspect to Persia as Conon and Evagoras and had concluded an alliance with Persia's Egyptian enemy, Hakori. Athens sent Chabrias with reinforcements to Cyprus, but for a moment Sparta was again supreme at sea, owing only to Persian help to which she did not desire to be indebted. The Peace of Antalcidas followed (386), in which all the warring states of Greece made peace with one another and with Persia, and Sparta cynically abandoned to the barbarian the mainland cities of Ionia which Athens had rescued for Hellenism. Evagoras, who had no formal alliance with but only the sympathy of Athens, was tacitly abandoned to the wrath of Artaxerxes. Egypt, which nine years before had been sought as an ally by Sparta and two years before had alliance with Athens, was not mentioned.

Artaxerxes was now free to strike at either Evagoras or Hakori or both, if he could. He chose first the land-attack on Egypt, which was delivered by the satraps Pharnabazus, Tithraustes, and Abrocomas between 385 and 383, but apparently without energy and decision, and certainly without success. The Athenian publicist Isocrates contemptuously refers to this war in his *Panegyricus* (140) as showing how little the barbarians could now do without Greek aid. Hakori had probably very few Greeks with him, and none of importance, or we should have heard more of this war: the Persians none. Other than that of Greek soldiers of fortune, the only help that the Cypriote and the Egyptian could invoke was one another's: Athens could only timidly and occa-

Vorgeschichte des Ptolemäerreiches; Klio xx, 1926, p. 273) retains without question (cf. *ib*. p. 278) Beloch's arrangement of these kings (*Gr. Gesch.* III, 2², pp. 121 *sqq*.), which is now known to be erroneous.

sionally do something to help her old friend and admirer, Evagoras, who now fought in a way to compel admiration not only from Athens but from all Greece. With unspecified help from Hakori he carried war into the enemy's camp, took Tyre and held Phoenician towns and raised revolt in Cilicia. The Athenians twice sent a fleet under the admiral Chabrias to the assistance of the allies. Hecatomnus the prince of Caria sent his subsidies. Hakori concluded a treaty with the Pisidian cities, probably arranging the hire of mercenaries. For ten years Evagoras defied the Persians, thus defending Egypt as well as himself, but was at last brought to bay, defeated at sea, and blockaded in his own island. The Persian generals were constrained to conclude peace (380) on condition that no further harm should be done to Evagoras, who was to pay tribute henceforth to Artaxerxes not as a slave to his master, but as one king might to another. Not long afterwards he fell a victim, with his son, Pnytagoras, to a conspiracy; and was succeeded by another son, Nicocles, who was as philhellenic as his father (see above, p. 58 *sq.*).

The whole episode of Evagoras I is a most interesting one, though it can only interest us here incidentally. The Greek element in Cyprus was always the predominant element in the island, as it is now. The Phoenician settlements were few in number, but made up for their numerical weakness by their importance: Citium was always an important place. But Assyrian and Babylonian control had never resulted in an increase of the Semitic element. The Cypriote Greeks, though cut off from their fellow-countrymen by a long sea-road, and exposed to strong Semitic and Anatolian influences from the mainland as well as the leaven of the indigenous peasant population (of Anatolian affinities), continued Greeks, albeit old-fashioned Greeks: in classical days their kings still went to war in chariots, which in Greece had been relegated to the games centuries before. The thirty-five years of Egyptian domination (*c.* 560–25 B.C.) under Amasis (see vol. III, p. 306) had introduced a strong Egyptian element in art, and possibly had some effect on the Cyprian culture. Then came the Persian domination and the rescue of the Cyprian Andromeda from the barbarian dragon by that gallant Perseus, Cimon, only to be followed by her abandonment to her fate by the Peace of Callias. Then followed after half-a-century the stirring episode of Evagoras. The prince of Salamis regarded himself as a Teucrid, and so of Attic blood; he was as civilized a Hellene as any other, certainly more civilized than a Macedonian prince, for instance; he aspired to make Cyprus a free Hellenic state.

Unsupported by Hellas, and with none but Athenian sympathy and none but Egyptian help, he went down in the struggle against Persian numbers, but with honour. He had helped Hakori by staving off renewed Persian attack for at least another ten years.

At this juncture Hakori died (378) and was succeeded by Nepherites II, who reigned only four months and left no monuments. The throne was now seized by the prince of Thebnūte (Sebennytos), Nakhtenbōf or Nakhtenēbef[1] (Nektanebos or Nectanebo I), who was said to have been a son of Nepherites I, the Mendesian, passed over in favour of Hakori fifteen years before, but as a matter of fact was the son of a certain general named Zedhōr (Tachōs). His predecessor Nepherites II was slain, and his son after him, according to tradition, no doubt by Nakhtenēbef. The new king and his two successors, Zedhōr (Tachōs) and Nakhthorehbe (Nectanebo II), formed the XXXth Dynasty, the last dynasty of native Egyptian kings to rule the whole land.

Artaxerxes was not able to attack Egypt at once on account of disaffection in the fleet. First revolted the admiral at Citium, Glōs, son of that Egyptian Tamōs who had escaped from Ionia to Egypt twenty years before, and therefore an Egyptian or half-Egyptian himself. Then, after he was suppressed and fled to Egypt, his successor (also, oddly enough, an Egyptian), named Tachōs (Zedhōr), himself revolted. Probably this was the result of Egyptian machinations. When the king's armament was at last got together and had been placed under the command of the now elderly satrap Pharnabazus, a new complication arose. Nakhtenēbef invited to his aid the Athenian admiral Chabrias with his fleet (377), and Chabrias, nothing loth, went to his assistance, without leave from the Athenian people. Pharnabazus immediately protested loudly at Athens in the name of the Great King, asking whether the Athenians deemed it prudent to provoke the resentment of Persia.

---

[1] Spiegelberg has shown (*Die sogenannte demotische Chronik zu Paris*, 1914, p. 6) that the generally accepted identification of Nectanebo I with Nakhthorehbe and Nectanebo II with Nakhtenēbef should be reversed, as Nakhtenēbef certainly reigned before Nakhthorehbe, who then, and not Nakhtenēbef, will have been the last native pharaoh. The fact is proved by the evidence from the temple of Hibis noted by de Garis Davies and quoted by Spiegelberg, *loc. cit.* Brugsch's argument for the priority of Nakhthorehbe to Nakhtenēbef (*Egypt under the Pharaohs*, ii, 307) drawn from the genealogy on the Berlin sarcophagus No. 7, is based upon an error; all that the inscription proves is that king Nakhtenēbef was the son of the general Tachōs, whose father is not mentioned; Nakhthorehbe does not appear in it at all (Jéquier, *Livre de ce qu'il y a dans l'Hadès*, 1894, p. 26, n. 4. The present writer owes the reference to Dr H. Schäfer).

The alarmed *demos* at once recalled Chabrias and furthermore, at the request of Pharnabazus, lent him the services of the famous officer Iphicrates, who in 390 had created such a sensation in Greece by his destruction by means of peltasts (light-armed troops whose use he developed and advocated) of a whole Spartan *mora* or battalion of hoplites outside the walls of Corinth (p. 51 *sq.*).

The Athenian general accordingly repaired to Asia, and joined the army of Pharnabazus, which now advanced through Palestine and in 374 delivered its attack. It is said to have comprised 200,000 Persians and other barbarians, 12,000 (or 20,000) Greeks under Iphicrates, 300 warships: all figures which cannot be checked and may be quite erroneous. The Mendesian mouth of the Nile was forced by the fleet on board which were Iphicrates and many of his men, and the way lay open southward to Memphis. Iphicrates wished naturally to press on and finish the campaign at a blow, but Pharnabazus, deeply distrustful of the Greeks, and suspecting them of a design to seize Egypt themselves in the manner of the Athenians eighty years before, refused to allow him to do anything until the arrival of the *gros* of the Persian army overland from Asia, when both forces would advance simultaneously on Memphis. Accordingly they waited, but the opportunity was lost, Memphis was fortified and garrisoned, and then towards summer the inundation covered the Delta with a sheet of water, and the invaders had hurriedly to decamp. Iphicrates, throwing up his command, departed secretly to Athens, and Pharnabazus had to make the best of his way to Asia and explain matters to his master as best he might.

Egypt was undisturbed during the rest of the reign of Nakhtenēbef, which lasted eighteen years, till 361. A record of his relations with Greece exists in the Stele of Naucratis, erected in his first year, which records the gift to Neith of Saïs of a tithe of all imports from Greece and of all products of Naucratis. The king took the opportunity, rare since the days of the Saïtes, of leaving some mark of his reign on the temples. In his sixteenth year, in consequence of a dream, he commanded the priest Petisi to restore the temple of Sebennytos. The deity Sopd, guardian of the eastern marches, was specially propitiated in order to secure his aid against the Persian danger, and his shrine at Ṣafṭ el-ḥennah in the Wadi Tūmilāt, excavated by Naville in 1884, is a remarkable example of the use of great masses of stone that is characteristic of the temple-architecture of this period, and also well exhibits their meticulous decoration, equally characteristic of the age. The cutting of the hieroglyphs and other figures is carried out in a precise and delicate style like the Saïte yet differing from it sensibly in details. He built not only in the Delta, but also at Abydos, Thebes and at Philae, where a graceful little temple commemorates his reign. The work of his architects is not untasteful. The green breccia sarcophagus of the king is at Cairo. His successor was his son Ze(d)ḥō(r), or Tachōs as the Greeks called him, the Teōs of Manetho: the name, meaning 'Saith Horus,' the symbol representing the human face being now used for the name of Horus (usually represented by the symbol of the falcon), was pronounced something like 'Žaḥō' or rather 'Tjaḥō,' and was a very common name at this time.

The accession of the new king was marked by a rude termination to the peace of the past twelve years. As before, the course of events was dependent on the kaleidoscopic changes of politics in Greece. The previous peaceful years had been contemporaneous with the dramatic contest between Sparta and Boeotian Thebes, immortalized by the names of Pelopidas and Epaminondas, which had ended the previous year in the battle of Mantinea and the death of Epaminondas (p. 101). 'After the battle,' says Xenophon, 'there was even more uncertainty and confusion in Greece than there had been before.' The attempt of Pelopidas to bring the Greeks to a general peace and agreement under the aegis of the Great King as universal mediator failed, and the Greek delegates came back from Susa profoundly disillusioned as to the wealth of Susa and the King: 'the famous golden plane-tree would not give enough shade for a lizard.' And now all Asia broke into revolt under various dynasts and satraps; Mausolus of Caria, whose person we know from his tomb-statue in the British Museum, Datames, Orontes of Mysia, Autophradates of Lydia, Ariobarzanes of the Hellespontine region, and others. The king's only weapon against them seems to be assassination. And then Tachos must needs join in the dance. He prepared an army to invade Syria, and as the modern Greeks get a French officer to reorganize their army and a British seaman to put their navy in order, so the Egyptian hired a Spartan to look after his army and an Athenian to take charge of his navy. They were respectively the old king Agesilaus and the admiral Chabrias, who, we are told, was always a lover of Egypt. Agesilaus came with the full consent of the Spartans, who were angered with Persia because Artaxerxes had approved at the conference at Susa of the freeing of Messenia by Epaminondas, and brought with him 1000 Spartans, a formidable reinforcement for Egypt in spite of its small numbers. Chabrias came at his own charges, and used his knowledge of

Egypt to advise Tachos to confiscate much of the temple-revenues to pay his troops, an act which, if it was carried out, was not calculated to enhance the popularity of the Egyptian king with his subjects. Agesilaus's appearance and his familiar camp-manners with his Spartans earned him only contempt from Tachos, but the Spartan king, though he was over eighty, had lost none of his vigour, and when after the arrival of the army in Phoenicia he found that he was utterly unable to agree with Tachos (who also was not loved by the Egyptians, who had revolted against him at home), he deposed him in favour of his relation the young prince Nakhthoreḥbe (359). Tachos fled to Susa. '*One changes left for right*'; said the oracle of Heracleopolis in the 'Demotic Chronicle.' 'To the right is Egypt, to the left is Phoenicia. That is to say they exchanged him who went to Phoenicia, which is left, for him who stayed in Egypt, which is right'; says the commentary.

The new king immediately abandoned the Asiatic expedition (a consequence that can hardly have been expected by Agesilaus) in order to secure his power at home, which he only did after severe fighting, in which Agesilaus acted, as before, as chief-of-staff, and guaranteed him victory. The native troops on either side, Egyptian or Persian, hardly count for anything now: all the real fighting is done by the Greek mercenaries on both sides, and no sensible king would go to war without employing the best Greek military specialist he could. Agesilaus, when peace was restored in Egypt, received great gifts and a fee of 230 talents to Sparta (which he distributed among his soldiers), and went home, only to die on the way. Chabrias followed him. These Greek military specialists remind us, not so much of medieval *condottieri*, with whom they have been compared, as of the German and other professional generals of the seventeenth and eighteenth centuries, men like Montecuculi, the von der Schulemberg who commanded the Venetians at Corfu, Marshal Schomberg, and the famous Maréchal de Saxe.

Two other experts had soon to be engaged by Nakhthoreḥbe to command his forces. In 359 the Persian prince Ochus, now associated with his father as king, had attempted to follow Nakhthoreḥbe and Agesilaus into Egypt, but had retired, probably owing to the death of his father (358), whom he now succeeded as king Artaxerxes III, Ochus. The confederacy of Anatolian satraps broke up partly owing to the defection of Egypt, and partly owing to treachery among their number. His position being assured, Ochus, hearkening to the prayers of the exiled Tachos, determined to reinstate the Egyptian as his tributary. In the resulting attack, which was defeated probably about 357 or 356, the Egyptian defending forces (mostly no doubt Greeks) were ably commanded by the Athenian Diophantus and the Spartans Lamius and Gastron. We hear no more of Tachos. Like Nakhtenēbef, Nakhthorehbe (Nectanebo II) reigned for some years now in peace, and also erected monuments like him at Thebes and elsewhere, notably at Edfu and at Hibis in the oasis of al-Khargah. Of Tachos there is little trace in Egypt. He does not appear to have been a person of much distinction. Both Nectanebos, however, come before us as kings of a certain nobility and dignity, and we hear no ill of them. They were both distinguished patrons of the arts, and the later Saïte renascence that marks the second half of the short sixty years of independence, and is so important as the prelude and incentive to the fine efforts of early Ptolemaic art and architecture, must have been due to their direct patronage as well as to the inspiration which renewed independence and even power had given to the development of the arts.

Artaxerxes Ochus was a man of proud and energetic nature, who could not brook the continual independence of a people which he regarded as subject to his ancestors and so rightfully subject to him. Persian policy too was obstinate in endeavouring to regain its hold over a country so wealthy as Egypt. The Greeks after all could contribute nothing to Susa's treasury: they had nothing to export but their philosophy and art and no ware that Persia wished to buy but their military science. They were really not worth troubling about except on the point of honour. But the Egyptians meant flesh-pots, corn, and gold to their ruler. Accordingly prematurely aged Persia must put forward her half-palsied arm again to try to coerce decrepit Egypt into submission to her. And this time Ochus, or his advisers, acted with some skill while Nakhthorehbe did not. For the Persian at last realized that without expert Greek aid his expedition must fail, while the Egyptian, whether because he would not or could not pay properly for the best advice, or because he thought himself a general, did not trouble to secure his professionals as he should have done, and was betrayed by them.

The immediate cause of the war was a revolt in Phoenicia and Cyprus led by the king Tennes of Sidon, to whom Nakhthorehbe in an evil hour promised help (344). He sent him 4000 Greek mercenaries under Mentor the Rhodian, who, when he heard of the approach of Ochus in person with his army, opened communication with the Persians in collusion with Tennes. Ochus nevertheless besieged Sidon, whose citizens knew nothing of the treachery of their king. When the Persians were admitted into the city by Mentor and Tennes, the Sidonians burnt themselves, their fleet and their houses in one great pyre. Forty thousand are said to have perished[1]. Tennes was cynically executed by Ochus, and Mentor with equal cynicism taken into his service. Cyprus was reduced for him by Idrieus, prince of Caria, the successor of Mausolus, helped by the Athenian admiral Phocion and the Salaminian king Evagoras II, who had been expelled from Cyprus and now returned.

In 343, strengthened by Mentor and his men, well acquainted with the eastern border of Egypt, and by Lacrates the Theban and Nicostratus the Argive, whom Ochus had specially engaged with their men from Thebes and Argos on payment of a subsidy to the two states, and 6000 Ionians besides, the Persian king moved southwards on Egypt. Nakhthorehbe defended the line of the isthmus of Suez with a considerable army, which is said to have included 20,000 Greeks, though this seems improbable. He had at least two Greek generals, Philophron and Cleinias of Cos, but they were not of the first rank; Lacrates and Nicostratus easily outclassed them, and Mentor's local knowledge stood the two chief commanders in good stead. Nicostratus forced the passage of the canals at Pelusium and beat Cleinias in the field and killed him; whereupon Nakhthorehbe, who had apparently no other Greek commander on whom he could rely, retreated to Memphis, leaving his Greeks to continue the fighting. After his disappearance from the scene they soon surrendered, and now the cities of the Delta had to open their gates to their conquerors. Bagoas the eunuch, the chief Persian commander, received their submission, and advanced with Mentor on Memphis, from which Nakhthorehbe fled with his treasure, as Taharka had done before him, to Ethiopia (see vol. III, p. 281). The finely wrought sarcophagus which had been prepared for his tomb, probably at Saïs, in his lifetime, and was never occupied by him, is in the British Museum, after having acted for long as a bath in some Alexandrian palace.

Ochus now arrived in Egypt, and, if we are to believe the chroniclers, celebrated his arrival in a way that outdid the outrages of Cambyses, stabling an ass in the temple of Ptah and having Apis slain to be roast for a banquet. This Persian king was no doubt very much of a savage, but we may doubt whether these are not a mere *réchauffé* of the tales against Cambyses, unless, of course, he purposely imitated the sacrileges of his predecessor,

[1] See on the date of the Fall of Sidon, pp. 22, 249.

which is not impossible. The archives of the temples, which had been carried off, had to be redeemed by the priests from Bagoas for large sums.

Pherendates (Frañadāta) was appointed satrap, and Egypt sank into an uneasy torpor of dazed submission to the 'Great Kings' who now ruled by the favour of Bagoas, and to their new satraps, until, only ten years later, she was awakened by the trumpet-call of Alexander. One can almost smile at the succession of unexpected shocks which the Greeks gave to the Egyptians during this catastrophic fourth century, but the last was certainly the most startling of all, though it turned out well for Egypt.

III. THE COMING OF ALEXANDER

The rumour of the coming of the Macedonian conqueror had preceded him, and the sieges of Tyre and Gaza had given the Persians in Egypt and the Egyptians plenty of time in which to make up their minds how to receive him. The Persians, cut off from all help, could do nothing; and the feeling of the Egyptians would certainly be in his favour; they would prefer a Greek, or *soi-disant* Greek, conqueror to a Persian. To them Alexander was a Greek as others before him. And though he might punish individuals, he would not oppress the whole nation or contemn its gods. Mazaces the satrap submitted, and, amid the acclamations of the Egyptians, Alexander sacrificed to the Egyptian gods and was hailed by the priests as the Son of Amon-Rē' the Sun-god, and king of Egypt (332). He had no time to visit Thebes, so went to the more romantic oasis-oracle of Ammon at Sīwah instead, where his divinity as king of Egypt was fully recognized and proclaimed[1]. If he was king of Egypt he could not avoid being the son of the sun-god, and indeed 'the good god' himself, even if he wished. His Macedonians could not understand the fiction and resented the assumption, while the Greeks mocked when they dared. The divinity of Alexander was due to no mad arrogance nor can it be proved that he believed it in the least himself, but it was a 'legal' necessity, so far as Egypt was concerned; it could be justified to the Greeks as the divinity

[1] Also the fact that the temple of Sīwah had been well known to the Greeks for two centuries or more owing to its proximity to Cyrene probably had something to do with its selection as the seat of Amon to which the king repaired. He was then not merely the son of the purely Egyptian Amon-Rē' of Thebes, but also of the Zeus Ammon whom the Greeks of Cyrene had long venerated, and whose oracle was well known to the Greeks (cf. Ehrenberg, *Alexander und Aegypten*, pp. 37 *sqq.* and below, p. 377).

of a 'founder-god,' θεὸς κτίστης, or at any rate the semi-divinity of a 'founder-hero,' ἥρως κτίστης, as the founder of Alexandria. And Iskander dhu'l-qarnain, 'two-horned Alexander,' with the ram's horns of Ammon springing from his head as on the coinage of Lysimachus[1], he has remained in oriental tradition till this day. Popular legend in Egypt soon busied itself with him after his death, and we have that marvellous tale, the 'Alexander Romance' of the Pseudo-Callisthenes: how Nectanebo, who was a great sorcerer, fled, not to Ethiopia, but to Macedonia, where he visited the queen Olympias in the guise of the ram-headed Ammon, and so he, not Philip, was the real father of Alexander, who was thus doubly the rightful pharaoh of Egypt. The Heracleopolite oracular description of the Greeks as 'the dogs' and of Alexander himself as 'the Big Dog' (see p. 157) who finds something still to devour, is not necessarily derogatory, although the nationalist priests of Heracleopolis cannot really have loved the 'dogs,' though they drove out the Persian oppressors: the idea is rather a neutral one, describing Alexander and his soldiers rather appropriately under the guise of their own Molossian hounds, chasing away the Medes and seeking everywhere for more to devour.

Alexander attempted to enlist the Egyptians themselves in the government of their country by appointing a noble, Petisis, as satrap, though solely with the power of a Minister of the Interior carefully checked both from the financial as well as the military side, the taxation of the country being entrusted to a Naucratite Greek, Cleomenes, with his colleague Apollonius, its military security to the Macedonian officers Peucestas and Balacrus and the Greek admiral Polemon. The Egyptian, however, declined his post and a certain Doloaspis, who had been associated with him, was appointed as sole satrap. This Doloaspis, judging by his name, was not an Egyptian, but a Persian, or possibly an Anatolian. Cleomenes got the last ounce of tribute out of Egypt for his master, and the reason for Alexander's diversion to Egypt after the fall of Tyre is evident. He had to secure the wealth of Egypt before pursuing his attack on Persia. He could trust the treachery, ineptitude, and incapacity of the Persians to leave his Anatolian conquest unattacked, his land line of communications uncut. Not, too, that he needed that much now. The possession of Phoenicia and her fleets gave him an invulnerable line of communication by sea, if he were cut off by land, and that of Egypt rendered the sea line absolutely safe from land attack, since it could be transferred at a moment's notice from Tyre and

[1] See Volume of Plates ii, 8, l.

Sidon to Naucratis and to the new port and city of Alexandria-
Rhacotis, which the conqueror established in the neighbourhood
of Naucratis at the west end of the Delta coast. Here alone there
was no fear of a silted-up harbour, since the Nile-flood drives its
silt eastward up the coast from the mouths in the direction of
the Serbonian bog, not westward towards Libya.

With the foundation of Alexandria the ancient history of
Egypt ends, and that of the new Hellenistic Egypt, ruled by Greek
pharaohs from the Greek sea-city and in continuous connection
with the Mediterranean world, begins. Had Alexander lived on as
Great King at Babylon or Susa, and founded a dynasty there, it is
doubtful whether his experiment in Egypt would have survived.
It was owing to the fate that confined Ptolemy Soter to Egypt
as his share of the empire of Alexander that his Macedonian
dynasty, circumscribed to Egypt and wholly identified with it,
survived, and Alexandria with it. The Ptolemies were in all
respects for their subjects Egyptian kings, residing in Egypt and
representing Egypt only, as the Persians had never been, and as
Alexander's dynasty, had it existed, would not have been. Therefore, on the whole, they kept the loyalty of their subjects.

The last native régime, which had made such valiant struggles
against the Medes, was, it is true, looked back to in Ptolemaic
days with regret. We read in the prophetic oracles of Heracleopolis (preserved in the 'Demotic Chronicle'), of the Mendesian
and Sebennytic kings: of Amyrtaeus 'the first after the Medes,'
of Naif'aurud 'the second after the Medes,' and so on to the
seventh, Nakhtenēbef, son of Naif'aurud, the eighth Zedhōr
(Tachōs) and then the tragic figure of Nakhthorehbe. '(The
chief who came after Zedhōr, eighteen years shall he reign....)
They have opened the gates of the veil (?), *they will open the doors of
the curtained place* (?); (they who came after him, the Madai
[Medes]....) *Our lakes and our isles are full of tears;* (the dwellings
of the men of Egypt have none in them at this time: that is to say,
at the time named it is meant that the Medes had taken their
dwellings in order to live in them)....*I love the first day of the
month more than the last:* (by which he would say: better is the first
year than the last in the times which they bring, namely the
Medes)....*I have arrayed myself from head to foot* (by this thou
wouldst say: I appear with the basilisk of gold which none shall
take from my head! He said this of king Nakhtenēbef.) *My
royal vestment is upon my back:* (that is to say, my royal vestments
shine upon my back: none shall take them from me.) *The
scimitar is in my hand:* (that is to say: the kingly office is in my

hands, none shall take it from me...the scimitar of victory!).'
But Nakhtenēbef's pride and splendour, the glory of the renewed
kingdom, were cast down into dust: '*the herds of the people of the
deserts have entered Egypt* (that is to say: the nations of the west
and east have entered Egypt. And they are the Medes!)....
O Gardener, do thy work! (that is: Pharaoh, do thy work:
by whom he meant king Nakhtenēbef) *O Gardener, may thy
planting remain!*' Such, according to the latest version[1], is the
style of this curious book of prophecies with their commentary
or interpretation (in brackets), which often seems to be a double
interpretation: a commentary on a commentary on the original text.

We seem also to read vague and veiled aspirations after the
coming of a saviour-king, who should come to Hermopolis
from Ethiopia, like Pi'ankhi long before (vol. III, p. 271), under
the auspices of the god Harshafi of Heracleopolis and his priests,
and end the Ptolemaic domination: '(for the Ionians who come to
Egypt, they rule Egypt for long) *The dogs, may they long live: the
Big Dog, he finds somewhat to eat*' (see p. 155). But no Ethiopian
deliverer ever came; intelligent Ethiopian princes like Ergamenes
(*c.* 220 B.C.) realized too well the power of the Ptolemies and the
civilization they represented to think of trying to conquer Egypt.
And though patriotic antiquaries and *litterati* might sometimes
sigh, in the characteristic old Egyptian fashion in times of
internal war or foreign domination, for a Messianic deliverer,
and though prophecy-mongering priests might do their best to
keep up the hope of a native monarchy in the minds of the people,
it never revived. Local dynasts in Upper Egypt, like Harmachis
and Anchmachis in the reign of Epiphanes at the beginning of the
second century, might arrogate royal regnal years to themselves
as long as they dared. But the nation as a whole desired no change.
The régime of the Ptolemies was a very different thing from that
of the Persians, and though Greeks might settle everywhere in
the country and penetrate into the life and being of the native
race to a remarkable extent, they did so as fellow-subjects of
kings who wore the Double Crown of Egypt and no other.

IV. RETROSPECT

When we look back over the eight hundred years of
Egyptian history since the days of the priest-kings, we shall
perhaps be struck by the great sameness that runs through the
whole story. The history of Egypt in many respects resembles

---

[1] Spiegelberg, *loc. cit.*

that of China. Both countries were and are inhabited by a sturdy peasant-folk of intensely conservative instincts, which for thousands of years has altered but little. Barbarians from outside, Scyths, Turks and Huns (Yueh-chi, Tü-chi, and Hiungnu), Khingans, Mongols, and Manchus in the case of China, Libyans, Ethiopians, Assyrians in the case of Egypt during this period, Hyksos and Philistines before it, have always flowed in, or tried to flow in from the surrounding bad lands into the desirable cultivation and amenity of the river-countries: they have in both China and Egypt conquered the native folk and given them an aristocracy and a royal house. We may very well compare the Libyans of the Twenty-second Dynasty not only with the Kassites in Babylonia but also with the Manchus in China. The conquerors have however always become absorbed in all essentials into the native race, while often retaining the mere insignia (in the way of names and so forth) of their alien origin. This phenomenon repeats itself in Egypt: we may compare the 'Great Chiefs of Ma' with the Manchu 'banner-men' in China. The pharaohs of the Nineteenth Dynasty may more than be suspected of being of Semitic origin, descended from some Hyksos princely family that remained behind in the Delta after the exodus of the Shepherds. Here we have the Arab-Canaanite filtering in from the east. In the case of the Ptolemies we have strangers from the sea (albeit Alexander came by land like the others) coming in to rule the patient race that made the wealth for them. But of all the foreign dominations that of the Libyan families was the most persistent. Under the Twenty-first Dynasty they began to dominate Egypt, under the Twenty-second they gave a royal house not only to Egypt but also to Ethiopia, and seven hundred years after the time of the Meneptah the princes of Saïs still bear the apparently Libyan name Psamatik[1]. The Egyptian military class was then largely of Libyan origin, the descendants of the followers of the Great Chiefs of Ma. It was the appearance of the Greek mercenaries and the Persian conquest that together wrecked the 'Hermotybies and Kalasiries,' and caused the final disappearance of the Libyan element, which under the Mendesians and Sebennytites no longer exists and has left hardly any trace except the popular proper name Sheshenḳ, which occurs in Ptolemaic and even in Roman days (as Sesonchosis).

We must now cease to think of the Ethiopian kings as very radically opposed to the Libyans of the north. It has been

[1] Vol. III, p. 291. Niku (Necho) is pure Egyptian, and an archaistic revival of an Old Kingdom name. Cf. Nekaurē' (vol. I, p. 279).

shown[1] that the Ethiopian royal house was of Bubastite origin and bore Libyan names. Yet there is no doubt that Nubian names occur among their queens, and there can be little doubt that the Ethiopian kings themselves soon became half Nubian. Taharḳa is represented by the Assyrians as having the visage of a negro: and, after all, Egyptian representations of him are negroid in appearance. He may in fact have had not a Nubian, but a negress, for his mother. The Saïtes of the Twenty-sixth Dynasty show no Ethiopian, much less negroid, traces in their portraits, so that there was probably no intermarriage with the Ethiopian royal house. We have an excellent portrait of Psamatik I on an intercolumnar slab probably from Saïs, in the British Museum, which is obviously faithful; it represents him as remarkably like the famous Lord Chancellor Brougham, with an almost equally characteristic nose[2]. One would say that the features were those of a west-European. The nearest Egyptian approach to his type is that of a Fourth Dynasty grandee from Gizeh, whose 'reserve head' (vol. i, p. 288) for the tomb was found by Reisner[3]. The ancient head is the nobler of the two. But the persistence of this 'European' type is interesting. There is certainly nothing of the Ethiopian about it, or Semite. Something of the same type, but more conventionally Egyptian in character, is the portrait of Nakhtenēbef, also on an intercolumnar slab in the British Museum[4]. Character in a Sebennytite portrait is not unexpected: it was not till the Ptolemaic period that the faces of royal statues again became characterless and conventional. Apries, on a slab also in the British Museum, has marked features though without the character of Psamatik I.

The Libyan admixture, apart from the royalties, was chiefly apparent in the upper class. We find it already under the priest-kings in the burly Masaherti (vol. iii, p. 256), who bore a Libyan name. It was probably on the whole a healthy admixture. The Semitic

[1] By Reisner, "Outline of the Ancient History of the Sudan" (*Sudan Notes and Records*), ii (1919), pp. 42, 66.
[2] See Volume of Plates ii, 14, *a*.
[3] Reisner, in *Boston Museum Bulletin*, xiii, 1915, p. 34.
[4] Volume of Plates ii, 14, *b*. A statue formerly attributed to Nakhtenēbef in the same collection (No. 44) has been assigned (by Miss M. A. Murray and Dr Evers) to Senusret I, of the Twelfth Dynasty, on grounds of style: the prenomens of the two kings are identical. The present writer is now convinced that the old attribution to Nakhtenēbef is an error. There is, it is true, unwonted energy in the face, battered though it is now; and there are other traits which must be taken to indicate that the statue is a genuine work of the Twelfth Dynasty.

and Anatolian admixture, however, which (apart from Semitic peasants in the eastern Delta) was probably now apparent chiefly in the cities, was by no means of the best, consisting probably (as it does now) of the riff-raff of Phoenicia and the Levantine coasts generally. This cannot have been any but a degenerate component in the new Egyptian race, to which Ethiopian and negro elements contributed nothing good except (like the Libyans) a certain amount of energy, without which the Egyptians would have been an even feebler folk at this period than they actually were. The effect of these doubtful foreign strains on the national type is perhaps seen in a particularly villainous cast of countenance that appears in certain portrait-heads of the Saïte period, which are almost too faithful representations of their subjects[1]. The negro and Nubian ('Berberine') elements in the population were probably more apparent than they are now; many of both races belonging to the armies of the Ethiopian kings would settle in Egypt in the eighth century, and Ethiopian types, often mixed with negro, would be seen then also among the upper classes, and most apparently at Thebes, owing to the long domination there of the southern kings. Yet Mentumeḥet (vol. III, p. 321) appears before us as in his portrait as a typical Egyptian of the old-fashioned broad-faced type which we know under the Fourth Dynasty. Fellah blood after all was but little contaminated, and the country gentleman would be fellah then as he is now. The degeneration was in the towns and among the ruling classes in the capital cities.

We have spoken of the Egyptians of this time as being a feeble folk. The fellah stock of the nation was not in itself feeble, but it was, as it always has been, pacific, except in regard to local quarrels between villages or parties, when the use of the *nabūt* or heavy staff was as common as now and as is the *lathi* among those other very simple peasants, the Jāts of the Punjab. The stronger stick prevailed then as now, and when it was in the hand of a resolute pharaoh or a foreign conqueror, the fellah submitted to his master in either case. It was only a strong pharaoh and a strong incentive that could get the fellahin forth of Egypt and away from their beloved fields to fight abroad; weak government and poverty meant that Egypt became indeed a broken reed, able to stave off conquest by a resolute aggressor only by means of the weapons of intrigue and chicane. The centuries of manœuvres of this kind must have had as bad an effect on the minds of the Egyptian ruling classes as it had on those of the similarly situated

[1] See Volume of Plates ii, 14, *c*.

Byzantines. Then, in Saïte times, the eclipse of the military class
by the foreign mercenaries, with the result that in the fourth
century the Egyptian armies were largely composed of foreigners,
reduced the manliness of the nation to a very low ebb. It cannot
be said that in classical times the Egyptian had a very savoury
reputation. At Rome he was usually the professor of religious
humbug and 'occult' quackery. But for a temporary revival, the
result of Islām, during the Middle Ages, the Egyptians have continued to be an unwarlike, albeit quarrelsome, race from Saïte
days to our own. And yet the nation had and has, like the Chinese
again, the solid virtues of its main stock, the sons of the soil. This
race is as fecund as ever it was. Its misfortune always has been
that it has so rarely been ruled by men of real light and leading,
of true credit and renown.

Of the condition of the farmer and the peasant class we hear
little that is new during the period. The foreign warriors that
were settled among them soon mixed with the native population.
The conditions of life were not altered for anybody: in Egypt they
are unchanging. Only a very high or low Nile makes any difference. We have documents from which something of the petty
details of the land and tax organization can be learned, but they
are marvellously dull reading, and of no interest to anybody but
specialists in law or language. All that need be said in a general
history is that traditional system was preserved with necessary
modifications, and that the complicated system of Ptolemaic and
Roman days was, so far as we can tell, already in existence in a
somewhat less elaborate form. The many trading documents of the
time of Darius I (p. 137) have already been mentioned. Trade with
Asia always flourished except in time of actual war; and nothing
shows the resilience of the Egyptians so well as the astounding
speed with which the traces of constantly recurring wars and
invasions disappeared from the daily life of the people.

Of other documents we possess letters of the Twenty-first
Dynasty in the shape of the correspondence of certain Theban
officials, the scribes Zaroiye and Thutmosis, the commander of the
guard Pi'ankhi, the scribe Buteha-Amon, the priestess or singer of
Amon Shedumedua, and others, that give a tantalizing impression
of the life of educated but not noble persons of that time, an
impression tantalizing because so much space in each letter is taken
up by compliments that there is little room left for information
which might be to us of priceless value. Here again we see a
parallel with old China. Both countries were in much the same
state of civilization, with a despotic ruler, a cultivated, literary,

and over-elaborate upper class, stupid and bad soldiers, and a long-suffering and silent peasantry.

It is difficult to judge from these letters whether the peasants are regarded as serfs or slaves or not. The letters are full of injunctions to be kind to the workmen, but, at the same time, 'Look after the people sharply every day,' writes Thutmosis to Buteha-Amon and Shedumedua, whose relations were probably conjugal; they appear to have stood in some subordinate relation to Thutmosis. 'Direct your attention to the people who are in the fields; make them do their irrigation work, make them do their irrigation work! and don't let the boys at school throw their books on one side! Look after the people in my house: make them dig ditches, but not too much!' It is much the same relation as that in India to-day between a zamindar and his rayats. The fellahin were not slaves any more than they are now: far less slaves indeed than most of other oriental peoples: the true slave was the negro and the war-captive, male or female. We possess interesting documents of a later period, the Saïte, relating to slavery, in the demotic papyri from el-Hibeh preserved in the Rylands Library at Manchester. From them we see that in the reign of Amasis Egyptians also could be held and sold as slaves, a practice that had probably grown up during the wars of the Dodekarchy. Under the Persians foreign mercenaries, like the Jews at Syene, could own Egyptian slaves[1]. After legal formalities a man could mortgage his own body for debt, and could also, if he willed, sell himself into slavery. Legal contracts, properly witnessed, were necessary for these proceedings.

The correspondence of Thutmosis and Buteha-Amon gives rise to the surmise whether these letters are not really model pieces of writing, intended for scholastic use? The reference to the bad boys casting aside their books looks very like it: one can hardly imagine Thutmosis troubling about the matter in real life, though perhaps the *litteratus*, Egyptian or Chinese, would be capable of mixing this matter up with irrigation. Such scholastic models were however common, and most of our copies of Egyptian literature are of this character: they are school exercises. But the letters, whether they are genuine or not, and whether Thutmosis and his friends were real persons or not, give some idea of the life

---

[1] Cowley, *Aramaic Papyri*, pp. 103 *sqq*. But it must be remembered that these Egyptians may have been Nubians or even negroes with Egyptian names, not genuine Egyptian fellahin. The names are Peṭosiri and Lilu (m.) and Tebo (f.). Lilu simply means 'child' and may not actually be a name.

of the time. The language is the altered common speech of the day, with many neologisms and foreign importations, which in the course of our period became the tongue of Ptolemaic days, practically identical with the later Coptic.

Under the Twenty-first Dynasty letters and all other documents were of course still written in hieratic and the same may be said of the Twenty-second. But in the time of the Ethiopians they begin to be, and from that of the Twenty-sixth Dynasty onwards they are always written in demotic, the new short-hand script that was evolved from hieratic and became popular somewhere about the beginning of the seventh century; after which time hieratic, written in a peculiar small, neat style, was used only for religious papyri. In fact our period might almost be called the 'Demotic Age' of Egyptian history, so characteristic of the period is the use of the older type of demotic writing, when hieratic had disappeared from ordinary use and Greek was not yet employed. Like the business documents and letters of all kinds now, the romances and prophecies which have been mentioned as written down in Ptolemaic and Roman times were written in demotic.

We have little literature in demotic script before Ptolemaic days. The stories were there, of course, in the mouths of the people, but had not yet been written. Notable among such tales that have not a direct historical bearing, and so have not yet been mentioned, are the stories of Setme Kha'muas, the great sorcerer, who is none other than an actual historical personage of old time, the prince Kha'muas, son of Rameses II, of whom there is a statue in the British Museum. He seems in his lifetime to have been a student of occult arts, and was high-priest of Ptah at Memphis; whence his later title of Setme, the name of the *Setme*-priest[1]. In the story, which was written down at the end of the Ptolemaic period, Setme Kha'muas has marvellous adventures with ghosts in a tomb into which he penetrates in order to obtain a book of magic deposited in it. Kha'muas plays draughts with the ghosts, the stake being the precious book. He goes down too into Hades and sees wonders there, and his son Si-Osirei, being still a child, but a reincarnation of a former sorcerer, defeats the sorceries of some Ethiopian magicians, who have the audacity to transport pharaoh himself by magic from Memphis to Ethiopia, there beat him in the presence of the 'Viceroy,' and bring him back to Memphis, all in the space of six hours. We hear of contests

[1] This, Mr Griffith thought, was the original of the Herodotean Sethōs or Sethōn (see vol. III, p. 278), the king in whose time occurred the famous destruction of the Assyrian host by the aid of the 'mice.'

between Egyptian and Ethiopian magicians exactly parallel to those between Moses and the Egyptian sorcerers in the Book of Exodus, and finally Si-Osirei disappears, having done the work for which he was reincarnated, the rescue of Egypt from Ethiopian magic. The whole story is curiously weird, and though occasionally it may read like a tale from the Arabian Nights, there is in it a macabre element that is very Egyptian and could only belong to the land of tombs and mummies in its old age.

It may be that the nation was becoming depressed by continued foreign rule and gloomier than it was in olden days. Certainly in late Roman times all joyousness seems to have departed from Egypt, when we seem to have reached an age of humourless, semi-idiotic religious delirium and fanaticism, and the dirtier, the stupider and the more delirious a man was the holier he was deemed to be by the murderers of Hypatia. That desperate time was however not yet, though perhaps we see premonitions of it already. In religion during our period we are greatly struck by the increase of the element of magic and obscure occultism. This element had of course always existed from the days of the predynastic medicine-men and of Dedi the magician of king Khufu. But now we find it very much to the fore, and manifesting itself in odd pantheistic figures and objects like the famous 'Metternich-stele,' which is of the time of Nakhthorehbe[1]. In the Egyptian religion the idea of sin and responsibility had but a small place: in fact consciousness of sin hardly appears till the Ramessid period, and is then no doubt a Semitic importation. Later we find religion sinking beneath the weight of formalism and mere superstitious observance of magical rites. Under the Saïtes a religious revival (if it may be so termed) among the priests, connected with the archaistic movement (vol. III, pp. 299, 317), led to a new recension and edition of the 'Book of Coming Forth by Day,' the 'Book of the Dead,' as we call it, which resulted in the fixing of the order of its 'mouths' or chapters. The primitive, barbarous and unintelligible Pyramid-texts of the beginnings of Egyptian civilization were revived in an even more unintelligible form, and their childish gabble, that of the 'Book of the Dead,' was much preferred to the splendid Eighteenth Dynasty hymns written when Egypt was really civilized in honour of Amon-Rē', the great god of the imperial period. The whole religion was becoming funerary in character, in accordance with the exaltation of Osiris at the expense of Amon.

We see the gradual retirement of Amon from his ancient pride

[1] See Volume of Plates ii, 16, a.

of place as the chief deity of the realm, though in the Saïte days he is still Amonrasonthēr, 'the king of the gods.' Under the Twenty-first Dynasty he is of course still all-powerful, with his wife Mut and his son the moon-god Khons, whose worship had developed so greatly under the Twentieth Dynasty. Under the Twenty-second Amon is still the chief god and war-lord. But alongside him in royal and popular estimation is now a form of Hathor, the cat-goddess Ubastet or Baste, the deity of Bubastis, the city of the court. The magnificent temple which the Bubastite kings built at Bubastis on the ruins of one that went back to the days of Khufu is well known in its formless ruin. But Baste was eclipsed with the Bubastite dynasty. Of course she still continued to be venerated, especially at Bubastis, but she is no longer to the fore. As the special patroness of dynasty and people she was succeeded by the war-goddess Neith, who was Libyan, but Libyan of a very early day, and had been naturalized as an Egyptian goddess long ago, in the days of the First Dynasty at least. Her position as the local deity of Saïs made her the special protectress of the Saïte kings, and names compounded with hers were common under the Twenty-sixth Dynasty. Probably the later Libyans of the days of the Ma identified their gods with those of Egypt wholly: Harshafi of Heracleopolis may have owed his popularity among them to identification with some Libyan Heracles, some Antaeus of the desert-caves.

Amon was soon to follow Baste, but to a more definite limbo of discarded gods, at any rate for a few centuries. The destruction of Thebes in 663 was probably the turning-point in his divine career. Osiris, the god of the dead, took his place in the popular mind as the universal lord whom all revered, and in Ptolemaic days Amon and Osiris were more or less confused with one another and with the deified sage Amenōthes or Amenōphis, son of Paapis. This was the historical Amenhotep, son of Hapu, vizier of Amenhotep III (vol. ii, p. 99 *sq.*), now regarded as a god, like Imhotep, the vizier of king Zoser (vol. i, p. 276), also now deified as the son of Ptah and patron of learning, the Imouthes of the Greeks. Officially Amon reappears under the Ptolemies as a royal god, owing to Alexander's special devotion to him, the ram-headed god whom he claimed as father. Alexander had to be son of Rē', but in the assumption of his pharaonic filial dignity it would appear that he was advised to become, or by chance became, son of Amon-Rē' of Sīwah rather than of Rē' of Heliopolis only. The imposing *panache* of the pre-Saïte Amon-Rē' suited the ideas of the Ptolemaic period, when men were inclined to revive the imperialistic spirit under the influence of the grandeur and foreign empire of such kings as Philadelphus. But to the common people Amon was no more than Amenophis or Osiris. The welding together, so far as it could be accomplished, of the Greek and Egyptian religions produced the curious phenomenon that we know well in classical days of Alexandrian religion with its worship of Sarapis (Osor-hapi, Osiris-Apis the funerary deity of Sinopion [Sinhapi], the necropolis of Sakkāra near Memphis), who was naturally identified with Hades, and with its Graeco-Egyptian 'fake' mysteries, which brought hierophants of Isis to Delos and to Rome, and made the great mother-goddess of a great and ancient people become one of the attractions of a second-rate Roman seaside resort like Pompeii. So Egypt perished, but *qualis artifex*! On her death-bed she was a sham and a *poseuse*: but what had she not been in her young days: the mother of the arts?

CHAPTER VII

THE INAUGURATION OF JUDAISM

I. THE HISTORICAL OUTLINES

THE little that is known directly of Syria and Palestine during the Persian age is almost wholly concerned with the Jews. Although these lands, constituting, as they did, part of the fifth of the twenty satrapies of the Achaemenids, were involved in the larger history of Persia and the West, the Jews alone preserved their national consciousness, and formed a link between the Assyrian and Babylonian age (vol. III) and the events leading up to the rise of Christianity. Jerusalem, so sequestered as not to command the attention of the curious Herodotus—who does not name the Jews—stands out by reason of an achievement which sealed the long development of the religion of Israel: the inauguration of 'Post-exilic Judaism.' This event, remote though it is from the main historical theme of the present volume, was destined ultimately to shape the world's history, and an account of it, so far as our scanty and difficult sources allow, must be given in this place.

A period which once seemed somewhat dull and lifeless is now found to be one of great permanent changes; and its most conspicuous monument is the Pentateuch. For, in the view of modern scholars, 'the Mosaic history is not the starting-point for the history of ancient Israel, but for the history of Judaism[1].' What

Note. The chief sources for this period are (1) the books of Ezra and Nehemiah (with 1 Esdras and Josephus), (2) a stock of contemporary papyri from a flourishing Palestinian military colony in Syene or Elephantine on the southern border of Egypt, (3) some contract tablets from an influential commercial colony at Nippur in the East, and (4) those portions of the Old Testament which on internal grounds are now commonly ascribed to the Persian age.

[1] The words quoted are the thesis of Wellhausen's *History of Israel* (1878) and define the standpoint of modern Old Testament criticism. The thesis is primarily a *literary* one (viz., of the relative dates of different sources of the Pentateuch, etc.), and it is distinct from the varying 'conservative' and 'advanced' reconstructions of the biblical *history* which have been put forth. How far, in the present writer's opinion, criticism has forced a restatement of the old traditional views has already been indicated in this work, period by period (vol. I, pp. 225 *sqq.*; vol. II, ch. XIV; vol. III, chs. XVII–XX).

was really a new stage in the religious development of Israel has been carried back and ascribed to the beginning of the tribal history, before the Davidic monarchy; and the Persian age is now the vantage ground from which the Old Testament viewed in the light of modern research becomes more intelligible.

The books of Ezra and Nehemiah, our main source, are an integral part of the 'Chronicler's History' (vol. III, p. 335), which passes from the capture of Jerusalem by the Babylonian Nebuchadrezzar (586 B.C.) to the return of Jewish exiles by the permission of Cyrus the first ruler of the Persian dynasty (538 B.C.). This history is that of the men who returned each to his own city, the rebuilding of the Temple in spite of continued opposition—the help of Samaritans being rejected—and the establishment of a distinctive community separated from the Samaritans and other strangers. The reader is looking at events through the eyes of uncompromising reformers whose horizon is strangely circumscribed. On the internal history of Palestine as a whole during the exile, on the prominence of the new Davidic scion Zerubbabel, and on the Messianic hopes of his supporters the 'Chronicler' maintains silence; though from the independent writings of the contemporary prophets Haggai and Zechariah (c. 520 B.C.) two facts emerge: (1) that no considerable or influential body of exiles could have returned, and (2) that Zerubbabel stands for a religious and political movement far more significant than our scanty narratives record. A renewal of the Davidic monarchy was evidently in the air (vol. III, pp. 409 sqq., 488). But some sixty years pass before the curtain is lifted again, and the Chronicler records that in the seventh year of Artaxerxes (458 B.C.) Ezra, a priest and scribe, receiving royal permission, returned accompanied by a body of priestly, temple and lay followers, with rich gifts for the temple, and extensive powers. His task was to inquire into the religious conditions, to instruct the people in accordance with the Law (Tōrah), and to appoint judges for all the Jews 'beyond the River.' His mission is represented as the first step in the inauguration of post-exilic Judaism.

This benevolent action of the Persian king is the outstanding fact in the inauguration of Judaism. It is in contrast to the inveterate jealousy and hostility of the neighbours of the Jews, and to the story of Esther and the escape of the Jews from massacre in the reign of the preceding king Ahasuerus or Xerxes[1]. How far such favour—which was also enjoyed by the colony at Ele-

---

[1] The Septuagint and Josephus read Artaxerxes; there is another reference to hostility to the Jews in the reign of Xerxes in Ezra iv, 6.

phantine—was influenced by merely political considerations it is difficult to say. Judah—Palestine in general—had traditional political relations with Egypt (whence the presence of the military colony in Elephantine), as also with Babylonia. Presumably it was affected by the revolts in Babylonia which compelled Xerxes to adopt a less conciliatory policy, as also by the intrigues of Inaros and Megabyxus in Egypt (pp. 3, 138 *sq.*). The foreign policy of the petty peoples was rarely if ever unanimous and the revolts outside their doors were usually accompanied by serious dissensions within. Yet, however that may be, it appears that Ezra's far-reaching plans with all the political consequences involved in them were frustrated, not by any political opposition, but by the internal conditions among the Jews themselves. There had been extensive intermarrying with strangers and, according to the narrative, almost his first step, instigated by the leading men in Judah, was to purge the community by the summary expulsion of the non-Jewish wives and their children (Ezra x).

At this point our narrative suddenly introduces us to quite another situation—the vivid story of Nehemiah's vigorous efforts to revive a prostrate and defenceless Jerusalem. Thirteen years have passed. It is the twentieth year of Artaxerxes (445 B.C.; or twenty-fifth year, so Josephus) and Nehemiah the cup-bearer of the Great King at Susa is overwhelmed with grief at the news of the lamentable condition of the city of his fathers' tombs—he was perhaps of royal ancestry. He gained the ear of the king—and of the queen: harem rule prevailed in Persia (p. 3), and it is thought possible that he was a eunuch. Leave was granted him to return to rebuild Jerusalem. Like Zerubbabel he firmly refused aid from outside, and succeeded in arousing his disheartened and indifferent brethren. Despite continuous intrigue and opposition, he sufficiently strengthened the walls in the short space of fifty-two days, and then the blow fell. Opposed to him was a strong party, Sanballat, the Ammonite Ṭobiah, Gashmu the Arabian, and their supporters and kinsmen among the Jews[1]. It was alleged that Nehemiah had bribed prophets to hail him king (Neh. vi, 7) —a charge which recalls the enthusiastic anticipations of Haggai and Zechariah for Zerubbabel[2]. No doubt there were fears of

[1] The names Sanballat (Sinuballiṭ, *i.e.* Sin gives life) and Ṭobiah (goodness of Yah[weh]) are interesting for the divine names which enter into them. Sanballat the 'Ḥoronite,' was of Beth-ḥoron in Samaria or of the Moabite Ḥoronaim.

[2] In several respects there is a similarity between the time of Nehemiah (the Jewish [? Davidic] governor who re-fortified Jerusalem) and the Davidic Zerubbabel the builder of the Second Temple.

some fresh political aggrandizement, and specimens of the utter-
ances of patriotic prophets may perhaps be recognized in Is.
lx–lxii, where, though there is no Messianic figure, the supremacy
of the holy city of Zion is awaited. But it was an empty city and
Nehemiah's task was to fill it[1]. At this point the story breaks off;
and Ezra suddenly reappears on the stage.

Now at last the Law is read, and in accordance with its pre-
scripts the 'seed of Israel' observed the national Feast of Tabernacles as never before 'since the days of Joshua.' They separated
themselves from strangers, and a covenant was solemnly drawn
up. Its chief terms were the avoidance of intermarriage with the
heathen, no Sabbath trading, the observance of the Sabbatic year,
the remission or rather suspension of debts every seventh year,
and various regulations for the maintenance of the Temple. That
the remarkable powers conferred upon Ezra by Artaxerxes were
fully utilized does not appear; but the occasion, as is shown by
the list of those who signed it, was regarded as epoch-making,
and it culminated in the determination never to forsake the 'house
of our God' (Neh. viii–x, Oct. 445 B.C.).

Again there is an abrupt change in the narrative—the city is
being re-populated, the newly built walls are dedicated, and Nehemiah makes arrangements for the temple ministrants. On the
strength of the Deuteronomic law (Deut. xxiii, 3–6) the Jews
separated themselves from Ammon, Moab and other strangers.
In some way twelve more years have passed, and Nehemiah, who
had returned to Persia, obtained leave in the thirty-second year
of Artaxerxes to revisit the city (433 B.C., Neh. xiii, 6). Grievous
sights met his eyes. The sanctity of the Sabbath was being pro-
faned by Jewish and Tyrian traders, the Hebrew language was
dying out owing to intermarriages, the temple service was crippled,
the high priest Eliashib was allied by marriage with the Ammonite
Ṭobiah whom he had installed in one of the temple-chambers,
and a son of Eliashib's son Joiada was son-in-law to Sanballat.
The zealous governor remedied matters in his own vigorous way,
and with his work in purging the priesthood and re-establishing
the temple organization, his lively story ceases with the prayer:
'Remember me, O my God for good.' A place must be found
somewhere in the history for a striking narrative, now strangely
inserted in the midst of the hasty rebuilding of the walls of the

---

[1] Neh. vii, 6–73 is the Chronicler's list of the Judaeans who returned
from exile in the days of Cyrus each man to his city (Ezra ii); cf. the identity
between the *family* of Jacob-Israel which went down into Egypt and the
subdivisions of the *tribes* who came out (Gen. xlvi, Num. xxvi).

city, where he tells of his generous measures on behalf of his poorer brethren, and his integrity and hospitality during a twelve years' governorship (Neh. v). The solidarity of the people had been broken by class-differences and reckless divorces (denounced by the evidently contemporary 'Malachi'), and a new social covenant also stands to his credit. Thus does the personality of Nehemiah stand out, more clearly than most characters in the Old Testament; and although, as will have been seen, the chapters relating to him do not furnish a simple outline of events, they afford the starting-point for any discussion of the history of the reign of Artaxerxes.

Certain facts can be clearly recognized: the fortification of Jerusalem, the re-organization of the Temple, its personnel and cult, the importance attached to the Sabbath; the introduction of the Law, the divorce of foreign wives and the separation from strangers, and the formation of an exclusive Judaean community, almost an ecclesiastical community[1]. But difficult problems at once arise. Thus Nehemiah's last step—the purging of the priesthood—appears to have some reference to the great Samaritan schism, when the intermittent hostility between Judah and Samaria led to the subsequent enmity of two closely-related though rival sects. So at least the Jewish historian Josephus understood the schism, although in his version it is placed about a century later, in the days of Joiada's grandson Jaddua and the invasion of Alexander the Great. According to this writer, at a time of fierce animosity between Samaria and Jerusalem, Sanballat, then an old man, sought to win over the Jews by marrying his daughter Nikaso to the priest Manasseh, the brother of Jaddua. This was bitterly resented in Judah, and at last Manasseh, with sundry priests and Levites who had married strangers, migrated to Samaria where Sanballat built a temple for them on Mt Gerizim. The story is circumstantial, but such was the ignorance which came to prevail concerning the Achaemenid dynasty that it is not easy to decide when the final separation actually occurred. Certainly the slumbering jealousy between north and south readily burst into flame as occasion offered, but the acceptance by the Samaritans of the Pentateuch, together with other evidence, points to one or more periods of *rapprochement*.

---

[1] However natural it may seem to say that Israel became a Church, it is preferable, in view of modern usage (as distinct from the days of the Papacy), to fall back upon the term 'theocracy' coined by Josephus (*contra Apion.* II, 7). He says: 'our legislator (Moses) ordered our government to be what I may call by a strained expression, a theocracy, attributing the power and the authority to God.'

Some light has more recently been thrown upon the age by the Jewish papyri discovered at Elephantine (mainly in 1904–8), and in particular by the appeals sent to Jerusalem and Samaria after the destruction of the local temple of Yahu (Yahweh) by the Egyptians in the reign of Darius II (411 B.C.)[1]. For some reason no notice was taken of the first appeal addressed to Jehohanan (John) the high-priest of Jerusalem and to Ostanes, whose brother Anani is specially mentioned, and may therefore have been Zerubbabel's descendant of that name (1 Chr. iii, 24). On the other hand, a sympathetic reply was received from one of the two sons of Sanaballaṭ (a more correct spelling of the name) and from the Judaean governor Bagohi. The events belong to the generation after Nehemiah. Sanballat is presumably represented by his sons, and these would be brothers-in-law of the renegade son of Joiada (the son of Eliashib, so Neh. xiii) or of Manasseh the son of Johanan (so Josephus) the leading figures in the two versions of the Samaritan schism. It is of course possible that there were two Sanballats, and certainly the name Bagohi was not a rare one[2]. Further, Josephus tells of a Bagoses a military commander (*strategos*), evidently of the time of Artaxerxes II (404–358 B.C.), who proposed to replace the high-priest John by his brother Joshua (Jeshua); and who, when John slew the latter within the sacred precincts, severely punished the crime, enslaving the people and imposing heavy tribute upon the daily sacrifices in the temple. Josephus, while condemning Bagoses for having 'polluted' the temple by entering it, does not conceal his abhorrence of the fratricide, which he places immediately before the Samaritan schism. Such an incident must reflect far-reaching political and religious differences between the governors and priests of Judah. The more exclusive policy of Nehemiah, like the failure of the Jerusalem high-priest to respond to the appeal from Elephantine, thus stands in contrast to the action of Sanballat and his two sons—both of whom have distinctly Jewish names—and of the Persian governor Bagohi. It would be tempting to speculate further upon the attitude of the Jews of Elephantine to Persia, and upon both the more exclusive and the more conciliatory tendencies which can so easily be recognized; but it is difficult to frame a consistent chronological reconstruction of the course of events and of the relations between Jews and Samaritans.

[1] See the Appendix (p. 559 *sq.*).
[2] Bagohi, Bagoi or Bagoas (the Hebrew Bigvai) is from the Pers. *Baga* 'god.'

The Jewish Canonical History ended with the significant reforms of Nehemiah, aimed at Samaritans and other non-Jews. But at a much later date the series of documents, Chronicles-Ezra-Nehemiah, was artificially divided and the halves transposed, so that in the Hebrew Bible Chronicles now stands after its sequel in Ezra-Nehemiah. In consequence of this division, the Bible of the scattered Jews of subsequent centuries ended appropriately on a happy note, with the rise of a new and friendly empire and the opportunity to return to Jerusalem to rebuild the Temple. On the other hand, the incomplete First Esdras of the Apocrypha—which breaks off in the middle of a sentence—has an order of its own, and represents the increasing tendency to place Ezra's work before Nehemiah's. This tendency grew, and Josephus places Ezra wholly before Nehemiah, and Ezra's work very fittingly ends, as has been seen, with the vow to cherish the Temple. Thus there are different tendencies and arrangements in order to give the first position to Ezra or to find some suitable climax, and in giving effect to this or the other intention alterations have been made sometimes of a very intricate character.

While Josephus has concentrated the chief events upon the coming of Alexander the Great, other late Jewish writers made Ezra the predominating figure. Not only is he supposed to re-write the Sacred Books which had been burnt with the temple, but others besides (24 canonical and 70 esoteric works). He also introduces a new script, the Aramaic ancestor of the 'square' Hebrew in the place of the older which was retained by the Samaritans (vol. III, p. 421). To him is also ascribed (by a dubious interpretation of Neh. viii, 8) the Targum or popular Aramaic version. In fact Ezra becomes a hated figure among the Samaritans for his activity in intensifying the differences between them and the Jews[1]. Here tradition has concentrated on one figure and on one age changes which were spread over a considerable interval; and the same possibility applies to the earlier tradition preserved in the biblical books.

In contrast with this exaltation of the priest Ezra the layman Nehemiah is the more important figure in earlier tradition, and Ezra is not named by Ben Sira in his list of post-exilic heroes (Ecclus. xlix, 11–13). Nehemiah, it was said, actually built the Temple and the altar, he resumed the sacrifices, and collected 'writings concerning the kings and the prophets, and the books of David and letters of kings about sacred gifts' (2 Macc. i,

---

[1] See 2 Esdras xiv, 44 *sq.*, Driver, *Samuel*, pp. 1 *sqq.*, Gaster, *The Samaritans*, p. 28.

18 *sqq.*, ii, 13). He is thus a forerunner of Judas Maccabaeus who collected the books that survived the ravages of war; and it is noteworthy that even in the Old Testament some building or repair of the temple is ascribed to the reign of Artaxerxes I (Ezra vi, 14). There is a growing consensus of opinion that the account of the work of Ezra presupposes that of Nehemiah: the soil has been prepared, the city is populous, conditions are more stable, the political opposition has been put down; religious changes alone remain to be carried out, and they are willingly effected. The work of Nehemiah, in turn, presupposes more disturbed conditions; the energetic layman seems to precede the priest. It is very generally agreed, therefore, that Ezra did not return before Nehemiah, though it is disputed whether to place the priestly scribe between the first and second visits of Nehemiah, or after Nehemiah and under the *Second* Artaxerxes, or even to reject the story of Ezra as a later invention.

Whichever of these views be adopted, we have still to seek the cause of the scenes of desolation and despair which confronted Nehemiah—must we look back nearly a century and a half to the Fall of Jerusalem (586 B.C.), or was it more recent? A valuable Aramaic fragment, now out of place in the account of the rebuilding of the *temple* by Zerubbabel in the time of Darius, tells of an important return of Jews in the reign of Artaxerxes to rebuild the *walls* (Ezra iv, 7 *sqq.*), though curiously enough the version in 1 Esd. ii, 18, 20 refers to the *temple*. Bishlam, Mithredath, Tābēl and other officials, it is said, wrote to the King to protest that these Jews were rebuilding a city which had a reputation for its intransigence, and that if this were done it would be a danger to the empire; Artaxerxes, having ascertained that Jerusalem had indeed been rebellious and the seat of powerful kings, gave orders for the work to be stopped forcibly until instructions were sent. So runs the fragment, which has been utilized to explain the cessation of the building of the *temple* between the reigns of Cyrus and Darius. By some it is thought to explain the unhappy conditions which confronted Nehemiah. But a better place for it would be after Nehemiah's return, at the point where the story abruptly ceases. The opposition probably reached its height with the allegation that political aims were on foot, and Nehemiah himself states, 'Tobiah sent letters to put me in fear' (vi, 19). Fortified though Nehemiah was with the King's authority, the accusation of disloyalty and rebellion might well alarm the King; and Tobiah, whose letters so disturbed the honest governor, has a name which is the Hebrew equivalent of

the Aramaic Tābēl who was among those who formally com-
plained to Artaxerxes. Nehemiah himself was obliged to return to
the King; and since he reappears on his second visit in a stronger
position, it may be assumed that Artaxerxes satisfied himself of
the governor's loyalty. But it is also possible that the fears of
Artaxerxes were aroused and that care was taken to preclude any
monarchical aspirations: certainly the later governor Bagohi
seems far less of a Jew than either Zerubbabel or Nehemiah.

In any case, the story of Ezra represents the sort of ecclesiastical movement that could follow the more primitive activities
of a Nehemiah who—if only perhaps by reason of his ancestry—
laid himself open to the suspicion of nationalistic activities: contrast Bagohi's association with the son of Sanballat. The story
of Ezra is also the prelude to the subsequent theocracy. It is
virtually the description of the inauguration of Judaism; and
when Ezra reads the Book of the Law, the narrator is evidently
referring to the Pentateuch as a whole, even as it was Deuteronomy which, according to an earlier writer, had been 'redis-
covered' in the reign of Josiah (vol. III, p. 396 sq.).

All the main traditions converge upon the reign of Artaxerxes I.
Thenceforth there is silence, unless, as some scholars urge, the
account of the favour shown by the King of Persia to Ezra belongs
to the reign of Artaxerxes II, in which case his return should be
dated to 397 B.C. The latter king is, however, notorious for his
recognition of Mithra and the goddess Anahita by the side of the
supreme god Ahura-mazda, and images of the goddess were set
up in the larger Persian cities, in Damascus, and as far afield as
Sardes. While there was much in the character of the ethical and
imageless All-Creator Ahura-mazda with which Jews could sym-
pathize, the addition of an intermediary and redeeming god
Mithra, and, in particular, the religious prostitution associated
with Anahita, a goddess of the Ishtar type, would inevitably provoke
the Jews who had come under the influence of the prophets and
the Deuteronomic reforming movement, and fierce opposition is
only to be expected. Direct evidence is wanting, although mention should perhaps be made of the view that the religious changes
led to a crisis in Judaism which forms the historical basis of the
highly embellished traditions of Jewish persecution and reprisals
in the book of Esther[1].

Later, the separatist movements in Egypt and the West shook
the Persian empire. The revolt of Evagoras (389 B.C.) extended to
Phoenicia and Palestine (p. 146 sq.), and the unrest of c. 366–60 B.C.

[1] So Hoschander; see the Bibliography to this chapter.

(p. 104), like the Phoenician revolts and the re-organization of Egypt 343–2 B.C., doubtless had their repercussion in Palestine. According to a late and rather dubious tradition, recorded by Eusebius, Jericho was captured and Jews carried off to Hyrcania and elsewhere[1]. In the romance of Judith, too, traces of historical events of the time of Artaxerxes Ochus (358–38 B.C.) have been conjectured. Not unnaturally has it been thought that those Old Testament passages which relate to the sufferings of the Jews and to the anticipations of deliverance, and which, on internal grounds, appear to be later than the sixth century B.C. and the time of Zerubbabel, really belong to this later period. In this way the age of Artaxerxes III and the advent of Alexander the Great, with all its promise of a new epoch, can, in the opinion of some scholars, be illustrated by passages which otherwise might seem to belong to the rise of the Persian Empire itself, when Cyrus was the expected saviour. In default of contemporary external evidence the most valuable criteria are to be found in the history of religious ideas and the literary growth of the Old Testament, although intricate problems of the development of thought are involved. But something will have to be said on these, so vital and suggestive are they; they serve to fill the gaps in the narrative, and the nature of these gaps will be realized when one looks back to the Fall of Jerusalem in 586 B.C., the scanty facts of Zerubbabel and the Second Temple (520–16 B.C.), and, travelling over the obscure history of Nehemiah and Ezra, passes through some two or three blank centuries before the historical narrative is resumed in the days of the Maccabees (Antiochus Epiphanes, 175 B.C.).

II. THE JEWS AND THEIR NEIGHBOURS

Leaving the historical narratives we turn, first, to a consideration of the general conditions. The satrapy of which Palestine was part included Syria, Phoenicia and Cyprus; Arabia was independent[2]. 'Transpotamia,' to give it a name (the Greek πέραν Εὐφράτου, Heb. 'ēber han-nāhār), extended from Posidium on the Orontes to the border of Egypt, and this single political unit, after the late writer in 1 Kings iv, 24, would correspond to Solomon's realm from Tiphsah to Gaza[3]. The constituent provinces enjoyed a certain freedom; each had its prince (nāsī) or governor (peḥah, tirshāthā) appointed by Persia, and one of the

---

[1] See Ency. Bib., col. 2202.

[2] See, on the satrapies, vol. IV, pp. 194 sqq.

[3] It is probable that other conditions of the Persian age are reflected in the late accounts of the first great kings of Israel and Judah.

Jewish families is even named after the governor of Moab (Pahath-Moab). The feelings of native states were so far considered that Zerubbabel, and possibly Nehemiah, were of the old dynasty; and, as was usual, for example in the Amarna age, the states would have their representatives at the suzerain's court. Samaria was in several respects of greater political importance than Jerusalem; but still more powerful was the north, *e.g.* Damascus, the seat of the satrap, Aleppo, and Hierapolis-Mabbog, famous later for its temple. The satrap, who travelled around maintaining order (like Tattenai in Ezra v *sq.*), seems to have had a seat at Mizpah, like Gedaliah of old (vol. III, p. 402 *sq.*). There was an elaborate organization for the collection of taxes, toll and tribute, and to control the supplies (*e.g.* wheat, wine, oil, salt). Babylonian and Persian names are conspicuous among the officials, whose titles become increasingly Persian. It is noteworthy that Shimshai, the Samaritan scribe or secretary in the time of Artaxerxes has, like the scribes at Elephantine, a Babylonian name, and that it is only an older form of that given to David's scribe Shavsha (see vol. II, p. 334). Although the tribute paid by Palestine was perhaps not heavy relatively, the land lay too near scenes of revolt and warfare to escape other burdens; the frequent passage of armies and warring-bands, taxation, debt, and bad harvests would crush the unfortunate peasants, forcing them to sell their children as slaves to their richer brethren. The officials were maintained by the royal purse, and a generous governor would refrain from exacting supplies and would entertain a large body of pensioners. Garrisons, as at Elephantine, received monthly payments in money or kind; passports and troops would guarantee a safe journey; letters of recommendation were in use, and special permits were necessary, for example, before timber could be obtained. There was an elaborate system of reports, and the formal procedure of the satrap Tattenai at the suspicious conduct of the Jews stands in marked contrast to the realistic account of the intrigues against Nehemiah. If Artaxerxes did indeed grant Ezra supplies of money, wheat, oil and salt, free the temple-personnel from taxes, and even permit him to set judges over all the Jews in Transpotamia, it is at least obvious that such remarkable generosity to the Jews and their temple at Jerusalem would provoke the keenest resentment and bitterness among their opponents. Needless to say the Persian administration was not without red tape, and the meticulousness, of which the Elephantine papyri give an extraordinary example, repeats itself in the fondness for specifications, attested by Ezra vi, 3, 17; vii, 22, and in certain portions of the biblical narrative and law now ascribed to the 'Priestly' source, commonly known as 'P' (see p. 193)[1].

The army was under a separate administration, and although aristocratic and landed families formed the governing class, a military type of settlement can be traced—at least in Elephantine. Here the garrisons lived a settled life, with land and houses of their own; and, as in P's accounts of the Israelite journey into the Promised Land, men were distributed by 'flags' (*degel*, cf. Num. ii) which, in the former case, are known by Persian or Babylonian names. The province (*medīnah*) was, as the word shows, the unit of jurisdiction; and although in Judah the priestly Levites come to be regarded as lawgivers, religious and civil cases (and in Elephantine military cases) would be kept separate. The Jews had their '*ēdah*, a 'Congregation' with superior powers; but the supremacy of the priestly over the secular officials is relatively late. Each had its own sphere; Nehemiah, as it would seem from Neh. vi, 10, had no right to enter the Temple, and Bagoses by his presence there was held to have polluted it (see above). The King and the governors would recognize and control the cults, as is evident from the acts of Nehemiah, Bagohi and Bagoses (if the last two are not identical); and it is in the name of no less than Darius himself that a document is sent in 419 B.C. to Arsames, and thence by one Hananiah to the priest Yedoniah at Elephantine, instructing them to keep the Feast of the Unleavened Bread[2]. Consequently even the more extravagant decrees in the Old Testament which purport to come from Cyrus, Darius or Artaxerxes, may have behind them genuine decrees of a more modest character; and the extent to which the cults were or could be patronized, regulated or controlled, however profitable to the Jews at times, would also strike at the religious freedom claimed by a community so proud of its religious prerogatives as was the seed of Israel.

Fragments of two copies of the Aramaic version of the inscription of Darius at Behistun have been found at Elephantine:

[1] In Cowley, *Aramaic Papyri*, no. 26 (a very obscure Aramaic papyrus) it would seem that A reports through B to C that a boat needed repair. C informed the military governor Arsames who gave instructions to an Egyptian personage (? an expert). The Treasury officials were ordered to inspect the boat and undertake the necessary repairs; and they, with the boat's carpenter drew up a list of necessaries (wood, nails, sails, etc.). Finally Arsames the secretary (or chancellor, Ezra iv, 9) had his scribe Anani draft the document in question, which was accordingly written by Nebo-'akab on the 13th of Tebeth, the twelfth year of Darius (412 B.C.).

[2] Cowley, no. 21 (fragmentary). The wording has suggested to some authorities that the Passover was also mentioned in the complete document.

a striking illustration of a procedure, utilized by the romantic writer of Esther (in the Apocrypha, xiii, 1; xvi, 1), which was calculated to weld together a vast empire. Aramaic was the *lingua franca*, it was becoming the language of the people (see vol. iii, p. 423). As an international language as far as Sardes and Elephantine, it united the disparate elements of the Persian Empire, and not least the widely-severed Jews; these were not lost sight of, and prophets could look for the return of exiles alike from Sardes and Syene[1]. Everywhere local types of culture would persist, but the fact that even at Elephantine the legal usages betray distinct Babylonian ancestry suggests that the Persians took over the judicial system of their predecessors. Moreover, Palestine itself would doubtless have similar laws for contracts, loans, building rights, dowries, etc., and consequently their almost complete absence from the 'Mosaic' legislation—in contrast to their presence in Talmudic literature—does not mean that they were unknown among the Jews of the home-land (see vol. iii, p. 481). In all the more important towns the population was mixed (for Samaria see Ezra iv, 9), and at Elephantine the 'Judaeans' (the older form of the word 'Jew')—or 'Aramaeans,' as they are more widely called—mingle with Babylonians, Persians and Egyptians (see p. 143 *n*.). The actual conditions in the towns and the inevitable intermarriages would be detrimental to the growth of Jewish exclusiveness, and the keen bitterness provoked in such circumstances by the forcible acts of separation that mark the inauguration of Judaism can be readily imagined. In fact the hostility would be the stronger in view of the free social intercourse and the distinctly higher position of women under the Persians.

At Elephantine the women hold and convey property, and carry on business, like the 'Virtuous Woman' of Proverbs (chap. xxxi). In the marriage contracts provision was made for divorce by either party, and the woman can formally 'divorce' (the word is 'hate') her husband in the 'Congregation.' The prophet's denunciation of the common divorce of the evidently less protected Jewish wives in Judah—sometimes in order that the husband could marry a stranger—will point to a rather different social environment (Mal. ii, 11 *sqq*.); while the abhorrence for the 'Canaanite' and other traders—such as the husband of the Virtuous Woman was—reflects a very characteristic feeling, but it is only a partial aspect of the many-sided life of the Palestinian world (Zech. xiv, 21; Joel iii, 17).

[1] Obad. *v*. 20 (Sepharad), Is. xlix, 12 (E.V. Sinim, *i.e.* Syene—Elephantine).

To judge from the personal names as a whole, the Jews in both Elephantine and Nippur formed a self-conscious community: it is worth noticing that at the former the custom of naming a child after the grandfather was already in vogue. The Egyptian priests are described, even in contracts, as *Kemārīm*, a term which, however inoffensive primarily, came to have a derogatory application among the Jews (2 Kings xxiii, 5, R.V. mg.). Whatever the cause of the outbreak leading to the destruction of the temple of Yahu, the religion of the colonists was not uninfluenced by its environment. Fervent worshippers of Yahu, the 'god of heaven,' they none the less freely recognized 'the gods,' and the personal names include foreign gods, like the local Khnub (Khnum), the famous potter-god, creator of the world. A woman, prominent in the business documents, in separating from her Egyptian husband, swears by Sati the great consort of Khnum; but the witnesses do not have Jewish names—the Jews perhaps held aloof[1]. But the Jews themselves took oaths by Ḥerem-bethel, by 'the shrine (*masgēda*) and by Anath-Yahu,' and a unique document of 419 B.C. divides the contributions to the Temple between Yahu, Ashima-bethel and Anath-bethel, in the ratio of $12\frac{1}{2}$, 7 and 12[2]. It is a remarkable triad, and it corresponds precisely to the local Egyptian triad Khnum, Anuki and Sati, where the last two were respectively nurse and mother-goddess (or concubine), representing the same social conditions as Abraham with his Sarah and Hagar. This not unexpected syncretism is enhanced when a late local Greek inscription identifies the Egyptian triad with Ammon (Zeus), Hera (Sati) and Hestia (Anuki), inasmuch as a tendency to equate Yahweh with Zeus arose under Greek influence, and a unique drachma (probably of Gaza) in the British Museum represents a solar Zeus who is explicitly styled 'Yahu' in Aramaic lettering of about 400 B.C. But whereas the ready identification of Zeus and Yahweh came to prevail in the Greek period, now it is that of Yahu (Yahweh) and Khnum which might well have provoked the Jews in Elephantine, even as the prominence throughout the Persian Empire of the majestic Ahura-mazda would cause resentment among the more nationalistic Jews. The marked favour shown to the Jews by the Persians must be regarded as of exceptional importance for the inauguration of Judaism, but the exalted character of the supreme Persian god brought new and difficult problems into the religion of Israel.

[1] Cowley, no. 14; dated 441 B.C.
[2] See vol. III, pp. 429, 430 *n*., and, for Anath, vol. I, p. 232; II, p. 347.

III. EDOM AND SAMARIA

Phoenician sea-power gave the coast-lands a political importance of which they were not slow to take advantage, although
rivalry among the ports precluded any lasting achievements. The
rivals Tyre and Sidon differed temperamentally. Tyre had its
age-long connections with Jerusalem; Sidon—temporarily eclipsed
when it paid the penalty for revolt in 345–4 B.C. (pp. 22, 153)—
was now the leader: wealthy, cosmopolitan and philhellene. The
influence of Phoenicia readily extended southwards along the
Philistine coast, and by sea to the Delta; and Phoenician jar-
handles, indications of the Sidonian wine-trade (cf. Herod. III, 6),
have been found as far south as Elephantine. From time to time
the closer political interrelations between Phoenicia, Philistia
and the South of Palestine (Edom, etc.) had vital consequences for
Israel and Judah, whose security depended upon the goodwill of
these dangerous neighbours[1]. Gaza held an important position
as the meeting-place of trade-routes to Syria, the Levant, Egypt
and Arabia. The 'Arabs' were always a force to be reckoned
with; but the precise application of the term is sometimes doubtful, as in the case of the 'king of the Arabs' who aided Evagoras
against Persia. More is now being heard of Arab tribes and
states (Dedan, Sabaeans, Minaeans, etc.), and various Old Testament passages testify to a steady pressure upon, if not rather a
penetration into, Southern Palestine and Transjordania (see vol.
III, pp. 393, 405 sq.).

In the Greek age the Nabataeans held sway in Transjordania
from Petra northwards to Damascus; and, like other Semitic
states with convenient bases (Jerusalem, Palmyra, etc.), were able
to exercise influence far beyond their own territory. Such are the
natural advantages of the Edomite area between Egypt, Palestine
and Arabia, and so established the valuable trade in gold, incense
and spices, that after the decay and downfall of the powerful
Judaean monarchy and before the age of the Nabataeans—who
come before us as the heirs of an old tradition—the Edomite area
must have played a prominent part in the political history. The
Minaeans and Sabaeans of South Arabia traded with Egypt and
Gaza, and at a Minaean colony of el-Öla, some 400 miles south
of Gaza, inscriptions of uncertain date refer to the male and female
temple-servants of the god Wadd, and their name (*lawi*[*at*])
strikingly resembles that of the Levites who are explicitly connected with the South of Palestine. Farther north of el-Öla lay

[1] Cf. the slave trade, Amos i, 6, 9, Joel iii, 4–8, and see vol. II, p. 380 *sq.*

Tema (Teima), also on a trade-route; it was the home for a few years of the Babylonian antiquarian king Nabonidus (vol. III, pp. 222, 407), and its Aramaic inscriptions, of the sixth or fifth century B.C., manifest the influence of both Babylonia and Egypt upon a culture which has an individuality of its own.

Thus it was in a busy world that Judaism grew up as an exclusive if not intolerant faith with its undying hatred of Edom and of Samaria. Relations between Judah and her neighbours naturally varied from time to time, periods of alliance and of enmity alternated. But it is difficult, as already seen in the case of the Samaritans, to trace with any precision the history of these 'canonical' animosities as they might be called. Now it is noteworthy that Nehemiah's Judah is remarkably circumscribed: Jericho, Mizpah, Keilah and Beth-ṣur are roughly its limits. The land has been stripped by envious rivals, and the question is a vital one—whether this was Judah's normal condition after the fall of the Monarchy. Its desolation is commonly ascribed to the destruction of Jerusalem no less than some 140 years previously. Much more probable, however, is the view that there was some quite recent disaster, although the incident in Ezra iv, 7–23 (see p. 174 above) can hardly be cited in explanation. About three centuries later there was some extension of Judaean territory, into Hebron and Lod or Lydda (1 Macc. v, 65; xi, 34); and under the ambitious Hasmonaeans the old glories of Israel seemed likely to revive. Certain late writings manifest a keen interest in a larger Israel (*e.g.* Psalms lxviii, lxxx; Zech. ix–xiv); and traditions in Chronicles (2 Chron. xxx, 10 *sqq.*) and the story of Judith suggest that Judah was politically not unimportant. On occasion the Samaritans would seize Judaean territory (Josephus, *Ant.* xii, 4, 1), and even the Maccabees appear to *regain* in Gilead and Galilee districts where Judaean influence had not had time to die out (1 Macc. v, 9). The Jews of the time of Alexander the Great were an influential body; and, after all, the wealth and importance of the Temple at Jerusalem point to an authority which was not merely spiritual. Whether or not Ezra was actually authorized by the Great King (Artaxerxes I or II) to appoint judges over the Jews throughout Transpotamia, Jerusalem had a reputation for unruliness, and extensive political combinations arise and fall with equal suddenness in the East. We may be sure that the Jews were as prompt to seize an opportunity for the extension of power as their enemies were ready to combine and crush them. In a word, the fall of the Monarchy (586 B.C.), the time of Nehemiah (445 B.C.) and the Hasmonaean period are too widely severed and the facts too scanty for us to base our conceptions of the fortunes of Judah upon them alone.

Whatever the internal conditions in Palestine after the Fall of Jerusalem in 586 B.C., later we may recognize closer relations between Judah and Israel—a new all-Israel, such that the subsequent bitterness between Judah and Samaria was the reaction after a closer alliance (cf. vol. III, p. 406 *sq.*). Direct evidence is wanting, but even the little that can be seen of the age of Zerubbabel is sufficient to emphasize the gap between the triumphant completion of the Sacred Temple under what seemed to be the beginning of a Second Monarchy and the desolation that overwhelmed the patriotic Nehemiah(vol. III, p. 412). Not unnaturally, therefore, has it sometimes been conjectured that there was a fresh disaster to Jerusalem arising out of the political and priestly rivalries of the time of Zerubbabel (see vol. III, pp. 413, 488).

The view that Nehemiah's Jerusalem was suffering from some recent catastrophe seems to be borne out by the 'Trito-Isaiah'[1]. This group of chapters reflects a disillusionment after earlier hopes. We have pictures of anguish and humiliation; there had been a new outburst of Yahweh's wrath: a short affliction (Is. lvii, 17, Greek version). Yahweh's attitude, as has been well remarked, is now less eager and enthusiastic, it is more reserved. There was sectional or sectarian strife, though it is difficult to identify the parties with certainty. There is poignant grief, which we may date, not at the Fall of Jerusalem, but after some later disaster. To the laments of the people comes the reply that their sins—their failure, for example, to observe the Sabbath—have severed them from Yahweh: there is a ritualistic note in the Trito-Isaiah. The people's confession leads up to Yahweh's intervention and the promise of a Redeemer, even as the Chronicler's History places the people's penitence for intermarrying with foreigners and Ezra's marriage reforms before the visit of Nehemiah. If the people are in despair, the approaching vengeance upon Edom is foreshadowed; if they feel neglected, the punishment of Edom proves that Yahweh hated Esau and loved Jacob (Mal. i). Edomite aggression is the keynote in several undated passages which seem to refer to events later than 586. Edomites even seized Judaean cities, and Edom's hostility to Israel is the more

---

[1] Instead of a Deutero-Isaiah (xl–lxvi) a further division, the Trito-Isaiah (lvi–lxvi), was first urged by Duhm (1892), and accepted and developed, with various modifications, by Cheyne (1898–9), and most scholars. The Trito-Isaiah is later, and may illustrate the age of Nehemiah.

treacherous by reason of the traditional brotherhood of Esau and Jacob.

What this kinship means is clearly seen from the genealogies of Judah[1], where a sadly decimated tribe, before the Monarchy— ? not of David but of Zerubbabel (see vol. III, p. 479 *sq.*)—has been largely reconstructed by means of Caleb, Jerahmeel and other more or less Edomitic clans of the South of Palestine. Such a Judah could not afford to throw stones at the mixed population of Samaria, and whereas the Chronicler's History tells of the work of re-organization by those of the old Judaean kingdom who returned to their cities (Ezra ii), traces of the Calebite or semi-Edomitic infusion can be found in the independent lists of the men who helped Nehemiah to rebuild the wall and to re-populate the city. On the other hand, very few of the names in these lists can be identified with the families who are supposed to have returned from Babylon[2]. That is to say, just as the sons of Jacob (Israel) go down into Egypt and return as the Israelite tribes, so Judah and Jerusalem are carried off into exile in 597 and 586, and their descendants are supposed to return and restore the continuity of history—and in each case the people of Palestine are ignored. Here are explicit artificial theories which give a one-sided conception of the history, and allowance has to be made for them. They obscure the importance of the native population; and we should probably recognize that it was a semi-Edomitic Judah, rather than the pre-exilic Judaean state, upon which the attack by the Edomites—perhaps forced by the pressure of the Nabataeans —would leave so lasting a memory of unbrotherly conduct.

Edom, it would seem, had taken advantage of Judah's extremity, and if Judah's sufferings were the consequence of a revolt against Persia and a punitive captivity it is possible to explain why characteristically Jewish names (in -*iah*, -*yah*) appear more or less suddenly in the Nippur contract-tablets of Artaxerxes I and Darius II[3]. In any case, the Trito-Isaiah depicts an oppressed Judah and Jerusalem, hemmed in on all sides and deserted. Neglected by Israel (Jacob) and by Abraham—the ancestral figure at Hebron, now in Edomite hands—they appeal to Yahweh. For 'a little while' only had Yahweh's holy people possessed their inheritance and now he had cast them off as those that had never

---

[1] 1 Chron. ii, iv, xi; cf. Gen. xxxvi; Benjamin can also be included.

[2] The significance of Neh. iii was first pointed out by Eduard Meyer (*Die Entstehung des Judentums* [1895], pp. 139, 152 *sq.*, 157), whose treatment of the history is, however, a conservative one.

[3] So Daiches (see the Bibliography).

been his. How different had he been when he brought them up out of Egypt, and 'the angel of his presence' saved them. Had he hardened their hearts as he had hardened Pharaoh's? Jerusalem was, as Nehemiah learns, 'in great reproach,' and well did the saviour of the city of his fathers' graves deserve his significant name of 'Yahweh comforteth'[1].

This Edomitic-Judaean phase in the history upon which we can lay our finger, thanks to the genealogical lists, is not wholly unique—a few centuries later the Idumaean Antipater founded the Herodian dynasty. But it is of the greatest significance, because all the evidence suggests that it belongs to a crucial stage in the growth of the Old Testament. It seems to explain various specifically South Palestinian features in the biblical narrative. At the outset, it is to be observed that, although the internal social changes due to captivity and immigration in and about the sixth century B.C. can hardly be reconstructed in detail, traces are to be found not only of aristocratic and military social organization, but also of local communities (as for instance Jericho, Neh. iii, 2) and, what is more noteworthy, of guilds[2]. Trades and professions were largely hereditary, and the scribes, to judge from their names, were Babylonian in Samaria and Elephantine, whereas in Judah there were families of scribes of Kenite, Calebite and semi-Edomitic origin (1 Chron. ii, 55). How far such facts would account for the Babylonian and for the South Palestinian lore in the Old Testament can scarcely be determined, but the presence of the latter can easily be seen. Thus, an Edomitic figure Othniel has been placed at the head of the 'judges' of Israel, and South Palestinian features are conspicuous in the accounts both of the patriarchs (Abraham and Isaac) and of the journey into Palestine. Moreover, in the Cainite (Kenite) and related traditions we can discern traces of an ambitious account of the origins of culture: Cain the first builder, Tubal-Cain the metal smith, Jabal probably the herdsman, Jubal the inventor of musical instruments, and Na'amah ('beloved'), probably a reference to the temple-women[3]. We have a far-reaching view of the rise of civilization—for the name Tubal refers to the Tabal and other iron-working tribes of Asia Minor—and although analogies to the scheme can be found in late Phoenician and, to a less degree, in Babylonian lore, it is a

---

[1] The interpretation of Is. lxiii, 7–lxiv, 12 is admittedly obscure.

[2] Mention is made of craftsmen, potters, workers in linen, perfumers (1 Chron. iv, 14, 21, 23; Neh. iii, 8, 31).

[3] Gen. iv *sq.*; see E. Meyer, *Israeliten u. ihre Nachbarstämme*, p. 218 *sq.*; also Skinner, *Genesis*, p. 123.

South Palestinian version of origins, which presumably owes its presence in our Old Testament to the prominence of clans and guilds from southern Palestine who were subsequently settled in and around Jerusalem. A Calebite Bezaleel is commemorated as the chief metal-worker in the Tabernacle in the wilderness, and not only would the Second Temple as naturally require skilled workmen as did the First, but portable sanctuaries were known, and the late Post-exilic and Priestly account of the Tabernacle may, amid much that—since the days of Bishop Colenso—has been found untrustworthy, reflect an acquaintance with actual usage among the desert peoples outside Palestine.

The interest in guilds and in the origins of culture is in accord with what we know of the Temple-personnel. The Chronicler's lists closely connect the Levitical classes of the Temple with South Judah and South Palestine, and they ascribe their origin to David, who himself is spoken of as a famed maker of musical instruments[1]. The Chronicler takes a peculiar interest in the Temple musicians and singers; and some of these guilds (e.g. Korah, Ethan) can be traced back to the south. Nor is this true only of music and psalmody; to the Kenite father-in-law of Moses was due a judicial system (Ex. xvii), and the Levites were also reputed teachers. Indeed, to the desert itself belongs all that was best in the sphere of wisdom (Jer. xlix, 7; Obad. 8); so that, although Palestine had a cultural history going back to the Amarna period and beyond, the influence of South Palestine, which was of course not confined to any one age, is most explicitly associated (a) with the account both of the beginnings of Israel and of the Davidic monarchy and temple, and (b) with the new developments of about the sixth century B.C. That is to say we have to deal with a literary phenomenon which can be co-ordinated with the vicissitudes of that age: and the problem of the literary analysis of the biblical narrative and the problem of the actual history in the sixth century are essentially one.

David and Levi—the monarchy and the temple—are coupled in the Chronicler's account of the rise of the *first* monarchy, and in the prophet's anticipations of the Messianic restoration (Jer. xxxiii, 17 *sqq.*); but, on various grounds, there is reason to suppose that this very interesting combination is a late one. It is not the one that prevails in the Old Testament. The evidence throughout is extremely intricate, it reflects struggle and defeat, victory and compromise between those responsible for this southern and Edomitic phase and their rivals and opponents. The Edomitic

---

[1] I Chron. xxiii, 5; 2 Chron. xxix, 26; cf. Amos vi, 5.

Caleb, once connected with Hebron—which becomes increasingly prominent in the later accounts of the patriarchs—must have played a far more important part than is allowed by those writers who have subordinated him to the Ephraimite Joshua, and Joshua to the High-priest (Josh. xv, 13; Num. xxvii, 21). For his faith Yahweh's 'servant,' Caleb, was promised the land he had once entered, whereas to the exiles—who plumed themselves on their superiority—the new inhabitants of the land (*i.e.* presumably these southern immigrants) were pagan interlopers. The latter, proud of their new inheritance, felt themselves to be the heirs of Abraham—though other writers denounce their irreligion. But the time came when those who had looked to their ancestors, Abraham and Sarah of Hebron, were overwhelmed with disasters, and felt that even Abraham had forgotten them[1].

Other vicissitudes are suggested by other details. The supremacy of the Jerusalem priesthood of Zadok over the faithless Levites is set forth in the priestly prophet's scheme (Ezek. xliv, 6–16), and is evidently reflected in the story of the degradation of Abiathar in favour of Zadok in the days of Solomon. But a compromise can be recognized when a list of the priestly courses allows eight to the family of Abiathar (Ithamar) as against the sixteen of the Zadokites (1 Chron. xxiv), and Zadok is made a descendant of Aaron. Aaron, however, is hardly prominent in the older narratives; the Levitical families are Mosaïte, and the tendencies to make them Aaronite and to elevate the 'priestly' Aaron over the more 'prophetic' figure Moses belong to the later stages in the growth of the Old Testament.

Meanwhile there are varying attitudes to the northern tribes and Samaria which are as difficult to interpret as those just noticed. The prominence of Shechem and the all-Israelite standpoint of the book of Deuteronomy are in marked contrast to the anti-Israelite and anti-Samarian treatment of the history of the divided monarchies in the books of Kings, where 'Israel' is used in a restricted sense[2]. The prophets' interest in (north) Israel contrasts both with the harsh repudiation of the Samaritans who desired to assist in rebuilding the Temple and with the insistence in later Deuteronomic literature upon Jerusalem as the only place where Yahweh could be worshipped[3]. Bethel and its priesthood

---

[1] So, at least, it seems possible to interpret Num. xiv, 24; Ezek. xxxiii, 24 (cf. the complaint in xi, 15); Is. li, 2, lxiii, 16.

[2] Cf. vol. ii, p. 355.

[3] Neither Deuteronomy nor the 'Deuteronomic' literature can be regarded as of one date or standpoint; see vol. iii, pp. 472, 482, 485.

naturally gained increased authority when Jerusalem was weak, and Aaron himself, as has been conjectured, was perhaps a Bethel- ite figure who came to be placed even above the Jerusalem Zadok. But this is not the place to enter into details, and it must suffice to remind the reader that prolonged analysis of the internal diffi- culties of the Old Testament has proved that important historical facts, on the nature of which one can only speculate, account for the complexity of our evidence. Much is quite uncertain and obscure, but the extreme exclusiveness which marks the isolation of Jerusalem and the inauguration of Judaism, though it has shaped the biblical narrative, did not have the last word.

IV. RELIGIOUS TENDENCIES

At its worst, Israelite or Jewish exclusiveness manifests an intolerance and vindictiveness illustrated in stories of Rechabite and Levitical reformers, the Deuteronomic theory of the invasion of Palestine and the destruction of its inhabitants, the story of the campaign against Midian (Num. xxxi), certain prophecies against the 'Gentiles,' and in Luther's bugbear Esther, with its 'too much heathen naughtiness.' But this megalomania always had its opponents, especially the prophets, the most uncompro- mising of anti-Semites, with their conviction that Israel had neither merits nor claims but depended upon Yahweh's grace. So too the beautiful idyll of Ruth the Moabitess, the ancestress of David, is best understood and becomes most telling when its conclusion is read in the light of the uncompromising aversion from foreign marriages. Also the Midrash, or didactic story, of Jonah culminates in an impressive question which a self-centred Judaism had to answer. No religion develops consistently. The merchants and foreign caravans that helped to enrich Jerusalem and its Temple also brought much that was distasteful to the stricter Jew, and Persian patronage itself, which was so powerful—and perhaps, as some scholars think, so indispensable—a factor in the growth of Judaism was not an unmixed boon.

The Persian Empire and its centralizing policy, and the wide- spread recognition of a God of Heaven, or Sky-god, combined to foster the belief in a Universal Deity. And Jewish universalism, indeed, shows itself in the conviction that Yahweh was not the god of Israel alone (Is. lxv, 1), and that his name was great among the Gentiles (Mal. i, 11). The supremacy of the Persian Ahura- mazda meant the supremacy of many fine ethical ideas, and in this syncretizing age there would be a tendency to relate one to another all the great gods—Yahweh, Khnum of Elephantine,

Baal of Phoenicia, Hadad of Syria and others (see p. 180). But whether there was one God with many names or many gods depended upon one's standpoint. Universalism has its price. A universal God cannot have a narrowly national history, and the wider became Yahweh's supremacy outside the Jews, the more were Jewish prerogatives endangered, and the weaker became the old characteristic bond between the worshipper and his god. The Jew would find that his God had no particular distinctive attributes, and there was the risk that the God who had hitherto been indissolubly connected with his nation would soon be fused with other gods.

The Jews, like the Semites in general, were virile, passionate, intense—men of great driving power. They prospered even in exile. Their financial ability was bound up with their religion (Deut. xxviii, 12, 44), and religion inculcated loyalty to their new homes (Jer. xxix, 7). Their prosperity and their extreme self-conscious claims provoked bitterness even in pre-Christian times. The Semite, more self-conscious than the Indo-European, tended to dogmas of exclusive rather than of universal gods; and the only natural compromise was a religious imperialism which led the Jews—especially (? or only) those of Judah—to see in Jerusalem the world's religious centre, an inviolable Zion whither should resort tribute-bearing monarchs and pilgrims in search of divine truth (cf. Is. ii, 2–4; lxii). So there are dreams of an Israel served by aliens, of a priestly people performing priestly service on behalf of the world. Jerusalem is a mystical centre—one might almost say a magical one: 'whoso of all the families of the earth goeth not up unto Jerusalem to worship the King, the Lord of hosts, upon them there shall be no rain'[1]. In harmony with this is the theory of the priestly ritual and its remarkable efficacy (see below). It is true that a prophet might dream of a grand alliance —Israel, Egypt and Assyria, a triple blessing to the world (Is. xix, 23–25); but this would destroy the unique status of a people, the 'peculiar (i.e. personal) treasure' of its god (Mal. iii, 17), and the versions with one consent paraphrase the sentiment away. Yet as a protest and a protection against contemporary religion a vigorously self-centred and self-conscious Judaism was as intelligible and as necessary then as it was later in the Maccabaean age. Isolation and concentration were necessary if Israel was to fulfil her destiny.

Licentious cults apparently continued to be practised at the

---

[1] Zech. xiv, 17. The reference is to the Feast of Tabernacles; and it implies that upon the cultus at Jerusalem depended the rain, and therefore the crops, and the existence of man and beast.

'high places' and under the trees. The cult of Anath, evidently still alive at Elephantine, was strengthened when Artaxerxes II officially recognized Anahita (Anaitis, Nanaea), a goddess like Ishtar and Astarte, whose name, only accidentally as it would seem, resembles that of Anath. Near by, Askalon was to become famous for the fish-goddess Derceto (Atargatis), and the cult of Semiramis was perhaps already familiar (? in the Levitical name Shemi-ramoth). The recognition of the redeeming solar god Mithra by both Artaxerxes II and Artaxerxes III would strike at Jewish monotheism as surely as the Assyrian cult of Marduk had done. Tables were spread, not to Yahweh, but to Gad, the god of Luck; and wine was poured out to Fortune (Měni), the equivalent of the later Greek Tyche. Children were slain (Is. lvii, 5)—perhaps to the grim Molek or Melek, the king-god; and there were mysterious cults in gardens ('behind one in the midst'), and strange rites connected with dogs and swine. If the reference is to mystic brotherhoods, it is tempting to recall the contemporary guild organization, the evidence for animal cults at the Temple (vol. III, p. 444), and the recurrence of animal names in South Palestine (for example Caleb, the 'dog'). In any case, the picture (Is. lvii, lxv *sq.*) is one of remarkable cults, and a religiosity which laid the emphasis upon ritual 'holiness,' thus justifying those who denounced a ritual which was illegitimate or indifferent, or which gave the second place to ethical demands. So the faithless are rejected, and a new community of 'Yahweh's servants' are to possess the land and be rewarded for their faith (Is. lxv, 13 *sqq.*).

The 'prophetical' teaching of the Deutero-Isaiah enhanced ideas of Yahweh's supremacy and paved the way for the more 'priestly' endeavour to ensure his transcendent holiness (vol. III, p. 489, cf. p. 485 *sq.*). Through the elevation of the national god, intermediary beings were more prominent; the 'angel of Yahweh' became a less intangible conception, and in time an elaborate angelology was developed. Here and elsewhere Judaism may have been influenced by Zoroastrianism, though the most striking examples occur in the literature after the Persian age[1]. While

---

[1] The seven eyes in Zech. iii, 9 have been associated with the seven Amesha-Spentas; and while the later festival of Purim (in the book of Esther) is Persian, a much earlier Persian trait has been suspected in Ezek. viii, 17 (the branch to the nose). Such antitheses as Light and Dark, Truth and Lie (Falsehood) have been classed as Persian; but it is necessary to con-sider (1) how far Zoroastrianism was indebted to Babylonia, and (2) how far Median or rather Iranian elements may have influenced Palestine long before the Persian period (see vol. II, p. 331). On the date of Zoroaster, see vol. IV, p. 616.

Zoroastrianism as a practical religion was for a pastoral and agricultural people, a general influence may be expected, and in particular we may point to the emphasis which that religion laid upon
Moral Right (*Asha*), of which Ahura-mazda was the source. *Asha*
was an eternal principle working in the Universe, and in the form
Arta—*e.g.* Artaxerxes means 'the true kingdom'—the term can
be traced back some eight or nine centuries to the age when
interrelated ideas of law and order and right can be recognized
over a wide area in South-west Asia (vol. ii, p. 400 *sq*.). But the
idea of an inflexible law, now as then, could take other than dis-
tinctively ethical forms, of far-reaching consequences for religious
and other thought. Moreover the very transcendence of the god
Yahweh led to the avoidance of the ineffable Name, and the use
of the less distinctive El and Elohim—names compounded with
El becoming more frequent—tended to alter the tone of the
religion.

The universalizing tendencies encouraged a rather colourless
theism and a somewhat international type of literature, distinctive
as regards neither age nor place, and inculcating practical worldly
wisdom in the conviction that good conduct, humanity and prosperity went hand-in-hand. Thus, in the famous Story of Ahikar,
to which reference is made in the Apocryphal book of Tobit, the
absence of any specific religious or national background is most
marked[1]. In the Old Testament, Wisdom is especially connected
with tribes and places which, though outside Palestine proper,
were, as has already been seen, not necessarily remote from the
culture of Egypt and Babylonia. Indeed, the recent discovery of
the teaching of an Egyptian sage Amen-em-ope has revealed what
was evidently the origin of a small section of the book of Proverbs
(xxii, 17–xxiii, 11). But the Hebrew scribe has ignored the
Egyptian gods and such distinctive Egyptian ideas as the Judge-
ment of the Dead, and he has adapted his material to Hebrew
metre and thought, as also did the original author of Psalm civ
who was perhaps acquainted with Ikhnaton's hymns (vol. ii,
p. 117 *sq*.). A similar free use of borrowed material characterizes
alike the formation of the North Semitic alphabet (vol. iii, p. 422
sqq.), and the Mesopotamian (Babylonian) myths of Creation and
Deluge, etc., in the Old Testament.

Typical of the many-sidedness of an age which was preparing
the way for Greek rationalism is the book of Job, noteworthy for

---

[1] See vol. iv, p. 520. Incidentally the story affords most interesting proof
of the scantiness of authentic history in the popular traditions of great
figures of the past.

its desert atmosphere. In this, one of the masterpieces of the world's literature, disillusionment and scepticism reach their depth, and Semitic religious intimacy takes its most striking form. The once rich and fortunate Job, suffering beyond endurance, and unconscious of offence, despite his friends' conviction that he is being punished for his sins, arraigns his God. It is not that there is no God—Job is no atheist—it is God's dreadful unfairness which overwhelms him. Yahweh's absolute and neutral 'right-eousness' as taught by the great ethical monotheists (vol. III, p. 471), has become to the sceptic an a-moral ruthlessness. Job had acted up to his ethical principles—and they compel admiration (xxix, xxxi); but God is not merely unfair (cf. Ezek. xxxiii, 17), His government of the world is non-moral. He shoots His arrows at Job as at a target, and there is no escape from his vindictiveness. Job's old fellowship with the Almighty is in bitter contrast to His determined hostility (xxix *sqq.*); God is Job's terrible friend. There is—there can be—no mediator or 'daysman' between God and man. If only God would be judge and not accuser; for though there is no justice on earth, there *is* justice! Yet the vindictive God is not *the* God: and behind Job's present unhappy experiences of God's ways there is the God of his early days, who would vindi-cate him in the future. Job's God is a twofold one—as in the Koran: 'there is no refuge from God but to Him.'

The solution of Job's problem recalls that of *Paradise Lost*—man's insignificance before God's omnipotence. The Semite has no selfless interest in the Universe; nature and history are inter-esting only from a narrowly personal point of view. And when God answers Job, it is to ask him what part had he taken in the creation of the world or in the processes of nature? What know-ledge had he of the mysteries of the world about him, or of the growth of the herbage on which the wild animals lived? Did he feed the lions or give the cubs their food? Could *he* do what God did? Had *he* the right to condemn a Universe in which he was so insignificant and helpless?

A Job whose 'righteousness' might be expected to benefit others was ranked with Noah and Daniel (Ez. xiv, 14); and in the prose Prologue and Epilogue his acquiescence in his lot is followed by his successful intercession on behalf of his friends and a twofold recompense. But the great drama is not content with so simple a solution. It does not inculcate the caution of the sage praying for neither poverty nor wealth (Prov. xxx, 2–9), nor has it the patience of the Psalmist (xxxvii): it is not that death will redress misfortunes (Ps. xlix), but that, even as the Psalmist's visit to the sanctuary brought home to him the justice of divine rule (Ps. lxxiii, 17), so Job gained some new insight into God's power in the world, and, no longer self-centred, found his consolation in his new knowledge. The book of Job has points of contact with the Deutero-Isaiah, and especially with the problem of the Suffering Servant: but the emphasis is different, and Job's drama may be interpreted as that of an Israel, once basking in the favour of Yahweh, unconscious of fault, and now unable to find a place in religion or philosophy for grievous misfortune. It is, it may be conjectured, an Israel for whose benefit all the processes of history are guided, a rather self-centred and spoilt Israel, with that narrowness of outlook that is rebuked in the story of Jonah. Both Job and Israel judge the world from their private conditions —it was incredible that a God who so loved his 'servant' or his 'son' (Hosea xi, 1) should give him up to death! It is the old-time problem, which began with Amos (iii, 2). But if this interpretation be right, and if Job be a type for an Israel, lamenting, as was her wont, her truly grievous disasters, the teaching, like that of the 'Servant of Yahweh' itself (Is. liii), can hardly be said to have been woven into the texture of early Judaism, and even 'Yahweh's servants' are promised most tangible blessings, while their enemies will fall by the sword and leave their name for a curse (Is. lxv, 13 *sqq.*).

V. THE PRIESTLY SOURCE ('P') AND THE PENTATEUCH

The outstanding feature of the age, one which set its mark upon the history of the religion of Israel, is 'P.' It is the work of a priestly body which succeeded in impressing itself upon contemporary life and thought. By P we mean the series of narratives and the groups of laws which can be readily distinguished in the Pentateuch, the narrative itself extending to the book of Joshua. P's record, from Creation to the settlement of the tribes in Palestine, is distinguished by a fondness for stereotyped phrases and formulas, by tables, numbers and specifications which give it a certain monotony. It is methodical and apt to fall into repetition, the worst examples being Num. vii, and Exod. xxxv–xxxix compared with xxv–xxxi. With an imposing and circumstantial chronological system and a schematic view of events, P is the 'groundwork' giving unity to the Pentateuch. History is divided into stages marked by the figures Adam, Noah, Abraham, Jacob (Israel) and Moses, and by steps in the self-revelation of God (Elohim, El Shaddai, Yahweh). It leads up to the Sinaitic legislation, the formation of the Israelite congregation and the 'theocracy.' The standpoint differs from, and the details often conflict with, the earlier sources ('JE,' see vol. III, pp. 473–8). The patriarchal figures become somewhat abstract types and their imperfections are ignored. Anthropomorphic features are reduced to a minimum, and are incapable of being misunderstood in a material, physical sense. Theophanies are not described. God 'speaks,' He creates by the 'word,' and things have a divine origin—like the pattern of the Tabernacle (Ex. xxv, 9). None the less, God abides in the midst of the people (Ex. xxix, 43–46; cf. Ezek. xlviii, 35). He is the God of the individual, there are no intermediaries, no dream or angel; but He is transcendent, apart, and hedged around. He is a Holy God amid a Holy People, and this holiness must be secured. Of supreme value, therefore, are the religious institutions, the priests and the sacrificial system; the immense claims of the priesthood and the elaborate sacrifices are characteristic of the period.

The interest in the priestly ritual was partly theoretical, partly practical, and it is due to this that there are noteworthy differences between the book of Ezekiel and P (e.g. as regards the Levites), and of a kind that seriously perplexed the Rabbis of old. But while Ezekiel (xl–xlviii) offers a programme for the future, the tendency reflected in P throws its ideas back into the past. The festivals are now due to divine commands, dates and quantities are fixed, and they are associated with the traditional history. The Sabbath is especially holy, and of immemorial antiquity. Circumcision is more symbolical than before; and here as elsewhere the teaching of the prophets has borne fruit. Uncleanness and purification are of fundamental significance, and moral and ritual offences are one (e.g. Ex. xxx, 33; Lev. x, 1–7). 'Morality was not indifferent to our legislating priests, but it was not, if one may say so, upon their agenda paper' (Montefiore). No secular ruler is contemplated, the High Priest stands at the head of the people, a priest with almost kingly powers, an echo of the former monarchy. The post is unique, much sought after, and, on occasion, the centre of intrigue; but it was not secured by any dynastic idea, except in so far as the holder was an Aaronite. A rigid line comes to be drawn between priestly and non-priestly Levites, and this development, like Ezekiel's elevation of the Zadokites, which P simply presupposes—it is a conspicuous difference between the two authorities—is only one of very complex vicissitudes in the later history of the priesthood, the details of which are still obscure (see vol. II, p. 363).

Judaism is a 'theocracy' which had its authority, partly—but not always—in the secular arm, but more especially in the impressive convictions of the power and value of the sacrificial system as a whole. The system had an almost magical potency. To withhold the tithes and temple offerings was dangerous (Mal. iii, 8–12; Judith xi, 13); the temple-ritual removed sin, and sin—ritual or ethical—precluded prosperity (vol. III, p. 447, cf. *ib.* p. 442). The sacrifices are centralized, and are less of a communal character. The burnt-offerings, which are made wholly to Yahweh, have a new importance; it is on this account that they were perhaps wanting at the new temple at Elephantine[1]. Sin and atonement hold a place that is not merely prominent, but, in a sense, even exaggerated. The High Priest replaces the earlier king as representative of the people, he bears the people's guilt, and his sin brings guilt on the people (Lev. iv, 2 *sq.*). The great Day of Atonement becomes the supreme day of the year, and there developed a more or less mechanical systematization as well as a deeply spiritual treatment of the ideas of sin and forgiveness. The problem of sin has been solved: God will no more destroy a wicked world (Gen. vi, 7, viii, 21 *sq.*), He has an eternal covenant with man (Is. liv, 9, cf. Jer. xxxi, 35 *sq.*), and sacrifice is 'the divinely appointed means for the preservation and restoration of that holiness in virtue of which alone the theocratic community of Israel can realize its true ideal as the people of a holy God' (A. R. S. Kennedy). Israel belongs to Yahweh, everything is already his (cf. 1 Chron. xxix, 14): hence the offerings of first-fruits, the surrogates for the first-born, the separation from the heathen—though proselytes are welcomed—and a practical social-religious organization which gave room for profound spirituality, extreme ritual scrupulosity, and a religiosity which, as among other Semites, permitted most incongruous types of conduct.

The priestly religion is, on the whole, rather shallow and abstract; we miss the depth, immediacy and warmth of the prophets and Deuteronomy (cf. vol. III, p. 483 *sq.*). Revelation is written rather than oral, as will be seen by a contrast of Ezekiel iii, 1 with Jeremiah i, 9. We have the religion of the book; and while the emphasis on ritual and the written word led easily to magic, and exclusiveness and spiritual arrogance had their dark sides, the priestly régime preserved Jewish monotheism even as Zoroaster's teaching may be said to have been secured by the ritual of the Vendidad.

The spiritual superiority claimed by the Jewish exiles in Babylonia[2] and their return to raise the level of a population of

---

[1] Cowley, no. 32; see the Appendix, p. 559 *sq.*
[2] Jer. xxiv, 1–10; Ezek. xi, 16–21, xxxiii, 25–29.

mixed blood, living on what they regarded as a lower religious plane, are the outstanding factors in the rise of Judaism. It is possible that life in some 'Congregation' remote from actual Palestinian conditions—like the colony of Levites in Ezra viii, 17 —will account for the rather doctrinarian character of some of the ideas of the priestly revolutionaries. But precisely what literature Ezra, or other exiles, brought back from Babylon is uncertain. The book of Ezekiel, for example, is marked by a certain scholarliness, and distinctive Babylonian traits have been noticed in it. Others also recur in the book of Job; and, although features of apparent Babylonian origin (*e.g.* the mention of months by their number instead of by their name) are more prominent in the sixth century and later, we have no right to assume that all Babylonian parallels necessarily come direct from Babylonia or belong only to this late period[1]. It is easy to exaggerate the debt of Judaism to Babylonia, or Egypt, or Persia; an antipathy to external culture may be said to characterize Judaism, and the differences prove more essential than the points of contact.

It is impossible, indeed it would be unjust, to attempt to limit Judaism by a formula. Not P but the Pentateuch is its charter, and the difference between the two is that between a caste religion and the religion of a people. 'The general principle of the priestly legislation surrounds the holy things of Israel by fence within fence, and makes all access to God pass through the mediation of the priesthood' (Robertson Smith). P is the true ancestor of the much later Book of Jubilees, which goes farther in carrying back the origins of Mosaism, or rather of Judaism, but won little favour and soon fell out of use. On the other hand, P, which of itself could hardly live apart from the Temple of Jerusalem and its priesthood, and as such was of local and temporal value, was preserved by the fact that it was combined with those earlier and fresher sources that have always been read with delight and edification (see vol. III, pp. 473 *sqq.*). The resultant Pentateuch with its diverse and even discordant elements was, intentionally or not, a compromise representing different needs, interests and attitudes, and corresponding to the many-sidedness of Judaism as a working institution. P's characteristic legalism was certainly a decisive phase, and legalizing tendencies persisted; yet, on the one hand, the Law was a joy and delight to its devotees, inspiring many Psalms[2], and, on the other, not only was it modified by the later

---

[1] See vol. II, pp. 377, 385, III, p. 391 (Assyria). Each case must be considered on its merits.

[2] Note *e.g.* the treatment of Jer. xvii, 7 *sq.* in Ps. i.

Scribes, but it never expelled tendencies of an anti-legalist nature. Outside Jerusalem synagogues were springing up; and, as apart from the more national religious organization with Jerusalem as its seat, a deeper personal religion was manifesting itself, of which the Psalms afford so many impressive examples.

In point of fact, the Pentateuch as a whole contained in narrative and in law, in precept and in example, a treasure upon which the worshipper of Yahweh, as an individual or as a member of the religious community, could draw inexhaustibly. The grand conceptions of the discipline of history which give unity to the Pentateuch have compelled admiration for their sweep and reverence for their profundity. And, as frequently elsewhere in the Old Testament, questions arise as to the historical circumstances that lie behind the great ideas. So, the deliverance from Egyptian bondage, the tedious journey into the Promised Land, the rivalries, the promises and covenants, the discipline of both people and leaders—these not only gain an entirely new interest when read in the light of the disintegration and constructive efforts of the sixth and fifth centuries B.C., but as has been seen, they are contained in very composite sources which were only then assuming their present form[1].

Further, the Pentateuch breathes a fine universalism when it opens, as it does, not with Yahweh and Israel, but with Elohim and Mankind; but the God who destroys a sinful world and undertakes never to repeat the catastrophe is, in the sequel, Yahweh, who is uniquely the god of Israel. And when mankind, a universal brotherhood, essays a fresh start, and, arrogantly striving to transcend human limitations, builds a tower to reach unto heaven, the races of mankind are scattered, and this new divine judgment prepares the way for the subsequent appearance of Abraham and the first beginnings of the history of a chosen people. Here, whether Israel—and who represented the true Israel was quite another question—was to be a prophet-people with a mission, or a priest-people with saving-rites, there are in either case sweeping conceptions of God, the Universe and Israel; and these come fittingly, not as part of the catastrophes of the early exilic age (at or shortly after 597 and 586 B.C.), but more probably after a new and unsuccessful attempt at reconstruction and a fresh calamity, at a rather later age, the age of (or after) Zerubbabel, and prior to the supremacy of the exclusive and legalizing priestly phase (p. 183 above). There are, at all events, facts to be explained, and the explanation, in the nature of the

---

[1] Cf. vol. III, pp. 496 *sqq*.

case, becomes increasingly hypothetical as one seeks to fill in the gaps; but it can safely be said that the complete Pentateuch *in its present form*, with P as its framework, belongs to the Persian age, and after the age of Nehemiah, and that its literary growth and the great events of the sixth and fifth centuries B.C. are linked together. This is the starting-point for reconstructing the history of Israel on the basis of the criticism of the Old Testament.

The Samaritans did not refuse the Pentateuch. Deuteronomy probably arose in the north (see vol. III, p. 482), and the Samaritans were eager to assist in rebuilding the Temple. But it is significant that, whereas on internal literary grounds we may speak of the 'Hexateuch'—the Pentateuch and Joshua—as a single unit, the line has been so drawn that the first part of the Jewish Canon ends, not with the solemn covenant of all Israel at the ancient Samaritan sanctuary of Shechem (Josh. xxiv), but more neutrally, after the death of Moses beyond the Jordan. Although the actual history of the kingdoms of Israel and Judah had been full enough of events to stimulate religious teaching and literary activity, the story of the monarchies leaves relatively little impression upon later generations; and the most impressive memories are of a neutral and much more remote age before the division of a united people. The religious history upon which psalms and prayers love to dwell is common ground to an All-Israel, and, so far as can be seen, both the biblical account of that past itself and the most pregnant ideas enshrined in it were of relatively recent inception.

The Pentateuch was the book of both Judaism and Samaritanism, rival sects which grew further apart until this book alone united them. And if Jewish exclusiveness—and Jerusalem—must be held responsible for this, the fact remains that the Samaritans who rejected the other writings which the Jews added to their Canon, played no part in history, and that Judaism was preserved by its exclusiveness, self-consciousness and intensive development. It was the nationalistic Jews who fought with indomitable courage and unquenchable enthusiasm to preserve the heritage of their fathers; and the stalwart fight of the Maccabees against tendencies which would have destroyed all that was best in Judaism forms the next chapter in the vicissitudes of an Israel jealous of its name, its past, and its destiny.

Thus does the history of a petty people hidden away in the vast Persian Empire raise the profoundest problems of national genius, its contribution to the world's history, and the price it has to pay. The genius of Israel showed itself in her prophets, story-tellers and psalmists, and in her ideas of religion and history.

Genius has its conspicuous defects: that of the Semites, and especially Israel, not least of all. Yet through her genius Israel's history was what it was; and she was able both to interpret and to shape her history in a way no other people has done or could do. No other people found and made their national history so supremely significant, so worthy of interpretation and of preservation. She alone of all peoples earned the right to set forth for mankind that which she had learnt at the cost of heavy sacrifices. Poignant experiences and their re-expression in a theistic exposition of history constitute Israel's unique contribution, and this gift becomes doubly precious as fuller knowledge of the facts of ancient history is bringing a re-interpretation of the past which is placing the Old Testament and the function of Israel in a new and larger framework[1].

[1] It may be convenient to summarize here some tendencies in recent criticism of the period covered by this chapter. (1) The historical criticism of the books of Ezra and Nehemiah, which was inaugurated by the Dutch scholar, Kosters (1894), and reached its most definitive form in Torrey's *Ezra Studies* (1910), leads to the conclusion that (a) the usual 'post-exilic' criteria hardly date as early as the return of Zerubbabel in 538 B.C., but point to some later disaster, (b) that the 'Priestly legalism,' though an epoch-making stage in the religion, does not by any means represent all the formative movements in Israel, and (c) that much more attention must be paid to the *internal* conditions in Palestine, as distinct from the subsequent activities of exiles who returned (notably in the reign of Artaxerxes I), and whose standpoint shapes the biblical narrative (see also vol. III, p. 415 *n.*). Further (2), as distinct from the work of analysis and the investigation of the greatest possible antiquity of the biblical material, there is increasing recognition of the significance of the sixth century (roughly) as a period of *rapprochement* and of a new All-Israel. Here the most important criticism (mainly the work of Kennett from 1905–6) has been chiefly on the date of the present Deuteronomy, and the *raison d'être* of the different compilations (J, E, etc.). These enquiries, more recently supplemented by the work of Hölscher and others in Germany, open up a new and fruitful approach to the problems of the Old Testament, the more especially so if, as is urged in this chapter, a distinctive semi-Edomitic phase may be recognized *after* the disasters to Judah (597 and 586 B.C.) and *before* the separative policy of those exiles who returned from Babylonia.

CHAPTER VIII

THE RISE OF MACEDONIA

I. THE GREEK WORLD AT THE ACCESSION OF PHILIP

IN the year 360 B.C. the position of Athens in the Greek world was, to all appearance, a very strong one (p. 106). The battle of Mantinea had put an end for the time to the rivalry of Thebes; the influence of Sparta even in the Peloponnese itself was held in check by the recently established powers of Messene and Megalopolis; the Athenians had made up their differences with the minor Peloponnesian states; there was no city which could at the moment compete with Athens in naval and military strength or in the number of its allies. Nevertheless there were difficulties which she had to face, and some of which were destined to test severely both her statesmanship and her military capacity.

The failure of one Athenian general after another in the hostilities against Cotys, king of the Odrysian Thracians, had led to a most unsatisfactory situation, which was complicated by the inconstant behaviour of the mercenary captains, Iphicrates and Charidemus, who were taking part in the operations. Iphicrates, indeed, though son-in-law to Cotys, did not forget that he was an Athenian, and would not assist his father-in-law except in defensive measures; and after the siege of Sestos by Cotys (probably at the beginning of 360) he refused to proceed with him against Elaeus and Crithote, which had come into Athenian hands about 364, and retired into temporary inactivity in Lesbos, where he was of no service to either side. Charidemus, on the other hand, was unashamedly treacherous. When Cephisodotus was sent

Note. The continuous ancient sources for the narrative in this and the following chapter are Diodorus XVI and Justin VII–IX, and except for certain special difficulties (mainly chronological) the story which they give appears to be substantially trustworthy. The speeches of Demosthenes and Aeschines and the writings of Isocrates supply much contemporary evidence. (Indications of the several occasions of these speeches and pamphlets will be found in the narrative.) There are many inscriptions which bear upon the period, and Plutarch's Lives of Demosthenes and Phocion are of some importance. For further information the reader is referred to the Bibliography.

from Athens in 360, in succession to a number of unsuccessful commanders, to protect her possessions in the Chersonese and to support Miltocythes, a prince who was in revolt against Cotys, Charidemus (who had been engaged for a year or two in trying to found a little kingdom of his own in the Troad, and was finding the attempt unlikely to succeed) wrote to Cephisodotus and offered to help the Athenians against Cotys, if he and his men could be transported across the Hellespont in Athenian ships. As it happened, circumstances enabled him to cross without this help, and he promptly joined Cotys at Sestos against Cephisodotus, besieged Elaeus and Crithote, and (now or later) married Cotys' daughter.

In other quarters also Athens was in difficulties. The dispute for the possession of Amphipolis was unsettled. Perdiccas III, though he had until recently been friendly to Athens, and (probably with a view to setting up some counter-influence to that of Olynthus) had helped the Athenians to establish themselves in the towns on the coast of the Thermaic Gulf, was not prepared to give up his claim to Amphipolis, and Timotheus had failed to take the place (p. 105).

Finally, the Athenian alliance was weakened by the retirement from it of Corcyra (about 361), and the discontent, which in two or three years led to the outbreak of war between Athens and her allies, must already have begun to show itself.

It is the development of these difficulties which we have now to trace.

Before the end of the year 360 Cotys was murdered, to avenge a private quarrel, by two Greeks from Aenus, who were crowned with gold by the Athenians for their action, and given the citizenship of Athens. He was succeeded by his son Cersobleptes, whom Charidemus supported, as he had supported Cotys. The request of Cephisodotus for the fulfilment of Charidemus' promises was met by fresh acts of hostility; Charidemus inflicted heavy loss on the crews of ten Athenian ships while they were breakfasting on shore at Perinthus; and when Cephisodotus was attempting to exterminate a nest of pirates at Alopeconnesus (on the western shore of the Chersonese), Charidemus marched to their assistance down the Chersonese. Finally, after some months of hostilities, he obliged Cephisodotus to conclude a treaty with him, in which, among other provisions dishonourable to Athens, the town of Cardia, the key of the Chersonese and already hostile to Athens, was handed over to Charidemus as his own possession. The

Athenians deprived Cephisodotus of his command, fined him five talents, and repudiated the treaty. Among the witnesses against him was the young Demosthenes, who had sailed in the expedition as trierarch, taking the General on his ship.

Cersobleptes was but a youth, and despite the support of Charidemus, his succession to the Odrysian kingdom did not go unchallenged. Two rivals, Amadocus, a prince of the royal house, and Berisades, whose origin is unknown, each claimed a portion, and each was supported by Greek generals whom they bound to them (as Iphicrates and Charidemus had been bound to the house of Cotys) by ties of intermarriage, Berisades being aided by Athenodorus, an Athenian who had a considerable estate in the Chersonese itself or not far off, Amadocus by Simon and Bianor. A miscalculation on the part of Charidemus himself helped their cause. Miltocythes was betrayed into his hands by a certain Smicythion. Instead of handing him over to Cersobleptes, who, true to the Thracian dislike of political murders, would have saved his life, he delivered him to the Cardians, who took him out to sea and drowned him, after killing his son before his eyes. This brutal act roused the feelings of the Thracians very strongly against Charidemus. Berisades and Amadocus joined forces, with Athenodorus as commander, and sent to Athens for aid; and Athenodorus was able to force Cersobleptes to agree to divide the Odrysian Kingdom with his two rivals, the eastern portion, from the Hebrus to Byzantium, going to Cersobleptes, the western, as far as the neighbourhood of Amphipolis, to Berisades, and the coast between Maronea and the Chersonese to Amadocus.

By the same treaty the Chersonese was to be surrendered to Athens, and Chabrias was sent from Athens with a single ship to receive the surrender. But, though it must have been obvious that the treaty would not be respected unless it were maintained by force, the Athenians, by failing to contribute the necessary funds to Athenodorus, obliged him to dismiss his army; and Chabrias was reduced to consenting to a revision of the treaty, in the same terms as those previously accepted by Cephisodotus. The Athenians again repudiated these terms, and sent commissioners to demand the formal renewal on oath of the treaty of Athenodorus; but, despite the repeated charges of bad faith made against them by Berisades and Amadocus, they still failed to supply men or money, and it was probably not before the latter half of 357—after the Euboean expedition, to be described shortly—that Chares sailed with a considerable fleet and enforced the surrender of the Chersonese to Athens, though Cardia still remained *de facto* in the hands of Charidemus.

In the meantime the deaths of three monarchs had taken place, bringing changes which were of great moment for the history of the next years. Artaxerxes Mnemon had died, and the Persian throne was ascended, probably in the year 358, by his son Artaxerxes Ochus (p. 21). Alexander of Pherae had been murdered by Tisiphonus, Lycophron and Peitholaus, the brothers of his wife Thebe, who had been alienated by his savagery and herself directed the plot. Perdiccas III of Macedon had also fallen; whether by assassination instigated by his mother Eurydice, or in consequence of a wound received in battle with the Illyrians, remains uncertain.

The new Persian sovereign was less inclined than his predecessor to submit to any encroachments upon his power either by his own satraps or by the Greeks; this will appear in the sequel. The despotism which had been exercised by Alexander was at first shared by Thebe and Tisiphonus, but a few years later Lycophron and Peitholaus appear as tyrants of Pherae, and the former is frequently mentioned alone. It appears also that the position of the princes of Pherae in Thessaly was no longer unchallenged, as it had been, and that the way was open for any external power to play upon the divisions which arose.

But it was the death of Perdiccas which was fraught with the most momentous consequences. His son Amyntas was an infant, and Philip, the younger brother of Perdiccas, and, like him, the son of Eurydice, assumed the regency as the infant's guardian. But there were five other actual or possible claimants to the crown —Archelaus, Arrhidaeus and Menelaus, half-brothers of Philip; Pausanias, also of royal descent, who had been prevented by Iphicrates from snatching the royal power from Perdiccas at his accession; and Argaeus, who was favoured by Athens. In view of these difficulties, as well as of the constant danger from neighbouring tribes, the Macedonians obliged Philip to take the monarchy himself. He at once put Archelaus to death; Arrhidaeus and Menelaus fled from the country; the chances of Pausanias were undermined by gifts and promises to the Thracians —probably Berisades and his subjects—on whom he chiefly relied; and the Athenians were weakened in their support of Argaeus by the skill with which Philip conducted himself towards them.

Argaeus had promised the Athenians Amphipolis, if he should succeed in getting the crown. Philip countered this promise by

actually withdrawing the Macedonian force with which Perdiccas
had garrisoned the town, and dispatched a letter to Athens,
asking for an alliance such as his father Amyntas had had with her.
Consequently the Athenians did no more for Argaeus than to
escort him to Methone with a considerable number of ships; and
when he attempted to make his way to the old Macedonian capital
of Aegae, he had but a few Athenian volunteers to reinforce his
mercenary troops and the Macedonian exiles who were with him.
The people of Aegae would have nothing to say to him, and he
attempted to return to Methone, but on the way was overpowered
by Philip. The Athenians who were captured with him were
treated with great generosity, and restored to Athens with polite
messages; and a formal peace was made, probably early in 358,
in which Philip admitted the Athenian claim to Amphipolis.

II. THE EARLY YEARS OF PHILIP'S REIGN, 359–356 B.C.

Such was the beginning of one of the most remarkable reigns
recorded in history. For it is the personality of Philip, now about
twenty-three years old, that dominates the course of events from
this time till his death. In 367 he had been taken to Thebes as a
hostage for the good behaviour of Macedonia towards Thebes,
and there, in the house of Pammenes, he had learned to know
Epaminondas and Pelopidas, and had acquired an unbounded
admiration for the former. It was doubtless from Epaminondas
that he learned, through precept and example, the value of new
ideas in military organization and tactics,—while at the same
time he came to appreciate that fine Hellenic culture which was
already in favour at the court of Perdiccas, but was still regarded
by the more warlike Macedonians as a form of degeneracy.
(Whether or not the Macedonians as a whole were closely akin
to the Hellenic stock is a question which will probably never be
settled. Demosthenes speaks of them, and of Philip, as barbarians, when he is in the mood to do so; but the royal house at
least was in part of Hellenic blood.) On his return from Thebes
after about three years' sojourn, Philip was entrusted with the
administration of a district in Macedonia, and he had organized
a military force there in accordance with his own ideas, when he
was called to the throne.

As soon as he had got rid of all possible rivals, it became necessary
for him to secure himself against the aggressions of neighbouring
tribes. The Paeonians, to the north, he had already bought off
temporarily by presents and promises, when they invaded Macedonia on the death of Perdiccas, and now, their king Agis having

died, he reduced them to subjection. Alarmed at this, the Illyrian king Bardylis, who had overrun a great part of Western Macedonia, offered to make terms on condition that each power should retain what it held at the moment. Philip refused, and a battle was fought, probably in the neighbourhood of the modern Monastir, in which Philip was victorious, his cavalry encircling the Illyrian left wing, and so attacking the Illyrian army in front and rear at once. After a very fierce struggle, Bardylis was forced to yield all the territory east of the lake Lychoridus (Ochrida); the semi-independent princes of the regions of Lyncestis and Orestis, who had helped the Illyrians, were reduced to definite subjection, and probably other district-princes were similarly brought within a definite organization.

The success of Philip against the Paeonians and Illyrians was probably due in the main to that re-organization of the Macedonian army which must have been one of his first undertakings on coming to the throne. It is not possible, indeed, to trace the steps by which the new model was brought to perfection, but its main features are clear. Before this time the strength of the army had lain in its cavalry, composed of the 'Companions' of the sovereign—a hereditary aristocracy of land-holders; the infantry had been an ill-organized mass. Philip retained the 'Companions,' and took special measures to attach the nobility to himself, surrounding himself in court and camp with the sons of the chief houses as his personal attendants, and forming an inner circle of noble 'Companions of the King's Person,' whose position was the most coveted of all. The 'Companions' also remained a most important part of the army; but there was now to be, in addition, a well-organized infantry. Part of this force, the Hypaspistae, are commonly thought to have been armed after the manner of Iphicrates' peltasts, who had become the model for mercenary troops generally, though the fact that Alexander employed them in the East as heavy infantry, no less than the phalanx, makes this somewhat doubtful. The phalanx itself, which became the most notable element in the Macedonian army, was certainly furnished with a weapon strange to Greek troops, the long pike or *sarissa*, which gave it the advantage of the first blow. Moreover, it was formed into a less dense mass than the conventional Greek hoplite force, its object being no longer to carry the day by sheer weight, but to give room for a more skilled play of weapons, and to keep the enemy's front engaged, while other troops won the victory by freer movements. To the new infantry was given the name of 'Foot-Companions,' which assimilated their position in relation to the king to that of the Companions, and so gave them a pride in their status and an incentive to loyalty. At the same time Philip consulted Macedonian sentiment by retaining within these larger units the territorial or tribal organization which was traditional. The armies of the Greek city-states were in the main composed of heavy infantry, though most of them had a small cavalry-corps, and the mercenaries whom they employed often possessed greater mobility. It was Philip who first created a national army on a broad basis, and planned out carefully the relation to one another, not only of cavalry and infantry, but of archers and all kinds of light-armed troops, so that he had at his disposal many mobile elements, which could be used in a great variety of ways in conjunction with the heavier phalanx.

Philip appears to have followed normally the principle, developed by Epaminondas, of strengthening one wing in particular for his main attack, and of using cavalry, in combination with infantry, for this purpose, as had been done both by Pelopidas at Cynoscephalae, and by Epaminondas afterwards; but he went far beyond the Theban generals in the tactical use of a very varied force for a carefully planned end. It was the elasticity which his new organization rendered possible that was so immense an advantage, as against the more rigid methods of ordinary Greek armies; and the infusion of a spirit of loyalty to himself gave his troops the inspiration which was so often lacking to the forces of the Greek city-states, particularly when composed, as they often were, largely of mercenaries.

Moreover Philip's army was kept constantly at work, and never allowed to fall out of practice; and though Demosthenes once hints that this continual labour was not exacted without arousing great discontent, there is no confirmation of such a view, nor any reason to believe that Philip overtaxed the loyalty of his men. The armies of most of the Greek states, which were only accustomed to operate during certain regular campaigning seasons, and were very unwilling to be away from home for long periods, could hardly hope to compete with one so trained.

The military re-organization of Macedonia seems to have been accompanied by a thorough re-organization of the internal Government, which, without departing from the territorial principle, effected a much greater centralization of political and financial control. Financial reforms had already been begun by Callistratus, who, when exiled from Athens, was called in to his aid by Perdiccas (p. 104). Security was given to the new order of things by the foundation of new towns or fortresses in various parts of the country.

It was not long before the advantages of the new régime in Macedonia were to be strikingly displayed in contrast with the characteristic vacillation and ineffectiveness of democratic Athens. Early in 357 Philip took advantage of the opportunity offered by some unfriendliness on the part of the Amphipolitans to lay siege to Amphipolis, which, a year or two before, he had acknowledged to be an Athenian possession. The Athenians had apparently been content with this acknowledgment, and had taken no steps to make good their claim by sending a garrison to the town. It is true that they had, at least for a short time, had other employment for their troops. For the Euboeans, who had been under the domination of Thebes since the battle of Leuctra, had grown restless, and on the appearance of a Theban army to crush their rising, had appealed to Athens. Timotheus supported the appeal in an energetic speech; the Athenians were roused to enthusiasm; volunteers came forward eagerly (Demosthenes among them) to serve as trierarchs; within five days a naval and military armament was ready; by the end of a month the Thebans had been forced to leave Euboea, and Chares, who had joined in the expedition with a mercenary force, was set free to go to the Chersonese, where, as has already been narrated, he brought Charidemus to terms. The Euboean cities became members of the Athenian confederacy.

But the expedition to Euboea took place only very shortly before Philip's attack on Amphipolis, and does not explain the neglect of the Athenians to garrison the town, nor their blind credulity in regard to Philip's assurances, when, to counteract the appeal made on behalf of the Amphipolitans to Athens by their envoys Hierax and Stratocles, he affirmed his intention of giving it up to Athens as soon as he had captured it. Negotiations followed, and an arrangement was made by which the Athenians were to receive Amphipolis, and were to hand over to Philip in exchange the sea-port of Pydna, which had been taken by Timotheus. But, as it was known that Pydna would not willingly consent to this, the arrangement was kept secret even from the Athenian Assembly, the Council only having cognizance of it. The arrangement was not carried out. Amphipolis resisted bravely, but in the latter half of 357 Philip obtained possession of the town with the aid of traitors from within, and got rid of his enemies there, while treating the inhabitants as a whole with kindness; but as the Athenians did not fulfil their part of the dishonourable bargain, he did not give them Amphipolis. So confident, however, were the Athenian statesmen even now in Philip's intentions, that they persuaded the Assembly to reject the overtures made by the inhabitants of Olynthus, who appealed to Athens in alarm at the evidences of Philip's power. Thus disappointed, the Olynthians thought it prudent to make terms with Philip himself, according to which neither side was to make a treaty with Athens apart from the other.

The Athenians were by this time involved in the war with their own allies, and Philip had no need to hesitate. Instead of waiting for the Athenians to give him Pydna, he seized it by force, again aided by treachery (early in 356). Then, assisted by the Olynthians, he took Potidaea, though not without trouble, and handed both it and Anthemus over to the Olynthians, who seemed so far to have derived nothing but benefit from their alliance with him. At the same time, Philip did not confess to any hostility to Athens; in the attack on Potidaea he professed to be acting as the ally of Olynthus, and the Athenian settlers captured in the town were allowed to return in safety to Athens. The Athenians themselves appear to have done nothing to oppose Philip's conquests, except to order an expedition to Potidaea when it was too late, though this at least showed that their faith in his friendship had at last been shaken.

The possession of Amphipolis was of the utmost value to Philip; for beyond the town stood the Pangaean Mountain, which was being developed as a field for gold-production by settlers from Thasos. A few years before this they had founded the town of Crenides as the centre of their operations, being accompanied and probably inspired by the exiled Callistratus, before the ill-advised attempt to return to Athens, which ended in his execution (p. 104 n.). Crenides was within the district which formed part of the kingdom of Berisades, and which, on his death in 357 and the distribution of his kingdom between his sons, fell to Cetriporis, the eldest of them. Cetriporis' ownership was already being threatened by Cersobleptes, when Philip came on the scene and occupied Crenides, settling large numbers of his own subjects there and re-naming it Philippi[1]. He at once began to produce gold on a very large scale, and before long derived as much as 1000 talents a year from this one source; while the forests of the neighbourhood gave him abundance of timber for ships. He was thus provided with the two things which he most needed—a

---

[1] This re-naming is attested by the coins, see Volume of Plates ii, 6, *l, m*.

large and steady revenue, and a fleet, with which he could annoy the Athenians on their own element. The Athenians were at present unable to retaliate, owing to the war with their allies, but they endeavoured to check Philip by making an alliance with Cetriporis in the summer of 356. Two other princes, the Paeonian Lyppeius[1] and the Illyrian Grabus, were joined with them in the treaty; but the alliance had little effect. Philip at once took military measures against both Paeonians and Illyrians, and it was doubtless the victory of his general, Parmenion, over the Illyrians in this campaign that was reported to Philip shortly after mid-summer, 356, along with the news of the birth of Alexander, his son by Olympias, and of the victory of his horse at Olympia. It was possibly at this time that the Nestus was made the recognized boundary between the Macedonian and Thracian kingdoms.

The gold-works on the Pangaean Mountain also enabled Philip to introduce a new coinage, in which were included both the gold staters, named after himself, and a silver coinage bearing a fixed relation to them. This new coinage not only helped to unify his own kingdom, but also to increase its economic importance, as against both Athens and Persia, the two states whose money had hitherto been most widely current in the Greek world[2].

III. THE WAR OF ATHENS AND HER ALLIES
357–355 B.C.

We must now return and consider the main cause of the failure of the Athenians to take any effective steps against Philip. In the latter half of the year 357, three members of the Athenian League, Chios, Rhodes and Byzantium, formed a separate alliance, in which they were soon afterwards joined by Cos. It may be that the seed sown by Epaminondas in his naval expedition in 364 was now bearing fruit, or that the allies had been alarmed by the establishment in 365 of Athenian cleruchs in Samos (which had remained outside the Athenian League till then), and their re-inforcement by new settlers in 361. The recent subjection of Ceos and Naxos to the jurisdiction of the Athenian Courts may also have had its effect in arousing suspicion. But the immediate cause of the revolt was probably the instigation of Mausolus, satrap of Caria, who gave it open aid.

[1] So Ditt. *Syll.*[3] 196. To judge from Paeonian coins, Lykkeios may be the more correct form of his name.

[2] For a full discussion of the relation between Philip's coinage and his policy see A. B. West, *Numism. Chron.* 1923, pp. 169 *sqq.*

Mausolus is one of the more striking figures of this period (pp. 24, 104). While nominally a satrap of the Persian king, he had virtually an independent princedom, founded by his father Hecatomnus of Mylasa, and extending not only over Caria, but over a considerable part of Ionia and Lycia. His own capital was at Halicarnassus, a more convenient base of operations than Mylasa; and, with a large fleet at his disposal, he had begun to threaten the independence of the Greek islands adjacent to the Asiatic coast. The union of the inhabitants of Cos into one community in 366–5 was probably a precautionary measure against his possible encroachments. Only the Athenian League appeared to stand in the way of his ambition, and in order to get rid of this obstacle, he determined to break it up by detaching from it its most powerful members. His intrigues succeeded, and the war of these allies against Athens (357–5 B.C.) was the result.

The fleets of the disaffected allies met at Chios, and Athens sent against them a large naval force, of which Chabrias was in command, and a considerable body of mercenaries under Chares. The latter landed at Chios and attacked the town, while Chabrias engaged the hostile fleet. Both failed, and Chabrias was killed while dashing ahead, apparently without adequate support from the rest of the Athenian fleet, which afterwards sailed away, taking Chares and his troops with it.

This disaster caused the revolt to spread more widely; Sestos and other towns joined the allies, and a fleet of 100 ships led by the Chians did much damage to Lemnos, Imbros and other places which had remained true to Athens, and (probably early in 356) laid siege to Samos. To meet the expense of the war, the Athenians passed a law proposed by Periander, providing a more businesslike and expeditious method of obtaining the funds required for the equipment of the fleet, by transferring the responsibility for trierarchy to twenty Boards or Symmories of sixty persons each. The new plan was open to abuses, since the wealthier members of each Board had the practical management, and did not act fairly towards their poorer associates in the apportionment of contributions; but it appears to have worked at least as well as the method of collecting the war-tax, on which it was modelled (see above, p. 74).

Chares, with only sixty ships, had been unable to oppose the 100 ships of the enemy; but apparently it was not till the middle of 356 that the Athenians sent out a large naval armament to join him, under the command of Iphicrates, his son Menestheus, and Timotheus. To divert the allies from Samos, and to secure the

route followed by the Athenian corn-trade, the combined fleet proceeded to threaten Byzantium. The allies left Samos, and came up
with the Athenian fleet in the Hellespont, but, when the Athenians
offered battle, withdrew again till they reached Embatum, in
the strait between Chios and Erythrae. Here the Athenian
generals arranged a plan of attack; but Iphicrates and Timotheus
were deterred by the stormy sea, and Chares unwisely led his
ships into battle without them, and was driven back. He at once
prosecuted his colleagues for treachery, alleging that they had
been bribed by the enemy to desert him, and he was joined in the
prosecution by Aristophon, who had been the leading statesman
in Athens since the fall of Callistratus. It is uncertain whether
the trial was concluded within the year, or whether it dragged on
until 354; but in the result, Iphicrates and Menestheus were
acquitted; their defence appears to have been both spirited and
businesslike; Timotheus, who was already unpopular in Athens
owing to his haughty demeanour, was fined the enormous sum
of 100 talents, and withdrew to Chalcis, where, in 354, he died.
The fine was never paid; but his son Conon, on spending one-
tenth of the sum on the repair of the fortifications of the city, was
granted a discharge from the debt. Iphicrates lived a few years
longer, but was never again given a command. In this way Athens
treated the two commanders of real genius whom she possessed.

Chares was now in sole command, but instead of taking further
steps against the enemy, he gave his services to Artabazus, satrap
of Hellespontine Phrygia, who was in revolt against the Persian
king and was being hard pressed by the other satraps whom
Artaxerxes Ochus had sent against him (see above, p. 22). Chares
won a great victory, and was richly rewarded and so enabled to
pay his troops. Moreover, in return for his services he appears
to have been given possession of Sigeum, and perhaps of Lampsacus also. But there were some who saw in his action an illustration of the excessive independence of mercenary armies, and
more who were not free from the dread of Persia; and when news
was brought that Artaxerxes, who had already dispatched strong
protests to Athens, was preparing an immense force, it was
assumed that its object was to take revenge upon Athens for the
action of Chares. Consequently the Athenians thought it prudent
to recall him and to come to terms with the allies; and in the
course of the year 355–4 peace was made, and the independence
of Chios, Cos, Byzantium and Rhodes was recognized.

Athenian feeling, however, was not unanimous. There were
orators who saw an opportunity for urging again the policy which

they liked to think of as traditional for Athens, and calling upon the Greeks to attack Persia in force. Fortunately the leading statesmen in Athens had the good sense to resist this suggestion, and it is interesting to find Demosthenes, who was now beginning to take part in public affairs, speaking on the side of prudence, and at the same time proposing (though without effect) some modifications of the Law of Periander, in order to get rid of the abuses which were possible under that law. Others, and particularly Isocrates, whose speech or essay *On the Peace* belongs to the year 355, thought that Athens should abandon all claim to maritime empire, and free herself and her allies from the evils attendant upon the employment of unreliable mercenary armies.

The war with the allies had in fact brought Athens to the verge of exhaustion. It had cost her over a thousand talents. Not only had she lost the allies who revolted, but others soon declared their independence—among them Perinthus and Selymbria, Mitylene and Methymna; and both her prestige and her revenues were very greatly diminished. Only Euboea, with the islands in the Northern Aegean and a few towns on the Thracian coast, now remained to her.

Yet it was not long before some of the allies themselves had reason to regret that they had listened to Mausolus, who, having rid himself of the Athenians, proceeded to act according to his plan. Within a year or two he had mastered Cos[1] and Rhodes, driving out the partisans of democracy, and establishing oligarchies obedient to himself. In Chios also there was an oligarchic revolution, and ultimately the island came under the power of the Carian dynasty. In 353 Mausolus died and was succeeded by his widow Artemisia, who reigned two years and then succumbed to her inconsolable grief for his loss, before even the magnificent monument was completed which has perpetuated his name in many modern languages. After her accession the exiled Rhodian democrats appealed to Athens for restoration, and were supported by Demosthenes, who spoke eloquently in the name of Democracy. But the Athenians could hardly forget that it was this same party that had led the revolt in 357, nor would it have been safe to underrate (with Demosthenes) the danger of hostile action by the Carian or Persian powers. Accordingly Rhodes was suffered to remain subject to the Carian house.

---

[1] The portrait of Mausolus appears on Coan coins of this period; see G. F. Hill in *Anatolian Studies presented to Sir Wm. Ramsay*, 1923, pp. 207 *sqq.*: and Volume of Plates ii, 8, *a.*

IV. THE SACRED WAR DOWN TO 353 B.C.

But long before the events last described, a new conflict had begun, which was fated to transform the whole aspect of the Greek world. The Council of the Amphictyonic League, originally a religious association which had the care of the temple and oracle of Delphi, was so composed that the Thebans and the leading Thessalians, with the insignificant neighbouring tribes who were virtually at their mercy, could, if united, determine its decisions; and they had little scruple about making use of the religious prestige of the Council for political ends. The so-called 'Sacred War' originated in such an attempt. Thebans and Thessalians alike were natural enemies of their Phocian neighbours, and it was probably by some of their representatives that a charge was brought before the Council against the Phocians in 357 or 356, to the effect that they had been cultivating part of the land which was consecrated to Apollo. Other charges may have been added, and a fine of many talents was imposed.

As this remained unpaid, the Amphictyonic Council resolved, probably early in April 355, that unless the debt were discharged, the territory of the Phocians should be confiscated and dedicated to the god. At the same time the Council ordered the payment of the fines which they had imposed upon other states, one of these being Sparta, which had been condemned to pay a large sum for the seizure of the Cadmea at Thebes in 382. Upon this, Philomelus of Ledon, a prominent Phocian, persuaded his fellow-countrymen, who could not pay so large a sum, not to submit tamely to the loss of their territory, but to retort by claiming from the Council, as by ancestral right, the control of the oracle of Delphi, and to appoint him general with full powers of action. This done he went to Sparta and interviewed the king Archidamus, urging that both Spartans and Phocians were in the same case, and promising that, if successful, he would get the Amphictyonic sentence on Sparta annulled. Archidamus would not at present promise open assistance, Sparta having traditionally taken sides with the inhabitants of Delphi in opposition to the claims of the Phocians; but he undertook to send funds and mercenaries secretly. With fifteen talents from Archidamus, and much more provided by himself, Philomelus hired a body of mercenaries; and with these and a picked band of 1000 Phocian peltasts he seized the temple, probably towards the end of May, 355. He destroyed the clan of the Thracidae, who opposed him, and confiscated their property. (Only the intercession of Archidamus prevented much greater brutality.) He compelled the priestess of the oracle to mount the tripod and to pronounce as to his future prospects, and while protesting against this violation of religious custom, she impatiently exclaimed that he could do what he liked. This utterance he proclaimed as oracular before the assembled Delphians, and declared that they need have no fears of him. He was further encouraged by a good omen—an eagle which chased and carried off some of the doves that flew about the altar of Apollo.

Upon this the Locrians of Amphissa and the neighbourhood (old rivals of the Phocians and friends of Thebes) attempted to drive Philomelus out of Delphi, and a battle was fought above the Phaedriades, the great cliffs by which Delphi is dominated. Philomelus was victorious, taking many of the enemy prisoners, and forcing others to throw themselves over the cliffs. About the same time he despatched messengers to the chief Greek states, and especially to Athens, Sparta and Thebes, to declare that he had no lawless intentions, but was asserting the ancient right of his people, proved by lines of Homer himself, to the possession of Delphi; he promised to be strictly accountable for the temple-treasures, and asked the states for military assistance, or, at worst, for neutrality. The formal appeal to the government of the states was probably combined with informal propaganda. In response to this appeal Athens and Sparta each made an alliance with the Phocians, though they did not follow it up by action, and the Athenians appear to have halted between the two sentiments of abhorrence of the sacrilege, and anxiety lest the Phocian people should be exterminated. On the other hand, the Thebans (to whom the defeated Locrians had also sent an appeal), together with the Locrians of the Eastern or Epicnemidian branch and some other tribes, resolved to oppose the Phocians in the name of the god of Delphi.

The next step, which was doubtless taken on the instigation of the Thebans, was to procure the formal declaration of war by the Amphictyonic Council against the Phocians. This probably was done at a special meeting, after midsummer in 355, and was followed by embassies from Thebes to the Thessalians and the smaller tribes who were members of the Amphictyonic League. These all declared war upon the sacrilegious Phocians, and in the meantime Philomelus, seeing that the danger was now serious, threw a wall round the temple-precinct, and collected as large a mercenary force as possible by offering half as much again as the ordinary rate of pay, at the same time enrolling all the fittest of the Phocians. His whole force amounted to some 5000 men.

He obtained funds by extorting all that he could from the most prosperous of the inhabitants of Delphi, and made clear that he would tolerate no opposition from them to the Phocian cause.

When his army was complete, probably in the autumn of 355, Philomelus invaded the territory of the Eastern Locrians, which lay upon the routes by which the Thessalians and Boeotians would naturally join forces. After devastating much of the country, he laid siege to a stronghold by a river, but, failing to take it, raised the siege, and in a battle with the Locrians lost twenty men, whose bodies the Locrians refused to give up, as Greek religious principles required, for burial, on the ground that they were those of sacrilegious robbers. Philomelus, however, in a further attack, killed some of the enemy, and refused in turn to give up their bodies till the Locrians consented to an exchange. Then, after over-running the open country and providing his mercenaries with plenty of plunder, he returned to Delphi for the winter. The Boeotians—whether because they were naturally slow to move, or because, as is likely, they were in financial difficulties—had taken no steps to oppose Philomelus in the field, but it was clear that they intended to do so with a great force; and, in order to be prepared to meet them, he now at last began to lay hands on the offerings dedicated in the temple, and with the proceeds to collect a larger mercenary army, composed, Diodorus tells us, mainly of unscrupulous men, on whom the impiety of his actions had no deterrent effect, and numbering 10,000 in all. With this force he again invaded Eastern Locris, probably in the spring of 354, and got the better of the Boeotian and Locrian troops in a cavalry battle. A force of 6000 Thessalians and other Northern Greeks was next defeated by the hill Argolas. Then the Boeotians confronted him with 13,000 men; 1500 Achaeans from the Peloponnese joined the Phocians, and the two armies encamped opposite each other at a short distance. After some acts of ferocity on both sides towards prisoners casually taken, both the armies shifted their ground, and the foremost troops in each suddenly found themselves entangled with one another in a rough wooded place by Neon, on the north side of Mount Parnassus. A general engagement followed, in which the Boeotians were victorious by weight of numbers; and in attempting to escape over precipitous ground many of the Phocians and their mercenaries were cut to pieces. Philomelus, after fighting with the courage of despair and sustaining many wounds, threw himself over a cliff and perished. His colleague Onomarchus took the survivors of the Phocian army back to

Delphi, and the Boeotians, thinking their victory decisive, also returned home.

The battle of Neon probably was fought about August, 354; but the whole chronology of the Sacred War is keenly disputed, owing to the contradictions between the ancient authorities, and the uncertainty as to the precise events to which some of them refer as the 'beginning' and 'end' of the war, and in relation to which other events must be dated. Accordingly the dates given in this chapter can be regarded only as probable. Some modern authorities[1] date the whole of the events just recorded about a year earlier, and place the occupation of Delphi by Philomelus in June, 356, rearranging the intervals between subsequent events in various ways in consequence. There is in fact no absolutely fixed date until we come to the trial of Aristocrates and the siege of Heraeon Teichos, and calculations based upon the length of time which certain expeditions 'must have taken' are very untrustworthy. But the general sequence of events is fairly certain and intelligible, and there are only one or two occurrences, the place of which in the series is really open to doubt.

The defeat of Philomelus gave those of the Phocians who had scruples about the war an opportunity of urging that peace should be made; but Onomarchus, who was one of those upon whom the fines imposed by the Amphictyonic Council would have fallen most disastrously, made a carefully prepared speech in defence of the Phocian claim to the temple, and secured a vote for the continuance of the war under his own supreme command. Encouraged by a dream, he at once began to fill up the depleted ranks of his army, and made free use of the temple treasures, turning the bronze and iron into armour, and the gold and silver into coin, which he distributed freely to the allied cities and their leading citizens[2]. He also used bribes to secure the support or the neutrality of some of those who, like Lycophron of Pherae, had been hostile to the Phocian cause. At the same time he arrested the Phocians who were opposed to his plans, and confiscated their property.

[1] *E.g.* Beloch, *Griechische Geschichte* III², 2, pp. 262–7, on the strength of the inferences which he draws from the inscriptions recording the meetings of the Naopoioi at Delphi. Other discussions of the chronology of the period are mentioned in the Bibliography. (That of Cloché is the most important.) Even if the earlier date for the seizure of the temple be accepted, there is much room for difference of opinion as to the exact dates of subsequent events up to 352 B.C.

[2] For Phocian coins bearing the names of Onomarchus and his successor, Phalaecus, see Volume of Plates ii, 8, *b, c.*

His preparations having been made, he invaded Eastern Locris once more, probably early in 353, and besieged and took Thronium, one of the towns commanding the Pass of Thermopylae, of which he must have obtained control. Then he made an attack upon Amphissa, and terrified the inhabitants into subjection, and next proceeded to overrun Doris, sacking the towns and ravaging the country. He then invaded Boeotia itself, and took Orchomenus, but failed in the siege of Chaeronea, and was forced to return into Phocis, probably about the end of August, 353.

His failure at the end of so successful a campaign was perhaps due to a division of forces which he had been led to make in consequence of the appearance of Philip in Thessaly.

V. PHILIP'S ACTIVITIES IN THRACE AND THESSALY DOWN TO 352 B.C. THE SACRED WAR CONTINUED

Our survey of Philip's actions was broken off at the point at which he had delivered his counterstroke to the Athenian alliance with Cetriporis, Lyppeius and Grabus, by a victorious campaign against the Illyrian and Paeonian members of the alliance (356–5 B.C.). We have no clear view of him again, until we find him, probably late in the summer of 354, capturing the Thracian coast-towns of Abdera and Maronea, and, apparently, intervening in the long-standing dispute between Amadocus and Cersobleptes, the latter of whom, supported by Charidemus, was as anxious as ever to extend his dominions at the expense of the other Thracian princes. On this occasion Philip appears to have favoured Cersobleptes, in so far as he accepted the pledges of friendship which Cersobleptes offered him by the hand of Apollonides of Cardia. Both Cersobleptes and the Cardians were enemies of Athens, while Amadocus was in friendly relation with her; and it is clear that the event would emphasize the increasing incompatibility of the interests of Athens in Thrace with those of Philip.

Cersobleptes is said to have given pledges at the same time to Pammenes, who had been dispatched from Thebes under somewhat remarkable circumstances. Artabazus, as we have seen, had lost the assistance of Chares in his revolt against the Persian king, and in his anxiety for a new ally he had applied to Thebes. The application probably came just at the moment when the defeat and death of Philomelus seemed likely to relieve the pressure of the war with the Phocians; and although the Thebans were generally on good terms with the Persian king (and indeed were so once more within three years or so of this time), it may have been the case that they were short of funds, and were glad to give Artabazus the use of Pammenes and 5000 men for a sufficient recompense. So Pammenes marched through Thrace, and met Philip, his former guest, at Maronea, where he joined him in accepting the overtures of Cersobleptes. When he arrived in Asia Minor, Pammenes won two victories over the satraps sent by the Persian king to quell the revolt of Artabazus; but he appears to have subsequently been suspected of disloyalty, and arrested by Artabazus himself. He was afterwards released, and doubtless was allowed to return home with his men; but it was not long before Artabazus was himself obliged to take flight, and we find him later at Philip's court in Macedonia (see above, p. 22).

Philip may have intended to proceed beyond Maronea; but his march was opposed by Amadocus, and, for whatever reason, he thought it better to return. At Neapolis, Chares, who had perhaps been sent in answer to an appeal from Neapolis some time before, endeavoured to intercept Philip's ships; but Philip evaded him by a ruse and got safely away. It must have been at about this time that Chares gained a victory over a body of Philip's mercenaries under Adaeus, a general who was nicknamed 'the cock,' and was ridiculed by the comic poets as a *Miles Gloriosus*. Chares had participated in the distribution of the Delphic treasures by Onomarchus, and used his share to feast the people of Athens in celebration of this victory.

Early in the spring of 353, Cersobleptes, perhaps disappointed at receiving so little aid from Philip against Amadocus, and distrustful of the king's future intentions, once more returned to Athens, and sent Aristomachus to declare the friendly feeling of himself and his general Charidemus towards the Athenians, and to promise that if Athens would elect Charidemus their general, he would capture Amphipolis for them from Philip. Possibly the former treaty between Athens and Cersobleptes was confirmed, by which the latter acknowledged the title of Athens to the towns of the Chersonese, with the exception of Cardia. An Athenian named Aristocrates went so far as to propose that anyone who killed Charidemus should be liable to summary arrest in any place within the dominions of Athens. Such a decree must necessarily have been taken as an unfriendly act by the other Thracian princes and their generals, against whom Charidemus had been fighting; and Aristocrates was indicted for the illegality of the decree by one Euthycles: its operation was suspended in consequence, and as the indictment did not come to trial for over a year later, the decree, in accordance with Athenian law, fell to the ground. Demosthenes spoke on behalf of the prosecution, and his speech is an invaluable source of information both as to events in Thrace, and as to Athenian policy. It is not known what was the result of the trial; but the action of Athens was not without its adverse effects; for when Philip appears again in Thrace, we shall find that Amadocus is in alliance with him against Cersobleptes. In the summer of 352 Chares re-occupied Sestos (which had revolted in 357 or 356) in the name of Athens, after meeting with stout resistance from the inhabitants, whom he proceeded to slay or sell into slavery. Shortly afterwards the Athenians sent cleruchs to occupy the town.

After leaving the Thracian coast in the autumn of 354, Philip may have returned to Macedonia. The next act of war on his part which is recorded is the taking of Methone, which fell after a long siege, probably in the early summer of 353. The inhabitants were expelled. Methone was the last Athenian stronghold on the Thermaic Gulf, and after its capture Philip virtually controlled the whole coast from Mount Olympus to the mouth of the Nestus. In the course of the siege of Methone he lost an eye.

It must again be noted that the chronology of these events is uncertain, and that the evidence admits of no more definite conclusions. It is possible that Methone fell a year earlier, before Philip marched against Abdera and Maronea, and there is some slight ground for thinking that it was at least threatened in the last days of 355. The mission of Pammenes to Asia and his meeting with Philip at Maronea may belong to the early spring of 353, though the meeting must have occurred before the overtures of Cersobleptes to Athens. But not much turns on the precise chronological order of these events, and whether he came immediately from Macedonia or Thrace or Methone, in the summer of 353 Philip appeared in Thessaly.

It seems that (probably ever since the death of Alexander of Pherae) Philip had taken the opportunity of fostering the divisions which already existed among the Thessalians; and now his aid had been invoked by Eudicus and Simus, the princes of Larissa, of the house of the Aleuadae, against Lycophron of Pherae, once the enemy and now, thanks to Onomarchus, the friend of the Phocians. Lycophron at once appealed for aid to Onomarchus, who sent his brother Phayllus to Thessaly with a force of 7000 men. Phayllus was defeated by Philip and ejected from Thessaly. Thereupon Onomarchus, probably soon after his retirement from Boeotia, went with his whole army to the aid of Lycophron, and being superior in numbers to Philip and his Thessalian allies, defeated them in two battles, in which the Macedonian troops lost so heavily that his mercenaries were inclined to abandon Philip. But he succeeded in reviving their spirit, and withdrew into Macedonia, as he said, 'like a ram, to butt the harder next time.' He did not fail to carry out his intention. Early in the spring of 352 Onomarchus again invaded Boeotia, and he had taken Coronea and Corsiae, when he was once more called away to oppose Philip in Thessaly. Philip had succeeded in persuading most of the Thessalians to abandon their mutual hostilities and make common cause against Lycophron's sacrilegious allies; and Onomarchus had only 20,000 infantry and 500 cavalry, to oppose a somewhat larger number of infantry and as many as 3000 cavalry. Philip inspired his men with a kind of religious zeal against the temple-robbers and decorated them with laurel as the champions of the injured god. In the battle which ensued Philip was victorious, thanks to the decisive action of his cavalry. The Phocian soldiers were driven to the sea with great slaughter. Some threw off their armour and tried to swim out to an Athenian squadron, commanded by Chares, which happened to be sailing past; but over 6000 perished, including Onomarchus himself, who, according to one account, was killed by his own men, as being the cause of the defeat; and the 3000 who were captured were thrown into the sea by Philip's orders, on the pretext of their impiety.

Philip now took Pherae, and besieged the important town of Pagasae. The inhabitants of Pagasae appealed to Athens, and an expedition was ordered to go to their relief, but did not move in time. The town passed into Philip's possession, as did the whole of Magnesia. He was now able to make such arrangements as would secure his control of Thessaly; but, when he advanced towards Thermopylae—probably about August, 352[1]—he found that the Athenians, at last aroused, had sent an expedition under Nausicles to defend the pass. History had shown that even a small force could hold the gates of Thermopylae against a very large one, and Philip, not wishing to face such a conflict, returned to Macedonia, and thence in the autumn marched once more along the Thracian coast.

The precise order of events is again uncertain; but in November, 352, he was besieging Heraeon Teichos, which (though its exact position is now unknown) was a stronghold of great im-

[1] Beloch, *loc. cit.*, dates the defeat of Onomarchus in the summer of 353, and places the capture of Pagasae before it, the capture of Pherae after it, and Philip's advance to Thermopylae late in 353.

portance in the neighbourhood of the Chersonese, and was now held by Cersobleptes. The Athenians once more had a fit of alarm, and resolved to send forty ships, carrying citizen troops, and to raise sixty talents by special taxation. But Philip fell ill and was obliged to raise the siege; a rumour of his death reached Athens; the armament was disbanded, and it was nearly a year before the Athenians took any further step.

So much is certain. It is also certain that in his hostilities against Cersobleptes Philip was now allied with Amadocus, as well as with Byzantium and Perinthus. The combined forces were victorious, and Cersobleptes was forced to give his son to Philip as a hostage. Philip also made alliance with Cardia, and the campaign served to make it plain that, unless some diplomatic settlement could be achieved, a struggle must almost inevitably take place between Philip and the Athenians for the control of the Chersonese. But in order to explain the policy of Athens during this period, it is necessary to go back a few years.

VI. ATHENIAN POLICY: ARISTOPHON, EUBULUS, DEMOSTHENES

After the banishment of Callistratus, about the year 361, the leading statesman in Athens was Aristophon, whose policy seems to have been in accordance with the imperialistic and militant predilections of the democracy, and to have been carried out, to a great extent, in conjunction with Chares, who was a hero to the masses. Thus he fought the disaffected allies, instead of meeting their suspicions in more peaceable ways, and when the allies were successful, he prosecuted the generals in true democratic style, and secured the condemnation of the unpopular Timotheus. When funds ran short, he had recourse to measures which would chiefly trouble the wealthier citizens, such as a commission to enquire into debts of the State, and the abolition of grants of immunity from taxation—a measure proposed by Leptines, but supported by Aristophon, and made more famous than its intrinsic importance would warrant by a striking speech of Demosthenes against it. Finally, when the Messenians, whose independence helped to neutralize the power of Sparta in the Peloponnese, applied to Athens for alliance (about the year 355, when Thebes, their old ally, was too much occupied with the Sacred War to attend to Peloponnesian affairs), it was probably Aristophon who secured that the request should be granted, though it might easily involve hostilities with Sparta.

But the failure of Athens against the allies, and the military and financial exhaustion which it entailed, gradually discredited the military party; and in the latter part of 355 Eubulus begins to come into prominence. His official position was that of a member of the Board which controlled the Theoric Fund. This fund consisted of the sums allocated for distribution to the people, nominally to enable them to attend the public festivals—a system which had been begun by Pericles, and was apparently renewed in the fourth century and then fused with the distribution of two obols a head to the citizens, instituted towards the end of the fifth century by the demagogue Cleophon (vol. v, p. 344). The mass of the people were naturally greatly attached to the distributions of festival-money; these not only ministered to their pleasure, but also symbolized the democratic principle that all alike were entitled to share in the profits of State-management; they were, as Demades called them, the 'cement of the democracy.' Now the aim of Eubulus was, above all, financial recuperation; and this required a change in the attitude of Athens to Hellenic affairs generally. The fact that the members of the Theoric Board held office for four years made some continuity of policy possible, and the reputation of Eubulus was such that his supporters came to fill most of the administrative posts to which appointment was made by election. This popularity Eubulus obtained by giving security to the theoric distributions. Much might be said against such a spending of public funds upon pleasures, even though some religious sentiment may still have attached itself to the festivals; and we find it said in strong terms by Demosthenes and by Aristotle. But Eubulus evidently thought it right to pay this price for the provision which he obtained thereby for the real needs of the State.

It appears that, according to the system in force, certain portions of the revenue were permanently allocated by the laws to the regular departments of State-expenditure. Whether these allocations under standing laws were supplemented by annual budgets, taking into account expenditure not covered by these laws, is uncertain. In any case, the allocations having been made, the surplus was at the disposal of the people, who could vote money from it at pleasure for military expeditions or for any object; and no doubt the Theoric Fund got its share when it was possible. Eubulus appears to have carried a law, perhaps two or three years after his election to office, that the whole surplus should always go to the Theoric Fund; but at the same time, by good administration and skilful budgeting, he secured sufficient funds to put the city into a thoroughly sound financial and military condition. He brought the number of the fleet again up to 300 triremes; he repaired the docks and fortifications; he took care, by exercising strict surveillance over officials, that the State should really receive the income to which it was entitled; he conferred benefits on trade and commerce by unobtrusive changes, such as a better procedure for the settlement of trading disputes; he improved the roads of Attica, and gave the city a good water-supply. (His predecessors had probably starved such public services in their anxiety to secure a large surplus for war.) But though he maintained a large fleet as a security for peace, he provided no funds for ambitious military designs. The Theoric Fund was to have the whole surplus; so that if any great war were undertaken, money would have to be raised by special taxation; and this also was to some extent a guarantee of peace.

The ascendancy of Eubulus, when combined with the great reluctance of the Athenians to serve in the army in person, except on short and sharp expeditions, explains in a great measure the failure of Athens to act energetically, or even to send mercenary forces to represent her, since mercenaries were very expensive. His policy was plainly justified by the condition in which Athens found herself at the end of 355. Whether it was compatible with a proper attitude towards Philip is another question; and it was upon this question that, from about 352 onwards, Athenian politicians were most sharply divided, until at last the opposite view to that of Eubulus once more prevailed.

At first Eubulus was successful enough. The peace with the allies was probably due to his influence, as well as the recall of Chares from Asia Minor, and the rejection of the appeal of the Rhodian democrats. Athens could not risk hostilities with Persia. Nor would it have been well for her to be led into war with Sparta. Consequently when the people of Megalopolis appealed to Athens for help, probably in the winter of 353–2, they met with a different reception from that which Aristophon had given to the Messenians. The cause of the appeal was an astute move made by the Spartans, who, seeing that Thebes, the chief supporter of the anti-Spartan States in the Peloponnese, was deeply involved in the Sacred War, made a proposal to the Greek States generally for the restitution of territory to its original possessors. The aim of Sparta was the recovery of her own control over Messenia and Arcadia, and she might well hope for support, not only from Elis and Phlius, parts of whose former territory were in the hands of the Arcadians and the Argives respectively, but above all from

Athens; for the Athenians had never ceased to resent the Theban occupation of Oropus, and the suppression of the Boeotian towns which had been friendly to her—Orchomenus, Thespiae and Plataea; and Athens was also an ally, at least in name, of the Phocians against Thebes. But these considerations could not weigh with Eubulus against the danger of unnecessary war with Sparta, and the people of Megalopolis went away unsatisfied. At the same time Eubulus was no undiscerning peace-fanatic. He was ready to acquiesce in Philip's conquests at Amphipolis and about the Thermaic Gulf; but Philip's approach to Thermopylae was another matter, and the expedition of Nausicles was sent promptly and with good results. The encroachments of Philip along the Thracian coast might be endured, and Cersobleptes, fortified by his understanding with Athens, might be left to resist Philip as well as he could; but the safety of the corn-route was of vital importance, and the recovery of Sestos was doubtless favoured by Eubulus, who appears to have been, on the whole, a wise and level-headed statesman, such as the time required.

It was during the early years of Eubulus' administration that Demosthenes came forward on to the political stage. He had made himself an orator by heroic persistence in overcoming his physical defects, and by persistent study of history and rhetoric; and he acquired practice in private cases, mostly of no political importance. A man of strong public spirit, he had already served twice as trierarch; and though he appears to have been personally unattractive, and was uncompromising both in his enthusiasms and his dislikes, he was filled with an intense belief in Athens as the champion of freedom—which meant, at that time, of democracy —whether against orators and generals whom he believed to be making profit for themselves instead of maintaining the traditions of the city, or against any who, like Philip and his supporters, appeared to threaten the autonomous city-state with what seemed like servitude; though men of wider outlook, like Isocrates, might see in the movement of events a progress towards the realization of Hellenic unity.

At first he seems to have supported Eubulus, so far at least as practical policy was concerned. He deprecated the idea of military preparations against Persia in 354; and, if the speech which has come down to us as the thirteenth in the Demosthenic Corpus is a true representation of his views, he had no objection in principle to the theoric distributions; in fact he himself joined in renewing them after the battle of Chaeronea, when the need for their suspension was over. But his whole bent was towards active measures: the very debate upon Persian affairs he made an occasion for suggesting (without success) a drastic reform of the trierarchic system, which would bear heavily upon citizens of substance; in the speech for the Rhodians he was ready to give active help to the exiled democrats, and was unduly confident that there was no need to fear embroilment with Caria or Persia; and throughout, while admitting the claim of the citizens to the funds of the State, he insisted that they should earn their share by practical work, and above all by service in the army. It is clear that his main object was to raise a standing army, ready to fight whenever it might be required, and throughout his early career he regarded the gratuitous distributions of festival-money as the great obstacle to this. In the matter of the appeal of Megalopolis he spoke, with an air of impartiality, but with complete conviction, in favour of the suppliants, and discounted the risk of war with Sparta; and in speaking against the law of Aristocrates he showed his desire to support the rivals of Cersobleptes, and so to neutralize the danger to Athenian interests from him and from Charidemus, whose untrustworthiness was abundantly proved. In both these speeches he made much use of the idea of the Balance of Power as the right principle of Athenian policy—the maintenance of an equipoise between Thebes and Sparta, between Amadocus and Cersobleptes—with armed intervention, if necessary, to adjust the balance. Prudence was clearly on the side of Eubulus; but when the danger to Athens from Philip seemed to be unmistakable, Demosthenes claimed to stand for a higher principle than prudence—the maintenance of the great traditions of Athens, and above all, of autonomy against tyranny. Whether he was right is a question which is not easily settled by argument; and we may conveniently return to the consideration of the course of events during the year 352.

VII. THE SACRED WAR CONTINUED, 352–347 B.C.

In the course of that year the Spartans invaded the territory of Megalopolis, perhaps some months after the rejection of the latter by Athens. The Megalopolitans, with troops sent to their aid by Argos, Sicyon and Messene, encamped near the sources of the Alpheus, and awaited the help which they had asked for from Thebes. The Spartans, on the other hand, received at once the aid of 3000 infantry from the Phocians—perhaps mercenaries who transferred their services to Sparta in the interval between the defeat of Onomarchus and the resumption of hostilities by Phayllus in the autumn of 352; and also of a small squadron of cavalry from Lycophron and Peitholaus, whom Philip had allowed to depart unharmed from Pherae. The combined Spartan army encamped near Mantinea, whence they made a surprise attack upon the Argive town of Orneae and took it, defeating the Argives who came to its assistance. The Thebans, perhaps because they had their eyes on the energetic preparations being made by Phayllus, had as yet made no move to help Megalopolis; and it was probably not until the spring of 351, when the hostility of the Phocians appeared to be less formidable, that Thebes sent 4000 infantry and 500 cavalry to join the Megalopolitans. After a doubtful battle, in which the superior numbers of the Megalopolitan and Theban army were neutralized by their inferiority in discipline, the Argives and other Peloponnesian allies of Megalopolis went home, and after storming Helissus in Arcadia, the Spartans also returned to Laconia. After an interval, hostilities were renewed; the Thebans defeated a Spartan division at Telphussa and gained the advantage in two other engagements. Then the Spartans won a considerable victory and made a truce with Megalopolis, which, however, retained its independence. The Theban forces returned to Boeotia, where they were once more required to deal with the Phocians.

Phayllus had succeeded to the command of the Phocian forces after the death of Onomarchus. Even the loss of 9000 men in the recent engagement seems not to have daunted him; the temple-treasures appeared to be inexhaustible, and he used them unscrupulously to obtain allies and mercenaries, even coining into money the blocks of gold dedicated by Croesus. From Sparta came 1000 men, from the Achaeans 2000, from Athens 5000 men and 400 cavalry under Nausicles. Lycophron and Peitholaus also joined him with 2000 mercenaries, and the gold given to the leading men in the smaller States brought its reward in troops. It was probably towards autumn (352 B.C.) when he invaded Boeotia. He was defeated with considerable loss near Orchomenus, and again in a battle near the Cephisus, and a few days later at Coronea. On this he seems to have changed his plan, and to have invaded Eastern Locris. After capturing all the other towns in this district, he was driven out of Naryx, which he had taken one night with the help of treachery. He then encamped near Abae, but the Boeotian troops inflicted great loss upon him in a night attack, and then, elated by their victory, proceeded to ravage Phocis itself and acquired rich booty. In the meantime he had renewed the attack on Naryx; the Boeotians, returning from Phocis, tried to relieve it, but were routed by Phayllus, who now took and destroyed the town. This, however, was his last success. He fell ill, and, after a long sickness, died in the course of the winter, leaving Phalaecus, the younger son of Onomarchus, in command, with Mnaseas as his guardian. But Mnaseas soon fell in a night affray, and not long afterwards (probably in the spring of 351) Phalaecus himself was worsted in a cavalry battle near Chaeronea. Little seems to have been effected by either side during most of the year, and we have seen that a Theban force was engaged in the Peloponnese. Late in the year Phalaecus succeeded in taking Chaeronea, but was expelled by the Thebans, perhaps after the troops sent to the Peloponnese had returned; and the Boeotian army once more overran Phocis, taking much plunder and destroying some of the local fortresses.

But both sides were more or less exhausted, and in the next year (350) only desultory fighting and occasional forays occurred. The Thebans, however, who were in great financial straits, sent ambassadors to Artaxerxes to ask for aid; he responded gladly, and sent them 300 talents. Evidently the expedition of Pammenes could be overlooked, and Artaxerxes, who was anxious to recover his lost empire over Egypt, Phoenicia and Cyprus, was doubtless eager for assistance from Greek troops, like that which had been so invaluable to the provinces in their revolt. Nor was he wholly disappointed (see above, p. 22).

We know little of the course of the Sacred War from this point onwards. Our chief authority, Diodorus xvi, 56 *sqq.*, crowds into the one year 347–6 events which certainly belong in part to the two years preceding. The Boeotians (according to his narrative) once more ravaged Phocis, and won a victory at Hyampolis, but were defeated, probably in 349, near Coronea by the Phocians, who, besides Coronea, held Orchomenus and Corsiae in Boeotian territory. Next we hear of the Boeotians destroying the standing corn in Phocis—this must have been in the early summer of 348 or 347—and of the Phocians ravaging Boeotia from the strongholds which they occupied; and Demosthenes also mentions engagements at Neon and Hedyleum. Phalaecus and his treasurer Philon seem to have outdone their predecessors in their disregard for the sanctity of Delphi, and Philon had actually begun excavations within the temple walls and beneath the sacred tripod in the hope of finding treasure, when a terrible earthquake, which was taken by pious minds to be a sign of the anger of Apollo, put a stop to the operations. But the concluding scenes of the Sacred War are so closely bound up with the movements of Philip that we must return to these.

VIII. THE OLYNTHIAN WAR

We have seen that in 352, and perhaps during some portion of 351, Philip was in Thrace. The order of events from the beginning of 351 to the end of 349 has been the subject of endless controversy, which the evidence is not sufficient to settle. It seems, however, that the Olynthians, who had agreed not to make alliance with Athens apart from Philip, had become mistrustful of him, and had not only begun to solicit the friendship of Athens, but had given an asylum to Arrhidaeus, who had been one of Philip's rivals for the throne, and his brother Menelaus. Philip is said to have warned them not to invite War and Violence within their borders, and he doubtless began to foster a Macedonian party within the city. He seems also to have marched through Olynthian territory on his way back from Thrace, thus making a demonstration, though one unaccompanied by hostile action; perhaps this took place in the course of a campaign against the Bisaltae, who overlapped the Chalcidic peninsula. Besides this, he was probably occupied for some time in establishing fortresses in Illyrian territory, and he made an expedition against Arybbas, king of the Molossians, by the subjugation of whom he became virtual master of a great part of Epirus. It was during the same period that his ships began to interfere seriously with the Athenians. They raided Lemnos and Imbros, and made prisoners of Athenian citizens there; they captured an Athenian fleet, carrying corn, off the south coast of Euboea; they even landed a force near Marathon, and took an Athenian state-galley on its way to a religious solemnity at Delos.

These events caused no little excitement in Athens. It may have been on account of them that in October, 351, Charidemus, now in Athenian service, was sent to the Hellespont with ten ships and five talents, with which to procure mercenaries and, no doubt, to secure the corn-route. Whether it was now or somewhat earlier that an agreement was made with Orontes, satrap of Mysia, who had already helped to supply the Athenian commanders with corn, cannot be decided. It is unsafe to conclude, with some historians, that Orontes must have been in revolt against Persia at the time of these communications; Eubulus was not anxious to provoke Persia to hostility, and Artaxerxes had every reason, at this period, for wishing to maintain peaceful relations with Athens. It is true that his enemies in Egypt had an Athenian commander to aid them; but in 350 Phocion, one of the most famous generals of Athens, was helping the Persian cause in

Cyprus; both of course were acting not as Athenians, but as captains of mercenaries. For the rest, the activities of the Athenians during 351 and 350 seem to have been confined to some rather trifling quarrels with Megara and Corinth, which led to two unimportant military excursions.

But the energy of Philip, the widening breach between him and the Olynthians, and the appeal of the latter to Athens, roused the party of action in Athens, and, perhaps in 351, perhaps not till the beginning of 349—the evidence is once more indecisive— Demosthenes for the first time took the lead in a public debate, with the speech which we know as the First Philippic. The speech is a passionate appeal to the Athenians to realize their danger from Philip, and to meet it by a consistent and energetic policy, and above all by the creation of a standing naval and military force, which could act at a moment's notice, without the delays involved in the preparation of a separate force on each occasion, under conditions which made it impossible for it to act in time. No army that Athens could create could meet Philip in the field; but such a force could make descents upon the weak points in his coast-line, blockade his harbours and protect the allies of Athens. It was, moreover, essential to his plan that the army should be composed of citizens, not of mercenaries who could not be counted upon. The fine patriotic zeal of Demosthenes must always command admiration, and on the present occasion the details of the scheme, as regards both recruitment and finance, were carefully worked out; but for the moment the speech can hardly have had more than an educative effect on the Assembly. Eubulus was evidently not prepared to act. It may be doubted also whether Demosthenes allowed sufficiently for the virtual necessity of a professional soldiery, in view of the recent developments in the art of war, the greater length of military campaigns, and the increasing pre-occupation of the Athenians with trade, which is liable to suffer heavily from the interruptions of military and naval service, and tends to require the specialization of the fighting profession. On the other hand, the habit of having their fighting done by proxy must itself have lowered the patriotic spirit of the Athenians, since there is no such stimulus to love of one's country as that which is given by fighting for it.

The appeal of Olynthus was renewed when, in the spring of 349, Philip demanded that the Olynthians should give up Arrhidaeus and Menelaus; and Demosthenes strongly supported the appeal in his first Olynthiac Oration, once more drawing a strong contrast between the persistent energy of Philip and the slowness of the Athenians both in decision and in action. While urging the preparation of a double force—part to defend Olynthus, part to carry on an offensive campaign against the Macedonian ports—he proposed that a sufficient war-tax should be levied, though he made it plain that the best course, if only the Athenians would consent to it, would be to suspend the theoric distributions and use the money for the war. Probably as the result of this debate, the alliance with Olynthus was at last made, and a considerable armament was dispatched under the command of Chares. This was to be reinforced later; but sufficient funds were not voted, and the expedition proved ineffective, probably because Chares had to raise funds by plundering friend and foe alike. That at least is what is suggested by the second Olynthiac Oration, which, delivered probably in the course of the summer of 349, appears to aim at meeting arguments which the peace-party had used, to the effect that Philip was too strong to be resisted. Demosthenes in reply maintained that power founded upon deception and aggression was essentially rotten, and drew a picture, which appears to have been almost wholly imaginary, of disunion among Philip's troops. He also returned to the attack upon the levity of the Athenians, and once more demanded of them that they should serve in person in the army and reform their financial methods.

In both the first two Olynthiac Orations Demosthenes speaks of the Thessalians as becoming restless under Philip's supremacy; his appropriation of their harbour- and market-dues bore hardly on them; and they appear to have thought of requesting him to restore the port of Pagasae to Pherae. The request may have been prompted by Peitholaus, who seems to have found his way back to Pherae; and it was necessary for Philip to go to Thessaly in person—the exact date of the expedition is uncertain—to eject Peitholaus and quiet the Thessalian unrest.

But Philip's main task was now the subjugation of Olynthus and the other towns of the Chalcidic League. Stagirus, the birthplace of Aristotle, whom Philip afterwards selected as the instructor of his son Alexander, was razed to the ground, and the Athenians did little to help the town. Chares was recalled and prosecuted for misconduct; but Charidemus, who was sent, in response to a further appeal, with eighteen ships and a large mercenary force, after making some excursions into territory which Philip had overrun and harrying Bottiaea (a district of Macedonia to the south of Pella), abandoned active warfare to indulge in gross luxury at the expense of the Olynthians.

At last the war-party in Athens ventured to demand un-ambiguously the surrender of the Theoric Fund for the purpose of the war. A decree was carried by Apollodorus that the Assembly should decide to which purpose the surplus should be applied; but the procedure which he followed was illegal; he was prosecuted and fined, and the decree invalidated. Demosthenes, with greater regard for legality, urged in the third Olynthiac Oration that the party of Eubulus should itself take the necessary steps for the repeal of the law which made the Theoric Fund inviolable, and that public funds should only be distributed to those who gave personal service, whether in the army or in administrative posts. The proposal seems to have failed, though it is evident that at the time when it was made—probably in the autumn of 349—the prospects of Olynthus had changed greatly for the worse.

The situation was now complicated by a movement against Athens in Euboea, the cities of which had been converted from the Theban to the Athenian alliance in 357. There can be little doubt that the change was due to intrigues on the part of Philip, who desired to divide the Athenian forces and distract them from the support of Olynthus. Plutarchus, the ruler of Eretria, an ally of Athens, found himself threatened by a rising under Cleitarchus, and asked the Athenians for aid. This aid Eubulus, supported by Meidias, a wealthy Athenian and a friend of Plutarchus, was prepared to give, doubtless on account of the importance of keeping control of Euboea. Demosthenes, on the other hand, opposed Plutarchus' application, the granting of which could only weaken the campaign against Philip; but in vain. A force was sent under Phocion, about February, 348, and at first fared badly, being hemmed in near Tamynae by the troops of Callias and Taurosthenes of Chalcis, who were aided by mercenaries sent from Phocis. (The circumstances under which they were dis-patched are not clear. Possibly Phalaecus had already conceived the hostility to Athens which he displayed strongly at a later period; or perhaps some of his mercenaries were allowed to occupy themselves in Euboea at a time when little fighting was going on on the mainland.) The Athenians sent some reinforce-ments, and, in view of the financial pressure, they were obliged to ask that those who could do so should undertake the expense of the trierarchy voluntarily; but the reinforcements did not start in time for the battle of Tamynae, which was brought on by a rash sally on the part of Plutarchus, and was only won with difficulty by Phocion. Callias betook himself to Philip's side; Plutarchus' conduct, and his flight before Phocion came into action, were condemned as due to treachery, and he was expelled by Phocion from Eretria. Phocion occupied the important stronghold of Zaretra, and reinforcements of cavalry arrived from Athens, probably at the beginning of April; but the campaign went badly under Molossus, who succeeded Phocion some time afterwards, and ended in the defeat and capture of Molossus, and the acknowledgment of the independence of all the Euboean towns except Carystus.

While the Euboean campaign was in progress, the Dionysiac festival took place; and Meidias, who was opposed to Demosthenes in regard to the campaign, assaulted him violently in the theatre. Demosthenes was serving voluntarily as choregus, and the assault at such a time was sacrilege, and was rendered worse by many other insults on the part of Meidias. Demosthenes obtained from the Assembly a vote of censure on Meidias, and gave notice of his intention to prosecute him for impiety. The speech which he wrote is an eloquent and uncompromising denunciation of the life-long insolence of Meidias; but (like Cicero's speech for Milo against Clodius, which it somewhat resembles) it was never delivered. The trial was postponed for more than a year, and by that time the political situation had changed. Demosthenes was then temporarily acting in harmony with Eubulus, and so was content to compromise, and to accept half a talent from Meidias in atonement of the injury.

While the Athenians were engaged in Euboea, Philip had not been idle. Throughout the early part of 348 he was taking the Chalcidic towns in quick succession, more by the help of his hirelings in each than by force. All the time he appears to have kept up the pretence that he intended no hostility against Olynthus itself, and his hired accomplices in the city, Euthycrates and Lasthenes, no doubt tried to foster the illusion; and it was not until he had taken Mecyberna, the port of Olynthus, and the important town of Torone, that he threw off the mask and told the Olynthians that their continuance in Olynthus was incompatible with his continuance in Macedonia. The Athenians, again appealed to, were in difficulties in Euboea, but the charges against Chares, which had not yet come to trial, were hurriedly dropped, and he was sent off with 2000 citizen foot-soldiers and 300 cavalry. Once more it was too late; the winds were contrary, and the traitors in Olynthus had done their work. They betrayed their cavalry to Philip on the field of battle, and in August, 348, the town capitulated. The inhabitants were sold into slavery; Arrhidaeus and Menelaus were put to death; lands, property and

captives were distributed among leading Macedonians and other
friends of Philip, and, according to Demosthenes' statement,
thirty-two towns in the peninsula were entirely wiped out. The
accounts which have come down to us may be somewhat exaggerated, and Philip was only doing on a large scale what Chares
had done on a small at Sestos in the name of Athens; but the
destruction was probably without a parallel in Greek history.
While the Athenians did what they could for the relief of the
fugitives, Philip held high festival in Macedonia, and celebrated
his conquests by games, dramatic performances and abundant
feasting.

IX. THE PEACE OF PHILOCRATES, AND THE END OF THE SACRED WAR

But Philip had for some time been anxious for peace with
Athens. Probably he intended to assert his supremacy in due
time over her and the other Greek states; but the time was not
yet, and the Athenian ships were in the meantime capable of
inflicting no little injury on his coasts and hindering his operations.
There was still something to be done before he could regard even
Thrace as a secure possession; and before he could claim the
overlordship of Greece, there would be much preliminary work
to do. So he proceeded to approach Athens, as he had once
approached Amphipolis and Olynthus, with professions of friendly
feeling. Some such messages were sent, even before the fall of
Olynthus, through an Athenian named Phrynon, whom he had
captured and released, and through Ctesiphon, who had been sent
to ask Philip for the return of the money paid for Phrynon's
ransom. The Assembly welcomed the messages, and on the
proposal of Philocrates it was resolved to allow Philip's representatives to come to Athens to propose the terms of an understanding. But about this time the fall of Olynthus and its attendant
horrors shocked the Athenians so greatly that, instead of sending
any such invitation, they resolved, on the motion of Eubulus
himself, to make an attempt to unite all the Greek States against
Philip.

The proposal was eloquently advocated by Aeschines, an
orator who now for the first time took a prominent part in public
life. A man of great natural gifts and good education, he had
once been obliged to follow somewhat humble callings—those of
schoolmaster, actor and clerk in a public office; but, with his
brother Aphobetus, he had for some time been a supporter of
Eubulus, and on the present occasion he took an active part in the

embassies which were sent to invite the Greek States to a congress, to discuss the measures to be taken against Philip. But despite the eloquent indignation of Aeschines the embassies failed; the natural disunion of the States, and a certain want of imagination (such as had on other occasions prevented the Spartans from anticipating any possible danger to themselves) led them to turn a deaf ear; and there was nothing for it but to make peace. Informal messages passed for some time, gradually becoming more definite, until (probably in the late summer of 347) one of the messengers, the Athenian actor Aristodemus, was awarded a crown by the Council on the motion of Demosthenes, who was now as much convinced as anyone of the necessity of peace, and was acting in harmony with Eubulus. Demosthenes even defended Philocrates, who had been arraigned by one Lycinus for the illegality of his original peace-proposal, and secured for him an easy acquittal.

But a new complication was introduced into the situation by the turn of events in the Sacred War (see above, p. 227). In the course of 347, if not earlier, dissensions had arisen in the Phocian ranks. Phalaecus was accused of appropriating the temple treasures to his own use, and the Phocian government deposed him from his command. Three generals, Deinocrates, Callias and Sophanes were appointed in his place, and his treasurer, Philon, was tortured till he revealed his companions in theft, and died miserably. Evidently, however, Phalaecus retained the support of a large body of mercenaries; he appears to have made his headquarters not far from Thermopylae: and the Thebans, suffering severely from loss of men and lack of funds, applied to Philip for aid. Philip was well content to see their humiliation; and, to lower their 'Leuctric pride' still further, he only sent a few soldiers—just enough to show that he was not indifferent to the sacrilege at Delphi. An attempt of the Phocians to fortify Abae was defeated, and a number of them who took sanctuary in Apollo's temple there perished in an accidental conflagration. Both sides now appealed for allies, the Boeotians once more to Philip, the Phocians—probably, that is, the home-government of Phocis, which had appointed Deinocrates and his colleagues—to Sparta and Athens. The Phocians offered to give into the hands of the Athenians the strongholds which commanded the Pass of Thermopylae, if the Athenians would assist them. In consideration of this, Athens sent Proxenus, probably in the autumn of 347, to take possession of the strongholds, and ordered the equipment of fifty ships with citizen troops. But Proxenus found

Phalaecus, and not a representative of the Phocian government, at Thermopylae, and Phalaecus repudiated the agreement with contumely; the ships, of course, were not sent. Archidamus, who was sent from Sparta with 1000 men, also received a rebuff and returned home. It seems to have been generally assumed that Philip was about to join forces with the Thessalians, and to settle the Sacred War adversely to the Phocians; but for the present he concealed his hand, doubtless waiting for the development of the Athenian inclination for peace, and watching for the right moment to intervene in the war. The only action which he is known to have taken about this time was in support of the Thessalian town of Pharsalus against Halus, which was on terms of friendship with Athens, and was probably assisted by the presence of Athenian ships.

The movement for peace came to a head in Athens early in 346. On the motion of Philocrates, it was resolved to send ten ambassadors, accompanied by a representative of the allies of Athens, to Philip. The ambassadors included several of those through whom the previous informal communications had passed, as well as Philocrates himself, Aeschines and Demosthenes. It was thus representative both of the supporters and of the opponents of Eubulus, both parties being temporarily at one as regards the peace. The ambassadors sailed with the least possible delay, landed at Halus, which was being besieged by Parmenion, Philip's ablest general, and then hastened overland to Pella, where Philip received them very graciously. Aeschines (according to his own account of the proceedings, which is the only one that we possess) devoted his speech mainly to the Athenian claim to Amphipolis; other speakers must have discussed the questions relating to the Chersonese, the Phocians and Halus; Demosthenes, who spoke last, broke down from nervousness. He was never a ready extempore speaker, and it is quite likely that the nine or ten earlier speeches may have left him at a loss for arguments.

Philip's reply was friendly in tone. The claim to Amphipolis, indeed, he must have plainly rejected; but he promised to take no hostile steps against the Chersonese while the negotiations were in progress, and offered to do great things for Athens, if he were granted an alliance with her, as well as the Peace. His manner, as well as his offers, made a very favourable impression upon the ambassadors, and particularly upon Aeschines, who had hitherto been one of his most outspoken enemies; and they did not fail to declare this impression to the Council and the Assembly on their return to Athens, though Demosthenes, who had fallen out with his colleagues, criticized them somewhat peevishly for their flattery, and simply proposed in unvarnished language that Philip's envoys should be received with the usual civilities, and that two days should be set apart for the discussion of the Peace in the Assembly.

The two debates were held about the middle of April, 346. The course of the proceedings is known only from the contradictory accounts given several years later by Demosthenes and Aeschines, at a time when each was eager to prove that he had had nothing to do with a Peace which had ended, as this was destined to end, in the sacrifice of the Phocians. But apparently there were two proposals before the Assembly, the one formulated by the Synod of the allies of Athens, that any Greek State (and therefore, of course, the Phocians and Halus) should have the opportunity of joining in the Peace within the next three months: the other put forward by Philocrates, who was no doubt closely in touch with Philip's envoys, Antipater and Parmenion, that the Athenians should make an alliance as well as a Peace with Philip, but that the Phocians and Halus should not be permitted to join in it. The Assembly was evidently anxious to save the Phocians; but in the interval between the two debates, the chief statesmen must have become aware that Philip would not agree to this, and apparently Antipater, when publicly interrogated by Demosthenes, said so plainly. The attempt was then made to get the Assembly to approve the Peace and the alliance, without any express mention of the Phocians or Halus being inserted in the terms, but with an assurance, given almost certainly by Aeschines, that Philip really intended to behave as the Athenians desired, though his close connection with the Thebans and Thessalians forbad him to say so expressly. There is no reason to doubt that Aeschines believed this, however severely he may be criticized for allowing himself to be deceived by Philip's conciliatory manner. But even this failed; and it was only when Eubulus pointed out that there was no alternative between simple acceptance and the renewal of war, and that the latter would involve the sacrifice of the festival-money to pay the expense, that the Assembly yielded. It was then agreed that peace should be made by Athens and her allies with Philip and his allies, each party retaining what they possessed at the time of the ratification. Thus Philip kept Amphipolis, the Athenians the Chersonese, except Cardia. A few days later, in the presence of Antipater and Parmenion, the Peace was sworn to by the Athenians and their allies. A demand made by a representative of Cersobleptes that his master should be

included among the allies was quite rightly rejected by Demosthenes, as president of the Assembly for the day; since
Cersobleptes, though on friendly terms with Athens, was not a
member of her alliance.

The ten ambassadors who had previously served were directed
to go once more to Philip, to receive the oaths of himself and his
allies, and to procure the freedom of the Athenians who were
prisoners in his hands. The differences which had sprung up
between Demosthenes and his colleagues on the first embassy
now made themselves felt more acutely. There is no doubt that
Aeschines and Philocrates, supported by Eubulus and his party,
desired a permanent settlement with Philip; while Demosthenes,
though convinced of the necessity of peace for the moment, was
still irreconcilable, and looked on the Peace simply as a breathing-
space, during which Athens could recover herself before renewing
what was, for him, the conflict between the free city-state and the
tyrant. In consequence he was anxious to give Philip as little
opportunity as possible of extending those possessions which
would be his from the moment of his taking the oath. Philip had,
in fact, been occupied, while the Peace was being discussed at
Athens, in the effectual subjugation of Cersobleptes, whose title
to participate in the Peace he had never recognized; and, probably
on the very day before the Athenians themselves swore to the
Peace, he had completed his occupation of a series of fortified
places in Thrace by the capture of Cersobleptes himself in the
stronghold known as the Sacred Mountain; any opposition which
Chares and his mercenaries may have offered was without effect;
and before the ambassadors obtained an interview with him, he
had taken possession of the Odrysian Kingdom, leaving Cersobleptes himself there as a vassal-prince, and retaining his son as
a hostage.

Demosthenes was naturally anxious that the ambassadors
should accomplish their mission with all speed; but it was
necessary for him to procure a special decree of the Council,
before they could be induced to move at all. They delayed on
the journey; they did not follow the instruction that they were to
join Proxenus and his ships, and cause him to carry them to any
place where they could find Philip; but, after meeting Proxenus,
they went to Pella, and waited there for about a month before
Philip arrived, having made his Thracian conquests secure. It
was fifty days since they had left Athens. Their object in delaying
their approach to Philip is unknown; Demosthenes imputed it to
deliberate treachery, conceived under the influence of presents

from Philip; but of this there is no further proof, nor is it clear that their greater haste would really have effected any change in Philip's plans, or that it could have availed to check his seizure of places in Thrace, even though they were defended in part by Athenian soldiers fighting, under the generalship of Chares, for Cersobleptes.

The Athenian ambassadors found envoys from many other Greek States assembled at Pella—Thebans, eager to secure Philip's immediate aid against the Phocians; Spartans, Euboeans, Phocians (though whether of Phalaecus' following, or of the party in power in Phocis, is unknown)—each with their own object, for which they desired his good-will, and each beguiled, with his characteristic skill, into thinking that they had attained it. Demosthenes differed strongly from his colleagues not only in his ultimate aim, but also in regard to the policy to be pursued at the moment. It followed from his desire to renew the struggle against Philip, when occasion offered, that he would not wish to weaken Thebes, or to take any step which might prevent an alliance of Thebes and Athens against Philip. His colleagues, who in this were in sympathy with the general feeling of the Athenians, were hostile to Thebes and anxious to save the Phocians; and when the ambassadors were granted an interview with Philip, Aeschines did all he could to promote this object, laying stress upon all that could be said against the Thebans in their conduct of the Sacred War, and pleading for a solution, not by armed intervention, but by a vote of the Amphictyonic Council, to be given after both sides had been heard. Demosthenes, who had spoken first, seems again to have cut a poor figure, hinting at the differences of opinion between himself and his colleagues, commending himself for the civilities which he had shown to Philip's envoys, and at the same time mocking his colleagues for the flattery which they had bestowed upon Philip. Philip was certainly not diverted a hair's breadth from his plan by the orators, but he seems to have led Aeschines genuinely to believe that he intended the Phocians no harm, and his air of friendliness was enhanced by lavish presents to the ambassadors, which all but Demosthenes accepted without misgiving. He declared his consent to the Peace, but did not take the oath until, accompanied by his army and escorted by the ambassadors, he had marched southward as far as Pherae. Here also the ambassadors received the oaths of Philip's allies, instead of visiting their cities for the purpose as they had been instructed to do. At some stage in the proceedings Philip must have made it clear that the Phocians and Halus were not included in the Peace, and in fact Halus was forced to surrender to him not long afterwards, and was treated with great severity. Demosthenes, being unable to act with his colleagues in regard to the Phocian question, had devoted himself chiefly to the interests of the Athenian prisoners, and these Philip promised to send home in time for the Panathenaic festival.

When Philip had taken the oath, the ambassadors returned home, sending before them a despatch announcing the results of the mission. Before they reached Athens, about July 7, Philip was at Thermopylae. The Athenian Council was so far impressed by the charges of breach of instructions which Demosthenes brought against his colleagues that it neither gave them the usual vote of thanks nor the complimentary feast which generally went with it. But the Assembly was carried away by Aeschines' declaration that in a few days they would see Thebes besieged by Philip and punished for the contemplated occupation of the temple of Delphi; Thespiae and Plataea would then be rebuilt, and (he hinted) Oropus would be restored to Athens. A letter from Philip was read, in which he took upon himself the blame for the ambassadors' failure to carry out their instructions literally, and offered to do anything that he could honourably do to satisfy the Athenians. Demosthenes (according to his own account) was refused a hearing, when he rose to express his disbelief in these assurances, and the Assembly laughed with delight when Philocrates cried, 'No wonder that Demosthenes and I disagree; he drinks water; I drink wine.' The Assembly passed the motion of Philocrates, thanking Philip for his righteous intentions, extending the alliance first made to his posterity, and calling upon the Phocians to surrender the temple to the Amphictyons and lay down their arms; failing which, Athens would take arms against them.

Clearly the Assembly must have been convinced that Philip intended to treat both the Phocians and Athens generously, and this impression must have been due to the assurances of Aeschines and his colleagues; otherwise its action, considering the favour with which it had always regarded the Phocians, is inexplicable. The same confidence was probably the reason for their declining Philip's invitation to them to send an army to join him at Thermopylae, and assist in the settlement of the matters which concerned the Amphictyonic powers, though Demosthenes and Hegesippus (a violent anti-Macedonian), who recommended the refusal of the invitation, may themselves have desired to avoid any such clash of Athenian and Theban policies at Thermopylae as would have rendered subsequent co-operation against Philip difficult. The refusal was almost certainly a mistake, since it deprived Athens of all influence in the settlement of North Greece.

However this may be, the Athenians were suddenly startled by the news that on the day after the resolution of Philocrates had been passed, Phalaecus had surrendered to Philip at Thermopylae. The news was brought by the ambassadors sent to inform Philip of that resolution, who had turned back in alarm on hearing it at Chalcis. For a moment the Athenians were panic-stricken, and thinking that Philip's next move would be against themselves, ordered defensive measures to be taken immediately, at the same time sending the ambassadors once more on their journey, to use such influence as they could upon Philip in his camp.

The surrender of Phalaecus was no doubt due to the disunion in the Phocian ranks, and the exhaustion of his funds. He was allowed to depart with a force of 8000 mercenaries. After various adventures, he perished towards the end of the year in Crete, where he and his men had taken part in a quarrel between Cnossus and some other Cretan towns. Those who survived of his army met their end in 343 in Elis, where they had sold their swords to some Elean exiles desirous of restoration. The historian Diodorus does not fail to draw a moral from the fate of the sacrilegious Phocians and their allies, and notes with satisfaction how Archidamus, who had once helped them, afterwards died in battle in Italy, where he had gone to help the people of Tarentum against their Lucanian neighbours (see p. 300).

On the surrender of Phalaecus, some of the Phocian towns capitulated to Philip, and those which did not were rapidly reduced. Many of the inhabitants fled to Athens and were welcomed there. Philip appears to have been both surprised and annoyed at the manner in which Athens had received the news of his action, and sent a letter, strongly worded, protesting that the Phocians had not been included in the treaty of peace, and that he was acting within his rights.

The fate of the Phocians was left to be determined by the Amphictyonic Council. After more barbarous proposals had been rejected, it was resolved that the Phocian towns should be dismantled, and the citizens dispersed into villages of not more than fifty houses each, with at least 200 yards' interval between one village and another; that they should repay the value of the temple-treasures by annual instalments, and should not bear arms or own horses until complete restitution had been made, and that the fugitives of the sacrilegious race should be liable to seizure in any country. The destructive part of the sentence was carried out by the Thebans, and Demosthenes, three years later, drew an impressive picture of the desolation which was caused, though, judged by Greek standards, their fate was not a specially cruel one, and the fact that the repayment to the temple began within three years, and proceeded without interruption, shows that they must soon have recovered some measure of prosperity. Some of the Phocian territory was occupied by Thebes; the Boeotian towns which had joined the Phocians against Thebes were destroyed and their inhabitants enslaved. The Phocians lost their votes in the Amphictyonic Council, and votes were now assigned to Philip and to the Delphians, who resumed charge of the temple. Sparta also is said to have lost her Amphictyonic rights, but the evidence of inscriptions leaves this very doubtful. Athens was deprived of her right to precedence in the consultation of the oracle.

To assert before the world his newly-acquired dignity, Philip was appointed to preside over the forthcoming Pythian games; but Athens and Sparta, by way of protest, refused to send the customary deputations to attend the festival. Accordingly Philip demanded from Athens a formal recognition of himself as a member of the Amphictyonic Council, and Aeschines argued in favour of this recognition, on the ground that the adverse action of the Council had been due to the preponderant influence of the Thessalians and Thebans. But the Assembly refused to give him a hearing, and it was not until Demosthenes himself, who saw that Athens could not at present resist the forces of Philip and his allies, recommended the Athenians to accede to Philip's request, that they submitted. In the speech *On the Peace*, which was delivered on this occasion, he professed to make light of the matter; but there can be no doubt that the Athenians felt their humiliation greatly.

Thus, by the autumn of 346, Philip had become by far the strongest power in the Greek world. His influence extended over nearly the whole of North Greece, and over all Thrace, with the exception of the Chersonese, and he was already entering into communication with some of the Peloponnesian States. There was good reason for Isocrates' anticipation that the day of small states was done, and that the Greek peoples could achieve well-being, if at all, only by subordination to such a controlling power as Philip. Whether he was right in the further view which he expressed in a pamphlet addressed to Philip just at this time, that they would achieve unity best by combining in a common enterprise against the Persian Empire, is perhaps less certain. Probably some such project was already in the mind of Philip; but the unity which the enterprise, when it was undertaken, did impose was but superficial.

The significance of Philip's success, apart from the proof which it gave of his own skill in planning movements and playing upon both individuals and peoples, was that it emphasized unmistakably the advantages of central and personal control, as compared with the Athenian method of government by discussion with its inevitable delays, its spasmodic activities, its fluctuations of policy, constant only in its assumption that the one thing that ultimately mattered was that the festival-money should not be interfered with; and there was also plainly to be seen the immeasurably greater efficiency of the united Macedonian army, when compared with the disconnected bands of mercenaries who for the most part represented the Greek cities.

Philip, no doubt, was aware of these advantages, and so was Isocrates, who, as a reflective spectator of events, was in some ways more clear-sighted than the politicians themselves. Demosthenes was also aware of them, and it was for that reason that he strove with all his eloquence to rouse his fellow-citizens to fight and act for themselves, and to act in accordance with some consistent policy; and for the same reasons he desired to bring about a combination between Athens and Thebes, such as alone could offer any hope of successful resistance to Philip. Clearly he did not despair of the free city-state. It was his detestation of what seemed to him to be foreign domination that animated all his efforts, and he claimed with justice to be upholding the traditions of which Athens was most proud.

Of his opponents, and in particular of Aeschines, it is less easy to speak with confidence. The charges of corruption which Demosthenes brought against Aeschines are certainly not proved. Philip did, it is true, use money freely to open the gates of cities and to foster Macedonian parties within their walls; but Demosthenes, with all his greatness, was one of those unfortunate persons who find it difficult to ascribe a good motive when they can imagine a bad one; and he saw corruption everywhere. There is no reason to doubt that Aeschines, after the example of his first political leader Eubulus, was convinced that a peace with Philip which secured the Chersonese for Athens, gave her freedom from war, and included (as it did) provisions for the suppression of piracy and the security of the trade-routes by the joint action of

Philip and the Athenians, was a compromise worth accepting, even if Amphipolis and most of the Thracian coast passed finally out of Athenian control. As for the Phocians, he had done his best to help them both at Philip's court and at the Amphictyonic Council; and it was by no means certain that Philip intended anything but friendship towards Athens. In truth, little substantial criticism can be passed upon the main policy of either party at Athens. The divergence between men with imperialistic sentiments and a pride in national traditions, and men whose instinct leads them to care most for peace, with economic prosperity and financial stability, is one which exists everywhere, and is not discreditable to either side. If criticism is to be passed it must be rather upon those faults of temper which marred the attempts of both sides to carry out their policy,—upon the rancour shown by Demosthenes both towards Philip and towards his political opponents in Athens, when a more reasonable demeanour might have secured better results even from his own point of view; upon the liability of Aeschines and his friends to be deceived by Philip's generosity and his well-timed assurances of good-will; and upon the readiness of both to distort the truth, whether in the Assembly or in the Law Courts. These defects will appear still more plainly in the years which form the subject of the next chapter.

CHAPTER IX

MACEDONIAN SUPREMACY IN GREECE

I. YEARS OF NOMINAL PEACE BETWEEN PHILIP AND ATHENS, 346–343 B.C.

AFTER the final ratification of the Peace and the consolidation of his latest conquests in Thrace, Philip devoted his attention to the carrying out of plans for the securing of his frontiers, and, in all probability, for the civilizing of all parts of his kingdom. His coast-line was already secure; but far inland there was always the menace of outbreaks by wild tribes, and, to counter this, he planted colonies in the frontier regions; and at the same time he settled the former inhabitants of Chalcidice and the Thracian coast in various parts of his kingdom, where they might be centres of hellenizing influence. His own court was always such a centre; the most eminent Greek poets and artists were made at home there; Aristotle was appointed as tutor to Alexander; and there is some evidence that Philip made a point of including influential Greeks among his 'Companions,' and of otherwise conferring distinction upon them.

His northern and western frontiers, however, continued to give trouble; and in 344 he was obliged to undertake an expedition against the Illyrians who were subject to Pleuratus. The pursuit of this king probably took him nearly to the Adriatic, and cost him a severe wound in the leg.

This done, he turned his attention to Thessaly, where, apparently with the good-will of the Thessalian peoples, he entirely changed the government of the country. In 344 he was appointed 'archon,' or ruler, of Thessaly for his life; the public revenues of the Thessalian states and regular contingents of Thessalian soldiers were placed at his disposal; the country was divided into four tetrarchies, each with a reliable governor, and the whole province seems to have been united in a personal loyalty to himself, which henceforth remained unshaken, and was sufficient to prevent the revival of the constant quarrels of former days between different regions and princes. Isocrates took occasion at this time to address a letter to Philip, in which he invited him to show the same tact in conciliating Athens as he had shown towards the Thessalians.

But Athens was in no mood for conciliation. Demosthenes had announced in 346 his intention of prosecuting Aeschines for corruption on the Second Embassy to Philip, and had only been caused to postpone the case by a successful counter-stroke of Aeschines, who secured the condemnation of Timarchus, Demosthenes' associate in the prosecution, for the immoral habits of his youth, and thus brought some reflected discredit upon Demosthenes himself. About the same time the Athenians had tried to re-open the question of the inclusion of Cersobleptes in the Peace, sending Eucleides to Philip for the purpose; and they had rejected Philip's attempt to win their favour by offering to cut a channel through the Chersonese, and so give them a defensible frontier against the Thracians.

In the Peloponnese an equilibrium seems to have been maintained, for about two years after the Peace of Philocrates, between Sparta and the peoples opposed to her,—the Messenians, the Arcadians of Megalopolis, and the Argives. But in 344 Sparta showed signs once more of a desire to interfere with them, and they appealed to Philip for support. Probably he had for some time been fostering parties favourable to himself in these States, and he now supplied them with money and mercenaries, and ordered Sparta to abstain from troubling them, threatening to march into the Peloponnese in person to their support, if the warning were disregarded. The anti-Macedonian party in Athens were naturally roused, and Demosthenes returned to the policy, which he advocated in 353, of supporting the minor states against Sparta, in the hope of persuading them that Athens, and not Philip, was their friend. He himself, as well as other orators, went to the Peloponnesian towns, and warned them in eloquent language that the fate which awaited them was that of Olynthus or of Thessaly, which they represented as having been subjugated by Philip by means of pretended kindness. But all this eloquence could not do away with the facts, that Athens and Sparta had been closely associated in recent years; that Athens had done nothing to help the Peloponnesian towns when she was appealed to previously; and that Thessaly had actually benefited greatly by the changes made by Philip. Instead, therefore, of breaking with Philip, the Arcadians invited him to be their welcome guest, whenever he wished, and set up his statue in bronze at Megalopolis; Argos voted him a golden crown; and Argos and Messene sent ambassadors to Athens to express their resentment of her attempt to weaken them in their resistance to the encroachments of Sparta. Philip also sent a formal protest against the orator's allegation that he had been faithless to his promises, and demanded its withdrawal. The Second Philippic of Demosthenes was delivered in one of the debates upon these protests. It was an attempt to prove that Philip, by his friendships with the Peloponnesians and Thebans, was aiming at isolating Athens with a view to her ultimate subjection, and that he was being assisted in Athens itself by the orators whom he had corrupted.

Philip's party appear to have made the most of the rumours (which would be welcome to the Athenians as a whole) that some coolness was springing up between Thebes and Philip, and that Philip was inclined to be more gracious to the Phocians, about whose overthrow Athens was still feeling very sore; and they may have quoted these rumours (which Demosthenes treats with contempt) as evidence of Philip's good intentions. It is at least possible that there was a real difference of opinion between Philip and the Thebans in regard to exaction of the repayment on account of the temple-treasures from the Phocians. This repayment had not so far been enforced, and Philip may have stood in the way of the Theban desire to enforce it. (This would not be the only case in history in which victorious allies have differed in regard to the exaction of reparations.) Moreover if Philip, though as yet the friend of the Thebans, intended to be their master in the end, he may not have desired to destroy utterly the Phocian people who might at some time be useful as a counterpoise to Thebes in North Greece. But any difference of opinion between them on this matter was not yet serious; and though the issue of the debate at Athens is not recorded, it is not likely that it was favourable to Philip.

That Philip was genuinely anxious to be on good terms with Athens, in spite of herself, is shown by an incident, small in itself, which occurred about this time. Athens was mistress of the sacred island of Delos, and the islanders appealed to the Amphictyonic Council for liberation from Athenian rule. Despite the fact that the anti-Macedonian Hypereides had been substituted by the Council of Areopagus for Aeschines as the Athenian advocate in the matter, the Amphictyonic Council, in which the influence of Philip was now preponderant, gave its decision in favour of Athens.

The anti-Macedonian party was not to be moved by any such courtesies. Hypereides now indicted Philocrates for corruption and deception of the people, and Philocrates withdrew from Athens before the hearing; he was condemned to death in his absence, and, if any reliance can be placed upon the statements of Demosthenes, he had in fact profited very largely by Philip's generosity.

Yet once more Philip attempted to conciliate the unwilling people. Early in 343 he sent Python of Byzantium, with some representatives of his allies, to express his good-will to Athens, his regret at the attitude which certain orators had led her to adopt, and his readiness to amend the terms of the Peace if good reason could be shown. Python, himself an eloquent orator, was supported by Aeschines, and the invitation to reconsider the terms of the Peace was accepted; but the alterations actually proposed by Athens were such as Philip could not possibly accept. They desired that instead of the clause which gave to each party to the Peace 'what they possessed,' there should be an agreement that each should retain 'what was their own'—a phrase which scarcely veiled the intention of the Athenians to claim Amphipolis and Potidaea once more, as well as Cardia; they wished also to include in the Peace all the Greek States (and of course Cersobleptes), and to arrange mutual guarantees between the States against aggression. The Athenian envoy Hegesippus who bore these requests to Philip made the situation worse by his violent language and bad manners. The proposals were of course rejected, and Philip must now have seen that all hope of a friendly understanding with Athens was over.

Even so, negotiations continued for some time upon minor points, and particularly in regard to the island of Halonnesus, to the north of Euboea, which the Athenians, who claimed it as their own, had allowed to become infested with pirates. Philip had expelled the pirates, and offered (after the discussion had gone on for about a year) to give it to Athens. The Athenians, on the proposal of Demosthenes, supported in intemperate language by Hegesippus, refused to take it unless he offered to give it *back*, and also declined to refer the matter to arbitration; and so the negotiations came to an end.

Before this a definite trial of strength had taken place between the two parties in Athens. In the summer of 343 Demosthenes renewed his prosecution of Aeschines for corruption when on the Embassy. But unpopular as the Peace was, disastrous as it had been to the Phocians, towards whom the Athenians seem to have felt a peculiar tenderness, and eloquent and impressive as was the speech which he delivered, Demosthenes failed to make good his case, and Aeschines was acquitted by a majority of 30 votes out of 1501. The support given to him by Eubulus (of whom we now hear for the last time) and by the honest and blunt-spoken general

Phocion must have told greatly in his favour; but in fact he was not only able to reply convincingly to many of the charges which were made against him, but was also able to show that it was he, and not Demosthenes, who had been the friend of the Phocians throughout; and the nobility of the principles to which Demosthenes appealed cannot blind us to the grossness of his distortions of the truth. The special emphasis laid by him on the misery of the Phocians may possibly be connected with the fact that now for the first time they were beginning to pay the instalments due to the temple. If Philip had abstained from enforcing these out of consideration for the feelings of Athens, he must have felt that there was no longer anything to be gained by doing so.

But the set-back to the anti-Macedonian party through the loss of this case was only temporary. They continued to direct the policy of Athens for some years from this time; and if we are to treat as typical the story of the arrest by Demosthenes of a certain Antiphon, on the pretext that he was a spy, and of the torture and execution of Antiphon by order of the Council of Areopagus, they even resorted to terrorism to quell opposition.

The behaviour of the Athenians appears to have led Philip to abandon, from 343 onwards, the attempt to conciliate them, and a series of events which occurred about this time, and which were very unwelcome to Athens, was, it cannot be doubted, due to his instigation. In the summer of 343 (probably after the mission of Hegesippus to Philip, but before the trial of Aeschines), the Macedonian party in Elis, aided by the Arcadians, asserted itself and gained the mastery; its opponents were massacred in great numbers. (It was in this affair that the last relics of the army of Phalaecus met their end.) At Megara, Perillus and Ptoeodorus, two of Philip's friends, aided by mercenaries sent by him, attempted to seize the power, and were only prevented by a hasty expedition from Athens under Phocion, who occupied the port of Megara and so gained control of the town. An alliance between Athens and Megara was then arranged by Demosthenes. It was much more serious that a great part of Euboea fell into the power of Philip's friends, through the overthrow of the democracy in Eretria by Cleitarchus, and in Oreus by Philistides. It was only a partial compensation for this that Chalcis, led by Callias and Taurosthenes, transferred its friendship from Thebes to Athens.

Philip was also active in Epirus. Late in 343 he expelled Arybbas from the Molossian kingdom, and replaced him by Alexander, the brother of Olympias. He also increased Alexander's kingdom by conquering and adding to it the region of

Cassopia. But when he threatened Ambracia and Leucas, which were colonies of Corinth, and the Corinthians appealed to Athens for help, the Athenians, who had already given a home and citizenship to Arybbas, sent a force to defend Ambracia, and promised also to assist Naupactus, which Philip proposed to take and hand over to the Aetolians, as the price of their friendship; and the move was so far successful that Philip did not think it well to proceed against either place, and returned to Macedonia.

The Athenians, at the same time, were using all the resources of diplomacy to detach from Philip his allies in Thessaly and the Peloponnese. In Thessaly there is no sign that they met with any success, unless the replacement of the Thessalian garrison, which Philip had left in Nicaea in 346, by a Macedonian force may be taken to show that he at any rate preferred to have the command of the Pass of Thermopylae in his own hands. But in the Peloponnese, where most of the leading orators of the anti-Macedonian party were active, they succeeded in renewing the former friendship of Athens with the Messenians, and in securing at least the nominal alliance of the Achaeans (whose colony at Naupactus had been threatened by Philip), the Argives, and the Arcadians of Megalopolis, though none of these peoples can be supposed to have abandoned in consequence their existing alliance with Philip.

II. THE RELATIONS OF PHILIP AND THE GREEK CITIES WITH PERSIA

The scene now changes to Thrace; but before pursuing the course of events there, it will be well to notice a somewhat significant event, which happened at about the same time as the mission of Python to Athens in 343. This was the arrival in Greece of an embassy from Artaxerxes Ochus, asking for alliance and friendship from each of the more important States. For many years the Great King had found it difficult to retain his hold upon his outlying dominions[1]. There had been repeated revolts of the satraps of Asia Minor; two attempts made by Ochus to recover Egypt had failed; the revolt of Sidon and the rest of the Phoenician dominions of the King had only been crushed by the help of the gross treachery which led to the surrender of Sidon in 345 or 344; Cyprus, which had also revolted, was reduced about the same time through the assistance given by Phocion and a

---

[1] For a more detailed account of these events, see above, pp. 21 *sqq.* The chronology is disputed; see especially Beloch, *Griechische Geschichte*, III², 2, pp. 284–7, and Cloché, *Revue Égyptologique*, 1919, pp. 210 *sqq.*

Greek mercenary force at the request of Idrieus, the satrap of
Caria, whom the King had requested to undertake the task. Ochus
was now anxious to make another attempt to recover Egypt, and
to do so with the help of those Greek troops and generals whose
value he well knew; for Nectanebo II, the reigning Pharaoh,
had gained his power largely by the help of Agesilaus, and had
repelled the second invasion by the army of Ochus mainly owing
to the aid of Diophantus of Athens and Lamius of Sparta; and
Greek mercenaries had taken an important part on one side or
the other in nearly all the conflicts in which the Persians had
recently been engaged. In answer to his overtures, the Athenians
replied that their friendship with the King would remain, so long
as he did not interfere with any Greek cities. This was another
way of saying that they did not intend to give him any active help;
this abstention from any Persian quarrel which did not involve
Hellenic interests was just the policy which Demosthenes had
advocated in 354 and 353, and he had evidently not changed his
view. Sparta also was unresponsive. But the Thebans, who had
received large subsidies from Persia in the Sacred War, as well as
the Argives, sent contingents to help the King, when he once
more invaded Egypt, after a temporary set-back owing to the
missing of the way in crossing the Serbonian marshes, and the
consequent loss of many of his troops. This time the invasion was
a complete success; in the winter of 343–2 Nectanebo was compelled to flee, and Egypt was re-organized as a Persian province.

At what time the Persian King became aware that Philip was
a power to be taken seriously is unknown. At a later date Darius
wrote to Alexander the Great, reminding him of Philip's friendship and alliance with Ochus; and, as early as the First Philippic,
Demosthenes speaks of a rumour that Philip had sent ambassadors
to the King. It is possible that Philip had wished to secure himself
against any interference on the part of Persia with his conquest
of Thrace; but the exact period of the negotiations must remain
uncertain. That Philip did not long regard any such alliance as
important is shown by his reception in Macedonia of the rebel
satrap Artabazus; while an incident which occurred in the winter
of 342–1 shows that the action of the Persian authorities was not
controlled by any special regard for Philip. The latter was on
terms of friendship with Hermeias, the 'tyrant' of Atarneus
(a well-fortified town on the Asiatic coast opposite Mitylene),
which he held, as well as Assos and a considerable district, in
independence of Persia. Hermeias had been a hearer of Plato and
Aristotle at Athens, and had welcomed Aristotle and established

him and his school at Assos after Plato's death. In view of the position of his dominions, his friendship was obviously of some political importance to Philip. But Mentor of Rhodes, to whose generalship the Persian reconquest of Egypt had largely been due, was now, it appears, put in charge of the Great King's interests in Asia Minor. He first obtained the King's pardon for Artabazus, and recalled him from Macedonia, and then proceeded to attack Hermeias. Securing his person by treachery, and the towns which he possessed by means of forged instructions, which he sealed with Hermeias' signet, he sent him to the King, who had him crucified; while Mentor quickly reduced to submission the disaffected parts of Asia Minor. We shall soon find the Persian King and his satraps openly taking steps adverse to Philip.

III. THE STRUGGLE IN THRACE AND
THE CHERSONESE, 342-339 B.C.

During the greater part of the year 342 B.C. Philip was in Thrace. Cersobleptes had become restive, and he, and the neighbouring prince Teres, had to be subdued. Their kingdoms were now taken from them in name as well as in fact, and were incorporated in the Macedonian Empire; and to secure his hold, Philip planted military colonies in the valley of the Hebrus (the Maritza), the most important of which, Philippopolis, still retains its name. The colonists are said to have been men of violent character, and it was suggested that the colony should rather be called *Ponēro-polis*—which may be translated 'Rogueborough' or 'Scoundrelton.' This extension of his kingdom pushed Philip's frontiers further north and east; and to secure these he made a friendly agreement with Cothelas, king of the Getae (a tribe dwelling between the Maritza and the Danube), as well as with a number of Greek towns on the coast of the Black Sea, two of which were Odessus (now Varna) and Apollonia (near the modern Burgas). The work of conquest was not completed until Philip and his army had passed through the severe hardships of a winter in Thrace. It was soon after this that, through the defection of Aenus to Philip, Athens lost her last ally on the south coast of Thrace.

In the meantime a fresh cause of dispute between Philip and Athens had arisen in the Chersonese. The Athenians had recently strengthened their position in the peninsula by sending a large number of new colonists. These colonists, while favourably received by the towns which were properly within the Athenian alliance, came into collision with the people of Cardia, which was

allied to Philip, and which declined to cede lands to them. The
Athenian commander in that neighbourhood, Diopeithes, was
ordered to support the colonists, and, having no adequate supplies
from Athens, paid his mercenaries by plundering ships indis-
criminately in the north of the Aegean, and levying contributions
from coast-towns and islands, either as blackmail or as the reward
for escorting their trading-vessels. The people of Cardia naturally
asked Philip to help them, and received a garrison from him; and
when Diopeithes not only invaded a district of Thrace which was
undoubtedly in Philip's territory, but actually held Philip's envoy
to ransom, Philip wrote a letter to Athens, early in 341, in which,
after a strong protest against the actions of Diopeithes, he stated
his intention of defending the Cardians.

Opinion in Athens was sharply divided. Diopeithes' conduct
was undoubtedly a defiance of all international morality, and this
point was strongly pressed by the party of Aeschines, who also
warned the people that a bellicose policy would endanger the
distributions of festival-money. Demosthenes replied that it
would be madness to get rid of the one commander who was
maintaining the interests of Athens; that Philip was really at war
with Athens, and, as a tyrant, was bound to be her enemy so long
as she was a democracy; that Athens was destitute of allies—
apparently the friendship of the Peloponnesians had already cooled
off;—and that so long as the people refused to show any interest
in their own affairs, beyond mere acclamation of fine speeches, or
to punish the corruption of the politicians who were acting as
Philip's agents in Athens, the position was hopeless.

There is no evidence to show whether any action followed this
debate, but probably it was not until a month or two later, and
mainly as the result of Demosthenes' Third Philippic Oration,
that the anti-Macedonian party succeeded in inducing the people
to take vigorous measures. The pessimistic tone which marks the
speech on the Chersonese, particularly in regard to the isolation
of Athens and the extent of the power which Philip had gained
by corrupting the politicians in the Greek States, is even more
marked in the Third Philippic; and he was now successful in
alarming or inspiring his fellow-countrymen sufficiently to obtain
their sanction for his proposals. Diopeithes was supplied with
men and money; Chares was soon afterwards sent north, and made
Thasos his headquarters; Proconnesus and Tenedos were garrisoned; and once more the orators undertook a great diplomatic
campaign, and achieved extraordinary success. Demosthenes
himself persuaded the people of Byzantium, who must by now

have realized that Philip's plans of conquest might affect themselves, to renew the alliance with Athens which had been broken
off fifteen years before; Abydos was also won over; the Thracian
princes who still remained were assured of Athenian support;
even the Illyrian tribes were visited. Hypereides went to Chios
and Rhodes: whether or not he secured the actual renewal of their
alliances with Athens is uncertain; but at least we find them in
the next year fighting with Byzantium against Philip. The friendship made in the previous year with Callias of Chalcis now became
a formal alliance; and the Athenian generals, Cephisophon and
Phocion, crossed to Euboea, drove out Philistides and Cleitarchus,
and restored the democracies of Oreus and Eretria. A Euboean
confederacy was formed, which was politically and financially
independent of the Athenian League, but was in alliance with it;
and though the enemies of Demosthenes made it a charge against
him that he had sacrificed the contributions which the Euboean
towns might have made to the Athenian League, there is no
doubt that he was wise, as well as generous, in refusing to place
the Euboeans in any kind of subordination to Athens.

Demosthenes and Callias now attempted to organize a Panhellenic league. In the Peloponnese their success was only
partial. Corinth, Megara and the Achaeans promised men and
funds; but other States, though they may not have been unfriendly
to Athens, were not prepared to break with Philip. On the other
hand, the Acarnanians were won over by Demosthenes; the fact
that their neighbours, the Aetolians, were friendly to Philip
probably helped his arguments. Ambracia, Leucas and Corcyra
had already been brought in; and early in 340 a congress met at
Athens, to arrange the details of the alliance. Still there was no
formal declaration of war, though many acts of hostility were
committed. Callias captured the towns on the Bay of Pagasae,
which were in the Macedonian alliance, and also seized some
Macedonian merchant-ships and sold the crews as slaves. The
Athenians not only lent him the ships which he used for these
purposes, but passed decrees in commendation of his action. The
island of Halonnesus was raided by the inhabitants of Peparethus,
who were allied with Athens, and this led to a series of reprisals
and counter-reprisals. Athenian officers arrested a Macedonian
herald, carrying despatches, on Macedonian territory, and held
him in custody for nearly a year; the despatches were read aloud
in the Assembly at Athens. A certain Anaxinus of Oreus came
to Athens on an errand from Olympias, and Demosthenes had
him arrested as a spy, tortured and executed. The feeling of the

Athenian people was unmistakably shown when, in March 340, Demosthenes was publicly crowned at the Dionysiac festival, in recognition of his services.

Events in Thrace at last led to open war. Byzantium and Perinthus were still nominally allies of Philip, and he demanded their aid against the Athenians in the Chersonese. They refused, on the ground that the terms of their agreement with him did not justify the demand; and in the summer of 340 his fleet sailed up the Hellespont. The Athenians, for whom the safety of the Hellespontine corn-route was vital, ordered their commanders to oppose his voyage, and he was forced to land troops on the Chersonese, which marched parallel with the fleet and so held any opposition in check. He at once besieged Perinthus. Athens does not seem to have helped directly in the defence, but the Byzantines gave all possible assistance, and a large force of Greek mercenaries, under the command of the Athenian Apollodorus, was sent by the Great King's satraps in Asia Minor to aid the beleaguered town.

Thus Persia declared openly against Philip. Already, in the Third Philippic, Demosthenes had proposed to send ambassadors to the Great King, though it is evident (from the Fourth Philippic) that some argument was still needed to justify a step which, even when its object was to secure Hellenic freedom, was yet discordant with the traditional feeling of the Athenians towards Persia. It is uncertain when the ambassadors went; but at first the King appears to have rejected their overtures openly, while covertly sending funds to Diopeithes, and perhaps (though this is quite uncertain) not long afterwards to Demosthenes himself. But at the siege of Perinthus the King's attitude was declared.

The siege proved to be a very difficult task. The town stood on a promontory, and could not be taken from the seaward side, on account of the steepness of the cliffs; but it was joined to the land by an isthmus about 200 yards wide and strongly fortified, while the houses rose steeply in terraces up to the highest point of the town, overhanging the sea. Philip gave the besieged no rest day or night. His engines constantly assailed the outer wall, and his sharp-shooters worked great havoc among the defenders of it. At last, after weeks of assault with battering rams, mines, siege-towers a hundred and twenty feet high, and every device of ancient warfare, the wall was taken, but to no purpose; for the Perinthians had joined up the first line of houses so as to form a defence as strong as the wall itself; the fear that they might be starved out was removed by the ample supplies sent by the Persian satraps; and there was every prospect that, since a new line of defence could be prepared at each terrace, the siege would be interminable. Accordingly, after it had been prolonged for perhaps three months, Philip suddenly called off half his troops from Perinthus, and laid siege to Byzantium, hoping to take it by surprise; and very shortly afterwards war was formally declared between him and Athens.

The immediate occasion was the seizure by Philip's ships of 230 Athenian merchant-vessels, which were waiting with cargoes of corn and hides in order that Chares with his war-ships might escort them safely towards Athens. But when Chares left the ships to confer with the Persian commander, Philip took the opportunity to capture them, with their cargoes and a great sum of money; the timber of the ships was used for his siege-works. In reply to a protest from Athens, he sent a letter which was in fact a declaration of war, and was so taken by the Athenians, who now destroyed the monument upon which the Peace of Philocrates had been engraved, and determined to exert all their strength. Demosthenes carried the reform of the trierarchic system which he had long had in mind; the liability of the members of the Boards by which the ships were maintained was made strictly proportionate to their wealth, and evasions were no longer possible. He was himself appointed to an extraordinary office to supervise the equipment of the fleet, and Chares was ordered to relieve Byzantium.

The siege nevertheless lasted through the winter. The Byzantines were suspicious of Chares, and he seems to have effected little; it was not until Phocion and Cephisophon were sent out that there was any satisfactory co-operation between the Byzantines and the Athenian forces. But Phocion was a personal friend of Leon, who directed the defence of the town; and together they organized a successful resistance, which was further aided by the arrival of ships from Chios, Cos and Rhodes. Phocion also secured the trade-route for the merchantmen of Athens, and corn was now actually cheaper and more plentiful in Athens than it had been during the Peace. Philip made a last great assault on a moonlight night of early spring in 339; but the barking of dogs betrayed the attack, and he soon afterwards resolved to retire. But his ships had been driven back into the Black Sea, and confined there by the Athenian fleet which held the Bosporus; and in order to release them, he wrote a letter to his general Antipater, giving instructions which, if known to the Athenian commanders, would certainly cause them to call off their ships from this vital point. It was arranged that the letter should fall into Athenian hands; the ruse succeeded; Philip's ships got safely through the

Hellespont, and they, or their land-escort, did some damage on the way to the Athenian colonies in the Chersonese, though Phocion afterwards made some successful raids, by way of reprisal, upon Philip's towns on the coast of Thrace. Philip's failures at Perinthus and Byzantium were the more remarkable, because the great Thessalian military engineer Polyeidus, who was employed by him, had used all the most ingenious resources of siege-craft, and the defence had proved equal to them.

Nothing daunted, however, by this reverse, Philip withdrew his forces, and started upon a long expedition against Ateas, king of the Scythian tribes who lived in what is now the Dobrudja, to take his revenge for the refusal of Ateas to help him with men or money against Byzantium, and for previous contumelious behaviour on his part. The expedition gave him vast numbers of slaves and live-stock, and Ateas himself, now in his ninetieth year, fell in battle with the Macedonians. But Philip's return to Macedonia was fraught with disaster. The Triballi, a wild Balkan race, attacked him and inflicted great loss, taking from him all his Scythian booty; he himself was severely wounded and he and his army fought their way home with difficulty.

IV. THE AMPHISSEAN WAR: CHAERONEA (338 B.C.)

On his arrival at Pella, probably in the spring of 339, Philip found that affairs in Greece were once more in a condition which he could turn to his advantage, and once more the train of events had started at Delphi. The Athenians had erected there in a new treasury, or chapel in which offerings were dedicated, some shields which they had captured in the Second Persian War, bearing an inscription (which they now regilded) in which they were described as 'taken from the Persians and Thebans, when they fought against the Greeks.' The new chapel had not been formally consecrated, and the action of the Athenians was therefore irregular, as well as offensive to the Thebans; and at the meeting of the Amphictyonic Council, late in the autumn of 340, a councillor who represented the Locrians of Amphissa demanded that Athens should be fined fifty talents, while another denounced the Athenians as the accomplices of the accursed and sacrilegious Phocians. The Amphisseans had been allied with the Thebans in the Sacred War, and the Thebans were doubtless at the back of the Locrian proposal. Aeschines, who was the Athenian envoy to the Council, and was no lover of Thebes, replied in great wrath by charging the Amphisseans with cultivating the plain about the harbour of Cirrha, which was sacred to Apollo, and exacting

harbour-dues for their own profit; and by the eloquence of his
indignation he so roused the councillors—men unused to oratory,
as Demosthenes contemptuously termed them—that they descended with the whole population of Delphi to the harbour and
destroyed it, at the same time burning some of the houses in the
place. The Amphisseans, however, retaliated in force, and drove
the assailants back to Delphi. Next morning a meeting of all
good worshippers of Apollo who were at Delphi was summoned
by Cottyphus of Pharsalus, the president of the Council, and it
was resolved to convene an extraordinary meeting of the Council
at Thermopylae to pass sentence on the Amphisseans for their
sacrilege, both in cultivating the plain, and in attacking the councillors, whose persons were sacred.

There can be no doubt that the adroitness of Aeschines had
averted a resolution of the Council, which might have led to an
Amphictyonic war against Athens, and his report was warmly
acclaimed by the city. He was eager that the Athenians should
themselves take the field against Amphissa, but there is no
evidence for his having conceived the design, sometimes attributed
to him, of a united war by Athens and Philip against Thebes.
Philip was still in Scythia. But from the point of view of Demosthenes the breach with Thebes which was actually threatened
was disastrous, since he relied in the last resort upon an alliance
with Thebes as the best hope of defeating Philip; he saw plainly
that if either Athens or Thebes should succumb to Philip, the
other would have little chance of effective resistance; and (by
whatever arguments, for his partiality to Thebes was still certain
to be unpopular) he succeeded in persuading the Council and the
Assembly to send no representative to the meeting at Thermopylae. Thebes also was unrepresented; it would have been difficult
for the Thebans either to join in a sentence against their friends,
or to appear to condone their sacrilege. So when the Council met
early in 339, war was declared against the Amphisseans; Cottyphus was appointed to conduct it, and messages were sent to the
Amphictyonic powers, bidding them send troops. The response
was slight. Cottyphus appears, indeed, to have inflicted a defeat
upon the Amphisseans, in consequence of which a fine was
imposed upon them, and they were ordered to banish their leading
politicians and recall their opponents; but evidently they did not
comply, and as Cottyphus could not obtain troops, the Council,
at its meeting in May or June, decided to invite Philip to undertake the conduct of the war. The invitation, which was proposed
by Cottyphus, may well have been prompted by Philip himself;

it gave him exactly the opportunity which he wanted, and it was at once accepted.

Having marched southwards, Philip first occupied Cytinium in Doris, which lay on the direct route from Thessaly to Amphissa[1]; and if he had had no other object than the punishment of Amphissa, he could have marched there without delay. But if, as appears certain, he intended now to make good his supremacy in Greece, it was necessary to make sure of Thebes; and it is probable that the attitude of Thebes towards him was less satisfactory than it had been. For the Thebans were the friends of the Amphisseans, and they had taken Nicaea, which commanded the Pass of Thermopylae, from the Macedonian garrison left there by Philip, and had garrisoned it themselves. (Whether this was really a sign of disaffection towards Philip, who at the time was in Scythia, is uncertain: it may have been prompted by a desire to help the Amphisseans indirectly, by securing that so vital a point should be in friendly hands.) Further, the friendly relations between Thebes and Persia may have rendered her a less trustworthy ally in the eyes of Philip, who had been opposed by Persian troops on the Hellespont, and possibly by Persian gold in Athens. Therefore instead of going straight to his ostensible goal, Philip suddenly diverged from Cytinium and marched to Elatea and fortified it, probably at the beginning of September[2].

The occupation of Elatea, which lay on the road to Thebes and Athens and was but three days' march from Athens itself, at first produced consternation in the minds of the Athenians, who expected an immediate invasion by the Macedonian and Theban armies. When, after a night of excitement, of which Demosthenes has left an incomparable picture, the Assembly met, the politicians at first appeared to be paralysed; but Demosthenes saw that the moment had come for carrying out the policy which had long been in his mind. Philip, he argued, would not have rested at Elatea, if Athens had been his immediate aim: his object was rather to turn the scale by his presence, as between the two parties in Thebes, and to force the Thebans to join him. The one chance, therefore, for Athens, was to frustrate Philip's intentions by herself making an alliance instantly with Thebes, and, as a proof of sincerity, sending a force into Boeotia without delay. His advice was accepted, and he went at once to Thebes, with other envoys, while a citizen-force marched as far as Eleusis, which was on the road to Boeotia.

[1] See map facing p. 213.
[2] Beloch, *Griechische Geschichte*, III[2], 2, p. 297, would date the event about three months later.

But Philip also had sent ambassadors to Thebes, representing himself and his Thessalian allies, offering to treat the Thebans as neutrals in the war against Amphissa, but demanding in return that they should either march with him into Attica, or at least give him a free passage through Boeotia. Nicaea he proposed to restore to the Locrians of Opus, to whom it had originally belonged, and who were on terms of friendship with Thebes. He held out before the Thebans the prospect of bringing home with them once more, as in the Decelean War, the slaves and flocks and herds of Attica; but if they refused, he threatened to plunder their own territory in the same manner.

Having heard Philip's proposals, the Theban Assembly gave audience to Demosthenes, who, in order to secure his aim, took the risk of offering terms more generous than the Athenians would even have considered a very short while before. The supremacy of Thebes over Boeotia was to be acknowledged, and, if necessary, supported by Athenian forces, even though this meant the abandonment of Plataea and Thespiae, and the loss of Oropus; in the war with Philip, Thebes was to command by land, Athens by sea; and two-thirds of the expenses of the war were to be met by Athens. The eloquence and generosity of Demosthenes carried the day, and both sides now tried to secure allies for the forthcoming struggle, the Athenians and Thebans doubtless emphasizing the peril to Greece as a whole, while Philip was studiously careful to describe his aims as entirely those of the Amphictyonic Council. Neither side, however, appears to have gained more support than was already assured. Nearly all the Peloponnesian States, having alliances with both Athens and Philip, remained neutral; Athens and Thebes were supported by the people of Euboea, Achaea, Megara, Acarnania, Leucas and Corcyra; Philip by the Thessalians and some smaller Amphictyonic tribes.

In Athens itself Demosthenes was now all-powerful. The measure which he had advocated in vain at the time of the Olynthian crisis, the transference of the festival-money to the war-chest, was carried without difficulty; the repairs of the dockyards and arsenal at the Piraeus, which had been begun after the Peace of Philocrates, were suspended; the financial administration passed under the control of Lycurgus, a very able man of business, and himself a distinguished orator; and despite adverse omens and deterrent oracles, the movement of troops into Boeotia was pushed forward with all speed.

The allies occupied all the passes by which Philip might

attempt to cross from Phocis into Boeotia, the chief of these being the Pass of Parapotamii, north-west of the plain of Chaeronea; and 10,000 mercenaries were sent with Chares to defend the road which led from Cytinium to Amphissa and to the Gulf of Corinth, across which Philip might wish to communicate with his Peloponnesian friends. In this region the Theban Proxenus was in command. Some minor engagements—which Demosthenes speaks of as the 'winter-battle' and the 'battle by the river'— took place during the following months, probably in consequence of tentative efforts on the part of Philip to dislodge the occupants of the passes. In these the allies were victorious, and there was great jubilation in Athens; Demosthenes was once more crowned at the Dionysia (in March, 338).

Philip's long postponement of more active operations is to be explained partly by a desire to wait for reinforcements from Macedonia and Thessaly, but partly, and more significantly, by political motives. There can be no doubt that at this time he was engaged in forwarding the restoration of the Phocian towns (which was wrongly ascribed by Pausanias to Athens and Thebes), and in the renewal of their federal government. No better move against the interests of Thebes could have been devised. And so we find the Phocian community once more mentioned in the Delphic records, and their compulsory payment to the temple of sixty talents a year reduced to ten talents. These measures were doubtless ratified by the Amphictyonic Council at their spring meeting, at which Philip and his Thessalian friends had the preponderant influence. Inscriptions[1] show that the Thessalian representatives on the Council were no longer Cottyphus and Colosimus, who had sat on it for seven years, but Daochus and Thrasydaeus, who had accompanied the Macedonian envoys to Thebes in 339, and who appear on Demosthenes' list of traitors in the Speech on the Crown. Moreover, the Council itself was reduced in importance by the appointment for the first time in the winter of 339 (probably at the November meeting) of a College of Treasurers of the temple-funds, in which also Philip's friends carried most weight. On the other hand, the Council appears to have acquired a new political status, and its coinage, as issued first in the spring of 338, bears the superscription not, as heretofore, 'Of the Delphians,' but 'Of the Amphictyons'[2]. Finally, Philip gained in moral influence through being proclaimed by the

---

[1] *B.C.H.* xxi (1897), pp. 322, 478; cf. P. Foucart, *Rev. Phil.* xxiii (1899), pp. 106–7.

[2] See Volume of Plates ii, 8, *d*.

Council as the champion of the god of Delphi. All these arrangements must have occupied a considerable time.

At last, however, Philip was ready for action, and he prepared the way by a ruse not unlike that which had enabled him to get his ships away from the Bosporus over a year before. He addressed a letter to Antipater, announcing his hurried return to Thrace, to crush a revolt there; the letter fell, according to plan, into the hands of Proxenus and Chares, who relaxed their vigilance, as Philip expected them to do. Then, without warning, he came through the pass from Cytinium by night with a great force, inflicted a severe defeat upon Proxenus and Chares, and took Amphissa without difficulty. Its walls were destroyed under an order of the Amphictyonic Council, and its leading statesmen banished. He also secured his communications with the sea and the Peloponnese by marching rapidly to Naupactus, and handing it over to his allies, the Aetolians. Then he returned to Elatea.

The position of the Athenian and Theban forces in Parapotamii and the parallel passes was no longer tenable, since Philip's troops could now cross the mountains by roads in their rear and threaten their retreat, and from this time onwards they executed many harassing movements, and ravaged the lands of Western Boeotia. Consequently the allied line was withdrawn to the plain of Chaeronea, and Philip was free to cross the Pass of Parapotamii and force a final battle.

Yet even now (unless indeed these negotiations belong to an earlier date, before the conclusion of the alliance between Athens and Thebes) he showed his desire for a bloodless settlement by messages sent both to Athens and to Thebes. In both cities there were those who were ready to listen—at Athens, Phocion, who was as fearless of unpopularity as of the enemy, and whose honesty and experience carried great weight, and at Thebes, the principal magistrates, the Boeotarchs, whom Philip may have attempted to corrupt. But both were met with violent language, as well as by argument, from Demosthenes, whose sarcastic request to the Thebans for a free passage for the army fighting against Philip shamed them into a renewed readiness for the conflict; while the Athenians were easily persuaded that it was better that the final struggle should take place as far away as possible from Athens.

On the seventh day of the month Metageitnion—probably 2 August, possibly 1 September 338—the battle of Chaeronea was fought. The great mound in which the Macedonian dead were buried determines approximately the site of the conflict. The opposing lines must have been drawn from the banks of the

Cephisus, about 200 yards from the mound, in a south-westerly direction across the plain, to the opening in the hill of Thurium, where the stream called Molos runs down into the plain, the allied left wing resting against the mountain-promontory which bounds this opening on the east[1]. On each side between thirty and thirty-five thousand men[2] were engaged. The allied front was composed of the Thebans, under Theagenes, on the right; the mercenaries and troops from smaller allied States in the centre; the Athenians, under Stratocles, Lysicles and Chares, on the left, on ground rising slightly above the plain. On the Macedonian side Alexander, now eighteen years old, and eager to display his prowess in the presence of his father, commanded on the left, where the best troops were placed, Philip himself on the right. On the left wing there was a fierce struggle from the first; but in the end, largely by force of his personal example, Alexander's men broke through the Theban ranks; the famous 'Sacred Band' of the Thebans, true to their tradition, stood their ground till all had fallen. Philip, on the other hand, at first gave way of set purpose before the Athenian onset, until he had drawn the Athenians, jubilant at their supposed victory, from their favourable position on to lower ground, while he himself probably brought his men up to a slightly higher level. Then he suddenly turned upon the Athenians and broke their line. Those who could, Demosthenes among them, escaped over the pass which led to Lebadea; but a thousand citizens of Athens were killed and two thousand captured; and the centre of the allied force was hopelessly cut up between the two victorious Macedonian wings which now converged upon them, the losses of the Achaean contingent being especially terrible.

The main cause of the defeat was undoubtedly the superior generalship of Philip, and the greater efficiency of his highly trained army. The Thebans alone were equal in any degree to the Macedonians in the necessary military qualities, and for that reason Philip had opposed to them his best troops under Alexander. It is plain that, throughout the campaign and in the battle, the allies were not directed by one commanding mind. Phocion,

---

[1] This view at least seems more probable than the older one, which thought of the battle-field as extending from just below the town of Chaeronea to the western spur of Mount Acontium. See Bibliography, p. 583. The arguments of Soteriades seem to be conclusive as against the view of Kromayer.

[2] For the computation of the numbers, see Beloch, *op. cit.* III[2], 2, pp. 299, 300.

who was probably the ablest Athenian general, was away in command of the fleet in the Aegean. Stratocles evidently lost his head at the apparent success of his men at the outset, and shouted hysterical exhortations to them to pursue the enemy to Macedonia. Stratocles may have fallen in the battle. Of the doings of Chares, in the battle and afterwards, nothing is reported. Lysicles returned to Athens, and was prosecuted by Lycurgus and condemned to death. The battle was a crowning proof of the inability of amateur soldiers and citizen-levies to cope with a well-trained professional army, combining units of all descriptions under a centralized direction. We do not indeed hear what part Philip's cavalry took in this particular battle, but they doubtless helped to complete the defeat of the enemy.

The battle also marked the fact that the independent city-states had had their day as disconnected units. Whether with or without their good-will, some other form of political existence must needs be found for them, if they were to play any but a small part in the world. To the experiments of combining them which were made under Macedonian leadership in the years which followed the battle of Chaeronea we shall shortly return.

V   AFTER CHAERONEA

The news of the battle came to Athens first by rumour, and then in its full gravity through the return of the fugitives. The city was at once prepared for defence against siege by land; the inhabitants of Attica were brought within the walls, and all citizens under sixty years old were enrolled to man the defences. Hypereides, who until the return of Demosthenes took charge of the preparations, even proposed the complete enfranchisement of all resident aliens, and the liberation of all slaves who would enlist; but these proposals were afterwards indicted as illegal, and their operation was thereby suspended. When, some time later, the indictment came to trial, Hypereides defended the admitted illegality on the ground that the danger had darkened his vision—'It was not I who made the proposals, but the battle of Chaeronea'—and the jury acquitted him; but the time for carrying out any such decrees had then gone by. Charidemus was given the chief military command; his long-standing hostility to Philip seemed to point him out as the man for the work. The details of the defensive operations and the financial provision for them were worked out on his return by Demosthenes, and his supporters proposed the decrees which ratified them.

But to the astonishment of the Athenians, their anxiety proved to be unfounded. Philip had, indeed, in the first orgy of triumph, refused even to give up the allies' dead for burial; but as an outspoken word from the orator Demades, who was one of his Athenian prisoners, caused him to break off his drunken revel, so he rapidly returned to the mood of far-sighted generosity which was both characteristic of his temper and conducive to the fulfilment of his plans.

For Thebes, indeed, the false friend, as for the Olynthians ten years before, there could be no mercy. The leaders of the anti-Macedonian party were executed or banished, and their property confiscated; an oligarchy of three hundred, whom Philip could trust, was appointed to govern; a Macedonian force occupied the citadel; the power of Thebes over the Boeotian League was taken away; Plataea, Thespiae and Orchomenus were restored. The Theban prisoners were sold as slaves, and it was only with difficulty that the Thebans obtained leave to bury their dead at the spot where the marble lion, which was erected in their honour, has once more been set up. In all this Philip only acted towards the Thebans as they would have acted to any city which they had conquered.

But towards Athens he showed himself in another light. His reasons were no doubt in part strictly practical. His experiences at Byzantium and Perinthus had shown him the difficulty of capturing a strongly defended maritime city, without the command of the sea; and if the project of a great campaign against Persia was now clearly in his mind, as it must have been, he would need both the ships and the goodwill of Athens. Further, Athens had not, like Thebes, pretended to be his friend (despite the alliance of 346) and then deserted him; nor was she, like Thebes, a likely centre of Persian influence in Greece. But to these reasons it must be added that Athens was the home of the highest artistic and literary culture of the Greek world; and if Philip's plans included not only the hellenizing of his own country, but also (as those of Alexander certainly contemplated) the spread of Hellenic civilization over the Eastern world, he would need the co-operation of Athens for higher purposes than those of conquest. And even if the ascription of such aims to him is no more than a very probable conjecture, there is no doubt of his own admiration for Athens and all that she stood for in the Greek world.

Be that as it may, the arrival of Demades from Philip's camp, and the account which he gave of the king's mood, quickly changed the plans of the Athenians. They no longer talked of resistance to the death, but, Phocion having been placed by the

Council of Areopagus at the head of the forces instead of Charidemus, they sent him with Demades and Aeschines to treat with Philip. The terms which Philip dictated were far better than they could have dreamed possible. He guaranteed to Athens freedom from Macedonian invasion by land or sea, and left her in possession of the chief of the islands of the Aegean,—Lemnos, Imbros, Delos, Scyros and Samos. The Chersonese he took from her, but he restored Oropus, her former possession on the Boeotian frontier. The Athenian League, of course, was dissolved, and Athens became his ally. There was to be freedom of traffic by sea, and Athens was to unite with Philip in the suppression of piracy. Philip sent Alexander to Athens, with two of his principal commanders, bearing the bones of the Athenians who had fallen at Chaeronea and had been burned there; and the Athenians in return gave their citizenship to both Philip and Alexander, and erected Philip's statue in their market-place. Demosthenes, to whom this reversal of the fighting-spirit which he had animated must have been more than painful, had accepted a mission to procure corn and funds from abroad, and was doubtless absent when these things were done.

Yet the heart of the people was with Demosthenes, and his own zeal for the public service, as he understood it, was unabated. It was he who was appointed to deliver the Funeral Oration on those who had died at Chaeronea; and it was he who, aided by the great financial ability of Lycurgus, superintended the continued repair of the fortifications and other public works; for these purposes he contributed largely of his own substance.

For some years a bitter war of prosecutions was waged between the party of Demosthenes and that of Philip. Success seems almost always to have fallen to the former. Lycurgus, in particular, was relentless in his pursuit of his opponents, and even of those who had so far despaired of the future as to leave Athens, with their families and their resources, when Philip's vengeance was supposed to be imminent and all the help that every citizen could give might well be needed. Hypereides, who was attacked, as has been narrated, for the illegality of his decrees, retaliated by indicting Demades for his proposal to confer honours upon Euthycrates, who had betrayed Olynthus to Philip. Demosthenes himself was, he tells us, 'brought to trial every day.' But the administration of Demosthenes and Lycurgus was both successful and popular. The theoric distributions, which had probably been suspended only for the duration of the war, were naturally resumed; great public works, among them the rebuilding of the

Dionysiac theatre, were worthily carried out; and there is no doubt that the decree proposed by Ctesiphon, that at the Great Dionysia in 336 Demosthenes should receive a golden crown, because he always did and advised what was best for Athens, would have been enthusiastically passed, had not Aeschines taken advantage of a technical irregularity in the proposal to bring an indictment against its mover. The trial of the issue was destined to be delayed for six years; but the feeling of Athens as a whole at the time of the proposal cannot be mistaken.

In the meantime Philip was taking steps to make his supremacy in Greece secure. To retain Northern Greece, he placed garrisons in Chalcis and Ambracia, as well as at Thebes, and he had the leaders who had favoured Athens expelled from Acarnania. The Aetolians and Phocians, and of course the Thessalians, were already his friends; Epirus was, as we have seen, virtually a dependency of Macedonia. Byzantium also made its peace with Philip about this time; but, like Perinthus and Selymbria, it must have preserved a certain amount of independence, since it continued to issue its own coinage.

The turn of the Peloponnese came next. Philip was welcomed on his way there at Megara, and also at Corinth, where he left a garrison to control the Isthmus. The Arcadian Confederacy, the centre of which was at Megalopolis, was re-organized; Mantinea and the neighbouring towns were brought within it; and Philip assigned to the Arcadians, the Argives and the Messenians, districts which had until now been in the hands of Sparta. For the Spartans, who had held aloof from the recent struggle, now declined to receive Philip, and preferred to suffer not only these losses of territory, but also the plundering of Laconia by the Macedonian army. Whether he really threatened to suppress the dual monarchy, as some have thought to be indicated by an expression in the paean of Isyllus, remains uncertain; in the end he left Sparta itself and its constitution intact, but greatly reduced in power and influence. The territorial arrangements which he had made proved, as a whole, to be lasting.

Philip had now dealt with the Greek States in detail. It remained to sum up his achievements by the creation of a single organization which should embrace them all. This was done at the Congress which met, on his summons, at Corinth, late in 338. The Greek States (with the exception of Sparta, which obstinately refused to send representatives) were united in a common league, and the terms which Philip laid down for the union show a broad-minded statesmanship, and a grasp of the condition of the Hellenic world, which had been greatly lacking in the politicians of the city-states.

The League was to be in alliance, offensive and defensive, with himself, and was to be represented by a council to which each State was to send delegates whose number varied with the importance of the State. The contingents which each was to provide for the common forces were settled. The Athenians, indeed, made a show of opposition when called upon to provide ships and cavalry; but the good sense of Phocion once more saved them from putting themselves in an impossible position. Any citizen of an allied State who took service with a foreign power against Philip or against the League was to be banished as a traitor, and his goods confiscated. But of far greater significance was the attempt to give internal peace and unity to Greece. The autonomy of the several States was guaranteed, as it had been nominally by the Peace of Antalcidas, which the Treaty of Corinth virtually superseded, with better hope of good results. The forces of the League were to protect the independence of each member; the existing constitutions of the States were to be undisturbed, and there were to be no violent interferences with private property. No tribute was to be exacted, and no garrisons planted in the cities, except (we must suppose) in so far as the military organization of the League demanded definite military centres. The seas were to be open for trade to all. The military command was, of course, to be in the hands of the Macedonian king, as well as the right to summon the Congress of the League, though doubtless it was to have its periodical meetings. The Amphictyonic Council was to be the supreme judicial Court in matters affecting the States which were included in the League.

Such was the first great attempt to combine the Hellenic States in an effectual political and military union. The chapters which follow will show how far it was successful. In fact the two States in which the spirit of the independent city was strongest, Athens and Sparta, do not appear ever to have entered wholeheartedly into any form of federal union, and they stood apart from the federations of the next century. But for the rest there can be no doubt that the work which Philip did was well done and was fruitful in good results.

The League was also given an immediate object for its activity —the same which had so often been advocated by Isocrates, who died, after inditing a warm letter to Philip, just at the moment when the king was giving substance to the old man's vision. This was the united campaign against Persia, which must long have been in Philip's mind. We do not know whether (as some historians assert) he himself represented it as an act of vengeance for the Persian invasion of Greece, a century and a half before; even if he was not of the romantic temper of Alexander, such an appeal to sentiment may well have been adopted by him as no less convenient than the appeal which he had twice made to religious feeling by professing to be the champion of the God of Delphi. Nor (as has already been said) do we know whether his own plans were confined to the liberation of the Greek peoples in Asia Minor from Persian rule, or whether, like Alexander, he entertained the vaster vision of the conquest and hellenization of the East. But the campaign was announced, and the needful forces requisitioned, at the Congress of Corinth, and arrangements were made to send the generals Attalus and Parmenion into Asia Minor with a Macedonian army to prepare the way for the great host which was to follow. The recent murder of Artaxerxes Ochus made the moment a peculiarly favourable one for the projected invasion.

VI. THE DEATH OF PHILIP. CHARACTERS OF PHILIP AND DEMOSTHENES

But Philip was not destined to see the fulfilment of his design. For a long time there had been little love lost between himself and his wife Olympias, the mother of Alexander. Monogamy, indeed, was not demanded by Macedonian ethics and six or seven wives of Philip are known by name, most of whom he had married since his wedding with Olympias; but Philip's wedding in 337 with Cleopatra, the niece of his general Attalus, was marked by an incident which led to an open rupture. Attalus, in proposing a toast at the wedding-feast, expressed the hope that Cleopatra would bear Philip a legitimate heir to the throne. Such an insult was more than Alexander could brook; a furious quarrel broke out on the spot between him and his father; Alexander threw his cup in Attalus' face; Philip dashed from his place, sword in hand, and would have tried to slay his son, had he not stumbled and fallen. After a jeer at the man 'who wanted to cross from Europe to Asia, and could not cross from one couch to another,' Alexander left the court, and his friends were sent into exile. He himself repaired to the country of the Illyrians, on whom he had the year before inflicted a defeat, which had been followed by an even more crushing one at the hands of Philip; but it may well have been Alexander's object to rouse the warlike tribes once more against his father. Olympias was already with her brother, Alexander of

Epirus; but as it was undesirable for Philip to leave that prince disaffected when he went to the East, a reconciliation was arranged, and Philip's daughter by Olympias, another Cleopatra, was offered in marriage to her uncle, the king of Epirus.

The reconciliation with Alexander, though he returned to the court, proved to be very hollow. The prince was disposed to marry the daughter of Pixodarus, satrap of Caria. Philip refused his consent, nominally because the alliance was not worthy of Alexander, really (we may suspect) because an alliance between his son and a nominal vassal of Persia might not be convenient on the eve of his Persian campaign.

However this may be, preparations were made to celebrate the wedding of Cleopatra with Alexander of Epirus with unheard-of magnificence. In July, 336, the festivities began. The statue of Philip was borne into the theatre with those of the twelve greatest gods; and he himself was walking alone, somewhat ahead of his guards, to display his confidence in the position which he held, when he was struck down by Pausanias, one of his guardsmen, in revenge, it was said, for his refusal to punish a gross insult which had been inflicted years before upon Pausanias by Attalus. There were, however, some who had no doubt that Olympias encouraged or even instigated Pausanias to do the deed. Her own fierce nature, and the subsequent murder by her order of Cleopatra (the niece of Attalus) with her infant son and many of her supporters, and that of Attalus himself at the bidding of Alexander, lend colour to the darkest suspicions[1]; but the evidence is contradictory, and no definite conclusion is possible.

Such was the end of the strongest of the few strong men who had appeared on the stage of Greek history since the end of the Peloponnesian War. With his private life history is not much concerned; he had his vices, and indulged in them freely; yet he was always master of himself, and could pass in a moment from extreme indulgence to the coolest and most calculating sobriety. His morality in public affairs was doubtless of a kind of which few statesmen would care to boast at the present day, though it may be suspected that the gap which separates him from many modern politicians is not so great as the picture drawn by Demosthenes might lead us to suppose. He was ready to use any means which was likely to effect his purpose, and he seldom miscalculated. If bribery or liberality would secure him agents, he would use bribery or liberality to secure them. If he could keep

[1] See Diodorus XVI, 93–4; XVII, 2–3; Justin IX, 6–7; Arrian I, 25, 1, and below, p. 354.

a city or an individual under the delusion that he was their friend,
until he was ready to fall upon them, he would do so. If it served
his purpose to inflict final and crushing disaster, he did not shrink
from it; but he was equally ready to be generous and forgiving,
if some larger purpose was served thereby, and his natural instinct
probably inclined him towards such a course. Whether he was
dealing with politicians or generals or masses, he had an unusual
power of divining the way in which the minds of others would
work, and he acted upon his conjectures with conspicuous success.
If on some particular occasion he was beaten, he accepted the
situation without hesitation, in the full confidence that he would
win in the end. Whether he chose to strike suddenly or to wait
patiently for the maturing of his design, his plans were laid on a
great scale, and based on an unerring and comprehensive view of
the facts. His personal courage was remarkable, and it seems to
have been accompanied by a certain light-heartedness, which is
reflected in a number of anecdotes, and which, with his fondness
for good-fellowship, his natural eloquence and his love of artistic
and literary culture, helps to account for the attraction which he
exercised both upon his own people and companions, and also
upon the representatives of the Greek States who came in contact
with him.

Of his great opponent, Demosthenes, it is difficult to speak
impartially. There has been a tendency in recent historical
writings to minimize his importance and to decry his personal
and political character. His importance was at least fully recognized by Philip himself, and it was not without reason that
in his revel on the night of Chaeronea the king constantly de-
claimed words of triumph over Demosthenes. That Demosthenes'
greatest title to fame rests upon his oratory, which at its highest
level remains unsurpassed and unsurpassable, may be admitted.
It must also be admitted that in regard to the worst practice of
democratic orators, modern as well as ancient—that of adapting
the facts to suit the impression which it is desired to create—
Demosthenes was as unscrupulous as any Greek; and that a
natural unsociableness, perhaps due originally to physical causes,
was reflected in a lack of generosity towards his opponents, and
the consequent misinterpretation, at times, of their motives. Yet
he stood unflinchingly, and without counting the cost, for a great
ideal,—that of the free city-state; and it must be added that in
this he was truly representative of the Athenian people. It was
upon the triumphant vindication of their freedom against Persia,
and its maintenance, despite the issue of the Peloponnesian War,

against all rivals in Greece, that their national pride was founded; and nothing proved the fundamental genuineness of their faith so conclusively as their constancy to Demosthenes after the battle of Chaeronea had occurred. To modern readers of ancient history, twenty-two centuries after the events, it may be clear that the ideal of Demosthenes and of Athens was a narrow one; that it was in the interests of humanity that it should be superseded by wider political and ethical conceptions; and that the Macedonian kings, whether by design or not, did a work for the world which the city-states, in their detachment and irreconcilability, could never have done. But no such considerations were or could be before the mind of Demosthenes. Despite all his faults, his noble championship of the losing cause must always command admiration; nor, when he is criticized for blindness to the signs of the times, should it be forgotten how near he came to success.

CHAPTER X

SICILY, 367 TO 330 B.C.

I. DIONYSIUS THE SECOND

ON the death of Dionysius I in the spring of 367 his empire passed to his eldest son, who bore his name (p. 134). The succession met with no opposition from the people of Syracuse and of other cities: what danger there was lay within the ruling house itself. We are told that, when Dionysius seemed likely to die, Dion, the husband of his daughter Arete and brother of his wife Aristomache, tried to influence Dionysius to designate as his successors Hipparinus and Nysaeus, the children of Dionysius and Aristomache. These were probably not yet of age, and, if Dion had had his way, the power would doubtless have remained in his own hands. But the court-physicians denied him access to Dionysius' sick-bed, and are said to have hastened the tyrant's end in order to ingratiate themselves with the heir. This story, however, is very likely groundless and invented some years later, after the younger Dionysius had quarrelled with Dion. If he had already shown himself disaffected in this way, it is improbable that the new ruler would have kept him in the position of a trusted minister, as he did for some months.

Dionysius II kept his power for ten years; but unfortunately the record of his actions during those years has almost completely vanished. We possess one or two scraps of information about his foreign and domestic policy and some general remarks on his character. But all that we know in any detail about his rule is the manner in which he lost it. In fact what we possess is really an account of the exploits of Dion, who overthrew him. The account exists partly in the biographies written by Plutarch and Nepos, partly in the history of Diodorus. It is in no way surprising that we should have these biographies, for Dion lived for nine years in Greece, where he became a well-known figure and in particular formed a close connection with the Platonic Academy, whose members did much to preserve his memory. What is more curious and disappointing is that the account of Diodorus hardly adds

Note. The main ancient sources for the narrative in this chapter are Plato, *Epistles* III, VII, VIII, which are now generally regarded as authentic, a series of sections in Diodorus XVI, Plutarch's *Dion* and *Timoleon*, Nepos' *Dion* and *Timoleon*. For further detail see the Bibliography.

anything, and is written from the same standpoint; the Sicilian historian has scarcely a word to say of events in Sicily between the exile of Dion, which seems to have occurred little more than a year after Dionysius' accession, and his return in the guise of liberator in 357 B.C. If, as we must suppose, he found nothing of interest to extract from Timaeus' record of these years, the inference is that they were in the main peaceful and uneventful.

What we are told of the character and actions of Dionysius confirms this. He was weak, dissolute, and unenterprising; in the eyes of Plato and the Academy he was crafty and treacherous, and utterly belied the fair hopes which they had conceived of him. Rigidly debarred during his father's lifetime from playing any part in affairs, he had taken up carpentry as a hobby; and on coming into power when less than thirty years of age his policy, so far as he had one, was to preserve and enjoy his inheritance. Peace was soon made with Carthage on the basis of the *status quo*, later also with the Lucanians after a war which had dragged on indecisively for some months. Two colonies were founded on the coast of Apulia, to protect the commerce of the southern Adriatic from pirates; Rhegium was restored under the name of Phoebia, and Tauromenium received as an addition to its mixed population the Naxians expelled by the elder Dionysius. This last act is described by Diodorus, who assigns it to the year 358–7 B.C., as being wholly the work of an eminent and wealthy citizen, Andromachus, father of the historian Timaeus; but it is plain that filial piety has exaggerated and that the new settlement was an act of the Syracusan state, that is to say, of the tyrant. We also hear of the return of political exiles and the remission of taxation. All these acts are best interpreted as measures designed to increase the tyrant's security and popularity. For a time they were successful; but we may believe that throughout these ten years hatred of the tyranny smouldered in the breasts of the Syracusans and the subjects of other Sicilian cities that had once been proud of freedom. The power of the elder Dionysius had been tolerated so long principally because he was a conqueror and a champion against the Punic foe; now that the danger from Carthage seemed at an end, the hatred of tyranny revived. Hence when a liberator, real or pretended, appeared in the person of a member of the tyrant's own family, he was welcomed with boundless enthusiasm, and his intentions were for the moment unquestioned.

When quite a young man Dion had met Plato on the occasion of the philosopher's first visit to Sicily in 389–8, and an attachment had sprung up between the two men which had not weakened twenty years later. Fired with enthusiasm for Plato's political ideas, Dion saw in the young Dionysius the possibility of fulfilling that essential condition without which, as Plato had declared, his Republic could not come into being: the king should turn philosopher (p. 315). It was of course a necessary antecedent to this conversion that the tyrant should turn king, that is to say, constitutional monarch; and in this lay the real crux of the matter, as the sequel was to show.

A pressing invitation from the tyrant, seconded by Dion himself, could not well be refused by Plato, ageing though he already was and reluctant to quit the professor's chair. If we may believe the evidence of the seventh Platonic letter, his decision to go to Syracuse was due not so much to any hopes of realizing Dion's aspirations as to his fear of being held untrue to his own philosophy. There were passages in his writings which seemed to contemplate just such a situation as had now arisen at Syracuse, if indeed Dion's account of the possibilities of reforming the young tyrant through education were true. Dion did not minimize the need of such reform; but he represented that it was still possible to remedy the evils due to the tyrant's upbringing, and he had himself begun to prepare the way. In truth Dionysius himself, who was athirst if not for philosophy at all events for a philosophical reputation, was eager to have Plato at his court; and for a time all seemed to go according to Dion's plan. In conformity with the regular Academic course the pupil was started on the study of mathematics, and geometry became the fashion at court. To this no one could object; but Plato's ethical and political teaching was not so harmless. We hear that on one occasion when sacrifice was being offered in the domestic chapel and the customary prayer for the safe continuance of the tyranny was recited, the tyrant, to the great consternation of his ministers, exclaimed 'Stop cursing us.' Philosophy then, it seemed, meant the end of the tyranny and the abasement of all who throve thereon. It is not surprising that Dion's plan aroused opponents, who prevailed upon the tyrant to recall from exile the historian Philistus, who had for many years been living at Hadria.

Philistus, in spite of his banishment, was still a strong supporter of the tyranny, which as we have seen (p. 112) he had helped to create; he set himself deliberately to thwart and discredit Dion. Rumours were spread that Dionysius was being induced to give up power, which would be assumed by Dion himself as regent for his nephews, the sons of Dionysius I and Aristomache; alarm was created by the suggestion that the national safety was being endangered by plans for military and naval disarmament. Finally a letter from Dion to the Carthaginian Government was intercepted: the peace had not yet been concluded and Dion had written urging that his own presence should be insisted upon at any peace conference. This advice doubtless implied no disloyalty, but the letter was invaluable to Philistus and his party, who convinced Dionysius that it meant that Dion was treacherously promising to secure better terms for the enemy in order to strengthen his position by foreign support. Without an opportunity of defence Dion was at once expelled from Sicily, probably before the end of 366.

But though expelled Dion was not yet openly disgraced. His friends and supporters were too numerous to be disregarded, and they prevailed with the tyrant to allow Dion to continue to enjoy the income from his estates, which were considerable, and to forward his movable property to Greece. He was thus enabled to support a magnificent establishment in Athens, which became his home for the next nine years (366–57). He kept in close touch with the Academy, and was particularly intimate with Speusippus its future head, to whom, on his return to Sicily in 357, he left an estate which he had bought in Attica. He also travelled to other cities, where his wealth and culture won him numerous friends. Amongst other marks of esteem he received the most unusual honour of Spartan citizenship, although Sparta was at this time in alliance with Dionysius, who had in 365 sent a contingent to assist her against Thebes (p. 94); it is however possible that Plutarch has misdated this event, and that Dion had received Spartan citizenship before his banishment, perhaps before the death of the elder Dionysius.

The reports which reached Syracuse of Dion's mode of life soon began to arouse the tyrant's suspicions; not unnaturally the connections that he was continually forming with prominent statesmen were interpreted as hostile to Dionysius. How far this interpretation was just it is hard to say, but it does not seem probable that Dion was from the first deliberately planning to recover his position by force of arms; he was a man of many interests, and doubtless his association with the Academy and with men of culture elsewhere was maintained for its own sake, and not merely as a means of disguising political plans. But it was inevitable that the sympathy and admiration so universally manifested towards the exile should foster resentment at his injuries, and awaken in him a sense that he was called to be the liberator of his countrymen; doubtless, too, these feelings were accompanied by the desire for power. Meanwhile the conduct of Dionysius constantly afforded further provocation; he postponed fulfilment of the assurance given to Plato that Dion should be recalled, he held back the revenue from Dion's property and sold part of it, he proposed to find his wife Arete another husband.

Plato, who had remained for a while at the Syracusan court after Dion's expulsion, had been vainly endeavouring to act as mediator. The attitude of Dionysius to Plato presents a curious mixture of sentiments: while admiring the philosopher, he disliked and distrusted the friend of Dion; and although Plato was unable to heal the ever-widening breach, yet his personal relationship to the two men had the effect of postponing the inevitable conflict. Dionysius feared that if he went to extremes in his treatment of Dion he would lose his hold on Plato, and this he wished to avoid, principally from motives of personal vanity. He believed himself proficient in philosophy, and it was his ambition to prove himself so; he even went to the length of composing a sort of metaphysical handbook purporting to give the substance of Plato's doctrine.

Plato had taken his measure after a very brief acquaintance; he knew that he had no real capacity for philosophy, and that his professions in favour of political reform were only the froth of an impulsive temperament; his sole reason for continuing to maintain relations with Dionysius was the belief that he might contrive the restoration of Dion. Hence, after one refusal, he was prevailed upon to make a second visit to Syracuse, early in 361, accompanied by Speusippus and other members of the Academy. Dionysius sent a trireme to fetch him, and when he arrived treated him at first with marked respect and deference. But he found the Syracusan court, with its atmosphere of suspicion and intrigue and its shallow culture, fully as uncongenial as he had expected. Particularly distasteful must have been the presence of Aristippus, the so-called Socratic who had twisted the teaching of his master into a theory of more or less refined hedonism. Aristippus had gone to Syracuse frankly to get anything he could out of a munificent patron of learning; he had found high favour with Dionysius, and now resented the higher favour accorded to Plato, whose refusal of the tyrant's bounties merely increased his rival's jealousy. Plato was unable even to raise the question of Dion's recall, and his repeated attempts to do so soon began to annoy Dionysius. The increasing estrangement was hailed with delight by Aristippus and other rival philosophers at the court; it is recorded that, when an eclipse of the sun had been predicted by Helicon of Cyzicus, Aristippus remarked that he too had a prediction to make; and that, on being asked what this was, he replied 'I predict that there will soon be a breach between Dionysius and Plato.'

Plato's visit was in fact quite useless, and in the end the wayward tyrant came to treat him virtually as a prisoner; indeed it needed the intercession of Archytas, the ruler of Tarentum, to procure his escape. Meanwhile Dionysius' conduct towards Dion had grown even more hostile: he sold the remainder of his property and gave Arete in marriage to Timocrates. It must be admitted that there were some grounds for this hostility. Speusippus had been sounding the populace, and predisposing them in Dion's favour, while Heracleides, a friend of Dion who co-operated in his subsequent enterprise, was suspected of engineering a mutiny of mercenaries which occurred during Plato's visit.

II. THE ENTERPRISE OF DION

By the summer of 360 B.C., when Plato met Dion at Olympia, it was clear, at least to Dion, that no satisfaction could be procured save by an appeal to arms, and we may believe Plutarch's statement that it was now that Dion definitely contemplated this course; the indignities to which the aged philosopher had been subjected perhaps turned the scale. Speusippus, who had taken pains to discover the sentiments of the Syracusans, had found them longing for Dion to come as their deliverer. With the aid of Heracleides, who had escaped arrest and fled from Sicily, Dion now set about collecting mercenaries, but it is probable that he found this a more difficult task than he had anticipated: he got together a force of 3000[1], and took three years in doing so. It was not until August 357 that the expedition was ready to sail; only 1500 accompanied Dion, the rest being left to follow later with Heracleides: the reason no doubt lay in difficulties of commissariat. Several prominent members of the Academy accompanied the force, but Plato himself held aloof, feeling perhaps that a private quarrel did not justify the spilling of Syracusan blood.

The destination had been kept secret: it was not until the last moment that the troops, at their rendezvous on the island of Zacynthus, learnt against whom they were to serve. Their dismay at the discovery was not unnatural, and they were only with difficulty reassured by being told that the whole Syracusan

---

[1] See Beloch, *Griechische Geschichte* III^2, 1, p. 257, n. 3.

population was ready to rise, and that they themselves would be used mainly as officers.

The enemy, however, was well informed. Philistus, the admiral of Dionysius, was cruising off the coast of Iapygia, ready to intercept Dion, whom he expected to take the ordinary route across the Adriatic and down the coast of Italy. Dion, however, wisely sailed direct to Sicily, and after a hazardous voyage landed at Heraclea Minoa, the Carthaginian outpost on the south coast. The resistance offered by the garrison was only nominal: Dion, doubtless, had an understanding with its Greek commander. After a short rest the troops started for Syracuse, leaving behind their surplus baggage and arms. Dion had counted upon greatly increasing his numbers on the march, and his expectations were amply fulfilled. Volunteers flocked to his standards from Acragas, Gela, and Camarina; Sicels too and Sicans, even it is said men from Messana and the cities of Italy; their number it is impossible to give, for Plutarch represents that on the way to Syracuse the original force had been increased by no more than 5000 recruits, while Diodorus makes them as many as 50,000; it is plain that nothing approaching the latter number could have been equipped, but Plutarch perhaps under-estimates in order to heighten the glory of his hero's achievement.

As they drew nearer Syracuse the inhabitants of the rural districts added their quotas. The last halt was made at the old Syracusan outpost of Acrae, about twenty miles west of the city. While encamped there, Dion received a welcome piece of news: the Campanian mercenaries, drawn from Aetna and Leontini, who guarded the fort of Euryalus had quitted their post, owing to a rumour spread by Dion's agents to the effect that his first objects of attack would be their own two cities. Dion was now able to enter Syracuse without opposition, amidst the acclamations of the citizens who welcomed their deliverer with divine honours. Only the Island fortress was held by the troops of Dionysius; the tyrant himself chanced to be absent on a visit to his Italian colony of Caulonia, and a despatch sent to him by Timocrates, whom he had left behind as his deputy, had miscarried, so that it was not until six days later that he returned to Ortygia. Timocrates meanwhile, after vainly attempting to prevent the desertion of the Campanians on Epipolae, had found it impossible to rejoin the garrison and had fled.

The festal entry culminated in a mass meeting of the liberated populace in front of the five gates which gave access to the Island from Achradina. Taking his stand on the sundial which Dionysius had erected on this spot, Dion harangued the assembly, exhorting them to grasp their liberty and select their leaders. The first cries were for Dion himself and his brother Megacles to act under the title of 'generals with full power'; such, in fact, was the faith of the masses that they had no hesitation in conferring on the liberators the office which had clothed the tyranny with a semblance of constitutional authority. But Dion was unwilling to accept a position which would in effect concentrate all power in his own single person; and his refusal must surely be interpreted as evidence that he had not returned, as some have supposed, simply to expel Dionysius and take his place. As a convinced adherent of Plato he could tolerate neither tyranny nor democracy; the alternatives were constitutional monarchy and aristocracy, and it is probable that the 'freedom' which he had come to win for Syracuse was intended ultimately to take the form of an aristocratic constitution. But he must have realized that for the present executive power must remain in the hands of a few persons upon whom he could rely. It was therefore arranged that, in addition to Dion and Megacles, twenty generals should be appointed, of whom ten were selected from the fellow-exiles of Dion who had returned with him; who the other ten were we are not told. No doubt the whole twenty were in fact selected by Dion himself rather than by the massed citizens. How far Dion really meant them to have a share in the government it is impossible to say: but they appear in the event to have been mere ciphers.

So far everything had been easy; but from the military point of view Dion's task was as yet hardly begun. The freedom of Syracuse was wholly illusory so long as Dionysius held the Island with his mercenaries and the sea with his fleet. Dion's first measure was to build a wall from the greater to the lesser harbour, barring off the Island from the rest of the city. Plainly, defensive action alone was possible on land: the only chance of defeating Dionysius effectively was by sea, and for this Dion had to wait until Heracleides should arrive with the second force. During the winter the Syracusans were active in building triremes, of which they had as many as 60 at their disposal in the sea-fight which ensued in the summer of 356 B.C.

Meanwhile Dion's difficulties were increasing. After the first outburst of enthusiasm his popularity rapidly waned: an aristocrat in behaviour, he lacked the arts of the popular leader, nor did he care to acquire them; the necessities of defence compelled him to act arbitrarily, to disregard his nominal colleagues, in fact to act to all intents and purposes as a tyrant. In these circumstances Dionysius was quick to seize every opportunity to increase his enemy's unpopularity. He first tried secret negotiations with Dion personally instead of with the Syracusan people, intending no doubt to repudiate his proposals after Dion had compromised himself by replying to them; but in this he was foiled, as Dion told him to address himself to the people; in other words, to make his proposals public. The tyrant's next trick was to send a letter purporting to come from Dion's son, in which he reminded Dion of his zealous services on behalf of tyranny, and suggested that it would be wiser for him to assume the tyranny now himself rather than abolish it: only so would he be safe from the vengeance of those who remembered him as the prop of tyrants. The contents of this clever document[1] somehow became known to the populace, as was of course intended by the writer, and convinced many that the deliverer was playing false. To supplement propaganda by force, an attack was launched on Dion's cross-wall, but was repulsed after sharp fighting in which Dion himself was wounded and showed conspicuous bravery.

It was at this moment that Heracleides arrived with his ships. His arrival was a great encouragement to the Syracusans, but a considerable embarrassment for Dion, whose opponents found Heracleides very ready to side with them. He accepted from the assembly nomination as admiral, but Dion insisted that this appointment was an infringement of his own position as 'general with full powers'; we hear nothing at this point of Dion's twenty colleagues. In his contention Dion had precedent to go upon, for under the régime of the elder Dionysius the office of admiral had undoubtedly been subordinate to that of the General from whom he received the appointment. The precedent was indeed the precedent of tyranny, yet Dion can hardly be blamed for resisting a measure which was plainly designed to undermine his position. Another assembly was convened in which Dion himself appointed Heracleides to the command at sea; in truth he had

---

[1] The story of this letter is somewhat perplexing. It is said to have been marked outside 'From Aretaeus (Hipparinus) to his father' and to have been sent along with other letters of appeal to Dion from Arete and Aristomache, who were with Dionysius on Ortygia. Dionysius must have known or guessed that it would be read out in the Assembly: otherwise there was no object in sending it. Probably the letters from Arete and Aristomache had actually been read out already, and the letter purporting to come from Aretaeus was sent later in the belief that it would be read out too. Dionysius calculated that a letter coming openly from himself would have been withheld from the public.

no choice but to do so, for the warships were already under Heracleides' orders.

In the naval battle which ensued in the early summer of 356 B.C. a decisive victory was won by the patriots; the ship of the enemy admiral Philistus was captured, and in his despair the aged warrior took his own life[1]. The virulence of hatred which made civil warfare so horrible in Syracuse, as indeed in all Greek cities, is brought home to us when we read how the corpse was subjected to outrage and mutilation; such conduct was unhappily very common throughout antiquity, but it comes as something of a shock to find the gentle and philosophical Plutarch remarking that it was 'perhaps pardonable' that those who had been wronged by Philistus should thus exact their vengeance.

Dionysius had suffered a severe blow. Not only had he lost a capable and trusty servant, but, what was even more serious, he had lost the command at sea and therewith the possibility of indefinitely sustaining the siege. He therefore offered to surrender the Island, together with his mercenaries and munitions[2], on condition that he should be allowed to retire to Italy in the enjoyment of the revenues from his private estate in Syracusan territory. This offer was however refused. Dionysius now cared for little but his personal safety, and contrived to get away by sea with a few friends and some of his possessions; he reached Locri, eluding the vigilance of Heracleides' fleet, and left his son Apollocrates to hold the Island. A storm of indignation burst upon Heracleides for his negligence, and in order to save himself he lent his sanction to the demands of the extremists amongst the opponents of Dion, the doctrinaire republicans who clamoured for equality—by which they meant a redistribution of land—as the complement of liberty. With the support of Heracleides this measure was carried in the assembly, and further it was decided to discontinue the pay of Dion's mercenaries, and to elect new generals in place of the existing nominees of Dion. Thus was the liberator's advice to the people to grasp their liberty accepted in full measure. The reaction from despotism is apt to be violent: to the newly freed, liberty may mean anarchy. So Dion had found

[1] According to Ephorus (Frag. 152 *F.H.G.* I, p. 274) and Timaeus (Diodorus XVI, 16). Plutarch (*Dion* 35) prefers the story of Timonides, an associate of Dion, who says that the Syracusans took Philistus alive and murdered him. It is possible that the letter of Timonides to Speusippus, on which Plutarch relies, was a forgery.

[2] So Plutarch. Diodorus (XVI, 17) says that the mercenaries and munitions were to be retained by Dionysius.

to his cost. He had no choice but to withdraw from Syracuse with his mercenaries, to the number of more than 3000. They came to Leontini, where Dion was received with honour and the soldiers were given citizen rights.

The garrison of Ortygia had by this time almost exhausted its provisions and had begun negotiations for surrender, when an unexpected relief appeared. Dionysius, who perhaps saw a chance of recovering his position now that Dion was gone, had contrived to secure a body of mercenaries, under the command of one Nypsius, a Campanian soldier of fortune. These were dispatched to Syracuse together with food and money for the starving garrison, and were accompanied by some triremes, sufficient in number to have a chance of coping with the Syracusan ships guarding the entrance to the harbour. The arrival of this force was a complete surprise to Heracleides and his colleagues, and men and stores were landed without opposition. The Syracusan admiral, anxious to atone for his negligence, went out to give battle; four of the enemy's triremes were captured, and in exultation over this success the whole population gave itself up to revelry. Discipline under the régime of the triumphant democrats was despised, and danger disregarded. In the night that followed, Nypsius' men carried Dion's wall and were let loose upon the city, sacking, plundering and murdering. In their extremity the miserable Syracusans had no choice but to send a deputation to Leontini, to implore aid from the men whom they had driven out. And they did not plead in vain. Dion and his 3000 men came back; we are told that they came slowly, that their advance was delayed by fresh messages from Syracuse. Nypsius had called back his troops to the Island at nightfall, and the democratic leaders, imagining that the worst was over, repented of their haste in agreeing to call upon Dion, whose attitude towards themselves they might well expect to be pitiless. It needed a second night of terror to convince them that it was better to trust to the doubtful mercies of a fellow-citizen than to abandon themselves, their women and children and all that they had, to the savagery of blood-thirsty barbarians. How great was the havoc wrought by fire and sword on that second night we cannot say, but we know that Nypsius, acting presumably on orders from Dionysius anticipating such a situation, sent forth his men not to conquer or to capture, but to burn and kill. It is to be supposed that some quarters of the city, probably Upper Achradina and Epipolae, escaped, and that some of the population in the lower town fled thither; otherwise there would have been none for Dion to save.

On the third day the brother and uncle of Heracleides, who him-self was wounded, appeared as suppliants before Dion, now eight miles distant; in hot haste Dion advanced at the head of his men and re-entered the burning city; through blood and fire and the masses of dead lying in the streets they fought their way, and at last overpowered the enemy, most of whom, however, escaped into their fortress.

It might have been expected that the position of Dion, now that he had rescued Syracuse a second time, would be secure, and that his democratic opponents would be permanently silenced. His biographers fail to give any adequate explanation why this was not so; but it seems plain that the leniency which he displayed on the morrow of the victory was a grave error of judgment. All the prominent demagogues had taken to flight except Heracleides and Theodotes, and Dion would have been amply justified in executing these two, as his friends advised, or at the least in expelling them from Sicily.

The *beau geste* of a free pardon was certain, as he might have realized, to have deplorable results. It was interpreted, naturally, as a sign of weakness, as in fact it was; but if we are surprised at this action it is indeed amazing to find Dion soon afterwards con-senting to the restoration or continuance of Heracleides' command at sea. We can hardly believe that Dion still preserved any faith in Heracleides, nor that a desire to conciliate the popular party could by itself have induced him to consent to the appointment. The probability is that the crews of the triremes were masters of the situation, and would tolerate no other commander: they had presumably not suffered like the townsfolk in the recent sack of Syracuse. While he gave way on this point, Dion insisted on the repeal of the popular decree for redistribution of land; and the odium which this aroused was sufficient to encourage Heracleides to resume his machinations.

The relations of Dion and Heracleides were now complicated by the momentary appearance of two enigmatic figures from Sparta, Pharax and Gaesylus who, perhaps in Dionysius' interest, sought to use against Dion the prestige of Sparta. The only result of their intervention was that Heracleides, who had intrigued with them in turn, was once more discomfited, and that Dion now felt strong enough to insist on demobilizing the crews of the triremes, pro-bably immediately after the capitulation of Apollocrates in 355 B.C. The son of Dionysius was at length starved out and his mercenaries were mutinying: he was allowed to depart with five triremes, but surrendered all his munitions and equipment.

Even now, when the deliverance from tyranny was completed, the dissensions amongst the Syracusan population continued with melancholy persistence and wearisome reiteration. Dion still fails to conciliate his opponents, and seeks advice and support from Corinth in his endeavour to establish his aristocratic constitution; Heracleides still intrigues until at last Dion connives at his assassination. According to the account of Nepos, financial difficulties forced him to impose heavy taxes upon the richer citizens, and consequently he lost their support. In the end he was murdered, in June 354, as the result of a plot devised by his former friend of the Platonic Academy, Callippus.

Dion had failed, as he himself fully realized before the end. His connivance at the murder of Heracleides was the act of one disillusioned and half distraught. Considering the provocation that he had suffered, we cannot blame him overmuch; but the action was fatal to his prospects, for it convinced all men that they had only exchanged one tyrant for another. Dion had indeed become a tyrant in spite of himself. His tragedy is the tragedy of an idealist who wholly lacks the ability to accommodate his ideals to the realities of time and place. Syracuse was not a favourable ground for the establishment of aristocratic government, for owing to the numerous changes of population which it had suffered it lacked a genuine aristocracy of birth. No one at Syracuse sincerely wished to realize the political ideals of Dion and of Plato, and hence Dion could never have formed a strong party to support his projects, even if he had been born with the gifts of a party leader. Moreover, generous, high-minded and patriotic as he certainly was, he could not win the affections of his fellow-citizens, for he was handicapped both by his kinship with tyrants and by his spiritual affinity with the philosopher who had for the common people nothing but contempt.

The murderer of Dion affected to be a liberator, and was the hero of the hour; but there is no reason to suppose him to have been anything but an adventurer who had seized his opportunity. After ruling thirteen months he succeeded in establishing a tyranny at Catana, but only at the cost of losing Syracuse, where he was displaced in 352 by Hipparinus, the elder son of Dionysius I and Aristomache. After two years the new tyrant met his end in a drunken quarrel, and his place was taken by his brother Nysaeus. Of the character of Nysaeus and his rule we know nothing, but the fact that he maintained himself for five years proves that he was a man of some ability. Finally in 347 he was expelled by Dionysius himself, who thus regained his power ten years after he had lost it. During all these years, since the murder of Dion, the condition of Syracuse seems to have been miserable in the extreme. A large proportion of the population had perished in the constant civil strife, poverty and destitution were widespread, and there seemed no escape from the series of hated tyrants.

Dionysius, who during his ten years' exile had ruled at Locri, had there displayed all the worst features of the despot, and his second period of power at Syracuse proved so intolerable that the despairing citizens appealed for aid to Hicetas, a Syracusan by birth, who now ruled at Leontini. At the same time danger threatened from abroad, for a Carthaginian force had made its appearance in Sicily, and it seemed likely that the last traces of Greek freedom would be obliterated. Indeed the condition of the island as a whole at this date was pitiable. The majority of the Greek cities had either been devastated and depopulated, or were crowded with Italian mercenaries who had been brought in by the tyrants and who constituted their effective support. So extensive had been the settlements of these foreigners that according to a contemporary writer[1] there seemed a real danger of the Greek language falling out of use, and being replaced by the tongue of the Oscan or of the Carthaginian.

III. TIMOLEON: THE DELIVERY OF SYRACUSE

It was in these circumstances that an appeal was made, probably early in 345 B.C., by the Syracusans to Corinth, their mother-city; we may suppose that it was made from Leontini, whither the followers of Dion, who had most to fear from the returned Dionysius, had fled for refuge. The selection of Corinth was natural, not only because she had a reputation for befriending her colonies but also because Dion himself had sought the help of Corinthians in his legislative reforms; Sparta, on the other hand, was mistrusted in view of the conduct of Pharax and of Gaesylus. It is not clear whether Syracuse expected or asked for troops or warships: in view of the disturbed state of Greece at the time it could hardly be thought likely that Corinth would be willing or able to supply troops in any numbers, but the main requirement was a commander who would inspire confidence and could not be suspected of harbouring personal ambitions.

According to Plutarch, it was the fear of an attack by the

---

[1] Plato, *Epistle* VIII, 353 E.

Carthaginians that occasioned this appeal. This may very well
be true, and it might be expected that assistance would more
readily be granted against a barbarian attack than against a Greek
tyrant. Nevertheless there was pressing need also for help against
domestic foes; for Hicetas was known or believed to be intriguing
with Carthage. He supported the appeal, but not in good faith;
for while ready enough to help the Syracusans to get rid of Dionysius, he intended to fill the vacant position himself. Doubtless he
felt, and not altogether without reason, that freedom and democracy in contemporary Syracuse were vain dreams, and that he
had as good a right as any other to rule; any commander sent from
Corinth could only appear to him a rival or an impediment. It is
doubtful whether he seriously contemplated enlisting Carthaginian help before the appeal to Corinth was suggested; in any
case, it was the threat of the interference of old Greece in Sicilian
affairs that moved Carthage to respond. Apart from that, it seems
likely that she would have preserved the non-aggressive policy
that she had followed since her conclusion of peace with Dionysius
II in 367 B.C. (p. 273). She had on that occasion acquiesced in
the Halycus frontier, and the little that we know of Carthaginian
history between 367 and 345 suggests that mercantile interests
now dominated her policy rather than schemes for territorial
expansion. In 348 B.C. she concluded the second treaty with
Rome[1], which, on the one hand, reiterated her claim to a *mare
clausum*, going beyond the first treaty by excluding Rome from
trade in Sardinia and the whole of Libya except Carthage itself,
and, on the other, embodied clauses for the restriction of piracy.
And at some time between these dates, or possibly a little later,
she had to suppress a dangerous attempt by Hanno to overthrow
the constitution and seize supreme power. The failure of Hanno's
coup may perhaps be interpreted as a triumph of the commercial
and peace-loving party over the landed aristocracy which had
come into prominence during the past century and favoured an
imperialistic policy.

The presence of a Punic army in the island in 345 B.C. was a
lucky accident from Hicetas' point of view: it was occasioned, so
far as we can judge, simply by the need of defensive or repressive
action in the Carthaginian province[2]. It would seem that the
town of Entella, occupied since the time of the elder Dionysius
by Campanian settlers, was heading an anti-Carthaginian movement in the province, and endeavouring to gain support from

[1] Polybius III, 24.
[2] So Meltzer, *Geschichte der Karthager*, I, pp. 315–18.

without its borders also. The attempt proved a complete failure: the Carthaginians laid siege to Entella, and a contingent of 1000 men, sent by the Sicels of Galaria, a town near the western slopes of Mt Aetna, was annihilated before reaching its goal. Help had been promised also by the Campanians of Aetna, but on the news of the Galarians' defeat their efforts were abandoned. It is probable that Entella thereupon capitulated: at all events we find the town once more in Carthaginian possession three years later.

Hicetas, who, as we have seen, joined in the Syracusan appeal to Corinth, seems to have expected that it would not meet with success; and he may have reflected that, in that case, his policy of calling in the national enemy might be acquiesced in by the Syracusans as the only remaining alternative to the tyranny of Dionysius. But his calculations were wrong.

On reaching Corinth the Syracusan envoys were sympathetically received, and the magistrates at once invited candidates for the honourable commission to submit their names for election by a popular assembly. Amongst others the name of Timoleon, son of Timodemus, was put forward, not by himself but by a humble admirer: it was received with acclamation and Timoleon was elected. The choice was abundantly justified by the event, but it was a strange one. Timoleon was a man of good birth possessed of sagacity and courage, but for the past twenty years he had lived under a cloud; his brother Timophanes, in or about the year 365, had abused his position as commander of a mercenary force employed by the city to make a bid for tyranny, and Timoleon, unable to deter him, had either slain him with his own hands or contrived his assassination. It was an act of pure patriotism, but men's minds were divided between admiration for a tyrannicide and detestation of a brother's murderer. Ever since, Timoleon had lived in mourning and seclusion; his response to the call from Syracuse was, we may conjecture, inspired by the feeling that divine favour now offered him an opportunity for wiping out the memory of the past. We are told that after his election a prominent citizen named Teleclides observed in the Assembly that if Timoleon should be successful in his enterprise his fellow-citizens would account him a tyrannicide, if he should fail, a fratricide.

The choice of Corinth must have seemed a curious one to the Syracusans; Timoleon, though his bravery in war was proved, had no reputation as a general: and a man long withdrawn from public life was likely to be a stranger to the diplomacies and duplicities necessary for securing the goodwill of the Sicilians and for coping with a Dionysius: in fact his reception when he first arrived in Sicily was far from enthusiastic. The task which he had set himself was formidable; it was not to be confined to securing the freedom of Syracuse; that was of course his first and main purpose, but other Greek cities had associated themselves with the Syracusan appeal, and Timoleon aimed at freeing the whole island from tyranny. To accomplish this he must of course mainly rely upon the Sicilians themselves, and it was by no means certain that he would inspire confidence or win active support: so dubious and complex were the political conditions in Sicily that the appeal which had reached Corinth could by no means be taken as representing a universal sentiment. Timoleon, however, set about his task with energy, uplifted by a belief in divine protection manifested in visible signs from the outset, and in a trust in his own good luck, a trust which was amply borne out by subsequent events and to which he gave expression in later days by building a shrine to a strangely impersonal goddess, Automatia.

The force with which Timoleon sailed in the spring of 344 consisted only of seven triremes supplied by Corinth, together with one from Leucas and one from Corcyra, sister colonies of Syracuse, and of some 1000 mercenary troops, most of whom had been recently employed by the Phocians in the Sacred War (ch. VIII). Unlike Dion, he took the ordinary route down the Italian coast instead of making direct to Sicily across the open sea. On arriving at Metapontum he was met by a Carthaginian trireme and warned to proceed no farther. Carthage, taught by Hicetas, saw in Timoleon the would-be restorer of Dionysius' empire, the opponent of that particularism in Sicily which suited her policy. Hicetas had shown his hand before Timoleon left Corinth, and had sent a letter to the Corinthians urging them to lend no support to Timoleon's venture; he had, he said, been forced by their delay in sending help to have recourse to the Carthaginians, and the latter would not allow Timoleon's force to approach Sicily. The threat had no effect save to increase the enthusiasm of the Corinthian people for Timoleon's venture. Disregarding the warning given him at Metapontum, the deliverer proceeded down the coast to Rhegium, now a democratic state. In their readiness to aid the cause of freedom, and in their cordial dislike of the Carthaginians as neighbours, the men of Rhegium had promised Timoleon assistance, and it was due to them that Timoleon now found it possible to elude the Carthaginians and cross over to Sicily. Twenty Punic triremes had sailed into the straits, and envoys from Hicetas were on board: their message was that Timoleon himself might if he wished give Hicetas the benefit of his counsel, but that, since the war against Dionysius was well-nigh finished, his ships and troops should be sent back to Corinth, more especially as the Carthaginians would not permit their crossing the straits. Timoleon affected compliance, but proposed that their compact should be made before witnesses, in the assembly of the Rhegines. His ruse, concerted with the Rhegine authorities, was to detain the Punic envoys by lengthy speeches, during the delivery of which Timoleon's ships should put to sea one by one. Waiting until news was brought to him that all his ships except one had got safely away, Timoleon slipped unnoticed through the crowd and put off on the remaining ship. To the Carthaginians, indignantly protesting at the trick that had been played upon them, the men of Rhegium expressed their astonishment that any Phoenician should be displeased at guile.

It was to Tauromenium, the newly refounded city just outside the Straits, that Timoleon's squadron sailed. Andromachus now ruled there, with the authority, it would seem, of a constitutional king rather than of a tyrant; the picture drawn by Plutarch of this monarch, the friend of liberty and bitter enemy of tyrants, may reflect something of the partiality of his son, the historian Timaeus; but the facts remain that Tauromenium was the only Sicilian city that had promised Timoleon support before his arrival, and that it was likewise the only one left under the control of a single ruler when Timoleon's work was done. To the Carthaginian envoy who now appeared and demanded the expulsion of the Corinthians Andromachus returned a spirited and defiant answer; and so for a time Tauromenium became Timoleon's headquarters. At first he could see little prospect of success. In the message from Hicetas which reached him at Rhegium there was this much truth, that Hicetas had three days earlier defeated Dionysius and become master of the whole of Syracuse except the Island of Ortygia, where the tyrant was now blockaded. He had now induced the Carthaginian fleet to enter the great harbour, so that in any attempt on Syracuse Timoleon was confronted by a threefold enemy. From the numerous tyrants that ruled in the other cities, such as Hippo of Messana, Mamercus of Catana, and Leptines of Apollonia he could only expect opposition. If any of the victims of these tyrants' oppressions had joined in the invitation which brought Timoleon to Sicily, they showed no sign of supporting him now that he had come. He might, they felt, after all be only another adventurer like Pharax or Callippus, or a half-genuine liberator like Dion.

But during the summer of this same year, 344, Timoleon won

a success which completely changed his prospects. In the small town of Adranum it was felt that the citizens must choose between Hicetas and the Carthaginians on one side, and Timoleon on the other: opposite counsels were favoured by opposite parties, and in the end each made its appeal. Hicetas and Timoleon were both prompt to respond, and reached the vicinity of Adranum at the same time. But Timoleon took Hicetas by surprise, and though his force is said to have numbered only 1200—one-fifth of his opponent's—he was completely successful, taking a large number of prisoners and capturing the enemy's camp. The pro-Carthaginian party at Adranum must have been extinguished by this event, for Timoleon now established his headquarters there. By what was accounted, and indeed almost was, a miracle, he escaped assassination at the hands of an agent of Hicetas, and the general belief in a special providence that watched over him gained ground. It was perhaps in part due to this belief that several cities now declared their adherence to his cause: amongst these were Tyndaris on the north coast, and Catana, where Mamercus was tyrant; it is doubtful however whether Mamercus was sincere in his profession of a change even for the moment; in any case he did not long remain so.

But the most important result of Timoleon's victory was the surrender of Dionysius. This came as a great surprise to Timoleon, but from the tyrant's point of view it was undoubtedly a wise and natural proceeding. He could not sustain a siege indefinitely, and he preferred to surrender to Timoleon rather than to Hicetas. The reason which Plutarch (and perhaps Timaeus) assigns for this preference is that he despised Hicetas for his recent defeat, and admired Timoleon: but we may guess that a more cogent reason influenced the tyrant's choice. He realized that his career in Sicily was now finally closed, and that the only chance of saving his life was to escape to Greece; Hicetas, even supposing him to be willing to accept anything less than unconditional surrender, had no ships at his disposal; nor, if he had, would his Carthaginian allies have tolerated an arrangement guaranteeing Dionysius a safe passage out of the harbour; but to Timoleon the possession of the Island without a struggle would seem so desirable that he might be expected to accept the offer on condition of facilitating the tyrant's escape. The details of that escape are not recorded; but it was of course by sea, and must have been on a ship provided by Timoleon. The risk of capture by the Carthaginian ships had to be faced, but it was probably not great, nor was this the first time that Dionysius had been successful in running a blockade.

Accompanied by a few friends he reached Timoleon's camp, which had probably been transferred to Catana since the adherence of Mamercus; thence he was sent to Corinth to end his days in beggary and to provide innumerable anecdotes for historians and moralists.

The surrender of the Island had taken place within fifty days of Timoleon's landing in Sicily, that is to say, towards the end of the summer of 344 B.C.[1] Timoleon had good cause to congratulate himself and to confirm his belief in his automatic deity: immense quantities of war material came into his possession, together with 2000 mercenaries. Best of all, he had justified the choice of the Corinthian people, who hastened to dispatch reinforcements to the number of 2000 foot-soldiers and 200 horsemen. Nevertheless his task was still considerable, with the Island blockaded on the land side by Hicetas and on the sea by the Carthaginians. His first measure was to smuggle in by sea, in small detachments, 400 of his own troops to take over the fortress and the munitions: without this step he would of course have no security for the fidelity of the surrendered mercenaries. But the great difficulty was to feed the large garrison; provisions had to be brought in small fishing boats from Catana, which found it possible, especially in stormy weather, to make their way through the wide gaps in the enemy's line of ships. All through the winter of 344–3 B.C. Timoleon laboured at this task, which must have become still more formidable when (probably in the spring) the Carthaginians greatly increased their fleet in the harbour. It is said that Hicetas induced Mago to bring up his whole fleet, to the number of 150 triremes, and at the same time to disembark 50,000 or 60,000 troops in the city. These numbers must be greatly exaggerated, but it is plain that Timoleon had to face heavy odds. Nevertheless, in spite of the despair with which the Syracusans witnessed the spectacle of their city converted into a barbarian camp, their deliverer in his camp at Catana, and Neon, the Corinthian commander of the garrison in the Island, did not lose heart. Before long the carelessness of their enemies supplied them with an opportunity that they were prompt to seize. Mago and Hicetas rightly decided that they must capture Timoleon's base at Catana; but, while their best troops were withdrawn on this expedition, the vigilance of those left at Syracuse was relaxed, and Neon in a successful sally captured Achradina, the defences of which he

[1] So Plutarch. Diodorus (XVI, 70) places this event in 343–2. For arguments in favour of the later date (which is not here accepted) see Beloch, op. cit. III², 2, p. 380.

forthwith strengthened and united with those of the Island. The Corinthian garrison now had ample supplies of grain, and no attempt was made to dislodge them by Mago and Hicetas, who had returned in hot haste, abandoning the attack on Catana.

Meanwhile Timoleon was awaiting the reinforcement from Corinth. We are not told how soon after Dionysius' capitulation they were dispatched, but it is unlikely that they left before the spring of 343; and their journey was beset with obstacles. On reaching Thurii they found that their advance by sea was rendered unsafe by a Carthaginian squadron patrolling the coast. They therefore proceeded by land, meeting with some opposition from the Bruttians, a people previously subject to the Lucanians whose yoke they had recently (356 B.C.) shaken off. So they came to Rhegium; but they might have found it hard to cross the Straits in safety had not the Carthaginian admiral been inspired with a foolish conceit. Believing that the Corinthian troops would not dare to attempt the passage—a storm was raging, but it seems to have had no terror for the Carthaginians—he dashed off to Syracuse to display to the garrison of Ortygia his ships decked with bunting and Greek shields, an exhibition intended to persuade Neon that the Corinthian reinforcements had been captured in the Straits, so that he might as well surrender the Island without more ado. This puerile ruse had an effect very different from that intended; for meanwhile the storm had suddenly subsided and the troops had crossed at their ease in fishing-boats. Timoleon was waiting them[1]; he promptly united his forces and marched on Syracuse, encamping by the Anapus. And now there ensued the most extraordinary piece of good fortune in Timoleon's fortunate career; suddenly the Carthaginians embarked their whole host and sailed away. No adequate explanation is given for this remarkable action: Diodorus ascribes it simply to fear of Timoleon's army: Plutarch has a not improbable story of fraternization between the Greek mercenaries in the service of Timoleon and those of Hicetas, which came to the ears of Mago and caused him to suspect Hicetas of treachery; a modern historian suggests that Mago intended to have a hand in the revolutionary attempt of Hanno at Carthage[2]. The only point that is clear is that the withdrawal was not ordered

---

[1] Plutarch (*Timoleon*, 20) adds that he now occupied Messana, but gives no details. Diodorus (xvi, 69) makes him 'recover' Messana after the capture of Syracuse. Probably both references are to a nominal adherence of the tyrant Hippo, who afterwards met his end at the hands of his own subjects (see p. 297).

[2] Holm, *Geschichte Siziliens*, ii, p. 203. But the date of this attempt cannot be exactly fixed: see Meltzer, *op. cit.* i, p. 314.

by the authorities at Carthage: it was a personal decision of Mago's. He killed himself to escape judgment and his fellow-countrymen crucified his corpse. Hicetas, thus deserted, could offer no effective resistance. Timoleon attacked the city from three sides simultaneously—from Achradina and from the north and south sides of Epipolae, and was completely successful, though we can hardly believe Plutarch's statement that he lost not a single man killed or wounded. Hicetas, however, escaped to Leontini, where for the time being he continued to rule unmolested.

IV. TIMOLEON: THE SETTLEMENT OF SICILY

It was now late in the summer of 343; Timoleon's first object, the deliverance of Syracuse from tyranny, was achieved. There was formidable work still before him in the extirpation of tyrants in other cities; there was the possibility, if not the certainty, of a further Carthaginian menace; and there was the resettlement of Syracuse. The last was perhaps the hardest task of the three, and it was to this that he now addressed himself. Would he succeed where Dion had failed? That question was assuredly in the mind of every citizen of Syracuse. Two things at least were in his favour: Dion's experience taught him what to avoid, and he had no past record as a tyrant's henchman to live down. Moreover the recent presence of a Carthaginian army in the streets of Syracuse, and the likelihood of its return, might be expected to revive a national spirit and to quench the passions of party hatred. The first step was to re-populate the depleted city. Allowing for some exaggeration in Plutarch's description of streets and market-place overgrown with dense grass where horses were pastured, we cannot doubt that during the recent period of civil disorder the population of Syracuse had very considerably diminished[1]: some had met a violent end, some were in exile, thousands must have been forced to seek other homes after the night when Nypsius had sacked and burnt. It was but proper that the invitation to new settlers should be issued from the city of Timoleon and of Archias, the first founder of Syracuse[2]; the Corinthians gave the greatest possible publicity to Timoleon's appeal, and from all quarters of the Greek world men came together to live as free citizens of the restored Syracuse. Of 60,000 immigrants, excluding women and children, it is said that 5000 came from Corinth itself, and as

[1] Plato, *Epistle* vii, 337 c, implies a population of not more than 10,000 in 354–3.
[2] Coins struck by Timoleon bear Corinthian types, and one issue shows what may be the head of Archias. See Volume of Plates, ii, 8, *e, f, g.*

many as 50,000 from Italy and Sicily; Diodorus adds that 10,000 were also settled in his own native town of Agyrium. The process of resettlement must have been a gradual one, and Agyrium at least cannot have received its immigrants until, some five years later, Timoleon had expelled its tyrant Apolloniades. At Syracuse a redistribution of land took place amongst old and new citizens alike, while the houses were sold so that the old inhabitants had a chance of purchasing their dwellings; a thousand talents were thus realized for the treasury, which was so depleted that it was found necessary to sell the public statues by auction, that of Gelon alone being excepted. Meanwhile Timoleon had lost no time in obliterating the outward and visible signs of despotism: the palace of Dionysius and his two strongholds on the Island were demolished, and courts of justice were erected in their place.

Our information as to the constitution established by Timoleon is meagre. His advisers in the work were two Corinthians, Cephalus and Dionysius. It is not likely that any Corinthian would contemplate an unlimited democracy, and the statement that the old laws of the democrat Diocles (p. 108 sq.) were emended to suit the needs of the time doubtless points to some form of restriction. All we can say is that Syracuse remained a genuine democracy down to the time of Agathocles' tyranny, although the influence of the wealthy made itself increasingly felt. When we come to resume the history of Sicily after the gap of about twenty years which follows the retirement of Timoleon we shall find an oligarchical club of 600 referred to in such terms as to suggest that organized opposition to Timoleon's constitution very soon made its appearance. The chief executive power was vested in the priest or *Amphipolos* of Olympian Zeus, whose sacrosanct person would be a check upon revolutionary plotters; he was to be chosen yearly by a mixture of election and lot, and it would seem that he must be a member of one of the three leading families. Military control remained in the hands of a college of generals, but we hear of a resolution to the effect that in any war against barbarians a generalissimo should be imported from Corinth. It is probable that the same type of constitution was established in the other Sicilian cities when Timoleon had freed them. A loose federation or alliance bound them together, but Syracuse does not appear to have been accorded any kind of hegemony[1]: she would nevertheless be felt as the predominant

---

[1] Meltzer, *op. cit.* I, pp. 336–7, argues that the clause in the peace with Carthage stipulating that all Greek cities east of the Halycus should be free (see below, p. 297 *sq.*) was intended to preclude any Syracusan hegemony.

partner, for her population must have far outnumbered that of any other city.

It was probably in the summer of 342 that Timoleon undertook a campaign against Hicetas, who after his escape from Syracuse had resumed his rule of Leontini. But his attack was unsuccessful, and he next marched against Leptines who controlled a number of Sicel towns in the north. Leptines surrendered and was sent to share the fate of Dionysius at Corinth. Returning to Syracuse, Timoleon dispatched troops to the Carthaginian province, and succeeded in detaching Entella and some other towns from the Carthaginians: considerable spoils accrued from this expedition, which was probably undertaken after news had arrived that Carthage was preparing another attack on a large scale.

Disgusted at the failure of Mago and Hanno, the Carthaginians had determined to abandon half-measures and to rely no more upon the co-operation of Greek tyrants; it is said that they were resolved to drive the Greeks out of Sicily altogether, but this perhaps does no more than reflect the exasperation which they felt at the moment against Hicetas and such other rulers as had supported or feigned to support them in the previous campaign. The force, 70,000 foot and 10,000 horse, with 200 warships, was not exceptionally large, but it was notable as including 2500 Carthaginian citizens, belonging to the so-called Sacred Band. It was seldom that Carthage allowed the blood of her own sons to be spilt in her wars, and the presence of the Sacred Band attests the serious view which was taken of this campaign; it was felt that the Carthaginian hold on Sicily was gravely menaced. For the rest, the troops were recruited from Libya, Spain, Gaul and Liguria: the commanders were Hasdrubal and Hamilcar. In May or early June of the year 341[1] the troops were disembarked at Lilybaeum, where they heard of Timoleon's raid; and the news determined their generals to attack with all speed. It is not clear whether they resolved to march upon Syracuse, or first to chastise the raiders, assuming that these were still in the west: in any case the site of the battle was decided by Timoleon's rapid march into the enemy's country. The total force of the Corinthians, as our authorities call them, was no more than 12,000[2], and of these only 3000 were Syracusans. Plutarch (or his source) ascribes this small figure to the terror felt at Syracuse in face of the formidable enemy, but it is perhaps more reasonable to believe that the

[1] For the date of the battle of the Crimisus see Beloch, *op. cit.* III[2], p. 383, whose view is here accepted.
[2] So Diodorus (XVI, 78). Plutarch (*Timoleon*, 25) says only 6000.

resettlement of the city had not as yet gone far enough to increase its population very considerably. Other cities no doubt furnished some citizen troops—Diodorus says that all the Greek cities and many Sicel and Sican cities[1] also readily put themselves under Timoleon's orders after his capture of Entella—but the greater part of the remainder were probably mercenaries. In the course of the march Timoleon was embarrassed by a mutiny of the mercenary troops, one thousand of whom were suffered to return to Syracuse, to be dealt with later. The battle was fought on the bank of the Crimisus, not far from Segesta. It resulted in a decisive victory for the Greeks, which was due to several causes: the presence of a heavy mist enabled Timoleon to surprise the enemy by an attack from high ground; a violent thunderstorm came on, which drove rain and hail straight in the face of the Carthaginians; and the heavily-armed warriors of the Sacred Band, who bore the brunt of the fighting, found themselves at a great disadvantage in face of the superior mobility of the Greek infantry; the torrent of rain rendered their equipment still heavier, and as the plain rapidly became a morass owing to the overflowing of the river and to the swollen streams which swirled down from the hillside they found it increasingly difficult to move. Large numbers were swept away down stream, the rest were slain or put to flight. As many as 10,000 are said to have fallen, including the whole of the Sacred Band; heaven, in a very literal sense, had aided the Corinthian leader in this great battle, which was fought in mid-June, 341: the spoils of the enemy's armour were very rich, and fine trophies were sent to adorn the temples of Corinth and to add to her renown.

The remnants of the defeated host took refuge within the walls of Lilybaeum. The Punic fleet still rode the waters off the west coast, and it was therefore out of the question for Timoleon to attempt the siege of that stronghold, or of Heraclea or Panormus; without a naval victory it was impossible to drive the Carthaginians out of Sicily. Timoleon therefore left some troops to plunder enemy territory, and himself returned to Syracuse, where his first act was the expulsion from Sicily of the thousand mercenaries that had deserted him; they are said to have crossed to Italy and been cut to pieces by the Bruttians.

It says much for the tenacity and spirit of the Carthaginians that after this crushing defeat they did not abandon the war. It says much moreover for their adaptability that they returned at

---

[1] Evidence of coinage suggests that the Elymian Eryx allied itself now with Timoleon. See Evans in Freeman, *History of Sicily*, IV, p. 351.

once to their former policy of co-operating with Greek tyrants. Mamercus of Catana, who had become an adherent of Timoleon after the battle of Adranum, Hicetas who had supplied him with troops at the Crimisus, and Hippo of Messana now reverted to their previous allegiance; all were mere opportunists in their alliances, and whereas they had recently thought their positions endangered by the Carthaginian invasion they had now more to fear from Timoleon.

The Carthaginians now recalled Gescon, a son of the revolutionary Hanno (see p. 292 above), from the exile to which he had been sentenced for complicity in his father's designs, and put him in command of a fleet of 70 ships which entered the harbour of Messana probably during the summer of 340 B.C. Troops were disembarked, consisting of Greek mercenaries, for Carthage had profited by the experience of the Crimisus. At first they met with some success, Timoleon's troops suffering one defeat near Messana and a second at Ietae in the west of the island; Hicetas even ventured on a raid into Syracusan territory, but was routed by Timoleon at the river Damyrias, probably near Camarina[1]; he fled to Leontini, but was pursued by Timoleon, surrendered by his own people, and executed as a traitor to the national cause. His wife and daughters were condemned to death by a vote of the Syracusan assembly; this is the one event in Timoleon's career which Plutarch, his biographer, deplores, but it is probable that he had no constitutional means of preventing it. Soon after this Catana was surrendered by Mamercus' own comrades, and he fled for refuge to Hippo of Messana. Timoleon laid siege to the town, and when Hippo tried to escape by sea he was captured by the Messanians and executed in their theatre, where even the school-children were admitted to witness the joyous spectacle. Mamercus then surrendered, and after a public trial at Syracuse was crucified like a brigand. With the expulsion of the tyrants of Centuripa and Agyrium[2] in 338–7 the emancipation of Sicily from despotism was now complete, though one monarch, Andromachus of Tauromenium, still ruled his people as a constitutional king.

Carthage meanwhile had not waited for the complete overthrow of the tyrants, but had made overtures for peace in 339 after Timoleon's victories at the Damyrias and at Catana. It was agreed that the Halycus should remain the boundary of the Punic

---

[1] So Beloch, *op. cit.* III[2], 1, p. 587, who thus emends the unknown Calauria of Plutarch, *Timoleon*, 31.

[2] The people of Agyrium now received Syracusan citizenship.

province, that Carthage should recognize the independence of all Greek cities east of that river[1], and allow any Greeks in her own province to migrate to Syracuse if they wished. Further, she gave an undertaking to refrain in future from alliances with Sicilian tyrants. Thus Selinus and Himera remained subject to Carthage, who also appears to have retained Heraclea Minoa, although this town stood on the east bank of the Halycus. It is at first sight surprising that terms so favourable to the defeated enemy should have been granted: the explanation is partly that the peace was made while the tyrants, though defeated, were still at large, and Timoleon was willing to pay a considerable price to detach the Carthaginians from their alliance; but it must also be recognized that the victory of the Crimisus, glorious as it was, had been due to favourable circumstances, and hardly represented a real superiority of the Sicilian Greeks over any strength that Carthage might put forth. It is possible too that the defeat at Ietae was more serious than our Greek authorities admit, and that it involved a reconquest of the whole Carthaginian province[2].

About two years after concluding this peace Timoleon withdrew from public life. His principal work during these years was the resettlement of Gela and Acragas[3], the famous cities which since their destruction by Carthage in 406 B.C. had only revived on a very small scale; now that Carthage had renounced all claim to south-west Sicily it was possible to restore both to some degree of importance and prosperity. Camarina too, which had suffered under Punic dominion, received a fresh body of settlers, but the population of Leontini—presumably descendants of the mercenaries settled there by the elder Dionysius—were transplanted to Syracuse. The Campanian mercenaries of Aetna were expelled, and, as we may suppose, replaced by Greeks.

How long Timoleon lived after his retirement we do not know[4]. His last years were clouded by the loss of his eyesight, but he retained the confidence and veneration of the people of Syracuse, and occasionally spoke in the Assembly when specially important measures were under consideration. To his funeral flocked many

[1] Beloch's (op. cit. III[2], 1, p. 588) interpretation of the words τὰς Ἑλληνίδας πόλεις ἁπάσας ἐλευθέρας εἶναι (Diod. XVI, 82) as referring only to Greek cities east of the Halycus, is here followed.

[2] So Meltzer, op. cit. I, p. 336. Polyaenus (V, 11) says that Gescon's appointment was followed by a change in the fortune of war.

[3] The share taken by Syracuse in the resettlement of these cities is reflected in their coinage. See Volume of Plates ii, 8, h.

[4] Diodorus (XVI, 90) puts his death in 337–6; this was probably the date of his retirement (see Beloch, op. cit. III[2], 2, p. 384).

thousands from all parts of Sicily: the proclamation over his pyre, recorded by Plutarch, tells in words of simple dignity what he had done: 'The Syracusan people here gives burial to Timoleon, son of Timodemus, of Corinth, at a cost of two hundred minae, and honours him for all time with musical, equestrian, and athletic contests, because he put down the tyrants, conquered the barbarians in war, resettled the greatest of the devastated cities, and restored to the Siceliotes their laws.' There were few perhaps amongst those that came to do honour to their country's saviour who guessed how soon his work was to be undone.

V. SOUTHERN ITALY

The course of events in southern Italy during these years offers a parallel to that in Sicily. Just as in the island the dissolution of the empire of the elder Dionysius had ultimately involved the renewal of the struggle with Carthage, so on the peninsula the Greek cities had to contend against the attack of native Italian peoples. But there is this difference to be noted, that whereas in Sicily Carthage had held her hand until the security of her own province in the north-west was deemed to be endangered by the support proffered to Syracuse by Corinth, in Italy the barbarians' advance was definitely aggressive and unprovoked. The most formidable of the aggressors were the Lucanians and the Bruttians. The Lucanians, as we have seen (p. 128), had combined with Dionysius I in an attack upon the people of Thurii and had decisively defeated them at Laus in 389 B.C. But although the Syracusan tyrant had been ready enough to use barbarian help in his warfare against the Italiotes he was nevertheless alive to the danger of allowing Greek civilization to be submerged by a barbarian flood. His project of a wall across the isthmus of Scylletium in order to meet this danger had never been carried out, but it would seem that so long as the Syracusan Empire stood firm the Lucanians felt it unsafe to attack the Greek cities. It was not until 356, after the expulsion of Dionysius II, that the first attack came: and it came not from the Lucanians but from the Bruttians. It was probably a false etymology that represented this people as consisting of the fugitive slaves of the Lucanians; they seem rather to represent a number of tribes previously subject to the Lucanians who now seized the opportunity presented by the weakening of the Syracusan power to throw off the Lucanian yoke, uniting themselves under a common name, perhaps that of the strongest tribe, with a federal capital which they named Consentia. Terina, Hipponium, the Sybarite settlement on the river Traeis (vol. v, p. 168) and a number[1] of other Greek towns fell rapidly into their power. From the Siris to the isthmus of Scylletium the Bruttians were for the next twenty years or more the dominant power: we have seen that in 343 B.C. they opposed the passage of Timoleon's reinforcements from Thurii to Rhegium (see above, p. 292).

Farther north, Tarentum had to resist the attacks of the Lucanians and Messapians, and, like Syracuse, she turned for help to her mother-city, Sparta. It was probably in 342, two years after Timoleon had come to Sicily, that Archidamus, king of Sparta, crossed to Tarentum with a force of mercenaries, mainly drawn, like Timoleon's, from the survivors of the Phocian army in the Sacred War. Just as his more famous father Agesilaus had in his old age fought for the revolted subjects of the Persian Empire in the hope of restoring Sparta's prestige and replenishing her treasury, so now Archidamus in the same adventurous spirit responded to the offer of Tarentine gold. Nor was the son more successful than the father: he seems to have struggled for some three years, only to be decisively defeated and killed in 338 B.C., on the very day, it was said, of the battle of Chaeronea. The final battle was fought at a place called Mandonium in Lucania.

About five years later the Tarentines were again constrained to seek help from old Greece. From Sparta nothing more could be expected, for she had been brought under the heel of Macedon, but a powerful champion was found in the person of Alexander, king of Epirus, the brother of Olympias and uncle of Alexander the Great. It was his ambition to emulate in the West the exploits of his nephew in the East, and for a while that ambition seemed in a fair way to be realized. He first attacked the Messapians and Iapygians, carrying his victorious arms as far north as Arpi and Sipontum: then turning against the Lucanians, he advanced to Paestum on the western sea, and defeated the united forces of the Lucanians and Samnites. Farther south he captured the Bruttian capital at Consentia, and recovered Terina. In short, he gained for a brief space the control of a great part of southern Italy, and perhaps the most notable evidence of his power is the alliance into which he entered with the Romans, who had by now been brought into conflict with the Samnites. It is possible that

---

[1] Diodorus (xvi, 15) adds Thurii. But, as Beloch, *op. cit.* iii², 1, p. 594, points out, Thurii appears as an independent state in the time of Timoleon and during the campaigns of Alexander of Epirus (*c.* 331 B.C.).

his designs extended to Sicily also[1]. It soon became plain to the
men of Tarentum that instead of a protector they had in fact
called in a conqueror. Unable to recognize the plain fact that
the Lucanian advance could only be permanently stayed by the
establishment of a strong military power such as that formed by
Alexander, they preferred to defend their independence and
turned against him. Supported by the lesser Italian cities, such
as Thurii and Metapontum, Alexander coped successfully with
the new enemy and captured the Tarentine colony of Heraclea.
But naturally the Lucanians and Bruttians seized the opportunity
for attack, and in a battle at Pandosia, in the valley of the Crathis,
the Epirote king was completely defeated and stabbed in the back
by a Lucanian exile serving in his own army; this was probably
in the winter of 331–30[2].

Although Alexander's far-reaching designs had thus been
shattered, yet the Italiote cities were for the present relieved from
further barbarian pressure. This was mainly due to the outbreak
of the great Samnite war (327–304), into which the Lucanians
were drawn as Rome's allies. Tarentum was to make two more
bids for independence, under the championship first of Cleonymus
of Sparta, secondly of Pyrrhus, before she became subject to the
great power which as early as at the death of Alexander was fast
advancing towards the control of all Italy.

<hr/>

[1] Evans in Freeman, *History of Sicily*, vol. IV, p. 339, notes that numismatic evidence suggests that Alexander was in alliance with Syracuse, and
also with Locri. See Volume of Plates ii, 8, *i, j, k*.

[2] For the date see Beloch, *op. cit.* III[2], 1, p. 598, n. 1.

CHAPTER XI

THE ATHENIAN PHILOSOPHICAL SCHOOLS

I. THE PHILOSOPHY OF SOCRATES

IN the imaginary conversation of the *Phaedo*, Plato makes Socrates tell how he had lost all interest in the physical science of his time. The 'nature of things' had been sought, as it were, by taking the world to pieces and imagining it formed either by differentiation out of some primitive stuff or by the combination of several unchanging elements—a mechanical process, innocent of design. Anaxagoras, indeed, had spoken of Mind giving the first impulse of motion; but, to Socrates' disappointment, this Mind was not employed to plan the universe, in all its parts, 'for the best.' It was as if the reason why Socrates was then in prison should be found, not in his resolve to abide the sentence of the law, but in the movement of the limbs that brought him thither. Socrates did not himself attempt what Anaxagoras had left undone. He turned from the world of things to seek wisdom in the world of discourse.

The result of this re-orientation of philosophy was that the two great systems of the fourth century, the Platonic and the Aristotelian, looked for the nature of things no longer in a simpler material out of which they develop, but in some final perfection of form towards which they aspire by a natural or divine impulse, comparable to the conscious purposes of man. The mechanical interpretation of Nature yields to the teleological. Socrates himself, as Aristotle says (*Metaphysics* I, 6), had no system of Nature; but the revolution which set the concept of design above mechanical and material causes followed naturally upon his pre-occupation with the intelligent guidance of man's life towards his proper good.

The external facts of Socrates' life have already been described (vol. v, p. 386 *sq.*). For our knowledge of his philosophy we depend upon three witnesses: Xenophon, Plato, Aristotle; for Socrates himself left no writings, and we learn nothing of his characteristic doctrine from the *Clouds* of Aristophanes (first performed, 423 B.C.). The Socrates of this comedy is a composite picture of at least three incompatible types: the head of a resident school of atheistical Ionian science; the wandering Sophist, lecturing on rhetoric, grammar, and other subjects to young men rich enough to pay his fees; and a ragged ascetic, neglecting his worldly interests to teach morals. The third figure only has something in common with the Socrates of Plato's *Apology* and the ideal philosopher of the Cynic School. The Sophist may be dismissed entirely. Our other evidence, above all the *Apology*, denies that Socrates ever taught physical science, though he may well have sought wisdom in that quarter and failed to find it. Aristophanes recognized in Socrates and Euripides the two most subversive exponents of the modern spirit, and he heaped upon them every trait that he condemned, never dreaming that posterity would mistake his masks for historical portraits (see vol. v, p. 142).

The bulk of Xenophon's *Memorabilia* (see vol. v, p. 386) is not, even in intention, historical; it belongs, with his *Oeconomicus* and *Symposium*, to a type of apologetic literature known as 'Socratic discourses.' There were many such works[1]. The writers were to some extent in competition, each correcting the others' views of Socrates, who is a problematic figure to us because he was so even to his followers. Aristotle classes these writings with the prose mime as a form of fiction. They were imaginary conversations, designed to show what the dead master was like; and, while preserving a general fidelity to his character, the writers felt free to indulge in anachronism and to express their own opinions through his mouth. All Plato's dialogues are subject to this convention. Aristotle must have known this literature, besides what he learnt from Plato in an intercourse of twenty years. His evidence provides the only means of fixing the point where Plato goes beyond his master; for Xenophon's work is not independent of Plato's, and of the other Socratic discourses only a few fragments survive.

No document takes us nearer to the real Socrates than Plato's *Apology*, which is not an imaginary conversation in fictitious circumstances. Its aim is to give a true account of Socrates' work. That the account is not only true, but substantially complete[2], may be inferred from the 'high tone' which Xenophon found in all reports of Socrates' speech. Plainly Socrates had not tried to

[1] The Stoic Panaetius (2nd century B.C.) 'accepted as genuine those of Plato, Xenophon, Antisthenes, and Aeschines (of Sphettus), was doubtful about those of Phaedo and Eucleides, and rejected all the rest.' (Diogenes Laertius II, 64.)

[2] This is consistent with the probability (see vol. v, p. 392) that Plato left out some parts of Socrates' defence. His own reply to the charges of irreligion and corrupting the youth was to be given in the Socratic dialogues.

make an effective defence: he would not slur over anything in his past that would tell against him. The misrepresentation of his character and work by the comic poets is repudiated in terms that would have been futile, as well as disingenuous, if the picture in the *Clouds* had been even a caricature of the real man. He goes on to give his own account of his mission to Athenian society.

The Delphic oracle had declared that no one was wiser than Socrates (vol. v, p. 388). Unconscious of any wisdom, Socrates set out to refute the oracle by testing the recognized leaders of thought and action. The statesmen he found to be unaware that they knew nothing worth knowing. The poets, popularly esteemed as authorities on religion and morals, could give no rational account of their poems; they wrote, it seemed, 'by some inspiration of genius.' But among the craftsmen, (if only the cobbler would stick to his last and not fancy he could govern Athens), Socrates found what he called knowledge. We can infer what Socrates meant—or at least what Plato, at this stage, thought he meant—by the wisdom which he always said he did not possess and could not impart. The craftsman knows what he is trying to do, and why, and how to do it. He can give an explicit account of his knowledge; all his actions are intelligibly related to his purpose. Socrates' ideal was to reduce conduct to an art of this type; hence he seldom discussed a moral question without referring to the mason or the carpenter. Statesmen and poets had no such knowledge of the true aim of public and private life; they did not even feel the want of it.

For himself, Socrates asserts that he has nothing to teach. Attempts have been made to provide him with a *Begriffsphilosophie*. They were based upon statements in Xenophon, now seen to be derived from Plato's dialogues, and upon a passage (*Metaphysics*, 1, 6) where Aristotle, describing Socrates' influence on Plato, observes that he tried to define moral terms. Socrates' essays in this kind had a practical motive. Clear notions, he thought, are needed for right action; no one can be consciously and consistently good unless he knows what goodness is. Aristotle gives no ground for ascribing to Socrates a speculative interest in concepts or universals, or any theory of their metaphysical status. In the *Apology* (30 A) Socrates describes the positive side of his mission thus: 'I have no other business but to go about persuading you all, both young and old, to care less for your bodies and your wealth than for the perfection of your souls, and telling you that goodness does not come from wealth, but it is goodness that makes wealth or anything else, in public or in private life, a good thing for men. If, by saying that, I am perverting the young, so much the worse; but if anyone asserts that I say anything else, it is not true.' The only positive doctrine professed by Socrates is that, of all the aims men pursue in life, only one has any value, namely, 'to make one's soul as good as possible.' This had never before been said in Athens; it was a paradox, hard to understand. What is it, to be good? The question could not be answered in the *Apology*; but our witnesses agree in formulating certain principles which, at first sight, seem to be either platitudes or obviously false. These Socratic propositions are: (1) Goodness (virtue) is knowledge; (2) Goodness cannot be taught; (3) No one does wrong willingly; (4) Happiness is the result of goodness.

(1) The word *aretē* (goodness) lacks some of the associations of 'virtue.' Linked with the notions of function and performance, it denotes the excellence of whatever is good for any work or end; in the plural it can mean 'achievements.' The 'goodness' taught by the Sophists was ability to manage affairs and to attain the aims of personal ambition. The Socratics do not depart from this usage; they differ only in their view of man's function, which determines the content of his 'goodness.' The soul's function, says Socrates in Plato's *Republic* (353 D), is 'to take thought and to govern'; more generally, it is 'living'; man's goodness is that which enables him to live well, and so to 'do well' in another sense—to be happy. The first Socratic proposition defines this goodness, on which right living and happiness depend, as knowledge. This hard saying means, as the *Apology* indicates, that there is, or should be, an art of living, whereby all our actions would be consciously directed to an aim clearly conceived—the good in which our function consists, the true end of life. If we are to be good, this end must be known.

(2) How is such knowledge gained? It cannot, in the common sense, be taught. If the end of life were health or riches or social success, we could learn the means from the physician, the business man, the Sophist. Or, if 'living well' meant conforming to the rules of conduct approved by society, this again could be learnt as matter of ascertainable fact. But current beliefs about right and wrong cannot be knowledge: they are not consistent even within any one society; and no belief accepted on mere authority can be knowledge. I shall not know that what others call right and good is really so, unless I can see it for myself; and if I can see it, what others think becomes irrelevant. My action must be

determined solely by my own conviction. The implied postulate is that every human soul has the power to discern, by direct intuition, what really is good. Once cleared of the mists of prejudice and false appearance, its judgment is infallible and beyond appeal. Socrates, accordingly, had no system of morals to teach. He spent his time inducing anyone who would undergo the test to examine his own beliefs, until their confusion and inconsistency led him to the conviction that he did not know the true end of life.

(3) Critics, ancient and modern, have raised the obvious objection: I may know what is good and yet fail to desire it; mere knowledge is not enough to determine the will. Socrates replied: No one does wrong willingly (or wittingly). The wrong-doer is misled; his sense of what is really good, and good for him, is obscured by a false appearance. The rival pleasure seems good, and he follows it. It is not true, then, that he knows, at the moment, what is good. If he knew this, in the full sense of 'knowing,' he could not desire anything else. In a conflict of motives the fault lies, not in desire, which is divided between the two objects, but in the failure to discern the true object from the false. Once we can do that, the whole current of desire must flow towards the true good. *Celui qui n'agit pas comme il pense, pense imparfaitement* (Guyau).

The *Charmides* of Plato contains a discussion of self-control, starting from the Delphic precept, Know thyself. The upshot is that self-control, like every other virtue, means the knowledge of good and evil; and we may infer that this is tantamount to self-knowledge—the recognition of a true self, at the core of our being, which claims control over all the rest of what we call our 'selves,' and is, in the last resort, the 'soul' we must care for. Both Plato and Aristotle accepted the belief in this inmost self, and held it to be the divine element in man. Its peculiar form of desire, always directed to the true good it can perceive, they called by a special name, 'Wish' (*boulēsis*). When we act wrongly, we do what we like, but not what we wish; the insight of the true self is for the moment obscured.

(4) Finally, happiness is the result of goodness. The sacrifice of pleasures that falsely seem good is not a sacrifice of happiness. There is no real conflict between duty and pleasure, because no pleasure is comparable to the satisfaction of the soul which follows the inward recognition of good. To live well is the same as to live happily. This doctrine could easily be misconstrued to mean that virtue is to be chosen for its reward in terms of worldly goods.

Xenophon constantly ascribes this vulgar 'utilitarianism' to Socrates. It must be remembered that Socrates was not usually engaged in setting forth the moral principles above formulated,— we owe the formulation to Plato—but in drawing out and criticizing other men's notions about conduct. No doubt he generally talked to them on their own level; he may often have recommended virtue as a means to health or social esteem. This would suffice to mislead a Xenophon; but the Socrates of Plato holds that worldly prosperity and honour are indifferent; what matters is 'to care for one's soul.' The unresting pursuit of moral goodness is happiness, though poverty, suffering, and death be the cost. We do not will the good in order to be happy; we are happy in willing it.

This simple and profound doctrine of the right way of life is the philosophy of Socrates. Upon the question whether it had, in Socrates' mind, a religious background or sanction Xenophon cannot be trusted; we depend entirely on the *Apology* and the earlier dialogues of Plato. One thing is clear: the moral doctrine is self-contained, requiring no support from theological beliefs. If the distinction between good and evil, right and wrong, is absolute, and can be known directly by the inward eye of every soul, no supernatural sanction for conduct is needed, though it might exist. In the *Euthyphro* Socrates discusses religion with a self-satisfied formalist, and, in the course of a subtle argument, makes him admit that right conduct cannot be defined as conduct pleasing to the gods. Their approval is, in logical terms, an accident; it does not make an action right. The action is approved because it is right, absolutely and without condition. Hence a theology professing to interpret the will of heaven as a guide to conduct is superfluous. Further, if happiness can be attained only by knowing and choosing what is good, it is attainable in this life, in proportion to our success in fulfilling the condition. No belief in rewards or punishments after death could influence conduct. The good man is happy now, the bad unhappy. If there is a future life, it will be the same then; if there is not, goodness is not to be renounced as unremunerative. This truth Socrates undertakes to prove in the *Republic*.

Whether, and in what sense, the historic Socrates believed in gods or in immortality is a doubtful question. Xenophon says that he sacrificed both publicly and in his own house; but conformity implied no acceptance of dogma. He prayed, we are told, though never for the satisfaction of particular wants. 'His formula of prayer was simple: Give me that which is best for me;

for, he said, the gods know best what things are good[1].' The Platonic *Apology* speaks of 'God' or 'the gods' in conventional terms, open to any interpretation. The attitude to immortality is definitely agnostic. 'To fear death is to think you are wise when you are not; it is to think you know what you do not know. No man knows whether death may not be the greatest good a man can have; yet men fear it, as if they knew it to be the worst of evils.... Were I to make any claim to be wiser than others, it would be because I do not think I have any sufficient knowledge of the other world, when in fact I have none' (29 A). Death may be either a dreamless sleep or the migration of the soul to another place. In either case it is certain that 'no evil can happen to a good man, and his concerns are not neglected by heaven' (41 C). If Socrates had professed any definite belief in immortality, no motive could have induced Plato to convey a false impression in the *Apology*[2]. To Socrates this question, like every other, was a question of knowledge; and an essential trait of his mind is the clear sense where knowledge ends and ignorance, with its un-tested beliefs, begins. That no evil can befall the good man is a rational conviction, following from the definition of happiness. The only evil that can befall anyone is the loss of moral goodness. The statement that the good man's concerns are 'not neglected by heaven,' expresses, in conventional terms, a conviction that the world is so arranged that goodness does bring happiness. No doubt Socrates believed this; but that 'the gods' had so arranged the world was not even a generally accepted belief; and we are not warranted in ascribing to Socrates either Plato's theory of a designing Mind or Xenophon's simple faith in a busy Providence. The master might have thought that both his dis-ciples were in danger of thinking they knew what they did not know.

If conduct is subject to no external authority, social or super-natural, what stands between my will and the satisfaction of any desire whose end I can compass? Are not all things lawful by natural right? Why not define 'goodness' as the effective ability to do what I like? In the age of the Sophists and Socrates this ultimate problem rose up to confront the discoverers of the inner world of freedom. Science before Socrates had moved outwards into the physical world, expecting, with innocent confidence, to surprise the secret of its birth and nature, and unaware that it was

[1] Xenophon, *Memorabilia*, I, 3, 2.

[2] Especially if the address to the court after the sentence cannot have been actually made (see vol. V, p. 392).

discovering a pattern of its own contrivance. This speculation seemed at first to have no bearing on conduct, which was regulated by law, custom, and belief. But the unsettlement of tradition after the Persian Wars turned some minds to explore the inner world, governed, as it seemed, by other laws than those of the outer realm of necessity, or perhaps by no laws at all. In sleep, said Heracleitus, every man turns aside from the common world into a world of his own. When the speculative mind turns inward, Nature will become *appearance*, the scenery of a private dream: what more can be known of the alleged 'nature of things,' which does not appear? Each mind, at the centre of its own dream, will claim freedom and lordship of the inner realm. The restraints of religion and custom, imposed by society, will be denounced as unnatural conventions. The individual will identify his nature with the instincts, which disown artificial constraint. Give him Gyges' ring of invisibility, let him either elude or overpower the watch-dogs of society, and he will do as he likes.

Protagoras, who denied the Parmenidean world of unapparent Being and started this train of thought, stopped far short of the conclusion (vol. v, p. 378). Plato was the first to see all that was implied in what he called Sophistry, and to find an explicit answer. Socrates' answer was rather implicit in his life, a secret that made him a riddle even to his own disciples. In his character seemingly opposite tendencies were held in lightly balanced harmony. His rationalism found the key to goodness in clear thinking, and claimed for the individual an autonomy over-riding every re- cognized authority, divine or human. It was not clear to his contemporaries why this assertor of individual freedom should not be antinomian; why he should be indifferent to his own interests and pleasures; why he should not repudiate, or try to subvert, social institutions. Yet he challenged no conflict with received religion or with the demands of the State. He conformed to the established cult, and his accusers could find no more damaging charge than that he sometimes spoke of warnings received from a 'divine sign.' He did not, like the later Cynics, insult the decencies of common life, or exalt a state of nature above the civilization of Athens. Though he kept aloof from politics, he fulfilled the duties of a citizen, held office, married, and brought up children. He was not a champion of natural rights, but upheld positive law and accepted the duty of passive obedience. He was content to find in Athenian society freedom enough to go about his chosen business, avoiding any serious breach without the least compromise of principle. Regarding pleasure, and even comfort, with complete indifference, he had not that fear of pleasure which makes the ascetic. He could take pleasures when they came; when they did not come, he never missed them. True, the Socrates we know is the Socrates whom Plato and Xenophon knew, a man between sixty and seventy. His self-mastery may have been won after a long struggle with a passionate temperament; but, as we see it, the harmony is perfect. The followers who founded the minor Socratic schools could not divine its secret; Socrates had lived by a knowledge that he refused to call knowledge because he could give no account of it. The Cynics mistook him for an ascetic, and fell into anti-social extravagance. The Cyrenaics, following another clue, sought peace of mind in a haven of agreeable sensation[1]. Plato alone saw Socrates whole, and he set himself to give an account of the knowledge his master had disclaimed, but must certainly have possessed.

The inquiry was to carry him further than he could then foresee. Aristoxenus, the Peripatetic, had an anecdote of an Indian who met Socrates at Athens and asked him about his philosophy. When Socrates said that he sought to understand human life, the Indian replied that man cannot know himself without knowing God. The story may show that the successors of Plato and Aristotle were aware how far these two had travelled beyond their master's explicit doctrine, when they saw that the recognition of goodness demanded by Socrates could not be separated from the recognition of Ultimate Being.

II. PLATO: THE EARLY DIALOGUES

Plato was born (428–7 B.C.) of a family noble on both sides. In boyhood he must have listened to the conversation of Socrates, and felt the effect described by Alcibiades in the *Symposium*: 'No Corybant's heart ever throbbed like mine when I hear him; his words make the tears pour from my eyes.' As Plato grew to manhood, he came, deeply and irrevocably, under this influence. The story goes that he burnt a tragedy which was to have been staged at the Dionysia; Socrates had condemned the mere inspiration of the poet's genius, unable to give a rational account of its meaning. But Plato was not only a student of philosophy. His mind was poignantly distracted by another vocation, the life of active statesmanship, for which he was marked out by his gifts

---

[1] The Cynic and Cyrenaic Schools, founded by Antisthenes and Aristippus respectively, will be treated in vol. VII, as precursors of the Stoics and Epicureans.

and social position. He never ceased to acknowledge this claim upon powers he could not contentedly suffer to fust in him unused.

After Socrates' death, Plato, with others of his closest friends, withdrew to join Eucleides at Megara, resolved to continue the master's work and defend his memory. The next twelve years Plato must have spent mainly at Athens. He is said to have served in the Corinthian War of 395–86 B.C.; and probably, at some time in this period, he visited Egypt and studied geometry under Theodorus at Cyrene. Meanwhile he composed the *Apology* and the imaginary conversations which form the earliest group of his writings. The order of the dialogues cannot be exactly determined. Plato may well have written more than one at a time. The *Republic* must have taken several years; others might have been composed in as many weeks. Happily, the methods of stylometry have laid some check upon the caprice of subjective criticism. There is now a general agreement to recognize three main groups, though the order within each group is still disputed. To the early group we shall here assign the direct defence of Socrates in the *Apology* and *Crito*; *Laches*, *Lysis*, *Charmides*, *Euthyphro*, illustrating the true character of Socrates' work; the *Shorter*, and perhaps the *Longer*, *Hippias*, *Protagoras*, *Gorgias*, in which the leading Sophists appear; and the *Ion*. Probably all these were written, and the *Republic* begun, before Plato founded the Academy. The *Apology* has already been mentioned. The *Crito* explains why Socrates, to the surprise of the public and possibly to the dismay of his accusers, declined to escape from prison before his sentence was carried out. The history of Plato's thought begins in what are sometimes called the Socratic dialogues.

The general purpose of the *Laches*, *Lysis*, *Charmides*, and *Euthyphro* is still apologetic: the first three show how far Socrates was from 'perverting the young men'; the last indicates his true attitude to conventional religion—the other count in the indictment. But Plato is not merely echoing his master. These dialogues are by no means realistic specimens of Socrates' conversation; they are closely knit works of art, grappling, sometimes obscurely, with fundamental thoughts. Plato was himself trying to grasp the Socratic philosophy of life and to make up his account with its implications. He was at this time in painful hesitation, whether or not to yield to the importunities of political friends, urging the claims of public life upon one in whom they must have seen the Alcibiades of his generation, with the same social advantages and far more brilliant intellectual powers. Alcibiades, in the first of two dialogues named after him[1], stands on the threshold of political life, and Socrates convinces him that he will not be fit to advise his country until he has gained self-knowledge, or the knowledge of good and evil. Plato may have felt that the Socratic conception of the meaning and end of life had opened a gulf at his feet. The Socratic dialogues were, perhaps, written partly to clear his own mind before deciding whether he could hold true to this philosophy and also serve Athens as an active statesman.

The four dialogues are constructed on a uniform plan. The conversation arises out of a scene of ordinary life described at some length. The theme is the definition of a virtue: courage (*Laches*), self-control (*Charmides*), piety (*Euthyphro*), friendship (*Lysis*). A series of definitions are elicited, criticized by Socrates, and finally rejected. No conclusion is reached, and the reader is left wondering what inference he is to draw. This peculiar form avoids making Socrates lay down and defend any positive doctrine; but the inconclusiveness is only apparent. At least one positive result is indicated—the central Socratic principle that virtue can be reduced to wisdom or knowledge, with its corollary that all virtues are one. The *Laches*, for example, disproves the common view that a man can be brave and at the same time unjust or intemperate. If virtue means a knowledge of what is good and bad, such insight will cover every field of conduct, and determine all desire and action.

The *Charmides* shows Plato's mind at work upon the problem which then faced him in a practical form and never ceased to occupy his thoughts: the bearing of Socrates' philosophy upon the government of society. The concept of self-knowledge leads to the question, how a man can know the limits of his own and other men's knowledge and ignorance. What is this knowledge —Socrates had seemed to possess it—which judges all other knowledge? It is not an omniscience embracing all the special branches of science and art. If we could conceive the possessor of such omniscience in supreme control, every department of life would be scientifically directed; but it is not clear that true welfare and happiness would follow upon increased efficiency. Pursuing the same ends as before, men would be richer, healthier, stronger in war; but would they be better? The ruler should possess, not technical omniscience, but 'a single kind of knowledge which

---

[1] It is disputed whether *Alcibiades* I was written by Plato or by an early member of the Academy.

has for its object good and evil'—a Sovereign Art, assessing the
values of minor ends and their contribution to the well-being of
the whole. The *Charmides* contains in germ the central doctrine
of the *Republic*: that the ills of society can be healed only when
political power is combined with knowledge of an absolute
standard of value. The inference for Plato himself was that he
could not become a statesman until he had become a philosopher.

Beside these studies of Socrates' identification of goodness
with knowledge, Plato has set some satirical exposures of the
professed teachers of 'goodness.' In so far as the Sophists merely
supplied an education in advanced subjects, they did not cross
the path of Socrates, who sent them pupils; but their claim to
teach the conduct of life to young men who were to guide the
destiny of Athens challenged examination. Did they know themselves what was good or evil? Two dialogues devoted to Hippias
(see vol. v, p. 380) amusingly exhibit the professor of omniscience
as unable to follow the subtleties of a Socratic argument. In the
Protagoras three of the four great Sophists, Protagoras, Hippias,
and Prodicus, are present with their admirers in the house of a
wealthy amateur; Gorgias is reserved for another occasion. Their
methods—the allegorical discourse, exegesis of the poets—are
parodied with the reserve of exquisite art. Socrates maintains
the unity of all the virtues; but the argument is interrupted.
Protagoras holds the centre of the stage, discoursing of education
as a socializing influence. The vital question, on what philosophy
of life sophistic education is based, is not raised till near the end.
The argument is so cleverly turned that critics have been misled
into imagining that Socrates here defends hedonism. The real
purpose is to lead the Sophists to confess that their philosophy is
the same as the ordinary man's who believes that 'good' means
'pleasant,' or that pleasure is the only good. When he says
that some pleasures are bad, he only means that they are out-
weighed by future pains: he has no standard of good save the
amount of pleasure or pain. All errors of conduct must, then,
be errors of judgment in the use of the hedonistic calculus.
Socrates ingeniously claims this as a confirmation of his own
doctrine: All wrong-doing is due to ignorance. This ignorance,
he blandly suggests, the Sophists would cure, if only the public
would send their sons to be taught. Charmed with this conclusion,
all the Sophists accept the whole argument: 'the pleasant is good,
the painful evil'; right action can be defined as action that secures
a pleasant and painless life. Thus the professional teachers of
goodness are revealed as willing to fall in with popular hedonism.

Their function is to teach men how to pursue efficiently the only end they recognize. If goodness can be taught at all, it is not taught by men to whom 'the good' means nothing but pleasure.

If the *Protagoras* was too clever and gave the impression that Socrates could uphold hedonism, the *Gorgias* leaves no shade of ambiguity. Conceived in a wholly different vein of passionate earnestness, this dialogue throws into sharpest contrast two ideals of life. Rhetoric is treated as the weapon of political power in civic assemblies, and so as including statesmanship. It claims to be the Sovereign Art, but knows nothing of the true end of power; its aim is the autocracy of the politician in control of a democratic machine. To Socrates tyrannical power is at best unenviable. Better suffer wrong than do it; better be punished for wrong-doing than escape chastisement. Callicles, a rich young aspirant to political honours, protests that, if this be true, 'the whole of human life is upside down.' He maintains the natural right of the strong to the lion's share and professes hedonism, which Socrates now openly refutes. The life of self-asserting ambition, exalted by Callicles above the life of the philosopher, 'whispering with two or three striplings in a corner,' is to Socrates the life of the enemy of society. Socrates claims to be the only true statesman; but if he should enter public life without stooping to flattery, he would be put to death.

The bitter passion of the *Gorgias* reveals Plato's nature stirred to its depths by a conflict that had not yet been solved. His *Seventh Letter* tells how, before the revolution of 404 B.C. and later, he had been attracted to public life and again repelled by the deeds of the men in power, culminating in the execution of Socrates.

The result was that I, who had at first been eager to take part in public life, when I saw all this happening and everything going to pieces, fell at last into bewilderment. I did not cease to think how all these things, and especially the general organization of the State, might be amended; but I was all the time waiting for the right moment for action. At last I perceived that the constitution of all existing States is bad and their institutions all but past remedy without a combination of radical measures and fortunate circumstance; and I was driven to affirm, in praise of true philosophy, that only from the standpoint of such philosophy was it possible to take a true view of public and private right, and that, accordingly, the human race would never see the end of trouble until genuine philosophers should come to hold political power, or those who held political power should, by some divine appointment, become philosophers.

It was in this mind that I first went to Italy and Sicily.

III. THE ACADEMY. DIALOGUES OF THE MIDDLE PERIOD

In the *Gorgias* Plato had resigned the hope of exercising the Sovereign Art in his own city. There remained the possibility of intervening in some State which could be reformed by a despot from above. This prospect opened before him on his first visit to Sicily (389–8 B.C.). A second, and (as it proved) more effective, means was to found a school of philosophic statesmen. Plato's own task would be to direct this school and to work out the Socratic philosophy on lines now taking shape in his mind, publishing his results in a form that would reach the educated public throughout the Greek world and attract students. The Academy was founded just after the first visit to Western Greece. At Syracuse Plato thought he had found in Dion, the brother-in-law of the reigning Dionysius, a young man who might become a philosopher-king; but to flatter a despot proved as impossible as to flatter a mob; and Dion, now deeply devoted to Plato, had to procure his escape by a ship which was conveying home the Spartan envoy, Pollis. According to Plutarch (*Dion*, 5) Pollis, acting on Dionysius' instructions, sold Plato into slavery at Aegina. Redeemed by a Cyrenian friend, Anniceris, he returned to Athens, probably in the summer of 388 B.C. Anniceris, it is said, refused repayment of the ransom, and the sum was used to buy a garden in the grove of the hero Academus. Here the school was founded on lines partly suggested by the Pythagorean societies Plato had seen in South Italy. He also found in Pythagoreanism the clue to the problem of knowledge. The discovery is unfolded in the dialogues of the middle group: *Meno, Phaedo, Symposium, Republic, Phaedrus.* Some outlying works may be mentioned here. The *Euthydemus* dissociates the dialectic of Socrates from the barren disputation which was infecting the Megarian School. The founder of this School, Eucleides, was an Eleatic, who declared the Good to be one thing with many names—Wisdom, God, Mind. The Zenonian dialectic of his followers was called by their opponents 'eristic' or 'anti-logic,' and they have little to their credit beyond the formulation of puzzles which gave an impulse to logical theory. The *Cratylus* disposes of the notion that philosophic truth can be deduced from the structure of language. The *Menexenus* (385 B.C.) contains a satire on the Periclean ideal—a Parthian shot at Athenian democracy.

The possibility of knowledge had become a problem when

Parmenides condemned as false the manifold world which 'seems' to the senses, and Protagoras had asserted, on the contrary side, that what seems to every man is real or true for him. Was there, or was there not, a world of true Being behind appearances and capable of supporting them? Protagoras' fellow-countryman, Democritus of Abdera, whose long life must have nearly covered the century 450–350 B.C., gave the materialist answer. The atomism he adopted from Leucippus (see vol. IV, p. 575) is an ideally mechanistic system. True Being consists solely of atoms of uniform quality and of the void in which they move. Sensation is due to the impact of atoms from outside upon the atoms of the soul. All sensible differences of quality must be consequences of the only real differences between atoms—in shape, size, and position. These secondary qualities are 'conventional,' not part of the objective reality which is inaccessible to the 'bastard knowledge' of the senses. But the 'genuine knowledge' that reveals the real nature of the invisible atoms is explained by the same mechanism. The soul atoms, being diffused all over the body, can, by a direct contact independent of the sense-organs, perceive the atoms outside as they are. Democritus, of whom Aristotle remarked that he reduced all the senses to touch, might be said to reduce all thought to an exceptional kind of sensation. Such is the final outcome of Ionian science, seeking the real 'nature of things' in the ultimate components of material bodies.

To a follower of Socrates the problem of knowledge presents a different aspect; it is, in the first place, the problem of that knowledge which is goodness. Plato was, at this stage, no more interested than his master in the world of Nature. He held to the doctrine, learnt in his youth from the Heracleitean Cratylus, that sensible things are always changing and cannot be known. The primary aim of the Platonic theory of Forms or 'Ideas' is to provide for the inner world a law to save the individual will from the nightmare of unlimited freedom. The sovereign knowledge of good and evil must have for its object standards that are universally and absolutely valid. Justice and the other moral conceptions that Socrates sought to define must be eternal objects, to be known by thought, though not by sense. They are not part of the furniture of anyone's private world, but form a common world independent of what 'seems' to any individual or to all. Plato did not reach this conclusion solely by reflection upon the methods of Socrates and the formula, Goodness is knowledge. Platonism, as Aristotle saw[1], is a form of Pythagoreanism, modi-

---

[1] Aristotle, *Metaphysics*, I, 6.

fied by Socratic influence. The *Gorgias* (507 E) already points in this direction, where Socrates describes justice and temperance as a principle of order and law in the soul, and connects this principle with the harmonious order of the universe and the structure of mathematical truth.

The *Meno* announces a further discovery: how knowledge of eternal objects, moral or mathematical, is acquired. It cannot be derived by any process of 'abstraction' from the dream-world of appearance; it comes out of the soul itself by Reminiscence. Perhaps through contact with the mathematicians of Cyrene and South Italy, Plato came to recognize that the objects of the mathematical sciences—the only organized bodies of knowledge that could be called 'science'—were not concrete things, and that the truths of mathematics neither hold good of sensible things nor can be proved by experience. To account for the *a priori* discovery of fresh mathematical truth, Plato postulates an impersonal memory, which, so far as it extends, is the same in all men, unlike the personal memory that registers the peculiar experience acquired during this life. All mathematical truth is stored in this impersonal memory, and, since reality is a coherent system, the soul which recalls one truth can proceed to rediscover all the rest, without recourse to experience. Unlike historical information, such truths are *recognized* at first acquaintance; they carry their own warrant of immediate certainty, and they are linked in a necessary sequence. In the *Meno* Socrates establishes the fact of reminiscence by experiment, eliciting from a slave, ignorant of geometry, the solution of a rather difficult problem. The theory is supported by further arguments in the *Phaedo*. In both dialogues it is associated with the hypothesis of the soul's pre-existence and the Pythagorean doctrine of reincarnation.

Plato held, moreover, that knowledge of the meaning of moral terms, such as Socrates had tried to define, was reached in the same way. The meaning of 'Justice' is an object of knowledge, as absolute and immutable as the meaning of 'Triangle.' Further, the world of moral truth, like the mathematical, is an intelligible and necessary system, at the apex of which the *Republic* places the Form (Idea) of Goodness itself. To trace out its structure was to be the function of an ideal dialectic. This new conception of knowledge and its objects takes Plato beyond Socrates, who had seen the ideal type of knowledge, not in mathematics, but in the practical intelligence of the craftsman. It also points to aristocracy. Theoretically, all knowledge is latent in every human soul; but few will recover enough to justify their taking control of society. The rest must be guided by 'true belief,' imparted by a philosophic lawgiver. This lower form of goodness can be taught; the higher can be attained only by rational intuition, after a long and laborious training of the intellect.

In the *Phaedo* the light of this discovery transfigures the meaning of life and death. The life of the lover of wisdom is a meditation of death, and the death of Socrates becomes a symbol of the death of every man. The objects of rational knowledge, set in clear contrast with the experience that comes to the bodily senses, are the unchanging Ideas, incomposite and indestructible. The immortal soul is akin to the Ideas, and knows them when it withdraws from the body 'to think by itself.' This withdrawal is completed by the severance of soul from body in physical death; but, even then, only the philosopher's soul is freed from all taint of the earthly.

Towards the end of the *Phaedo*, the theory of Ideas is formally stated for the first time. Reminiscence accounts for our knowledge of mathematical and moral Ideas; but here the theory has assumed a much wider application. It is announced as superseding all earlier explanations of the becoming and change of concrete things. At the same time it appears, at least to the modern reader, to be intended as a logical theory of propositions in general. This logical aspect is not distinguished from the metaphysical, and it must be remembered that no science of Logic existed. Since, however, the two aspects of the theory appear to lead to incompatible conclusions, of which Plato later became aware, it may be well to present them separately.

In Logic, the 'Form' or Idea (*eidos*) is a common character of any number of things called by the same name; for every common name there is a Form (which is, in one sense, the meaning of the name), and a corresponding class of things. The theory states (1) that there are Ideas such as Beautiful, Good, Large, etc. 'just by themselves,' and (2) that 'if anything else (*i.e.* any individual thing) is beautiful, it is so for no other reason than that it partakes of that "Beautiful."' Logically construed, this amounts to an analysis of the proposition '*This thing is beautiful*' into (*a*) *this thing* (a particular subject), (*b*) *Beautiful* (a universal or predicate), and (*c*) *is* (the subject-predicate relation, 'partaking,' which every particular has to some universal). The proposition means the same as '*This thing partakes of* (*the*) *Beautiful* (*itself*).' Considered simply as an analysis of the type of proposition which has a particular subject and a universal predicate, this theory marks a brilliant discovery in Logic. Unfortunately it is extended to other types of proposition, such as '*A is larger than B*,' which do not in fact contain a predicate or the subject-predicate relation. It is probable also that a confusion of the proposition '*This thing is beautiful*' with '*This beautiful thing exists*,' partly accounts for the failure to distinguish the logical theory from a metaphysical explanation of the causes of existence, becoming, and change in time.

Under this other aspect, the theory is stated in the same context as follows: 'What *makes* a thing beautiful is nothing but the *presence* of that "Beautiful" or its *communication*, however it may occur; for I do not insist on that, but only say that it is by the Beautiful that all beautiful things are beautiful' (100 D). This appears to mean that the fact corresponding to the proposition 'This thing is beautiful' is the presence in the thing, either of the Idea (εἶδος) 'Beautiful' itself, or of a character (ἰδέα, μορφή) imparted by the Idea to the thing. When a beautiful thing begins to exist, or a thing becomes beautiful, what happens is that the Idea somehow either comes to be present in the thing or imparts its own nature to it. When the thing ceases to exist or to be beautiful, this presence or character is withdrawn, for neither the Idea itself nor the character can cease to exist or change. Thus the theory becomes a metaphysical account of 'the causes of becoming and perishing,' which is to supersede all mechanical and materialistic doctrines.

When we try to reconcile the two aspects of the theory, difficulties at once occur. In Logic common names, such as 'red' or 'dirty,' are on the same footing as 'just' or 'triangular'; but can we suppose that redness and dirt are eternal Ideas, to be known *a priori* without reference to sensible experience? How, again, can an eternal and unchanging Idea impart its character to a thing at some moment of time and withdraw it at another? The metaphysical relation between the supersensible Idea and the perceptible thing, whether called 'partaking' or 'presence' or 'communication,' does not appear to us to be the same as the logical relation between subject and predicate, and it remains mysterious.

Elsewhere Ideas are often described as 'models' (*paradeigmata*) or types, which are copied or reflected in sensible things; and it is suggested that the imperfect things of sense are striving to realize in themselves the perfection of their models (*Phaedo* 74 D). On this view, the moving cause which *makes* the thing (imperfectly) like the Idea lies, not in the Idea, but in the thing which, as it were, desires to reproduce its character. This suggestion bears fruit in Aristotle's doctrine of the Form as moving and final cause. An alternative suggestion is latent in the earlier passage where Socrates calls for a teleological explanation of existence, recognizing an Intelligence which designs the world, in all its parts, 'for the best.' What exists in time is not to be accounted for by mechanical antecedents or by an analysis of things into material elements. The ground of all existence must be sought in the real world of perfect Ideas. These may be conceived as the models, with reference to which the divine Artist fashions an imperfect world of appearance. A cosmology of this type, in which the moving cause is the divine Mind, was to be outlined later in the *Timaeus*.

Meanwhile Plato's thought was still bent upon the reform of society. What were the least changes which would enable a Socrates to replace the Callicles of the *Gorgias* and to put in practice the sovereign art of philosophic statesmanship? The *Republic* studies the problem of harmonious organization in the analogous cases of the State and of the individual soul. Conflict and disharmony arise because the competing motives characteristic of groups of men in society and of 'parts' of the soul—love of knowledge and goodness, love of power, and love of pleasure —are not reconciled, and their relative values are not determined. A perfect society can exist only where the men who know what is really good are in complete control. In the perfect character the discord of motives must be so resolved that it cannot break out again, because all ends are seen in true proportion and no part of our nature is thwarted of its true satisfaction. The social and individual problems are intertwined throughout the *Republic*. Their solutions meet in the doctrine that political power must rest with the perfect character, the philosopher.

The commonwealth described is a reformed city-state, whose citizens are classed according to their natural dispositions and abilities. The lowest class minister to economic needs; next comes the executive and fighting class; and above them the philosophic rulers, who possess true wisdom and virtue. The cardinal virtues, which in the Socratic dialogues had all been reduced to wisdom, are now separately defined. Justice and Temperance are virtues of the citizen as such, and pervade the whole community. The principle of justice, that each should do the work he is naturally fit for, replaces the principle of 'equality' in existing democracies, where every man was held to be capable of all social functions. Temperance unites all classes in harmonious agreement on the question where power should lie[1]. This principle of government by consent replaces the democratic 'freedom' of every man to do as he likes. To understand the secret of this harmony we must turn to the economy of the individual soul.

The division of the soul into three 'parts'—reflective, spirited, and appetitive—is not meant as an exhaustive classification of faculties. It is established by analysing states of mind containing a conflict of motives; and, as Aristotle observes, the element of desire is distributed among all three parts, each of which has its own desires and pleasures[2]. The reflective part desires knowledge; the spirited, honour; the appetitive, money as a means to sensual enjoyment. There are three corresponding types of character, each preferring its own kind of pleasure. The pleasures of knowledge are the truest; but the lower parts, by following reason, find the truest pleasure they can have; they are not sacrificed. The three forms of desire are characterized by differences in their objects, as if desire were a single energy which can be diverted from one channel to another (485 D). This analysis corrects an impression left by the *Phaedo*, which was concerned with the significance of death and opposed the soul, as the thinking thing, to the body, as the seat of emotion and desire. From that standpoint, an ascetic type of morality treats the inward conflict as a struggle between passionless reason on the right side and naturally evil desire on the wrong. The *Republic* recognizes the element of desire as appearing in all three parts of the soul. Desire is not to be crushed as evil in itself; the moral problem is to be solved by bringing the competing desires into a stable agreement. Hence Temperance is defined as 'a harmony and solidarity of all three parts of the soul, when they all consent to the rule of the reflective part, and there is no faction among them' (442 c).

This conception of desire (*Erōs*) as the single moving energy of the soul is developed in the discourse which Socrates, in the *Symposium*, says that he heard from Diotima, a wise woman of Mantinea. The name Eros has been misappropriated to one species of desire; but the love of honour and the love of truth are manifestations of the same energy, which in itself is neither good nor evil, but takes its value from its object. 'All are in love with the same thing always,' namely with a happiness that consists in the possession of beauty and goodness, and the possession of

---

[1] *Republic*, 431 D, 'In our city, above all others, rulers and subjects will share the same conviction as to who ought to rule.'

[2] Aristotle, *De anima* III, 9. Plato, *Republic*, 580 D.

them for ever. Thus Eros is a passion for immortality, reaching out beyond the individual life and its pleasures. Even in sexual desire the mortal creature seeks the immortality of the race. The love of honour aims at undying glory, for which the individual will sacrifice enjoyment and life itself. A third form is the passion to beget spiritual children, seen in the creative artist and in the educator, who plants his thoughts in living minds.

Such an educator was Socrates himself. Diotima here pauses to tell him that, though he might be initiated into these Lesser Mysteries of Eros, she doubts if he is capable of the perfect revelation. Plato may wish to imply that the vision of the eternal world, in the Greater Mysteries that follow, was denied to the historic Socrates, unless we should rather say, the Socrates of the earlier Platonic dialogues. Immortality in the three forms above mentioned is the immortality in time attainable by the mortal creature, who can only perpetuate his race, his fame, his creative work, his thoughts, in other mortal creatures. In the higher stages, next described, Eros is detached from the individual object and from physical beauty. It passes on to moral, and then to intellectual, beauty, becoming the philosophic passion for eternal truth. The final object, embracing all these forms, is an absolute and divine Beauty. The soul united with it in knowledge becomes divine and immortal. The energy which wings the soul to this highest flight is the same that appeared in the instinct to perpetuate the race and in the lower forms of ambition. It is the single moving force of the soul; and in the *Phaedrus* soul is defined, no longer as the thinking thing, opposed to the body with its emotions and desires, but as the self-moved source of all motion. If Eros is the energy of the self-moving soul, the division of the soul into 'parts' may be understood as the temporary diversion of some of this energy from its proper object to ends incidental to incarnation in a mortal body. The temperate harmony of the perfect character is to be reached, not by the suppression, but by the re-orientation, of desire.

The conversion of Eros from its lower forms to the passion for wisdom lifts the philosophic natures, whose training for the government of society is described in the *Republic* VI–VII, above the lovers of sensible beauty, immersed in the dream-world of appearance. The virtue they must possess consists in a knowledge whose object is Goodness itself, the principle of all truth and being, as the sun in the visible world is the source of all light and life. The discovery of the world of Ideas has immeasurably deepened Plato's conception of the knowledge which is virtue.

It means no longer a rational art of conduct, but a recognition of the final significance of the universe. The supreme object of knowledge, which 'every soul seeks after, divining that it exists, but unable to say what it is,' lies beyond even the intelligible world. The eye of the soul must be turned away from the idols of the Cave—a symbol of the world of appearance—and accustomed to the light of intelligible truth, until it can bear to look upon the Sun.

The faculty exercised is the Reason; and Plato here distinguishes two complementary phases of its activity: Intellect (*dianoia*) and Intuition (*noēsis*). The procedure of Intellect is that deductive and discursive reasoning which operates in the mathematical sciences. Geometry, for example, assumes certain premisses, as if they were self-evident, and proceeds to deduce an indefinite series of necessary conclusions. But the Reason is also capable of a movement in the reverse direction, upwards from the consequence to the premiss that implies it. The assumptions of Geometry are not really ultimate. The branches of pure mathematics form a single chain of necessary truths, deducible from the ultimate premiss of the science of numbers (arithmetic), which we may perhaps formulate as 'the existence of unity[1].' Unity is one aspect of the Good. The upward movement is due to a power (as it were) of divination, which apprehends a prior truth by an immediate act of Intuition.

The Reason is first to be trained in the deductive arguments of mathematics. But mathematical concepts are not the only objects of knowledge, nor is unity the only aspect of the ultimate principle. There are the other Ideas, which culminate in the same principle under its aspect as the Good, though they also share with the mathematical structure the attributes of beauty and truth. From mathematics the philosophers will pass to Dialectic, the study of moral concepts, with a technique developed from the Socratic conversation aiming at the definition of moral terms. Here the deductive reasoning of Intellect has only a subordinate place, being employed in the criticism of 'hypotheses,' the tentative definitions advanced by the respondent and tested by the consequences to which they lead. The 'hypothesis' is reached by an effort of Intuition to perceive the content of an Idea. If the consequences prove the suggestion to be one-sided, too narrow or too wide, it will be rejected, and the respondent will frame a new

---

[1] *Parmenides* 143 suggests that the whole series of numbers is deducible from the postulate: 'the One exists.'

definition, which should more nearly coincide with the true meaning. The criticism of Intellect will again be applied, and so the process will be continued by Intuition and Intellect in alternating rhythm, until the Idea, which has all along been dimly in view, is fully apprehended. Even when an Idea is known, however, this knowledge is only a part of the whole system of truth. Intuition must mount higher still to the summit, from which the partial truth can be seen in relation to all the rest of truth—the knowledge of Goodness itself. If this unconditional principle can ever be reached, the Intellect may then proceed to a complete deduction of the structure of reality[1]. The philosopher, could he ever achieve this quest, would see the world as God might see it, and become as God, knowing good from evil. If virtue is knowledge, nothing short of this is perfect knowledge; and the man who can reach it should be enthroned as absolute lawgiver. Then the perfect commonwealth might see the light of day.

In the *Phaedo* and the *Republic* the sensible and intelligible worlds are sharply distinguished, and the relation between them is obscure. If Dialectic is concerned wholly with Ideas 'apart from all the senses,' how does the power of thought gain its first foothold to 'mount upon and spring from'? The theory of Reminiscence replies that the memory of an Idea seen before birth is awakened by the perception of its imperfect copies in the world of sense. The mythical encomium of Eros, delivered by Socrates in the *Phaedrus*, identifies this act of reminiscence with what we might call a process of 'abstraction.' Man, and man only, has Reason, enabling him to 'understand by way of the Form (Idea), a unity gathered by reflection from many acts of perception; and this is recollection of the things formerly seen by the soul, when it travelled in the divine company, despising the things we now call real and looking upwards to true reality' (249 B). Further we are told that, of the three aspects of the

---

[1] *Republic,* 511 B, 'Understand,' says Socrates, 'that by the second (higher) division of the intelligible world (the sphere of Dialectic), I mean that which reasoning by itself apprehends by the power of Dialectic, treating its hypotheses not as ultimate principles, but as "hypotheses" in the literal sense—things "laid down," which reasoning can, as it were, mount upon and spring from (the upward movement of Intuition), in order that, proceeding right to that which is unconditional, the first principle of the universe, it may apprehend that; and then, turning back again and holding to the consequences derived from that principle, it may thus descend to a conclusion, not availing itself of any sensible object whatsoever, but of Ideas, through Ideas, to Ideas, and ending with Ideas.'

divine—Beauty, Goodness, and Truth—Beauty alone is visible through the bodily eyes, as an 'indwelling light' in its likenesses on earth. The perception of Beauty in the individual causes the distraction of Love, a form of 'divine madness' compared to the inspiration of prophecy, religious enthusiasm, and poetry. This madness is exalted above rational sobriety; the influx of Beauty causes the wings which Psyche must receive from Eros to grow for the higher flights of philosophic intuition.

The theory of Reminiscence is here set in a new light. The Idea, a unity shared by a manifold, is intuitively discerned as beauty; as if the perfect type were revealed within, or through, the imperfect copy. The first apprehension is dim and confused. It is clarified by Dialectic, which, in the *Phaedrus*, is described as consisting of two complementary processes, Collection and Division, ending in the Definition. The Definition is a complete and explicit statement of the content of the 'indivisible species.' For this procedure the Ideas are conceived as forming a hierarchy, in which a higher term is related to the lower as genus to subordinate species. Collection is an act of Intuition, 'surveying together' the specific Form to be defined and a number of others that may be 'widely scattered,' and divining the single generic Form under which they must all be gathered. Everything will depend upon the correctness of this intuition; but it is an act of insight, not a method for which rules can be given. The genus is then systematically divided 'where the joints naturally come,' down through intermediate classes and sub-classes, each with its specific difference, to the indivisible species. This lowest term is a Form which cannot be further divided, because it has nothing below it but an indefinite number of individual things whose Form it is—the members of the species, unknowable in so far as they contain anything more than their common specific Form. This is the very Form that was dimly apprehended in the initial act of intuition. What is gained by the dialectical process is an explicit statement of its content; and, moreover, the Form so defined is set in its proper relations to kindred Forms. The definition consists of the generic term and all the specific differences of the intermediate classes. This method is later illustrated at length in the *Sophist* and *Statesman*. It exhibits the alternating rhythm of Intuition and Intellect, which in the mathematical sciences are employed to divine the premisses and to deduce the conclusions of demonstrative proof.

This description of Dialectic indicates that the intelligible world of Ideas includes a hierarchy of natural kinds, or 'types fixed in Nature.' Such a structure points to a possible object for a science of Nature; and we learn from a fragment of Comedy that the method of Division was applied in the Academy to the classification of natural species. The belief in the existence of a limited number of eternally existing real kinds was perpetuated as a fundamental postulate in the philosophy of Aristotle.

Towards the end of the *Phaedrus*, the written word is disparaged as no better than the bastard brother of the living and breathing word that can be written with understanding in the learner's mind. Plato speaks as if the dialogues we have reviewed were pastimes to amuse the leisure of the head of the Academy, whose serious work lay elsewhere, in living intercourse with his students. He may have laid aside his pen for some years. His time was also to be taken up by another essay in practical reform. On the accession of the younger Dionysius at Syracuse in 367 B.C., Plato was led by a sense of duty and by the more sanguine hopes of Dion to attempt once more the conversion of a despot to philosophy (pp. 274 *sqq.*). This unsuccessful journey may have interrupted the composition of the series: *Parmenides, Theaetetus, Sophist, Statesman.*

IV. THE LATER DIALOGUES

The newly discovered world of Ideas had yet to be explored and conquered. Complete conquest would mean the deduction of a rational and coherent system of the universe from an absolute principle. If Plato had moments when the way seemed clear, he could not communicate a finished result. The *Parmenides* opens with a searching criticism of his own theory of Ideas, formulating difficulties ignored in the *Phaedo* and perhaps brought to light by discussion in the Academy. (1) Can an Idea, like a thing, be the subject of propositions and have many predicates without loss of unity? (2) The extent of the world of Ideas becomes a problem, if Logic is to recognize universals such as 'mud' or 'dirt,' which Metaphysics can hardly admit to be eternal forms of reality. (3) No intelligible account of the relation between an Idea and its group of synonymous things has yet been found. The problem cannot be evaded by regarding Ideas as mere thoughts in our minds, or by recognizing only the relation of likeness between Idea and thing. The gap between the Ideal world and the sensible threatens to remain unbridged. Modern critics dispute whether the exercises in abstract dialectic which fill the rest of the dialogue offer more than some hints towards an answer to these problems. But the necessity of some answer is stated with emphasis: Ideas are indispensable to thought.

This conclusion is negatively reinforced in the *Theaetetus*, by a proof that knowledge is not to be found in sensation or sense-perception, or in 'true belief,' which can be produced or shaken by persuasion. Sensation is infallible, but does not apprehend reality; the immediate objects of the senses are qualities which only arise in a process taking place between the sense-organ and the physical thing. Nor can it yield truth; for this is a property of judgments, and every judgment must contain at least one term which is not a sense-object. The discussion of the claims of true belief shows that empiricist views of the mind as a mere passive receptacle of impressions from without cannot explain how we can ever make a false judgment. Incidentally Plato refutes the doctrines he ascribes to Protagoras: that what appears real to each man is real for him, and what he thinks true is true for him. He also rejects the extreme Heracleitean view which denies any stable Being, though he still holds that sensible objects are in perpetual change and cannot be known. The dialogue defends the old position that there can be no knowledge without the Ideas.

This criticism of the world of appearance and its champion, Protagoras, is followed by a dialogue defining the Sophist as a denizen of that world and himself a creator of illusions. The attempt involves a discussion of what is meant by an unreal appearance and by falsehood in speech and thought. The treatment of the former question does not solve the problem of the relation between an Idea and the things described as partly unreal copies of it. We find only a review of theories of the real, leading to a criticism both of the materialists, who believe only in tangible body, and of the 'friends of Ideas,' who admit only the reality of 'intelligible and bodiless Forms.' It is asserted that at least some perfectly real things must be capable of life and intelligence, and therefore of change. The friends of Ideas must not suppose that immutable Forms can be the whole of reality. Plato seems here to provide for the reality of the divine Mind, of that element in the human soul which knows truth, and, perhaps, of non-human intelligences, such as govern the movement of the stars.

The logical discussion which follows clears up some fallacies about negative propositions, and deals, for the first time, with propositions about Ideas, which are here treated as 'kinds,' arranged in a hierarchy[1]. The dialectician, by means of Collection and Division, will make out their relations. All discourse depends on the combination of Ideas with one another. False speech and judgment are now explained. A judgment (*doxa*) is the conclusion of the process of thought, the silent dialogue which the mind holds with itself. Speech is the utterance of a judgment in a significant combination of words. It is false when it states about its subject something other than what is. 'Appearance' (*phantasia*), in the psychological sense, is defined as 'a mixture of sensation and judgment,' with the implication, apparently, that the element of falsity it may contain is due to the judgment. This demonstration of the possibility of false speech, judgment, and appearance justifies the definition of the Sophist as a species of image-maker, practising an art of deceit.

The *Statesman* continues the conversation begun in the *Sophist*. It defines the scope of the sovereign art of statesmanship, dismissing theocracy as not for this world. The ideal is still the philosopher king, ruling without laws; but, in his absence, laws such as he would approve must be framed. Plato undertook this task in the *Laws*, his last work. He there finds the practical solution in a mixture of constitutional monarchy and democracy.

The series of critical dialogues is inconclusive: problems are raised that are not solved. The *Sophist* and *Statesman* seem to promise a further dialogue, the *Philosopher*, in which Socrates would have taken the lead once more. If projected, it was never written. In its place we have another unfinished trilogy. The *Timaeus* opens with the creation of the world and of man; the *Critias* (a fragment) was to exhibit a commonwealth like that of the *Republic*, identified with pre-historic Athens, saving the Mediterranean world from an invasion of the inhabitants of Atlantis, and then swallowed up by flood and earthquake. The *Hermocrates* (never written) would, perhaps, have described the rise of existing society after the catastrophe, and the establishment of a second-best constitution. Plato may have abandoned his scheme as too vast, and recast his material in the *Laws*.

---

[1] Plato selects, for purposes of illustration, 'some of the widest (*or* most important) kinds': Being, Sameness, Otherness, etc. He does not say they are '*the* highest kinds' in the hierarchy, or call them 'categories,' or indicate that they are in any way to supersede the Ideas of the earlier dialogues. Nor does he make any clear distinction between relations and predicates, but still speaks as if 'A is other than B' meant, or implied, that A 'partakes of the Form Otherness' (255 E). But the language throughout is so loose as to make interpretation very uncertain.

The cosmology of the *Timaeus* is a preface to the projected survey of human history and social institutions; it culminates in the description of the moral and physical nature of man. It is framed in conscious opposition to the mechanism of the Pre-Socratics and Democritus. Plato held that motion can be origin-ated only by the principle of life, or 'soul,' and that the soul, or souls, which cause the motions of the universe must be governed by Reason, purposing ends that are good. The *Laws* (966) declares that on these two discoveries rests the faith, indispensable to society, in gods whose providence is concerned with the good and evil of mankind. Thus metaphysical, religious, and moral considerations combine to dictate a type of cosmogony which is creational, rather than evolutionary, though nothing is created, in the later sense, out of nothing. The world is the work of a divine Artist, who, being good, desired that all things should be, so far as possible, like himself. An artist works upon existing material, and with reference to a model. The divine model is at first presented as the eternal world of Ideas, the existence of which is asserted throughout the *Timaeus* with all the old emphasis. The material is described as the visible principle of Becoming, whose orderless movement is reduced to order and harmony by the fashioning of a living universe with a reasonable soul and a body.

The World-soul itself is a compound of the two principles of Being and Becoming, or 'the Same and the Other.' It is ordered in the numerical ratios of a musical harmony; and its substance is divided into the two circles, equatorial and ecliptic, of the celestial sphere. The circle of the Other is subdivided into the planetary orbits. Here the allegorical or mythical form of ex-position masks an inexplicable transition from the purely logical order to the physical, which is characteristic of this part of the *Timaeus* and recurs in the construction of the body of the universe. Visible and tangible body is reduced to atoms, with the forms of four of the regular geometrical solids; these forms themselves are decomposed into elementary triangles, and triangles can be expressed in relations of number. Matter appears sometimes as an indeterminate substance bounded by these forms, sometimes as mere Space. Elsewhere it seems to be ultimately reduced to a logical principle of 'Otherness' or multiplicity, as if the physical dispersion of objects in space were derived from the logical Form of Otherness, which (as the *Sophist* showed) separates the Ideas themselves, since each of them *is not* (is other than) all the rest. Thus the cosmogony, which cannot here be followed in detail, still leaves in obscurity the old problem, how to relate the eternal world of Ideas to the mutable things of time and space. The mechanism of the visible heavens and the living creatures of earth emerge from a mysterious background of logical entities, itself concealing the Power whose word becomes flesh.

That this scheme is, in some sense, 'mythical' has always been recognized; and it is commonly assumed that the mythical form is an allegorical disguise which can be stripped off, so as to unveil a coherent theory of the universe. Plato, it is believed, chose to wrap in misleading, and even contradictory, imagery, a rational doctrine which might have been set forth in literal and prosaic terms. But the interpreters who reverse this proceeding arrive at conflicting and arbitrary results. In Plato's thought about God, the universe, and the soul there is an irreducible element of myth. This word has more than one sense. 'Mythos,' meaning 'account,' 'story,' is used by Timaeus himself to describe the physical theories which fill a large part of the dialogue. These seem to embody the best results of contemporary speculation in astronomy and medicine. But for Plato 'the actual physical world, just because it cannot be completely analysed into combinations of logical concepts, but involves a factor of irrational sensible fact, is incapable of being an object of science proper. Any conclusions we may form as to its structure and history must be put forward not as proved results of science, but as, at best, a "probable account"' (mythos)[1]. Such an account might be in the plainest prose; the element of falsity lies, not in the mode of exposition, but in the object described, which is only a fleeting image of the real. This sense of mythos does not imply the use of poetical imagery. Plato also recognizes an allegorical type of myth. The Guardians of the Ideal State will fabricate myths to convey to the unphilosophic citizens religious truths beyond the reach of their intellects. Here the element of falsity resides in the allegorical form; but the truth it contains is assumed to be known and deliberately disguised. Now, the myths in Plato's dialogues are partly allegorical; but those which deal with God and the soul cannot be completely transposed into rational and prosaic terms. They contain an element of that non-rational poetic thought, which the Phaedrus acknowledged as yielding intuitions of truth inaccessible to the sober intellect. When the imagery of Timaeus' creation myth is dissolved by the allegorical method of interpretation, with it disappears the element which Plato in his old age

---

[1] A. E. Taylor, Plato, p. 51.

valued more and more—the belief in 'a Maker and Father of this universe,' who not only designed the world but cares for the destinies of man.

The *Philebus* contains Plato's last word upon the nature of human happiness, occasioned perhaps by an Academic controversy between Plato's colleague Eudoxus, a hedonist, and others who denied that pleasure was a good at all and identified happiness with wisdom. Happiness is declared to consist in a mixed life combining all forms of knowledge with innocent and pure pleasures. The mixture owes its goodness to the qualities of beauty, truth, and measure. Judged in respect of these qualities, pleasure is declared, on metaphysical grounds, to be inferior to Reason and knowledge.

From Aristotle we learn something of a latest phase, in which Plato developed the Pythagorean doctrine that all things represent numbers. He distinguished the numbers Two, Three, etc., which are Ideas, not only from collections of so many things, but also from an intermediate kind of numbers which occur in mathematical propositions, such as $2 + 2 = 4$. An Ideal Number is unique, cannot be added to itself, and does not consist of units. Such Numbers are derived from a formal principle, the One, and a material, the 'great and small,' or 'Indeterminate Duality,' so called because 'the indefinite is held to proceed to infinity both in the direction of increase and in that of diminution.' The principles are called, in the *Philebus*, by the Pythagorean names, Limit and Unlimited. In the physical world the Unlimited is exemplified by 'hotter-and-colder,' or 'higher-and-lower' in sound. The Limit is represented by 'whatever has the ratio of one number or measure to another' ($\frac{1}{1}$, $\frac{2}{1}$, etc.). The union of the two principles produces 'a mixed being which has become,' *e.g.* health, musical harmony, temperate seasons, etc. Plato seems to have held that Numbers themselves can be analysed into corresponding principles. Ideal spatial magnitudes form a class of more complex Ideas, in which Numbers serve as the formal principle, and the material is space. Below these again are the mathematical numbers and magnitudes, and finally physical atoms in actual space. It appears, further, that Plato regarded all Ideas as in some sense 'Numbers,' composed of corresponding principles. Here the formal principle may be identified with the One in its aspect of the Good. The material is the principle of multiplicity in the Ideal world. Ideas so formed serve as the principle of Limit to sensible things.

We hear also of an unpublished lecture on the Good; but if the notes preserved by Plato's pupils had come down to us, it is not likely that we should understand them. Indeed, we have Plato's own assurance that we should not. On his last visit to Syracuse (361 B.C.) he had told Dionysius something, but by no means all, of what was in his mind with regard to the ultimate questions of philosophy. Dionysius afterwards composed a treatise and gave it out as his own doctrine. Of this essay and others like it Plato writes that their authors could not understand anything of the matter.

There is not, nor shall there ever be, any writing of mine on this subject. It is altogether beyond such means of expression as exist in other fields of knowledge; rather, after long dwelling upon the thing itself, in a common life of philosophic converse, suddenly, as from a leaping spark, a light is kindled, which, when it has arisen in the soul, thenceforward feeds itself. Yet of this I am sure: that, if these things were to be written down or expressed in words, I could express them better than anyone; I know too that if they were set down in writing badly, I should be the person to suffer most. If I thought they could be adequately set forth to the world in speech or writing, in what nobler business could I have spent my life than in writing a work of great service to mankind and revealing Nature to all eyes under the light of day? But I do not think that a statement of what has been attempted in this field is a good thing for man, unless it be for the very few who can be enabled, by a slight indication, to make the discovery for themselves. Of the rest, some would be puffed up with an entirely offensive spirit of false superiority; others, with a lofty and presumptuous conceit of understanding some great matter (*Ep.* VII, 341 C–E).

From these words we may infer that there were moments when Plato seemed to himself to have gained a luminous vision of reality, in which the claims of logical intellect and poetic intuition were reconciled, and the world appeared both rational and harmonious. All that he could give to others was a 'slight indication,' such as might enable a few to discover for themselves the knowledge which, as Socrates had said, cannot be taught.

V. ARISTOTLE

Aristotle joined the Academy in his eighteenth year (367 B.C.), about the time of Plato's second visit to Sicily, and worked there till Plato died in 347 B.C. He was born at Stagirus in the Thracian peninsula, a Greek colony from Andros and Chalcis, the home of his mother's family. His father, Nicomachus, was a physician, attached to the court of Amyntas II of Macedonia. The intellectual influences of Aristotle's early years came from medical and physical science, untouched, in that quarter of the Greek world, by the philosophic revolution begun by Socrates at Athens.

The natural bent of his mind was always towards the study of empirical facts; he collected them with enormous industry and sought to fit them into an encyclopaedic system of the universe. But during the twenty years he spent at the Academy, as the pupil and colleague of Plato, he became, once for all, a Platonist. His life-work was a gigantic effort to force the apparatus of Platonic thought to account for the natural world revealed by observation.

It is impossible as yet to trace closely the development of Aristotle's thought. Of the dialogues he wrote at the Academy, only fragments survive. His collections of material have perished almost entirely. The extant works form a corpus of treatises, mainly intended for the School and little known outside it until they were published by Andronicus of Rhodes in the time of Cicero. Some parts consist of lectures written out in more or less summary form; others seem to be compilations of essays, of various dates, collected either by Aristotle himself or by his pupils after his death. When criticism has made out the stratification of these writings, it may go on to construct the history of Aristotle's thought. A great advance has been made by W. Jäger, whose *Aristoteles* supersedes earlier biographies. Other scholars are pursuing the same line; but some of the results are still in dispute, and a long controversy may be expected before agreement is reached.

The dialogues written at the Academy were, like Plato's, intended for the educated public. Some, it would seem, were closely modelled, both in style and contents, upon the works of Plato's middle period. In others the dramatic manner was dropped; and a new form, later used by Cicero, appears, in which a series of speeches are made upon some theme proposed by a chairman, who sums up at the end. The treatment of immortality in the *Eudemus*, dated by the death of the Platonist Eudemus of Cyprus in 354 B.C., reproduced the conception of life and death expressed in the *Phaedo*. At this date Aristotle regarded the soul as a substance, not as a form inseparable from the matter of the body, and still held the theory of Ideas—a proof, incidentally, that the doctrines of the *Phaedo* had not been abandoned by their author. Another work of this period, the *Protrepticus*, reveals Aristotle's sympathy with that impulse which tempted Plato throughout his life to withdraw from the tasks of practical reform into religious contemplation of truth. It was an exhortation, after the pattern perfected by Isocrates, recommending the philosophic life to a reigning prince, Themison of Cyprus.

After Plato's death and the appointment of his nephew, Speusippus, to preside over the Academy, Aristotle may have felt that he could not continue his work under a man of inferior powers. With Xenocrates, who was later to succeed Speusippus, he withdrew to Assos in the Troad, where two Platonists, Erastus and Coriscus of Scepsis, were in friendly relations with the local despot, Hermeias of Atarneus, himself a former member of the Academy. Aristotle married Hermeias' niece, Pythias. In this Platonic circle he stayed for three years, and then taught for a short time at Mitylene in Lesbos, the country of his collaborator and successor, Theophrastus. In 343 B.C. he was invited by Philip of Macedon, who may have known him as a boy, to undertake the education of Alexander, then thirteen years of age.

In this second period of his life, Aristotle still called himself a Platonist; but death had freed him from the duty to respect the feelings of a venerable master; and, as the leader of an independent school, he was bound to formulate his own doctrine. The native bent of his mind now asserted itself in clearer antagonism to the mystical metamathematics of Plato's latest thought. The lost dialogue *Concerning Philosophy*, perhaps the programme of the School at Assos, attacked the Platonic Ideas, and, in particular, the theory of Ideal Numbers, distinct from the numbers of mathematics. It opened with a review of ancient wisdom, oriental as well as Greek, fragments of which Aristotle believed to have survived the catastrophes that, from time to time, had overwhelmed civilization. The cosmology set forth at the end had a theological character as marked as that of the *Timaeus*. The mythical Creator and his ideal model are, however, eliminated. The world is without beginning or end. The movement of the stars is the voluntary motion of their directing intelligences. God is already conceived as the Unmoved Mover, a pure unchanging Form, separate from the world. Some of the oldest parts of the extant treatises must date from this period.

VI. FORM AND MATTER, THE ACTUAL AND THE POTENTIAL

With Aristotle's rejection of the Platonic Ideas, the centre of reality is shifted back to the natural world of time and change. A science of Nature, such as Plato could not recognize, is possible, if the world given in experience contains objects that are real in the fullest sense. For Plato the world of immaterial Forms contained the true 'nature of things' and the objects of knowledge. In the hierarchy of Ideas, the method of Division led to the defi-

nition, by genus and differences, of the lowest object of knowledge—the indivisible essence of a natural kind. The problem
was to find an intelligible relation to link the specific Form in the
Ideal world to the individual members of the species. Aristotle
tried to evade it by denying independent reality to the Idea. The
specific Form, actually realized in each individual, is primarily
real, and is the nature of the things possessing it. The real world,
then, is no longer a world of universals, but of concrete things
which we perceive. Although these things become and perish in
time and suffer change, they contain a constant reality. Nature
is, in the first place, a kingdom of specific Forms realized in
matter; and every such Form is an invariable and limited set of
characteristics, which can be defined and known. The main
purpose of science is to define these essences and to demonstrate
universal truths about them. The Aristotelian philosophy has its
centre here. Its apparatus of concepts is designed to explain the
nature of the individual substance, and how it can come into
existence and undergo change.

The objects of physical science are things which have sensible
matter and movement. These two characteristics distinguish
them from the objects of the other theoretical sciences, mathematics and metaphysics. The objects of mathematics do not,
indeed, exist apart from sensible matter; number and geometrical
form exist only as determinations of physical things, though they
are studied by mathematicians in abstraction from them. But,
as thus abstracted, they are incapable of motion, and possess only
'intelligible matter,' a principle of individuation distinguishing
entities that are conceptually identical (e.g. two circles). This
'intelligible matter' is geometrical space, which is not imaginary,
but an abstraction of the same kind as mathematical objects.
The study of objects which are not only incapable of movement,
but wholly immaterial, is the field of metaphysics, also called
theology, because the chief among such objects is God. Since
Aristotle's theology is an appendix to his philosophy of Nature,
we must seek the kernel of his thought in the analysis of the
central objects of physical science.

In the *Physics* 'natural objects' are declared to be 'animals and
their parts, plants, and the simple bodies—earth, fire, water, and
air.' Inorganic Nature consists of the simple bodies and lifeless
compounds of them; organic Nature, of the living creatures,
grouped in species. The individual living creature can be analysed,
in the first place, into its specific Form, its other attributes, and
its Matter.

The specific Form is an immaterial principle of structure, which cannot exist apart from the appropriate matter embodying it. Its content is conceptually identical in all the individuals, and is expressed in the definition by genus and differences. It is the true 'nature' or 'essence' of the thing, or 'what it is to be' a thing of that kind. It constitutes, as it were, the permanent and invariable core of the individual's being. Round it are grouped the other attributes, divided into properties and accidents. A property is an attribute which belongs to all members of a given species and only to them, but is not part of the essence; thus the capacity for laughter is confined to men, but not essential. An accident is an attribute which may or may not belong to a thing, and may belong also to things of other species.

All these determinations, essential or not, are, in a wider sense, the Form of the individual substance at any given moment; but the substance is not simply the sum of them. It also contains an element determined by them, an unknown something which has the qualities and undergoes the changes that occur in the thing. This element is called 'Matter.' Matter and Form, however, are relative terms. In relation to the essential nature, the matter of a living creature is its body; but relatively to the organs of the living body, the tissues composing them are matter; relatively to the tissues, the simple bodies are matter; and these bodies themselves are logically analysable into the primary contrarieties (hot and cold, dry and fluid) and ultimate Matter. Ultimate or pure Matter is an abstraction of thought, not any kind of thing that can exist by itself. The lowest level on which Matter exists is the simple bodies. The name 'Matter' is applicable to anything indeterminate, but capable of determination. The history of this conception goes back through Plato's Indeterminate Duality, to the Pythagorean 'Unlimited'—the void womb of becoming, informed by the principle of 'Limit' (vol. IV, p. 551).

It is, further, a given fact of experience that individual substances begin and cease to exist. Natural objects, as distinct from artificial things, are defined as having *in themselves* a source of movement or rest. A living creature is born, grows to its full development and then ceases to grow, produces another individual of the same kind, and at last decays and dies. These phenomena cannot be accounted for either by the unimaginable operation of a changeless Platonic Idea, or (as the Pre-Socratics had supposed) by mechanical interaction of the lowest forms of matter. Aristotle sees the moving cause in the goal of development—the specific 'nature' realized in each individual. In the highest types of living creatures—and the lower is to be explained by the higher —the Form is impressed by the male parent, in the act of generation, on matter supplied by the female. From its latent condition in the germ it develops to full perfection, this stage being marked by the capacity to reproduce the Form in another individual. Thus the cycle begins again, the perfection or 'end' of one individual acting as the 'beginning' of another. The 'final cause' and the 'moving cause' coincide with the 'formal cause.'

The impulse of life, manifested in the growth of the living organism from the germ to perfection, is often spoken of as if it were an impulse of desire directed to the end, analogous to the artist's desire to produce in his material the form he has before his mind. In the language of personification, 'Nature' is said to work to an end. But 'Nature' is not a soul, capable of desire or purpose, but merely a collective name for the natures of all natural things. The personification is only a literary device, expressing the given fact that the development of the living germ follows a definite course that seems to be pre-determined: it can develop into the specific Form of its own kind and of no other. This fact is conveniently conceived by the analogy of conscious purpose, but not explained; for Aristotle's system admits neither a designing Creator nor a World-soul which might be the seat of such purposes.

The same fact is also expressed by saying that the germ has the power to develop into its destined perfection, or is 'potentially' what it later comes to be actually. In connection with processes of becoming and change Actuality (*energeia*) and Potentiality (*dynamis*) correspond to Form and Matter, and are similarly relative terms: what is actually bronze is potentially a statue. The notion of potentiality is obscure. *Dynamis* is the substantive answering to the auxiliary verb 'can,' and covers several meanings: (1) the mere *possibility* of anything that may or may not be; (2) *capacity* to pass through a change of quality, quantity, or locomotion; (3) the *potential existence* of something that may develop into actual existence; (4) the *power* to effect a change, the *faculty* of producing something or of manifesting activity. *Energeia* has the corresponding senses: (1) reality, (2) actualization, (3) actuality, (4) activity. These ambiguities sometimes cover a confusion, and often render the thought obscure. What, for instance, is meant by saying that the seed is 'potentially' a tree? In relation to the full-grown tree the seed is matter, but not, of course, pure matter capable of any determination. It has the capacity of becoming a tree, if nothing hinders it; and this capacity must be due to the actual Form it already possesses—certain properties confining its development to the course that will end in the perfect Form of its own species. But this is not all; a lifeless piece of bronze has actual properties which fit it to be made into a statue, but it will never become a statue of itself. The seed, as a natural object, must contain 'a source of movement within itself'—a force that will carry it to its fulfilment. But, though 'power' is one of the meanings of *dynamis*, this moving force resides, not in matter, but in the specific Form. Usually the 'moving cause' is said to be the specific Form as actually existing in the fully developed parent; but, in the act of generation, transmitting this Form to a new individual, the power or force must also be transmitted. Hence we must say that the specific Form, bearing this force, exists already in the seed; and since it does not exist in full actuality until the new tree is grown, it is said to exist 'potentially,' and conceived as containing a latent power, whose energy will effect the development. Finally, when the actualization of the Form is complete, this 'first entelechy' is endowed with faculties, to be further expressed in the activities or functions of life, such as nutrition and reproduction.

In this analysis the word *dynamis* shifts through all its meanings. The whole is a description, rather than an explanation, of the mysterious force of life, whose operation we witness but cannot understand. Characteristic of Aristotle is the notion that this force resides in the specific Form, conveying it in unbroken succession from one perishable individual to another. His merit lies in the caution which keeps him from going further beyond the observed facts of life to seek an 'explanation' in unverifiable and insufficient hypotheses. On the other hand, the specific Forms, considered as everlasting and invariable constituents of the natural order, are a metaphysical heritage from Plato, involving the dogma that the natural order itself is without beginning or end. A new species cannot be created or 'evolved' from another species; though, when a species becomes extinct, on Aristotle's principles the natural order must be impaired—a consequence he never faces.

The concepts of Matter and Form, Potentiality and Actuality, above illustrated from their primary application to living creatures, are used as master-keys to explain all phenomena. A few examples must suffice. In order to make the Form the moving cause in artificial production, the Form of a statue is declared to pre-exist in the sculptor's mind and to set in motion the desire leading to its realization. The material is moved by the tool, the tool by the craftsman's hands; his hands are moved, in an appropriate way, 'by his knowledge of his art and by his soul, in which is the Form' (730 *b* 11). In the analysis of changes other than the generation of substances—changes of quality, quantity, and place—the same concepts are used; and motion generally is defined as 'the actualization of that which is potentially.' In this context 'matter' figures as the subject which undergoes and persists through change. Aristotle tries to solve the old problem, How can what is come out of what is not? by remarking that Form (*A*) cannot come simply out of its privation (*not A*), but only from privation in a substrate (*x*) which has the new form potentially. Even in the case of locomotion, Aristotle speaks of 'local matter,' which is to be found, without the matter presupposed in other kinds of change, in the capacity for rotation of the heavenly spheres. Beyond this is 'intelligible matter' or spatial extension, and finally 'ultimate matter.' In the conceptual world, the genus is called 'matter' in relation to the species, which has a higher degree of determination. Aristotle can hardly be defended against the charge that concepts of such bewildering ambiguity are chiefly useful for making his system appear more complete and coherent than it is.

VII. THE OBJECTS AND METHODS OF SCIENCE

The belief, inherited from Plato, in the indivisible specific Form as the kernel of reality carried with it the old problem of the relation between the universal objects of knowledge and the particular things existing in time. Aristotle held to the doctrine that only the universal can be defined and known; but the most real things in his world are not universals, but individual substances, for the independent existence of the Platonic Ideas has been denied. When the specific Form is thus transferred from the intelligible world to actual existence in sensible matter, what it gains in substantial reality is offset by the danger that it may cease to be knowable. If the Platonic Idea is a universal, it can be known, but cannot exist; if it exists, it is an individual, and cannot be known. But the Aristotelian Form is open to the same dilemma. The world revealed to experience consists of individual existents. If these constitute the real, and the individual is indeed unknowable, the problem of finding real objects for knowledge, which the Theory of Ideas was to solve, seems to become insoluble.

On the other hand, if the problem appeared in this light to Aristotle, to us the reality of the specific Form may seem more doubtful than its knowableness. These invariable Forms, which are to stiffen the unstable world of Heracleitean change with a structure of constant fixity, are metaphysical figments. The actual Form of an individual substance is declared to be the most real of entities; but this Form, numerically different from the Form of any other individual, perishes; it is not transmitted to descendants. The alleged specific Form which never begins or ceases to be, but only comes to be 'actualized' in fresh individuals, and exists 'potentially' in the germ, is not a thing that really persists and travels unchanged through the succession of individuals. Though Aristotle attacks Plato for giving independent existence to Ideas, he is in fact guilty of the same offence; the difference is that he makes the Idea exist within and throughout the flow of time and change. It is still the Platonic Idea, with a better claim to be knowable than to be real; for it retains the essential of an object of knowledge—a determinate, unvarying, definable content. Having persuaded himself that it exists everlastingly in the natural world, Aristotle is left with the problem, how to make this object of knowledge accessible to experience which must enter through the gate of the senses. The senses show us individual things, each with a numerically different Form of its own, involved with a mass of necessary or accidental attributes. It remains to give some account of the process by which the universal is disengaged from the particular.

Aristotle's term *Epagogē*, though usually rendered by 'Induction,' rather denoted a process of abstraction. Starting from the animal faculty of perception, 'the first stage in the development from sense to knowledge is memory, the "remaining of the percept" when the moment of perception is over. The next stage is "experience," or the framing, on the basis of repeated memories of the same kind of thing, of a conception, the fixation of a universal[1].' It appears, further, that by a similar process we ascend from particular judgments to universal judgments and to the first premisses (definitions, axioms etc.) of all science. Aristotle recognizes, throughout all the stages, the operation of Plato's faculty of intuition (*noēsis*). It is ultimately this highest human faculty that guides the entire procedure by its power of penetrating to the Idea and to ultimate truths. Induction is 'the process whereby, after experience of a certain number of par-

---

[1] Ross, *Aristotle*, p. 54.

ticular instances, the mind grasps a universal truth which then
and afterwards is seen to be self-evident. Induction in this sense,
is the activity of "intuitive reason."' It is 'a process not of
reasoning but of direct insight, mediated psychologically by a
review of particular instances[1].' In Plato intuition 'collects' the
generic Idea from a review of the species; in Aristotle it also
arrives at the specific Form from a review of individuals; Plato,
indeed, had already made the sensuous intuition of beauty in
the individual the starting-point of philosophy[2]. On the lowest
level of knowledge, in perception itself, there is an element of
intuition, grasping the whole nature of the individual in a single
immediate act.

Possessed by intuition and 'induction' of its universal objects
and premisses, demonstrative science can proceed to its task of
proving universal truths. Since the belief in the primary reality
of the specific Form is as much the kernel of Aristotle's logic as
of his metaphysic, the typical purpose of science is to define such
Forms and to show why they possess properties which are necessary but not parts of their essence. Definition, as in Plato, is by
genus and specific differences; but Aristotle does not accept the
Platonic method of Division. An indivisible species is to be
defined by collecting attributes common to all individuals of the
species, and separately, but not collectively, shared by other
species of the same genus. Since we cannot examine every individual, we are once more thrown back upon intuition; and it
is not clear how essential attributes can be distinguished from the
properties which demonstration will prove to be necessarily
derived from the essence. Aristotle's whole discussion of this
subject is obscured by two pre-suppositions. In the first place,
he takes the existing structure of the mathematical sciences as
the pattern of all science; and in geometry, for instance, 'having
angles equal to two right angles' is taken to be a demonstrable
property of the triangle, but not part of its definition. The other
source of confusion is his belief that the syllogism—a discovery
of which he was proud—is the structure common to all reasoning,
and he tries to force the processes of scientific enquiry into this
mould. The perfect syllogism, to which other 'figures' are to
be reduced, is the figure with a universal affirmative conclusion.
It is assumed that every proposition in a syllogism contains the
subject-predicate relation, and the predicate in one premiss must
be a term which can stand as subject in the other. An account of

---

[1] Ross, *ib.*, p. 217, p. 41.   [2] See above, p. 324.

the process of reasoning which is subject to these limitations is necessarily incomplete and distorted.

Further, when the subject of inquiry is the cause of a class of events (such as eclipses of the moon), Aristotle tries to reduce this to an inquiry for the definition of an attribute. An eclipse is regarded as an attribute of the moon, and the 'cause' (the interposition of the earth) becomes the middle term of a syllogism: 'Loses its light' is always true of a body which has another body between it and its source of light; being such a body is true of the eclipsed moon; therefore 'loses its light' is true of the eclipsed moon. This can be recast into the definition: Eclipse of the moon is loss of light due to the earth's interposition. Aristotle did not, however, imagine that the causes of events could be discovered by demonstration. The discovery of the 'middle term' stating the cause is made, after a number of experiences of the fact, by an 'instantaneous guess' of intuition. He admits that the syllogistic statement does not even prove that the cause we have guessed is the true cause. What lies behind these logical contortions is the conviction that the 'cause' of a thing or of an event is to be found in its essential nature or Form. Aristotle holds true to the tradition that the aim of science is, not to establish laws of succession among phenomena, but to discover the 'nature of things.' Hence the relation of cause and effect is replaced by the notions of Form and Matter, or actuality and potentiality. An effect is a potentiality actualized by its cause, or 'Matter' of a certain kind determined by a certain Form. The Matter individualizes the Form, which in itself is universal.

The method of definition by genus and specific difference implies the acceptance of Plato's hierarchy of Forms, extending upwards from the indivisible species, through intermediate kinds, to highest genera, which must be simple and indefinable. The genus and intermediate kinds are less determinate than the lowest species, and so related to it as 'Matter'; every difference adds an element of Form. Accordingly, as we move upward towards the highest genera, we are not, as Plato supposed, approaching the ultimate cause of all existence, but receding ever further from the primary reality of the concrete thing. The highest genera appear to be identical with the 'categories' which figure everywhere in Aristotle's works, but are nowhere formally deduced. The authenticity of the treatise called *Categories* is disputed. It contains the famous list of ten: substance, quality, quantity, relation, place, date, position, state, action, passivity—apparently an inventory of the ultimate classes of things that are meant by words. They are the terms arrived at when we push the question, what a namable thing *is*, to the last point. But they stand at the farthest remove from the reality of the individual substance. To find anything that can rank as a higher kind of reality, we must look in another direction. There we find certain Forms which are declared to be without Matter, though they are all individuals. They are: the active Reason in man, which has no bodily organ, but is eternal and immortal or 'divine,' and enters the body 'from without'; the Intelligences which move the spheres; and God, the Prime Mover. The divinity of the active Reason is a dogma inherited from Plato and earlier religious thought. The Intelligences and God are required to explain the motion of the universe. The First Heaven is moved directly by God; the other spheres, having different motions, are moved by subordinate immaterial Intelligences.

VIII. COSMOLOGY

Aristotle's universe is a system of concentric spheres, with the earth at rest in the centre, and at the outside the 'First Heaven' of the fixed stars. The mathematical spheres, imagined by Eudoxus and Callippus to account for the apparent motions of the sun and moon and the five known planets, were converted by Aristotle into a mechanism of actual rotating spheres, each moving by contact the sphere next inside it. The number of spheres down to the moon was raised to 55. The heavenly bodies consist of a fifth element, incapable of any change except circular motion.

The existence of God is deduced from the eternity of the world and of motion. It is necessary, and sufficient, to suppose one eternal source of motion; but this cannot be itself moved. Already in the treatise *Concerning Philosophy*, Aristotle had declared God to be incapable of change; he is not a soul, or a creator, or even conscious of the world's existence; the activity in which his life consists can be nothing but intuitive contemplation, without any element of desire or action. He is without parts or magnitude; and although in one place he is said to be outside the universe, he cannot really be in space. He can cause motion only as the final cause, or object of desire, which moves without itself being moved. The subject of this desire must presumably be the soul animating the body of the First Heaven; but the operation of the Intelligences is left in obscurity. Aristotle's God thus holds a position like that of the Good in the *Republic*; and his efficacy is still illicitly imagined not merely as a source of mechanical motion propagated throughout the spheres, but also as an attraction to which life responds with its mysterious impulse to rise from the potentiality of Matter to the actuality of Form. The tendency to think in this way appears where personified Nature is represented as striving towards perfection. But, as we have seen, the system admits no soul in Nature that might be the seat of such desire. Aristotle's mind is still haunted by the Platonic doctrines of the Good and of Eros; but his God is the object of a desire for which he provides no subject.

A striking feature of the cosmology is the distinction between the celestial region and the sublunary, to which all becoming and all change, other than rotatory locomotion, are confined. Here are the four elements, which, as natural objects, 'contain within themselves sources of motion,' manifest in their tendency to move towards their natural places in four spheres—a notion which goes back to Anaximander (vol. IV, p. 540). Each element contains two of the primary qualities (hot, dry, cold, fluid), whose interaction explains the transformation of the elements into one another and the production of intermediate natures by combination. The elements are the material cause of the generation of substances. The efficient cause, as we have seen, resides in the specific Forms; but the alternation of birth and growth, decay and death, in the life of individual creatures is due to the rhythmical approach and retreat of the sun in its annual course, causing transformation of the elements and the seasonal alternations of heat and cold, drought and rain. The *Meteorologica* contains a further study of the combinations and mutual influences of the four elements, and deals with the 'meteoric' phenomena of the sublunary region.

IX. BIOLOGY AND PSYCHOLOGY

Biology is the department of science in which Aristotle's characteristic concepts are most at home, and the treatises on natural history are still admired by those men of science who are aware that they exist. They contain a large collection of observations of the structure and habits of some five hundred animal species. The theory of classification is carried to a point beyond which, it is said, no advance was made before Linnaeus. The principle observed in explaining organic Nature is teleological, in the sense that the process by which an organism and its parts come into being is to be explained by the Form of the perfect creature—'becoming is for the sake of being'—and the Form itself by its function or 'activity.' The phenomena cannot be accounted for by the casual play of mechanical causes, though these may suffice to produce some characters which are not essential. This teleology has, however, no firm metaphysical basis; it is an inverted mechanism, which cannot show how the end is to cause the beginning.

Natural history culminates in Psychology, for this science has for its object the specific Form, the vehicle of life. What has so far been studied morphologically as the structure characteristic of a species is now seen as the living essence embodied in the individual, informing its material parts. It is nothing else than the soul, which is related to an organic body of a certain constitution as Form to Matter. Thus soul and body are two inseparable aspects of one thing, and soul is defined as 'the first entelechy (or actuality) of a natural organic body,' the second, or further, actuality being the activities it displays in waking life. This interesting view of the relation of soul to body avoids the difficulties that arise when soul and body, or mind and matter, are conceived as entities of different orders, whose interaction has to be accounted for. All psychic phenomena which occur in plants and animals generally are not merely accompanied by physiological changes; they are the formal aspects of these material processes. Anger, for example, is on the physical side, a boiling of the blood; on the mental, a desire for retaliation. The mental aspect gives this phenomenon the Form of anger, which distinguishes the physical change from boiling that might be mechanically produced by the application of heat. Neither aspect can strictly be called, in the modern sense, the cause or the effect of the other; each is a 'cause' in the Aristotelian sense, the one formal, the other material. The psychologist, in defining anger, must mention both.

From this definition of soul it follows that no individual soul can exist apart from the body it informs from the moment of generation to the moment of death. On the other hand, the human soul contains an element, the active Reason, which is declared to be pure Form with no bodily organ, and to exist eternally. This is none other than that 'true self' which Socrates had believed in and Plato had held to be the rational part of the soul, whose impersonal memory contains all knowledge of reality. In Aristotle, as in Plato, it is immortal or 'divine,' and includes no element of personality, such as distinguishes one individual from another. More than once in the *Ethics* Aristotle explicitly calls it the 'self[1].'

---

[1] *Nicom. Eth.* x, 7, 9. 'This (Reason) would seem, too, to be each man himself, since it is the authoritative and better part of him. It would be strange, then, if he were to choose not the life of his self, but that of something else.... Reason more than everything else *is* man.' (Ross.) Cf. also ix, 8, 6.

As life rises in the scale of Nature, one layer of soul is super-imposed on another. The lowest form of life, in the plant world, consists of the faculties of nutrition and reproduction. To this is added in animals the sentient life, including sensation and perception, feelings of pleasure and pain, desire and conse-quent movement, and at least some rudimentary emotions. On the physiological side sense-perception involves the assimilation of the organ to the objectively existing qualities perceived; this 'reception of the Form without the Matter' has its mental aspect in the awareness of the quality. Imagination (*phantasia*) is the faculty which preserves images of former objects of perception, on which depends memory—the complex act of recognizing an image as the image of some past object. Imagination is also active in free imagery and in dreams.

In addition to these animal faculties, man has Reason, making him capable of thought and moral action. This faculty, though it can exist and exercise its activity of pure contemplation apart from the mortal soul, combines with the soul during life in such a way that its activity penetrates the lower functions. Even on the level of perception, while the senses receive only the Form of the sensible qualities, Reason, by its peculiar power of intuition, apprehends the essential nature of the individual. It thus receives the 'intelligible Form' of the indivisible species, in an immediate act occupying an undivided time. Again, we are told that the Reason 'thinks the Forms *in* the images' which, Aristotle holds, are present to the mind in all thinking. The Reason has thus the same function as in Plato: it is the power which apprehends the primary realities. Aristotle finally draws his distinction of Form and Matter, actual and potential, within the Reason itself: there is an active Reason and a passive. Some of his expressions suggest that, like Plato's rational part with its impersonal memory, the active Reason is always in possession of all truth, which it recovers by an act of recognition. In the process of gaining knowledge, potential knowledge is raised to actuality. This seems like a translation into Aristotelian terms of Plato's theory of reminis-cence. Aristotle, however, is embarrassed by his conviction that the objects of knowledge exist in the physical world, so that the intelligible Forms must pass into the soul through the channel of sense-perception and imagination, and be received from that quarter by the 'passive Reason.' The obscurity of this part of his psychology is, perhaps, due to his having to combine this doctrine with a conception of Reason and knowledge that was more like Plato's than he cared to admit.

X. ETHICS AND POLITICS

Aristotle's theory of Ethics is dictated, no less than other parts of his philosophy, by his central doctrine of the specific Form. The first object of ethical inquiry is to discover the good or final cause of man's existence. It is a foregone conclusion that this will be found among the activities of man's specific Form or essential nature, which the Psychology has identified with his soul. The 'good for man' or happiness (as all agree to call it) must be some activity of soul, in which his peculiar nature finds its fullest realization. Every other species has a corresponding 'good'; but man's business is to realize his own nature. The moralist, however, cannot admit that all activities of life are good in themselves or ethical ends. Aristotle's only discussion of the meaning of 'good' (*Nic. Eth.* i, 6) is confused and contradictory; but he recognizes that some things are good in themselves and such as ought to be desired, whether they are desired or not. He further holds, with Socrates and Plato, that the divine Reason or 'true self' has the power to discern what is really good, and always 'wishes' for it; its judgment is the only guide and is infallible. Happiness, then, must consist in activities recognized by this faculty as good in themselves. Aristotle describes such activities as those which are 'in accordance with virtue (goodness)' adding (without justification) 'or, if there be several virtues, in accordance with the best and most perfect.' But since the goodness or excellence of anything is that condition which enables it to perform its function well, virtue may equally well be defined in terms of good activities; it is a state of the soul from which good activities result, and analogous to bodily health (*Nic. Eth.* ii, 6, 1–3).

Man's nature is complicated by the presence in his soul of the divine Reason—the part which 'possesses a rational principle (*or* rule),' by virtue of its power of directly and infallibly perceiving what is good and 'wishing' it. In moral conduct, good or bad— an activity peculiar to man, since neither God nor the lower animals are capable of it—the operation of Reason is combined with the instinctive mechanism of action, namely the group of faculties we share with animals; sensation, perception, feelings of pleasure and pain, and the consequent desires and motions. The desires of this part, when left to itself, have for their object pleasure, or 'what appears good'; having no rational principle, this part cannot tell good pleasures from bad. In man, however, the lower faculties are interpenetrated by Reason, and hence this part is amenable to Reason. In the perfect character the harmony is complete; but there are less perfect types, in whom a conflict of the higher and lower motives still occurs; according as the higher or the lower usually prevails, they are called 'continent' or 'incontinent.' In perfect vice, the battle has been finally won by the lower nature.

Moral Virtue is acquired by habituation. Children are still irrational, and conduct judged to be right by their rational elders is imposed upon them from without. As the habit of acting in certain ways is established and the Reason develops, the conduct becomes virtuous in the full sense: besides acting from a fully formed habit, the agent is then aware of the nature of good action and acts from his own deliberate choice. He is now governed by the rational principle within himself. The ends of action are intuitively determined by the Reason, and Aristotle speaks as if this process involved no deliberation about the relative values of alternative ends. Deliberation is only the process of thinking out the chain of means which will lead to an end, and the object of 'choice' is the first link in this chain—an act we can at once perform. Choice thus involves a decision reached by deliberation, affirmed by desire, and issuing in corresponding action. Upon the question of free will Aristotle makes no clear pronouncement.

The famous doctrine that Virtue is a mean state between two vices, of excess and defect, is derived from the medical analogy of health, as a balanced or 'proportional' mixture of contrary physical qualities, which may be upset by extremes of heat or cold, dryness or moisture, etc. This was itself an application of the Pythagorean view of 'goodness' as due to the imposition of Limit on an Unlimited (vol. IV, p. 548). In moral Virtue the 'unlimited' factor is emotion, the affective phase of the instinctive mechanism. Emotion is held to vary in degrees of intensity; physiologically, it actually is a change in the amount of a quality in the direction of one or the other extreme. The habit which is Virtue or Vice is, from this standpoint, a certain range, somewhere in the scale, which determines the intensity of emotional reaction. If it is fixed too high or too low, the reaction will habitually be too intense or not intense enough. The mean state, which will be 'relative to us' (i.e. vary somewhat with differences of temperament), is Virtue. There are obvious objections to this theory; but the doctrine of the mean has attracted more attention than it deserves; and Aristotle himself recognizes that quantitative differences of emotion are only one factor in the determination of right conduct. We must feel and act 'on the right grounds, at the right time, towards the right persons, for the right end.'

Under all these heads the Reason of the virtuous man is the sole and infallible judge of what the occasion demands.

After a long analysis of the particular moral virtues, Aristotle passes to the intellectual virtues of the rational part. They fall under two main heads: theoretical and practical wisdom. The first includes scientific knowledge of necessary truth, the intuition of first principles and demonstration. The highest form of activity is, not discursive reasoning or the discovery of truth, but the contemplation of truth already possessed—the only activity possible to God or to the disembodied Reason. The life of the philosopher has foretastes of this mode of consciousness, which possesses every attribute of felicity and answers to the definition of happiness as the activity of the soul in accordance with the best and most perfect of virtues. It is, however, a divine, rather than a human, activity, for the animal part of our nature has no share in it. Accordingly, the 'good' or happiness of man as a composite being lies in the other mode of activity peculiar to man, moral action. This involves the lower intellectual virtue of practical wisdom, exercised by Reason in its control over the in-stinctive nature. Though Aristotle quarrels with the statement of Socrates' doctrine, 'Virtue is knowledge (or wisdom),' he accepts it in substance; for he declares that all the moral virtues are one, and that they cannot exist apart from practical wisdom, nor practical wisdom apart from them.

The *Nicomachean Ethics* opens with a picture of human activity portioned out into the several 'arts,' each with its end. Some of these ends are only means to the ends of higher arts; at the head of all is the art of Statesmanship (Politics), with its ultimate end, human happiness. Thus Aristotle inherits Plato's view of States-manship as the sovereign art, controlling all the other branches of human activity by virtue of its knowledge of good and evil. Ethics, which defines the supreme end and indicates the way to attain it, is 'in a sense' this very science or art; and the treatise on Politics, or the study of man in society, follows immediately. It consists of a collection of writings which were never welded into a consecutive whole. The earliest stratum may be the theory of the Ideal State, since this is closer to Platonic tradition; the later parts are enriched by the industry of Aristotle and his School in compiling studies of 158 Greek constitutions. The *Constitution of Athens* alone survives. The political doctrine is discussed else-where (see below, pp. 519 *sqq.*).

The three books on *Rhetoric* and the fragment of the *Poetics* complete the Aristotelian corpus.

XI. THE PERIPATETIC SCHOOL AT ATHENS

Soon after the accession of Alexander (336 B.C.), Aristotle, now fifty years old, returned to Athens. At the Academy Xenocrates had succeeded Speusippus in 339. Aristotle rented some buildings just outside the city in the grove of Apollo Lyceus and founded a rival school. The name 'Peripatetic' was derived from the walks (*peripatoi*), where the master discussed philosophy with his students. A large library was collected, with maps and a museum of objects to illustrate the lectures. Aristotle discoursed on the more abstruse subjects in the morning, and delivered popular courses to a wider public in the afternoon. He was also engaged in revising and adding to the writings of the previous period, and in organizing research. He ranks as the creator of a new kind of science of observation and description, amassing collections of facts of human and natural history, descriptions of animals, plants and minerals, materials for chronology in lists of the victors at the Pythian games and the Athenian Dionysia, the studies of 158 Constitutions, and innumerable smaller monographs. The first history of science was compiled by Theophrastus, Eudemus of Rhodes, and Meno, who respectively undertook physics and metaphysics, mathematics, and medicine.

A passage from the introduction to *The Parts of Animals* (1, 5), shows that young men accustomed to the discussion of abstract ideas and formal rhetoric were not easily induced to study the anatomy of worms and insects.

It remains to treat of the nature of living creatures, omitting nothing (so far as possible), whether of higher or of lower dignity. For even in the case of creatures, the contemplation of which is disagreeable to the sense, Nature, who fashioned them, nevertheless affords an extraordinary pleasure to anyone with a philosophic disposition, capable of understanding causes. We take delight in looking at representations of these things, because we observe at the same time the art of the painter or sculptor which created them; and it would be strange and unreasonable that the contemplation of the works of Nature themselves should not yield a still greater satisfaction, when we can make out their causes. Accordingly, the consideration of the lowlier forms of life ought not to excite a childish repugnance. In all natural things there is something to move wonder. There is a story that, when some strangers who wished to meet Heracleitus stopped short on finding him warming himself at the kitchen stove, he told them to come boldly in, for there also there were gods. In the same spirit we should approach the study of every form of life without disgust, knowing that in every one there is something of nature and of beauty. For it is in the works of Nature above all that design, in contrast with random chance, is manifest; and the perfect form which anything, born or made, is designed to realize holds the rank of beauty.

This manifold activity was cut short by an outbreak of anti-

Macedonian feeling at Athens upon the death of Alexander in 323 B.C. The conqueror's former tutor was assailed with the usual charge of impiety and withdrew to the home of his mother's family at Chalcis, leaving the school to the charge of Theophrastus. Aristotle may have hoped to complete his life's work by a final revision of his writings; but in the next year he died, at the age of 63. After the death of Theophrastus the intellectual supremacy passed from the Academy and the Lyceum to Alexandria.

Aristotle's best work was done in the fields of Biology and Ethics, where teleology is more illuminating than mechanism. Our brief review of his system has shown how it revolves round the doctrine, inherited from Plato, of the specific Form of the natural kind. In this context his apparatus of concepts possesses its full meaning. The farther he moves from this central point, the less appropriate the concepts become. When he passes below the level of the living organism to penetrate the constitution of the inorganic, the notions of Form and Matter, the actual and the potential, are strained till they trail off into verbal distinctions, all but meaningless save for illicit associations with their proper use. His work is inferior to that of the Atomists, whose strength lay precisely here, while their weakness was that they levelled down the phenomena of life to the plane of the inanimate. Again, when he passes upward from the sublunary sphere of living Nature to the celestial region, the Intelligences, and the first source of motion, he becomes a doctrinaire, ready to prove *a priori* that there cannot be more than one world or five elements, or that the earth must be at rest in the centre of the universe. Several causes combined to hold him back from reaching the standpoint of modern science. For better or worse, he could never shake free from the commanding influence of Plato, though in later life his natural inclination towards the study of empirical fact carried him ever farther from the Academy. He had, moreover, an exaggerated respect for tradition, founded on the notion that fragments of ancient wisdom had survived the cataclysms which destroyed civilization from time to time, and were embedded in proverbial thought or in the sayings of the older sages. Finally, he inherited the Pythagorean and Academic tendency to see the pattern of all science in mathematics and to believe that the divine faculty of Reason can, with unerring intuition, ascertain the premisses of all knowledge and deduce the whole structure of reality. This faith in the infallibility of the soul, when she 'withdraws to think by herself,' was to cost the scientific world many centuries of illusion and disillusionment.

CHAPTER XII

ALEXANDER: THE CONQUEST OF PERSIA

I. ALEXANDER'S EARLY YEARS

ALEXANDER III, son of Philip II and the Epirote princess Olympias, was born in summer 356, and was twenty when in 336 he succeeded to the throne of Macedonia. Though both his parents claimed Greek descent, he certainly had from his father, and probably from his mother, some Illyrian, *i.e.* Albanian, blood. When his son was thirteen, Philip invited Aristotle to

Note. In this chapter and the next our information derives from three main currents: the 'good' tradition, the 'vulgate,' and the anti-Alexander traditions. Of the five extant late writers—Arrian, Diodorus, Plutarch, Curtius, Justin—who give the connected story, Arrian's *Anabasis*, whose main source was Ptolemy, represents the good tradition; Ptolemy used the official *Journal* and other official material and his own notes and recollections, and with rare exceptions is trustworthy. (Further official material is supplied by contemporary inscriptions, which have preserved some of Alexander's rescripts, and by the Alexander-coinage.) Arrian also largely uses Aristobulus, a contemporary writer, independent and often sound, but with certain affinities with the vulgate; the vulgate itself he normally quotes as λεγόμενα, 'so they say.' Arrian's Ἰνδική in the historical part reproduces the trust-worthy Nearchus. The vulgate derives from Callisthenes and lesser writers, from elements of the good tradition, and from every sort of floating account and story; its form was ultimately fixed (in the writer's opinion not before 280–70 B.C., but many believe earlier) by an historian who is represented for us most directly by Diodorus XVII and who is usually identified with Cleitarchus of Alexandria; its aim was to glorify Alexander in its own fashion, and it long held the field. The traditions which, in more than one form, aimed at belittling Alexander represent the Greek opposition, and essentially go back to the attack made on him by the Peripatetics after his death. Plutarch, in his *Life of Alexander*, used every sort of material, good and bad, and produced an amazingly vivid picture which no one has yet attempted to analyse. Curtius also is difficult; while he chiefly used the vulgate, anti-Alexander material, and worthless school rhetoric, he does occasionally draw on a very good source, which was Macedonian, not Greek, and might be Ptolemy. Justin, who is worth little, used the vulgate and an anti-Alexander tradition. The modern historian's main problem is how far to use the vulgate, and it should be said that many recent historians rely on it in a way which the writer feels quite unable to do; while behind the good tradition itself lies a perhaps insoluble question—the relation of official truth to the truth. For the remaining material readers are referred to the Bibliography.

Macedonia to be his tutor; and, so far as his character was influenced by others, it was influenced by Aristotle and Olympias,
by a philosopher who taught that moderation alone could hold a
state together and by a woman to whom any sort of moderation
was unknown. Olympias was proud and terribly passionate, with
an emotional side which made her a devotee of the orgiastic worships of Thrace; but she kept her son's love all his life, and, though
he inherited from Philip the solid qualities of capacity for affairs
and military talent, his nature was largely hers, though not his
mind. For if his nature was passionate, his mind was practical;
he was found, when a boy, entertaining some Persian envoys by
questioning them about the routes across Asia. For physical
pleasures, except hunting, he cared little; but he read much
poetry, and shared Euripides' dislike of the professional athlete.
His heroes were his traditional ancestors Achilles and Heracles,
and he kept under his pillow a copy of the *Iliad* which Aristotle
had revised for him. Aristotle taught him ethics and metaphysics,
and some politics; later he wrote for him a treatise on the art of
ruling, and another on colonization. He also gave him a general
interest in philosophy, scientific investigation, and medicine. The
last two bore fruit in Alexander's care for his army's health in
Asia and in the great contributions he made to the knowledge of
geography, hydrography, ethnology, zoology, and botany; the
first is illustrated by the philosophers who accompanied him to
Asia, and by the treatise on kingship written for him by Xenocrates, while his admiration for Heracles may have been quickened
by the Cynic teaching which was already making of Heracles the
ideal king, labouring incessantly for the good of mankind. In
appearance, Alexander was fair-skinned, ruddy, and clean-shaven;
Lysippus' portrait-statues rendered famous the inclination of his
head to the left side and the soft, upturned eyes. For the rest, he
was at his accession easy to persuade but impossible to drive;
generous, ambitious, masterful, loyal to friends, and above all very
young. His deeper qualities, for good or evil, remained to be
called out by events.

At sixteen he had governed Macedonia in Philip's absence and
defeated a Thracian rising; at eighteen he had commanded
Philip's left at Chaeronea, and broken the Sacred Band of Thebes.
At nineteen he was an exile. Relations between Philip and Olympias had long been strained, for Olympias was not the woman to
tolerate Philip's harem; and the trouble came to a head when, in
337, Philip married Cleopatra, niece of his general Attalus.
Philip, it was said, doubted whether Alexander were really his

son—possibly a story spread by Attalus' friends; and at the wedding feast Attalus requested the company to pray for a legitimate heir to the throne. Alexander flung his cup in his face, took his mother, and fled to Illyria. Philip banished Alexander's friends, including Harpalus prince of Elymiotis and Ptolemy son of Lagos, both related to the royal house, and Nearchus, a Cretan settled at Amphipolis; finally Demaratus of Corinth acted as peace-maker, persuading Philip to recall his son and Alexander to return.

Next year Philip was assassinated. It was the official belief at the Macedonian court that the assassin was in Persian pay; it is possible enough. Antipater's attitude absolutely acquits Alexander of complicity. Olympias may have been privy to the plot; but the only evidence against her is Antipater's subsequent enmity to her, for our tradition on the subject derives from Cassander's propaganda later. Some in Greece believed that the conspirators meant to set on the throne Alexander son of Aeropus of Lyncestis; were this true, Olympias is acquitted. Aeropus' younger sons were certainly among the conspirators, but the eldest cleared himself for the time by being the first to hail Alexander as king. The usual confusion consequent on a change of ruler threatened; but Philip's generals Antipater and Parmenion declared for Alexander, and the new king acted with determination; he secured the army, put to death all the conspirators who did not escape to Persia, and executed Attalus for treasonable correspondence with Athens; he had no further trouble. Olympias is said to have murdered Cleopatra and her infant on her own account. It was her last public action in Macedonia while Alexander lived; though devoted to her, he was determined that she should not interfere in affairs, and in 331 she retired to Epirus.

Alexander had still to establish his position outside Macedonia; Philip had had no time to consolidate the League of Corinth, and the Greeks regarded their treaties with him as terminated by his death. Athens was rejoicing over his murder, Ambracia expelled his garrison, Aetolia recalled her exiles, there was excitement in Thebes and the Peloponnese; even in Thessaly the anti-Macedonian party for a moment seized power. Northward the Balkan peoples were flaming up; Macedonia might find herself between two fires. Alexander turned first to Greece, as more necessary to him and more dangerous; in late summer 336 he hurried south, turned Tempe, which the Thessalians were holding, by cutting steps—'Alexander's ladder'—up the flank of Ossa, and regained control of Thessaly without fighting. He was elected head for life of her league in Philip's place, and thus secured her all-important cavalry; for Thessaly was a country of horse-breeding landowners ruling a serf population, and cavalry was her natural arm. Greece was not prepared for resistance; he overawed Thebes, forgave Ambracia and Athens, and at a congress of the League states at Corinth was elected general of the League in Philip's place for the invasion of Asia, Sparta of course still abstaining: among the provisions of the new Covenant were that all League states should be free and self-governing and that their internal constitutions should not be interfered with. On his way back to Macedonia he visited Delphi.

In spring 335 he turned against the Triballi, a people whom pressure from the advancing Celts had driven eastward across the Isker into northern Bulgaria, whence they were threatening Macedonia. Alexander took the coast road eastward from Amphipolis, turned Rhodope, went north, roughly, by Adrianople, and after a sharp fight crossed the Haemus, probably by the Kajan or Koja Balkan pass, though the Shipka is possible. He broke the Triballi in a battle, and reached the Danube somewhere between Sistovo and Silistria; but the Triballi had sent their families to an island in the river called Peuke, and, though some Byzantine warships joined him, he could not take it, while the Getae, famous for their belief in immortality, were gathering on the northern bank to aid the Triballi. Between warships and log canoes he got 5500 men across the Danube, dispersed the Getae, and burned their town; this bold action caused the Triballi and their neighbours to surrender, and brought him an embassy from their enemies the Celts of the upper Danube, who swore alliance with him in a form still used by the Irish Gaels 1000 years later—'We will keep faith unless the sky fall and crush us or the earth open and swallow us or the sea rise and overwhelm us'; they added that, of the three, they only feared the sky falling[1]. Alexander now heard that Cleitus of Illyria had allied himself with Glaucias of the Taulantini (south Illyria), invaded Macedonia, and captured the border fortress, Pelion; while the Autariatae of southern Serbia were ready to fall on his flank as he went west. But his friend Longarus of the Agrianes on the upper Strymon, whose people furnished some of his best troops, undertook to hold the Autariatae, and Alexander, notwithstanding the great distance to be covered, reached Pelion before Glaucias joined Cleitus. He meant to blockade it; but Glaucias closed in on his rear, and he was not strong enough to

[1] This oath was brilliantly reconstructed by H. d'Arbois de Jubainville, *Les premiers habitants de l'Europe*, II, p. 316. But his Irish parallel shows it was not in form an *imprecation*, as he thought.

fight on two fronts. His own audacity and his men's discipline extricated the army from its dangerous position; then he turned and thoroughly defeated Cleitus. News from Greece prevented him doing more, but seemingly Illyria did not trouble him again; possibly fear of his Celtic allies counted for something.

A report had reached Greece that Alexander was dead, and the threatened defection was serious. The Theban democrats, exiled by Philip, had returned and seized power, and were attacking the Cadmea; Aetolia, Arcadia, and Elis were inclining to support them. Athens had voted help to Thebes; and though she had made no actual move, and had refused a subsidy of 300 talents offered by Darius, Demosthenes, it seems, had personally accepted the money—a dubious act, which was freely misconstrued—and with it was providing Thebes with arms. Alexander was afraid of a possible combination of the four chief military states of Greece—Thebes, Athens, Aetolia, and Sparta. But he showed, for the first but not the last time, that his speed of movement was worth an army; his campaign had already been sufficiently strenuous, yet fourteen days after the news reached him at Pelion he stood under the walls of Thebes, having collected the contingents of Phocis and Boeotia on the way. His presence checked any further developments, and the other Greeks waited on the event. He himself hoped Thebes would submit; he wanted a peaceful and contented Greece behind him and waited for overtures, but none came; Thebes meant to fight. Naturally he intended to take the city if accommodation failed; that Perdiccas began the attack without orders is immaterial. The Thebans sallied out but were defeated, and Alexander's men entered the city with the fugitives, whom the Phocians and Plataeans massacred in revenge for their former wrongs. Alexander nominally left Thebes' fate to the League, but the only delegates with him were Thebes' enemies; Phocis and Boeotia indeed voted the city's destruction, but the responsibility lies with Alexander. Thebes was razed, the temples and Pindar's house alone being left; Macedonia's partisans and other classes were released, and some Thebans escaped to Athens, but many were sold as slaves—perhaps 8000, if the recorded price be true[1]. Orchomenus and Plataea were fully restored, and the Boeotian cities divided up Thebes' territory. Thebes suffered what she had inflicted on Plataea and Orchomenus, and what other Greek cities had suffered at the hands of Greeks; but that does not acquit Alexander, and it is said that his own conscience troubled

---

[1] The 30,000 of tradition is a stereotyped figure, which recurs at Tyre.

him later. But the blow produced its effect; every Greek state
hastened to submit, and he showed general clemency; and though
he demanded the leading statesmen from Athens, he withdrew
the demand on the appeal of Phocion and Demades, the irreconcilable Charidemus alone being exiled; for he greatly desired a
contented Athens. He retained Philip's garrisons in Corinth,
Chalcis, and the Cadmea.

II. THE PREPARATIONS FOR INVADING PERSIA

In autumn 335 Alexander returned to Macedonia to prepare
for the invasion of Persia, and for this purpose recalled Parmenion from Asia, whither Philip had sent him in 336 with an
advance force. Parmenion's successor was defeated by Memnon,
who commanded Darius' mercenaries, but retained the all-important Dardanelles bridge-heads. Darius seems to have thought
that Parmenion's recall and Memnon's success had removed any
possibility of invasion; he made no preparations, and did not even
mobilize his fleet or appoint a commander-in-chief on the coast.

The primary reason why Alexander invaded Persia was, no
doubt, that he never thought of *not* doing it; it was his inheritance.
Doubtless, too, adventure attracted him; and weight must also be
given to the official reason. For officially, as is shown by the
political manifesto which he afterwards sent to Darius from
Marathus (p. 373), the invasion was that Panhellenic war of revenge which Isocrates had preached; and Alexander did set out
with Panhellenic ideas: he was the champion of Hellas. Later
tradition indeed asserted that he had read, and was influenced by,
Isocrates' *Philippus*. But Isocrates had envisaged the conquest of
Asia Minor only; and certainly Alexander did not cross the Dardanelles with any definite design of conquering the whole Persian
empire. There is a story that Aristotle once asked his pupils what
they would all do in certain circumstances, and Alexander replied
that he could not say until the circumstances arose; and, so far as can
be seen, he intended at first to be guided by events, and naturally
found that each step forward seemed to lead inevitably to a
fresh one. To discuss the morality of the invasion, and to call
Alexander a glorious robber, is a mere anachronism. Of course,
to the best modern thought, the invasion is quite unjustifiable;
but it is equally unjustifiable to transfer our own thought to the
fourth century. Greeks certainly objected to barbarians—'lesser
breeds without the Law'—attacking themselves, but the best
thought of the time saw no reason why they should not attack

barbarians whenever they liked; Isocrates warmly advocated it, saying barbarians were natural enemies, and Aristotle called it essentially just and told his pupil to treat barbarians as slaves. It was to be left to Alexander himself to rise to a higher level than Aristotle.

In the spring of 334 Alexander crossed the Dardanelles, as commander-in-chief of the army of Macedonia and the League of Corinth, with something over 30,000 foot and over 5000 horse. He left Antipater with 12,000 foot and 1500 horse as his general in Europe, to govern Macedonia and Thrace, supervise the Greeks, and keep Olympias quiet, a more difficult task. Of Alexander's infantry, 12,000 were Macedonians, viz. the phalanx, 9000, in six territorial battalions, and the hypaspists, 3000, in three battalions; and 12,000 were Greeks, composed of allies (League hoplites) and mercenaries (partly peltasts). The remaining infantry were light-armed: Agrianian javelin-men, Cretan archers, and Thracians. Generally speaking, the League infantry was used mainly for garrisons and communications; but the Cretan archers, who were not League troops, were as indispensable as the Agrianians themselves, and their loss of four commanders successively in battle shows how heavily they were engaged. The phalanx was a far more flexible body than the later phalanx, and their spears resembled those used by the Macedonian lancers. The hypaspists probably differed somewhat in armament, but shared the heavy infantry work; one of their battalions, the *agēma*, was Alexander's guard. Of the cavalry, the most important body was the Companions, drawn from the Macedonian upper classes, and divided into eight territorial squadrons; a little later they were 2000 strong. The 1800 Thessalians ranked next; there were also some Greek allied horse, who acted with the Thessalians, four squadrons of Macedonian lancers, and small bodies of Paeonian and Thracian horse. The advance on traditional Greek warfare was to lie in the combination of arms, and more especially in the use of a mass of heavy cavalry, acting in small tactical units, as the striking force; Alexander always struck with the Companions from the right, to cover the infantry's unshielded side. But though he usually led the Companions, he led other corps if occasion required—twice the phalanx, twice the hypaspists, and once the archers.

His officers were as yet largely Philip's. Parmenion was second in command; his son Philotas commanded the Companions, and another son, Nicanor, the hypaspists. Five of the phalanx-leaders were prominent later: Craterus, Perdiccas, Coenus, Amyntas, and

Meleager. Cleitus 'the Black' commanded the first squadron of the Companions, called the Royal; Harpalus' cousin Calas commanded the Thessalians, and Antigonus, the future king, the Greek allies. Of Alexander's Staff, the so-called Bodyguards, thirteen names are known, but many were appointed later; Ptolemaeus, Arybbas, Balacrus, and probably Demetrius, were among the original members. Beside the Staff, Alexander had about him a body of men of high position to whom the name Companions properly belongs and after whom the Companion cavalry was called, probably about 100 in number[1]; these acted as an informal council, and formed his general reserve both for special duties and for filling all high offices, whether military or administrative, such as satrapies. They included his personal friends Hephaestion and Nearchus; the future kings, Ptolemy son of Lagos, Seleucus, and Lysimachus; and a few Greeks like Demaratus, Stasanor, and Laomedon, who could speak Persian and was to have charge of the prisoners; but Cassander remained with his father Antipater, and Harpalus, who was physically unfit for service, accompanied the army as a civilian.

The army had a siege-train, and engineers for constructing pontoons and siege-machines, the chief engineer being Diades, who invented (or improved) portable siege-towers and rams on wheels. There were sappers, well-sinkers, and a surveying section (bematists), who collected information about routes and camping grounds and recorded the distances marched; their records, which were checked by Alexander, for long formed the basis of the geography of Asia. There was a baggage train; as for commissariat, supplies were collected in each district as conquered and used for the next advance. The secretarial department was under Eumenes of Cardia, who wrote the *Journal*, the daily official record of the expedition, probably checked by Alexander. There was a corps of Royal Pages, lads training to be officers, who watched before Alexander's sleeping quarters; and several philosophers and literary men accompanied the expedition. Aristotle himself retired to Athens, but sent with Alexander in his stead his nephew Callisthenes of Olynthus, philosopher and historian; there were also Anaxarchus a Democritean, and his pupil Pyrrhon, who founded the Sceptic school, and the historians Aristobulus and Onesicritus a Cynic. With them were geographers, botanists, and other scientific men, who among other things collected information

---

[1] To avoid repetition, the term 'Companions' throughout this chapter and the next means the Companion cavalry unless otherwise stated.

and specimens for Aristotle; but many of these, with poets and artistes, came out later. More important, however, than the professed literary men was Ptolemy son of Lagos, for to the use by later writers of his history, based on the *Journal* and other official material, we owe the best of our knowledge of Alexander's career.

Putting aside independent tribes and dynasts, and temple states, Asia Minor, as Alexander found it, was divided between two different land-systems: the Greek cities of the coast and the Iranian and native baronies of the central plateau. Each Greek city ruled its own 'city-land,' which was often cultivated by the native pre-Persian inhabitants, living in villages; sometimes these were serfs, bought and sold with the land, as the Phrygians at Zelea; sometimes hereditary occupiers paying taxes to the city, as the Pedieis at Priene; sometimes their villages had even a kind of corporate organization, as the Thracians at Cyzicus. Outside the city-lands the whole soil was King's land, often granted out to great landowners, who lived each in his stronghold, ruling his domain, which was cultivated by the native inhabitants of the villages, always apparently serfs. As regards the natives, therefore, the Greek system was somewhat more liberal, a matter of importance when we come to the city-foundations of Alexander and his successors. But for the moment, to Alexander, the King's land with its land-tax was the important matter, for he was bankrupt. He had only 70 talents in his treasury, and his subscription toward the new temple at Delphi was only 2100 drachmae; he owed 1300 talents, while the army's pay required 200 talents a month, with another 100 for the Graeco-Macedonian fleet of the League. The story that, before starting, he gave away all the royal domains in Macedonia to his friends, retaining only his hopes, is untrue, for King's land does not vanish from Macedonian history; but he did bestow some estates, the gift to Ptolemaeus the Bodyguard being known.

The Persian army was conditioned by the Persian land-system, which obtained not only in Asia Minor but in northern Syria and Armenia, and probably throughout all Iran. The Persians had abandoned their native system of warfare, which had consisted in disordering the enemy by archery fire and then charging him with cavalry; and the Persian archers had become a subordinate arm. The empire had plenty of good cavalry, for each landowner maintained a cavalry troop of retainers; but infantry meant either half-armed serfs, with no interest in fighting, or hill tribesmen, brave but undisciplined. Some attempt had been made to form a professional heavy infantry, called Cardaces; but the empire had really come to depend for infantry on Greek mercenaries. The course of Alexander's battles, and the large number of mercenaries still available for him to recruit, show that Darius most certainly had not the 50,000 Greeks of tradition; but Memnon probably had at least 20,000, a large force, though many would be peltasts.

III. GRANICUS AND ASIA MINOR

While Parmenion brought the army across the Dardanelles[1], Alexander, in imitation of Achilles, landed at Ilium, sacrificed in the old temple of Athena, and brought away the sacred shield which was to save his life. He declared Ilium free, restored democracy, and abolished the tribute paid to Persia; then he rejoined his army, and marched up the coast past Lampsacus, to meet the force which the coastal satraps, Arsites of Hellespontine Phrygia and Spithridates of Lydia, with Mithrobarzanes of Cappadocia and Atizyes of Phrygia, had hastily collected to oppose him. Tradition gives them 20,000 cavalry and 20,000 Greek mercenaries; but Alexander's small losses at the Granicus show that there were certainly not 20,000 well-trained Greeks there. The greater part of Memnon's 20,000 Greeks had in fact been assigned to the fleet, while strong bodies garrisoned Miletus and Halicarnassus. The satraps and the barons with them had their own cavalry, strength unknown, a small body of Greeks still with Memnon, who had joined them, and some native infantry. Memnon proposed to retire before Alexander, waste the country, and wait for Darius; that he also advised carrying the war into Greece is unlikely, for he did not do this when later he had the power; it represents what the Greek mercenary commanders hoped. Arsites however refused to allow his satrapy to be laid waste. The Persian leaders had in fact a very gallant plan; they meant if possible to strangle the war at birth by killing Alexander. They massed their cavalry on the steep bank of the lower Granicus, put the Greeks behind them, and waited. It has often been explained since that this was not the way to hold a river-bank; but that was not their intention.

Alexander's army was in what became his regular battle-order; on the left, Parmenion with the Thessalian, Greek, and Thracian horse; then the phalanx, then the hypaspists; on the right, himself with the Companions, lancers, Paeonians, Agrianians, and Cretans. Parmenion advised caution; but Alexander saw the disparity of strength, and rejected the advice. The ensuing battle

[1] See map to illustrate the march of Alexander, facing p. 357.

was fought mainly by his right wing. He ordered some cavalry across, and then charged through the river himself, conspicuous by the white wings on his helmet. The Persian leaders concentrated on him and threw away their lives freely in a desperate attempt to kill him; at one moment they almost succeeded, and Cleitus' promptitude alone saved Alexander from Spithridates' scimitar. Finally the Persians broke; their men, armed only with javelins, were unequally matched with Alexander's heavy cavalry, who (except the lancers) used short spears. The rest of the army had crossed, and Alexander surrounded the Greeks and killed all but 2000, whom he sent in chains to forced labour in Macedonia as traitors to the League; among them were some Athenians. Eight Persian notables of high rank were killed; Memnon escaped. Alexander lost 25 Companions and 90 other arms; and he emphasized the fact that he was general of the League by sending 300 Persian panoplies to Athens, with a dedication from 'Alexander and the Greeks, except the Spartans.' He left Calas as satrap of Hellespontine Phrygia, with a force of Greek allies, to secure the Dardanelles crossing; gave the vacant command of the Thessalians to Alexander the Lyncestian; and turned southward towards Ionia.

The Persians ruled the Greek towns by means of tyrants or friendly oligarchies, with occasional garrisons—precisely the method which Antipater, in Alexander's interest, was using in Greece. Alexander in Asia adopted the opposite method, the support of free democratic government. Partly this was due to circumstances: Persia's foes were his friends. But it must also have been due to conviction, for he never altered his policy when he could have done so. Consequently we get here, for the first time, the opposition between the two ways of treating Greek cities, the way of Antipater and the way of Alexander, which was to divide the Macedonian world till 301. Alexander now gave out that he had come to restore democracy; and in city after city the democrats overthrew the pro-Persian government. He himself occupied Ephesus; Priene admitted Antigonus; troops were detached to secure the Aeolian towns; Sardes was surrendered by the governor Mithrines. Alexander made Asander satrap of Lydia, and garrisoned Sardes; but he restored to the Lydians the right to be judged by their own native laws. At Miletus however the garrison closed the gates and stood a siege. The Persian fleet, said to be 400 strong, at last appeared off the city; but the fleet of the League, 160 ships, anticipated it by three days and blocked the harbour. The Persians offered battle; Parmenion advised

Alexander to fight, and offered to lead the fleet himself. But Alexander would not risk the moral consequences of defeat; he said he would not throw away his men's lives, but would conquer the Persian fleet on land. Miletus he took by assault; 300 mercenaries escaped to an island, and he gave them terms and took them into his service. He already saw that the purely Panhellenic policy of Granicus would not do. The Persian fleet retired to Halicarnassus, and Alexander dismissed his own, except the Athenian contingent; it served no purpose, and he had no money.

At first sight it looks as if, with the Persian fleet commanding the Aegean, Alexander was engaged in a mere gamble; Memnon, who was soon after appointed commander-in-chief of the fleet and the coast, might cut his communications at the Dardanelles, or raise Greece. But in fact Alexander, in this critical decision, showed fine judgment. His communications were not seriously endangered; galleys, with limited cruising powers and helpless at night, hardly ever prevented troops crossing the sea. To raise Greece was, he judged, impossible. Memnon might raise Sparta; but Sparta was as unpopular as Macedonia, and could be dealt with by Antipater. To raise Greece meant first winning Athens, the only city which might form a large combination; and Alexander judged the situation at Athens correctly (p. 443 *sq.*). Moreover, he held as hostages 20 Athenian ships and his Athenian prisoners, while in the allied troops he virtually had hostages for every state in the League. But there was more than this. In deciding to conquer the Persian fleet on land, he did not merely mean depriving it of bases; it might seize a base, as it did at Mitylene. But his proclamation of democracy had shaken the Greek half of the fleet to its foundations; for each city's squadron was manned from the poorer democrats, and would slip away home when its city was freed. And, thanks to Ochus, the Cyprians and all the Phoenicians except Tyre were disaffected (p. 22). Memnon's hands were tied; possibly the Tyrian was the only really loyal contingent he had. Alexander judged that if he secured the coast cities the fleet would die of dry rot; and it did.

He next entered Caria, where he was welcomed by Ada, Idrieus' widow and Mausolus' sister. She had been dispossessed of her authority by her brother Pixodarus; she adopted Alexander as her son and put her fortress of Alinda into his hands. But Alexander was held up by Halicarnassus, where Memnon himself commanded the garrison; with him were Orontopates, satrap of Caria, Pixodarus' successor, and some Macedonian exiles. Alexander had to bring up his siege-train and attack Halicarnassus in form. The besieged fought well; in various sallies they burnt part of the siege-train, and killed Ptolemaeus the Bodyguard and other officers; and when the town finally became untenable, they fired their magazines and escaped, Memnon to the fleet, Orontopates to the fortress of Salmacis. Alexander restored Ada to her satrapy and left Ptolemaeus son of Philippus, a squadron-leader of the Companions, with 3200 mercenaries to reduce Caria, where Orontopates still held several places. The Carian satrap, possibly with help from Agis of Sparta, made a good fight; he was defeated shortly before Issus by Ptolemaeus and Asander, but the reduction of Caria was not completed till 332.

Winter had now begun. Alexander sent home the newly married men of the army on furlough, a most popular measure; detached Parmenion with the heavy cavalry, the allies, and the siege and baggage trains, to await him in Phrygia; and himself with the rest of the army undertook a winter campaign in the mountains of Lycia and Pisidia. It became his usual practice to attack hill tribes in winter, when the snow confined them to the valleys and made them manageable. He first entered the Milyad, received the surrender of the Lycian towns, and was welcomed by Phaselis in Pamphylia. There he heard that Darius had offered Alexander of Lyncestis the crown of Macedonia and 1000 gold talents to kill him; whether the report was true or not, the Lyncestian could not be left in command of the Thessalians. Craterus' brother Amphoterus made his way to Parmenion through the hill tribes with a native guide, and the Lyncestian was arrested and imprisoned.

Alexander made Nearchus satrap of Lycia and Pamphylia, garrisoned Phaselis to protect it from the Persian fleet, sent part of his force to Perge by the famous Climax or Ladder—rock-steps cut in the hill—and went with the rest by the direct way along the coast. Here the cliffs of Mount Climax came down to the sea; with a north wind it was feasible to go by the beach, but with a south wind the sea made this impossible. The wind, which had been south, shifted at the right moment, and he had a swift and easy passage, though the men had to wade; the shifting of the wind was regarded as a sign of divine favour, like Cyrus' passage of the Euphrates (p. 6). He received the adhesion of Perge, Aspendus, and Side, and then entered the mountains of Pisidia, making for Termessus, the fortress which commanded the passes from Phaselis into the Milyad. To attack it without siege-engines was however, he saw, impossible. He fought his way north through the tribes, and took and razed Sagalassus and some forts; but he did not reduce Pisidia, though he nominally added the western half to Nearchus' satrapy; eastern Pisidia he never saw. Leaving the hills, he marched by Lake Buldur to Celaenae. Its Carian garrison agreed to surrender, if not relieved by a certain day; he left Antigonus as satrap of Phrygia with 1500 mercenaries to watch Celaenae, which surrendered, and in spring rejoined Parmenion at Gordium. Here was shown the chariot of Gordias, founder of the old Phrygian monarchy, with the yoke lashed to the pole by cornel-bark in an involved knot; local legend said that the man who untied the knot would rule Asia. The story that Alexander cut the knot with his sword is famous; but it is poorly attested, and hardly even expresses Alexander's character. The men on furlough now rejoined, bringing 3000 Macedonians and 650 horse as reinforcements; and ambassadors came from Athens to request the return of the prisoners. Alexander would not part with his hostages while the Persian fleet was in being; he told the Athenians to ask him again when things were more settled.

They were by no means settled as yet, for Memnon with the fleet was showing considerable activity; he had partisans in every city, and a fair force of Greek mercenaries. The oligarchs had put Chios into his hands, and he was besieging Mitylene. Some believed that he would cross to Greece; but this is improbable, for he was doubtless well-informed as to the policy of Athens. Probably his aim was to recover what cities he could and perhaps capture the bridge-head at Abydos, thus compelling Alexander to detach troops which he could not spare. Then Memnon died. Whether this meant much to Alexander cannot be said, for Memnon's capacity has to be taken on trust, and his nephew, Artabazus' son Pharnabazus, who succeeded him, knew his plans. Mitylene surrendered, on terms that she was to become Darius' ally according to the Peace of Antalcidas; Pharnabazus garrisoned the city, set up a tyrant, and levied a war contribution. He also recovered Tenedos and the rest of Lesbos, and set up a tyrant in Methymna. Alexander was forced to take measures to counter him, and sent Amphoterus and Hegelochus to the Dardanelles to collect ships from the allied cities and re-form the fleet. The decision however came from Darius, who was at last collecting an army; he confirmed Pharnabazus' command, but also sent Mentor's son Thymondas to bring him the mercenaries from the fleet. Thymondas shipped them to Tripolis in Phoenicia, and they joined Darius, leaving Pharnabazus crippled; he had only 1500 men left, and his fleet began to break up.

From Gordium Alexander proceeded to Ancyra (Angora), and there received envoys from Paphlagonia, now independent; they asked him not to invade their country, and offered formal submission. Alexander, whose aim was to meet Darius, had no intention of invading Paphlagonia; he added the country nominally to Calas' satrapy, and turned south. Ariarathes, the independent Persian dynast of northern Cappadocia, was not disturbed, and though Alexander marched through southern Cappadocia he made no attempt to conquer it; he left as 'satrap' one Sabiktas, possibly a local baron commissioned to do what he could, and pushed on towards the Cilician Gates. Properly held, the pass was impregnable. But Alexander hurried on in advance with the hypaspists, Agrianians, and archers, and reached it long before he was expected; the defenders had a panic, and he captured the Gates without the loss of a man. Through the Gates he descended into Cilicia, and hearing that the Persians meant to destroy Tarsus he galloped straight there with the cavalry and reached it in time. Here his exertions, or a bath in the Cydnus when heated, brought on a severe fever. His friend and physician, Philippus of Acarnania, was about to administer a draught when a letter arrived from Parmenion warning Alexander that Philippus had been bribed by Darius to poison him. Alexander, whose confidence in his friends was as yet unshakeable, handed Philippus the letter to read while he drank; Philippus read it and merely remarked to Alexander that he would recover provided he followed his advice.

IV. THE BATTLE OF ISSUS

Alexander, after his recovery, sent Parmenion forward to occupy the passes—Kara-kapu leading from Cilicia into the little plain of Issus, and the 'pillar of Jonah' leading out of that plain towards Syria; whether he also occupied the Syrian Gates beyond Myriandrus is uncertain. Alexander himself took over the Cilician cities, and campaigned for a week in the foot-hills of Taurus to secure his flank; then, hearing that Darius was at Sochi in Syria, beyond the Syrian Gates, he left his sick and wounded at Issus, joined Parmenion, crossed the Jonah pass, and entered Myriandrus. For some reason unknown his intelligence was at fault; he believed Darius to be still at Sochi.

Darius was not at Sochi. He had waited some time, and had concluded that Alexander, of whose illness he was ignorant, meant to halt in Cilicia; against the advice of the Macedonian exile Amyntas he decided to go and look for him. He sent his warchest and encumbrances to Damascus, crossed the Amanus by the

Amanic Gates while Alexander was crossing the Jonah pass, and came down on Issus, where he butchered Alexander's sick and wounded and learnt that Alexander had gone on to Myriandrus. He had come right across Alexander's communications, and could compel him to fight with his face toward his base. The Persian command at once saw that a drawn battle was to them as good as a victory. They took up a position on the river Pinarus (probably the Deli, the distance from hills to sea being less than to-day) with their back to the Amanic Gates, their right resting on the sea and their left on the hills, and waited.

Darius' army consisted of no more than his home and household troops (*i.e.* his guard and the Persian cavalry and archers), with the Greeks, Cardaces, and some light-armed. It did not number 600,000 men, and did not include 30,000 Greeks. When two Greek cities fought, each knew the other's approximate strength; but to the Macedonians a Persian army was guesswork, and both camp gossip and literary men made flattering guesses, such as seemed appropriate to the territorial extent of the Persian empire. Alexander's Staff doubtless got true figures later from the surrendered satraps, but the silence of Ptolemy, *i.e.* of the *Journal*, shows that they never gave them out; the moral effect on the army of the belief that it had broken a vast host was too good to forego. Persian numbers and losses are throughout unknown; but the right way to regard Darius' armies is to remember that the greatest force raised by Antigonus when king of Asia west of Euphrates was 88,000 men, partly Europeans, and that in 302–301, when every state was making a supreme effort, Macedonia, Greece, Thrace, Egypt, and Asia west of India, with mercenaries, pirates, and Illyrians, had some 230,000–240,000 men under arms, of whom probably half were Europeans. Darius' army at Issus was somewhat larger than Alexander's, but not too large to cross the Amanus in one night, and there were enough Greeks to handle one wing of the phalanx severely, but not to defeat the phalanx; as at least 10,000 Greeks got away, there may have been some 12,000 altogether. The Greeks under Amyntas and Thymondas were placed in the centre, with the Cardaces on either side; their front was palisaded where the banks were easy; they had only to hold the line, and Alexander's career was ended. The cavalry under Nabarzanes the chiliarch was massed on the right as a striking force. As Alexander was also expected to strike with his right, the archers were put on the left in front of the Cardaces, while on the extreme left the light-armed were thrown well forward along the foothills, to attack Alexander's flank and rear and prevent him charging. Darius and his guard were behind the centre. It was a good enough plan, had the infantry been all Greeks; but the Persian command had to use what it had got.

Alexander could not believe that Darius was behind him till he had sent a ship to report; then he hastened to secure the Jonah pass, camped, and next morning advanced towards the enemy (Oct. 333), deploying from column into line as the plain opened out. His army was smaller than that which had fought at Granicus. Many of the allies had been left with Calas, and 4700 mercenaries in Caria and Phrygia; allowing for the known reinforcements, and for losses and garrisons, he may have had from 20,000 to 24,000 infantry in action; but he probably had 5000 horse. Out of bow-shot he halted to rest the men. His line was in its usual formation; but on the right the lancers were next the hypaspists, with himself and the Companions before the lancers, a deep column of horse. The mercenaries and allies were behind the phalanx. Behind the lancers, to meet the threat of the advanced Persian left, was a flanking force, including the Agrianians; these began the battle by driving the Persian light-armed up the hill and out of action. With this danger removed, Alexander set his line in motion, and once within bow-shot he himself charged. The archers and Cardaces crumpled up before him; Darius turned his chariot at the sight and fled. But his guard stood, and gave Alexander a battle, and meanwhile the phalanx was in trouble; in crossing the river it had lost its cohesion, and the Greeks had thrown themselves at the gap. It was a battle of the two peoples. Part of the phalanx suffered heavily, and one battalion lost its commander; but the hypaspists swung round on to the exposed left flank of the Greeks and compelled them to retire. On Alexander's left Nabarzanes had charged across the river and driven back Parmenion's cavalry, but not decisively enough to take the phalanx in flank; and on the news of Darius' flight he too retired, and the retreat became general. Alexander is said to have lost 450 killed, and was himself wounded. The Persian loss was doubtless out of proportion, as that of the vanquished usually was; but they had a fair line of retreat, and as the battle was fought late in the afternoon, darkness must have soon checked the pursuit; they only lost five notables, while part of the army escaped into Cappadocia, brought it over to Darius, and possibly even attacked Antigonus. Two thousand Greeks rejoined Darius later. The main body, 8000 men under Amyntas, got away in good order; but they had seen enough of Darius. They marched back to Tripolis and sailed to Egypt; there Amyntas was killed trying to conquer the country, and his army subsequently took service with Sparta, to fight again at Megalopolis under a better king (p. 445).

Balacrus the Bodyguard was now made satrap of Cilicia; Menes succeeded him on the Staff, and Polyperchon, the future regent, got the vacant battalion of the phalanx. Darius' chariot and bow were captured, and his splendidly appointed tent gave the Macedonians their first glimpse of oriental luxury. 'This, I believe, is being a king,' said Alexander, as he sat down to Darius' table; and it was not entirely sarcastic. As he dined, he heard the wailing of women, and learned that it was Darius' mother, wife, and two daughters, who had been captured and were weeping for his death. He sent Leonnatus to tell them that Darius was not dead, and that they were quite safe; they would have the same rank and treatment as heretofore. He himself never set eyes on Darius' wife, or allowed her beauty to be alluded to before him; but he showed kindness to Darius' mother, and ultimately married one of the daughters. Later writers never tired of embroidering the theme of Alexander's treatment of these ladies; their praise of what he did throws a dry light on what he was expected to do.

V. THE ADMINISTRATION OF ASIA MINOR

Alexander's arrangements in Asia Minor may here be considered. The conquest of that country was only half finished, and Alexander did not wait to complete it. Calas perhaps subdued the Mysians, but he had not the force to conquer Bithynia and Paphlagonia; whether he attempted Paphlagonia is uncertain, but later he invaded Bithynia, which was never conquered by anybody, and was killed. Southern Cappadocia again obeyed Darius; Ariarathes probably annexed it after Gaugamela. Lycaonia was nominally part of the Phrygian satrapy, but whether Antigonus conquered it till much later is uncertain. Pisidia was still independent; Balacrus of Cilicia tried later to conquer eastern Pisidia and met his death. Alexander at present only controlled the central plateau west of Cappadocia and the south and west coastlands, with the through route into Cilicia; the north was open for an Iranian reaction, which duly came.

The Persian satraps, as Alexander found them, combined all powers, military and civil, and could coin (see vol. IV, pp. 197 *sqq.*); and the Persian financial system had a military basis. In the eastern provinces Alexander was to attempt to separate the three powers, civil, military, and financial, but in Asia Minor he constituted no separate civil authorities; all the satrapies embraced unconquered territory, and his satraps were primarily Macedonian generals with troops. But he made the great innovation of depriving them of the control of finance, and setting up separate financial superintendents. Possibly the Persian military subdivisions of the satrapies, called 'chiliarchies,' were maintained and utilized as smaller fiscal districts, under subordinates responsible to the financial superintendent for the satrapy. Whether the limits of his financial provinces coincided with the satrapies is unknown; at any rate there was in Asia Minor a double authority in each satrapy. The coinage Alexander kept in his own hands; the business of the financial superintendents was to collect and manage the taxes, which involved the management of the King's land; and as everything outside the city and temple territories was King's land, they obviously exercised much of the civil power. The financial basis of the Persian empire was that the peasants and serfs on the King's land—the 'King's people'—paid their taxes (in theory) to the King, in cash or in kind. Probably however the great landowners actually collected the taxes from their domains and paid the satraps a fixed amount, and the satraps deducted their costs of administration and remitted the balance to the King; there were thus endless opportunities for oppression and leakage. Alexander altered all this; his financial superintendents had to collect the taxes direct from the peasants and remit them to the Treasury, and also see to the assessment, which was retained unaltered on the ancient customary basis. The superintendents presently introduced the Greek system of granting cultivation leases. Probably however the only King's land as yet directly managed by Alexander's officials was that in the coast provinces of the west and south; the great landowners of the plateau for the present remained undisturbed, Alexander merely claiming their domains and taxes as overlord. Philoxenus was appointed over the taxes for the whole of Asia Minor north of Taurus; probably he was the superior of, and co-ordinated, all the provincial superintendents.

The Greek cities had also paid taxes (tribute) to the king. The Persian rule, though apparently not severe, was naturally unpopular; and Alexander's proclamation of democracy at once brought over to his side every city where the tyrant or garrison was not strong enough to prevent it. At Zelea the citizens captured the citadel and expelled the tyrant, thus earning Alexander's pardon for having, before Granicus, aided the Persians under duress; Lampsacus was similarly pardoned, it is said on the appeal of the historian Anaximenes; Erythrae came to an agree-

ment with its garrison, and raised money to send away the mercenaries and destroy the citadel-fort; many simply opened their
gates. In every city in which he or the people restored democratic
government he abolished the hated tribute. The liberated cities
became his free and independent allies; at Mitylene and Tenedos,
for instance, the treaty of alliance was engraved and set up;
Miletus made Alexander its eponymous magistrate for 334–3;
Ilium perhaps named a tribe after him. As allies, they probably
became members of the League of Corinth. There is nothing to
show that Alexander restored the Ionian League or formed the
Ilian; these sectional Leagues belong to the rule and the policy of
Antigonus. The effect of this liberation can be seen in the series
of treaties with other cities at once made by Miletus with a view
to restoring her commercial prosperity; and the cities continued
to coin on any standard they pleased.

But the restoration of democracy and recall of the exiled democrats did not quite end matters. Aristotle had said that a king
must hold the balance even between parties; and Alexander wanted
the support, not of a faction, but of united cities. When therefore
the restored democrats inevitably began to murder their opponents,
he at once interfered; he did not intend to permit reprisals.
At Ephesus he not only stopped the slaughter as soon as the
tyrant and his son had been killed, but punished the democrats by
refusing to abolish the tribute; he ordered however that it should
be paid, not to himself, but into the treasury of Artemis, whose
temple was being rebuilt, *i.e.*, the punishment was to make the
Ephesians pay for their own temple. He had been born on the
night that the old temple was burnt, and he greatly desired to have
his name on the new one as founder, but the Ephesians refused,
though he offered to bear all expenses of rebuilding; he did however enlarge the area of the temple's right of asylum. His action
at Chios, which had been betrayed to Memnon, was similar; after
the people had a second time overthrown the Persian sympathizers,
and Alexander had decreed the restoration of the exiles and democratic government, he ordered that a commission should revise
the laws and submit the revision to himself, and he garrisoned the
city until the Chians 'should be reconciled together'; presently he
ordered that the imprisoned pro-Persians should be released on
payment of a fine, and that no one in future should be accused on
the ground of Persian sympathies. The two exceptions he made
were of tyrants and traitors. Thus he ordered that those who had
actually betrayed Chios to Memnon, and had escaped, should be
outlawed from every city of the alliance and, if taken, should be

tried by the council of the League; while all the tyrants he took were handed over for judgment to their respective cities.

One other preliminary matter Alexander hastened to settle was the boundary between city land and King's land, in places where (like Priene) this was disputed; here he drew the bounds by his own fiat. It was vital to him, for till after Issus he was in financial straits, and the taxes from the King's land were his only source of revenue. But once the preliminary settlement of the disturbed affairs of the cities was over—and this was a war measure—he neither claimed nor exercised any further authority, beyond what the League gave him, and sent no more orders or rescripts, save the formal documents which accompanied the tyrants handed over for judgment; and the cities were of course not under his satraps. The limits he imposed upon himself are shown by his refusal to interfere with the working of the severe city-law of Eresus against the descendants of tyrants, and by his arbitration of the old boundary dispute between Samos and Priene without employing his powers; while the temporary garrison at Chios (and doubtless those elsewhere) was called, as it was, a 'defence force,' to avoid objectionable implications. Possibly after 330 the cities gave him, as was courteous, his royal title, as Delphi did in 329; but this has no bearing on their position. In fact, his Greek allies had a greater measure of freedom than those of fifth-century Athens, though later he was naturally confronted with the same problem as she had been:—How were you to exercise authority, when necessary, over free but weak allies? Meanwhile, as allies, the cities took part in the war. They did not apparently furnish troops, but Chios, and doubtless all the maritime cities, supplied ships; while for the tribute was substituted a 'contribution' of smaller amount, which officially counted as voluntary. These matters probably did not exceed the competence of the Commander-in-Chief of the League. In one case at least, Priene, even the contribution was remitted; if this was done because Priene allowed him to put his name as dedicator on her new temple of Athena Polias, possibly he paid it himself. The contribution, being an extraordinary and temporary war-measure, was doubtless paid into the war-chest direct and not through the financial superintendents, who had nothing to do with the cities.

All the Greek cities of Asia Minor, however, did not become his allies. He took no notice of the cities on the northern coast, which he never visited, it being useless to the Persian fleet; Cyzicus was the farthest ally in this direction. So Cius remained subject to the Persian dynast Mithridates, and Heraclea to its diplomatic tyrant Dionysius; with Chalcedon and Sinope he had no relations; the story that he restored democracy at Amisus is impossible, though there may have been a revolution in his name. In the south he was confronted with cities which (except Phaselis) were not of pure Greek character and speech, and coined on the Persian standard; and no clear rule appears. Phaselis and Selge became allies, but Side was garrisoned. Aspendus, which made an agreement with him and broke it, he punished like a subject town; it was fined 100 talents, placed under the satrap of Lycia, and ordered to pay tribute. At Mallus, where the democrats rose in his favour, he remitted the tribute, *i.e.* treated it as a Greek town; but Soli, which had aided Darius, he fined and garrisoned, though afterwards he remitted the fine and restored democracy, *i.e.* apparently full Greek rights. The native towns of Asia Minor were of course subject to satraps or fortress-governors; even at Sardes the people had no definite constitution, though they could act as a body for the purpose of commercial arrangements with other towns.

VI. TYRE AND EGYPT

It was probably after Issus that Alexander first thought definitely of conquering the Persian empire. The alternative was to follow Isocrates' advice and hold Asia Minor; this meant a defensive war, for Persia was bound to try and recover the sea-provinces. With Phoenicia and Egypt known to be disaffected, Alexander inevitably decided for the offensive, as his temperament dictated. He did not follow Darius; his immediate objective was Phoenicia and the ruin of the Persian fleet. He refounded Myriandrus, terminus of an important trade-route, as an Alexandria (to-day Alexandretta), and advanced to Marathus, which with Aradus was peaceably put into his hands; thence he detached Parmenion and the Thessalians to take Damascus. It was occupied without fighting and much booty secured, including Darius' baggage and war-chest; Alexander's financial troubles were now over. Parmenion also captured the families of many prominent Persians, and some Greek envoys to Darius; Alexander released the Thebans and the Athenian, but imprisoned the Spartan, as Sparta was threatening war. At Marathus he received a letter from Darius, asking him as king to king to release his family, and offering friendship and alliance. In reply Alexander sent the political manifesto already referred to (p. 357). It began by emphasizing the wrong done to Macedonia and the rest of Hellas by

Xerxes' invasion; it was to avenge this that Alexander, as Commander-in-Chief of the League, had crossed the Dardanelles, but not till after Ochus had begun war against Macedonia by invading Thrace and aiding Perinthus. Moreover, Persia had procured Philip's assassination, and was attempting to raise Greece and destroy the League's peace, and was subsidizing Sparta; while Darius, having assassinated Arses, was not even the lawful king. In conclusion, it claimed that Alexander was already king of Asia; if Darius wanted anything he must write as a subject to his lord. This claim was only put in to induce Darius to fight; but it shows what was in Alexander's mind. He did not really claim to be king of Asia till after Darius' death, or at least not before Gaugamela; otherwise he must have treated the satraps in arms as rebels, which he did not yet do. Besides, he knew that he had not yet met the levy of the empire.

Leaving Marathus, he received the surrender of Byblus and a hearty welcome from Sidon. Envoys from Tyre met him and offered a general form of submission; as a test, he asked leave to enter the island city and sacrifice to his ancestor Heracles (Melkart). The Tyrians were really loyal; they were not yet satisfied that Alexander would ultimately be victorious, and they were satisfied that Tyre was impregnable, as after its thirteen years' siege by Nebuchadrezzar they had a right to think (vol. III, p. 214). They replied that they were not receiving any strangers in the city, either Persians or Macedonians, but that there was a famous shrine of Melkart at Old Tyre on the mainland which would satisfy the requirements of his piety. Alexander at once prepared for a siege; he is said to have told his men that the fall of Tyre would mean the final dissolution of the Persian fleet, a prophecy which was fulfilled before Tyre fell. The city stood on an island half a mile from the coast, and Alexander set about building a mole to it from the mainland. Progress at first was easy; it was when the deep water near the island was reached and the workers came within shot of the walls that trouble began, while winter gales and the Tyrian warships alike hindered the work. Alexander got two siege-towers out to the end of the mole, their sides protected against blazing arrows by coverings of skins; but the besieged prepared a fire-ship, fitting long yards to the masts with baskets of inflammable matter depending from the ends. They weighted down the stern to raise the bows above the mole, grounded her successfully, and set her on fire; the crew swam away, and the yards burnt through and discharged their cargoes on to the towers, which also took fire. The arrows from the Tyrian warships prevented any rescue, and the besieged, swarming out in boats, tore down the mole. Alexander began to build it again much broader, to avoid a similar mishap; but he saw that without a fleet he must fail, and went personally to Sidon to collect ships.

His success at Sidon surpassed his hopes. The news from Phoenicia had finally disintegrated the Persian fleet, and Pharnabazus was stranded in the islands. Alexander was joined at Sidon by all the Phoenician squadrons except the Tyrian, and some ships from Rhodes, Lycia, and Cilicia; soon after came the Cyprians, led by Pnytagoras of Salamis; in all he collected 220 warships, from quinqueremes to small vessels. Azemilk, the king of Tyre, brought his own squadron successfully into his city; but Alexander was far stronger now than Tyre at sea. He collected engineers to help build new machines, shipped part of the hypaspists on his fleet, took command of the Phoenician wing himself (the prerogative of the Great King), sailed to Tyre, and offered battle; but his force was too great, and the Tyrians refused to come out. He stationed Pnytagoras north of the mole to blockade the northern harbour, and the Phoenicians south of it, where his headquarters were, to blockade the southern. As soon as his new machines were ready—towers, rams, and catapults—he placed some on the mole, some on Sidonian transports or warships lashed together in pairs, and attacked the wall.

The Tyrians however were ready for him. They had raised towers on the walls, whose fire worried the ships, and had made near approach to the island impossible by dropping rocks into the sea. Alexander brought up merchant ships to sweep for the obstacles; the Tyrian warships attacked them and cut their anchor-cables. He covered the sweepers with warships; Tyrian divers cut the cables under water. Then he anchored the sweepers by chains; the Tyrians had no reply, and he got the rocks out. As a last resource, the Tyrians manned 13 warships, attacked the Cyprian fleet when the crews had landed for dinner, and destroyed Pnytagoras' flagship and other vessels; but Alexander, who was watching, manned some Phoenician ships, rowed round Tyre, and cut off two of the returning squadron. The way was now open for a great combined assault. Part of the wall fell, and Alexander brought up the two transports which carried the storming party and bridges; on one was Coenus' battalion of the phalanx, on the other himself with a battalion of the hypaspists; their operations were covered by fire from the fleet. Both ships got their bridges placed successfully, and Alexander and Coenus captured their sections of the wall, while the Phoenicians and Cyprians forced the two harbours. Then the Tyrians broke; the Macedonians, embittered by the Tyrians having murdered their comrades taken prisoners, could not be held in; and the rest was massacre. Eight thousand fighting men were killed, and, as at Thebes, many men, women and children sold as slaves. Some were saved by the other Phoenicians, and a few found asylum in the temple of Melkart, among them some Carthaginian religious envoys, whose presence started a legend that Carthage had been preparing to help her mother-city. This horrible business of selling captives was the strict legal right of the victor, which Alexander exercised twice again, at Gaza, and at Cyropolis (where his men had been murdered); but it is to his credit that his expedition apparently produced hardly any effect on the world's slave-markets[1]. Tyre fell in July 332, after holding out for seven months. Its capture was possibly Alexander's greatest feat of arms; and he offered his sacrifice to Melkart after all, surely the most costly that that deity had ever received. Tyre became a Macedonian fortress, and Sidon again took the lead in Phoenicia, which dated a new era from Issus.

Before Tyre fell, Alexander received Darius' reply. Darius now offered 10,000 talents ransom for his family, and as the price of peace the hand of his daughter and the cession of everything west of Euphrates, *i.e.* nearly all the country which ultimately became hellenized. The story went that Alexander put the offer before his generals, and Parmenion said that were he Alexander he would accept; Alexander replied that he too would accept were he Parmenion. The story may indicate the first rift between Alexander and the old Macedonian party, who desired only what of Asia could be governed from Europe; but it is more probably untrue. Alexander's reply to Darius was a refusal to negotiate. Darius in fact offered hardly anything which he had not already, except Egypt; and Egypt could not be saved in any case. Once Tyre had fallen, Alexander did not wait to settle Syria; he left Parmenion to supervise the country from Damascus, and advanced towards Egypt by the immemorial route through Palestine; Egypt, once it was his, would be an impregnable bastion which he could hold from the sea. Nothing delayed his march till he reached Gaza, which resisted desperately, and cost him a severe wound before he could take it. The story that he visited Jerusalem and sacrificed in the Temple belongs to legend.

He reached Egypt late in November 332. The Persian satrap hastened to submit, for the temper of the people was

---

[1] G. Glotz, *Ancient Greece at work*, p. 350.

unmistakable: they saw in Alexander their avenger. He went upstream to Memphis, very wisely sacrificed to Apis, was accepted
as Pharaoh, and returned to the coast. There, on the shore near
the village of Rhacotis, he traced out the lines of what was to be
one of the greatest cities of all time, Alexandria; it was subsequently laid out by Deinocrates, the man who proposed to carve
Mount Athos into an heroic bust of Alexander. Alexander's immediate object was to create a great trade emporium to replace
Tyre in the Mediterranean; but, looking at the position chosen,
he may already have given some thought to a sea which was not
the Mediterranean. There now came to him his commanders from
the Aegean, Amphoterus and Hegelochus, who had settled the
last Persian resistance in the islands; Pharnabazus had escaped,
but they had recovered Lesbos, Tenedos, Chios, and Cos, garrisoned Rhodes, and captured and brought with them the tyrants
Pharnabazus had set up and those Chian oligarchs who had betrayed their city to Memnon. Alexander imprisoned the Chians
at Elephantine; the tyrants he sent back that their respective cities
might deal with them. Amphoterus was ordered to secure Crete
against Agis, and to take in hand the pirates who had aided Pharnabazus; but this was never done, for the war with Sparta diverted
Amphoterus' fleet to Greece.

Alexander himself with a few followers, perhaps including
Callisthenes, now made his famous expedition to the oracle of
Ammon (oasis of Siwah). Ammon had for centuries ranked, with
Delphi and Dodona, as one of the three great oracles of the Greek
world; Pindar had written a hymn for him, and the Athenians had
recently built him a temple (p. 442), and in connection with this
had perhaps already renamed the sacred trireme Salaminia Am-
monias[1]; and Alexander consulted Ammon as naturally as he had
consulted Apollo of Delphi, the two visits being coupled in the
tradition. Cambyses' attempted expedition to Siwah also weighed
with him; for he had begun to beat the bounds of his future empire
in proper Oriental fashion, and henceforth he does everything
which any Persian king had done. He certainly did not go to
Ammon to be recognized as a god for the Greek world; to suppose
that he was yet thinking of divinity is an anachronism, to suppose
that he arranged a comedy beforehand with the priests an absurdity. He did not however take either of the regular routes,
from Cyrene or Memphis; and this fact enabled his journey to be

---

[1] Usually connected with Alexander's deification in 324. But Athens
deified him unwillingly.

worked up into an adventure. He went along the coast to Parae-
tonium, where he received and accepted Cyrene's offer of alliance,
and thence struck across the desert. The guide lost his way, and in
the tradition the party made the last stage guided either by two
snakes[1] or by the birds returning to the oasis, as Columbus met
American birds before sighting land. Alexander entered the
shrine alone, and refused to divulge what the oracle told him,
except that he was pleased; later he disclosed that Ammon had
told him to what gods to sacrifice when in trouble, as Apollo told
Xenophon. It is certain however that the priest greeted the new
Pharaoh as son of Ammon; he could do no other, for every Pharaoh
was officially son of Amon-Rē'. It was also part of the regular
Amon-ritual that the priest in Pharaoh's name asked of the god
rule over all living, and the god granted this; from this ritual arose
the story that Ammon had given Alexander (as he gave many
other Pharaohs) 'the' dominion over the whole world. Whether
Alexander actually went through the ritual is unknown; but in any
case it was of no importance outside Egypt. He returned to Memphis by the usual route, and for years nothing more was heard of
the matter (see pp. 398, 419, 423).

At Memphis he arranged the government of Egypt on enlightened lines. He retained the native officials, and instead of a
satrap appointed two native governors for Upper and Lower
Egypt. His financial superintendent, Cleomenes of Naucratis,
was not to collect the taxes direct from the peasantry, but through
the smaller native officials, as was customary; doubtless the native
governors were to protect both officials and peasantry against
extortion, with an appeal to Alexander. One of the governors
however declined to act, and Cleomenes subsequently became the
real power in the country; conceivably Alexander enlarged his
authority. A small army of occupation was left, but under three
commanders; Alexander was impressed with the natural strength
of Egypt and the ease with which a strong general might revolt,
and the same idea occurred to his friend Ptolemy. He also
appointed a commander and other officials for 'the mercenaries.'
As he cannot have settled mercenaries there himself, with Gaugamela still to fight, these must represent Darius' garrison, who
had sometimes received allotments of land; probably the fourth-
century Pharaohs had made similar settlements. The story that
Alexander sent an expedition to the Upper Nile to discover the

[1] As this story is Ptolemy's, they conceivably represented the Alexandrian
serpents Thermouthis and Psois; for Psois—fortune deified—became identified with Ptolemy's new god Sarapis, who thus aided Alexander

cause of the annual flood is probably unfounded, for the cause was already known to Aristotle. In the spring of 331 he returned to Tyre, and settled Syria, appointing a Macedonian satrap with a financial superintendent; he also received envoys from Athens, Chios, and Rhodes. As the Persian fleet no longer existed, he withdrew his garrisons from the two islands, and granted Athens the return of her prisoners; it was politic to conciliate her, with Sparta threatening war. Parmenion had been ordered to bridge the Euphrates at Thapsacus, where Mazaeus, the ex-satrap of Cilicia, was holding the farther bank with cavalry and the remaining 2000 Greeks, as the advance-guard of Darius' army.

VII. THE BATTLE OF GAUGAMELA

The Persian command had been making a serious effort to get together an army that might have some chance of defeating Alexander. It was a hopeless task to improvise in a year and a half a force fit to meet a professional army commanded by a genius; but they made a creditable attempt, though they could not take the most necessary step of all, the removal of Darius from command in the field. The levy of the empire was called up, and the best of the cavalry re-armed with spear and shield instead of javelins. Their difficulty was infantry. Greek mercenaries could no longer be obtained; the Cardaces had been a failure; they had learnt that Alexander would simply ride through archers. Their obvious course was to avoid a pitched battle, and try to wear Alexander down with their fine cavalry; but as the dignity of the Great King demanded a formal encounter, and they could not win that with cavalry alone, they had perforce to fall back on the only weapon left them against the phalanx, the long-neglected scythed chariots. Efficient drivers, drilled to act together, could not be trained quickly; still, when chariots did succeed, their success was terribly complete; doubtless some remembered how Pharnabazus by the aid of two chariots had once destroyed 700 Greek hoplites.

In July 331 Alexander joined Parmenion and crossed the Euphrates at Thapsacus, Mazaeus falling back before him as he advanced. He crossed the Tigris unopposed, turned southward, and moved towards the village of Gaugamela, 18 miles N.E. of Mosul, where, as he had learnt from prisoners, Darius had taken position. The Persians had selected a perfectly flat plain, levelling any obstacles before their line, in order to give the chariots every chance. Their order of battle was subsequently captured. Darius was in the centre, with the 1000 Persian cavalry of the guard, the Indian horse from the Paropamisus, and the Carian settlers. The left centre included the Cadusians and the rest of the Persians, horse and archers; the left wing was formed of the excellent eastern horse, Bactrian, Sogdian, and Arachosian, with 1000 mailed Sacaean horsemen, Darius' allies from the Jaxartes, thrown out before them. The right centre included the Medes under Atropates and the Parthian horse under Phrataphernes; the right wing was formed of the best of the western horse, Armenians, Syrians, and the Cappadocians, later so famous, under the dynast Ariarathes, Darius' ally. It was thus a mixed line of cavalry and infantry, with a powerful striking force of cavalry massed on each wing. The 2000 Greeks were behind the centre, and with them some infantry, Babylonians and hill-men, probably worthless, and fifteen elephants from Arachosia. Judiciously posted, the elephants might have prevented Alexander charging, as untrained horses will not face them; but probably they could not be put in line, the Persian horses also not being trained to them. In front of the line were drawn up the scythed chariots, on which so much depended; the course of the battle shows that there were nothing like the stereotyped 200 of tradition. It was a larger army than that of Issus, large enough to make Alexander certain that both his flanks, at least, must be turned. Bessus, satrap of Bactria and Sogdiana, of the blood royal, commanded on the left; with him was Barsaëntes, satrap of Arachosia. Mazaeus commanded on the right.

Alexander is said to have had 40,000 infantry and 7000 cavalry. The latter might be accurate, for he had two new formations of mercenary horse, under Menidas and Andromachus. But the former must be exaggerated; the only new infantry formation mentioned is Balacrus' javelin-men, and his known formations do not approach 40,000. Doubtless he had been recruiting mercenaries, though only 4000 under Cleander are mentioned. But his system of reinforcements is obscure; probably he received an annual draft of recruits from Macedonia, and before his death he and his satraps had enlisted the whole available supply of Greeks; these perhaps about sufficed to meet losses and supply his armies of occupation, leaving his field force roughly a constant quantity[1]. His first line was shorter than usual; Parmenion on the left had the Thessalians and half the allied horse, then came the phalanx and hypaspists, on the right the Companions. Craterus' battalion was on the left of the phalanx that day, and next him Amyntas',

---

[1] Discussed by Beloch, *Griech. Geschichte*, III², 2, p. 322 *sq*

commanded (he being absent recruiting) by his brother Simmias. As Alexander expected to be outflanked, he drew up a deep column behind each wing, who were to form front outward if required; on the left, half the allied horse, the Thracian horse, and Andromachus' squadron; on the right, the lancers and Paeonians, Menidas' horse, half the Agrianians, half the archers, and Cleander's mercenaries. The army therefore formed three sides of a square. Before the hypaspists he threw forward the rest of the Agrianians and archers and Balacrus' javelin-men, as a screen against the chariots. The rest of the mercenaries formed a second line behind the phalanx, with orders, if the army were surrounded, to form front to the rear and complete the square. Behind were the baggage and prisoners, guarded by the Thracian foot.

Alexander gave his army a good dinner and sleep; but the Persians stood to arms all night, a needless strain on the men. Having made all his dispositions, he himself went to sleep and slept well into the morning. The day was 1 October 331. As he led his army out, he found that the Companions were opposite the scythed chariots; he therefore inclined to the right, bringing the chariots opposite the hypaspists. The battle opened on his right with the Saca horse riding round his flank and attacking; Menidas met but could not hold them, and Alexander sent in the Paeonians and Cleander's mercenaries; Bessus in reply sent in the Bactrians. At this point the scythed chariots made their charge. But the Agrianians and javelin-men, thrown well forward, broke the charge up, transfixing and tearing down horses and drivers; few chariots reached the line, and the hypaspists opened their ranks to let them pass through; the damage done was not great, and all were finally brought down. Meanwhile in the fight on the flank Alexander had gained the better position, for he was holding the enemy without using the Companions. Finally he threw in the lancers; their shock gained so much ground that Bessus, to restore the battle, had to send in all his cavalry that remained, and still the Companions were intact. The Persian line had begun to advance, but the left centre now stretched out to support Bessus, and a gap opened; Alexander at once ordered his infantry to advance, and with the Companions charged the gap, followed by the nearest battalions; the weakened Persian line broke, and, as at Issus, Darius turned and fled.

On the left, meanwhile, Mazaeus had outgeneralled Parmenion, and the battle was going badly for Alexander. The weaker flanking column on this side was driven in by the Cappadocians, and the Thessalians, attacked both in front and flank, were in trouble. Craterus and Simmias had to support them with their battalions of the phalanx, and when Alexander's order to advance came, both were fully involved and could not move; but the other battalions went forward, and a gap opened between Simmias and Polyperchon. Into this gap the Persian cavalry of the guard flung themselves, followed by the Parthians and some Indian horse; they rode right through the phalanx from front to rear, cutting it in half; for the moment Mazaeus must have thought he was victorious. But the Persians were out of hand, and instead of taking the phalanx in rear they rode on through the mercenaries, made for the baggage, drove off the Thracians, and began to free and arm the prisoners; the mercenaries in turn re-formed and drove them off. Parmenion however lost his nerve, and sent a message to Alexander for help. It reached him just after Darius fled; he turned the Companions and rode back. On his way he met the returning Persians and Parthians, and barred their retreat. A desperate fight followed, and Alexander lost 60 Companions; finally the Persians broke through, and he rode on to the help of Parmenion. But he was no longer needed. Darius' flight had become known, the Persian line was in disorder, and Mazaeus' cavalry had lost heart; the Thessalians with fine courage had come a second time; and when Alexander joined them he had little to do but order a general pursuit. On the other wing Bessus and the Bactrians retired as a unit, undefeated, sullen, and ready for mischief; the Greeks also got away intact; but the rest of the army broke up. Alexander's views of what constituted a victory were those of Nelson; men might drop and horses founder, but he kept up pursuit till dark, rested till midnight, started again, and never drew rein till he reached Arbela, 56 miles from the battlefield. He was determined that the enemy should never re-form as an army.

VIII. THE DEATH OF DARIUS

Gaugamela uncovered the nerve-centres of the empire. Alexander rested his army, marked out the sites of two cities, Alexandria near Arbela (Erbil), and Nikephorion, the city of victory, and advanced on Babylon, where Mazaeus had taken refuge. The city was not defensible, the great walls having long since been destroyed, and Mazaeus thought he had done enough for a king who ran. He came out to meet Alexander, and was received with the honour that was his due. The Babylonians welcomed Alexander; he reversed Xerxes' acts, restored all native customs, and

made Mazaeus satrap, his first appointment of a Persian. He
did not however give him the military command, but appointed a
Macedonian general to the satrapy as well as a financial superintendent; and henceforth, whenever he appointed a Persian satrap,
he divided the three powers, civil, military, and financial, the
Persians never having military power. But in one way Mazaeus'
position was unique; he was the only satrap permitted to coin,
doubtless for the convenience of Babylonian trade. At Susa
Alexander deposited Darius' family, and appointed another Persian satrap. He sent Mithrines, who had surrendered Sardes, as
nominal satrap to Armenia (which however was never conquered),
and Menes the Bodyguard to Phoenicia to take command of his
sea-communications between Phoenicia and Europe and arrange
for any support Antipater might require against Sparta. The Staff
vacancies occasioned by Arybbas' recent death and Menes' appointment were filled by Leonnatus and (probably) Hephaestion.
Amyntas now returned, bringing large reinforcements.

For the invasion of Persis Alexander as usual divided the army,
sending Parmenion with the Greeks, baggage, and siege-train by
road, while he himself entered the hills, it being mid-winter. He
reduced the Uxii, one of the pre-Aryan tribes displaced by the
Iranians and living by brigandage, and so came to the formidable
pass into Persis called the Persian Gates, strongly held by the
satrap Ariobarzanes. His frontal attack was repulsed; he left
Craterus to hold the defenders' attention, and with a mobile force
and three days' food struck into the snow-hills, relying on a
prisoner as guide. He took tremendous risks, but came down
successfully on the enemy's rear; caught between two fires, Ariobarzanes gave way. Alexander pushed on with all speed for Persepolis, and reached the great palaces on their rock terrace before
Ariobarzanes had time to carry off the treasure. Between Susa,
Persepolis, and Pasargadae, he secured probably 180,000 talents
in coin and bullion, nearly £44,000,000, beside vast booty in kind,
such as gold and silver plate and purple dye; such wealth seemed
fabulous to the Greek world. At Persepolis, against Parmenion's
advice, he deliberately fired Xerxes' palace, as a sign to Asia that
E-sagila was avenged (see above, p. 1) and Achaemenid rule ended.
The well-known story of Alexander's feast, with Thais inciting
him to the burning, is legend, invented for the dramatic effect:
it had needed Xerxes and his myriads to burn Athens, but now
an Athenian girl could burn Persepolis. Alexander stayed at
Persepolis till in spring 330 he received the news of Sparta's
defeat; then, after appointing a Persian satrap of Persis, he entered

Media, occupied Ecbatana, and there in the gold and silver palace sat down to take stock of an altered world.

So far he had been Alexander of Macedon, general of the League for the war against Persia. That task was ended; as an empire, Persia would fight no more; the League had no concern with the new Great King establishing his marches. He therefore sent home the Thessalians and all his Greek allies, and probably remitted the 'contributions' of the Asiatic Greek cities. As to his own position, Mazaeus' appointment shows that he had already made up his mind. Aristotle had taught him that barbarians were naturally unfitted to rule; he meant to see. Aristotle had said they must be treated as slaves; he had already learnt that here Aristotle was wrong. He had seen the immemorial civilizations of Egypt and Babylon; he had seen the Persian nobles in battle; he knew that barbarians, like Greeks, must be classified according to merit, and that the best ranked high. But one other thing which Aristotle had taught him was sound; it was as difficult to organize peace as to make war, but it must be done, or military empires must perish. He had conquered the Persians; he now had to live with them, and reconcile them both to his rule and to the higher culture which he represented. That culture too had its rights; but he hoped to spread it, not by force, but by means of the cities which he would found. But then the cities also must be an integral part of the empire, and not mere enclaves. How he was to unite in one polity Greek cities, Iranian feudal barons, and tribes who practised group-marriage and head-hunting, he did not know. But he knew the line he would take; he was not to be a Macedonian king ruling Persia, but king of Macedonians and Persians alike; he was to mediate between the Greek and the barbarian,—in Plutarch's phrase to mix them as in a loving-cup. No one had thought of such a thing before; no one living (unless Hephaestion) could as yet understand what he meant. Here begins Alexander's tragedy; the tragedy of an increasing loneliness, of a growing impatience with those who could not understand, of a failure which nevertheless bore greater fruit than most men's success.

He now appointed Persian satraps for Media and Media Paraetacene, and emphasized the new position of things by one great change; Parmenion's cavalry had gone home, and Parmenion, Philip's man, was left in Media with some Thracians and mercenaries as general of communications. His first task was to collect all the treasure and hand it over to Harpalus. Harpalus had done something before Issus which made him fear Alexander's anger, and had fled; Alexander, with his usual loyalty to his friends, had forgiven, recalled, and reinstated him. Philoxenus was presently transferred from his financial office to the command of the sea-communications between Asia Minor and Greece, and Harpalus became head of the civil service, *i.e.* of all the financial superintendents everywhere, responsible only to Alexander.

Darius after Gaugamela had escaped to Ecbatana, and had been joined by Bessus and his Bactrians, Barsaëntes of Arachosia, Satibarzanes of Aria, Nabarzanes, Artabazus, and others, including the 2000 Greeks; but on Alexander's approach they had left Ecbatana and retired towards Bactria. Eastern Iran had always been somewhat distinct in feeling from western, and it did not recognize Gaugamela as decisive. Alexander now heard that Darius was collecting reinforcements and decided to follow him (midsummer 330). Having decided, he acted with amazing speed. Exactly what he did cannot be ascertained; but apparently the tradition made him cover the 400 miles to Damghan in eleven days, excluding rest days, based on a belief that he could maintain the extraordinary average of 36 miles a day. He covered the 200 miles from Ecbatana to Rhagae (Rei near Teheran) by forced marches; there he learnt that Darius had passed the Caspian Gates, and rested his men. He then did the 52 miles to the Gates (so it is said) without a halt. There Mazaeus' son came into his camp with news: Bessus, Barsaëntes, and Nabarzanes had deposed Darius and held him prisoner. Nabarzanes as chiliarch must have led the charge of the Persian guard at Gaugamela, and all three probably felt that they personally had not been defeated. The only comment to be made on their action is that it was too late; they should have done it after Issus. Darius had twice deserted brave men who were dying for him. That Bessus was not man enough for the work he undertook is immaterial; had he succeeded, history would have justified him as a patriot.

Alexander recognized the need for yet greater haste; he took the Companions, lancers, Paeonians, and some infantry, with two days' food, and started for Bessus' camp. He was hampered by the infantry; but he had the 2000 Greeks in mind. Even so he marched 36 hours with one brief rest, but found Bessus gone; he heard however that the Greeks, and Artabazus, had left him. He pushed on for another 16 hours and reached a village where Bessus had halted the day before; there he learnt of a short cut, but across desert. The infantry could do no more; he decided to chance the truth of the news about the Greeks, dismounted 500 horsemen, put phalangites on their horses, and started across the desert.

They suffered from thirst; a little water was found for Alexander, and he refused to drink; the weary troopers bade him lead where he would and they would follow. They rode 50 miles that night, and at dawn, near Damghan, they saw the dust-cloud which meant the fugitives. Bessus was in no condition to fight; Barsaëntes and Satibarzanes stabbed Darius and left him dying, and they rode for their lives. A Macedonian gave Darius a cup of water; he died before Alexander came up. It was Alexander's one piece of mere good fortune; he was saved the embarrassment of dealing with his rival. He covered the body with his purple cloak, and sent it to Persepolis for burial. Darius 'great and good' is a fiction of legend. He may have possessed the domestic virtues; otherwise he was a poor type of despot, cowardly and inefficient. The wonderful loyalty of his satraps up to Gaugamela was devotion to the Persian idea, called out by the presence of the foreign invader.

CHAPTER XIII

ALEXANDER: THE CONQUEST OF THE FAR EAST

I. ALEXANDER, PHILOTAS, AND PARMENION

ALEXANDER was now Great King by right of conquest; in his dedication at Lindus this same year he calls himself Lord of Asia, while about 331 the lion-gryphon of Persia[1], and in 329 the title of King (which he never used on his coinage minted in Macedonia), begin to appear on some of his Asiatic issues. He consequently claimed, when he so desired, to treat all still in arms against him as rebels. He did not follow Bessus; for a group of Darius' adherents had taken refuge in Tapuria, and he had first to secure his rear. He sent his baggage by road via Shahrud, and struck into the Elburz mountains with two mobile columns commanded by Craterus and himself, which united at Bandar Gäz on the Caspian and thence proceeded eastward to Zadracarta, the royal residence of Hyrcania. His operations produced their effect, and all those still in arms came in, some to Gäz and some to Zadracarta, and submitted: Autophradates satrap of Tapuria, Phrataphernes satrap of Parthia and Hyrcania, Nabarzanes, Artabazus, and delegates from the Greek mercenaries. Artabazus, once Philip's friend, was received with honour, Nabarzanes pardoned, and the two satraps confirmed in their offices; Alexander desired to show that prompt submission to the new ruler would bring its reward. While waiting for the Greeks, he reduced the Mardi in their forest fastnesses in the hills south of the Caspian; he probably went as far as Amol, and added the country to Tapuria. Then all the Greeks came in, bringing the ambassadors who had been with Darius. Though Great King in Asia, Alexander desired to emphasize the fact that to Greeks he was still President of the Hellenic alliance, and he settled matters by the touchstone of the League. The Greeks who had been in Darius' service prior to the Covenant of the League, and the envoys from Sinope and Chalcedon, which were not members, went free; the other mercenaries were compelled to enter his service, and he imprisoned the envoys

---

[1] See G. F. Hill, *Alexander the Great and the Persian Lion-Gryphon*, J.H.S. XLIII, 1923, p. 156 and Volume of Plates ii, 8, *m, o*.

from the League towns, Athens and Sparta, as being traitors. Sparta was beaten, and the sea secure; he had no further need to give Athens special treatment.

Alexander had now reached a part of the world where towns were almost unknown. The true Iranian type of country knew only villages, fortresses, and 'royal residences,' a royal residence being a palace with pleasure grounds, a citadel, and an ancillary village, serving as a satrap's seat. The great non-Greek towns of the west of the Empire all belonged to older civilisations than the Persian; and if Bactra was really a town, tradition at least made it pre-Iranian. A royal residence might have a name of its own, like Zadracarta or Maracanda, or Persepolis, seemingly a corruption of Portipora; but it was often called by the name of the province, as 'the Arachosians.' If Alexander wanted cities in eastern Iran he must build them.

From Astrabad Alexander started to follow Bessus, who had gone to Bactria, while Satibarzanes and Barsaëntes had returned to their satrapies to collect troops preparatory to joining him. Alexander went up the Gurgan river and by Bujnurd into the valley of the Kashaf-Rud. At Meshed he received and accepted the submission of Satibarzanes, who was not yet prepared for resistance, and confirmed him in his satrapy, sending Anaxippus to him as general but with an inadequate force. Doubtless he was trying a policy of trust; at the same time he had evidently no idea of the feeling in Aria. He also heard that Bessus, supported by the Bactrians, had assumed the upright tiara and called himself Great King. From Meshed he followed the regular road towards Balkh; he may have reached the Murghab river when he heard that Satibarzanes had risen and killed Anaxippus and his force, and was collecting troops; Arachosia was also in arms. He could not invade Bactria with Aria up behind him; he had to turn. Leaving Craterus to follow with the army, he hurried south with a small force, and in two days reached the royal residence, Artacoana; Satibarzanes was surprised, and barely escaped to Bessus. Alexander marched through Aria, and, as he thought, subdued it; near Artacoana he founded Alexandria of the Arians (Herat). He appointed another Persian, Arsames, as satrap; he did not yet understand that eastern Iran was fighting a national war. Then he entered Drangiana, which was part of Barsaëntes' satrapy. Barsaëntes fled to the Indians in eastern Arachosia, and was handed over to Alexander, who put him to death; as Nabarzanes and Satibarzanes had been pardoned, it is clear that he was executed for rebellion and not for Darius' murder.

Alexander halted at the royal residence, Phrada, possibly near Nad Ali, site of the later capital, Faranj, which preserved the alternative name, 'the Zarangians'; and here occurred the execution of Parmenion's son Philotas. In estimating what happened, Alexander's position among his generals must be borne in mind. Olympias once rebuked him for making these men the equals of kings; and indeed they were little less. Some were princes of old lines; most were as proud and ambitious as himself, and intoxicated with victory and its material fruits. Many of them had high military ability; a few were to be great administrators. Of things like the sanctity of life they thought little; they lived hard and took their chances in a world full of wonderful chances. And scarcely one of them could understand Alexander. The ancient world had never seen such a group of men; and Alexander, who was twenty-two when he crossed the Dardanelles, had to drive them as a team. He did drive them with success till he died; but his success was not as yet a foregone conclusion.

There seems to have been a conservative element among the generals, men who did not care for Alexander's position as Great King, or his Persian policy and satraps. Their ideal was a national king like Philip, first among his peers; they disliked the notion of a king without a peer. Philotas, an overbearing man, may have represented this element; but more probably the motive of his treason was personal, not political. For Parmenion's family had held too much power; but now his son Nicanor was dead, and Parmenion himself had fallen out of favour. Since crossing the Dardanelles Alexander had uniformly disregarded his advice and had uniformly been successful; Parmenion too had failed at Gaugamela, and his enemies, including Callisthenes, were hinting that he had not particularly desired Alexander's victory. Since then Alexander had left him on communications, and Craterus was fast taking his place as second in command. Is the explanation of Philotas' action to be found in a belief that the star of his house was setting and his own position insecure?

Philotas' loyalty had already once been called in question; but Alexander had simply passed the matter by, as he had done with Harpalus. But at Phrada a plot was discovered against Alexander's life. The ringleader was an obscure person, but he claimed the support of Amyntas the phalanx-leader and Demetrius the Bodyguard. The plot came to Philotas' ears; on his own admission, he knew of it for two days and did not tell Alexander. Then Alexander heard. If Philotas, general of the Companions, were a traitor, it was necessary to strike hard and quickly. It was

Macedonian custom that in a trial for treason, where the king was virtually a party, the State was represented, as it was when the throne was vacant, by the Macedonian people under arms, the army; and Philotas was properly put on trial before the army. Nothing further is known beyond Ptolemy's statement that the proofs of his treason were perfectly clear; the army condemned him to death, and carried out its sentence according to Macedonian custom. It was rough and ready justice; but the army gave a fair trial according to its lights. For, after Philotas, Amyntas and his brothers were tried; all were acquitted and continued in their commands. Demetrius was subsequently cashiered, and Ptolemy son of Lagos replaced him on the Staff. It is said that Alexander the Lyncestian was now put to death; it has been thought that the conspirators meant to make him king.

There remained Parmenion. There was no evidence against him, but he could not be left in charge of Alexander's communications. But neither could he be removed. That a great general could be relieved of his command and retire quietly into private life would probably have seemed impossible to every Macedonian. There were only two known alternatives: he must rebel or die. Alexander decided that Parmenion must die. He sent Polydamas with swift dromedaries across the desert, bearing letters to Parmenion's generals in Media, Cleander and Menidas of the mercenaries and Sitalces of the Thracians. Polydamas travelled faster than rumour; the generals carried out Alexander's orders and killed Parmenion. Philotas' execution had been perfectly judicial; Parmenion's was plain murder, and leaves a deep stain on Alexander's reputation. But he had shown his generals that he was master; he struck once, with terrible effect, and the lesson went home; he never had to strike again.

II. THE CONQUEST OF TURKESTAN

It was clear that no subject must again hold Philotas' power; and the Companions were re-organized as two hipparchies, each of eight half-squadrons (nominally 1000 men), under Hephaestion and Cleitus as hipparchs. Alexander founded a city at Phrada which was, perhaps later, named Prophthasia, 'Anticipation,'— a curious allusion to the conspiracy. He apparently never took winter quarters at all in the winter of 330–29 B.C.; he was anxious to reach Bactria, and he had to ensure Bessus' isolation from the south. He went on from Phrada to the Helmund, where he found a people (perhaps the almost extinct Reis tribes) called the Bene-

factors, because they had once aided Cyrus with supplies. They
are represented as an innocent folk enjoying a golden age of righteousness, and he exempted them from satrapal rule and tribute
for helping his predecessor Cyrus. The satraps of Carmania and
Gedrosia now sent their submission; but Arachosia was master-
less and unconquered. Alexander separated Drangiana from it
and added it to Aria; then he followed up the Helmund and the
Argandab into Arachosia, where at the royal residence he founded
Alexandria of the Arachosians (Candahar); he left Menon to
reduce the country, pushed on up the Tarnak, and founded another
Alexandria, probably Ghazni. Thence he crossed the mountains
into the Cabul valley (spring 329). The troops suffered from cold
and snow blindness, and were glad to shelter at night in the bee-
hive huts which the natives built with a hole in the roof to let out
the smoke; but the natives had plenty of animals, and tradition
may have exaggerated the sufferings of the march, though Alexander possibly crossed too early in the year. In the Cabul valley
he founded another city, Alexandria of the Caucasus (Opian near
Charikar), appointed a Persian satrap of the country (Paropamisadae), and prepared to cross the Paropamisus or 'Caucasus'
(Hindu Kush) into Bactria.

Bessus was holding Aornos (Tashkurgan) with 7000 Bactrians and a force of Dahae from the desert; with him were the
great barons Oxyartes of Bactria and Spitamenes of Sogdiana.
The regular route across the Hindu Kush into Bactria probably
ran by one of the lofty Kaoshan group of passes; but all roads
joined at Anderab, and Bessus had wasted the country there right
up to the mountains. Alexander on leaving Charikar bore northward, and crossed by the lower but far longer Panjshir-Khawak
pass, 11,600 feet high. The army suffered from lack of food and
firing, and lived on raw mule and silphium, but they got across
with little loss; Persian armies must have crossed the Hindu Kush
before them. Alexander however did not take the direct road from
Anderab through the defile at Tashkurgan, as Bessus expected;
he bore north again, reached Drapsaka, and turned Bessus' position. Bessus fled across the Oxus; the Bactrians submitted, and
Alexander occupied Tashkurgan and Zariaspa-Bactra without
resistance, and made the veteran Artabazus satrap of Bactria. At
last too Aria was settled. Satibarzanes, with Arsames' privity,
had returned and raised the country again while Alexander was in
Arachosia, but had been defeated and killed by a force sent under
Erigyius. Alexander now sent as satrap Stasanor, of the royal
house of Soli in Cyprus, with orders to remove Arsames. The

national war had forced upon Alexander a change in his Persian policy; but in Stasanor he had found the right man, and Aria had peace.

From Bactra Alexander marched to the Oxus opposite Kilif, the army suffering from thirst in the summer heat; Bessus had destroyed all the boats, but the troops crossed native fashion, lying flat on skins stuffed with rushes and paddling. (The famous story, which occurs here, of Alexander's massacre of a harmless community of exiles from Branchidae for their ancestors' supposed treachery toward Apollo, is a clumsy fabrication, invented to glorify Alexander.) Word now came from Spitamenes that Bessus was his prisoner and that he was ready to surrender him. Ptolemy was sent to take the surrender; but after a forced march he learnt that Spitamenes had changed his mind and gone, leaving Bessus behind. He captured Bessus, who was put in the pillory and shown to the army, publicly flogged, and sent to Bactra to await judgment. Alexander then occupied Maracanda (Samarcand), the summer royal residence of Sogdiana, and pushed on by the usual route into Ferghana past the fortress of Cyropolis to the great southward loop of the Jaxartes, where Persian rule had ended; on the way he was wounded in the tibia and lost part of the bone. He left garrisons of mercenaries in Cyropolis and in the seven fortresses between Cyropolis and the Jaxartes which the Persians had built for protection against the nomads; and from there, at the end of the known world, he summoned all the Sogdian barons to a durbar in Bactra. He thought Sogdiana had submitted; but it was merely waiting for a lead, and the invitation to the durbar, which could mean nothing good, kindled the torch. The whole country flamed up behind him; his garrisons in Cyropolis and the seven fortresses were killed, and he had to reduce these places one after the other; at Cyropolis, which he razed, he was again wounded. He showed considerable severity; cut off from information, he thought he was dealing with a local revolt which severity might suppress.

At last he got news; Spitamenes had risen and was besieging the citadel of Maracanda. He could not spare many men to relieve the place, for a host of Turcomans was gathering on the Jaxartes; he sent 2300 mercenaries and 60 Companions, under the command of his interpreter Pharnuches, a Lycian; probably he scarcely realized that things were serious, and thought there might be negotiations. Meanwhile he decided to found a city on the Jaxartes as a defence against the nomads. In 20 days the mud walls were finished and the city settled; it was called 'Alexandria the Farthest,' to-day Chodjend. It was not founded to control the Silk Route from China across Chinese Turkestan, for Alexander knew nothing of the existence of Chinese Turkestan or of any Silk Route (if indeed the latter yet existed); beyond the Jaxartes was 'Europe.' All the time that the city was building the Turcomans patrolled the farther bank, challenging him to cross. They were beyond his marches; but he wished to prevent them helping Spitamenes, and he did not mean to be mocked by 'Scythians' as Darius I had been. He ranged his catapults on the bank and began shooting. The Turcomans were alarmed by the power of the strange weapons, which could kill them across the river, and retired out of shot. The army then crossed as it had crossed the Oxus, Alexander with the archers leading; once landed, he kept a clear space for the army to land behind him. Part of his heavy cavalry then attacked; the Turcomans tried desert tactics, riding round them and shooting; Alexander mixed the Agrianians and archers with the cavalry, and these succeeded in stopping the encircling tactics of the enemy. Once this was done, Alexander made his usual charge, and the Turcomans broke. He pursued them a long way, though very ill from drinking foul water; finally he had to be carried back to camp. The battle is notable, for it shows Alexander, who had never seen desert or 'Parthian' tactics before, meeting them with complete confidence and certainty; had he been an inferior general, he might have suffered the fate of Crassus at Carrhae.

What might have happened to Alexander did happen to the troops sent to relieve Maracanda. Spitamenes, beside his own Sogdian horse, had found allies in the nomads of the Kirghiz steppe west of the Polytimetus river; he retired down the river and drew the relieving force after him into the desert. There he attacked, using desert tactics. Pharnuches was not a soldier, and the mercenaries' leaders would not take the responsibility. The men formed square and fought their way back to the river, but at the sight of safety discipline gave way; there was a rush to cross, and Spitamenes practically annihilated the force. When Alexander heard, he realized at last that he was face to face with a national war and a national leader. He had apparently quitted Chodjend, and (taking the bematists' stade as about three quarters of the Greek[1]) was some 135 miles from Maracanda. He took the Companions, Agrianians, archers, and some picked phalangites, and according to tradition reached Maracanda in a little over three

---

[1] Marquart, *Phil.*, Supp. Bd. x, p. 1.

days and three nights; if allowance be made for better climatic conditions than to-day, for it being late autumn, and for Alexander's terrific driving power, it can hardly be pronounced impossible offhand, if the cavalry carried the spears and shields. Spitamenes was again besieging Maracanda; again he retreated to the desert. Alexander went as far as the battlefield and buried the dead, but he did not follow Spitamenes; he turned and retraced his steps up the Polytimetus, wasting its rich valley from end to end to prevent the enemy again attacking Maracanda. Thence he returned to Bactra, where he wintered; the victorious Spitamenes, with his headquarters in the winter royal residence of Sogdiana, Bokhara, was left undisturbed till spring. Alexander held little north of the Oxus but Chodjend and Maracanda; but the army had had no rest for two strenuous years, and winter quarters were an absolute necessity.

There was a great gathering at Bactra that winter (329–8). Phrataphernes and Stasanor came bringing in Arsames and other partisans of Bessus; large reinforcements arrived from Europe; the western satraps brought fresh drafts of mercenaries. Bessus was brought out and judged; his ears and nose were cut off and he was sent to Ecbatana for execution. He was condemned, not for the murder of Darius, but for having assumed the tiara; Alexander, in mutilating him, treated him as Darius I had treated Fravartish (vol. IV, p. 179). On the best Greek standards the mutilation was probably indefensible; still, Greeks used torture, and the best of them could on occasion advocate worse things than mutilation. There also came Pharasmanes, ruler of Chorasmia (Khiva); he offered Alexander his alliance and was also understood to have offered to guide him by some northern route to the Black Sea, thus linking up Bactria with Thrace. The Caspian was at this time joined to the Aral by one or more salt-water connections; and Alexander thought that the sea which he had seen in Hyrcania (the Caspian) was Aristotle's Hyrcanian lake, and that what it joined must really be the Maeotis (Sea of Azov)[1], the Jaxartes, like Aristotle's Araxes, being identified with the Tanais (Don), dividing Asia from Europe. Pharasmanes presumably was taken as confirming this view, for evidently the Black Sea was not far off. Possibly the subsequent expedition made by Zopyrion, Antipater's general in Thrace, who crossed the Danube, perhaps reached Olbia, and was killed by the Scythians, was an attempt to link Thrace with Bactria. Had Alexander lived, he

[1] The Aral was doubtless taken for Aristotle's Caspian lake.

might have attended to the Black Sea and its problems; but for the present, while accepting Pharasmanes' alliance, he told him that he must next go to India.

Sogdiana however had first to be reduced. In spring 328 Alexander left Bactra and again crossed the Oxus; by the river he found a spring of petroleum (he was the first European to discover it), and offered sacrifice to avert the evil consequences of the prodigy. The army he divided into five columns, which swept the plain country and reunited at Maracanda. Spitamenes could not face them; he crossed the Oxus southward, and went to the Massagetae of the desert. Alexander ordered Hephaestion to build fortified posts at various points, and continued to sweep the country. But Spitamenes was not yet beaten. He persuaded the Massagetae to help him, overwhelmed one of the border forts of Bactria, and a few days later appeared before Bactra itself, behind Alexander's back. The king had left Craterus with a strong force to patrol Bactria and prevent a rising, but in Bactra there were only details and the sick. The commandant of the hospital led them out; Spitamenes ambushed and annihilated them. Craterus came up in haste, but Spitamenes escaped into the desert with little loss. It had taken Alexander much of the campaigning season of 328 to reduce about half of Sogdiana, and still Spitamenes was at large; but the country was now a network of fortified posts and garrisons. He left Coenus in charge of western Sogdiana with two battalions of the phalanx, some Companions, and the newly raised Bactrian and Sogdian horse, the first Asiatic troops in his army; he himself made his headquarters at Nautaka, possibly to rest the army for the winter campaign and attend to administration, but there is a lacuna here in the story. Spitamenes was sadly hampered by the fortified posts, but by the promise of plunder he roused the Massagetae to another effort; they gave him 3000 horse, and with these and his own Sogdians he attacked Coenus. But Coenus had mastered his tactics, and he too had light horse. Spitamenes was decisively defeated, and his Sogdians left him and surrendered; the Massagetae lost heart, cut off his head, and sent it to Alexander. He was the best opponent Alexander met. His blood was continued in the line of the Seleucid kings; for Alexander subsequently married his daughter Apama to Seleucus, and she became the mother of Antiochus I.

III. CLEITUS, CALLISTHENES, AND ALEXANDER'S DIVINE DESCENT

This same summer saw the murder of Cleitus the hipparch at Maracanda. The dry climate of Turkestan, and the bad water, induced in the army much use of strong native wine. Alexander himself, as is quite clear, habitually drank no more than other Macedonians; he sat long at dinner, but chiefly for the sake of conversation; the stories of his excessive drinking were first put about after his death by Ephippus of Olynthus, a gossip-monger who was not with the army, and were afterwards spread by the New Comedy. However, at this particular banquet Alexander did get drunk, as did Cleitus; but the conversation in which the quarrel originated cannot be reconstructed with any certainty from the varying versions. It seems probable that some Greek recited a sarcastic poem about the mercenaries' leaders defeated by Spitamenes, and that in some way Parmenion's name was brought up, probably with a suggestion of failure; Cleitus, who had been Philotas' principal lieutenant, thought Alexander approved, and began to defend Parmenion and Philip's men generally, and went on to compare Philip with Alexander, whose Persian innovations he was known to dislike. Alexander became angry, possibly at being belittled, but possibly too at the indecency of such a comparison; Cleitus, too drunk to understand, went on to assert that Alexander owed his victories to Philip's Macedonians. What he seems to have been trying to express was, that Alexander was slighting the men whose bravery alone had raised him to a position in which he *could* slight them. Alexander made some effort at self-control; he turned to two Greeks beside him and said 'Don't you feel like demigods among beasts?' But Cleitus could not be restrained; he thrust out his hand towards Alexander and said 'This saved your life at the Granicus,' and continued to taunt him. Then Alexander's temper gave way utterly; he sprang up and snatched a spear from a guard, but some held him down, while Ptolemy pushed Cleitus out of the hall. He broke away, however, and hearing Alexander shouting his name rushed back, crying 'Here is Cleitus, Alexander.' Alexander ran him through on the spot.

When the king came to himself his remorse was bitter. He shut himself up for three days, taking no food, and calling on the names of Cleitus and his sister Lanice, who had been his nurse and to whom he had made such a fine return. The army became alarmed;

they might be left leaderless at the end of the earth. At last his friends persuaded him to eat; the soothsayers gave out that Cleitus' death was due to the anger of Dionysus for a neglected sacrifice, and the army passed a resolution that Cleitus had been justly executed. The philosopher Anaxarchus is said to have told Alexander roughly not to be a fool: kings could do no wrong. One hopes it is not true, though Aristotle had said much the same: when the supreme ruler did come, he would be above all laws. But he had meant human laws. Terrible as the incident seems to us, it probably affected the generals very little; life was cheap and you took your chances; Cleitus (as Aristobulus says) had only himself to thank. Arrian's kindly verdict is, that many kings had done evil, but he had never heard of another who repented.

While at Nautaka Alexander removed Autophradates from Tapuria and added it to Phrataphernes' satrapy, and restored Darius' former satrap Atropates to Media; these two men were loyal to him throughout, as they had been to Darius. Artabazus was permitted to retire on account of his age, and a Macedonian, another Amyntas, was made satrap of Bactria and Sogdiana; it was obviously an impossible post for any Persian. But Alexander had not yet conquered all Sogdiana. He held the plain country; but four great barons, Oxyartes, Chorienes, Catanes, and Austanes, were still in arms in the hills of Paraetacene. In January 327 Alexander attacked Oxyartes' stronghold, the 'Sogdian rock,' perhaps near Derbent; Oxyartes was not there, but his family were. The snow was so deep, and the rock so precipitous, that the garrison told Alexander he would never take it unless he found men who could fly. Alexander called for volunteers; 300 answered and went up with ropes and iron pegs; 30 fell and were killed, but the rest climbed the crag overlooking the fortress and hoisted the agreed signal. Alexander told the garrison to go and look at his flying men, whereon they surrendered. Among the captives was Oxyartes' daughter Roxane, whom Alexander married. It was a marriage of policy, intended to reconcile the eastern barons and end the national war. Tradition naturally represents him as in love with her; but she had no child for four years, and it is doubtful if he ever cared for any woman except his terrible mother. On hearing the news Oxyartes came in, and accompanied Alexander to the siege of Chorienes' stronghold, on the Vakhsh river south of Faisabad. The 'rock' was protected by a deep cañon, at the bottom of which ran the torrent; the garrison thought it could never be crossed. But Alexander set the whole army to work day and night making ladders; with these they descended the ravine on a broad front, fixed pegs in the rock, and bridged the river with hurdles covered with earth. Choarienes took fright, and Oxyartes secured his surrender by enlarging on the clemency and good faith which Alexander had shown toward the defenders of his own stronghold. Alexander then left Craterus to reduce Catanes and Austanes and the land east of the Vakhsh, which he accomplished successfully, while he himself returned to Bactra to prepare for the expedition to India. During his stay in Bactria he refounded Bactra as an Alexandria, and caused to be founded another Alexandria at Merv, subsequently destroyed by nomads. He also arranged for the education and training in Macedonian fashion of 30,000 native youths.

At Bactra there came up the question of Alexander's divine descent. The man who publicly brought it forward was the philosopher Callisthenes. He was anxious to please Alexander, as he hoped to secure from him the rebuilding of his native city Olynthus; he also had an exaggerated opinion of his own importance as the self-constituted historian of the expedition; he is reported to have said that Alexander's fame depended not on what Alexander did but on what Callisthenes wrote. Some time after 330 he had sent to Greece for publication his history of Alexander, so far as it had gone; he must have read it to Alexander and others, and it was doubtless well known. It was written to advertise Alexander, with an eye to the Greek opposition; he has been called Alexander's press agent. It contained some very extravagant inventions. He said that what the oracle of Ammon had told Alexander was, that he was not Philip's son at all, but in actual fact (and not merely officially) the son of Zeus-Ammon himself; that the oracle of Apollo at Didyma, so long silent, had again spoken and declared that Alexander was son of Zeus; that a prophetess at Erythrae had confirmed his divine origin; and that in his passage along the Pamphylian coast at Mount Climax the very waves had prostrated themselves before the son of Zeus (p. 364). Whether he thought this would please Alexander, or whether Alexander was deliberately using him to prepare his way in Greece, may never be known; his rôle in either case was equally inglorious. But as all knew that Philip was supposed to have doubted Alexander's legitimacy, the seed he sowed fell on fertile ground. True, he apparently made Alexander son of a god only, and not a god; but it can be seen from Timaeus and others that many Greeks now made no distinction on that head. Whatever blame accrues to Callisthenes must however be shared by others; for Isocrates had said that, if Philip conquered Persia, nothing would be left him

but to become a god, and Aristotle, not content with telling
Alexander that he had no peer, had written, with Alexander in
mind, that the supreme ruler when he came would be as a god
among men.

Alexander, on his side, had, since Darius' death, adopted on
State occasions Persian dress and Persian court ceremonial, and
had made Chares the historian chamberlain. He now resolved to
introduce the Persian custom of prostration (*proskynēsis*) for all
those approaching the king. Here arose a difficulty. To Persians
it was only a ceremony; the Achaemenid kings had not been gods,
and prostration in Persian eyes did not imply worship. But to
Greeks and Macedonians it did imply worship; man did not prostrate himself save to the gods. Alexander knew perfectly how
Greeks must interpret prostration, and must therefore have had
some strong reason for adopting it; *i.e.* the reason was not ceremonial but political. He had to settle how the autocrat of Asia,
without playing the autocrat, was to exercise such authority over
free Greek cities as might be necessary to unite Greeks and Persians in one empire, and safeguard that empire's access to the
Aegean; and we must suppose that he had already some idea of
the solution of 324: officially, he must be the god of his Greek
allies. This does not mean more than 'officially.' Alexander never
thought that he *was* a god; he was ironical on the subject in private,
and in public regularly alluded to his father Philip. The thing to
him was simply a matter of policy, a pretence which might form a
useful instrument of statecraft. What first put the idea into his
head is uncertain. It may have simmered there ever since the
greeting of the priest of Ammon; or it may really have been put
there by Callisthenes, as some afterwards believed. With prostration he began to feel his way. He had the support of Hephaestion and other Macedonians, possibly including Lysimachus; and
both he and Hephaestion believed that Callisthenes would aid
them, as was natural after his story of the sea prostrating itself before the king; some indeed asserted that Callisthenes had promised.
But when prostration was actually introduced, events took an unexpected course. Some of the Macedonians did not even oppose;
they laughed. But Callisthenes opposed in good earnest and asked
Alexander to confine this Asiatic custom to Asiatics. Alexander
did so perforce in future; but he was furious with Callisthenes.
He had counted on his influence as an aid to his policy, and
Callisthenes had failed him.

The reason for Callisthenes' change of attitude is obscure. In
the Peripatetic literature drawn on by Plutarch he figures as a

lover of liberty opposing a tyrant[1]; he was of course the same Callisthenes, the man who, Aristotle said, had no sense. Doubtless, as Aristotle's pupil, he despised barbarians and objected to Persian ceremonial; but the time to think of that was before he wrote about Mount Climax. To say that he had Panhellenic ideas, and wished to make of Alexander a god for Greeks but not for Persians, is no explanation; for deified men were unknown in Persia, and there was no question of Alexander becoming a god for Persians. One must suppose that he had only meant to write up Alexander in extravagant terms, and suddenly found himself (as he thought) faced with the terrible consequences of what he had done; the god he had made meant to act as such; it was no longer rhetoric but sober earnest. He tried to draw back, too late.

Then came the Pages' conspiracy. One of the royal pages, Hermolaus, had anticipated Alexander at a boar-hunt; he was deprived of his horse and whipped, apparently the usual Macedonian custom. He and some friends thereon conspired to kill Alexander; they were detected and put to death. This act of personal revenge had no political import, but it involved Callisthenes, who had been Hermolaus' tutor. Whether he was formally a party to the conspiracy is uncertain; but he had indulged in some wild talk to the boys on the virtue of killing tyrants, and Ptolemy says the boys confessed that this talk lay at the bottom of the whole business. Alexander put Callisthenes to death, presumably for conspiracy; to relieve him of odium, Chares spread a story that Callisthenes died naturally in prison. The verdict of the historian Timaeus may be recorded: Callisthenes deserved his fate, for he had made of a man a god, and done all in his power to destroy Alexander's soul. How far the verdict is true will probably never be known. But Callisthenes had his revenge; and Alexander paid. He incurred the hostility of Aristotle's school; Theophrastus in a pamphlet lamented Callisthenes' death and branded Alexander as a tyrant, and Demetrius of Phalerum presently carried the school over to Alexander's enemy Cassander; and the two philosophers worked out a doctrine of Chance, which was applied to Alexander. Thus from the Peripatetic school, of which Callisthenes had been a member, arose that debased portrait of Alexander against which Plutarch so passionately protested, and from which history for long could not shake itself free—the portrait of a despot whose achievements were due to luck, and who was ruined at the end by the excess of his own fortune.

[1] As the worthless Demades subsequently became a martyred hero; Crönert, *Anzeiger Akad. Wien,* 1924, No. VIII, on Berlin Papyrus 13045.

IV. INDIA: FROM BACTRA TO THE JHELUM[1]

Alexander received large reinforcements while in Bactria, and re-organized his army for the invasion of India. He separated the Royal Squadron from the Companions, and under the name of the *agēma* made it his personal command, doubtless because he had incorporated in it sons of a few great Persian nobles. Of the Companions he made four hipparchies instead of two, each of 1000 men; the hipparchs were Hephaestion, Craterus, Perdiccas, and Demetrius, one of the original squadron leaders. The original 2000 Companions were much reduced in numbers, and Alexander was yet to form a fifth hipparchy in India; the hipparchies therefore now contained only one Macedonian squadron apiece, and were filled up with Bactrian, Sogdian, Sacaean, and Arachosian horse. What invaded India, therefore, was not Macedonia but the Empire; and the army had already become a school for the fusion of races. The phalanx was raised to 10 battalions; of the old leaders, Coenus, Polyperchon, and Meleager alone remained; among the new were Alcetas, Perdiccas' brother, Attalus, afterwards Perdiccas' general, and Cleitus the White, the future admiral. Seleucus now commanded the hypaspists[2], whose numbers were unchanged, while Nearchus led one of the battalions. The Bodyguards were now Hephaestion, Perdiccas, Leonnatus, Ptolemy, Lysimachus, Peithon and Aristonoüs. Alexander already had a corps of horse-javelin men, and he now formed a corps of 1000 horse-archers from the Dahae; but the lancers and Paeonians were left behind. He cannot have taken many mercenaries with him, for he had been leaving them in every satrapy and newly-founded city, and of necessity he left a large body, 10,000, with Amyntas in Bactria, besides 3000 horse. He may have invaded India with some 35,000 fighting men; his known formations render any much greater number impossible. But the Macedonians had their native wives and their children with them, and there were scientific men and experts, camp-followers and traders; with the auxiliary services, the seamen, and the contingents supplied later by Indian princes, there may well have been (as tradition suggests) 120,000 souls in camp on the Hydaspes. The army

---

[1] For an account of the following operations, written more particularly from the Indian point of view, see also *Cambridge History of India*, vol. I, chap. xv.

[2] The 'Royal' hypaspists are the hypaspists, identified in Arrian I, 8, 3 and 4; IV, 24, 1 and 10.

had become a moving state, a reflection of the Empire; and provision was made for training the soldiers' children.

To understand Alexander's invasion of India we must discard all ideas later than 327 and try to see 'India' as he then saw it[1]. He never knew of the existence of northern or eastern Asia—of Siberia and Chinese Turkestan, China and further India; to the end of his life, 'Asia' meant to him, as to everyone, the empire of Darius I. He never knew of the Ganges or eastern Hindustan, which were unknown to Greeks prior to Megasthenes, or of the Indian peninsula, though later Nearchus and Onesicritus collected dim reports of 'islands' further south. There is no evidence that he even knew of the Rajputana desert, which Herodotus had known. 'India' to Alexander, when he invaded it, meant the country of the Indus, which, following Aristotle, he thought was a broad-based peninsula jutting *eastward* into the sea from the land mass of Iran. Along the north side of it, like a backbone, ran a chain of mountains, Aristotle's 'Parnassus' (*i.e.* Paropanisus); the rest was a plain, traversed by the Indus and its tributaries. Ocean, which was near the Jaxartes, washed the northern base of these mountains, and flowed round the eastern end of the peninsula. As to the south side, he began by sharing the perplexities of Aristotle, who at one time thought, like Aeschylus, that 'India' had land connection with Ethiopia (making the Indian ocean a lake), and at another believed that the sea separated them.

'India' had once been fairly well-known. Darius I had ruled the Cabul valley and Gandhara, and had subsequently conquered Sind and probably further parts of the Punjab; his admiral Scylax was said to have sailed down the Indus and back to Egypt, and though the truth of this has been doubted, Darius had made some use of the Indian ocean (vol. IV, pp. 183, 200). The Indian punchmarked silver coinage had been struck on the Persian standard and perhaps represented the Achaemenid coinage for India[2]; the official Aramaic writing of the Achaemenids had been introduced at Taxila (Takshaçilā), to become the parent of the Kharoshthī script. Taxila itself had an Iranian mercantile quarter, where Zoroastrian customs prevailed. But the fourth century had forgotten these things. To Ephorus, Indians were as shadowy as Celts. Herodotus was no longer much read; even Callisthenes could neglect him, and there is no sign that Alexander knew him at all, not even his account of Scylax' voyage. On the Persian side,

[1] Aristot. *Meteor.* 1, 13, p. 350 a, l. 18, and the *Liber de inundacione Nili*; both prior to Alexander's invasion.
[2] Decourdemanche, *Journal Asiatique*, 1912, p. 117

the Achaemenids had lost the satrapies of India, Gandhara, and probably the Paropamisadae; Alexander meets no Persian officials east of the Hindu Kush. Ochus had even believed that India joined Ethiopia and that the Indus was the upper Nile; this theory influenced Aristotle and, through him, Alexander, who started by believing it, though he soon learnt the truth. 'India' had become dim to the West.

But 'India' had been part of the empire of Darius I; and Alexander's invasion was only the necessary and inevitable completion of his conquest of that empire. It had nothing to do with any scheme of world-conquest; indeed it could not have, for in the far East the 'world,' like 'Asia,' only meant the Persian empire; nothing else was known. Possibly Alexander did not know, any more than we do, exactly how much of the Punjab Darius I had ruled; on the other hand, with his known interest in Cyrus, he possibly believed Xenophon's mistaken statement that Cyrus had ruled all 'India' to the eastern ocean; in either case he naturally meant to reduce the entire province, like any other satrapy. He had already, while at Bactra, formed some political connections there; a chief from Gandhara, Sasigupta, who had helped Bessus, had come over to him, and he had been promised aid by the powerful rajah of Taxila, who was having difficulty in withstanding his neighbour Porus and turned naturally to the new King of Persia, whose forerunners had once been Taxila's suzerains. Incidentally, Alexander greatly desired, as did Aristotle, to solve the problem of Ocean and the relationship of 'India' to Egypt. He meant therefore to explore the southern sea with a fleet; for this purpose he took with him to India rowers and shipwrights from Phoenicia, Cyprus, Caria, and Egypt, and had already decided that his friend Nearchus should be admiral. That is why Nearchus was recalled from his satrapy and given an interim command in the hypaspists, an apparent reduction in rank which must have puzzled those not in the secret.

In early summer 327 Alexander started from Bactra. He recrossed the Hindu Kush—local tradition says by the Kaoshan pass, 14,300 feet high—and reached Alexandria of the Caucasus, which was in disorder; he left Nicanor as governor to organize the city, and soon after made Oxyartes satrap of Paropamisadae. On his way to the Cabul river he was met by the local chiefs and the new ruler of Taxila, Ambhi (officially called Taxiles), the son of the old rajah, who was dead. They gave Alexander 25 elephants which they had with them (he did not, however, use elephants except for transport), and Taxiles put himself and his kingdom at his disposal. There Alexander divided his army, and sent Hephaestion and Perdiccas with Taxiles and the baggage through the Khyber pass to the Indus, with orders to build a bridge of boats; he himself with part of the Companions, seven battalions of the phalanx, the hypaspists, archers, Agrianians, horse-javelin men, and the siege-train, intended to march through the hills to the north of the Cabul river, to secure Hephaestion's northern flank from attack, his southern flank being protected by the nature of the ground.

Breaking camp about November, Alexander followed the old route through Laghman, ascended the Kunar river, and crossed into Bajaur, whose warlike people the Greeks called Aspasii. He attempted to prevent their concentration by the speed of his movements; he had much hard local fighting, was again wounded, and took several towns, including the capital Arigaion (Bajaur), which he settled; but he could not prevent the tribes concentrating for battle. He attacked their army in three columns, led by Ptolemy, Leonnatus, and himself, and after a severe fight broke them, taking many prisoners and cattle; he was so struck by the beauty of the cattle that he sent the best to Macedonia. He then left Bajaur, crossed the Landai river below the junction of the Panjkora and Swat, and entered Swat, the country of the Assaceni, who had concentrated before their capital Massaga; with them were a body of mercenaries from beyond the Indus. They did not wait to be attacked, but attacked him themselves. Alexander, who led the phalanx, feigned flight to draw them from the walls; but though he defeated them they reached the city with little loss, and in trying to rush the place he was wounded in the ankle. He brought up his siege-train, but failed to breach the walls or to enter by a bridge, as at Tyre; and the garrison held out till their chief was killed, when they surrendered upon terms. The Indian mercenaries left the town and camped outside; in the night Alexander surrounded them and cut them to pieces. The official explanation was that they had agreed to enter his service and were meditating desertion and he found it out. The explanation is unsatisfactory, for it omits the real point: had they taken the oath to Alexander or not? If they had, and were really meditating desertion, he was within his rights, though the death of the ringleaders might have sufficed. If they had not, it was massacre. Probably they had not, or the official explanation must have said so; the thing may have been some horrible mistake due perhaps to defective interpreting and to Alexander's growing impatience.

It was in Swat, in the district of the Kamdesh Kafirs, near Meros (the triple-peaked mountain Koh-i-Mor), that he found a town which the Greeks called Nysa, inhabited by people who, like their modern descendants, did not resemble the surrounding tribes; they worshipped some god (? Siva) who could be identified with Dionysus, especially as the ivy growing on the mountain made the Macedonians home-sick. Alexander welcomed the identification, for to suppose that Dionysus had been there and that he was going farther than the god encouraged the army; and he declared the Nysaeans, who probably really were immigrants from the west, independent of his satrap. Before leaving Swat he took and garrisoned two other towns, Ora and Bazira, and then came down through the Shāhkōt pass into the Yusufzai country, which Hephaestion had failed to reduce; he pacified it and received the surrender of the capital Peucelaotis. Here he reconstituted the country between the satrapy of Paropamisadae and the Indus, part of the old satrapy of Gandhara, into a provisional satrapy, which he gave to Nicanor. He next halted at a place not far from a mountain called by the Greeks Aornos, on which many Indians had found refuge. Heracles (Krishna) was said to have failed to take it, and Alexander decided to do so.

Aornos should be between the Cabul and Buner rivers; but geographers have sought it in vain[1]. It has possibly not been conclusively proved that it is not Mahaban[2]; but the mountain will never be satisfactorily identified till geographers know what they are looking for. Its alleged height and circuit, and the amount of plough-land and water at the top, are given by Arrian merely as stories with which the natives entertained Alexander beforehand; Curtius' 'ravines' were invented later in some school of rhetoric. None of these things appear in the simple narrative of Ptolemy, who was there[3]. Aornos to him was a *ridge*, difficult of access, and broad enough to camp on; at one end of the ridge was the 'rock' (a fortress, partly artificial), and the slopes were wooded. Alexander took the hypaspists, Agrianians, archers, Coenus' battalion of the phalanx, and a few horse for communications, and reconnoitred the path up to the rock; some natives offered to guide him to the ridge by another track. He sent Ptolemy up the track with the light-armed; they reached the ridge and palisaded themselves.

---

[1] It is now reported that Sir A. Stein believes he has found Aornos at Pir-sar, north of the Buner river. Further details, but not as yet the complete topography, have been published since this chapter was revised.

[2] Sir T. H. Holdich, *The Gates of India*, pp. 107 *sqq.*

[3] These points have to be taken into account in any proposed identification of the site.

Next day Alexander tried to force his way up the path and was beaten back; the Indians then attacked Ptolemy's camp but were repulsed. Alexander sent a message up to Ptolemy by an Indian deserter that he would attempt the track next day, and Ptolemy must take any defenders in the rear; the plan worked, and Alexander fought his way up and joined Ptolemy; how he got his catapults up is not recorded. He decided that the rock itself could not be stormed; there was, however, between him and it a hillock, of equal height. He began building a sloping embankment from Ptolemy's camp toward this hillock, dragging his catapults up the inclined plane as the work grew; some Macedonians seized the hillock, and Alexander completed the embankment up to it. Thereon the Indians, seeing that his catapults would now command the rock, gave up, and Alexander stormed the rock as they fled. He left Sasigupta to hold it.

From Aornos he pursued a chief still in arms through Swat to Dyrta; the locality is unknown, but it is unlikely that he entered Chitral. He then joined Hephaestion on the Indus. Hephaestion had bridged the river at Ohind, 16 miles above Attock, and had built in sections a number of boats, including some triakontors (light warships of 15 oars a side); while Taxiles had sent 30 elephants. Alexander crossed the Indus in early spring 326, and at Taxila, now partly excavated, his army for the first time saw a great Indian city. It was both a commercial centre and a famous university town, a headquarters of the teaching of the Brahmans. Taxiles gave Alexander 56 more elephants and some information. He was at war with the Paurava king (Porus), whose country lay in the plains between the Hydaspes (Jhelum) and the Acesines (Chenab), and who had allied himself with Abisares, ruler of the hill states of Rajauri and Bimber, both now included in Kashmir. Porus, however, had himself an enemy beyond the Chenab, the 'free nations' or Aratta (kingless ones), who were too strong for him to conquer; these peoples, the Cathaei, Oxydracae, and Malli, were confederations of village communities under oligarchic rule. Alexander left a garrison in Taxila, appointed Harpalus' brother Philippus as satrap, and advanced to the Hydaspes at Jhelum, which he probably reached early in June. He had now formed a fifth hipparchy under Coenus, and Antigenes took over Coenus' battalion of the phalanx; it had apparently been the crack battalion, picked for the attacks at Tyre and Aornos, and it continued to bear Coenus' name.

V. INDIA: FROM THE JHELUM TO THE BEAS

The river was not yet at its full size, but the rains would soon begin; and Porus with his army, including many elephants, held the farther bank. Alexander had the flotilla from the Indus brought across in sections, and made ostentatious preparations for crossing to hold Porus' attention, though he knew that the cavalry could not cross in face of the elephants. Under cover of these preparations he reconnoitred the bank, and selected a place 18 miles above[1] Jhelum, at the great bend of the river, where was a wooded island in mid-stream. The rains had begun, and there was need of haste. The boats were brought to the selected point and put together; meanwhile Alexander made numerous feints at crossing elsewhere, keeping Porus perpetually on the move; the Indian finally grew weary of meeting threats that never materialized. Shortly after the summer solstice, Alexander joined his flotilla by a wide detour, leaving Craterus at Jhelum with his hipparchy and part of the army; his orders were not to cross unless Porus were defeated or the elephants withdrawn from the bank. The following night was exceptionally stormy.

Alexander had with him the agema of the Companions, the hipparchies of Hephaestion, Perdiccas, Coenus, and Demetrius, and the horse-archers, nominally 5250 horse. Of infantry he had the hypaspists, two battalions of the phalanx—Coenus' (Antigenes') and Cleitus'—the Agrianians, archers and javelin-men; even if all the corps but the hypaspists were much below strength, he had at least 8000 foot; more probably he had over 10,000. Ptolemy's statement that he had under 6000 foot is, for once, demonstrably wrong; if taken from the *Journal*, it was given there simply with the object of minimizing the effect of the enemy's elephants. In the morning the force crossed to the island; but as soon as they left it they were seen by Porus' scouts. They landed safely, only to find themselves on another island; with great difficulty they waded ashore, and Alexander at once advanced downstream towards Porus' position, on the way defeating and killing Porus' son, who had been sent forward with 2000 horse to reconnoitre. Porus himself, leaving a few elephants to prevent Craterus crossing, had followed, and drew up his army on the sandy Karri plain, to avoid the mud so far as possible. His centre was formed by 200 elephants; behind and between them the

---

[1] Frontinus I, 4, 9 proves that the crossing was made *above* Porus' camp.

infantry were drawn up, with a body of infantry on each wing unprotected by elephants. His best infantry, the archers, carried huge bows capable of shooting a long arrow with great force; but one end of the bow had to be rested on the ground, and the slippery mud handicapped them badly. On either flank were his cavalry, some 3000–4000 altogether. Possibly his left rested on the quicksands of the Sookaytur, and he faced diagonally towards the Jhelum, with the purpose of driving Alexander into it.

Alexander had his heavy infantry in line, with the light-armed on either flank, Seleucus leading the hypaspists and Antigenes the phalanx; he himself with all the cavalry was on the extreme right. Out of bowshot he halted, to breathe the infantry; and Porus, seeing the massed cavalry, brought all his own cavalry round to his left. Alexander began by sending his horse-archers to attack the infantry of Porus' left wing outside the elephants and keep them occupied; his own infantry had orders not to attack till he had defeated Porus' cavalry. He desired to draw that cavalry away from the elephants; he therefore ordered Coenus to take two hipparchies and move off toward Porus' right (Alexander's left); then, when the Indian cavalry, seeing the force opposed to them, should charge, his orders were to take them in rear[1]. If Alexander knew that the Indian cavalry, a weaker force than his own, would charge him, this could only be because he intended to make them do so; the inducement was the division of his force; they would imagine Coenus was going to support the horse-archers, and would see only two hipparchies with Alexander. The plan worked; the Indians attacked Alexander's two hipparchies, and while Alexander met them Coenus swung round and took them in the rear; after a sharp fight they were driven to take refuge behind the elephants. Then the Macedonian line advanced and the elephants attacked them. There was a terrific struggle, but at last the Macedonians won; many elephants were killed, the wounded broke back, and the battle was over. The pursuit was taken up by Craterus, who had crossed the river. Porus, who had fought to the last and was wounded, rode leisurely off on his huge elephant; when finally he surrendered, and Alexander asked him how he would be treated, he replied 'Like a king.' Alexander's losses were carefully concealed, but there is a conclusive proof of the desperate nature of the battle with the elephants—its effect on the minds of the generals (as seen later) and especially on that of Seleucus, who had actually fought with them; when king, he ceded whole provinces in order

[1] A. Bauer (*Festgaben für Max Budinger*, p. 71), by a correct interpretation of Arrian's text (v, 16. 3 *sqq.*), has explained Alexander's manœuvre.

to obtain enough war-elephants, and they became the special arm and symbol of his dynasty[1].

As after Gaugamela, Alexander founded two towns after his victory, Bucephala, named from his horse which died there, and Nicaea on the battlefield; and later a coin was struck to commemorate the battle, showing Alexander pursuing Porus' elephant[2]. Porus became his ally, a protected native ruler; Alexander reconciled him to Taxiles, and greatly enlarged his kingdom. He had already enlarged Taxiles' kingdom, which now stretched to the Jhelum, and relieved him of subjection to Philippus; he meant the two rajahs to balance each other. Abisares, who had not helped his ally, sent envoys and 40 elephants to Alexander, who threatened him with invasion unless he came in person. Alexander now decided that, after reaching the end of 'India,' he would return down the Jhelum and Indus, reducing Sind; he left Craterus with troops to build a fleet and finish the new cities, and himself advanced to the Chenab, keeping near the hills to avoid wide crossings. It was early July, with the rains at their full and the Chenab rising; it flooded him out of his camp, and he had some losses crossing. He left Coenus to bring the transport across, sent Porus home to recruit troops, and advanced to the Hydraotes (Ravi), leaving garrisons along his line of route and detaching Hephaestion southward to conquer the kingdom of Porus' recalcitrant nephew (between Chenab and Ravi), and place it under Porus' rule. He then crossed the Ravi and entered the country of the Cathaeans.

The Aratta generally were regarded as the best fighters in the Punjab; and the Cathaeans had gathered for the defence of their capital Sangala (unidentified; not Sagala-Sialcot), and had formed a triple lager of wagons outside the town. Alexander attacked the lager, himself commanding on the right and Perdiccas on the left; cavalry being useless, he led the phalanx on foot. The lager was taken, but the defenders took refuge in the town; he had to build siege-machines, and ultimately stormed the place and razed it to the ground. The desperate nature of the fighting is shown by the unique admission that Alexander had 1200 wounded, for only the seriously wounded were ever counted. Porus was ordered to garrison the country, and Alexander pushed on to the Hyphasis (Beas), which he probably struck somewhere near Gurdaspur. It

[1] See Volume of Plates ii, 10, b.

[2] A second specimen, recently acquired by the British Museum, shows that the horseman is Alexander. See G. F. Hill in *Brit. Mus. Quarterly*, 1926, no. 2, p. 36, and Pl. xviii b; and Volume of Plates ii, 10, a.

is not certain if it then joined the Sutlej at all; the Sutlej may have helped to form the Hakra, the great lost river of Sind. Possibly the Beas had been the boundary of Darius I[1]; it would agree with what happened.

For at the Beas the army mutinied and refused to go farther. They were tired. The rains had told heavily on them, and they had been shaken by the severe fighting on the Jhelum and at Sangala. Report said that across the Beas was another Aratta people (possibly the Oxydracae are meant) with an unexampled number of very large and brave elephants; after their experience with Porus they had no desire to meet those elephants. But they were even more tired in mind than in body. They had understood the conquest of Persia; but now they did not know what they were doing or where they were going; they wanted to go home.

It was a severe blow to Alexander. True, he could not have gone much farther in any case; half his army was on his communications with Taxila, and he was using Porus' troops for garrisons. But he thought there was not much farther to go; his desire still to advance with his reduced force proves that clearly enough. The intention of conquering the Prasii, *i.e.* the great kingdom of Magadha on the Ganges, with which tradition has credited him, is a later legend; for he knew nothing of the Ganges or Magadha. Undoubtedly traders and students from the east came to Taxila; but the Achaemenids had not known of the Ganges, and any information Alexander obtained, filtered through two interpreters via Persian, would be no clearer to him than what he had got at Bactra from Pharasmanes, whose information about the Aral merely confirmed Alexander's Aristotelian geography. In fact, as the gazetteer of 324–3 conclusively shows, Alexander learnt clearly only of one more (unnamed) river, the Sutlej (or Sutlej-Hakra), and vaguely of one kingdom beyond it, the Gandaridae, which he probably thought lay near the river[2]; and then came, he supposed, the end, *i.e.* Ocean. To turn back meant, not only failure to secure the entire province of 'India,' but failure to solve the problem of Ocean, and above all to provide for the Greeks, in his continental empire, necessary access to a new sea to replace the

---

[1] As suggested by A. V. Williams-Jackson, *Cambridge History of India*, vol. 1, p. 341.

[2] The 'vulgate' identified this river and kingdom with Megasthenes' Ganges and Prasii (Magadha), thus placing Magadha *beyond* the Ganges, leaving out most of Northern India, and transferring to the Ganges Alexander's real intention of crossing the Sutlej. See the writer in *J.H.S.* XLIII, 1923, pp. 93 *sqq.*

home sea they would long for. Once the design of reaching the eastern ocean failed, we see Alexander giving little further thought to the Punjab, and concentrating instead on a second-best plan, the colonization of the Persian Gulf. How much he cared is shown by this, that almost his last act when dying was to discuss Ocean with Nearchus. He would have failed of course even without the mutiny; it was centuries too early, and Ocean was not where he thought. But it was a great dream.

VI. INDIA: FROM THE BEAS TO PATALA

Like Achilles, Alexander retired to his tent, and waited for three days for the army to change its mind; but the army was as stubborn as he. Then he took the omens for crossing, which naturally were unfavourable; he yielded to the gods, set up by the Beas 12 altars, one for each Olympian, at which Chandragupta afterwards sacrificed, and turned back amid the acclamation of his troops. But the actual clash of wills ended in a draw. They had stopped him going forward, but they did not get their desire, an easy return home; he went back by the way he had intended to go all along, and gave them some of the hardest fighting and worst marching of their lives. But he left his arrangements in India an unfinished sketch, to be sponged off the canvas the moment he died. He merely handed over all the country up to the Beas to Porus; and when, in spite of his threats, Abisares still did not come to him, he accepted his excuses, confirmed him in his kingdom as a (nominally) tributary prince, and gave him authority over the neighbouring ruler of Hazāra. Clearly Alexander no longer cared very much what happened east of the Jhelum.

On the Jhelum he completed his half-finished fleet—80 triakontors and some smaller warships, with horse-transports, supply vessels and numerous native boats carrying food; they were organized in divisions, and the flotilla reached the imposing total of 800. Nearchus commanded, and in the simple straightforward Cretan, most honest of chroniclers, Alexander had the right man; Onesicritus steered Alexander's ship. The expenses of equipment were borne by 33 trierarchs—24 prominent Macedonians, 8 Greeks, and one Persian. Before the start Coenus died, a loss to the army. Alexander took on board his favourite troops, the hypaspists, Agrianians, Cretans, and the agema of the Companions; the rest marched in three armies, Craterus on the right bank, Hephaestion with the elephants on the left, and Philippus following; they were accompanied by the contingents of the Indian princes, and a great train of women and children, camp-followers and traders. The start was made early in November 326, with the north wind. Alexander, standing on the prow of his ship, poured libations from a golden cup to his ancestor Heracles and to Ammon; to the rivers, Jhelum, Chenab, and Indus; to the gods of the sea, Poseidon, Amphitrite, and the Nereids; lastly to Ocean himself. Then his trumpets sounded; the wooded banks rang to the shouts of the rowers and the beat of oars; and the vast procession started down the Jhelum towards the sea.

Below the confluence of the Jhelum and the Chenab the armies camped, and Alexander prepared for his last important campaign, that against the Aratta people called Malli (Mahlava), who lived on the lower Ravi. They were said to be in arms, and confederate with the Oxydracae (Ksudraka), who lived eastward along the Beas; but if so they were very ill prepared, and were not barring his road. It is, however, quite probable that their country had been within the Persian sphere. He planned a great drive; he was to cross the waterless Sandar-Bār to the Ravi and work south, driving them on to Hephaestion, who was sent forward; Ptolemy was to guard against a break-back westward. He took his favourite troops, crossed 50 miles of desert, and surprised the first town; the men outside had not their arms, and were simply slaughtered; the town was then taken and no quarter given; Perdiccas took another town and slaughtered the fugitives. But most of the Malli broke eastward across the Ravi; Alexander followed, slew many, and took a town of Brahmans, which resisted desperately; he had to mount the wall first, and practically all the garrison were killed. Their other cities he found empty; he sent out detachments to scour the woods, worked round the main body, drove them back across the Ravi, fought a battle at the ford, and shut up some of them in a town on the west of the river (not Multān). The town was easily taken, but the Indians retired to the citadel; the Macedonians hung back, and Alexander snatched a storming-ladder and went up the wall himself, followed by his shield-bearer, Peucestas, and Leonnatus; Abreas, a corporal, mounted another ladder; then both ladders broke, leaving Alexander and the three on the wall. He leapt down into the citadel, and fought single-handed with his back to the wall till the three joined him; Abreas was killed, and Alexander was shot through corselet and breast by a long arrow. Peucestas covered him in front with the holy shield of Ilium and Leonnatus on one side; a tree prevented attack on the other; they kept the enemy off till the army broke in and slew every living creature there. Alexander was carried out fainting; Perdiccas cut the arrow out with his sword and he fainted again; the report went forth that he was dead. As soon as he could be moved he had himself carried on to a ship and shown to the army.

Among Alexander's campaigns this is unique in its dreadful record of mere slaughter. The explanation probably is that the army hated it; they had no wish to fight, but as they had to, they gave no quarter; they did not mean to be turned back from their way home to quell a fresh rising. Twice Alexander had to mount the wall first to get the men to follow; it was indeed time to go home. Indirectly, this, the least creditable of his campaigns, was to cost him his life, for the wound left him weakened; while it seems to have been among the Brahmans of the Punjab that the reaction started which placed Chandragupta on the throne of a united Northern India, and blotted out nearly every trace of Alexander's rule east of the Indus. For the time being both the Malli and Oxydracae formally submitted.

The progress of the flotilla down the Chenab and the Indus cannot be traced, or the places mentioned be identified, because all the rivers, more especially the Indus, have since altered their course many times. No one can say for certain where the Indus then ran; but most probably it joined the Hakra, and discharged into the Ran of Cutch. Alexander built a few more ships, and founded two Alexandrias on the Indus, one at the confluence of the Indus and the united stream of the four rivers, and another lower down; and he secured the submission of the tribes and rulers he passed, though, as among the Malli, the Brahmans were irreconcilable. At last, about the end of July 325, he reached Patala, where the Indus then bifurcated, and halted to prepare the last stage of the journey. Craterus with the baggage and siege-train, the elephants, the sick and wounded, and those troops not left with Alexander, had been already sent off homeward through the Mulla pass.

Alexander's Indian satrapies may here be noticed. There were Indian peoples west of the Indus; the satrapy of Gandhara, and parts of those of Paropamisadae, Arachosia, and Gedrosia, were of Indian blood. Alexander made separate governments of this Indian belt. Nicanor was apparently dead, killed perhaps in suppressing a revolt in Swat, and his satrapy of Gandhara, with parts of Paropamisadae and of Arachosia, was made into one big satrapy for Philippus, with his seat at the northern Alexandria on the Indus; Eudamus with Thracian troops was left to support him. Philippus, who was related to the royal house, was also called satrap of the Malli and Oxydracae; generally speaking, he represented Alexander's authority in the Punjab, being, as regards

the protected native kings, a kind of Resident. South of his satrapy, another Peithon (not the Bodyguard) was satrap of the rest
of the Arachosian belt, and of the Indus valley and Sind as far as
the sea; his seat was probably the southern Alexandria. The
Indian Oreitae of Gedrosia were presently made a separate satrapy.
The Indian belt west of the Indus was thus divided among three
satraps; its limits westward cannot be defined, but it was these
three satrapies, which contained territory carved out of the old
satrapies of Paropamisadae, Arachosia, and Gedrosia, which
Seleucus later ceded to Chandragupta.

At Patala Alexander began to build a great harbour and docks,
to secure sea connection with the west; he also explored the two
arms of the Indus. The coast of the Delta then ran some 50 miles
north of its present line, and the Ran of Cutch was an estuary. He
first sailed down the western arm, where the fleet was caught by
the bore, the dangerous tidal wave that runs up some Indian
rivers. Naturally alarm was caused, and some ships were destroyed; but he mastered the nature of the phenomenon, sacrificed
as Ammon had taught him, and sailed out into the Indian Ocean;
there he sacrificed and poured a libation to Poseidon and flung his
golden cup into the waves, praying that the sea might bring
Nearchus and the fleet safely home. He then explored the eastern
arm to lake Samārah, ascertained there was no bore, and began to
build a harbour on the lake as a starting-point for Nearchus.
Nearchus, for his voyage to the Persian Gulf, took the triakontors
that remained and some smaller vessels, perhaps 100–150 ships.
The crews would be some 3000–5000 men; he carried a few
archers and mercenaries, and some catapults to cover a landing.
He had no supply-ships; the fleet could carry food for ten days
only, and water at a pinch for five, but practically he had to land
daily for water. There was no question of the *possibility* of reaching
the Gulf, and his instructions were entirely practical, framed with
a view to establishing regular communication by sea between
Indus and Euphrates: he was to examine the beaches, harbours,
islands, and water-supply along the coast, explore any gulfs, find
out if there were any cities, and report what land was fertile and
what barren. In September 325 he dropped down the eastern arm
of the Indus to its mouth. He was timed to start with the N.E.
monsoon (late October); but the local tribes were so threatening
that late in September he put to sea, cutting through the sand-bar
at the mouth. He met contrary winds, and was delayed 24 days at
'Alexander's harbour,' near Kurachi, till he got the monsoon.

VII. GEDROSIA AND SUSA

In September Alexander started for his famous march through southern Gedrosia (the Mekran). He had with him the hypaspists, Agrianians, archers, and seven battalions of the phalanx; the agema of the Companions, the Macedonian squadron from each hipparchy, and the horse-archers, the other native cavalry being sent home. There was nothing foolhardy about it. His object was to support the fleet, which was not self-supporting, by digging wells and forming depôts of provisions; he knew the difficulties, but counted on an increased water-supply after the summer rains. Crossing the Arabis, he received the submission of the Oreitae of Las Bela, founded an Alexandria at their principal village Rhambakia, and made Apollophanes satrap, with orders to collect and forward supplies; with him he left Leonnatus with a strong force, including the Agrianians. He himself returned to the coast and formed a depôt at Cocala. As soon as he left, the Oreitae rose; Leonnatus defeated them, but Apollophanes was killed, and consequently no provisions were forwarded, which upset Alexander's arrangements. He had with him 12,000–15,000 fighting men, beside women, children and camp followers. At first he followed the coast; provisions were not plentiful, and, though he tried to form another depôt, his troops broke his seals and ate the food. But the real trouble began at the river Tomeros. He did not know of the Taloi range; it compelled him to leave the coast and strike inland. The guides lost themselves, and 200 miles of suffering in that desolate country followed. They marched only by night, because of the heat; they ate the baggage-animals and burnt the carts for firewood; all who straggled died. Alexander displayed his greatest qualities as a leader; he sent back his horse and went on foot, and refused water when there was not enough for all. He lost his personal baggage; the hardships endured are illustrated by the disorganization of his surveying section. At last he reached the sea at Pasni, and found enough water, and from Gwadur got the regular route to the royal residence, Pura, where he was able to rest his men. He had extricated the army without great loss, but the mortality among the noncombatants was severe. From Pura he followed the Bampur and Halil Rud rivers to Gulashkird in Carmania, where Craterus rejoined. Craterus had probably come by the Mulla pass, Candahar, and the Seistan lake, and had crossed the Lut by the ordinary route via Nazretabad. How Leonnatus got back is unknown.

Meanwhile Nearchus had left Kurachi. At Cocala he met Leonnatus, obtained provisions from the depôt, and put all shirkers ashore and got fresh men. Thenceforth the log of the fleet resolves itself into the daily search for food and water along the inhospitable coast. Often they only got fish-meal and wild dates; sometimes they ran clean out, and Nearchus could not let the men ashore for fear of desertion. But they had some adventures. They found an enchanted mermaiden's island (Astola); they were alarmed by a school of whales, whom they charged in battle-order to the sound of the trumpet, giving thanks when the frightened monsters dived; and they discovered the Fish-eaters, the first savages any Greek had seen—a hairy stone-age people with wooden spears, who caught fish in the shallows with palm-bark nets and ate them raw or dried them in the sun and ground them into meal, wore fish-skins, and if well-to-do lived in huts built of the bones of stranded whales. At last the fleet sighted Ras Mussendam in Arabia, passed up the straits of Ormuz, and after an 80 days voyage anchored in the Amanis river; they had only lost four ships. Nearchus landed, and after various adventures found Alexander, who had been terribly anxious about the fleet, for he knew what his failure to establish depôts might mean. The reunited army and fleet forgot their hardships in a round of feasting and athletic sports, a necessary holiday, which legend perverted into the story of Alexander, dressed as Dionysus, reeling through Carmania at the head of a drunken rout. An Alexandria was founded at Gulashkird; then both army and fleet proceeded to Susa, which was reached in spring 324.

It was time that Alexander returned; his empire could not function by itself, and he found it in great confusion. Some satraps had enrolled mercenaries and acted as independent rulers; some of the Persian satraps had ill-used and murdered their subjects. Pretenders had appeared in Media and Carmania. The tomb of Cyrus and several temples had been plundered, and two-thirds of the enormous royal stud of horses in Nisaea stolen; three of the generals in Media had joined in the campaign of wrong-doing. Cleomenes in Egypt had been guilty of many abuses; Harpalus had acted as though king, and had already fled to Greece. Alexander was determined not to permit oppression of subjects, and he struck very hard. He put to death the Persian satraps of Persis, Susiana, Carmania, and Media Paraetacene, and also the three generals in Media, including Cleander and Sitalces, who had killed Parmenion. Craterus had already captured the Carmanian pretender; Atropates now brought in the Median, who was executed. Aristobulus was commissioned to restore Cyrus' tomb; and all satraps were ordered to disband mercenaries enlisted for their private service. The vacant satrapies were perforce given to Macedonians. Tlepolemus received Carmania, and Sibyrtius three satrapies, Arachosia, Gedrosia and the Oreitae; the Indian satrapy of Philippus, who had been murdered, was entrusted provisionally to Eudamus and Taxiles. The most important matter was to quiet the minds of the Persians; Peucestas was made a Bodyguard and appointed satrap of Persis and Susiana. Peucestas was ready to carry out Alexander's ideas as he understood them; he adopted Persian dress, learnt Persian, and became extremely popular with his people. One trouble, a revolt of Greek mercenaries in Bactria, was not really overcome; Amyntas was replaced by another Philippus, but the discontent simmered till Alexander died.

At Susa a strange incident happened. Alexander was supposed, while in India, to have been interested in some ascetics, living in meditation in the forest, who told him that his conquests meant nothing at all, and that he owned precisely what they owned, as much ground as you could stand on. One of them, Calanus, accompanied the army, and is said to have taught Lysimachus; but, if his teaching was to master yourself and not others, Lysimachus did not profit by it. At Susa Calanus fell ill, and told Alexander that he desired to live no longer. Alexander demurred; but Calanus had his way, a pyre was built, and the Indian burnt himself alive in the presence of the army, while the trumpets sounded and the elephants gave the royal salute. He was said to have prophesied Alexander's death; he took farewell of the generals but not of Alexander, only saying to him 'We shall meet again at Babylon.'

At Susa too a great feast was held to celebrate the conquest of the Persian empire, at which Alexander and 80 of his officers married girls of the Iranian aristocracy, he and Hephaestion wedding Darius' daughters Barsine and Drypetis. It was an attempt to promote the fusion of Europe and Asia by intermarriage. Little came of it, for many of the bridegrooms were soon to die, and many others repudiated their Asiatic wives after Alexander's death; Seleucus was an honourable and politic exception. At the same time 10,000 of the troops married native women. Alexander undertook to pay the army's debts, and invited all debtors to inscribe their names. It is significant of the growing tension between him and his men that they at once suspected that this was merely a trick to discover those who had exceeded their pay; he thereon paid all comers in cash without asking names. But the tension grew from another cause. The governors of the new cities came bringing for enrolment in the army the 30,000 native youths who had received Macedonian training; this inflamed the discontent already aroused among the Macedonians by several of Alexander's acts, the enrolment of Asiatic cavalry in the hipparchies and of Persian nobles in the agema, and the Persian dress worn by himself and Peucestas. Alexander, they felt, was no longer their own king, but an Asiatic ruler.

VIII. ALEXANDER'S DEIFICATION AND DEATH

It was now that Alexander issued his decree for the return to their cities of all Greek exiles and their families, except the Thebans. His object was twofold. He wished to remove the danger to security involved in this floating mass of homeless men, ready to serve anyone as mercenaries; in this sense the decree was the logical outcome of his order to his satraps to disband their private troops. He also entertained the impossible idea of putting an end to Greek faction-fights, with their accompaniments of banishment and confiscation, and securing unity in the Greek world, even at his own expense; for, just as in the Greek cities of Asia he had for this purpose restrained his friends the democrats, so he now proposed to recall, among others, his enemies, the democrats exiled through Antipater's measures. Antipater had been interfering with the form of government, and the Greek democracies hated him. The story that, after Gaugamela, Alexander had ordered him to abolish his tyrants may not be true; but certainly a necessary condition of unity in Greece was his supersession. The attempt, however, to show that there was bad feeling between Alexander and Antipater is only later propaganda; there was in fact complete mutual loyalty, though doubtless Antipater wearied Alexander with his complaints, however well-founded, about Olympias; Alexander said Antipater could never understand that one tear of Olympias' would outweigh all his despatches. But a new policy required a new man; and Alexander arranged that Craterus and Antipater should change places.

The recall of the exiles was in itself a wise and statesmanlike measure. But it was also a breach of the Covenant of the League of Corinth, which forbade interference with the internal affairs of the constituent states. Of course Alexander's mere existence was a continuing breach of the Covenant, for in some cities his name was keeping a minority in power; the dead pressure on the League due to its President being also the autocrat of Asia was severe. That he could not help. But for his active breach of covenant he contemplated the strange remedy already foreshadowed by his attempt at Bactra to introduce prostration. The Covenant bound Alexander of Macedon; it would not bind Alexander the god; the way therefore to exercise authority in the cities was to become a god. The cities adopted this view, deified Alexander, and thereby, in form, condoned his breach of covenant. Subsequent events, however, seem to show that their action was in many cases an unwilling one, due to fear. If we look at facts, therefore, and not forms, we must conclude that Alexander was not justified in what he did; it was simply the old trouble of the world, doing wrong for a good end. There is nothing to show that he had any intention of doing away with Greek freedom; Craterus' instructions to supervise the freedom of the Hellenes show that the exiles decree was treated as an exceptional measure and that the League was to continue as before. But Alexander had taken the first step on the road of interference in the internal affairs of the cities; and he had sworn not to interfere. That the interference was badly needed does not mend the matter. What it might have led him to, had he lived, cannot be said; we shall see to what it led Antigonus.

It is somewhat uncertain whether Alexander requested the Greek cities to recognize him actually as a god, or only as a son of Zeus. But though the two things had certainly once not been identical, there are sufficient indications that many men no longer drew distinctions between them; and probably Alexander did not. The matter was probably brought before the League states by his partisans in the several cities, but certainly the initiative came from him and not from the Greeks; Hypereides' evidence seems conclusive, and in any case Athens (for instance), irreconcilably opposed to the exiles decree, would not of her own motion have conferred on Alexander the means whereby he could carry that decree into effect without a formal breach of the Covenant (see p. 451). But the fact that the initiative came from Alexander has no real bearing on his character, for his deification had no religious import. To educated Greeks the old State religions were spiritually dead, and Alexander's deification was a product, not of religious feeling, but of disbelief; while to Alexander himself it was merely a political measure adopted for a limited political purpose, to give him a foothold in autonomous Greek cities[1]. Greek cities had deified living men before; and no one now objected except his

---

[1] W. S. Ferguson, *American Historical Review*, 1912, p. 32.

political opponents, or a few old-fashioned people like Antipater, who really thought it impious. The Macedonians themselves were not affected, one way or another; and they were ready enough, at Eumenes' suggestion, to worship Alexander once he was dead.

It was soon afterwards, at Opis, that the discontent in the army came to a head. Alexander was not trying to oust the Macedonians from their ancestral partnership with him, but they thought he was; he only wished to take it up into something larger, but they distrusted the changes entailed by a new world, and especially his Persian policy. The occasion was his proposal to send home with Craterus any veterans past service. The whole army except some of the hypaspists broke into open mutiny; all demanded to go home. Alexander's temper rose; after ordering the hypaspists to arrest the ringleaders, he passionately harangued the troops, and ended by dismissing the whole army from his service: if they wished to go, let them go, every one of them, and boast that they had deserted Alexander. Then, after shutting himself up for two days, he called the Persian leaders to him and began to form a Persian army. This broke down the Macedonians; they gathered before his quarters, crying that they would not go away till he had pity on them. He came out and stood before them, with tears running down his face; one began to say 'You have made Persians your kinsmen,' and he broke in 'But I make you all my kinsmen.' The army burst into wild cheers; those who would kissed him; the reconciliation was complete. He made a banquet for 9000 men of the army, at which the Macedonians sat above the Persians and next himself; and after the libations he prayed for a union of hearts and a joint commonwealth of the two peoples. Those veterans who desired (10,000) were then sent home with large presents under Craterus' leadership.

That autumn at Ecbatana his friend Hephaestion died, a severe blow to the king. Hephaestion was hardly popular; he had feuds with Craterus, Eumenes, and Olympias; but Alexander clung to him as his second self, the one man who could understand. He had revived for him the Persian office of chiliarch (vizier), which to Asiatics made him the second man in the empire, and had probably, after returning from India, collected what remained of the original Companions into one hipparchy, and given him the command. He now ordered that a royal pyre should be built in Babylon and Hephaestion be honoured as a hero. Hephaestion's command was not filled up; his hipparchy was to bear his name for ever. No new chiliarch was appointed, but probably Perdiccas did the duties of the office. Alexander relieved his sorrow by a successful winter campaign in the hills of Luristan against the Cossaeans, who perhaps had demanded their customary black-mail for passage through their land. In the spring of 323 he returned to Babylon, which was destined for his capital; there envoys came to him from the Libyans and from three peoples of Italy—the Bruttians and Lucanians, who feared vengeance for the death of Alexander of Epirus, his brother-in-law, and the Etruscans, who desired freedom of the seas for their piracies.

He now again attacked the secret of the ocean. He sent Hera-cleides to explore the Hyrcanian sea, and ascertain if it might not after all be a gulf of Ocean—an old theory, known to but discarded by Aristotle; the project was abandoned on his death. He himself turned his attention to the Persian Gulf. He took steps to ensure better communication between Babylonia and the sea by removing the Persian obstacles to free navigation of the Tigris and founding an Alexandria on the Gulf, which, refounded later as Charax-Mesene, became an important trade centre; and he began to build a vast harbour-basin for merchantmen at Babylon. He also planned to colonize the eastern coast of the Gulf, along which Nearchus had sailed, and sent 500 talents to Sidon to be coined for the hire or purchase of sailors and colonists. This would help to establish the already explored sea-route between India and Babylon; but he meant to complete the sea-route from India to Egypt by exploring the section between Babylon and Egypt and circumnavigating Arabia, possibly as a preliminary to still more extensive maritime exploration in the future. He therefore planned an expedition along the Arabian coast, and for this purpose had a few larger warships, including quinqueremes, built in sections in Phoenicia, carried to Thapsacus, and floated down the Eu-phrates. It was to be primarily a naval expedition, though supported by troops, and the *Journal* shows that he himself was going with the fleet; it was reported that he did not mean to make Arabia a province under a satrap. He knew little of Arabia except the districts bordering on Babylonia and Syria, once subject (rather nominally) to Persia; Nearchus had sighted Ras Mussendam, but it might have been an island. Being ignorant of its size, he attempted a preliminary circumnavigation from both sides; he sent a ship south from the gulf of Suez which reached the incense-land of Yemen and heard of the Hadramaut, and three triakontors down the Persian Gulf. One discovered the island of Bahrein; Hieron of Soli, whose orders were to sail round to Suez, followed the Arabian coast down to Ras Mussendam, and wisely reported that Arabia must be nearly as big as India.

While the fleet was preparing, Alexander sailed down the Euphrates to study the Babylonian canal-system, and especially the Pallakopas cut, which carried off the flood water of the river; it was not working well, and he devised a better method for keeping the Euphrates at the proper level for irrigation; he also founded a city on the Chaldean side of the lower Euphrates as an outpost toward Arabia. The story was told that on the voyage his diadem blew off and lodged on a rush; a sailor swam out for it, and to keep it dry placed it on his head; later a legend grew up that the man who for a moment had worn Alexander's diadem was Seleucus. On his return to Babylon Alexander is said to have remodelled the phalanx, incorporating Persian light-armed, a step in which some have detected a knowledge of the Roman legion; later tactical manuals mention its occasional employment. Antipater's eldest son Cassander now came to him, to answer accusations against Antipater made by some Illyrians and Thracians. Also there came many envoys from Greece, with petitions on innumerable questions raised by the exiles decree; they came garlanded, as though they had been religious envoys sent to a god.

They set the stage for the final scene. For in the midst of his preparations for the Arabian expedition Alexander was struck down by a fever, which his constitution, weakened by overexertion and wounds, could not throw off. The *Journal* relates that for some days he continued his preparations, offering the usual sacrifices and discussing the coming expedition with his generals and Ocean with Nearchus, till he became too ill to move; then he was carried into Nebuchadrezzar's palace, already past speech. The army insisted on seeing him, and would take no denial; in silence the veterans filed through the room where the dying man lay, just able to raise his head in token of recognition and farewell. That night several of the generals inquired of some Babylonian god[1] if Alexander should be brought into his temple; the oracle replied that it would be best for him where he was. Two days later, at sunset, he died; for that was best. He died on the 13th of June 323; he was not yet 33 years old, and had reigned twelve years and eight months.

---

[1] It is not the *Journal* but Ptolemy who, for his own purposes, calls this god Sarapis.

IX. ALEXANDER'S CHARACTER AND POLICY

He was fortunate in his death. His fame could hardly have increased; but it might perhaps have been diminished. For he died with the real task yet before him. He had made war as few have made it; it remained to be seen if he could make peace. He had, like Columbus, opened up a new world; it remained to be seen what he could do with it. No man since has possessed so unquestionably the strongest power upon earth; had he desired, he could have conquered Carthage or Rome, just as (so Chandragupta said) he could have conquered northern India. But he could have done nothing with them had he conquered them; he could do nothing even with the Punjab. But there is no reason to suppose that he had formed any design of world-conquest; the belief that he had rests on a late and unauthentic compilation which passed as his 'Memoirs,' and attributed to him a scheme for the conquest of the countries round the Mediterranean, a scheme which the Romance afterwards made him carry into effect. In fact, he had not yet completed the conquest of the one-time Persian empire; a great block of territory stretching from Heraclea to the Caspian—Paphlagonia, Cappadocia, Pontus, Armenia, the Cadusii of Gilan—had become independent. His desire to reach the eastern Ocean had, as already noticed, nothing to do with world-conquest, *i.e.* with a desire to round off his empire on all sides with Ocean; had it had, he would not have turned at the Jaxartes, where (with Aristotle) he thought Ocean quite close, and he would have sent Heracleides to conquer, and not explore, the Caspian. He never even, like the Achaemenids, called himself King of Kings. That he aimed at world-dominion, as many believe, is a legend which derives ultimately from the Amon-ritual, in which Amon promised to many Pharaohs the dominion of the earth; it can only be supported, if at all, on the ground that, if Alexander desired to fuse the peoples under his rule in a common polity and culture, he must necessarily have desired so to fuse all peoples. As a theory this is open to belief, like any theory; but history has no right to attribute any such ideas to Alexander[1]. What he would have aimed at, had he lived, we do not know; we can only try to see what he was and what he did.

His personality was adequate to great tasks. Aristotle had presumably taught him that man's highest good lay in right activity of the soul; he had modified this for himself into strenuous energy of soul and body both. He had crowded as much into his short life as

[1] This view has been defended by the writer in *J.H.S.* xli, 1921, pp. 1 *sqq*

he could; when he died, his body was half worn out. But his vitality of mind was unimpaired; and his mind could generally make his body do what it chose. For, as Plutarch says, he thought it more kingly to conquer himself than others; and he gives a strangely vivid impression of one whose body was his servant. This is the key to his attitude toward women; apart from his mother, he apparently never cared for any woman; he apparently never had a mistress[1], and his two marriages were mere affairs of policy. When he called his beautiful Persian captives 'painful to the eyes,' what he meant is, in Plutarch's narrative, fairly obvious[2]: women were merely incitements to the rebellion of the body. The phenomenon has since become well known; but it made Alexander, to his contemporaries, seem either more, or less[3], than a man. It meant a will of iron; but even his will was inadequate for one end, the control of his temper. The son of Olympias was bound to be shaken by devastating gusts of passion; but though this showed in impatience, in irritability, in decisions repented of later, only once, apparently, did he absolutely lose control; then his wrath swept to its goal in total disregard of every other consideration, human or divine. The murder of Cleitus gives a fearful glimpse of the wild beast in him that he had to keep chained; his anguish after the deed was perhaps not only for his friend but for himself. It gives too a glimpse of the power of will that could usually keep such a beast chained. But if his temperament led him sometimes to grievous acts of injustice, it led him also to acts of justice far in advance of his time, like his unheard-of step of ordering Parmenion to put two Macedonians on trial for rape and kill them like animals if convicted. What his force of character was like can be best seen, not in his driving power, great as it was, but in his relations with his generals. Here was an assembly of kings, with passions, ambitions, abilities, beyond those of most men; and, while he lived, all we see is that Perdiccas and Ptolemy were good brigade-leaders, Antigonus an obedient satrap, Lysimachus and Peithon little-noticed members of the Staff; even on the masterful Cassander he so imposed himself during their brief acquaintance that Cassander, when king himself, could not pass a statue of Alexander without shivering.

[1] For 'Barsine,' see the writer, *J.H.S.* XLI, 1921, p. 18. Their sons' ages show that Thais was Ptolemy's mistress when at Persepolis: Dittenberger, *S.I.G.*[3] 314; *Justin* XV, 2, 7.

[2] That the words *may* be a quotation does not affect the sense in which they were used.

[3] Theophrastus and others in Athenaeus X, 434, F *sq.*

These are some of the things that seem to stand out most clearly in his picture. But there was another side, which cannot be overlooked; a romanticism which was kindled by the exploits of Achilles and Heracles, Semiramis and Cyrus, and burst into flame under the glamour of the East; something too of the mystic which set him apart from others as the man whom Ammon had counselled, and who possibly felt himself an instrument of the gods. From this side of him, obscurely as we see it, sprang what was probably the most important thing about him: he was a great dreamer. To be mystical and intensely practical, to dream greatly and to do greatly, is not given to many men; it is this combination which gives Alexander his place apart in history. There were of course terrible crimes in his record—the destruction of Thebes, the murder of Parmenion, the Massaga massacre—the sins of a young and imperious man who meant to rule because he could. None need palliate them; perhaps those only who have known the temptations of power can judge.

That he was a great general is certain; Napoleon's verdict suffices. The few who have doubted have either believed the fantastic legend which makes the Persian armies huge useless mobs, or have suggested that his success was due to Parmenion and the Staff. Alexander started of course with the advantage of Philip's army; but Parmenion's death made no apparent difference, while his Staff in Turkestan and India were men he had trained himself. Probably he was not tested to the full, unless at Tyre and on the Jhelum; but that he would have been equal to almost any test is shown by the manner in which he met every opponent with different but appropriate tactics; he handled the unknown foe—desert Turcomans, Indian hill-tribes, Porus' elephants—with the same certainty as Greek hoplites or Persian cavalry. If he charged himself, so did every general before Hannibal; the use of reserves was practically unknown, and the moral effect all-important (see however p. 16). In fact, he did use something like reserves at Gaugamela, and did not charge there till they were all in. He was a master in the combination of various arms; he taught the world the advantages of campaigning in winter, the value of pressing pursuit to the utmost, and the principle of 'march divided, fight united.' He marched usually in two divisions, one conducting the impedimenta and his own travelling light; his speed of movement was extraordinary. It is said that he attributed his military success to 'never putting anything off.' He understood absolutely how to keep his men's affection; and though their moral broke at the Beas, he had maintained it intact during eight strenuous years. He discovered the value of amusements in this respect, and held athletic and musical contests at every important halting-place. The enormous distances traversed in unknown country imply a very high degree of organizing ability; in ten years he had only two serious breakdowns, his intelligence before Issus and his commissariat in Gedrosia, the latter partly due to the bad luck of Apollophanes' death. The truth is, that his success was too complete. Perfect success invariably looks easy; but had a lesser man attempted what he achieved, and failed, we should have heard enough of the hopeless military difficulties of the undertaking. Did Crassus or Antony find the invasion of Persia easy?

Whether he was a great statesman is a more difficult question. Our information is inadequate, and his work was only beginning when death cut it short; no formal answer is possible. Something was wanted to divert his energy whole-heartedly from war and exploration to administration. The chaos in his empire when he returned from India should have called out his powers in this direction; but he was pre-occupied with the completion of the sea-route from India to Egypt, and he merely hanged some satraps and appointed others. Unless in the Punjab, he had nowhere gone beyond the boundaries of Darius I; and he naturally retained the Persian system of satraps. But it does not follow that that system would have been his last word. He abolished it in Egypt, and substituted an arrangement more enlightened than that which the Ptolemies subsequently adopted; he partially abolished it in the Punjab, where his satrap was only a Resident. Even in Iran it may have been largely provisional. For if, as is probable, the Alexandrias were meant to be satrapal seats, then there were too many of them, e.g. three in Bactria-Sogdiana and two in Arachosia. The separation of the Indian districts west of the Indus, and the formation of little satrapies like those of Media Paraetacene and the Oreitae, coupled with the number of Alexandrias, suggest that he may have meant ultimately to break up the great satrapies into smaller and more manageable units, a gain to centralization. In any event he greatly restricted the satraps' powers; they lost the right to collect taxes and (except at Babylon) to strike coins, while the chief fortresses were held by governors directly responsible to himself. Any subject who was wronged could, as in Macedonia, appeal to Alexander direct. For anything but satrapal government in some form Asia was not ripe; whether it would ripen must depend on the measures adopted to that end, and time. It will be convenient to consider Alexander's measures for his empire generally under four heads: finance, cities, fusion, and the general question of co-ordination. His dealings with the Greek cities have already been considered (p. 355, p. 371). To treat the Greeks as free allies was indeed a most statesmanlike policy, which offered the one chance of Greek unity, had the Greeks been willing to co-operate; but the policy was largely originated by Philip.

X. FINANCE AND THE NEW CITIES

Alexander's financial superintendents were a new and important thing, and the system survived his death. Probably they and their district subordinates were meant to form a comprehensive Civil Service, with Harpalus at its head, which would link up king and peasant. Unfortunately we do not know in what relation they stood to the satraps, or how the latter obtained the necessary funds for administering their satrapies. Harpalus' position however was superior to that of any satrap; he could give the satraps orders, and this explains how he tried to lord it as king during Alexander's absence, an extraordinary phenomenon in a civilian without military powers. His successor Antimenes introduced the first known scheme of insurance. The system should have benefited the peasantry by preventing indiscriminate exactions; and we hear of no complaint that taxes were too high. But during Alexander's absence it did not work well. Harpalus, himself corrupt, was not the man to repress exactions; the satraps, by ways familiar in Asia, got money enough to raise private armies; and a surviving document gives rather a lurid account of the sins of some of the financial officials. It may be liberally discounted, for it represents an attempt by some Peripatetic to belittle Alexander's administration; but the doings of the worst offender, Cleomenes, are corroborated from better sources. True, his famous corner in grain did not hurt the Egyptian cultivator, to whom he paid the usual price, even if his prohibition of any export but his own half ruined the Egyptian middleman; and he probably thought it clever to make huge profits out of Greek cities for the benefit of Alexander's treasury. That Alexander for other reasons condoned his proceedings is one of the most disappointing things about him.

Of great importance was the coinage. The problem was to reconcile the decimal coinage of Persia (1 gold daric = 20 silver sigloi) with the duodecimal of Philip II (1 gold stater, Attic standard = 24 silver drachmae, Phoenician standard). Alexander did it by reverting to a silver monometallism and adopting the Attic standard, thus making the stater = 20 silver drachmae, which, though lighter than sigloi, were accepted in Asia. He thus refrained from competing with Athens' coinage, and practically made her a trade partner; but he demonetized the Persian gold, for as the hoarded treasures of Darius began to circulate gold fell below Philip's basic ratio, and the daric became bullion. The uniform coinage powerfully promoted trade, but whether the credit for the adoption of the Attic standard as an auxiliary in conquering Asia belongs to Alexander may be doubted; for as he adopted the new standard the moment Philip died, it may be that Philip had already decided on the change. Only two countries disliked the new coinage—conservative India, and the Balkans, which Alexander had neglected. He continued to use nearly all the existing Persian mints, except Tyre and Gaza. But his principal mint was at Amphipolis, with Babylon second in importance; next came the Phoenician group (Sidon, Byblus, Ake, Damascus), the Cilician (Tarsus and Alexandria by Issus, with the independent Cyprian mints), and Alexandria in Egypt; there were many others, including Pella and Sicyon. His mints must have been controlled by royal officials, but to whom these were responsible is unknown; Tarsus however became the financial centre for Asia Minor and the eastern Mediterranean, and Harpalus had his seat there as well as at Babylon. But Alexander showed his wisdom by not forcing the new coinage wholesale on the great trading centres, Phoenicia, Cilicia, and Babylon; there he still permitted the old coinage to be struck also, as a temporary measure.

These were two great financial reforms. But the treasury still remained identical with the king's privy purse; and when Alexander's natural generosity and his enormous expenditure are considered, one wonders whether, had he lived, he would have been able to balance his accounts. He gave 2000 talents to the Thessalians and allies, and a talent each to the 10,000 discharged Macedonian veterans; 20,000 talents were used to pay the army's debts, and 15,000 for gold crowns for the generals; at the marriages at Susa he gave dowries to 80 noble Persian girls and 10,000 women of the people; he allocated 10,000 talents to Hephaestion's pyre and (possibly) 10,000 to restore temples in Hellas; and there were presents for Indian princes, artistes, and learned men, including 800 talents for Aristotle's researches. He had too an amazing programme of works in hand when he died; it included many unfinished cities; the new docks and harbours at Patala and Babylon; improved harbour-works at Clazomenae and Erythrae; the rebuilding of E-sagila, destroyed by Xerxes, where the arduous work of merely clearing the site of ruins was still going on in 310; the restoration and amelioration of the Babylonian canal system; the draining of Lake Copais. Except Hephaestion's pyre, most of this expenditure was justifiable in itself. The army was entitled to share Darius' gold; the dowries were part of a great policy; the Indian princes gave as much as they received; most of the works would have been remunerative, and E-sagila was provided for by special local taxation. But if we add the expenses of the war, and the money squandered and stolen by Harpalus, the tradition may be correct that, in spite of Alexander's large (unknown) revenue, out of all the treasure he had secured only 50,000 talents remained at his death.

We come to the cities. Isocrates had advised Philip to build cities in Asia; and Alexander was the greatest city-builder of all time. He is said to have founded 70; some 25 are known for certain. The conditions of foundation varied greatly. There were absolutely new cities, like Alexandria in Egypt and Chodjend; royal residences or old sites turned into cities, like Candahar and Herat; existing towns enlarged and hellenized, like Alexandretta. Besides these, there were towns that failed and were refounded by others, like Merv; towns that he planned and others built, like Smyrna; towns that other builders attributed to him or that attributed themselves; lastly, towns given him by romance, like Samarcand and Sian-fu. In this respect his successors carried out his policy whole-heartedly; all caught his inspiration and became great builders. He initiated what became a vast scheme of colonization in Asia, differing from the older Greek colonization in that it was deliberately planned, that many cities were not on the sea, and that the settlers were not drawn from single cities but were mixed. The typical Alexandria was settled with Greek mercenaries, traders, natives, and a few Macedonians. But this was only to start with. For the Greek mercenaries had native wives, and were not the best medium for the spread of Greek culture; Alexander probably meant to send out further settlers, and above all European women; otherwise the towns would soon have become simply Asiatic, for nationality depends primarily on the mother. That Asia was not more hellenized than it was arose simply from there not being enough Greeks in the world. They had to be collected into comparatively few towns; they never spread over the country. It has been suggested that it would have been better for Greek civilization had Alexander confined his conquests to Asia

Minor, which could have been governed from Europe, and attempted a more intensive hellenization. In this event, however, Greeks would not have secured a share in the great trade routes; they could not do both.

Simple hellenization, moreover, was not his object; and he did not, like Eumenes and possibly Antigonus, propose to oust any Iranian landowners. As his marriage to Roxane had guaranteed her class, and he meant the Iranian landowners and the new towns to co-exist, it cannot be supposed that his ultimate aim was an empire divided up into city states; for, as the new towns were designed to promote the fusion of Europe and Asia on a basis of Greek culture, they were probably not autonomous Greek cities (or they must have possessed city-land), but a new mixed type. Except for Doura-Europos, founded by Antigonus I's general Nicanor after Alexander's model, much of what we know about Alexander's towns relates to Alexandria in Egypt, and there it is impossible to distinguish what is original and what not; but the *type* was doubtless due to Alexander, for Ptolemy I's foundation Ptolemaïs was an autonomous Greek city. A provisional sketch of one of the Alexandrias under Alexander may therefore be attempted. It was founded on King's land, and the succession law of Doura-Europos shows that the land given it for settlers' allotments remained King's land, the king retaining the right of escheat; it had no city-land. The town itself would consist of a Greek corporation and probably other national corporations —Thracians, Persians, etc.—each possessing certain quasi-autonomous rights; probably also a few privileged Macedonians, and some local natives. The Greek corporation was much the most important; they were 'the citizens,' 'the Alexandrians.' The constitutive law of the city, given by Alexander, created officials of Greek type and prescribed their duties; these must have acted for the whole city, *e.g.* the astynomi would look after *all* the streets, whatever the nationality of the householders. It seems probable that there was neither Council nor Assembly; but there were autonomous Greek law-courts which, independently of the king, administered a body of private law formed by royal rescripts and the 'city law,' this last a code based on, or taken bodily from, that of some leading Greek city. This code may have been settled by a commission (nomographi) appointed at Alexander's instance; but doubtless in the more remote foundations he merely ordered that some well-known code should be adopted. The important thing is that *all* the inhabitants were in practice subject, not only to the king's rescripts, largely based on Greek legal conceptions, but

probably also to the 'city law[1],' which was in principle the personal
law of the Greek 'citizens'; at Doura the succession to all allotments was regulated by Greek law. Thus there might develop a
territorial law embracing the whole city; and possibly Alexander
deliberately meant to use Greek law, rather than political rights,
as one means of unifying these mixed city populations. One recalls that his financial superintendents leased King's land in Asia
according to Greek law.

Politically these towns, unlike the Greek cities, were subject to
governors appointed by Alexander, and possibly to his satraps.
They thus approximated somewhat to the native subject towns;
and it is related that the Greeks settled in the far East refused to
regard this mixed system as Hellenic 'life and training.' Whether
Alexander intended that these towns should, after a period of pro-
bation, acquire full autonomous Greek rights cannot be said;
possibly some did later. The gift of King's land to a number of
towns would diminish the royal revenue; probably therefore the
allottees paid an equivalent in taxes, whether directly or through
the towns.

XI. THE EMPIRE: ALEXANDER'S PERSONALITY

Next, Alexander's policy of the fusion of races. It was a great
and courageous dream, which, as he planned it, failed. Greek
blood had once been mixed with Asiatic (Carian) in Ionia with
good results, and Alexander might fairly suppose that a Graeco-
Persian blend would be successful; he could not guess that the
intermarriage of Europe and further Asia would often result in the
loss of the good qualities of both. But it is doubtful whether, even
had he lived, he could have carried out his idea of a joint commonwealth; for his system of Iranian satraps had broken down before
he died. Of eighteen appointed, two soon died, one retired, and
two are not again heard of; but ten were either removed for
incompetence or executed for murder of subjects or treason,
and were replaced by Macedonians. The three who alone held
office when Alexander died were doubtless good men; nevertheless Atropates certainly, and Oxyartes possibly[2], ended by
founding independent Iranian kingdoms, while from Phrataphernes' satrapy of Parthia-Hyrcania came later the main
Iranian reaction. In fact, Alexander had come into conflict

[1] The Jewish community in the Egyptian Alexandria was subsequently
an exception.
[2] A. de la Fuye, *Revue Numismatique*, 1910, pp. 281 *sqq.*

with the idea of nationality, which was exhibited, not merely in the national war fought by Sogdiana, but in the way in which, even during his lifetime, independent states like Cappadocia and Armenia under Iranian rulers arose along the undefined northern limits of his empire. But of course, owing to his death, his policy never had a fair trial. The Seleucid kings indeed, half Sogdian in blood, were a direct outcome of that policy, and they did carry out parts of it; they transferred Europeans to Asia, employed, though sparingly, Asiatics in high position, and produced a marvellous mixture of east and west. But it was not done on Alexander's lines or in his spirit; the Macedonian meant to be, and was, the dominant race. What Alexander did achieve was again done through the cities, both his own and those which he inspired Seleucus to found, and it was a great enough achievement; the cities radiated Greek culture throughout Asia till ultimately the bulk of the upper classes over considerable districts became partially hellenized, and for the second time certain Hellenic elements crossed the Hindu Kush from Bactria into India. What he did succeed in ultimately giving to parts of western Asia was not political equality with Greece, but community of culture.

Lastly, we have to consider the question of the co-ordination of the empire. That empire was even more complicated than the British. In Egypt Alexander was an autocrat and a god. In Iran he was an autocrat, but not a god. In the Greek cities he was a god, but not an autocrat. In Macedonia he was neither autocrat nor god, but a quasi-constitutional king over against whom his people enjoyed certain customary rights. In Thessaly he was the elected head for life of the Thessalian League; in the Amphictyonic League a man who owned two votes. The greater number of the Greek cities of Asia and Europe (outside Italy and Sicily) were his free and independent allies, in respect of whom his rights and duties were formulated and limited by the Covenant of the League of Corinth; but many Greek cities both in Europe and Asia had no relations with him at all. The Phoenician kings were subject allies; the Cyprian kings were free allies, who coined gold, the token of independence. Persepolis possibly kept her native priest-kings, from whom was to spring the Sassanian dynasty; the High Priests still governed Judaea according to the Law; the temple states of Asia Minor retained their strange matriarchal and theocratic social system unchanged. To the Iranian land-owners he was feudal superior. In Lydia and Babylon he had voluntarily limited his autocracy by native custom; Caria retained her native league of Zeus Chrysaoreus; part of Seistan was autonomous. With the peoples of the Punjab he had no point of contact; their real organization was the village community, and Alexander was merely the suzerain of certain rajahs who happened to be ruling certain groups of villages. The co-ordination of this heterogeneous mass of rights was not going to be achieved by Alexander claiming (as some believe he claimed) to be the divine ruler of the inhabited world.

Fortunately there is no reason for attributing to him any such idea. He was deified in 324 by and for the Greek world only, as a limited political measure; Greece apart, his deification had no bearing on the co-ordination of his empire. He did not claim to be the only god, or even the supreme god. There is no trace of any common official cult of himself in his empire; his head does not (as it would then have done) appear on the Alexander-coinage; his successor in the empire, Philip III, was not even a god at all, except in Egypt. That Alexander, like every Pharaoh, was divine in Egypt has no bearing on the matter; the point is, that he was not divine in Iran. Zoroastrianism knew nothing of, and had no place for, deified men; and it is noteworthy that on the coins which Agathocles of Bactria struck to commemorate his predecessors, though the Greeks Diodotus and Euthydemus are gods, Alexander is not[1]. We cannot read back into the tentative events of Alexander's life considerations which, if they arise at all, arise from the more extended worship of him under his successors and from the phenomena of Roman Imperialism.

Whether indeed he ever meant to try to co-ordinate his empire, and if so how, we do not know. It is unlikely that he had any cut and dried theories on the subject; but he had initiated various measures which, in their degree, made for unity, and he would probably have gone on in the same way, step by step, taking things as they arose. Trade, the coinage, the new mixed cities, might do something; something more might be done by inter-marriage, by training native youths in Graeco-Macedonian fashion, by giving Persians a share in the government. Babylon was probably selected for capital as being neutral ground between Greek and Persian, though it is not certain that Alexandria in Egypt was not meant to be a joint capital. But the true unifying force was lacking; there was no common idea, or ideal. The United States has turned men of many countries into Americans by force of the American idea. Britain and the Dominions are held together by a common idea stronger than any formal bond. There

---

[1] See Volume of Plates ii, 10, c.

was no equivalent in Alexander's empire; there was no common
term even between Greek and Persian. To two of the great contributions made by Greece to the world's progress, freedom of
action (so far as it went) and freedom of thought, Persia was a
stranger; and to incorporate Persia in the empire at all Alexander
had to diminish Greek freedom of action; his new cities were
probably not autonomous Greek foundations, and with the Greek
cities themselves he began to interfere. But if Persia could only
be incorporated by lowering Greek political values, then politically the empire stood condemned from the start.

Security of course it could and would have given, had Alexander lived; and behind that shield it might have developed those
possibilities of ethical and intellectual progress which constituted
Alexander's greatest gift to Asia, and might, given time enough,
have achieved complete unity of culture and therefrom created a
common idea. But all this was hypothetical, and dependent on
a single life; and, as a fact, up to Alexander's death, the empire
was held together solely by himself and his (mixed) army; that is,
it resembled the empire of the Hapsburgs. And a further source
of weakness was that the ultimate care of everything—the army,
administration, law,—fell upon himself personally, entailing a
stupendous amount of work; probably only his habit of occasionally sleeping for 36 hours kept him going; certainly toward the
end he was growing more impatient and irritable. His one attempt
at comprehensive delegation turned out unhappily, owing to
Harpalus' unworthiness. Nevertheless, had he lived his full term,
and trained a son, his empire, for all its defects politically, might
well have achieved a cohesion beyond our belief; it needed the
supreme shock of all history to break up that of the Hapsburgs,
and we have to reckon, as a moulding force, with Alexander's
astounding personality.

For when all is said, we come back at the end to his personality;
not the soldier or the statesman, but the man. Whatever Asia did
or did not get from him, she *felt* him as she has scarcely felt any
other; she knew that one of the greatest of the earth had passed.
Though his direct influence vanished from India within a generation, and her literature does not know him, he affected Indian
history for centuries; for Chandragupta saw him and deduced the
possibility of realizing in actual fact the conception, handed down
from Vedic times, of a comprehensive monarchy in India; hence
Alexander indirectly created Asoka's empire and enabled the
spread of Buddhism. Possibly his example even inspired the
unification of China under the first Han dynasty. Both flanks of the
Hindu Kush are still crowded with the imagined descendants of

the man who left none to succeed him; in Chitral, Gilgit, Hunza, and elsewhere on the Indian side they cluster thick, in places intermarrying only with each other; the white Kafirs are his Macedonians; in the middle ages his line still ruled even at Minnagara in the Indus Delta. Northward his descendants are found in Wakhan, Darwas, Karategin, Badakshan, and Ferghana; in Margelan of Ferghana his red silk banner is shown, and his tomb honoured as a shrine; the Mirs of Badakshan used to cherish a debased Greek patera as an heirloom, and their very horses descended from Bucephalas. Along the Indian frontier innumerable traditions attach to his name. But all the countries claimed him as theirs. In Persian story he became a son of Ochus by Philip's daughter; in Egyptian, a son of the last native Pharaoh, the magician Nectanebo, who in the guise of Ammon had deceived Olympias. In Jewish legend he was the Two-horned, the precursor of the Messiah; and as Dhulcarnein, the Two-horned, he became one of the heroes of Islam. The Bedouin thought that Napoleon was Iskander come again; in France he ended as a knight of chivalry, in Abyssinia as a Christian saint.

Hardly was he dead when legend became busy with his terrible name, and strove to give him that world-kingdom which he never sought in life. Around him the whole dream-world of the East took shape and substance; of him every old story of a divine world-conqueror was told afresh. More than eighty versions of the Alexander-romance, in twenty-four languages, have been collected, some of them the wildest of fairy-tales; they range from Britain to Malaya; no other story in the world has spread like his. Long before Islam the Byzantines knew that he had traversed the Silk Route and founded Chubdan, the great Han capital of Sianfu; while the Graeco-Egyptian Romance made him subdue both Rome and Carthage, and compensated him for his failure to reach the eastern Ocean by taking him through the gold and silver pillars of his ancestor Heracles to sail the western. In Jewish lore he becomes master of the Throne of Solomon, and the High Priest announces him as ruler of the fourth world-kingdom of Daniel's prophecy; he shuts up Gog and Magog behind the Iron Gate of Derbend, and bears on his shoulders the hopes of the whole earth; one thing alone is forbidden him, to enter the cloud-girdled Earthly Paradise. The national legend of Iran, in which the man who in fact brought the first knowledge of the Avesta to Europe persecutes the fire-worshippers and burns the sacred book, withers away before the romance of the world-ruler; in Persian story he conquers India, crosses Thibet, and subdues the Faghfur of China with all his dependencies; then he turns and goes northward across Russia till he comes to the Land of Darkness. But Babylon, as was fitting, took him farthest; for the Babylon-inspired section of the Romance knows that he passed beyond the Darkness and reached the Well of Life at the world's end, on the shores of the furthest ocean of them all.

The real impress that he left on the world was far different; for, whatever else he was, he was one of the supreme fertilizing forces of history. He lifted the civilized world out of one groove and set it in another; he started a new epoch; nothing could again be as it had been. He greatly enlarged the bounds of knowledge and of human endeavour, and gave to Greek science and Greek civilization a scope and an opportunity such as they had never yet possessed. Particularism was replaced by the idea of the 'inhabited world,' the common possession of civilized men; trade and commerce were internationalized, and the 'inhabited world' bound together by a network both of new routes and cities, and of common interests. Greek culture, heretofore practically confined to Greeks, spread throughout that world; and for the use of its inhabitants, in place of the many dialects of Greece, there grew up the form of Greek known as the *Koinē*, the 'common speech.' The Greece that taught Rome was the Hellenistic world which Alexander made; the old Greece counted for little till modern scholars re-created Periclean Athens. So far as the modern world derives its civilization from Greece, it largely owes it to Alexander that it had the opportunity. If he could not fuse races, he transcended the national state; and to transcend national states meant to transcend national cults; men came to feel after the unity which must lie beneath the various religions. Outwardly, this unity was ultimately satisfied in the official worship of the Roman Emperor, which derived from Alexander's claim to divinity; but beside this external form there grew up in men's hearts the longing for a true spiritual unity. And it was Alexander who created the medium in which the idea, when it came, was to spread. For it was due to him that Greek civilization penetrated western Asia; and even if much of the actual work was done by his successors, he broke the path; without him they would not have been. Consequently, when at last Christianity showed the way to that spiritual unity after which men were feeling, there was ready to hand a medium for the new religion to spread in, the common Hellenistic civilization of the 'inhabited world'; without that, the conquests made by Christianity might have been as slow and difficult as they became when the bounds of that common civilization were overpassed.

But if the things he did were great, one thing he dreamt was greater. We may put it that he found the Ideal State of Aristotle, and substituted the Ideal State of Zeno. It was not merely that he overthrew the narrow restraints of the former, and, in place of limiting men by their opportunity, created opportunities adequate for men in a world where none need be a pauper and restrictions on population were meaningless. Aristotle's State had still cared nothing for humanity outside its own borders; the stranger must still be a serf or an enemy. Alexander changed all that. When he prayed for a union of hearts and a joint commonwealth of Macedonians and Persians, he proclaimed for the first time, through a brotherhood of peoples, the brotherhood of man. True, it perhaps meant to him only a brotherhood of certain aristocracies, though he is reported to have said that all men were sons of one Father; but he, first of all men, was ready to transcend national differences, and to declare, as Paul was to declare, that there was neither Greek nor barbarian. And the impulse of this mighty revelation was continued by men to whom it did not mean a brotherhood of aristocracies; for Zeno, who treated his slave as himself, and Seneca, who called himself the fellow-slave of his slaves, would (though Alexander might not) have understood Paul when he added 'there is neither bond nor free.' Before Alexander, men's dreams of the ideal state had still been based on class-rule and slavery; but after him comes Iambulus' great Sunstate, founded on brotherhood and the dignity of free labour. Above all, Alexander inspired Zeno's vision of a world in which all men should be members one of another, citizens of one State without distinction of race or institutions, subject only to and in harmony with the Common Law immanent in the Universe, and united in one social life not by compulsion but only by their own willing consent, or (as he put it) by Love. The splendour of this hopeless dream may remind us that not one but two of the great lines of social-political thought that have divided the world since go back to Alexander of Macedon. For if, as many believe, there is a line of descent from his divine kingship, through Roman Emperor and mediaeval Pope, to the great despotisms of yesterday, despotisms 'by the grace of God,' there is certainly a line of descent from his prayer at Opis, through the Stoics and one portion of the Christian ideal, to that brotherhood of all men which was proclaimed, though only proclaimed, in the French Revolution. The torch Alexander lit for long only smouldered; perhaps it still only smoulders to-day; but it never has been, and never can be, quite put out.

CHAPTER XIV

GREECE: 335 TO 321 B.C.

I. THE FEELING IN GREECE

WHEN Alexander crossed to Asia, he left behind him a Greece formally regulated by the League of Corinth, but in fact cowed by the destruction of Thebes (p. 356). In 335 he had been afraid of a general combination against him. That danger was past; his rear was secure, and in the allied contingents he held hostages for the good behaviour of the League states. But it is well to consider what those states were feeling.

In form, the League had united a Greece disunited by nature and traditional sentiment. Its strong point was that it gave the small cities proportionate rights over against the large ones. Its weak points were that it stereotyped the actual, not the ideal, position, and that its President was, in Greek eyes, a foreigner. Many Greeks refused to regard it as a unification, or anything but an instrument of foreign control; the delegates met under the shadow of the Macedonian garrison on Acrocorinthus. Alexander might treat the cities as free allies; he could not alter this feeling. Many Greeks too resented the loss of an independent foreign policy. For the war with Persia they cared nothing; their hearts were with their fellow-countrymen in Darius' service, and they hoped for Darius' success. Matters were not improved by the man whom Alexander had left to govern Macedonia and supervise Greece. Antipater was a strong character, capable, honest, and loyal; but he was narrow and unimaginative. He had no sympathy with Alexander's policy of treating the Greeks as free allies; and he probably had no liking for the League, regarded as an instrument to secure the freedom of all Greek cities, great and small, subject to such restrictions as the Covenant

Note. There is no connected narrative extant for this chapter till we reach the Lamian war in Diodorus XVIII. For the earlier part, some episodes are related by the Alexander-historians, notably Diodorus XVII (see p. 352 n.); but better material is supplied by speeches of the contemporary orators, of which a list is given in the Bibliography, and by inscriptions. Some information of varying value is scattered about elsewhere, among which may be mentioned Plutarch's Lives of Demosthenes and Phocion, and the life of Lycurgus in the *Lives of the Ten Orators* which passed as Plutarch's.

imposed. It might have its uses in his eyes as an instrument to maintain the position of the possessing classes and crush the threat of social revolution; for some of the possessing classes were his friends. But what he regarded as his real business was to keep the League's peace. His own method of keeping the peace would have been to dispense with Leagues, garrison selected points, and support the oligarchs against the democrats. This last he did; but, as to garrisons, it cannot be shown that at first he did more than maintain Philip's original detachments in Corinth, Chalcis, and the Cadmea; the Covenant provided for 'no garrisons,' and he meant to do his duty by the Covenant, though he gave it its narrowest interpretation. For instance, it provided that no constitution in force at its date should be altered. Obviously this meant forcibly altered from without, for it also provided that the internal affairs of the cities should not be interfered with; but Antipater took the words literally, and restored certain tyrants who had been expelled,—those of Pellene and Sicyon, and Philiades' sons at Messene,—on the ground that they had been ruling at the date of the Covenant. To many Greeks 'the Macedonian' soon became the best-hated man in the peninsula.

To many, but not to all. To get a true perspective, we must avoid looking at Greece exclusively through Athenian eyes; we must admit that all free cities, big or little, cultured or the reverse, had an equal right to their own lives, and that the alternating supremacies of the three great cities, Athens, Sparta, Thebes, had infringed that right. That right was now secured by the Covenant of the League; and there were cities who regarded the Covenant as a charter of liberty. Fortunately the view of one group of them has been preserved by the Arcadian Polybius. We find ourselves in a different world from that of Demosthenes. Macedonia is far away; she may be a pre-occupation to Athens, but to Arcadia the pre-occupation is Sparta. Demosthenes might call those who did not see eye to eye with Athens traitors; it was a base libel (says Polybius) on some of the best men of the Peloponnese, including those very sons of Philiades. These men knew that the interests of their own cities and those of Athens were not identical; far from being traitors, they had by means of Macedonia secured safety from their secular terror, Sparta, and given to their homes revived freedom and the possibility of leading their own lives undisturbed. The Arcadian view may not have been the highest view, but it must be considered. It explains why Argos was a base for Macedonian influence no less than Thessaly, and why Alexander could use his Peloponnesian horse in the first line.

Athens felt very differently. She still felt that supremacy in Greece was hers by right; she lived in the hope of a second chance. Meanwhile there must be no open breach with Alexander; it was too dangerous. There were really four parties in the city. There were the oligarchs, led by Phocion, a man of personal worth, but one who believed that Athens' day was done and favoured a policy of resignation to the will of Macedonia. There were some propertied moderates, represented by the clever Demades, a creature worthless and corrupt, but able by that very fact to render Athens service with the Macedonians, who knew that he could be used and were willing to favour his requests. There were the radicals, led by Hypereides, the man who after Chaeronea had proposed to arm the slaves; they hated Alexander and were ready to fight at any time. Last, and most important of the four, was the great bulk of the democratic party, rich and poor alike, the men who had followed Demosthenes. They were now led by Lycurgus; for Demosthenes had recognized that, for Athens' sake, he must efface himself for a time. Both men were fully convinced that Athens must and would fight again; both were equally convinced that she must await a favourable opportunity, and that meanwhile all good patriots must work to strengthen and restore the city internally. Thus three of the four parties desired peace, though for different reasons; and an arrangement, tacit or express, was come to under which the pro-Macedonians, Phocion (who was annually elected general) and Demades, managed external affairs, *i.e.* kept the peace with Alexander, while Lycurgus had a free hand in internal matters. The radicals did not at present oppose this arrangement.

II. LYCURGUS AND ATHENS

During the twelve years following Chaeronea (338–326) Lycurgus was the most important politician in Athens. He was a pupil of Plato and a friend of Xenocrates, now head of the Academy; he might call himself a democrat, but his ideal was Sparta, and his régime was not particularly democratic; most of the offices still went to the well-to-do. Stern and pitiless, a hard worker and quite incorruptible, he was efficient rather than attractive. His sphere was finance; and the combination in one person of the chief finance minister and the leading orator of the city was as powerful as the phenomenon of a financier with a moral mission was strange. That mission was to purge and uplift the city and stamp out treason. It was said that against wrongdoers (in his sense) his pen was dipped in blood, not ink; he rarely failed in a prosecution, for the juries believed that, though merciless, he was not unjust. The great wrong-doing, in his eyes, was to have despaired of the State, or failed in her service; thus he secured the death of Lysicles, general at Chaeronea, and of one Autolycus, who had left the city after the battle. His qualities are shown in his speech for the prosecution (in 330) of a wretched trader named Leocrates, who had left Athens after Chaeronea but had returned. Contrary to Greek practice, he did not seek to vilify Leocrates' private life; he treated the man impersonally, as a mere embodiment of that treason to Athens which would wreck the city if not remorselessly suppressed.

For twelve years he controlled Athenian finances; but what office he actually held is uncertain. Most probably the existing financial offices, those of the theoric commissioners and the military steward, were filled by his nominees, while he himself held an extraordinary commission and pulled the strings. He is described informally as head of the administration; the later office of Superintendent of the Administration, seemingly created in 307, which presently gathered to itself all financial power, was probably modelled upon his activities. Athenian trade was as yet unimpaired and ready to take advantage of the openings Alexander was creating, and Lycurgus, it is said, raised the revenue of Athens from 600 to 1200 talents a year; this does not mean double the income, for money was fast depreciating in value. He used this revenue, as he used his advocacy, to strengthen Athens for the future war. The renovation of the walls had already been begun; brick was replaced by stone, and a ditch dug to prevent the approach of rams. The military commands were further specialized, and generals might now be elected from the whole people without reference to tribes. The fleet was remodelled, and triremes as they wore out were replaced by larger vessels; by 325 B.C. Athens had 50 quadriremes and 7 quinqueremes in addition to 360 triremes. Of course she could not man 417 ships; probably her effective fleet was about 200. Lycurgus also accumulated arms and ammunition, and doubtless formed a war fund.

He carried out at the same time a great building programme; it adorned Athens as she had not been adorned since the time of Pericles, though his object was still the practical one, the strengthening of Athens for war. By means of a special tax he completed Philon's magazine and his half-finished docks, and he finished the Panathenaic stadium, for which voluntary subscriptions were received. The Dionysiac theatre was converted into a stone building, as were the old gymnasium in the Lyceum and its palaestra. By 332 Philon was at work on his portico at Eleusis. Lycurgus thus provided the material; it remained to form the men. The stadium and gymnasium might train the body; Plato's pupil thought also of training the mind. Far the most important measure of the time—it may have been instituted about 335— was the remodelling of the Ephebate. It became a system of compulsory military training; the lads enrolled (ephebes) had to pass a judicial examination of their claim to serve, and served for two years, the 19th and 20th; the system produced some 800 recruits annually. The first year was spent in training and exercises; at the end of it the ephebes received shield and spear from the State, took the oath, and spent a year on garrison duty in the Attic forts. But the prime importance of the system was that it was designed to train the mind no less than the body; the ephebes went through a course of study, and beside the military instructors stood a *kosmētes* and ten *sophronistai*, one for each tribe, whose names are eloquent: the lads were to learn order, temperance, and self-control. These were to be the foundations on which Athens should be built afresh.

Connected with this were Lycurgus' religious measures; in 334 he took in hand the re-organization of the public cults, and also created a new state fund, the *dermatikon*, from the sale of the skins of sacrificial victims; from this and other monies he replaced on the Acropolis the seven missing Victories of solid gold, thus restoring the Periclean ten (vol. v, p. 355), and provided many ornaments for the religious processions. But any attempt to restore the *spirit* of the State religion was bound to fail; for to the educated the worship of the Olympian gods no longer had much meaning. Nor was philosophy yet ready to take its place. There was indeed a great philosopher in Athens; Aristotle had returned to the city from Macedonia when Alexander crossed to Asia. But Aristotle of Stagirus was foreign in feeling to the Athenian democrats; his friendship with Alexander, and still more that with Antipater, whom he made executor of his will, estranged them; he and Lycurgus had nothing in common. And anyhow Aristotle had nothing with which to replace the old state-worship; scientifically he might be the precursor of the future, but ethically he belonged to the past; for a new quickening principle men had to wait for Zeno's enunciation of duty. With the state-religion wanting, and philosophy without counsel, the only alternative was to turn to the more intimate worships of the East. Whether Lycurgus did so is quite uncertain. In 333 a State temple of Ammon was ceremoniously opened in Athens; but Ammon had already a long connection with Athens as an oracle, and there is nothing to connect his temple specifically with Lycurgus. Certainly in the same year Lycurgus carried a resolution to grant the merchants of Citium a site for a temple of the Cyprian Aphrodite, and it was probably through his instrumentality that, shortly before, a site for a temple of Isis had been granted to some Egyptian merchants. Probably however his aim was merely to encourage corporations of foreign merchants, *i.e.* to benefit trade; but this would serve the same purpose as all his acts, the strengthening of Athens.

In addition, two of his laws deserve notice. One provided that official copies of the plays of Aeschylus, Sophocles, and Euripides should be made and kept, and that no other versions should be acted; the other forbade Athenians to purchase as a slave any free man taken in war. This humane law may have influenced those cities which in the next century bound themselves not to enslave each other's nationals.

Greece had not ceased to be an effective force because Athens and Thebes had been defeated at Chaeronea and a new state had entered the circle of Greek culture. The great days of several Greek cities, as Rhodes and Megalopolis, and some of the best of the history of Sparta, lay in the future, as did the Athens of the philosophers. Greece for long was to remain the most important country in the world; and if we feel—and justly feel—that during Alexander's lifetime Greece has lost importance, that depends, not on military defeat or Alexander's conquests in Asia, but simply on the fact that Athens had, for the moment, lost to Alexander her primacy in the world of ideas; it was Alexander who was now opening up new spheres of thought. For Aristotle, though in, was not of, Athens; he is a lonely figure, out of touch with Athenian democracy, and fast losing touch with Alexander, who in some ways was passing far beyond his outlook. But science was his; and he claimed that Wisdom, whose representative on earth he was, was as great a power as Alexander himself. Even if we regard the future as lying with Alexander, we must try to appreciate the very different points of view of Aristotle and of Athens.

III. AGIS III OF SPARTA

Alexander's dealings with the Persian fleet show that he knew that Athens would only wait and watch; and if Athens was not above indulging in pin-pricks,—if she sent envoys to Darius and even in 334 permitted his fleet to provision at Samos,—Alexander

could afford to smile. From 335 to 331 Athens had in fact no
foreign policy. But another city was preparing for war. Agis
of Sparta had in 333 sent envoys to Darius, and had opened communications with the Persian admirals, whom he met at Siphnos,
with a view to securing the aid of the Persian fleet. The news of
Issus interrupted their conference; the Persian admirals had to
look to themselves, but they gave Agis 30 talents and 10 ships,
with which he made an attempt on Crete, a fine recruiting ground;
Alexander had to send his fleet under Amphoterus to protect the
island. Agis also made some attempt to support those Persians
who were still in arms in Caria. He subsequently took into his
service the 8000 mercenaries who had escaped from Issus, and
by 331 he had definitely decided upon war. It was known that
Persia was making a great effort, and some in Greece thought
they ought to fight while Darius' power still stood; also Antipater
was involved in Thrace, where his general Memnon had revolted,
perhaps with native support.

Agis now sought to win over Athens. Some were ready to
subscribe money toward a war; even Demosthenes seems for a
moment to have thought that the time had come, though his common sense soon reasserted itself. The radicals of course heartily
supported Agis, and one of them, in the speech *On the treaties
with Alexander* (if it was delivered), called on Athens to join him.
The speech itself is an attempt to show, by an enumeration of
Antipater's misdeeds, that Macedonia had consistently broken
the Covenant of the League, and that Athens had a duty to intervene. In particular it was emphasized that Antipater had re-
established tyrants in certain Peloponnesian cities, though it was
conveniently forgotten that five years previously Athens had
honoured Cleomis, tyrant of Methymna—a tyrant was not so bad
if he were in your own interest. It was also alleged that Alexander
had detained Athenian merchantmen in the Dardanelles. If true,
it was probably some subordinate's excess of zeal; for Alexander
had never wavered in his policy of conciliating Athens since he
had sent her the spoils of Granicus, and about the time of this
discussion at Athens (summer 331) he released the Athenian
prisoners taken in that battle, in order to secure her good-will,
though he gave her warning not to interfere by reinforcing
Amphoterus, who was watching events in Greece, with 100 ships,
probably raising his fleet to a larger force than Athens could
mobilize. The government at Athens kept their heads and kept
the peace, and crowned Alexander for releasing the prisoners.
Agis' enterprise was indeed foredoomed from the start. The

presence of his fine army at Chaeronea, or even before Lamia, might have altered history; but to neglect to support Athens and Thebes in 338, and then to fight Macedonia single-handed, was merely throwing away men's lives to no purpose. Possibly however he was actually co-operating with Darius; the story of his attempt rests on scanty and inferior evidence.

Agis could only secure Elis, Achaea, and part of Arcadia as allies, and quite failed to disturb the grouping in the Peloponnese that was to become traditional; Megalopolis, Messene, and Argos, Macedonia's watchdogs, held to Antipater. In summer 331 Agis moved north with an army of 22,000 men,—presumably the usual Spartan levy of 6000, his 10,000 mercenaries, and 6000 allies,—defeated a force which Corrhagus, probably the Macedonian commander in Corinth, collected to oppose him, and besieged Megalopolis. Antipater patched up matters in Thrace and hurried south, gathering the League troops on the way; it may have been now that he garrisoned some places in Thessaly, where there was unrest, and in Malis. He entered Arcadia in late autumn 331, shortly after Alexander's victory at Gaugamela, and Agis raised the siege and met him near Megalopolis. The Spartan army gave Antipater a hard fight; but the Macedonian victory was complete and Agis died on the field. Antipater was too wise to drive Sparta to extremities. He treated his success as the success of the League; he merely demanded as hostages 50 noble Spartans, whom he sent to Alexander, and entrusted the decision with regard to Sparta to the congress of the League. Sparta appealed from the hostile League to Alexander; he forgave all but the chief leaders, but directed payment of 120 talents to Megalopolis as compensation. The defeat crippled Sparta for years, and probably she now had to enter the League. Antipater sent to Alexander what remained of the 8000 mercenaries of Issus (see p. 456); possibly they formed part of the force subsequently left by him in Bactria, and there sowed disaffection among their fellows which bore fruit later.

IV. THE PROSECUTION OF DEMOSTHENES

Though Gaugamela and Megalopolis had paralysed the desire for war, Agis' attempt put an end to the truce which had reigned in the internal affairs of Athens. Passions had been roused on both sides which found their outlet in the law-courts. Lycurgus prosecuted Leocrates, as a demonstration that his anti-Macedonian policy remained unaltered, and Polyeuctus in prosecuting one Euxenippus alleged against him pro-Macedonian sympathies. Hypereides defended Euxenippus, the first sign that the radicals were passing definitely into opposition; they had desired war, and thought that the government had neglected a favourable opportunity. In Leocrates' case the votes were equal, and he was acquitted. Probably the jury felt it unfair to call the man to account after eight years had passed; but their verdict encouraged the friends of Macedonia. These were already, in various cities, prosecuting members of the war party; and they now instituted at Athens a far more important prosecution than that of Leocrates. After Chaeronea one Ctesiphon had proposed, and the Council had decreed, that a gold crown should be bestowed upon Demosthenes in the theatre at the Dionysia in commemoration of his services to Athens, *i.e.* against Philip. Aeschines had indicted the proposal as illegal; and though on the news of Philip's death the indictment had been dropped, it had suspended the operation of the decree, and the crown had not been given. Aeschines now renewed his prosecution of Ctesiphon, whose defence Demosthenes of course undertook. Aeschines thought that the time had come to try and crush his rival; for everyone well understood that what was really on trial was not Ctesiphon but Demosthenes and his policy up to Chaeronea. The trial came on in spring 330, and the speeches of both Aeschines and Demosthenes have been preserved.

It has recently become a fashion with some writers to treat Aeschines as a far-seeing statesman and Demosthenes as a demagogue; but this view of Aeschines derives no support from his speech against Ctesiphon. It was a weak speech. On the juridical aspect of Ctesiphon's proposal—that it was illegal to crown an official still liable to scrutiny and illegal to confer a crown in the theatre—Aeschines had a good case, and Demosthenes could not really answer him; but the jury would care little for the technical points of law, as Demosthenes well understood. But when he came to the substance of the charge, Aeschines adopted the extraordinary course of fighting Demosthenes on the latter's own ground. He made no attempt to show that the line of policy taken by Demosthenes was wrong; he only argued that Demosthenes had not carried out that policy either thoroughly or successfully. Doubtless he realized that most of the jury had approved of the war with Philip; and it may have been clever and prudent to contend that Demosthenes was really rather pro-Macedonian, and had neglected many good chances against both Philip and Alexander. But the prudence was uncommonly like timidity, and the cleverness that of the small attorney. Even on the lines he himself selected he handled the matter inadequately; he dealt only with details, and did not attempt to expose the basic flaws in Demosthenes' activity,—the neglect of any thorough attempt to secure Sparta, and the failure to understand the military importance of Aetolia, which flanked Philip's communications,—the things in fact which Alexander had afterwards been afraid of. But had he had the mind and the courage of a statesman, he might have expounded that alternative policy which some believe he saw. He need not have said 'We were bound to keep friends with Philip at any price'; he could have argued that the League of Corinth was a great constructive conception, and that Athens should have co-operated with Philip, abandoning dreams of empire, working for a united Hellas in a league where all alike, small and great, would be free, using the great strength of such a league to check any subsequent encroachment upon autonomy by Philip, should such there be. It may not have been the right policy for Athens; but it would have been an honest alternative to put. Instead, he stultified himself completely by expressing regret for Athens' lost supremacy; if he really felt that, he had no right to have worked against Demosthenes. Naturally he failed to carry the jury with him; there was nothing in the attitude he adopted to influence anybody, and the absurdity of treating Demosthenes as secretly friendly to Alexander was patent.

Demosthenes lifted the debate on to a different level. His speech *On the Crown* is generally considered to be one of the greatest speeches of the ancient world, even if it has not the fire of some of his own attacks on Philip, or the peculiar glamour of the Funeral Oration in Thucydides. But a modern man, knowing only the repute of the speech and actually reading it for the first time, would probably be somewhat puzzled. He would be repelled by the consistent egoism of the speaker (even if he recognized that this was partly forced upon him), and more than repelled by the unworthy personal abuse of Aeschines and, still worse, of Aeschines' mother. Parts of the defence of the speaker's policy are effective; but, granted the policy, it was an easy one to defend, and its real defects, which had not been pointed out by Aeschines,—the neglect of Sparta and Aetolia,—might easily slip out of sight, covered up by the undeniable achievement of winning over Thebes. One line of defence however,—that the speaker had never made a move except in answer to one of Philip's, —was very poor; it was clap-trap for the gallery, and invited a crushing retort. Putting aside the technical skill of the speech as

an oratorical exhibition, its fame really rests on its patriotism. It
does indeed glow throughout with a white heat of patriotism;
but again a modern reader will note, with a certain anxiety, that
the expressed aim of the speaker was not so much the freedom of
Athens as her supremacy; the speech is shot through with regrets
that Athens had ceased to be the first power in Hellas. Yet, for
all that, the speech deserves, and more than deserves, its accustomed repute, though perhaps not quite for the accustomed
reason. For in one way it is unique among extant Greek orations;
it is the panegyric of failure, the triumph-song of the men of the
lost battle. What matters in a man is not what he achieves, but
what he intends and aims at. To have striven to the uttermost for
a great end, even if in vain, is the highest thing given to him;
success or failure rests with God. That is the keynote of the speech;
and that is the glory of Demosthenes. Perhaps only once before
had any Greek reached such a level; some hearer of the speech *On
the Crown* may have recalled the wonderful drama in which, in
an older Athens, Euripides had written

> There is a crown in death
> For her that striveth well and perisheth.

The result of the trial was the complete vindication of Demosthenes; Aeschines failed to obtain a fifth of the votes, and went
into exile to Rhodes, where he died. The pro-Macedonians gave
up further useless attacks on the Nationalists; the co-operation
of all parties except the radicals was restored; any idea of a foreign
policy was again abandoned. The reconciliation of the parties is
shown by Lycurgus and Demades serving together in 330 in the
sacred mission sent to Delphi for the dedication of the new temple,
while in 329 Lycurgus, Demades, and the pro-Macedonian oligarch Thymochares were appointed among the commissioners to
supervise the games at the Amphiaraum at Oropus, and were
thanked on Demosthenes' motion.

The time was rendered difficult by a food shortage which began
in 330 and lasted till 326[1]. Doubtless the harvests failed in many
places; but Alexander's requirements must also have drained the
world of its floating supply of corn, and the trouble was aggravated
by Cleomenes in Egypt (p. 427). Cleomenes, by forbidding
anyone to export corn from Egypt except himself, had succeeded

---

[1] An inscription from Cyrene (S. Ferri, *Alcune Iscrizioni di Cirene*,
no. 3) now shows that this famine affected Greece generally and also
Epirus. Cyrene gave 805,000 medimni of corn to alleviate the distress,
including 100,000 to Athens.

in monopolizing that important source of supply; he had a good system of information, and diverted his cornships to wherever prices at the moment were highest. Athens, who depended absolutely on foreign merchants and sea-borne corn, suffered heavily; the price of wheat rose from the normal five drachmae a bushel to sixteen drachmae. The foreign merchants in Athens seem to have behaved well; we hear of firms who offered to the State 10,000, 12,000, even 40,000 bushels of wheat at the normal price. Traders in Phoenicia and Cyprus also rendered assistance, and Harpalus, the head of Alexander's civil administration, sent some corn and was rewarded with citizenship. But the famine got beyond any private efforts; and in 328 a Corn Commission was appointed with Demosthenes as Commissioner. To provide funds a subscription, nominally voluntary, was called for; Demosthenes himself gave a talent. With the proceeds corn was purchased at the prevailing high prices and re-sold to the citizens at a low one. It was the first time this had been done; it marked a stage on the road to free distribution. Apparently too the people were rationed. In 326 some of the new quadriremes were used to convoy cornships; it may have been on account of pirates, but the adventures of Heracleides of Salamis, whose ship was seized by the Heracleotes, rather suggest that the cities were not averse from stealing each other's corn supplies. By 325 the scarcity seems to have been over. Athens however had been thoroughly alarmed, and in 324 she sent a strong fleet under Miltiades, a descendant of the victor of Marathon, to the Adriatic to found a colony there 'in order that Athens might at all times have her own supply of corn.' The colony was to serve as a naval station from which to deal with the Etruscan corsairs who were menacing Athenian trade; but in this attempt to tap the rich lands at the head of the Adriatic, Athens was probably also seeking a field of supply beyond the reach of the activities of Alexander, who controlled Egypt and could, if he wished, by his hold on the Dardanelles, fetter the Black Sea trade.

In 326 Lycurgus was not re-elected, and was succeeded by a personal enemy, Menesaechmus. Probably the connection of events is, that few believed Alexander would return from India; that the war-party, the radicals, were already becoming active by way of anticipation; and that Menesaechmus procured the rejection of Lycurgus by the aid of that party. But the reason may only be that Lycurgus' health was failing; he died soon after 324. He took little further part in affairs, though when Menesaechmus impeached his accounts he had himself carried to the Council

Chamber and completely vindicated his integrity. Menesaechmus pursued him even after death, and had his children imprisoned; Demosthenes, then in exile, procured their release by representing the bad effect abroad of such ingratitude for Lycurgus' services. Lycurgus' retirement left Demosthenes alone at the head of the democratic party when the crisis came which is known as the affair of Harpalus.

V. THE AFFAIR OF HARPALUS

Harpalus had shared the common belief that Alexander would not return, and had squandered the Treasury funds on every sort of luxury. But he had gone far beyond riotous living. He had acted as though king, and had had his successive mistresses, Pythionice and Glycera, treated as queens; when Pythionice died he raised elaborate monuments to her in Babylon and near Athens, and set up a temple to Pythionice Aphrodite; Glycera lived in the palace at Tarsus and was called queen, and those who approached her had to prostrate themselves as though before the wife of the Great King. Then, late in 325, came news that Alexander was on his way back. Harpalus fled, and in spring 324 appeared off Sunium with 30 warships, 6000 mercenaries, and 5000 talents in gold which he had stolen. It was feared that he might try to seize the Piraeus; and, on Demosthenes' proposal, Philocles, the general in command at the Piraeus, was charged not to admit him. Harpalus then sent his fleet and troops to Taenarum, and with two triremes and part of the gold requested admittance as a suppliant. It was difficult to refuse admittance to a citizen who came as a suppliant; and Philocles let him in[1]. Harpalus thereon offered Athens the aid of his forces for war against Alexander, asserting that many of the satraps were disaffected and would rise in support; it was evidently not yet known in Athens how sternly Alexander was dealing with the disaffected, or that all the satraps had had to disband their private troops. Undoubtedly too Harpalus began a campaign of bribery. The radicals, it seems, were anxious to accept his offer, thinking the occasion propitious for war; but Demosthenes and Phocion, who had throughout acted together, gauged the position more correctly. Then Philoxenus, in command of Alexander's sea-communications, sent to Athens and demanded Harpalus' surrender; and it was rumoured that Alexander was preparing for a naval attack on Athens if she refused. The situa-

[1] It is now certain that Harpalus entered in 325–4; for in 324–3 Philocles was cosmetes and Dicaeogenes general in Piraeus, Ἐφ. Ἀρχ. 1918, p. 76.

tion was dangerous, for public opinion was against surrendering a suppliant; finally, on Demosthenes' proposal, it was resolved to detain Harpalus in prison and take charge of the gold till Alexander sent for it. In reply to a question, Harpalus said that he had brought 700 talents; it does not follow that he told the truth. Demosthenes was among those charged to convey the money to the Parthenon; when deposited and counted it was found to be only 350 talents. This fact however was not made public. It does not appear that Demosthenes was the person whose obligation it was to make it public, though doubtless he could have done so. But everyone believed that Harpalus had been distributing bribes wholesale; and Demosthenes carried a proposal that the Areopagus should inquire into the matter and report who had taken Harpalus' money. About this time Harpalus escaped. It was easy to escape from prison at Athens, but who aided him is unknown. He went back to his troops, and was subsequently murdered by his lieutenant Thibron.

The situation was now further complicated by the arrival of Alexander's decree for the return of the exiles, which affected every city of Greece, and with it the request for divine honours for himself (pp. 418 *sqq.*). The exiles decree excited uncompromising hostility among Athenians, not because it was a breach of the Covenant, but because they had expelled the Samians from their lands and colonized the island, and it meant that they would have to restore Samos to the Samians. The grant of divine honours was also opposed by Demosthenes and Lycurgus no less than by the radicals. In September (324) Nicanor of Stagirus, Aristotle's son-in-law, appeared at the Olympia bearing Alexander's decree; he read it out to 20,000 exiles who had assembled to hear it, and who naturally received it with enthusiasm. Demosthenes was at Olympia as head of the Athenian religious envoys, and he had a conversation with Nicanor which apparently affected him greatly; he saw that Alexander was in earnest, and that the risk in opposing him was serious. To accept the exiles decree was indeed impossible, in the face of public opinion at Athens; but it might placate Alexander if what seemed at the moment the less important demand were granted. Consequently, when the convenient Demades formally proposed that Alexander should be a god, Demosthenes gave a contemptuous assent: 'Let him be son of Zeus, and of Poseidon too if he likes.' Thereon Alexander was deified at Athens (p. 419), though the story that he became a particular god, Dionysus, seems unfounded. The other cities, even Sparta, made no difficulty about his deification; and most of them prepared to receive back their exiles, glad that this would at any rate entail the supersession of Antipater, and started to decide the notoriously difficult question of what proportion of their former property should be restored to them, Alexander having apparently indicated the main lines on which decisions should be founded. At Tegea, for instance, the exiles recovered half, claims being adjudicated by a commission from another city. But one other people beside Athens was irreconcilable; the Aetolians had taken Oeniadae from Acarnania shortly before, and had no intention of restoring it. Early in 323 many embassies from Greece started for Babylon, partly to congratulate Alexander, partly to submit to him questions arising out of the exiles' return. Whether Athens requested the retention of Samos is unknown; Perdiccas' action later shows that Alexander did not grant the request, if made.

Meanwhile at Athens excitement had been growing over the Harpalus case, and the whole city rang with charges and counter-charges of corruption. Demosthenes was accused among others, and proposed a second decree ordering that the Areopagus should inquire into his case; he offered to submit to the death-penalty if found guilty. At last the Areopagus, who had delayed in the hope that matters would blow over, were forced by public opinion to issue their report (winter 324–3), six months after the institution of the inquiry. The report gave neither evidence nor reasons; it was merely a list of names with a sum of money against each. Demosthenes' name appeared with 20 talents against it; others named were Demades, Philocles, Phocion's son-in-law Charicles (who had previously superintended for Harpalus the erection of Pythionice's monument), and the orator Hagnonides. Demosthenes had acted throughout in conjunction with Phocion, who, though known to be incorruptible, was affected through Charicles; and as Demades also was involved, it meant that the radicals (whom Harpalus had not needed to bribe) were the only party not under suspicion. Thereon the radicals carried the Assembly, which appointed their leader Hypereides and nine others to prosecute those named in the report. The prosecutors were not an imposing body; the only well-known names among the nine were Menesaechmus, who was to disgrace himself by his treatment of Lycurgus' children, Pytheas, who became a creature of Antipater's, and Stratocles, of evil notoriety later. Hypereides alone gave weight to the prosecution. Though immoral in private life, he was in his public life honest, sincere, and patriotic; but he was headstrong and impulsive. He probably believed quite genuinely that a good opportunity to fight had been lost, and by Demosthenes' fault. It leaves an unfortunate impression that he should prosecute Demosthenes, after their close association at the time of Chaeronea; but they had steadily drifted apart, for he had no sympathy with Demosthenes' view that Athens must not fight unless a favourable chance offered; and he probably thought that he was putting country before friendship.

Demosthenes' case was heard first, as a test. The speech of Stratocles, who spoke first, is lost; possibly he outlined the evidence on which the prosecution relied, but there is nothing to show. Demosthenes' speech is also lost; we really therefore know almost nothing of the case made by either side. All we possess is parts of Hypereides' speech, which took the line that Demosthenes had disgraced democracy, and a bitter speech written by Deinarchus for one of the prosecutors, which argued that Demosthenes was a pro-Macedonian. The jury condemned Demosthenes to a fine of 50 talents; he could not pay, and went into exile to Aegina. Demades and Philocles were also condemned; Demades paid his fine and stayed in Athens.

The question of the guilt or innocence of Demosthenes has been passionately argued ever since; but in fact we have not the material to arrive at a conclusion. Two things may first be set aside altogether. One is Pausanias' statement that Philoxenus obtained from Harpalus' confidential slave a list of those bribed, and Demosthenes' name was not among them. The source of this is unknown, and Pausanias is poor historical authority; but, even if true (and Harpalus' slaves apparently *were* sent to Alexander), it is susceptible of more than one explanation. The other is the common belief that Demosthenes was not bribed, but that he did take the money, though for the Theoric fund and not for himself,—a belief based on Hypereides' statement that Demosthenes admitted having done so. Now Hypereides was counsel for the prosecution, and a statement by counsel is not evidence; and if this be so to-day, when counsel for the prosecution only states what he hopes to prove, far more was it so at Athens, where it was habitual to attempt to create prejudice. It is true that, if counsel for the prosecution deals by anticipation with the defence, he must for his own sake state it correctly, if he knows it; in the absence of written pleadings he sometimes does not know it. But in fact Hypereides does not even say that this was Demosthenes' defence. He believes that that defence was to be a denial by Demosthenes that he ever had the money, and a plea that he was being sacrificed to appease Alexander; and he adds, as an argument of his

own, the statement that Demosthenes had stultified that defence
by a previous admission of guilt. And he does not make even this
statement without reservation; he qualifies it by saying 'so I
believe.' This statement is not evidence for anything; neither is
Hypereides' further assertion that Cnosion confirmed Demosthenes' admission; what we want is Cnosion's evidence, and particularly his cross-examination, had such a thing been known.
There is absolutely nothing to justify the belief that Demosthenes
admitted taking the money for patriotic purposes, to help form a
war fund. Incidentally, of what use were 20 talents for a first-class
war? He could have had the whole 5000 openly, had he wished.

To come to what is known. We know neither what proof the
prosecution offered, nor Demosthenes' defence. We do know
that the prosecution drew such a vague indictment that Demosthenes very properly asked for particulars; this does not argue
any special confidence on their part. The fact that the jury convicted means nothing, for they admittedly treated the matter as
res judicata, decided by the Areopagus' report; but the further
fact that, when they could have inflicted the death-penalty or a
fine of 200 talents, they fined Demosthenes 50 talents only, does
not suggest any great measure of conviction on their own part.
We are really thrown back simply on the report of the Areopagus,
which, be it remembered, Demosthenes had himself called for.
All we know about it is this. They searched the houses of the
accused for the money. They *apparently* questioned Demosthenes,
and therefore presumably others also. They desired, but failed,
to let the matter blow over. And they gave no reasons in their
report. Was that report a judicial finding based on evidence, or
was it a piece of politics, a sacrifice offered to Alexander? That is
the whole question; and we do not know, and probably never
shall know.

VI. THE LAMIAN WAR

This trial dealt the final blow to the coalition government at
Athens; the radicals, supported by most of the democrats, controlled the Assembly, and Hypereides henceforth held the real
power. He got rid of Demades by three prosecutions for illegality, which disfranchised him; later on he attacked Pytheas,
who fled to Antipater. Then in the summer of 323 came the report
of Alexander's death. Some refused to believe it; were it true,
said Demades, the whole world would reek of the corpse. But
the excitement was great; and Phocion in vain tried to gain time
for reflection by suggesting that if Alexander were really dead

to-day he would also be dead to-morrow. Hypereides and the war party were in no mood for reflection; and even before the news was confirmed they sent for Leosthenes. Leosthenes the Athenian appears in the tradition as a mystery. He *may* be the Leosthenes who was general in 324–3, but his previous career is nowhere revealed; even in the *Funeral Oration* Hypereides only says of him that Athens needed a man, and the man came. But he appears as one with special influence among mercenaries and with an unquestioned military reputation, and there can be little doubt what he really was: he had been a commander of mercenaries under Alexander and had learnt in his school. Some 8000 mercenaries, largely veteran troops discharged by Alexander's satraps, were camped at Taenarum, the usual rendezvous of mercenaries awaiting employment; possibly Leosthenes had brought them from Asia himself. He now received 50 talents, and undertook to make sure of the 8000. Then, about September, came eye-witnesses of Alexander's death; and the Assembly met to decide on peace or war. Phocion pleaded hard for peace; but Leosthenes' assurance carried the day. The Assembly voted war; they declared that the aim of the People was the common freedom of Hellas and the liberation of the cities garrisoned by Antipater, and they ordered the mobilization of 200 triremes, 40 quadriremes, and all citizens under 40; three tribes were to guard Attica, and seven to be available for service abroad. Harpalus' gold was appropriated for the war fund, and Leosthenes was supplied with arms and money and told to begin operations.

With this decree the Hellenic (commonly called the Lamian) war was fairly launched, and Lycurgus' twelve years of patient work bore their fruit. It is natural now to feel that Athens should have waited for the war between the Successors to break out; but that could not be foreseen. Athens took the right course of applying at once to Aetolia, who concluded an alliance with her. But as usual only two of the four chief military states could be brought into line; Sparta could not or would not move, and Thebes no longer existed. One would like to treat this war as simply a struggle for Greek freedom; but it is unfortunately probable that Athens and Aetolia were thinking a good deal of Samos and Oeniadae, and that the exiles decree counted for much in the movement. The returning exiles, Macedonia's enemies, of course counted for something also; thus at Sicyon one of them, Euphron, expelled the tyrant's garrison and brought Sicyon, first of the Peloponnesian cities, over to Athens. But probably the mercenaries counted for more. The great rising of Greek mercenaries in

Bactria after Alexander's death may well be connected with this war; but if the two movements were really one, then Leosthenes and the other leaders of the mercenaries must have begun to plan that movement before Alexander died, perhaps even as early as the confusions of spring 324; we may possibly have before us a general attempt by the world of mercenaries to reverse the verdict of Issus, especially if the surviving mercenaries from Issus were in Bactria. It is all hypothetical; but Hypereides treats Leosthenes as author of the *policy* which resulted in the Lamian war; and if there were really a greater plan as early as 324, and Hypereides knew of it, his desire to accept Harpalus' offer and his prosecution of Demosthenes would assume a new aspect.

The Hellenic alliance took months to form; but the states which ultimately took part in the war, beside Athens and Aetolia, were:—Thessaly and all the peoples north and west of Boeotia, except most of Acarnania and certain cities like Lamia and Heraclea, which Antipater had probably garrisoned; Leucas; Carystus and perhaps Histiaea in Euboea; and, in the Peloponnese, Sicyon, Elis, Messenia, Argos, and the neighbouring coast cities. Some Illyrians and Thracians offered help; but Seuthes was probably kept occupied by Lysimachus. Sparta's neutrality neutralized Arcadia, who dared not send her men north with Sparta uncertain; for the same reason it is improbable that Messenia sent troops. Antipater's garrisons in Corinth, Chalcis, and the Cadmea held Corinth, Megara, and most of Euboea to him, while Boeotia was heartily on his side, for the Boeotian cities had divided up the Theban territory, and they feared that Athens, if victorious, would restore Thebes. No island joined the alliance. The allies tore up the Covenant of the League of Corinth, and formed a new Hellenic League, with a Council and delegates; but its organization is unknown, and the Council may have been only a war council. One unhappy consequence of the war was that Aristotle had to leave Athens and retire to Chalcis, where he died next year, a homeless man.

Antipater was in a difficult position. Macedonia had been drained of men, and he had only 13,000 foot and 600 horse. He sent word to Craterus, who with his 10,000 veterans had reached Cilicia, to hasten his march, and applied for help to Leonnatus, now satrap of Hellespontine Phrygia, which suited Leonnatus very well, as he dreamt of the throne of Macedonia. Antipater himself after some delay entered Thessaly, where 2000 cavalry, many of them Alexander's veterans, joined him under Menon, Pyrrhus' maternal grandfather. But Leosthenes had made good use of the delay. He had shipped his 8000 mercenaries to Aetolia, where 7000 Aetolians joined him, and had seized Thermopylae; Phocis and Locris then rose, and Delphi cancelled the honours previously paid to Aristotle,—a natural enough step to take against Antipater's friend, but none the less regrettable, though there were precedents. Athens now sent 5500 citizen troops and 2000 mercenaries to join Leosthenes; but their way was barred by the commander of the Cadmea garrison with a force of Boeotians and Euboeans. Leosthenes hurried back with part of his army, joined the Athenians, and defeated the enemy; a little later a force from Chalcis was landed at Rhamnus, but defeated by Phocion. Leosthenes, after his victory, advanced through Thermopylae to meet Antipater, who gave battle; Menon and the Thessalians rode over to the Greeks, and Antipater was defeated and shut up in Lamia. About November Sicyon joined the alliance, and Athenian envoys were active in the Peloponnese; Antipater had sent Pytheas there to try and save Arcadia, and Demosthenes on his own account went to Arcadia to try and obtain its alliance. He could only secure its neutrality; but the Athenians in gratitude voted his recall and sent a trireme to fetch him. He landed at the Piraeus, and was met by all the magistrates and a great crowd of people; his entry into Athens was a triumphal progress. The State paid his fine.

The blockade of Lamia lasted through the winter, Leosthenes having no siege-train; Alexander would have made one. Antipater offered to treat, but Leosthenes demanded unconditional surrender; possibly he did not know that Peithon had crushed the rising in Bactria. It was the crucial point of the war; for Antipater could and would have kept any terms he made, and complete freedom might possibly have been secured. Then Leosthenes was killed in repulsing a sally, a heavy blow; Antiphilus, who succeeded, was competent, but did not carry weight enough to keep all the allies together; the Aetolians went home during the siege through some 'national necessity,'— presumably the usual Acarnanian invasion[1],—and other allies also. Early in 322 Leonnatus crossed the Dardanelles, gathering reinforcements as he came; he had 20,000 infantry, partly Macedonians, but only 1500 horse. Antiphilus with 22,000 foot and 3500 horse, having raised the siege, met and defeated him, thanks to the Thessalian cavalry, and Leonnatus was killed; but Antipater, who had followed Antiphilus, succeeded in joining the

[1] Certainly not to hold the Assembly; neither meeting was held in winter.

beaten army. He had however not cavalry enough to risk another engagement, and retreated into Macedonia to re-organize and await Craterus; and the campaign ended on a note of triumph for the Greeks, reflected in the *Funeral Oration* spoken by Hypereides over Leosthenes and the dead.

The Hellenic League should have easily raised 40,000 men, including the mercenaries; but it never did. Some Aetolians possibly rejoined before Crannon; but it does not appear that the other allies, apart from Aetolia, ever furnished more than some 7000–8000 men. The brunt of the war was borne by Athens, Thessaly, and the mercenaries; one Athenian fleet watched the Dardanelles, and won over Abydos, and another possibly co-operated with Leosthenes. But Antipater had 110 ships of Alexander's, and he had been reinforced by part of the Imperial fleet, presumably including quinqueremes, under Cleitus; and in spring 322 Cleitus severely defeated the Athenian fleet under Euetion off Abydos. Soon after Craterus crossed with his 10,000 veterans, 1000 Persians, and 1500 horse, and joined Antipater, to whom he conceded the supreme command. The shattered Athenian fleet had returned home; by a great effort Athens again manned 170 ships, metics helping to supply rowers (probably slaves), and Euetion took station at Samos, presumably to intercept reinforcements coming to Cleitus from Phoenicia. Off Amorgos Cleitus met him with 240 ships, probably about July, and defeated him with heavy loss. It was more than the decisive event of the war; it was the end of Athenian sea-power. Athens' navy never recovered from the blow; the Aegean henceforth becomes Macedonian. Cleitus made his triumphal offerings on Delos, and must have at once blockaded the Piraeus[1]. In the summer Antipater and Craterus again invaded Thessaly with over 43,000 foot and 5000 horse (possibly an exaggeration); Antiphilus and Menon met them at Crannon with 23,000 foot and 3500 horse. They expected further reinforcements; but, with the sea lost, the Peloponnesians could not pass the Isthmus, and the blockade of the Piraeus prevented them waiting. The position was that only a crushing victory, leading to Antipater's surrender, could save Athens from strangulation. Thanks to the Thessalians, the actual battle of Crannon, fought in August on the anniversary of Chaeronea, was little more than a draw in Antipater's favour; but it sufficed, and the Greek leaders had to make terms. Antipater declared that he would not treat with the Hellenic League, but

[1] Whether he destroyed another Athenian squadron in the Malian gulf is problematical.

only with the separate states, and the League thereon broke up;
the smaller states hastened to make their peace, though some
Thessalian towns, and subsequently Sicyon, where Euphron died
fighting, had to be stormed.

Once again Athens called on Demades for help. His civic
rights were restored, and with Phocion and Demetrius of Phalerum, an oligarch now coming into prominence, he went to
Antipater, who had entered Boeotia. Antipater in his turn demanded unconditional surrender, but agreed, out of personal
respect for Phocion, not to invade Attica. The position at sea left
Athens no choice, and Phocion returned to make submission;
Demades apparently wrote secretly to Perdiccas for help, but got
no satisfaction. Antipater proceeded to dictate his terms. The
constitution was to be drastically altered, and a Macedonian
garrison was to occupy Munychia; Athens was to pay the costs
of the war (a payment remitted later on Phocion's appeal),
receive back her exiles, hand over Oropus to Boeotia, and surrender the orators, who were regarded as the authors of the war;
Samos was referred to the kings, and Perdiccas restored the
Samians. In brief, Antipater applied to Athens his system of
maintaining in power an oligarchy friendly to Macedonia, supported by a Macedonian garrison; it seems that many other towns
were similarly treated. His aim was to secure peace by making
the individual towns dependent on Macedonia; and he attempted
no comprehensive system, though one account says he had a
governor in the Peloponnese. In September 322, on the first day
of the Eleusinian mysteries, the foreign garrison under Menyllus
entered Munychia, not to quit it for fifteen years.

But Aetolia, though isolated, fought on. Antipater and
Craterus invaded the country, but were recalled in winter by
events in Asia; and in 321 the Aetolians, now Perdiccas' allies,
again raised Thessaly, and had some success. But they were
called home by the usual Acarnanian invasion; and Polyperchon,
whom Antipater had left in charge of Macedonia, defeated the
Thessalians, Menon falling in the battle, and recovered Thessaly;
this victory over the renowned Thessalian cavalry gave him a
great reputation. But Aetolia itself remained unconquered, the
one refuge left for Antipater's enemies. Outside Sparta and
Aetolia, there was little enough liberty now in Greece.

At Athens, though the oligarchs at once took control and
honoured Antipater as a benefactor of the city, the new constitution probably did not come into force till 321. The franchise was
restricted to those who had 2000 drachmae, *i.e.* to the three

classes liable to hoplite service; this reduced the citizen body to
9000, a narrow oligarchy of wealth, and disfranchised 22,000.
It was treated as a return to Solon's constitution. The jury courts
were emptied, and surpluses were no longer distributed, there
being no poor citizens. There were not indeed citizens enough
to fill all the offices, and many were abolished; rotation by tribes
ceased, and probably election by lot also. The astynomi and the
eleven vanished, their duties being transferred to the agoranomi
and the Areopagus respectively; possibly too the financial boards,
the apodectae and the theoric commissioners, were abolished, and
only the military steward retained, but there is really nothing to
show how finance was administered. Many of the disfranchised
went into exile; Antipater offered land in Thrace to those who
would, and some later joined Ophellas in Cyrene.

Demosthenes, Hypereides, and their friends had fled from
Athens when she surrendered, and the people, on Demades'
motion, condemned them to death. A nominal death-sentence,
coupled with voluntary exile, was a well-understood form, which
they probably thought would satisfy Antipater. But the Macedonian was in earnest; he took the death-sentence literally, and
proceeded to execute it himself. Hypereides was taken and put
to death; Hagnonides' life was saved by Phocion. Demosthenes
took refuge in the temple of Poseidon at Calauria, where he was
found by Antipater's agent Archias, the 'hunter of exiles,' who
tried to induce him to leave the sanctuary. Demosthenes asked
for time to write a letter, and took poison which he carried in his
pen; he then attempted to leave the temple to avoid polluting it,
but fell dead by the altar (12 October 322). The great orator had
not been an attractive character; and his faults,—his deceptions
of the people by falsifying what had happened, his bitterness, his
ungenerous attitude toward his opponents,—had not been small
ones. But one supreme thing he had done. Amid all the difficulties
created by the constitution of his city, and in the face of very superior
force, he had fought to the end, unwavering and unafraid, for
his ideal, the good of his country as he saw it. Undeterred by the
defeat of Chaeronea, he had aided Lycurgus soberly and patiently
so to strengthen Athens that a second attempt should be practicable;
and when that second attempt was made by others, he was high-
minded enough to put himself aside and work with the man who
had impeached and exiled him, for Athens' sake. His very faults
all sprang from the excess of his loyalty and devotion to his
country. He failed; but the gods gave him one of their highest
gifts, to fail greatly in a great cause.

CHAPTER XV

THE HERITAGE OF ALEXANDER

I. THE QUESTION OF THE SUCCESSION

ALEXANDER left no heir to his empire, but Roxane was shortly expecting a child. He had made no arrangements for carrying on the government if he died. Perdiccas, who was senior hipparch and probably acting chiliarch (vizier), called a council of generals; he proposed that they should await Roxane's confinement, and if the child were a boy make him king. Peithon supported him; the others acquiesced, and Meleager, as senior phalanx-leader, was sent to carry the proposal to the infantry. The generals had no constitutional power in the matter; for, as the throne was vacant, the crown was in the hands of the whole Macedonian army, which would include Antipater's army in Europe and Craterus' 10,000 veterans. Meleager was the only survivor of Alexander's original phalanx-leaders who had never received promotion; probably he had a grievance. He stirred up the infantry to revolt; they would have a national Macedonian king and not the child of a barbarian woman. They chose as king Arrhidaeus, an illegitimate son of Philip II, who was a half-witted epileptic, re-named him Philip, and made Meleager his guardian. It came to a struggle between cavalry and infantry; Meleager tried to murder Perdiccas; Perdiccas with the cavalry and elephants left Babylon and blockaded the approaches. The infantry however shrank from open war, and Eumenes effected a compromise. Philip (III) and Roxane's child, if a boy, were to be joint kings. Craterus was to be executive of Philip's kingship (not 'kingdom')[1], *i.e.* his guardian in lunacy, with the custody of

Note. The narrative material for most of this chapter is excellent. The main story is that given in Diodorus XVIII–XX (which unfortunately breaks off just before Ipsus), reinforced in the earlier part by the fragments of Arrian's Τὰ μετ' Ἀλέξανδρου; both are largely derived from the contemporary and very trustworthy historian Hieronymus of Cardia. The contemporary inscriptions (which include some rescripts of Antigonus), the coins, and the Babylonian documents mentioned in the Bibliography, also supply valuable evidence, while Plutarch's Lives of Eumenes and Demetrius (based on Hieronymus, Duris, and other material), and that of Phocion, are useful. For further information see the Bibliography.

[1] R. Laqueur, *Hermes*, LIV, 1919, p. 295 *sq.*

his person and seal. Who was to be guardian of the infant is uncertain; possibly Perdiccas and Leonnatus jointly. Antipater was to remain general in Europe. Perdiccas was to be formally appointed vizier, and command the army in Asia, with Meleager as second in command. No regent of the Empire was appointed, and the effect of the arrangement was to put the regency in commission; Perdiccas had the effective power in Asia, but could only lawfully act on the counter-signature of Craterus, as representing Philip. Weak points about the scheme were, that the relation of Perdiccas' authority to that of Antipater, who had not been consulted, was left undefined, and that Perdiccas and not Craterus actually obtained possession of Philip's person. The Lamian war, which called Craterus to Europe, prevented the arrangement from ever coming into force, and left Perdiccas in unfettered control of Philip and of Asia. Soon after, Roxane gave birth to a son, Alexander IV, who was hailed by the army as king; but as orders naturally went out, and coins were struck, in Philip's name alone, contemporaries, as the inscriptions show, were frankly puzzled as to whether there was one king or two.

The story of the Successors, in the tradition, is the story of a struggle for power among the generals. War went on almost without intermission from 321 to 301 B.C.; and, except for the brief episode of Antipater's regency, the conflict was one between the centrifugal forces within the empire, represented by the satraps (territorial dynasts), and whatever central power stood for unity. The conflict falls into two divisions; in the first the central power represents the kings, but after 316 it means Antigonus, who claimed personally to stand in Alexander's place. But though the actors changed, the issues were the same throughout; the end was complete victory for the dynasts. But the protracted war, which caused much loss and misery, was in reality the birth-pangs of a new order of civilization; the period was essentially one of construction, though we see little of the process, only the result later. It is worth trying to realize the men who were to be the chief actors in the struggle.

The principal generals at Babylon were Perdiccas, Ptolemy, and Leonnatus. Perdiccas, of the princely line of Orestis, was brave and a good soldier; he was probably loyal to Alexander's house, and meant to keep the empire together; but he saw that someone must exercise the actual power, and he meant it to be himself. He was, however, unconciliatory and inordinately proud, and probably difficult to work with. Ptolemy, deep-eyed and eagle-nosed, wiser and more popular than Perdiccas, knew exactly what he meant to do, and did it; he believed that the empire must break to pieces, and for twenty years he did his best to make his belief come true; he meant to be independent ruler of a definite fraction. Leonnatus was, like Ptolemy, related to the royal house; showy and unstable, he wanted to be a king and could not wait. The other Bodyguards were Peithon, able, overbearing, and ambitious of power; Lysimachus, a man of long views, content to go slowly till he felt solid ground under his feet; Aristonoüs, loyal to the royal house; and Peucestas, satrap of Persis and Susiana, very popular with the Persians, but too small-minded for a leading part. Beside the Bodyguards, there were in Babylon three men of the first importance: Seleucus, commander of the hypaspists, who could hold a bull by the horns, perhaps less cruel than most of his contemporaries; the Greek Eumenes of Cardia, Alexander's chief secretary, absolutely loyal and a fine general; and, undistinguished as yet, Antipater's son Cassander, ruthless and devoid of sentiment in politics, but with the makings of a statesman. Nearchus, strangely enough, played no further part in affairs; he was apparently content to serve Antigonus. But several of the most important men were not at Babylon. Antipater in Macedonia, the last of Philip's men, had high claims. Craterus, Alexander's second in command, handsome, experienced, reasonable, and popular with the army, had reached Cilicia with his 10,000 veterans; with him was the former phalanx-leader Polyperchon, of the princely line of Tymphaea, a good soldier but nothing more. Antigonus the One-eyed, an older man than anyone except Antipater, was in his satrapy of Phrygia. His ambition was limitless, and his capabilities almost sufficient for his ambition; harsh, cruel, and overweening on occasion, magnanimous and conciliatory when he chose, he was to be a considerable statesman and the first general of the time; he could get almost as much out of his men as Alexander. With him was a boy of thirteen, of extraordinary personal beauty, his son Demetrius, who, had his character been adequate to his gifts, might have been Alexander's truest successor.

There were already certain definite groupings among the generals. Antipater and Antigonus were good friends, while Antipater's irreconcilable hostility to Olympias had made him the enemy of Eumenes, whom he probably suspected of influencing Alexander against him; and as Eumenes was friendly, and Antigonus unfriendly, to Perdiccas, this tended to throw Perdiccas and Antipater into opposition. Ptolemy would oppose whoever held the central power; but the firmest friendship of the time, that between Lysimachus and Cassander, was hardly yet formed. Both Perdiccas and Antipater stood for the kings; but the fact that Perdiccas opened negotiations with Olympias, who was governing Epirus as regent for the young Neoptolemus, accentuated the rift between Antipater and himself. Beside Olympias, there were two women of the royal house to be reckoned with. One was Alexander's sister Cleopatra, widow of Alexander of Epirus; she had selected Leonnatus for her hand, and with her aid he hoped to become king of Macedonia. The other was a girl of fourteen, Adeia (afterwards called Eurydice), betrothed to Philip. Her father Amyntas, a son of Perdiccas III of Macedonia, had been executed by Alexander for conspiracy; her mother Cynane was an illegitimate daughter of Philip II. She had thus a claim to the crown in her own right, and no love for Alexander's family.

II. PERDICCAS

Perdiccas at the first opportunity put Meleager to death. He then, alleging Philip's orders, called a council of generals, at which he allotted the satrapies. There must of course have been a good deal of bargaining. Ptolemy's price for recognizing Perdiccas' authority was Egypt, which he obtained, Cleomenes, who was virtually in control, being subordinated to him. Leonnatus, with an eye on Macedonia, took the vacant Hellespontine Phrygia. Lycia and Pamphylia were added to Antigonus' satrapy, if indeed they were not his already; Asander's successor Menander retained Lydia; Caria was given to another Asander, Syria to Laomedon, and Babylon to an unknown man, Archon; Perdiccas possibly meant Babylon to be his own seat. The eastern satraps were retained unchanged, as were Taxiles and Porus in India; but the fiction of an Armenian satrapy was abandoned, the hereditary Persian dynast Orontes, formerly Darius' satrap, being really independent. There remained the two men who had helped Perdiccas after Alexander's death. Peithon desired and obtained Media. As however Atropates was Perdiccas' father-in-law, Media was divided, and Atropates acquiesced in his restriction to an undefined and unconquered district to the north, where later he founded the kingdom of Atropatene (Azerbaijan). Eumenes received Cappadocia, with Paphlagonia and Pontus, a large territory, which had however first to be conquered from Ariarathes, who had been in possession since Gaugamela. In Europe, Thrace (where Seuthes, the powerful king of the Odrysae, had regained his independence after Zopyrion's disaster) was withdrawn from Antipater and given to Lysimachus. Seleucus accepted the command of the hipparchy which comprised what remained of the original Companion cavalry; it must however have soon broken up, for from its ranks must have come many of the 'Friends' who began to gather round the leading satraps. Harpalus' office was abolished, and though apparently Alexander's financial superintendents were retained, they were made subordinate to the satraps, whose increased authority is shown by the fact that Archon at Babylon[1] and some of the eastern satraps began to strike coins.

Alexander had left 13,000 Greek mercenaries in Bactria, who were homesick and simmering with mutiny even before his death; on the news they rose, and were joined by their compatriots from the other far-eastern provinces; together they formed a veteran army of 20,000 foot and 3000 horse, whose purpose was to go home and rejoin their own people. The possible connection of this movement with the Lamian war has already been noticed (p. 456). The danger was vigorously met; while Craterus supported Antipater, Perdiccas sent Peithon eastward with 3800 Macedonians and an order on the eastern satraps for 10,000 foot and 8000 horse; his army thus included the native cavalry which had fought for Alexander in India. Peithon's orders were to destroy the mutineers. But he had his own plans; he hoped to win them and by their aid make himself master of all the eastern satrapies; and when treachery and his overwhelming cavalry compelled them to surrender, he merely disarmed and took an oath from them and dismissed them to their settlements till required. But his Macedonians had no mind to lose their plunder; they surrounded and massacred the Greeks, a severe blow for Alexander's eastern cities. Peithon returned to Perdiccas, to whom he was henceforth a source of weakness, both from his reputation and his double-dealing.

Perdiccas had had perforce to abandon Alexander's Arabian expedition and many of his public works; but he was properly anxious to complete Alexander's half-finished task in Asia Minor, and he ordered Leonnatus and Antigonus to furnish troops for the conquest of Eumenes' satrapy of Cappadocia. Antigonus took no notice; Leonnatus sent for Eumenes and attempted to win his support for his project of marrying Cleopatra; Eumenes refused, and Leonnatus then tried to murder him. Leonnatus' death in the Lamian war ended Perdiccas' difficulties in that

[1] See Volume of Plates ii, 10, d.

quarter (p. 458); but as it was vital to him to secure a strong position for Eumenes, the one man on whom he could absolutely rely, he invaded Cappadocia himself in the spring of 322 with Philip and the Imperial army, defeated and hanged Ariarathes, and gave his satrapy to Eumenes, who in this campaign had probably revealed his quality as a general. Perdiccas then detached Alexander's armour-bearer Neoptolemus, of the Epirote house, to attempt the conquest of Armenia, and himself invaded eastern Pisidia, where Balacrus of Cilicia had met his death (p. 369). He took Laranda and Isaura, after a horrible struggle; for the Isaurians refused to survive their freedom, and at the end fired their town and died in the flames. He then sent his brother Alcetas, the phalanx-leader, to occupy western Pisidia; Alcetas for his own purposes worked on different lines, and secured for himself the strong friendship of the tribes, especially the unconquered Termessians.

Perdiccas had achieved notable success, and he began to reconsider his position; he secured from his army his appointment as executive of the kingship of both kings, a function he was actually exercising; it was virtually the regency. That he was aiming at the throne is unlikely, as it would have involved a breach with his ally Olympias; but in fact, under the primitive customs of Macedonia, a regent in command of the army was virtually king. Antipater, who naturally did not recognize a position conferred by Perdiccas' army alone, became alarmed. He had from the first tried to strengthen himself by the aid of his numerous daughters; he had married Eurydice to Ptolemy, and Phila, a noble and capable woman who helped him with affairs and whose judgment he greatly valued, to Craterus, and had offered another daughter to Leonnatus. He now sought to safeguard himself by inviting Perdiccas to marry his daughter Nicaea; at the same time Olympias proposed that he should marry Cleopatra, who left Macedonia and came to Sardes. Eumenes, who saw what must come, advised Perdiccas to take Cleopatra; but he chose Nicaea. Soon after, Cynane set out from Macedonia to bring her daughter Eurydice to Philip and combine their claims to the throne; she successfully defied Antipater, who was occupied in Greece, and reached Asia. Perdiccas then sent Alcetas to stop her; his men would not fight against Philip's daughter, but in some way he procured her death. Then his Macedonians mutinied and took Eurydice under their protection, and Perdiccas had to consent to her marriage with Philip. In spite of this set-back, however, he now felt himself strong enough to call Antigonus to account for his disobedience. Antigonus fled to Antipater and Craterus and sought their help; he accused Perdiccas of murdering Cynane, and told them that he was aiming at the throne and meant to turn Antipater out of Macedonia. Antipater believed him, while Craterus felt that Perdiccas had usurped his office. The two were attempting to conquer Aetolia; they broke off the invasion, prepared to cross to Asia, and applied to Ptolemy for help.

Ptolemy had taken possession of Egypt without incident, and had attracted to himself, by his reputation for generosity and fair dealing, a considerable number of Macedonians; he had a moderate force of mercenaries. In 323 civil war had broken out in Cyrene, and the vanquished oligarchs sought Ptolemy's aid; in 322 his general Ophellas conquered Cyrene, and Ptolemy added it to his satrapy. More important to Perdiccas was the matter of Alexander's corpse. The meeting of the generals at Babylon had decreed the provision of a magnificent bier, and Ptolemy had been strong enough to secure the nomination of his partisan Arrhidaeus to superintend the funeral arrangements. The army doubtless expected the body to be taken home to Macedonia; and whatever Perdiccas' earlier views may have been, this now suited his ambition, for a new ruler in Macedonia was expected to confirm his title by burying his predecessor. Ptolemy however meant to confirm his own position by burying the body himself. He made sure of Arrhidaeus, and he spread or adopted a plausible report that Alexander had desired to be buried at Ammon. Late in 322 the funeral procession left Babylon, and took the road, not to Macedonia, but by Damascus to Egypt. Perdiccas sent his general Attalus after Arrhidaeus, but failed to stop him; and Ptolemy received the body and buried it at Memphis, pending the provision of a fitting tomb at Alexandria.

Ptolemy had now annexed a free ally of the empire, and stolen Alexander's body; Perdiccas must take up the challenge or abdicate. Ptolemy of course hastened to accept Antipater's proffered alliance; and Perdiccas was faced by war on two fronts. The spring of 321 B.C. saw the opening of a struggle which, though its nature altered after 301, was not closed for forty years, and engaged the entire military strength of the empire, both Macedonian and Asiatic, as well as large forces of Greeks. The cavalry employed in Asia were largely Asiatic, and the infantry mercenaries of every nationality, European and Asiatic, who easily changed sides; but every general tried to secure a nucleus of Macedonian infantry. With the Macedonian troops the war was unpopular; they would have held to the royal house if they could but as between the contending generals they cared little, and their apparent ficklenesses and desertions were really attempts to end the struggle in favour of the side which for the moment seemed victorious.

Perdiccas spent the winter of 322 in preparation; he allied himself with the Aetolians, still in arms against Antipater, and replaced Archon of Babylon, who was disaffected, by Docimus. He also decided to repudiate Nicaea and marry Cleopatra, which meant that he openly claimed Macedonia, and early in 321 he sent Eumenes to Cleopatra at Sardes with presents. Soon after, Antigonus started with part of Antipater's fleet for Cyprus, where Nicocreon of Salamis, Nicocles of Paphos, and other kings had joined Ptolemy; thither too Perdiccas sent part of his fleet under Aristonoüs. On his way Antigonus landed in Caria; both Asander and Menander of Lydia were his partisans, and in a raid on Sardes he nearly caught Eumenes, who was only saved by Cleopatra's warning. Perdiccas had decided to stand on the defensive against Antipater and attack Ptolemy; but he had lost valuable time by sending Eumenes, who was to conduct the defensive, to Sardes, for Eumenes' army was not ready. He now gave Eumenes a battalion of Macedonians, and purported to give him the satrapies of Leonnatus, Antigonus, Asander, and Menander, *i.e.* nearly all Asia Minor, together with the supreme command in that country. Eumenes hurried to his own satrapy and raised some native infantry and 5000 excellent Cappadocian horse, but he was too late at the Dardanelles; Antipater and Craterus, with Lysimachus' aid, had corrupted the troops on guard and crossed with 32,500 men, chiefly Macedonians. Perdiccas had ordered Neoptolemus from Armenia and Alcetas from Pisidia to join Eumenes; both had some Macedonians. Alcetas refused; Neoptolemus came, but meditated treachery. Eumenes discovered this, attacked and defeated him, and took over his troops; Neoptolemus with 300 horse escaped to Craterus.

Eumenes now had 20,000 foot beside his 5000 horse; among his generals were Pharnabazus, once Darius' admiral; Phoenix, who was one day to betray Antigonus; and his fellow-countryman Hieronymus of Cardia, the great historian to whom we ultimately owe most of our knowledge of this period. Antipater after crossing divided his force; he himself pushed on south with 10,000 men to help Ptolemy, leaving Craterus with 20,000 foot and 2800 horse to crush Eumenes, who could hardly, he thought, face Macedonians. In the opening cavalry engagement, however, Eumenes' Cappadocians were victorious on both wings, and

Craterus and Neoptolemus were killed; Eumenes, who was wounded, then negotiated with the 20,000 Macedonian foot, whom he dared not attack with his mixed infantry, and received their surrender. In the night, however, they marched off to rejoin Antipater, and he got little from his victory but a great name.

Meanwhile Perdiccas, accompanied by the kings and the rest of his fleet under Attalus, had invaded Egypt. Ptolemy had secured 8000 talents by putting Cleomenes to a not undeserved death, nominally for favouring Perdiccas, and was prepared; Perdiccas failed to force the river line, and the two armies raced upstream to Memphis, where Perdiccas again failed to cross, losing many men drowned in the Nile. Thereon his Macedonians mutinied, for they thought he had no further chance of success, and under the lead of Peithon, Seleucus, and Antigenes, Alexander's former phalanx-leader who now commanded the hypaspists, they killed him in his tent. Next day they offered Ptolemy the regency; but that was not at all what he desired, and on his advice they made Peithon and Arrhidaeus joint-regents (one representing each army), pending Antipater's arrival. The day after came the news of Eumenes' victory; had it come two days sooner it might have saved Perdiccas. Its only result now was that the army condemned Eumenes and Alcetas to death. Attalus with the fleet retired to Tyre.

III. ANTIPATER'S REGENCY

The regents brought the army and the kings back to Triparadeisus in Syria, perhaps near Riblah, where Attalus, professing submission, joined them. Eurydice was seeking with considerable success to win the Macedonians and the actual power for Philip, *i.e.* herself, and the position became threatening. At last Antipater and Antigonus arrived; Peithon and Arrhidaeus laid down their office; and the Macedonian army, united for the last time, elected Antipater regent of the Empire. But Eurydice, with Attalus' support, merely turned her agitation, which aimed at abolishing the regency, against Antipater, and at her instigation the army of Asia, led by the hypaspists, demanded certain rewards promised them by Alexander. Antipater tried to temporize, and was nearly stoned; he was saved by Antigonus and Seleucus, and escaped to his own troops. But he had not fought half his life with Olympias for nothing; he finally mastered the situation, and 'persuaded Eurydice to keep quiet.' Having established his authority, he distributed certain satrapies afresh. Ptolemy was confirmed in possession of Egypt and of all conquests westward, *i.e.* Cyrene. It was a dangerous step; it condoned disobedience, and definitely reversed Alexander's policy, for as yet no Greek city had been subjected to a satrap. But it accorded with Antipater's policy in Greece; and henceforth till 315 the satraps garrison Greek cities where they can. The others who had helped to pull down Perdiccas were well rewarded. Seleucus received Babylon, Arrhidaeus Hellespontine Phrygia, Antigenes Susiana, and Antigonus' partisan Nicanor Cappadocia, while Peithon obtained his desire, the general command over the eastern satrapies. In the east Philippus was transferred from Bactria to Parthia, and the competent Stasanor from Aria to Bactria. Stasanor's compatriot Stasander received Aria; probably he was his brother, as similarly formed pairs of brothers' names occur elsewhere. Antigenes was ordered to bring the royal treasure from Susa to Kyinda in Cilicia, to be nearer Europe; as escort he was to take his 3000 hypaspists, henceforth called the Argyraspids (Silver Shields), which removed these turbulent troops from the army. Antigonus was made general of the royal army in Asia, with Menander as second in command, and commissioned to subdue Eumenes and Alcetas; the vacant Lydia was given to Antipater's admiral Cleitus, the victor of Amorgos. Antipater gave Antigonus 8500 Macedonians and 70 of Alexander's elephants, and also gave him his daughter Phila, Craterus' widow, as a wife for Demetrius, now fifteen; but as some check on Antigonus he made his own son Cassander chiliarch. He then, with the kings and the rest of the Macedonians and elephants, set out for Europe; he thus again reversed Alexander's policy, broke up the joint empire, and made Asia a dependency of Macedonia.

The events of Antipater's regency are largely lost. Attalus again had to fly, and joined Alcetas in Pisidia; they successfully invaded Caria, but their fleet was defeated in an attempt on Rhodes, and again off Cyprus by Cleitus and the Athenian Thymochares[1]. Finally, Alcetas and Attalus lost everything but Pisidia, where they were joined by Docimus, whom Seleucus drove from Babylon. In Pisidia they had nearly 17,000 men, and the goodwill of the tribes; but their cause was ruined by Alcetas' refusal to co-operate with Eumenes.

Eumenes after his victory entered Lydia, hoping that Cleopatra might pronounce in his favour; but her attitude was studiously correct, and Eumenes, who had meant to intercept

---

[1] Aristonoüs, who next appears in Macedonia (p. 481), must have joined Antipater.

Antipater as he returned, yielded to her request not to make her appear to the Macedonians as an author of civil war, and retired to Celaenae in Phrygia, where he wintered. He was now an outlaw, trying to keep together an army which he could not even pay; but he devised a scheme which tided him over the winter. Phrygia was Antigonus' country, and was still in the hands of its Iranian barons. Eumenes, as representing their overlord (the kings), sold their estates to different companies of his troops, to whom he lent siege-machines to reduce the barons' strongholds; the troops repaid themselves from the plunder, while their officers replaced the Persian landowners. Antigonus meanwhile recruited troops, and in the spring of 320 crossed the Taurus, detached a force to watch Alcetas, and invaded Cappadocia with 10,000 infantry, 2000 cavalry, and 30 elephants. Eumenes had double his numbers; but his men had small desire to fight against authority and elephants for a lost cause and an outlawed leader. He was defeated at the Orcynian fields, most of his army going over to Antigonus; but he and Hieronymus escaped to the impregnable fortress of Nora on the Cappadocian border. Antigonus recovered Cappadocia and Phrygia, but failed to win over Eumenes, and invested Nora. He then reunited his forces, preparatory to reducing Alcetas; with the troops taken from Eumenes he now had 40,000 foot, 7000 horse, and 65 elephants. After a wonderful march he surprised and defeated Alcetas; Attalus and Docimus were taken, and Docimus presently entered Antigonus' service, to betray him seventeen years later. Alcetas escaped to Termessus, where he committed suicide; Antigonus brutally refused him burial, but his body was buried by the Termessians. So ended the house of Perdiccas. Antigonus incorporated Alcetas' troops; he had now a very large and victorious army, and had become the strongest force in the empire. No enemy of Antipater's remained except Eumenes.

Then, in the spring of 319, Antipater died. With him died all legitimately constituted authority. The kings,—an infant and an idiot,—were powerless of themselves; the Macedonian army could never again be united for the election of a legitimate regent. During his two years of rule he had held the empire together for the kings; but this had depended solely on the personal respect felt for him by the various satraps. And, even so, he had only achieved it by abandoning Alexander's joint empire of Europe and Asia, and by permitting the aggrandizement of the chief disruptive forces in the state, Antigonus and Ptolemy. The moment he was dead the forces of disruption burst their barriers. Ptolemy, since his defeat of Perdiccas, had treated Egypt as 'spear-won' territory, which means that he regarded the King's land, with its taxes, as his personal possession; he must have ceased to remit those taxes to the Treasury, if indeed he ever did so. He now invaded Syria, captured the satrap Laomedon, and annexed the whole country. Antigonus set about conquering the remainder of Asia Minor; he expelled Cleitus from Lydia and took Ephesus, and tried to eject Arrhidaeus from Hellespontine Phrygia on the ground that he had attacked Cyzicus, a free ally of the kings.

IV. POLYPERCHON AND GREECE

Antipater's army, on his recommendation, had elected Polyperchon regent, thanks to the prestige of his reconquest of Thessaly (p. 459). The election, not being that of the whole army, was not valid and was not recognized by the satraps, but it was recognized in Macedonia and of course gave Polyperchon many advantages; he secured Antipater's army, 65 elephants, all the fleet not with Antigonus, and the power to issue orders over Philip's seal, which were sometimes obeyed even by the Macedonians in Asia. He meant to do his best for the kings—probably the reason why Antipater recommended him; but he was not a wise or strong character. Antigonus however knew that he would fight, and again tried to win Eumenes; he asked that Hieronymus might be sent to him, and through him he proposed to Eumenes friendship and alliance. Eumenes welcomed the chance of escaping from Nora. He accepted the proposed truce which Hieronymus brought; but he did not take the oath as Antigonus tendered it. Antigonus had sent a form of oath which indeed named the kings, but would have bound Eumenes to himself personally. Eumenes amended the oath into one which bound him to be the ally of Olympias and the kings, as well as of Antigonus, and submitted this form to the Macedonians of the investing force for their opinion. They saw no harm in an oath to the kings, whose general Antigonus professedly was; they allowed Eumenes to take the amended oath and go free. It was very sharp practice on Eumenes' part; he had accepted Antigonus' truce, and was bound therefore to submit the amended form to him. Antigonus was furious when he heard, but it was too late; Eumenes was again at large, and bound by oath, not to the man Antigonus, but only to the kings' general.

Polyperchon's immediate pre-occupation, however, was not Antigonus. Antipater's death had unchained many forces; among

the greatest of them was his son Cassander. Cassander, left with
Antigonus in 321, had quarrelled with him and returned to
Macedonia. He had expected the army to give him the regency
on his father's death, and he had no intention of acquiescing in
Polyperchon's rule in Macedonia; he returned to Antigonus and
asked for assistance, representing that he could help him by
keeping Polyperchon busy. Antigonus agreed, and gave him
35 ships and 4000 men; Ptolemy also joined their alliance.
Polyperchon realized that a struggle with Cassander would be
no small matter; Cassander, for his father's sake, had many
partisans, and Antipater's garrisons controlled many Greek cities.
But Greece was in a ferment with the news of Antipater's death,
and Polyperchon's camp was full of envoys praying him to deliver
their cities from Antipater's garrisons. He saw that capital might
be made of this, and in Philip's name he issued a proclamation
which reversed Antipater's policy. It asserted that Philip III had
been anxious to carry out the policy of Philip II and Alexander,
and that Antipater was solely to blame for the troubles of Greece
since the Lamian war; it then restored the constitutions of the
cities as they had existed under Philip II and Alexander, recalled
all those exiled by Antipater, and fixed a date in March 318 for
their return; all who opposed Philip (*i.e.* Polyperchon) were to
be banished. With this proclamation Polyperchon made himself
a party in Greece. It did not resemble Alexander's recall of the
exiles (p. 418); that aimed at promoting peace and unity, this was
a preparation for war. In one case it threw over Alexander's
policy altogether; it gave Samos back as a sop to Athens, though
this was never carried out. It was not a proclamation of freedom;
Philip frankly gave orders as master. But it gave Polyperchon
what he wanted, a weapon against Cassander; the democrats in
many cities were henceforth his, and he encouraged them to
attack Cassander's friends the oligarchs. But he did not withdraw
the garrison from Corinth.

Having taken measures against Cassander, Polyperchon sent
Eumenes letters from the royal family praying for his help
against Antigonus; he himself offered Eumenes the choice of
returning to Macedonia to share the regency or remaining as
supreme commander in Asia, and put at his disposal the royal
treasure at Kyinda and the Silver Shields. Eumenes decided that
his oath only bound him to Antigonus so long as Antigonus supported the kings, and that the royal family's appeal justified him
in treating Antigonus as a traitor; he declared his loyalty to the
kings and accepted the command in Asia. Some have condemned

his action; but any unfavourable verdict on this remarkable man's character must be based on the transaction at Nora, and on that alone, for by the terms of his oath, once that oath was taken, his action was undoubtedly justified. Antigonus, though he still posed before his army as the duly-appointed general of the kings, and though Polyperchon had no legal power to revoke his commission, was in fact as much a rebel as Ptolemy, and no longer concealed from his friends that he was following his own ambition. Polyperchon now made two mistakes. He neglected to procure from his own Macedonians (and it would have carried weight) a reversal of the death-sentence on Eumenes; and he invited Olympias to return to Macedonia as guardian of her grandson. The old queen showed more sense than the regent; she asked Eumenes' advice, and Eumenes, who knew her, replied in haste, begging her to remain in Epirus and let her generals manage matters. For the moment she complied; but she began to give orders as though regent, and threw herself heartily into the propaganda war. This war had been going on for years; Theophrastus' pamphlet *Callisthenes* was directed against Alexander (p. 400), and the earliest version of Alexander's 'Testament' is a scarcely veiled attack on Antipater. But it was now intensified; Olympias and the royalists attacked Cassander, while his friends the Peripatetics, embittered against Alexander's house because of Callisthenes' death, championed his cause. Both sides fought with poisoned weapons. Olympias revived the story, perhaps originally her own, that Antipater and Cassander, with Aristotle's help, had murdered Alexander, and gave circumstantial details; the opposition retorted that she had procured the death of her husband Philip, and gave details no less circumstantial (see p. 354). This propaganda war, nourished by forged or doctored letters of Alexander's[1], set its mark on history; we ultimately owe to it, among other things, the caricature of Alexander as the spoilt child of fortune, and doubtless parts of the traditional portrait of Cassander.

As soon as Eumenes' decision was known, Antigonus sent Menander against him. Eumenes, who had raised only 2500 men, retired across the Taurus to Kyinda, where he found Antigenes and the Silver Shields; the 'gold of Kyinda' was put at his disposal and he soon recruited an army, and though Ptolemy and Antigonus both attempted to win over the Silver Shields, he managed to secure Antigenes and his men. They were the last body of Alexander's veterans who had kept together as a unit;

---

[1] *E.g.* the two letters in Plutarch, *Alexander* 55, one forged by either side.

popular opinion regarded them as invincible. But they had joined
in condemning Eumenes to death, and could feel no personal
loyalty to him; and to meet the difficulty he declared that it had
been revealed to him in a dream that the deified Alexander was
still present with them in spirit as their real leader. He had a royal
tent prepared, in which on a golden throne lay Alexander's sceptre,
diadem, and arms; there he and the other generals sacrificed to
Alexander as their divine leader, and held their councils as though
in his presence, Eumenes claiming no superiority over the others.
The device held the Macedonians to Eumenes for two years; but
it somewhat impaired the efficiency of his force by substituting a
council for a commander-in-chief, and threw on Eumenes the
burden of perpetual diplomacy to get his own plans carried out.
His first step, as Antigonus held Asia Minor, was to invade Phoenicia and attempt to secure a fleet to keep open his communications with Polyperchon. Polyperchon on his side had part of the
imperial fleet, again commanded by Cleitus, who had fled to him
when driven from Lydia.

We must return to the affairs of Athens (see p. 459). In 319,
during Antipater's last illness, Demades went to Macedonia to
petition for the removal of the garrison of Munychia. But his
letter to Perdiccas in 322 had been found in the royal archives;
and Cassander, who received him in Antipater's stead, arrested
him and sent him to Athens to be tried for treason. The Athenian
oligarchy obediently condemned him to death, and Cassander
executed the sentence. Worthless as Demades was, he had rendered some service to Athens; but men only saw in his death a
just retribution on one who had moved the death-sentence upon
Demosthenes. Phocion met his fate soon after. Cassander understood the importance of Munychia, and, alleging Antipater's
orders, secured its transfer from Menyllus to his own partisan
Nicanor (not Aristotle's son-in-law). The Athenian populace
believed that Nicanor next meditated attacking the Piraeus, and
the Assembly ordered Phocion as general to take the necessary
steps for its defence; but Phocion, who trusted Nicanor, refused or
neglected to do so, and Nicanor captured the Piraeus. Then the
day for the return of the exiles arrived; led by Hagnonides, they
poured into Athens, mastered the Assembly, and called the
government to account. Demetrius of Phalerum and other oligarchs took refuge with Nicanor in the Piraeus; Phocion escaped
to Polyperchon. But Polyperchon was determined to get rid of all
who might support Cassander, and sent Phocion to Athens under
Cleitus' escort to be tried for treason. The trial of Antipater's

friend before men half-mad from their past sufferings at Antipater's hands was a farce, though Cleitus' disapproval saved
Phocion from torture; Hagnonides moved the death-penalty on
the man who had once saved his life, and Phocion was executed
(May 318). He had pursued a policy of hopelessness and resignation, and had definitely betrayed his trust in the matter of the
Piraeus; he was condemned as Antipater's tool by men who,
whatever their faults, had not like him despaired of the State.

Hardly was Phocion dead when Cassander returned from Antigonus to the Piraeus, and prepared to attack Athens, now again
democratic and friendly to Polyperchon. Polyperchon, with 24,000
men and 65 elephants, attempted to recover the Piraeus but failed.
He then entered the Peloponnese, expelled some of Antipater's
partisans, and made sure of Corinth, henceforth his stronghold.
Megalopolis however resisted, and he tried to storm it; but the
people raised a general levy, armed the slaves, and fought so
heroically that they beat him off with much loss of reputation.
In autumn, threatened by Cassander's success, he returned to
Macedonia.

V. EUMENES AND ANTIGONUS

With this summer (318) the new war was well under way; on
the one side were Eumenes in Asia and Polyperchon in Europe,
who stood for the kings; on the other Antigonus in Asia and
Cassander in Europe, who, supported by Ptolemy and others,
were attempting to pull down the new central power as Perdiccas
had been pulled down. Contemporaries regarded it as the continuation of the war against Perdiccas, interrupted by the episode
of Antipater's regency. The war lasted for nearly two years; we
may first follow events in Asia to their conclusion and then return
to Europe.

Antigonus had mastered most of Hellespontine Phrygia, but
Arrhidaeus still held some cities. He might, if supported, prevent
Antigonus crossing to Europe, and Polyperchon sent his fleet
under Cleitus to aid him. Nicanor with Cassander's squadron
followed and took over Antigonus' ships, bringing his fleet up to
130 vessels. The two fleets met in the Bosporus; Nicanor was
badly defeated, and lost some 60 ships. But Antigonus, with the
friendly help of Byzantium, got part of his army across in the
night; he then shipped good troops on Nicanor's remaining
vessels, and at dawn surprised Cleitus' fleet when drawn ashore
and caught it between two fires. It was Aegospotami repeated.

Nicanor captured nearly the whole fleet; Cleitus, who escaped, was killed by Lysimachus' people; Arrhidaeus vanishes from history. By this bold stroke Antigonus really decided the war; it gave his side command of the sea, and cut communication between Polyperchon and Eumenes. He at once hurried south to drive Eumenes out of Phoenicia before he could create a new fleet. Eumenes could not face him; nothing was left him but to strike eastward and raise the upper satrapies.

The position there was favourable for him. Peithon of Media had attempted to enforce his command over the eastern satraps and had killed Philippus of Parthia; the rest, under the lead of Peucestas of Persis and Susiana, had combined against him, defeated him, and driven him back into Media, where he was seeking help from Seleucus. Polyperchon had already written in Philip's name to the eastern satraps, ordering them to support Eumenes. With 15,000 foot and 2500 horse Eumenes reached Babylonia and summoned Seleucus and Peithon to aid the kings against Antigonus. Seleucus asserted his loyalty, but refused to treat with an outlaw; whereupon Eumenes captured and garrisoned the citadel of Babylon (October 318), and apparently secured the alliance of the eastern satraps. Next spring he advanced to the Tigris; there Seleucus and Peithon flooded his camp by cutting a dyke, but he cleverly extricated himself. They then called for help upon Antigonus, who had followed Eumenes and reached Mesopotamia, while Eumenes, who had crossed into Antigenes' satrapy of Susiana, was joined by Peucestas and the eastern satraps, who had kept together their victorious army; the only satrap who was not either present or represented was Peithon of Sind. They brought 18,700 foot and 4000 horse, practically all Asiatics; the small amount of cavalry they could raise beyond that requisitioned by Perdiccas throws much light on Darius' armies. Half the force was supplied by Peucestas; but Eudamus from the Punjab, who had assassinated Porus, brought 114 of Porus' elephants. Elephants were highly valued as an arm; and as Antigonus had part of Alexander's elephants, Eudamus' help meant much to Eumenes. He now had a larger army than Antigonus, who had left part of his troops in Asia Minor; but he suffered from the unwieldy council in the Alexander-tent and the jealousy of Peucestas. Peucestas was at variance with Antigenes, to whom he naturally had no wish to surrender Susiana; also he desired the supreme command.

Before Eumenes could compose these differences, Antigonus, who had with him Peithon, Seleucus, and Nearchus, settled the

question of Susiana by crossing the Tigris and occupying Susa,
where he installed Seleucus as satrap; when Seleucus recaptured
Babylon is unknown. Eumenes retired behind the line of the
Pasitigris (Kuren); but he had talked Peucestas round, and when
in summer Antigonus attempted to cross the Koprates (Ab-i-Diz)
he out-generalled and smartly defeated him. Antigonus, whose
troops had suffered from the heat, decided to retire into Media
and refit. Disdaining Peithon's advice to buy a passage according
to Achaemenid custom, he fought his way through the Cossaeans
and suffered terrible loss, a fact which illustrates Alexander's skill
in handling mountaineers. The disaster affected his army, and he
nearly met the fate of Perdiccas; but conciliation and lavish
presents, aided by the plentiful supplies which he energetically
collected in Media, averted the danger. Eumenes saw a great
chance; he proposed to turn westward, secure Asia Minor and
communication with Polyperchon, and cut off Antigonus from his
allies and bases. Antigenes supported him, but the other satraps
refused to follow; they had no mind to leave Antigonus at large
among their satrapies. Eumenes had to yield, and withdrew into
Persis; there Peucestas lavishly entertained the army, seeking to
win its favour for himself. But by unwearied tact Eumenes kept
the troops to their allegiance and even for the time won over
Peucestas and reconciled him to Antigenes; they had a joint guard
(*agēma*), and shared the command during Eumenes' illness. But
more than tact was needed, and Eumenes took the bold step of
bringing Sibyrtius of Arachosia, who secretly favoured Antigonus,
to trial before the Macedonians. Sibyrtius only avoided a death-
sentence by flight, and for a time Eumenes had no more trouble.

In the autumn of 317 Antigonus threatened to invade Persis;
Eumenes advanced to meet him and took up a strong position.
For four days the armies lay watching each other; then Antigonus
broke camp and started for Gabiene, a district full of supplies
where both generals desired to winter; Eumenes followed, and in
Paraetacene, near Ispahan, it came to a battle. Eumenes had
35,000 foot, barely half of them heavy-armed and only the 3000
Silver Shields Macedonians, 6100 horse, and 114 elephants.
Antigonus had 28,000 foot (chiefly heavy-armed, including
8000 Macedonians), 8500 horse, and 65 elephants; his 'Companions' were commanded by his son Demetrius, fighting his first
battle. Each had his cavalry on either flank of the infantry, the
usual formation of the time, with his elephants in detachments
before the line; each meant to strike with his right, where he
commanded in person; Eumenes also had some cavalry in reserve.

Diodorus however has transcribed his source very imperfectly, for the battle proceeds as though no elephants were there. Eumenes' right and centre were successful; but their advance opened a gap in his line, into which Antigonus flung his cavalry, threatening Eumenes' left so seriously that he had to recall his men from pursuit. The armies re-formed, and manœuvred for position till midnight, when both halted from weariness. Antigonus returned to the battlefield, but dawn revealed the fact that his loss was far the greater; he dared not wait, while Eumenes was across his road to Gabiene; he withdrew into Media, and Eumenes buried the dead, the sign of victory, and took up winter-quarters in Gabiene.

In midwinter Antigonus boldly attempted to surprise Eumenes by a nine days march across desert country. But the cold compelled his men to disregard his orders to light no fires; this gave Eumenes warning, and he was able to assemble his army for the final battle of Gabiene. Antigonus had now only 22,000 foot, but had 9000 horse against 6000 of Eumenes. Again the Silver Shields were victorious; but Eumenes' left was defeated, Peucestas treacherously leaving the line, and Antigonus' cavalry captured his camp, together with the wives, families, and treasure of the Silver Shields. The defeat was far from conclusive, and Eumenes desired to renew the battle; but the Silver Shields mutinied, seized him, and handed him over to Antigonus in exchange for their wives and children. Antigonus executed Eudamus, for which his murder of Porus would provide excuse, and burnt Antigenes alive, a piece of savagery for which no reason is apparent; the other satraps escaped. Finally, after some hesitation, he put Eumenes to death, though Demetrius and Nearchus tried to save him. Eumenes had tricked Antigonus at Nora; but he had been a gallant foe, and Antigonus' execution of the old partisan death-sentence was one of his worst acts. But he did justice on the Silver Shields; he divided them among Sibyrtius and other satraps, with orders to use them up in frontier warfare so that none should set eyes again upon the home-sea. Among the wounded was Hieronymus, who subsequently served Antigonus' house during three generations.

Eumenes stands out sharply from his Macedonian rivals. Doubtless, as a Greek, his only choice had been loyalty or self-effacement; but, his choice once made, he had stood firm in a shifting world, and his loyalty had never faltered. Given a fair chance, his power of handling men and his fertility in resource might perhaps have pulled Alexander's house through, even against Antigonus; but after Perdiccas' death, with little personal following, he had to work amid the perpetual plottings and jealousies of allies who demanded of him victory even while they made victory impossible. Any man's courage might have given way; but for four whole years, through sheer determination and military talent, he had faithfully upheld a losing cause with tools which he knew might at any moment break in his hand.

VI. CASSANDER AND THE COALITION

Polyperchon's defeat at Megalopolis had brought many Greek cities over to Cassander; and late in 318 Cassander seized Panactum. Discouraged by the loss, and unable to recover the Piraeus, which meant starvation, the Athenians sought peace; they opened negotiations with the oligarchs in the Piraeus, and Demetrius of Phalerum undertook to approach Cassander. Cassander's price for the Piraeus was high. Athens was to be his ally, all who possessed less than 1000 drachmae were to be disfranchised, and he was to garrison Munychia till the war was ended and keep a governor in Athens, an Athenian nominated by himself. He nominated Demetrius of Phalerum (January 317). That the franchise was more liberal than Antipater's mattered little, for Demetrius really governed Athens as a tyrant with Cassander's support; but apparently the only reprisal was the execution of Hagnonides for Phocion's death. The possession of the great city quite altered Cassander's position, especially as he procured from his army a death-sentence on Nicanor, whom he suspected of treachery, and garrisoned Munychia with his own men. By spring 317 he was strong enough, with the aid of Antipater's friends, to invade Macedonia and drive out Polyperchon, capturing some elephants. Polyperchon sent Roxane and her son to Olympias, but Eurydice and Philip escaped and joined Cassander. Eurydice in Philip's name now purported to abolish the regency, depose Polyperchon, and make Cassander Philip's minister; Cassander had found some one he could work with, and is said to have thought highly of her. He left her, supported by his brother Nicanor, to govern Macedonia, and again invaded Greece; he won Thessaly and much of central Greece, attacked Polyperchon's stronghold the Peloponnese, and took Epidaurus; but he was held up by the resistance of Tegea.

Then Polyperchon played his last card; he called on Olympias for help in good earnest, and she came. Supported by him and by her cousin Aeacides of Epirus she invaded Macedonia; Eurydice met her with the Macedonians, but they refused to fight against

her, and she mastered the whole kingdom without striking a blow.
Then what Eumenes had feared came to pass. Olympias abandoned all restraint. She murdered Nicanor and a hundred of
Cassander's friends, and imprisoned Philip and Eurydice; she
made her grandson sole king, with his title on the coinage; then
in his interest she murdered Philip, and sent Eurydice a rope, a
dagger, and a bowl of poison. Eurydice made no useless lament;
she composed Philip's limbs, prayed that Olympias might receive
the like gifts, and hanged herself in her girdle. A tribute of admiration may be permitted for the courage with which this girl,
left alone at fifteen, had thrown her throw for Alexander's empire.

Cassander at once broke off the siege of Tegea and hurried
north. Polyperchon's allies the Aetolians barred his path at Thermopylae; he shipped his army to Thessaly on rafts. He raised a
revolution in Epirus, turned out Aeacides, brought the country
over to his side, and made his general Lyciscus governor; he corrupted Polyperchon's men and left him helpless. Then he entered
Macedonia. Olympias' savagery had produced a revulsion of
feeling; the Macedonians again went over to Cassander, and
Aristonoüs, who commanded for her, could only save Amphipolis.
Olympias with the elephants and some mercenaries threw herself
into Pydna; with her were Roxane and her son, Thessalonice an
illegitimate daughter of Philip II, and the child Deidameia,
Aeacides' daughter and Pyrrhus' sister, betrothed to the young
Alexander. Olympias at the end showed herself Alexander's
mother. Cassander blockaded Pydna, which was ill provisioned;
but she held out till the elephants, fed on sawdust, all died, and
the mercenaries took to cannibalism, and only surrendered (spring
316) on terms that her life should be spared. She also ordered
Aristonoüs, who had had some success, to surrender Amphipolis;
Cassander promptly procured his assassination. Then he put
Olympias on trial for treason before his army. She did not appear.
Perhaps Cassander saw to this, for he dreaded the effect on the
Macedonians of an appeal from her; but it seems also that she
disputed the competence of the tribunal and claimed a trial before
the whole Macedonian army, now scattered far and wide. Whether
her absence were voluntary or otherwise, Cassander's army condemned her to death unheard. The difficulty was to execute the
sentence, for the troops he sent dared not touch her; finally she
was killed by relatives of the men she had murdered. She died
with the same defiant courage she had shown throughout her
stormy life.

Master of Macedonia, Cassander at once declared his future

policy, while he allowed full scope to his enmity to Alexander and his works. He gave Philip and Eurydice a royal funeral at Aegae, that is, he claimed to be the successor of the old national kings, Perdiccas III and Philip II, whose types he revived on his copper coinage[1], while his royal style after he became king was 'King of the Macedonians'; in effect he treated Alexander as an illegitimate interloper, though he continued for utility's sake to strike his silver coinage. He married Thessalonice, Philip's daughter, and imprisoned Roxane and her son. He founded himself a new capital, Cassandreia, on the site of Potidaea; the name shows that he treated Alexander IV as formally deposed. Alexander had refused to rebuild Olynthus, so Cassander settled the surviving Olynthians (amongst others) in Cassandreia; possibly he was worshipped there, and the peninsula still bears his name. He also by a comprehensive synoecism founded Thessalonica (Salonica), his greatest monument; his wife perhaps was honorary 'founder.' Both cities were organized in tribes and demes on the Greek model; and Cassandreia at least was a purely Greek, not Macedonian, foundation. Cassander governed his foreign possessions, such as Epirus and the Peloponnese, through generals, and the Greek towns which he controlled were practically subjects, not allies. Like most of the great Macedonians, he was a cultivated man; he knew Homer by heart and patronized the rationalist Euhemerus, who said that the gods were only men, while Aristotle's successor Theophrastus perhaps wrote for him a treatise on the art of government. It was possibly from Euhemerus that Cassander's crazy brother Alexarchus got the idea that he was the Sun; Alexarchus refounded Sane as Uranopolis, 'Heaven-town,' invented a new speech for the citizens, his 'children of heaven,' and obtained permission for them to strike coins[2]. Having settled Macedonia Cassander turned to Greece, and with the consent of the Boeotians refounded Thebes, which Alexander had destroyed. He collected the scattered Thebans; the Athenians built most of the wall, but the city was not finished for years, and subscriptions continued to be sent from many countries and dynasts. Then he turned Corinth by shipping his army and elephants to Epidaurus, took Argos and other places, and at the end of 316 returned to Macedonia to winter.

The death of Eumenes left Antigonus in virtual control of Asia, with overwhelming power; his armies amounted to over 60,000 men, he had secured 25,000 talents in bullion, and had

[1] See Volume of Plates ii, 10, *e*.

[2] Coins of this community reflect its fanciful character. Volume of Plates ii, 10, *f*.

an annual revenue of 11,000 talents. His aim was to obtain the
whole empire for himself without reference to the royal house;
and Alexander's lion-gryphon now vanishes from Athena's helmet
on the Alexander coinage. But he kept up appearances; Babylonian documents date by him as general only, not as king; he
claimed to act for Alexander's son, and his army made him regent.
He spent the summer of 316 in disposing of possible adversaries.
Peucestas was turned out of Persis; possibly he entered Demetrius' service. Peithon saw, too late, that he had been Antigonus'
tool; he meditated revolt, but Antigonus anticipated and killed
him. He could not displace the satraps of Bactria, Carmania, and
Paropamisadae without difficult campaigns, while Sibyrtius and
Peithon of Sind were his partisans; but he removed Stasander
from Aria. Then he entered Babylonia, and called on Seleucus
for an account of his revenues. Seleucus protested that he owed
no account to anyone; Antigonus insisted, and Seleucus saw
Peithon's fate before him; he left Babylon by night and rode for
his life to Egypt. Antigonus made Peithon of Sind satrap of
Babylonia, and brought Nicanor from Cappadocia to be general
of the upper satrapies. Then he gave his first intimation that he
stood in Alexander's place and meant to imitate his measures; he
appointed Persians to the satrapies of Media and Susiana, of
course without the military command. In the autumn of 316 he
returned to Cilicia, where he secured 10,000 talents at Kyinda,
and wintered.

The old central power was dead; but it had merely been replaced
by another, far more energetic, ambitious, and businesslike, and
controlled by a single brain. The opposition between Antigonus'
and Cassander's policies was becoming patent; and Seleucus
persuaded Ptolemy, Lysimachus, and Cassander, that Antigonus'
ambition threatened their very existence, and the three rulers
formed a definite alliance. Cassander, in possession of Macedonia, Epirus, Thessaly, Athens, and much of Greece, was far the
strongest of the three. Ptolemy had in Egypt an impregnable
fortress, but he depended on mercenaries from Greece and ship-
timber from Syria and Cyprus. Lysimachus had only a small
army, and had so far failed to conquer Seuthes, though some of
the Greek cities on the Thracian Black Sea coast had accepted his
garrisons(see above, p. 464); but he held the Dardanelles crossings,
which gave him importance. He had married Cassander's sister
Nicaea, Perdiccas' widow, and he and Cassander were now united
in an unwavering friendship and confidence. The history of
the next four years, 315–312, is that of the first war between
Antigonus and the coalition.

VII. ANTIGONUS' FIRST STRUGGLE FOR THE EMPIRE

Early in 315 the coalition sent Antigonus an ultimatum, claiming a division of the spoil taken from the central power: Syria for Ptolemy, Hellespontine Phrygia for Lysimachus, the restoration of Babylonia to Seleucus, and for Cassander Cappadocia (which included Paphlagonia) and Cilicia[1]. Antigonus would thus have been completely cut off both from inner Asia and the Black Sea, and restricted to part of Asia Minor. Cassander, whose territory would have joined Lysimachus' at one end and Ptolemy's at the other, had undertaken to hold the barrier against him, and followed up the ultimatum by sending a force, with Lysimachus' aid, to Cappadocia. Antigonus saw that his real struggle was with Cassander, the man he had made; and his objective throughout the war was Macedonia. But he could not invade Macedonia with Ptolemy in his rear; his plan therefore was to stand on the defensive in the north till he had crushed Ptolemy, meanwhile keeping Cassander and Lysimachus busy at home. His far-reaching combinations doubtless embraced Glaucias of Illyria and Seuthes, as well as Epirus.

In the spring of 315 Antigonus opened his attack. He sent his nephew Polemaeus to Cappadocia, and Aristodemus to Greece; detached a force to guard the Dardanelles; and himself with his main army invaded Syria. He was too strong to resist; Ptolemy garrisoned Tyre, took all the Phoenician warships, and retired into Egypt; Antigonus occupied the whole country, including Gaza, and began the siege of Tyre. Meanwhile both his diversions had been successful. Polemaeus drove Cassander's troops out of Cappadocia and advanced along the coast, bringing Heraclea, Bithynia, and Chalcedon into Antigonus' alliance; Aristodemus won over Polyperchon and his son Alexander, and Antigonus took over Polyperchon's elephants and made him his general in the Peloponnese. Polyperchon's base was the all-important Corinth, which he held with his own mercenaries. Cassander indeed invaded Greece, added part of Arcadia to his possessions, and in autumn brought Alexander over to his side and made him his general in the Peloponnese; but he could not

---

[1] Cassander's title to Cilicia in 301, and geography, show that 'Lycia' in Diodorus XIX, 57, 1 is a scribe's error for Cilicia. The confusion of the two names is common; e.g. MSS. of Diodorus XVIII, 39, 6 and XX, 19, 5; Dexippus frag. 1 (Antigonus' satrapy).

gain Polyperchon or take Corinth, for though Alexander's defection detached Polyperchon from Antigonus, he did not join Cassander.

Antigonus now took two steps of the first importance. He began shipbuilding in Phoenicia on a considerable scale, with a view to commanding the sea and severing Cassander from Ptolemy; and he issued a proclamation against Cassander, the effects of which were not exhausted for many years. It enumerated Cassander's crimes against Alexander's house and policy, and declared him a public enemy unless he released Roxane and her son, razed Thebes and Cassandreia (as representing Olynthus), and obeyed Antigonus as regent and general of the Empire; and it declared that all Greek cities everywhere should be free, ungarrisoned, and self-governing. That is, Antigonus asserted that he was fighting for the legitimate king, a pretence useful for his own army and for Macedonian opinion; and he revived Alexander's policy of treating the Greek cities as free allies. He cared nothing for Greek freedom; but he was among the first to realize the power of public opinion, and he desired enormously to have Greek opinion on his side; and to win this he did for years carry out his proclamation with honesty and thoroughness. He did win it; the whole Greek world, except the Cassandrean oligarchs, regarded him as its champion. The policies of Alexander and Antipater had thus come to an open conflict; Antigonus stood for Alexander's, while Cassander, with his oligarchies and garrisons, represented Antipater's, and drove the Greeks to give to Antigonus the confidence they had denied to Alexander. Asander of Caria, who had been garrisoning Greek cities, now naturally joined the coalition, while Delos and Lemnos seemingly took advantage of the proclamation to revolt from Athens[1].

It took Antigonus thirteen months to reduce Tyre, against Alexander's seven. Meanwhile he secured the alliance and fleet of Rhodes, and with his new ships he had by autumn 314 a fleet of 240, including several great *heptereis* (probably galleys of seven men to an oar), a new invention. He was not ready in time to prevent Ptolemy's fleet, commanded by Seleucus, from reducing some of the Cyprian kings; but he secured the Cyclades. All Greek cities, as they became 'free,' were expected to join him as his independent allies, bound however to furnish 'contributions' for the common war against Cassander, exactly as they had done for Alexander. In Greece, Aristodemus secured the alliance of

[1] It is possible that Delos was free by 318; P. Roussel, *Journal des Savants*, 1924, p. 106.

the Aetolians, natural enemies of Antipater's son, and campaigned against Polyperchon's son Alexander, who was murdered that summer, while Cassander was kept busy by Glaucias. Here, however, Cassander was successful; he took from Glaucias Apollonia and Epidamnus, and part of southern Illyria, where he founded Antipatreia; he also collected the Acarnanians along the border into strongholds, notably Stratus, for defence against Aetolia. In the autumn, to prevent Antigonus crossing to Europe, he sent a force to Caria; but Polemaeus, who had come right round the Ionian coast freeing the cities and establishing Antigonus' alliance, defeated it completely. Once Tyre had fallen, Antigonus left his son Demetrius at Gaza, with Nearchus and Peithon as his generals, to watch Ptolemy, and returned to Celaenae to winter; he had hit Ptolemy hard, and proposed in 313 to stand on the defensive at Gaza and begin his real offensive against Macedonia.

Ptolemy had sought to counter Antigonus with a proclamation of his own that the Greeks should be free; but this obvious imitation merely embarrassed the coalition, seeing that Cassander was carrying out its exact antithesis. Cyrene, however, took the proclamation seriously and revolted against Ptolemy's governor Ophellas. Ptolemy quelled the revolt; but he lost most of the critical season of 313, though his fleet conquered Antigonus' partisans in Cyprus, where he made Nicocreon of Salamis his governor. Antigonus himself, before attempting to cross to Europe, desired to draw off Lysimachus from the Dardanelles by creating trouble in his rear, and to ensure that Cassander should not again attack his flank in Caria. He therefore in 313 sent out three expeditions. One went to support the Thracian Black Sea cities, which, led by Callatis, and possibly united in a League, expelled Lysimachus' garrisons, and were joined by Seuthes. The second, under Docimus, once satrap of Babylon, and Antigonus' admiral Medius of Larissa the historian, freed Miletus and other cities, and reduced Caria; Asander vanishes, and Miletus celebrated the restoration of democratic government. The third, under Antigonus' nephew Telesphorus, attacked Cassander in Greece and freed the whole Peloponnese, except Corinth and Sicyon, which were held by Polyperchon; Epirus, too, revolted against Cassander and recalled Aeacides, while Glaucias, with Corcyra's help, recovered Apollonia and Epidamnus.

Cassander was alarmed, and made overtures for peace; but Ptolemy, very naturally, interfered. Negotiations having failed, Cassander displayed his usual energy; he sent an army to Epirus which killed Aeacides and recovered the country, and he himself invaded Greece and besieged Histiaea in Euboea, which had revolted. Antigonus thereon sent 5500 men to Greece under Polemaeus and his fleet under Medius; Polemaeus was joined by the Boeotians and attacked Cassander's principal stronghold, Chalcis. Possibly Cassander believed that this was the main attack; he quitted Histiaea and hurried to Chalcis in force. As soon as Antigonus thought that he was fully involved, he attempted his real offensive; he recalled his fleet to the Dardanelles, marched his army to the Bosporus (autumn 313), and sought from Byzantium, where he had many friends, alliance and a crossing. But he had delayed too long. Lysimachus had had a successful summer, defeating Antigonus' expeditionary force, conquering Seuthes, and recovering all the Greek cities except Callatis; he was back at the Dardanelles with greatly increased prestige. He sent envoys to Byzantium in Cassander's name and his own; they overawed the city, whose lands were at Lysimachus' mercy, and it declared strict neutrality. Faced by Lysimachus and Byzantium Antigonus could not cross; he retired foiled, the decisive event of the war. He had, however, compelled Cassander to leave Chalcis and fly back to Macedonia, and Polemaeus in an autumn campaign swept central Greece; he took Chalcis, and left this vital point free and ungarrisoned,—an extraordinary proof of Antigonus' honesty,—freed most of Euboea and of Phocis, took the Cadmea and brought Thebes over to Antigonus, restored Oropus to the Boeotian League, and finally invaded Attica and compelled Demetrius of Phalerum to ask Antigonus for an alliance, which was, however, never concluded.

Thus by the end of 313, if Antigonus was foiled, Cassander was badly shaken; he had lost most of Greece south of Thessaly, even Athens was threatened, and Lysimachus might not hold Antigonus a second time. He represented to Ptolemy that he must do something to take off the pressure from him. Seleucus was urgent in the same sense, for his own purposes; and in the spring of 312 Ptolemy with his full force attacked Demetrius at Gaza. His combatant army was 18,000 foot and 4000 horse, Macedonians and mercenaries; his auxiliary services were manned by Egyptians. Demetrius was outnumbered; he had 12,500 foot, of whom only 2000 were Macedonians, 4600 Asiatic cavalry, and 43 elephants. Ptolemy used a moveable barrier made of iron stakes and chains to hold up the elephants, and won a complete victory; Peithon and probably Nearchus were killed, 8000 mercenaries surrendered, and Demetrius fled with a few horse to

Cilicia. Ptolemy took Gaza, recovered all Syria and Phoenicia, and settled the surrendered mercenaries in Egypt and some Jews in Alexandria. The battle, however, did more than relieve Cassander; it opened the road eastward, and Seleucus with 1000 men made a dash for Babylon, where he had been popular. He collected 2000 more men on the way, occupied Babylon, and stormed the citadel; and when Nicanor attacked him with 17,000 men, he ambushed him in the marshes, surprised and defeated him by night, and enlisted most of his troops. The Seleucid era, beginning (in Syria) October 312, from which the Seleucid kings reckoned, dates from Seleucus' return to Babylon. He presently reduced Media, and also Susiana, where Antigonus' Persian satrap Aspeisas had claimed independence and put his name on the Alexander coinage[1]; and Antigonus had now a new enemy in his rear.

The rest of the year 312 advanced matters little. Antigonus recovered Syria and Phoenicia, Demetrius retrieving his reputation by smartly capturing 7000 Ptolemaic troops at Myus; but the price was the abandonment for the season of his attack on Europe, where otherwise matters had promised well; for Cassander was fully occupied with a revolt of Epirus under its new king Alcetas, and it took Lyciscus three battles before Alcetas was beaten and Epirus reduced. Meanwhile Ophellas in Cyrene had made himself independent, perhaps with Antigonus' aid; and Antigonus spent the rest of the season in attempts to damage Ptolemy's position in Egypt itself. He sent two expeditions against Petra of the Nabataeans, the second under Demetrius, with a view to denying to Egypt the great Petra-Gaza caravan route; but both failed. He sent another under Hieronymus to the Dead Sea, to corner the bitumen which Egypt required for embalming; but the local Arabs, who drew great profit from the bitumen-fishery, defeated him in a battle on the lake. Lastly he sent Demetrius, with a strict time-limit, to raid Babylon and attempt to capture Seleucus; Demetrius temporarily occupied Babylon, but Seleucus was in Media, and nothing came of this extraordinary raid.

By 311 it was clear that, as things were, neither side could defeat the other, and peace was made between Cassander, Lysimachus, and Antigonus; subsequently Ptolemy also made peace. Possibly he tried to obtain terms for Seleucus; but Seleucus was not included, as Antigonus refused to relinquish his claim to Babylon. Antigonus made excellent propaganda for Greek opinion

---

[1] See E. S. G. Robinson in *Num. Chron.* 1921, p. 37; and Volume of Plates ii, 10, *g*.

out of the negotiations: it was only, he said, through his anxiety
to give rest to the Greek cities, worn out with the war, that he
had first accepted Cassander's onerous proposals and then refrained from crushing Ptolemy when isolated. The terms of peace
were, that Cassander was to be general of Europe till Alexander
IV was old enough to rule; Lysimachus was to rule Thrace,
Ptolemy Egypt, and Antigonus Asia; all Greek cities were to be
free and ungarrisoned. The first term was a direct invitation to
Cassander to murder Alexander's son; the second marked the
break-up of the Empire; the third secured Antigonus' position
with public opinion, and gave him an excuse to begin war again
when he chose. The results of the war were, that Cassander had
lost much of Greece, but had retained Epirus and consolidated his
position in Macedonia, while his friendship with Lysimachus had
stood the test. Lysimachus had greatly improved his position.
Ptolemy had lost Syria and Cyrene; but he had restored Seleucus
and secured Cyprus, and Egypt was untouched. Antigonus had
in effect lost the eastern satrapies, but had obtained Syria, Phoenicia, and Caria instead; his realm, if not so extensive, was more
compact and probably stronger. At sea there had been only minor
actions, and the command of the sea was left undecided; and as
Antigonus' main army had never been engaged, the question
whether he could achieve his ambition was merely postponed.

VIII. ANTIGONUS' KINGDOM

Antigonus' realm, with its capital at Celaenae, comprised Asia
Minor up to Armenia (except Bithynia and part of western Pisidia,
which were independent), the whole of Syria, and probably Mesopotamia. He had governed the provinces beyond the Euphrates,
while he held them, by satraps, nominally those of Alexander IV;
but there are no traces of satraps in his kingdom after 311, only
extensive generalships; his method of government is really unknown, but his subjects, it is said, found his rule unexpectedly
mild. He had an informal council of 'Friends,' which became
usual in all Macedonian kingdoms, and a secretarial department
to draft his decrees. Like Alexander, he retained in power various
dependent dynasts, e.g. the Phoenician kings, and Mithridates of
Cius; in 302 he executed Mithridates for treason, but his son
escaped to be the ancestor of the kings of Pontus. He continued
the process of eliminating the Persian landowners from the King's
Land, doubtless a boon to the peasantry, and made grants to
Macedonians; but he apparently preserved Alexander's financial

officials and arrangements, and continued to strike Alexander's money; Ake dated a new era from his conquest of Phoenicia in 315, but in 307 he restored Tyre as a central mint, and Ake's brief prosperity ended.

The Greek cities began by being his free allies, as they had been Alexander's, though he too never freed Cius, or Heraclea, still ruled by the tyrant Dionysius. As free allies, the cities signed the peace of 311 (p. 488); as such, Cnidus attempted to mediate between Antigonus and Rhodes in 304, and Colophon voted help to Athens in 307; like Alexander, Antigonus allowed Eresus freely to enforce its law against tyrants. But though in much Antigonus copied Alexander, he made one innovation. He could not re-form the League of Corinth while Cassander dominated Greece; he therefore saw to the creation of sectional Leagues. The Ionian League was revived; a League of the Aeolian cities was formed, with its centre at Alexander's favoured Ilium; and the Ionian Cyclades were grouped into the League of the Islanders, with its centre at Delos, seat of Apollo the god of the home-sea, which none might rule save in his name. Antigonus desired sea-power; and this League, dependent on himself, was his solution of the problem of leaving Delos free while preventing Ptolemy from gaining control of Apollo. Here again, however, as elsewhere, freedom was at first a reality: Delos in 310 received offerings from Ptolemy's admiral Leonidas without Antigonus objecting. These peculiar Leagues were not full sovereign States. They had no civil head, no assembly, no military or judicial powers, and apparently no coinage; business was transacted by a council of delegates from the constituent cities. Their chief business was the administration of the federal festivals, though probably they had some economic functions; their revenues were small, and extraordinary expenses were thrown on the several cities. The Ionian League possessed its own federal temple, the Panionion; but the federal festival of the Ilian League was the festival of Athena at Ilium, re-named the Panathenaea, jointly managed by the League and Ilium. The Island League held its federal festival, the Antigoneia, at Delos, and, like the later Thessalian League, possessed the extraordinary power of granting citizenship in its constituent cities. Antigonus was worshipped as a god by the Islanders, and probably by the other Leagues also (though after Ipsus the Ionians worshipped Alexander); for Scepsis in the Ilian League was worshipping him by 310. By this means he obtained a footing in free cities, just as Alexander had done (p. 419).

Antigonus also founded a number of cities. Carrying out Alexander's plan, he refounded and rebuilt, though he did not complete, Smyrna, his most enduring work; he founded Antigoneia Troas, another Antigoneia on the Ascanian lake, famous later as Nicaea, and a third, which received many Athenian settlers, on the Orontes. He may have founded Pella (later Apamea), Gadara, and other cities in Syria; his general Docimus founded Docimeum as a centre for the export of the famous marble; and his general Nicanor founded Doura, afterwards called Europos, in the Euphrates valley. Doura was presumably a mixed city of Alexander's type, as its land remained King's Land; but in the west, as was natural, Smyrna and Troas certainly, and Antigoneia-Nicaea apparently, were fully autonomous Greek cities.

Antigonus exacted heavy war 'contributions' from the Greek cities, though he never taxed them as Demetrius was to do. But with the assumption of divinity he began to interpret 'freedom' as entitling him to interference. In the Ionian cities he laid down much-needed rules for judicial procedure; and he simplified the import and export arrangements of various Asiatic Greek cities, to promote trade and prosperity. This was very well. But many of the Asiatic Greek cities could not feed themselves; and Antigonus forbade the oversea import of corn on the ground that this ran them into debt, and, as the taxes he drew in kind from the King's Land made him a great corn merchant, made them buy corn from himself, though he declared that he gave them the corn at cost price. Then he began to synoecize two or more towns into one; seven went to form Antigoneia Troas (about 308). He did not indeed *order* if he could avoid it; he let his wishes be known, and left the cities to carry them out, as Teos and Lebedus did when they united in 302; probably the Leagues had been thus formed. But his wishes were law, as the Scepsians found, even if a good law; for he ended the secular warfare between Scepsians and Cebrenians by moving both to Troas. These synoecisms, however, involved in turn a mass of minute regulations as to lawsuits, property, and building; and Antigonus took power to prevent the passing of new laws against his interests, and to punish their proposers, just as he prevented the cities from borrowing money if he thought it inexpedient, or sent judicial commissions from one city to another. And though he desired to promote prosperity, his continual wars and war contributions had the opposite effect; many cities were in debt; at Ephesus, when he died, mortgages on land had become so heavy and purchasers so scarce that a special law had to be passed compelling mortgagors and mortgagees to value and divide the land, to prevent innumerable foreclosures and complete disorganization. Finally, after he took the royal title, he reached the last inevitable stage; he tried to compel Rhodes by force to become his 'free' ally, and he garrisoned cities on the ground of military necessity, just like Cassander; thus he garrisoned some Dardanelles towns, in spite of the petitions of the Ilian League, and in 302 Lysimachus solemnly 'freed' Lampsacus from the champion of Greek freedom, and 'liberation' became a mere counter in the political game.

IX. CASSANDER AND PTOLEMY

The peace of 311, though only an uneasy truce, marked the beginning of the dissolution of the Empire into independent states, a process completed ten years later. The dynasts did not yet call themselves kings, and continued to strike Alexander's money; but they emphasized their independence by founding capitals in their own names, though all but Cassander waited till Alexander IV was dead. Seleucus built Seleuceia on the Tigris, replacing Opis; Lysimachus in 309 founded Lysimacheia near Gallipoli, of which Cardia became a village. Antigonus did not found his new capital, Antigoneia on the Orontes, till he became king in 306. Ptolemy already had Alexandria, where Alexander was worshipped; but subsequently he built Ptolemaïs as capital of Upper Egypt.

The events of the years 310–308 are obscure. Cassander was probably somewhat exhausted by the war, and also knew that Macedonia's crying need was recuperation after the efforts of the last twenty-three years; he was loth to fight again, and was concerned with methods of restoration. He secured the friendship of Audoleon of Paeonia, which had become independent, by defeating the Autariatae of Serbia, after which he settled 20,000 of them on his Thracian frontier to replace the men Macedonia had lost; and he fostered trade with his northern neighbours, who disliked Alexander's money, by reissuing Philip's tetradrachms. He also achieved the feat of effecting a permanent reconciliation, based on territorial adjustments, between Thebes and Plataea, Thespiae, and Orchomenus; and Thebes, though with diminished territory, resumed her place as head of the Boeotian League. There could, however, be no real reconciliation between himself and Antigonus, and, although they did not fight, each was willing to damage the other if opportunity served; thus in 310, when

Polemaeus, who now governed Hellespontine Phrygia, thinking himself slighted, revolted from Antigonus, Cassander accepted him as an ally.

Cassander, however, had a domestic problem: Alexander IV was now nearly thirteen, and some Macedonians were saying it was time he began to rule. Cassander thereon murdered Roxane and the boy (310 or early 309). He reaped the odium; but all the dynasts except Seleucus (who was not party to the treaty of 311) were in fact equally guilty, and all shared the benefit; for the fiction that they were the king's satraps was now at an end. But it gave Antigonus an opening. Polyperchon, though now only a soldier of fortune, was still holding Corinth and Sicyon; and Antigonus showed him a chance of recovering his position, supplied money to raise an army to attack Cassander, and sent him a youth from Pergamum to play the part of pretender; under the name of Heracles he was to figure as a son of Alexander by one of his captives after Issus[1]. No one had heard of such a son, and the boy was five years too young; but the Macedonian people were content to take Polyperchon's word, and welcome a scion of Alexander. Between mercenaries, Macedonian royalists, and Antigonus' allies the Aetolians, Polyperchon raised 21,000 men and in 309[2] invaded Macedonia. Cassander was threatened with wholesale defection; but he obtained an interview with Polyperchon, convinced him that, if he succeeded, he would merely become Antigonus' servant, and bribed him with the generalship of the Peloponnese and a share of power in return for the pretender's death. Polyperchon killed Heracles, and entered Cassander's service. But, as Cassander foresaw, he could not confess that he had raised the Macedonians on false pretences; thus he could never again be a rival, for he had, it seemed, murdered a son of Alexander who trusted him.

Antigonus had attacked Cassander by deputy, because since the summer of 311 he himself had been engaged in an attempt to recover Babylon from Seleucus, who seemingly had the support of some eastern satraps and perhaps of the Cossaeans; Antigonus ravaged Babylonia in 310 and 309, and half ruined Babylon, but failed to subdue Seleucus. In 310 Ptolemy, as in honour bound,

---

[1] This view of Heracles is defended by the writer in *J.H.S.* xli, 1921, pp. 18 *sqq.*

[2] Diodorus' date; but perhaps really 308, if Cassander concealed the death of Alexander IV (Diodorus xix, 105, 2); this might explain why neither Polyperchon nor Cassander opposed Ptolemy in 308, and why one Babylonian document gives Alexander IV a *tenth* year (from April 308).

declared war again on Antigonus on Seleucus' behalf, but with
an ulterior object also, the acquisition of a share of influence over
the Greek world. His fleet attempted Cilicia, and was repulsed
by Demetrius, commanding for his father in Asia Minor; it then
sailed to Cyprus. Nicocreon was dead, and Nicocles intriguing
with Antigonus; he had fortified Paphos, and put his name on the
Alexander-coinage[1]. Ptolemy's generals besieged Paphos, and
compelled Nicocles and his family to commit suicide; and Cyprus
became an Egyptian possession, governed by Ptolemy's brother
Menelaus. Next year Ptolemy himself seized some bases in
Caria and Lycia. But late that year, 309, Demetrius made peace
with him; perhaps Ptolemy represented that his real enemy, like
Antigonus', was now Cassander. This peace implies that Antigonus also made peace with Seleucus; he could only use part of
his strength, and Seleucus and his allies had ultimately defeated
him. Seleucus kept Babylon, but Antigonus did not give up his
claim to Alexander's destined capital[2]. For nearly two years
Antigonus remained at peace.

Ptolemy spent the winter of 309 in Cos, where in spring 308
his mistress Berenice bore him a son, the future Ptolemy II; and
Polemaeus left Cassander and joined him, only to be executed for
alleged treason. Ptolemy now aimed at controlling Greece. This
involved challenging Cassander; but the two had drifted apart.
Cassander must have resented seeing his sister Eurydice neglected
for Berenice, which would estrange him from Ptolemy, while
Berenice's influence with Ptolemy would be thrown against
Cassander; perhaps too Ptolemy felt that Cassander had deserted
him in 311. To strengthen himself Ptolemy proposed to marry
Cleopatra, which meant definitely repudiating Eurydice. Cleopatra, weary of her virtual captivity at Sardes, agreed; Antigonus
promptly had her murdered by her women, whom he then executed for the crime. But Ptolemy persevered; in the spring of
308 he crossed the Aegean, freed Andros from Polemaeus'

---

[1] See Volume of Plates ii, *h*, and E. T. Newell, *Nicocles King of Paphos*,
Num. Chron. 1919, p. 64.

[2] This war between Antigonus and Seleucus rests on Otto's hypothesis that
in the Babylonian *Chronicle concerning the Diadochi* the first Alexander year
was 317/16; it seems the most probable view, though, like every other, it
involves difficulties. Polyaenus IV, 9, 1 clearly belongs here, as Droysen
guessed. In an astronomical table published by Kugler, *Von Moses bis Paulus*,
p. 305, the year 302 (see p. 503) is reckoned as Antigonus' fourteenth (or
fifteenth) year at Babylon, *i.e.* he preserved his claim. See now on the
whole question S. Smith in *Revue d'Assyriologie* XXII, 1925, p. 179.

garrison, landed at the Isthmus, and announced that he had come in the cause of Greek freedom. Polyperchon was absent, and his daughter-in-law Cratesipolis handed over Corinth and Sicyon to Ptolemy, who in the cause of Greek freedom garrisoned them. He then himself issued the usual religious invitations to the Isthmian festival; he *may* have thought of restoring the League of Corinth under his own presidency. But the Greek states took no notice of him; Antigonus had been first, and they were satisfied of his good faith; of Ptolemy's they were not. Ptolemy could do nothing, and as an opportunity offered of recovering Cyrene, where Ophellas had fallen a victim to Agathocles, he made peace with Cassander; the two might quarrel, but they were necessary to each other while Antigonus lived. Ptolemy did recover Cyrene, and made Berenice's son Magas governor.

X. ANTIGONUS' SECOND STRUGGLE FOR THE EMPIRE

Antigonus was roused by Ptolemy's attempt to steal his thunder. The story of the next six years is that of his second struggle to secure the empire for himself. Had he been younger, the story might have had another ending; but he was nearly eighty and becoming unwieldy, and he left much of the actual conduct of operations to Demetrius. Demetrius was now twenty-nine, and his extraordinary powers had ripened. His energy was hardly inferior to Alexander's; his majesty and attraction were unrivalled; he was great alike as leader, mechanician, and admiral. Also he had ideas, and was as yet chivalrous and full of generous impulses; unlike Antigonus, he really believed in Greek freedom and a union of hearts. The complete affection and confidence between his father and himself were about the best things the time could show. But with his brilliance was conjoined a character fundamentally impossible. Vanity and ostentation, a licentiousness which scandalized even that age,—these were not necessarily fatal; but he had no sense of duty, and was to be ruined by his instability. Antigonus gave out that he intended to free Greece, enslaved by Cassander and Ptolemy. But he abandoned the idea of crossing the Dardanelles. His new plan was first to raise Greece; then, while Cassander's hands were full, crush Ptolemy and gain command of the sea; then invade Macedonia in force from Greece. Given Macedonia and Greece, everything else would follow. Naturally he began with Athens.

For ten years now Athens had been ruled for Cassander by

Demetrius of Phalerum, with the vague title of 'governor.' He had acted entirely in the interests of the wealthy; from their point of view Athens had never been governed so well, for there was peace and prosperity, though maintained by foreign spears. Demetrius, a man of learning and ability, was a Peripatetic; under him Aristotle's school was all-powerful, and he obtained for the alien Theophrastus the right to purchase land and form the school, like Plato's, into a legally constituted association. He translated into law many of the ideas of Aristotle and Theophrastus; the basis of his legislation was the dogma that citizens cannot make themselves but must be moulded by the lawgiver, the source of all the trouble between the idealist philosophies and the democracy. His code of laws caused him to be ranked as the third lawgiver of Athens. Of loose and luxurious life himself, he favoured moderation and decency in others; he passed a body of sumptuary laws which cut down expenditure on marriages, feasts, and funerals, possibly prohibited the formation of new clubs, and regulated women's dress and their deportment in public, and in Aristotle's spirit appointed a board (*gynaeconomi*) to see that these provisions were observed; concurrently he revived the censorial powers of the Areopagus. He did something toward clarifying titles to real property and mortgages, and reformed the jury-courts in the interest of the well-to-do. He transferred the guardianship of the laws to a committee of seven 'guardians of the laws,' whose business was to see that existing laws were enforced and that no new ones illegal or objectionable to the government were proposed; they recall the guardians of Plato's *Republic*. This committee really controlled the Assembly, which for ten years hardly passed a decree. As a counterpoise he reduced the obligation to military service, which pleased the poor; but he also neglected the fleet and abolished the trierarchy, a measure which relieved the rich. He himself regularly held the office of general till 309, when he took the archonship for the sake of reforming the public festivals; again in the interest of the wealthy he abolished the private provision of choruses and threw the expense on the State, and appointed an annual official (*agōnothĕtes*) to conduct public festivals out of the public funds. He took a census of Athens, which showed a total of 21,000 citizens and 10,000 metics, say perhaps 120,000 souls, with an unknown number of slaves; the reduced number of citizens had brought Athens back to where she stood in 403. It was to his credit that he observed the general amnesty with which he began his rule, and under him extreme democrats like Stratocles and Demosthenes' nephew Demochares lived in Athens undisturbed. But the outstanding event of his ten years was the arrival in Athens of an obscure Phoenician from Cyprus named Zeno, who was to found the Stoic philosophy.

In June 307 Antigonus' son Demetrius sailed to Athens with 250 warships and transports, found the booms up at the Piraeus, entered the harbour, and from his flagship proclaimed to the people that he came to give them back their freedom and their ancestral constitution, the usual phrase for the overthrow of a tyrant. The garrison withdrew to Munychia; Demetrius of Phalerum surrendered Athens and retired with a safe-conduct to Thebes, and afterwards to Egypt, where he helped to found the Museum and perhaps made laws for Ptolemy. Demetrius then stormed and razed Munychia, and made his entry into a free Athens. Save for a brief moment in 318 the people had not tasted liberty for fifteen years; and the sudden revulsion brought out all that was worst in the Athenian character. A shameless demagogue, Stratocles, came into power, and some of the men who had fought the Lamian war, and whose sons were to fight the Chremonidean, lost their heads and gave themselves to slavish adulation of their liberator. They hailed Antigonus and Demetrius as kings; they worshipped them as 'Saviour gods,' with altars and religious festivals, and set up their gilded statues on the forbidden site beside those of Harmodius and Aristogeiton; they decreed that their portraits should be woven on Athena's mantle, and that they should be approached only by religious envoys, like the gods of Olympus; on the spot where Demetrius alighted from his chariot an altar was raised to Demetrius the Descender, and he was asked to give oracles like a god. Two new tribes, Antigonis and Demetrias, were created, and an Antigonis and a Demetrias were added to the sacred triremes.

There was fortunately another side. The laws of the Phalerian were treated on their merits; the 'guardians of the laws' and the *gynaeconomi* were abolished, but the liturgies were not restored and the *agonothetes* was retained; the changes entailed by two new tribes were quietly carried out; above all, Demetrius saw to it that the revolution was unstained by bloodshed, though Cassander's principal supporters were exiled. Stratocles, who had once impeached Demosthenes, nevertheless posed as the successor of Lycurgus' policy, and passed a long decree in his honour; it was probably now that the office of Superintendent of the Administration, modelled on Lycurgus, was created. The superintendent had a wide control of the state finances; the first occupant of the post, appointed in 307, was Lycurgus' son Habron. At the same time the judicial examination of the claims of candidates for citizenship was abolished, though it was re-imposed in 303 in consequence of indiscriminate grants of citizenship to Demetrius' followers. Measures were, however, taken against the Peripatetics; with Demetrius' approval one Sophocles carried a law that no philosopher should teach in Athens without permission of the Council and Assembly, and Theophrastus was exiled. He was Cassander's friend; but he was also the most learned man living. Fortunately for Athens' repute, Sophocles' law was declared illegal next year, as contravening the law as to associations, and Theophrastus was recalled; Epicurus also came from Lampsacus to Athens and set up his school. Meanwhile Lemnos rejoined Athens, and Antigonus sent the city 150,000 bushels of corn and timber to build 100 warships. Demetrius ordered all 'free' cities in Greece to support Athens, and having thus equipped the city for its destined war with Cassander returned to Asia to attack Ptolemy.

In the spring of 306 he sailed to Cyprus with 118 warships, many transports, and 15,400 men; he believed that Ptolemy must fight for Cyprus. He summoned Antigonus' former ally Rhodes to join him with her fleet; but the Egyptian trade was too important to the Rhodians, and they declared neutrality. Mene-laus in Cyprus had sixty warships and 12,800 men; Demetrius landed, defeated him, and shut him up in Salamis. As he an-ticipated, Ptolemy put to sea with his whole remaining fleet, 140 warships and transports carrying 10,000 mercenaries, to relieve Salamis. Demetrius blockaded Menelaus in the bottle-necked harbour with ten warships, and stood down the coast with 108 warships and 57 armed transports to meet Ptolemy, who, though superior in number of warships, had nothing larger than quinqueremes. Demetrius' right was inshore; he therefore massed his best ships,—the Phoenician, including seven heptereis, and 30 Athenian quadriremes,—on the left wing, where he com-manded in person on his hepteres. In the ensuing battle he crushed Ptolemy's right and then successfully turned on his centre, driving his fleet ashore; Ptolemy lost 120 warships, while trans-ports carrying 8000 mercenaries were captured; Salamis and the 60 ships there surrendered, and the question of the command of the sea was settled for twenty years. Aristodemus with the flagship carried the news to Antigonus, and hailed him king; Antigonus thereon assumed the royal title,—a frank usurpation, though confirmed by his army,—and conferred the like title on

Demetrius. It meant, not that Antigonus was king of his section of Asia, but that he claimed to be monarch, jointly with Demetrius, of Alexander's empire; their dated Tyrian didrachms show that they claimed the empire as from Alexander's death. Demetrius' coins also show that he commemorated his success by a statue of Victory standing on the prow of his flagship[1]; he became a god of the Island League, and a tribe Demetrias appears at Samos, where he and his father were also worshipped. Ptolemy lost Cyprus and his bases in Asia Minor, and ceded Corinth, which he could no longer reach, to Cassander. He could now no longer get ship-timber except through the merchants of Rhodes.

Antigonus thought that Ptolemy might now be finished off; he invaded Egypt with 88,000 men and 83 elephants, the largest army in Greek history commanded by one of Greek speech, while Demetrius with the fleet kept pace with him. But it was November, and too late for galleys. Many ships were wrecked in a storm off Raphia; and the army, too huge to be easily provisioned, suffered in crossing the desert south of Gaza, and was already discouraged when it reached the Nile. The river line could not be forced; the fleet, scattered by a second storm, could give no assistance; Ptolemy began seducing Antigonus' troops, provisions ran out, and Antigonus had to lead his army back to Syria. Again Egypt had proved impregnable from the north. Ptolemy after his victory also took the title of king (305), and was followed by Cassander, Lysimachus, and Seleucus. The title affirmed their independent rule in their respective territories; Antigonus of course did not recognize this, and Demetrius' friends professed to treat them as officials of Demetrius' empire. Ptolemy dated his reign as from Alexander's death, and instituted in Egypt an official State-worship of Alexander.

Antigonus had suffered a severe set-back; he was to suffer another in 305, when an attempt to bring Rhodes into his alliance failed. Why he stultified all his professions and wasted an invaluable year over the siege of Rhodes is incomprehensible; for, even if the Rhodians did carry ship-timber to Egypt, the loss of Cyprus had deprived Ptolemy of his last reserve of good seamen, a far more important matter. In the spring of 305 Demetrius sailed to Rhodes with 200 warships and 170 transports, carrying 40,000 troops and 30,000 navvies; he was aided by the irregular Aegean sea-power, the pirates, who hated Rhodes for her attempts

[1] See Volume of Plates ii, 10, *k*. It is now generally considered improbable that this was the famous Victory from Samothrace.

to suppress piracy. The Rhodians raised a general levy, armed the slaves, and the whole city set to work. Demetrius first attacked the harbour with warships behind a floating ironclad boom, and seized the mole; but two assaults were beaten off, and the Rhodians destroyed his boom and recaptured the mole. Demetrius then levelled the ground up to the wall, and brought up his 'Taker of Cities' (Helepolis), a huge armoured tower built in nine stages, greater than any yet known, with mechanically controlled ports to shoot through, and full of stone-throwers and catapults; it was supported by eight enormous 'tortoises' or shields to protect sappers, reached through covered galleries, and by two armoured rams 180 feet long, worked under penthouses. But the grand assault failed; the Rhodians had built two inner walls, and managed to set fire to the Helepolis. They fired 2300 great missiles the final night. Lastly, Demetrius tried a silent surprise, which also failed; then he sat down to a blockade. But his galleys, with their limited blockading powers, could not prevent Rhodian cruisers from destroying his supply-ships, or Ptolemy from running in provisions and mercenaries. Cnidus and Athens each tried to mediate; finally Antigonus told Demetrius to make peace, and an Aetolian embassy, arriving at the right moment, had the honour of settling the matter (spring 304); the terms, that Rhodes should be free and be Antigonus' ally except against Ptolemy, could have been reached without fighting. Demetrius gained nothing but much enjoyment, a showy reputation, and the name of Besieger. The famous siege was remarkable for its chivalry; there was a convention between the belligerents for ransoming all prisoners on either side at fixed rates; the Rhodians refused to destroy Antigonus' statues, and Demetrius spared works of art. Demetrius later gave a tenth of his spoil as a contribution to Thebes; the Rhodians sold his abandoned machines and with the money erected the Colossus, the heroic statue of the Sun which towered over their harbour. They also honoured Ptolemy as a saviour god.

Athens meanwhile had been fighting the Four Years War (307–4) against Cassander, who was hampered by the loss of Epirus (where Glaucias had in 307 restored Aeacides' young son Pyrrhus as king), and by the necessity of safeguarding Macedonia. At first Athens did well; Antigonus sent 150 talents, Demochares energetically armed the city and secured help from Aetolia and Boeotia, and in 305 the Athenian Olympiodorus defeated Cassander at Elatea. But after Antigonus' failure in Egypt Cassander could use his strength; in 304 he secured Boeotia, and, the Aetolians having gone home, invaded Attica, took Panactum, Phyle, and Salamis, and besieged Athens, while Polyperchon was reconquering the Peloponnese for him. The danger to Athens compelled Antigonus to make peace with Rhodes; and Demetrius hurried across the Aegean with 330 warships and transports. His energy soon retrieved the position. He landed at Aulis in Cassander's rear, compelled him to raise the siege and retire northward, followed and defeated him at Thermopylae, freed Euboea, regained Boeotia, renewed the Aetolian alliance, and retook Panactum and Phyle and restored them to Athens.

He spent that winter in Athens, a winter long remembered, in a round of feasting and debauchery; he took up his quarters in the Parthenon, saying that as a god he was Athena's younger brother; the Maiden's temple became a brothel, and one of his mistresses, the notorious Lamia, was worshipped as Aphrodite. Stratocles was now nothing but Demetrius' instrument, and the better elements among the democrats began to form an opposition. From this time Demetrius' own character seems to deteriorate. He had expected too much, and was disillusioned. He began to despise the very men who worshipped him; he ultimately ceased to believe in a union of hearts. He started interfering in the affairs of Athens, first with the course of justice, presently with the government; in 303 he suppressed a democratic revolt against Stratocles, and Demochares was exiled. The servility of Stratocles' party then culminated in a decree that whatsoever Demetrius ordered should be right for men and well-pleasing to the gods. But it is darkest before dawn; and in two years' time Zeno was to begin to teach in Athens.

In the spring of 303 Demetrius, having liberated practically all Central Greece, started to reconquer the Peloponnese. He freed Sicyon, where he was worshipped, drove Cassander's general Prepelaus out of Corinth, and recovered Achaea, the Argolid, and all Arcadia except Mantinea, districts which he was to hold permanently. At Argos he married Pyrrhus' sister Deidameia, which meant that he claimed to stand in the place of Alexander's son, to whom she had been betrothed, and then proceeded to carry out his father's great plan: he called a conference of the Greek states at the Isthmus, and renewed the League of Corinth on Panhellenic lines, its congress being designed to meet at the four Panhellenic festivals; the chief absentees were Thessaly, Sparta, and Messenia. Unlike Philip's League it was based on democratic governments in the constituent states. The League elected Demetrius general in Alexander's seat, but for a war against Cassander's

Macedonia; and the Corinthians requested him to garrison Acrocorinthus till the war was ended—a garrison which was to remain for sixty years. Demetrius put his father's name and his own, each with the royal title, on the Alexander coinage[1].

XI. DEFEAT AND DEATH OF ANTIGONUS

The loss of Greece, added to that of Epirus, rendered Cassander's position serious, and he made overtures to Antigonus; Antigonus demanded unconditional surrender. In this emergency Cassander displayed real greatness. He called Lysimachus to a conference; they decided on a plan of campaign and on a request to Ptolemy and Seleucus for help, explaining precisely what would happen to them if Cassander fell. Ptolemy was convinced; the difficulty was to communicate with Seleucus, as Antigonus held all the routes. Ptolemy undertook the task, and sent men on swift camels across the Arabian desert to Jauf, whence they reached Babylon. The four kings renewed the coalition of 315, but this time not to bridle Antigonus but to destroy him. Cassander probably knew, though the world did not, that in Lysimachus they now possessed a general who might be Antigonus' match. Lysimachus had conquered Callatis, solidified his power in Thrace, and acquired an important recruiting ground; his military strength was now very different from that of 315.

In spring 302 Demetrius invaded Thessaly with 57,500 men, —8000 Macedonians, 15,000 mercenaries, 25,000 League troops, 8000 pirates, and 1500 horse; it was the main attack to which Antigonus had been working up. In face of the danger, Cassander, risking everything on his judgment, sent part of his army under Prepelaus to Lysimachus and allowed Lysimachus to recruit Autariatae; no other king would have so trusted an ally. He himself met Demetrius with 31,000 men, took up a strong position, and left the rest to Lysimachus. Demetrius camped in face of his army, and looked for an opening. Given time, he must have conquered Macedonia; but he could not regain the year lost at Rhodes. Before an opening came, there came the news from Asia on which Cassander had counted. Antigonus sent to recall his son; for Seleucus was moving westward with 500 elephants, and Lysimachus had crossed the Dardanelles. Seleucus since 308 had acquired the eastern satrapies, partly by persuasion, partly by force, Stasanor of Bactria having to be conquered, and had finally crossed the Indus. There he became involved in war with Chandragupta, an illegitimate scion of the house of Magadha, who with the help of the Brahmans had consolidated all India north of the Deccan into the Mauryan empire; his capital was Pataliputra (Patna) on the Ganges, recently excavated. He was too strong for Seleucus, who made peace, ceding the Cabul valley and the governments west of the Indus which Alexander had formed out of the Indian districts[1]. In return he obtained 500 war-elephants, a lasting friendship with the powerful Mauryas, and possibly commercial advantages. He was back at Babylon when Cassander's message reached him.

Antigonus was holding a festival at Antigoneia on the Orontes when the news came that Lysimachus had crossed. How he crossed is unknown; probably through treachery. Antigonus had garrisoned some Dardanelles cities, and there was disaffection; Lampsacus and Parium went over to Lysimachus. But, beside this, two of Antigonus' generals in Asia Minor, Docimus of Phrygia, once the friend of Perdiccas and Alcetas, and Phoenix of Lydia, once Eumenes' lieutenant, were traitors; after many years Antigonus' severities recoiled on his head. The strange fact that Docimeum was named after Docimus attests his importance; very possibly both Phrygias and the Dardanelles were in his charge. A comet which appeared when Lysimachus crossed helped to unsettle Antigonus' subjects, already rendered superstitious by the earthquake which had shaken Ionia the year before. Lysimachus sent Prepelaus along the coast to Ionia; he took the Ionian cities one after another, including Ephesus, and Phoenix handed over Sardes. Lysimachus himself invaded Phrygia, where Docimus and his lieutenant Philetaerus, who afterwards founded the Pergamene kingdom, handed over Synnada and other fortresses, and the treasure there. Antigonus sent a small force to occupy Babylon behind Seleucus' back, on the chance of making Seleucus turn, and with his main army hurried to Phrygia, hoping to crush Lysimachus while isolated. Lysimachus played for time. He took a strong position and kept Antigonus before it till his supplies were cut off; then he slipped away by night and stood in Dorylaeum (Eshkisher), impregnable and well provisioned. Antigonus drew lines round the town; when they were almost complete Lysimachus again slipped away in a storm, and took winter quarters near Heraclea, ruled by

---

[1] See p. 414 and *Cambridge History of India*, vol. i, pp. 430 ff., 472.

Dionysius' widow, the Achaemenid Amestris; he married her and thus secured a fine base. He had kept Antigonus employed throughout the season; and Seleucus was wintering in Cappadocia.

Demetrius, on his father's summons, made a truce with Cassander; both knew that the decision must now fall elsewhere. He left Deidameia and part of his fleet at Athens, and sailed to Asia with Pyrrhus, whom a revolution had again driven out of Epirus; he recovered Ephesus and the Dardanelles cities, secured Byzantium's friendship, and held the straits in force when it was too late. Cassander sent his brother Pleistarchus with 12,000 men to reinforce Lysimachus, but Demetrius' fleet caught him crossing the Black Sea and sank part of his transports. Demetrius wintered at Ephesus, where he received many honours. In spring 301 Ptolemy invaded Syria, but returned to Egypt on a false report of Lysimachus' defeat; but Lysimachus, his army now swollen to at least 40,000 men, moved out from Heraclea, and in north Phrygia effected his junction with Seleucus. Demetrius too joined his father, and at Ipsus near Synnada the two great armies met in the 'battle of the kings.' Antigonus had 70,000 foot, 10,000 horse, and 75 elephants; the allies had 64,000 foot, 10,500 horse, 120 chariots, and 480 elephants. Demetrius opened the battle with a cavalry charge which scattered Seleucus' horse, but he pursued too far; the elephants cut him off from return, and Antigonus was defeated and killed, with the pathetic cry on his lips 'Demetrius will come and save me.' The struggle between the central power and the dynasts was ended, and with Antigonus' death the dismemberment of the Graeco-Macedonian world became inevitable. Demetrius fled to Ephesus, while Lysimachus and Seleucus divided Antigonus' kingdom. Cassander was recognized as king of Macedonia; he desired nothing in Asia himself, but (as in 315) he claimed Cilicia and (instead of Cappadocia) Caria, with Lycia and Pamphylia to connect them, which were made into a kingdom for Pleistarchus. The victors gave Antigonus a royal funeral. But later, under Lysimachus' harsher rule, a Phrygian peasant paid him a finer tribute; he was found digging a pit on his farm, and, when asked what he did, replied sadly 'I seek Antigonus.'

CHAPTER XVI

GREEK POLITICAL THOUGHT AND THEORY IN THE FOURTH CENTURY

I. THE POLITICAL THOUGHT OF THE FOURTH CENTURY

A DISTINCTION may perhaps be drawn, which is based on a real difference, between political theory and political thought. Political theory is the speculation of individual minds (though it may well become, and in the process of time often does become, the dogma of a school); and, as such, it is an activity of conscious thought, which is aware both of itself as it thinks and of the facts about which it thinks. Political thought is the thought of a whole society; and it is not necessarily, or often, self-conscious. It is an activity of the mind; but one naturally thinks of it as a substance or content rather than as an activity. It is the complex of ideas which is entertained—but not, as a rule, apprehended—by all who are concerned in affairs of state in a given period of time. It is such thought which makes history; and history is the mirrored reflection, or the reverse side, of such thought. Political thought and history are two aspects of one process—the process of the human spirit: they are two sides of a single coin. There is thus a political thought which is immanent in each historical process; and there is a political theory which is distinct from the process, and yet—because it cannot but be influenced by the process, either in the way of attraction, or in the way of repulsion—is part and parcel of it. It is easy to think of political thought as the active and determining maker of history, and to regard political theory as a speculation of the detached mind, remote from the motive forces of events. Such a distinction is perhaps nowhere true. Thinking which is directed to human conduct becomes a factor in human action; speculation that seems airy may bring down an abundant rain of events; the theory of Rousseau, for example, was a stuff which made and unmade states. The distinction is certainly untrue if it is applied to ancient Greece. Here political theory was conceived as a 'practical science'—a theory, indeed, or speculation, but not a mere theory or speculation, which left things as they were because they could not be otherwise. It was regarded as dealing with those human things which 'might be otherwise than they were,' and charged with the duty of showing how they might become otherwise in the sense of becoming better. Because it was practical, it was idealistic; because it was concerned with making men and states better, it issued in the construction of ideal states, which were meant to be realized—immediately and directly realized. Political theory in the modern world only becomes active and practical when it becomes political thought, and the many are converted to the teaching of the few. We submit, as it were, to a mediation between theory and action. The note of Greek political theory is immediacy. It moves directly to action; Plato, for instance, seeks at once to realize his 'republic' in Syracuse. If we reflect on the two divisions which we may make in the political theory of the fourth century—the politico-oratorical, represented by Isocrates, and the politico-philosophical, represented by Plato—we see that this immediacy is common to both. We see, too, that immediacy does not of itself command success. In the ancient world, as in the modern, the theory that becomes general thought, or reflects general thought, is the theory that succeeds. The spirit of Isocrates, by the end of the fourth century, might rejoice in the success of Isocratean theory. Whether it ought to have succeeded and whether it was better for the world that it should have succeeded, is another question.

The political thought immanent in political action, at the beginning of the fourth century, still owed allegiance to a belief in the sanctity of the self-governing and self-sufficing city-state; and here it agreed with political theory, which was always inspired by this belief. During the fifth century Athens had attempted a unification of cities: her far-flung Empire had embraced the shores and islands of all the Aegean Sea. Her policy had failed; and it had failed because both she and her allies, equally trammelled by the thought of the city-state, could not rise to the conception of a great non-civic state united in a common citizenship. On her side she could not extend her citizenship to them, because her citizenship meant—and could only mean— Athenian birth and a full participation in Athenian local life and ways and temper: on their side they could not have accepted the gift if it had been offered, because their citizenship of their cities meant just as much to them[1]. Without any common cement,

---

[1] A common citizenship would have been to the religious consciousness of all concerned (for the cult of the city-state was in effect a religion) 'an intolerable monotheism.' Political polytheism was the Greek creed; and that creed overthrew the Athenian Empire. It is curious to reflect that as religion

and based ultimately on force, the Empire collapsed before the thought of civic autonomy which inspired both the revolting 'allies' and the Peloponnesians who supported their cause. But the victory of the thought of civic autonomy over the thought of a unity of cities in some wider form of polity was only apparent; or at any rate it was only temporary. The fourth century moves (deviously; sometimes with halts, and sometimes with regressions) towards some scheme of unity. It begins with a Spartan Empire in Greece—for the champion of autonomy did not disdain an Empire—and with a Syracusan Empire, under Dionysius I, in Sicily and Magna Graecia: it passes into an hegemony of Thebes; it ends with a Macedonian Empire. The principle of autonomy indeed survives: it receives abundant lip-service: it is sometimes made effective, not for its own sake, but to satisfy a grudge and to appease a rancour. We see the lip-service in the clause of the Peace of Antalcidas, which provides that 'the Greek cities, great and small, shall be left autonomous,' and again in the renewal of the same provision in the peace of 374 (p. 76); we see actual effect given to the principle, under the terms of the first of these treaties, when in order to satisfy the Spartan grudge against Thebes the Boeotian cities are made autonomous, and the Boeotian League is dissolved. But in spite of constant lip-service and occasional homage, the principle of autonomy recedes gradually and reluct-antly into oblivion; and over the Greek world the city-cells seem to be moving and clustering together in this or that sort of union with this or that degree of permanence.

We may roughly distinguish two sorts of unions—the one based on isopolity, the other on sympolity. Where the union is based on isopolity, each city gives to the other its own citizenship, but each remains a separate and autonomous state, and no new co-ordinating authority—no new and embracing community, with its own citizenship distinct from that of its members—comes into being. Such a form of union is not in itself federal, but it is a preparation for federation. Where the union is based on sym-polity, each city still keeps its own citizenship; but a new authority and a new community of a federal character arise, and every man has a double citizenship—the one in his own city, and the other in the new federal community. Such a form of union was perhaps first suggested by Thales of Miletus early in the sixth century, if indeed he did not go further still, and propose the institution of

(the religion of the city) was the ruin of the Athenian Empire, so religion (in the sense of a common worship by all cities of a deified ruler) was the basis of the Empire of Alexander among the Greeks.

a single unitary state, in which the Ionian city-states would have become mere demes or centres of local administration. In a union based on sympolity the cities remained equal, or at any rate followed a system of proportionate equality, under which each exercised an influence in federal affairs corresponding to the number of its citizens, and each, again, retained its autonomy, though each remitted to the federal authority which it helped to constitute a large control of common affairs, and each admitted the direct action of that authority upon its citizens in the sphere of those affairs. The new Boeotian league, which came into existence after 379, was constructed on this basis (p. 70); and on the same basis, at an even earlier date, a Chalcidian confederacy had grown round the nucleus of Olynthus (p. 61), and an Achaean league had established itself in the north of the Peloponnese[1] (p. 95, *n.*). The second Athenian league was organized on lines of dualism rather than of sympolity: the Athenian Assembly and the synedrion of the allies were equal partners, with equal rights of initiative, and the measures accepted by either required the assent of the other to attain a common validity. But the Arcadian league, which arose after 370 B.C., was a sympolity in the Boeotian style; and about the same time, and on the same model, Thessaly also became a federation—a federation of a peculiar type, in which the constituent members were not city-states, but territorial divisions which were themselves federations of cities (p. 87).

Yet all these federations—alike in Boeotia, in Chalcidice, in Achaea, in Arcadia and in Thessaly—were but partial: none of them ever showed signs of expanding beyond its own territory; at the best the Boeotian federation attained some acceptance as a general model in the days of the Theban hegemony. Nor were they long-lived. If the Thessalian federation lasted till the end of Thessalian history, the Chalcidian confederacy soon succumbed to the enmity of Sparta (always a foe of federations), and the Arcadian league within ten years of its foundation had split into two separate and hostile halves. Partial in scope, and short-lived in time, the spontaneous federal movement within the Greek pale could not give unity to a country desperately resolved on division; and it was from the Macedonian North, and by violence, that unity finally came. One service, indeed, was rendered by the federal principle in the very moment of the death of Greek inde-

---

[1] The right of coinage is often an index to the seat of sovereignty, or at any rate to the tendencies of political development. Both in the Chalcidian confederacy and in the second Boeotian league the right of coinage was reserved to the federal authority.

pendence. It became the coffin of the corpse. The Macedonian supremacy disguised itself in federal forms: a nominal Hellenic confederacy, meeting in federal congress at Corinth, was made to elect Philip its general plenipotentiary against Persia, and to vote federal contingents by land and sea for the Persian War. After crushing federal Boeotia at Chaeronea, Philip installed the form of Boeotian federalism at Corinth. In fact, as distinct from form, Macedonian supremacy was as hostile to federalism as Spartan supremacy had been before. *Divide et impera* was its policy: scattered 'autonomous' cities suited that policy better than federal groups; in 324 B.C. Alexander, the head of the Greek confederacy, commanded (if we may trust the statement of Hypereides) the dissolution of Greek federations.

The political thought of the fourth century is thus one of unity, which expresses itself partly in the fact of hegemonies and empires, and partly in the fact of small federations; but it is a thought trammelled and thwarted by the survival and vigour of the counter-thought of the autonomous city—so much trammelled, and so much thwarted, that in the event it is no inner thought, but an external force, which achieves a factitious unity. The value of the national unification which Greece eventually achieved may easily be overestimated. The great state of Alexander certainly generalized culture—of a sort: it made economic intercourse easier: combined as it was with the Persian expedition, it made possible a movement of population from the overcrowded cities of Greece to the new lands of the East. But some German writers (under the glamour of their own unification), and some of their English followers, have been too apt to laud the great state, to deplore the tardiness of its coming, to lament the *Kleinstaaterei* of Plato and Aristotle, and to attack the anachronistic policy of a Demosthenes who sought to postpone the day of greater things. This is short-sightedness. Greek unification, in the form in which it was achieved, meant the purchase of material progress at the price of moral regression. Freedom is not a fetish: it is a fruitful mother of high accomplishment. The freedom of Athens in the fifth century had produced unbounded and unstinted political energy; witness the inscription of 459 B.C.—'of the Erechtheid tribe these are they who died in the war, in Cyprus, in Egypt, in Phoenice, at Halieis, in Aegina, at Megara, in the same year.' It had produced a great and unexampled art and literature (one may cite the calculation of a German writer, that for the popular festivals of that one free city, in that one century, there were produced at least 2000 plays, and from 4000 to 5000 dithyrambs):

it had stimulated the spirit of man in every reach and to every range. Chaeronea, fatal to liberty, was fatal also to its fruits. This has been nobly recognized by a great German classical scholar, whose words are worth remembering[1]. 'Let us recognize the tragedy of the fate of Greece, even if it had been deserved: let us not proclaim the wisdom of an Isocrates who, false to ideals he had often loudly proclaimed, hastened to greet the coming master. We must not refuse a human sympathy to those patriots who, in Thebes and Sparta and Athens, refused to believe that the strength for freedom had vanished out of their states. The Greek needed a self-governed commonwealth as the breath of his being...; in spite of all the light that falls on a Ptolemy or an Antiochus, and of all the shadows that lie on the doings of Athens, the democracy of Solon and Pericles represents a higher type of State than the Macedonian monarchy.' The free city-state is not built for long endurance in the world of politics. But who can deny the achievements of its short span, whether in ancient Greece, or in the Italy and Flanders of the Middle Ages? And who, reflecting on these achievements, can feel otherwise about the great State than that it was a 'cruel necessity'?

Yet whatever we may feel about the city-state at its best, and however we may lament the tragedy of its fall, we must not idealize the city-state of the fourth century. The old solidarity of the city—the reciprocal nexus of city and citizens, which meant that the city gave its citizen a scope for complete fulfilment, and the citizen gave a devoted energy to his city in return—these were vanished things. The political thought which determines the action of the fourth-century Athens is also a tragedy. There was a reaction against the high demands and the severe strain of the Periclean conception, which involved constant service in law-court or Assembly at home, and in the army or navy abroad. Defeated Athens began to ask 'Why?': her citizens relaxed into a slacker fibre: they took for their motto the perverted saying, that it is more blessed to receive than to give. The citizen army began to disappear: the fourth century B.C. in Greek history, like the fifteenth century A.D. in Italian history, was an age of mercenaries; and it was vain for Demosthenes in the one century, as it was vain for Machiavelli in the other, to preach the grand style of an earlier age. Mercenaries involved taxation: taxation could not be levied, even for objects on which the Assembly had solemnly resolved by its vote: the straits to which the Athenian general Timotheus was

---

[1] Wilamowitz-Moellendorff, *Staat und Gesellschaft der Griechen* (2nd edition), pp. 141, 171.

reduced in 373 B.C. were the inevitable result (pp. 77, 106). While giving diminished, receiving grew. It was a little thing, and it was defensible, that in order to provide a quorum at the meetings of the Assembly the principle and the practice were introduced of paying each citizen for his attendance. This might be regarded as a consideration for services rendered; but it was a pure gift, and a serious declension, when the state began to provide free seats at the theatre and to distribute doles among its citizens. The city was ceasing to be a partnership in high achievement and noble living: it was becoming a commercial association for the distribution among its members of dividends which they had not earned; and the principle of a social contract, which makes the state 'a partnership agreement in a trade, to be taken up for a little temporary interest,' took the place of the old principle of organic solidarity and reciprocal nexus of service. Democracy ceased to mean a system of collective control of a common life: it came to mean rather the absence of such control, and the freedom of each individual 'to live his own life.' The prominent Athenian of the fourth century is apt to be a free-lance who marries a Thracian princess: if he is not that, he is a steady and plodding administrator of the Theoric Fund which ministers to the citizens' wants.

Individualism has cosmopolitanism for its natural associate. Those who admit and welcome the claim of a particular group on their allegiance will draw a distinction between members and strangers: the enfranchised individual can afford to greet all men as brothers. Athens in the fourth century was not yet cosmopolitan, but she was less Athenian, and more Hellenic, than she had been in the previous century. She was more of a mart of general Greek trade: she was more of a centre of general Greek culture. In spite of autonomy and particularism, the conception of Greek unity gained ground. Plato in the fifth book of the *Republic* recognizes the existence of a common society of Greek states, in which war is indeed possible, but in which it must be mitigated by the observance of rules peculiar to the members of the society; Isocrates, in the *Panegyricus*, a few years afterwards (380 B.C.), proclaims that the Greek world has come to find unity less in blood than in a common education and a common type of mind. Here we touch the finer side of the movement towards unification which marks the century. Whatever it suppressed, and whatever the violence by which it came, it expressed a general sentiment, and it rested on something of a voluntary adhesion. This unitary sentiment is the other side of civic decadence; it is the conjunction of this sentiment and that decadence which explains and excuses the collapse of the city and the foundation of the great state.

If we add to this unitary sentiment two other factors—the factor of monarchism and the factor of anti-Persian prejudice—we shall have constituted the triad of forces which caused the fourth century to issue in the unification of Greece, on a monarchical basis, for the purpose of conquering Persia. Not only is the century marked by the figures of actual monarchs—Dionysius I of Syracuse, Jason of Pherae, Philip and Alexander: it is also a century of monarchist opinion. Plato writes of philosopher kings in the *Republic*, and of the 'young tyrant' in the *Laws*: Xenophon, half a Socratic and half a soldier, preaches the virtue of a wise sovereign, such as Cyrus, ruling over a state organized in the fashion of an army: Isocrates longs for the coming of the commander-in-chief who shall lead a united Greece to the East; and even Demosthenes can admit, with a reluctant admiration, the superiority of monarchy in secrecy of counsel and energy of execution. This monarchism found its plea, and alleged its justification, in the need which was often proclaimed for a strong hand that should not only repress civic strife in Greece, but should also guide all its cities in union to the common war against barbarism. The cause of monarchy was connected with the idea of a Crusade: a new Agamemnon was needed for a new war of retribution across the seas. Just as the idea of a League of Nations in modern Europe was for centuries based on the need of union against the Turk, and just as modern sovereigns long used the plea of a Crusade to cover their policy, so the idea of a united Greece was throughout the fourth century based on the need of union against Persia, and so the would-be sovereigns of Greece—Jason of Pherae, Philip and Alexander—used the plea of a Persian war to excuse their ambitions. There was a general feeling, which is already expressed in the opening pages of the history of Herodotus, that there was a rhythm and a recurrence in the relations of East and West, and that repayment was due to fourth-century Greece for the wrongs inflicted by the fifth-century Persia. An economic motive reinforced this romantic sentiment. The Greeks stood in need of a new colonial ground. The colonial expansion of earlier centuries must be resumed, under new auspices and in new regions, if provision were to be made for men who could find no place in their cities, and were falling into a life of roaming vagrancy. This is a theme which recurs in the speeches of Isocrates. It was the work of Alexander to satisfy this economic motive, and to find a field for this colonial expansion. His foundation of Greek cities all over his Empire, even in the parts of farthest Asia, will show how thoroughly he did the work. And in this sense the new monarch of these days, like the new monarch of the sixteenth century A.D., was justified by his solution of urgent social problems.

II. THE POLITICAL THEORY OF THE FOURTH CENTURY

Such was the political thought which went to determine the historical process of the fourth century. The political theory of the century, as distinct from its political thought, may be found partly in the field of oratory, and partly in that of philosophy. Oratory, in its nature, lies closer than philosophy to active politics; and oratorical theory, if we may speak of such a thing, is at its best an explication of the deeper political thought implicit in the movement of a period, and at its worst an exposition of current political commonplaces. Isocrates mingles the two, with a good deal of confusion: he is a mixture of a patriotic Athenian democrat, who would somehow reconcile democracy with the good old days of the Areopagus, and a devout Panhellene, who could at one and the same time believe theoretically that monarchy belonged only to barbarians or to countries on the verge of barbarism (such as Macedonia or Cyprus), and welcome in practice any monarch who would guide a united Greece against Persia. He is doubly inconsistent; but he was too much of a voice for his time, which was full of conflicting thoughts, to be otherwise than inconsistent. He was a journalist rather than an orator, who wrote his speeches not for delivery but for publication; and like a journalist he reflected the contemporary world in all its confusion. Demosthenes, a real orator, determined to sway rather than to reflect the movement of events, seems consistent enough—and just for that reason one-sided. He is the apostle of civic autonomy against the northern enemy; he has little regard for Greek unity or common Greek action. But he too had his inconsistency. He lived in a fourth-century Athens: he spoke and he acted as if he lived in the Athens of Pericles. In a city which was based on the principles of a commercial association, he preached a loyalty and demanded a service which would only have been possible in a city grounded on an ancient solidarity. It is one of the notes of the theory of the fourth century, at any rate in Athens, that it is always returning in aspiration, and in a spirit of antiquarianism, to the days of a vanished past. Isocrates would hark back to the Areopagus: Aristotle himself would return to an 'ancestral constitution.'

Demosthenes, too, turned his face backwards. The difference was that he acted as if the present were actually the past. Others were content to sigh, and to wait and to hope for the past to return.

It may be argued that the theory of Plato and Aristotle has its affinities with the oratory of Demosthenes. Plato, it is true, has a tinge of monarchism—but his monarch is only a civic monarch: he has a belief in the existence of a common Greek society—but his society is an international society, composed of sovereign states which are cities. His political philosophy, like that of Aristotle, remains a philosophy of the *Polis*—self-governing and self-sufficing: included in no form of union, and dependent on no external assistance. It illustrates the hold of civic life on the Greek mind, and shows how external and indifferent to that mind were sympolities and symmachies and all unions of cities, that in a century full of these things the two great philosophers should simply neglect their existence. We have to remember their conception of the real nature of the city. It was a home of moral life: it was a moral institution, designed to make its citizens virtuous. As such, and as such alone, it caught their attention. Their political philosophy was a part of ethics—or rather ethics was a part of their political philosophy; and the politics they studied were what we should call by the name of social ethics. Unions were only machinery: they existed for material objects, and not for moral purposes: they did not belong to a political philosophy which meant a study of the social ethics of a civic community. Neither Plato nor Aristotle (and least of all Plato) was blind to the signs of the times; but the signs which they studied were the signs which were connected with their studies. It was the signs of an inner moral decay, and not those of any external political expansion, which their point of view led them to seek; and these signs they saw only too abundantly. They are both critics of the democratic city which had turned itself into a loose commercial association, and has cast away moral purpose and moral discipline. They are thus, at one and the same time, prophets and critics of the Greek city-state; at once conservatives and radicals. Believing in the city-state as it should be, they disbelieved in it as it was; disbelieving in it as it was, they sought to show how it might become what it should be.

Plato, anxious for the reign of 'righteousness' (δικαιοσύνη), was supremely anxious for the reign of that wisdom on which he believed that righteousness depended: he saw salvation in the rule of a civic magistracy trained for its calling in philosophy, and devoted in an austere purity, by a renunciation of property and family life, to its high and solemn duties. The price of righteousness is wisdom: the price of wisdom is that a man should give all that he has, and leave wife and child to follow it. This ideal, as it is set forth in the *Republic*, is one for which no antiquity can furnish a precedent: Plato leaves the ground of the city, not to return to the past, but to voyage into the future. Aristotle, too, builds an ideal state where righteousness shall reign; but it is a pedestrian sort of ideal, and little more than a pale copy of that second-best ideal which Plato had constructed in his later days in the *Laws*. More attractive, and more genuinely Aristotelian in essence, is Aristotle's picture of the mixed constitution which, purging democracy from its dross, adds the best elements of oligarchy to make an alloy. But even the mixed constitution of Aristotle is hardly original. In theory it had already been anticipated by Plato in the *Laws* (which thus furnishes Aristotle alike with his picture of an ideal, and his principle of a mixed constitution): in fact it seems to approximate to that moderate type of oligarchy (ὀλιγαρχία ἰσόνομος) which had been practised in Boeotia during the fifth century, and attempted at Athens in the revolution of 411 B.C. (vol. v, p. 340). Indeed it may almost claim Solonian warrant; and it may thus come to be regarded as the 'ancestral constitution' of Athens.

III. XENOPHON AND ISOCRATES

Whether oratorical or philosophical—or to speak more exactly (for Isocrates also claimed to be among the philosophers) whether it takes the form of amateur or that of real philosophy—the political theory of the fourth century is derived from Socrates. Xenophon and Isocrates, Plato and Aristotle, are all heirs, directly or indirectly, and in a greater or less degree, of the Socratic tradition. Hence the common theses which they propound— that the State exists for the betterment of its members and the increase of virtue: that virtue depends on right knowledge, and is inculcated by a process of education rather than by the restriction of law; that statesmanship is wisdom, and the only true title to office is knowledge. Such positions occur in their simplest and naivest form in the writings of Xenophon. In him the Socratic tradition was mixed with Persian experience, military training, and Spartan leanings, to produce the blend we find in the *Cyropaedeia*. Here he draws a picture of ancient Persia, with a pencil borrowed from Socrates, according to a model furnished by Sparta. Its institutions were directed to the training of men to do right rather than to the prevention of wrong-doing: 'the Persian youth go to school to learn righteousness, as ours go to learn the rudiments of reading, writing, and reckoning.' At the head of the State, supported by an aristocratic class of ὁμότιμοι or 'peers' (here Xenophon copies the Spartan ὅμοιοι), stood Cyrus, the man born to be king, better and wiser than all his subjects, and devoted in his virtue and his wisdom to their betterment. Before such a kingdom and such a king, Cyaxares and the Medes were unable to stand: the state which is based on virtue and ruled in wisdom is not only happy within its borders, but irresistible without. Perhaps Xenophon wrote these things as a parable, holding that the Persians, now fallen into decay through the corruption of their kings, were as the Medes had been before, and that out of Sparta might come an impulse and a leader for a Greek conquest of fallen Persia. Of this, however, there is no certain indication in his pages: nor can we be sure, in spite of his praises of Cyrus, that he had any belief in the superiority of monarchy. Cyrus is a limited monarch in Xenophon's conception: he has made a pact with his people, promising to maintain their liberty and constitution, if they will maintain his throne: the aristocratic body of 'peers' are his free coadjutors; in a word, he is a king after the Spartan kind—and Spartan kingship was no monarchy. Yet Xenophon also wrote a dialogue called *Hiero*, in which he made a former tyrant of Syracuse discourse on the benefits which the absolute ruler could confer on his people. But this may be an academic exercise; and in this matter it is safest to say of Xenophon, that his views are not clear to us, because they were not clear to himself.

Xenophon was a general who had settled down to the life of a country gentleman, and used his leisure to recount reminiscences and to preach what he thought to be a philosophic conservatism. Isocrates, for more than fifty years, from 392 B.C. to the year of the battle of Chaeronea, was the head of a school of political oratory at Athens. The instruction which he gave was not only literary, in the sense of being concerned with style, or psychological, in the sense of teaching the methods of affecting and influencing an audience: it was also political, in the sense of conveying opinions and views about general political principles and contemporary political problems. Greek cities were governed by oratory: to teach the secrets of oratory was also to teach the secrets of government. For this reason Isocrates gave the name of philosophy to what he taught: it was a guide to life, and a clue to its problems. He was an empiric philosopher, who based his views on generally received opinion, which he considered to be the best guide in practical affairs; and here he diverged from Socratic tradition, and set himself against the Platonic demand for exact and grounded knowledge. His philosophy was entirely a political philosophy; but in that philosophy the internal ordering of civic affairs, which we may call 'legislation,' was assigned a lower place than the conduct of external policy, which he identi-fied with 'statesmanship' proper. His empiric leanings, and his view of legislation, are illustrated by a passage in his *De Antidosi*, in which it is maintained that the task of the legislator is simply to study the mass of existing laws, and to bring together those which have found a general acceptance, 'which any man might easily do at will.' Aristotle, at the end of the *Ethics*, very naturally rejoins that it argues a total ignorance of the nature of political philosophy to maintain that 'it is easy to legislate by bringing together the laws which have found acceptance'; for selection demands the gift of comprehension, and the use of a right criterion is crucial—and difficult.

In two of his speeches—the *Panathenaicus* and the *De Pace*—Isocrates dealt with matter of legislation, and discoursed of the internal affairs of Athens; but his wisdom was not profound. In the former he argues, like Xenophon in the *Cyropaedeia* (and like Plato in the *Republic*), that the training of men to do right by education is more important than the prevention of wrong-doing by legislation; and then, taking an antiquarian flight, not into ancient Persia, but into pre-Periclean Athens, he seeks to show how education throve, and men were wise and good and happy, in the days of the moral tutelage of the Areopagus. To go back to the days before Pericles would seem to involve a going back upon democracy; but Isocrates preserves a form of belief in the democratic faith (he could hardly do otherwise in Athens), and only suggests that election should be substituted for the use of the lot in the choice of magistrates, and that the desert of the better should thus be given that reasonable chance of receiving a higher reward which ensures a true or proportionate equality. This is the doctrine of limited democracy, or the mixed constitu-tion, which Aristotle also professed. And as he would purge demo-cracy of the use of the lot, so too Isocrates would purge it of maritime empire and of over-seas dominions. This is the argument of the *De Pace*; and it also recurs in other speeches. A supremacy over other states, which is based on naval power, will run to despotism and corrupt its possessor. One may date an ἀρχὴ κακῶν for Athens from the day when she assumed an ἀρχὴ θαλάσσης: she laid the foundation of trouble when she founded a maritime power.

But it is the higher 'statesmanship,' which transcends legislation and internal affairs, and is concerned with the conduct of external affairs and international policy, that exercises the mind of Isocrates most vigorously and continuously. Others might teach the art of legislation: he would teach the art of foreign policy. Partly, perhaps, he believed that its themes were ampler and more majestical; partly he felt that the inner troubles of Greek states—overcrowding, pauperism, vagrancy—could best be cured, not by remedial legislation, but by a policy of colonial expansion in which all states must join together under a common chief. The foreign policy which Isocrates was thus led to preach was a natural subject for oratory. When the Greeks gathered together for their common games, and felt themselves one people in spite of all their cities, it was easy for orators to rise and strike the note of Greek concord. Gorgias at Olympia had counselled concord in a famous oration (408 B.C.), and had sought to turn the Greeks against the barbarians by his eloquence. The orator Lysias had followed his example: at Olympia in 388 B.C. he had exhorted the Greeks to end civil strife, and to join in liberating Ionia from the Persian king and Sicily from the Syracusan tyrant Dionysius. Isocrates could not but embrace the same theme; and he wrote in 380 B.C., and published without delivering, an Olympic oration under the title of *Panegyricus*. He said nothing new; but he has the merit of having steadily preached for forty years a line of policy which he was perhaps first led to expound by the fact that it was simply the recognized staple of oratorical effort before a Panhellenic assembly. Others also preached the same sermon: we hear of one Dias of Ephesus, who urged Philip of Macedonia to be the Greek leader, and the Greeks to furnish him with contingents; 'for it was worth while to serve abroad if that meant living in freedom at home.' But Isocrates preached most steadily (one can hardly say most effectively; for there is no evidence to show that his pamphlets exercized any effect); and he preached to the principalities and powers of his day—to Dionysius I and to Archidamus of Sparta as well as to Philip of Macedon. It was not that he sought a monarch, or believed in monarchy. He sought only a new Agamemnon, commander-in-chief of the forces of a new Greek symmachy; monarchy, he thought, was an anachronism in the Greece of the fourth century, except in the nominal form in which it existed at Sparta; it was only where there was a large non-Hellenic population (in Macedonia, for example, or in Cyprus) that an active monarch could exercise a real authority. The symmachy of his dream would thus have been a military *entente* of autonomous cities under a generalissimo who might be king in his own country, but among his allies was simply a chosen commander.

IV. PLATO AND ARISTOTLE

To Plato and to Aristotle it is legislation and the internal cure of internal evils that are first and foremost, as they are also last and uttermost. Plato, as we have seen, has a certain Panhellenism: Aristotle, though he criticizes Plato for failing to treat of the external relations of the city he builds in the *Laws*, is even more civic in his outlook than Plato. Both, again, depart from Isocrates in regarding political theory as a matter of first principles and high philosophy, and not of current opinion and generally accepted views; though Aristotle is often Isocratean in his respect for experience and current opinion, and dismisses the communistic novelties of Plato on the ground that they have no warrant in either. Both find their real enemy not in Isocrates (Plato refers to him with a certain tenderness), but in the principle of individualism, whether preached by the sophist or practised by the Athenian citizen of their century; both are apostles of the organic life of the civic community, in which alone man rises to the measure of humanity, and finds himself and enjoys his rights by giving himself and discharging his duties to his city. Both believe that the moral life demands a civic association, because such an association supplies, in its organization and its law, a field for moral action and the content of a moral rule, and furnishes, through its scheme of education and the force of its social opinion, the stimulus and the impulse which can carry men upwards into steadfast action according to the rule of its life. Plato is more of the idealist, and Aristotle more of the realist: Plato would merge men utterly in the common life; Aristotle, the defender of private property and of the integrity of the family, would allow a large scope for the rights of individual personality. Plato, for all his idealism, is the more practical, the more eager for the realization of his ideal—ready to plunge into the ordeal of Syracuse, and prepared, if only success can be purchased by such surrender, to subdue the glowing scheme of the *Republic* into the paler colours of the *Laws*: Aristotle, for all his realism, is the more theoretical, the more academic, the less torn by conflict between the impulse towards action and the impulse towards pure thought. But whatever their differences, they are at one on the fundamental question. The political theory of both is a study of that system of social ethics, based on the *Polis*, which is the foundation and the condition of individual morality. 'It was not prophets and priests, but poets and philosophers, who sought in ancient Greece for the moral perfection of men; and the best of the Greeks— and above all Plato and Aristotle—believed not in a church, but in their city-state, as the institution charged with the service of this high aim[1].'

Plato and Aristotle thus believe in the small state. The state of the *Republic* is to contain 1000 warriors (Plato does not mention the number of the members of the farming class, which would be larger): for the state of the *Laws* 5040 citizens are suggested: in the ideal state of the *Politics* the citizens, who are to know one another and to be addressed by a single herald, must not exceed the number which makes it possible to satisfy these conditions. This limit of size is imposed on the state by its purpose: being a church, it cannot be a Babylon. Small as it is, it is complete: it is self-sufficient, in the sense that it meets from its own resources —from its own accumulated moral tradition and the physical yield of its own territory—all the moral and material needs of its members; and as it does not draw upon others, so it is not conceived as giving, or bound to give, to others, or as having to make its contribution to general Hellenic advancement. A complete whole, with a rounded life of its own, the small state rises to a still higher dignity than that of self-sufficiency: it is conceived as 'natural'— as a final and indefeasible scheme of life. In this conception of 'nature' we touch a cardinal element in the theory of both Plato and Aristotle; and it must therefore receive its measure of investigation.

A distinction between 'nature' and 'convention'—between institutions which existed by nature and those which existed by convention—had already been drawn in the preceding century by several of the sophists. The conventional was regarded as that which might or might not be; which owed its being, if it actually was, to the making or convention of a group of men, and was thereby opposed to the natural, which always and invariably was. It was easy to go still further, and to regard the conventional as that which ought not to be, on the ground that it defeated and over-rode the obvious tendency of nature; and in this way nature was extended to signify not the mere fact of regular recurrence,

[1] A. Bauer, *Vom Griechenthum zum Christenthum*, pp. 27–8.

but the sovereignty of a supposed and ideal tendency or rule. On such a view the state might readily be regarded as conventional in all its customary forms; and nature might be argued, for instance, to demand a form of state based on the good old rule and simple plan that the strong man armed should rule the weak for his own particular benefit. Such a view involves that theory of 'natural rights' which has long haunted political philosophy— a theory of rights 'inherent' in the individual as such, apart from society, whether the supposed individual be only the strong man armed, and the rights be only his right of domination, or each and all of us be held to be individuals, and the rights be the supposed rights of each and all to life and liberty.

It was the work of Plato and Aristotle to answer this view; and they answered it, as it must always be answered, by the contention that the individual could not be distinguished from political society; that he lived and moved and had his being in such society, and only in such society; that political society, necessary as it was to the life of the individual, was rooted and grounded in the constitution of human nature; and that, so rooted and grounded, it was perfectly and entirely natural. This is the answer implied in the argument of the *Republic*, that the state is a scheme, and that each of its members finds himself by discharging his function in that scheme: it is the answer explicitly propounded in the opening pages of the *Politics*. Such an answer, it is obvious, does not imply the view that the state is natural because it has *grown*. Plato has nothing to say of growth; and if Aristotle uses the language of growth in the beginning of the *Politics*, and speaks of the growth of household into village, and of village into state, he does not rest his belief in the natural character of political society on the fact of such growth. What makes the state natural is the fact that, however it came into existence, it is the satisfaction of an immanent impulse in human nature towards moral perfection, which drives men up through various forms of society into the final political form. As a matter of fact, Aristotle—like all the Greeks, who thought of politics as a sphere of conscious making in which legislators had always been active—would appear to believe in a creation of the state. 'By nature there is an impulse in all men to such society; but the first man to *construct* it was the author of the greatest of benefits.' There is no contradiction in such a sentence; for there is no contradiction between the immanent impulses of human nature and the conscious art which is, after all, a part of the same nature. There is no necessary gulf fixed between what man does in

obedience to the one, and what he does in the strength of the
other. Human art may indeed controvert the deepest and best
human impulses: it may construct perverted polities, based on
the pursuit of mere wealth or the lust of mere power, which
defeat the natural human impulse to moral perfection. Equally, and
indeed still more, it may help to realize nature. Nature and convention are not in their essence opposites, but rather complements.

The state is therefore natural because, or in so far as, it is an
institution for that moral perfection of man, to which his nature
moves. All the features of its life—slavery, private property, the
family—are justified, and are natural, because, or in so far as,
they serve that purpose. If Plato refuses private property and
family life to his guardians, it is because he believes that both
would interfere with the moral life of the guardians and therefore
with the moral life of the state: if Aristotle vindicates both for
every citizen, it is because he believes that all moral life requires
the 'equipment' of private property and the discipline of family
life. But both for Aristotle and for Plato there is one end; and
the end is the measure of everything else. That end is ruthless.
In the *Republic* it not only deprives the guardians of property
and family: it also deprives the labouring class of citizenship,
whose high calling cannot be followed by men engaged in getting
and spending. In the *Politics* it serves to justify slavery, which
can afford the citizen leisure for the purposes of the state; and it
excludes from real membership in the state all persons other than
those who possess that leisure. The end justifies: the end con-
demns: the end is sovereign. It is easy to glide into the view that
the state and its well-being are thus made into an end to which
the individual and his free development are sacrificed. Generally
stated, such a view is erroneous: it is really a return, in another
form, of that antithesis between political society and the individual
which Plato and Aristotle refuse to recognize. The state (they
believe) exists for the perfection of man: the fulfilment of the
individual means a perfect state: there is no antithesis. But this
is only true, after all, of the man who is citizen and the individual
who is a member of the body corporate. The rest *are* sacrificed:
they lose the development which comes from citizenship, because
citizenship is keyed so high. Rich things have a high price. A
lower ideal of citizenship, purchasable at a price which the many
can afford to pay, is perhaps a more precious thing than the rare
riches of the Platonic and Aristotelian ideal.

The state which is intended for the moral perfection of its
members is an educational institution. Its laws are intended to

make men good: its offices ideally belong to the men of virtue who have moral discernment: its chief activity is that of training the young and sustaining the mature in the way of righteousness. That is why we may speak of such a state as really a church: like the Calvinistic Church, it has a presbytery, and it exercises a 'holy discipline.' Political philosophy thus becomes moral theology, and sometimes pure theology. Plato in the *Republic* is the critic of the traditional religion of Greece: in the *Laws* he enunciates the canons of a true religion, and advocates religious persecution: in both he is the censor of art and poetry and music, and the regulator of all their modes of expression. Aristotle is less drastic: of religion he does not treat; but he would exercise a moral censorship of plays and tales, and he would subject music to an ethical control. The 'limit of state-interference' never suggested itself to the Greek philosophers as a problem for their consideration. They would regulate the family, and the most intimate matters of family life, no less than art and music. Plato's austerities are famous; but even Aristotle can define the age for marriage, and the number of permissible children. Whatever has a moral bearing may come under moral regulation. Neither Plato nor Aristotle allows weight to the fundamental consideration that moral action which is done *ad verba magistri* ceases to be moral. The state should promote morality; but the promotion of morality by act of state is the destruction of moral autonomy. The good will is the maker of goodness; and the state can only increase goodness by increasing the freedom of the good will. That is why modern thinkers, bred in the tenets of Plato and Aristotle, would nevertheless substitute the formula of 'removal of hindrances' for the formula of 'administration of stimulus' implied in the teaching of their masters. But after all we do an injustice to the theorists of the city-state if we compare them with the theorists of the great modern state. Their state, we have to remind ourselves, was a church as well as a state; and most churches believe in moral guidance and stimulus. And there is a stage of moral growth, when the good will is still in the making, at which it is a great gain to be habituated by precept in right-doing. Any state which is an educational institution, like every parent, must recognize the existence of this stage. Yet it is but a stage. The grown man must see and choose his way. Plato and Aristotle perhaps treated their contemporaries too much as if they were 'eternal children' (ἀεὶ παῖδες).

If these are the general principles of politics which Plato and Aristotle assume, we can readily see that they will naturally tend to the construction of ideal states, in which such principles, no-where purely exhibited in actual life, will find their realization for thought. The building of such ideals, whether on the quasi-antiquarian lines which we find in Xenophon and Isocrates, or on the bolder and freer lines traced by the imagination of Plato, was a staple of Greek political speculation. It accorded with an artistic temper, which loved to shape material into a perfect form, and would even, in the sphere of politics, assume a perfect material (in the sense of a population ideal in disposition, endowed with an ideal territory, and distributed on an ideal social system) in order that it might be the more susceptible of receiving an ideal form. It accorded, too, with the experience of a people accustomed to the formation of new colonial cities, on which the 'oecist' and legislator might freely stamp an abiding mark. Plato's ideal, as it is sketched in the *Republic*, exhibits the philo-sopher's demand upon civic life exhibited in its pure logic; yet he hoped that his contemporaries might rise, and in Syracuse he sought to raise Dionysius II, to the height of his demand. Of that ideal nothing need here be said: it is a common and eternal possession of the general human mind. The lower and more practicable ideal which is painted, with a rich and exact detail, in the *Laws*, has been less generally apprehended; but in practical experience, and perhaps in actual immediate effect (the training of the *ephebi* suggested in the *Laws* by Plato seems, for example, to have been actually adopted at Athens within a few years), the *Laws* transcends the *Republic*. Aristotle's ideal state, as we have seen, is largely a copy of the state of Plato's *Laws*: it is also a torso; and the profundity and the influence of Aristotle's thought are rather to be traced in his enunciation of general principles than in his picture of their realization. He is the master of defini-tion and classification; and it is the terse Aristotelian formula which has always influenced thought.

Ideals serve as judges and measuring-rods for the actual. The Greek states of the fourth century came to judgment before the bar of Plato's and Aristotle's ideals. Plato in the *Republic* first constructed his ideal, and then in the later books showed why, and in what degree, actual states were a corruption of that ideal. Aristotle seems to follow a reverse procedure when, early in the *Politics*, he examines actual states in order that their merits and their defects may throw light on the requirements of an ideal state; but in the issue he too uses ideal principles to criticize and classify actual states. Three results seem to follow from the application of the ideal as a touchstone to the actual—first, an elucidation of the principles on which offices should be assigned, and constitutions should therefore be constructed (for 'a constitution is a mode of assignment of offices'); secondly, a classification and a grading of actual constitutions; and, finally, a criticism of that democratic constitution which in the fourth century had become general (Thebes herself, the pattern of an 'oligarchy under a system of equal law' in the fifth century, had turned democratic after 379 B.C.), and which, in the populous states of his day, Aristotle regarded as inevitable.

The assignment of office, we are told, must follow the principle of distributive justice. To each the state must assign its awards in proportion to the contribution which each has made to itself; and in estimating the contribution of each we must look to the end of the state, and measure the contribution to that end. Logically, this would seem to mean the enthronement of the virtuous, or an ethical aristocracy: in the last resort, it would involve the enthronement, if he can be found, of the one man of supreme virtue, or an absolute and 'divine' monarchy. Practically, Aristotle recognizes that there are various contributions which directly or indirectly tend to the realization of the end. Besides virtue, there is wealth, which is necessary to the end in so far as perfect virtue requires a material equipment; and besides wealth there is 'freedom'—freedom not only in the sense of free birth, but also in the sense of liberty from that dependence on others and that absorption in mechanical toil, which distract men from the free pursuit of virtue. This is one of the lines along which Aristotle moves to the theory of the mixed constitution, which recognizes various contributions, and thus admits various classes to office. A classification of constitutions readily follows on this line of speculation: its terms, traced already in the speculation of the fifth century, and deepened and broadened by Plato in the *Politicus*, are firmly established by Aristotle in the third book of the *Politics*. The criticism of the democratic constitution follows in its turn. It has abandoned 'proportionate' for 'absolute' equality: it awards the same honour and the same standing to each and every citizen. It is based on recognition of one contribution, and one only—that of 'freedom'; and that contribution is by no means the highest or weightiest. Nor is this all. Not content with the freedom which means a voice for all in the collective control of common affairs, it has added a freedom which means the absence of control, the surrender of moral discipline, and the random life of chance desires. But this is anarchy: it is the negation of the city-state as it was conceived by Plato and

Aristotle. It is this fact, and not aristocratic leanings—it is a dislike of what they regard as anarchy, because anarchy is blank negation—which makes them both the critics of democracy.

We can understand the rigour of their criticism; but we can hardly admit its justice. Democratic government in the fourth century did not mean anarchy. The Athenian citizens had their defects: they loved the free theatre almost more than the free city; yet the last days of Athenian freedom were not a disgrace, either to the city-state or to the democratic constitution, and the career of Demosthenes was an answer to the strictures of Plato and Aristotle. Discipline and order were abroad in the days before Chaeronea: the cautious Eubulus was no demagogue; and, indeed, the statesmen of the fourth century in general stand as a proof that the Athenian people had some sense of merit and its desert. Nor can Aristotle's censure upon 'extreme' democracy, that it means the overthrow of established law by temporary decrees of the sovereign people, be justified at the bar of history. It is a misconception of the facts. Apart from this misinterpretation Aristotle is, on the whole, less critical of democracy than Plato. He recognizes, towards the middle of the third book of the *Politics*, that there is, after all, much to be said on behalf of the mass of people. They have a faculty of collective judgment, which hits the mark, alike in questions of art and matters of politics; 'for some understand one part, and some another, but take all together, and they will understand all.' They know again, from their own experience, how government and its actions pinch; and that knowledge has its value, and deserves its field of expression. These things suggest that the people should have their share in the government of the state; and Aristotle would assign to them those functions of electing the magistrates, and of holding the magistrates to account at the end of their term of office, which their faculty of judgment and their experience of the pressure of government fit them to discharge. Plato never goes so far as this. It is true that in the early part of the *Laws* he assigns to his 5040 citizens the two functions of serving as an electorate and of acting as a judicature; but it is also true that by the end of the *Laws* he enthrones a 'nocturnal council' which is very like the philosopher kings of the *Republic*; and even in the early part of the *Laws* he contends, in a sense which is the opposite of that of Aristotle, that the masses cannot judge art or politics, and that 'theatrocracy' and democracy are twin disasters. The conception of politics as a field reserved for the higher wisdom of the few is one which Plato cannot shed.

There is a similar difference between the view of law which we find in Plato and that of Aristotle. Anxious for a free field for the higher wisdom, Plato will have no laws in the state of the *Republic*. The eternal Ideas matter more than laws; and those who have apprehended these Ideas must be free to stamp them at discretion on the state. At the most Plato lays down a few fundamental principles—articles of belief rather than laws—to bind and guide the ruler: the state, for example, must never be allowed to exceed its due size, and its citizens must always be kept to the due discharge of specific functions. In the *Laws*, as the title indicates, law comes down to earth: philosophy only remains in the shape of 'prefaces' attached to each law for the purpose of explanation and persuasion. It is this admission of law (rather than the surrender of communism, which is by comparison a subsidiary matter), that makes the state of the *Laws* a 'second best.' At the same time, there is a fine philosophy of law in the dialogue; and there is an exact articulation and systemization of law—both criminal and civil—which represents the first real Greek attempt at codification, and influenced the growth both of Hellenistic law and, through it, of the law of Rome. Aristotle rendered less service to law: on the other hand he was, in general and in principle, a steady and consistent advocate of its sovereignty. 'It is better that law should rule than any individual: if individuals must bear rule, they must be made guardians and servants of law.' The Aristotelian thesis of the sovereignty of law, and the conception of government as limited by law, had a long history, and was a potent influence through the Middle Ages. The law which Aristotle thus enthrones is no code: it is the custom, written and unwritten, which has developed with the development of a state. Aristotle has a sense of historic development, which is as implicit in his general philosophy as the demand for radical reconstruction is imbedded in the philosophy of Plato. The growth of potential 'matter' into actual 'form' or 'end,' which is the general formula of his philosophy, leaves room for a large appreciation of history and the value of moving time: the Platonic conception of the impress of a timeless and eternally perfect Idea upon a receptive matter, which may take place at any moment when that Idea is apprehended, is inimical to any belief in gradual development. In the same way the Aristotelian formula involves some recognition of progress—though Aristotle believed that progress, alike in poetry and politics, had attained its conclusion and perfection in his time, and he had none of that looking-forward to an unending and unresting progress which is a mark of modern thought. The

Platonic conception leaves no room for progress: we may even say that Platonism and a belief in progress cannot live together: the process of movement in time is away from the ideal, or back towards the ideal, but never absolutely forward.

In modern times we distinguish between state and society. The one is the area of politics proper, of obligatory rule and involuntary obedience: the other is the area of voluntary co-operation, conducted in and by a variety of societies, educational, ecclesiastical, economic. It would be difficult to apply any such distinction to ancient Greece. The state was the one organization that embraced and contained its citizens: such groups as there were—small religious societies for the worship of Dionysus or the Orphic mysteries, or trade associations with a common hero or god—were insignificant. The *Polis* included everything; and in the same way the theory of the *Polis* included studies to which we should now give a separate existence—in particular the theory of economics, and (we may also add) the theory of education. There is much writing on 'economics' in the fourth century. It dealt partly with household management (the literal meaning of οἰκονομία), and partly with public economy or state finance. There is the *Oeconomicus* of Xenophon, which gave inspiration to Ruskin; there is an *Oeconomica* falsely ascribed to Aristotle; there is a treatise by Xenophon *On the Revenues of Athens*; there is economic theory in the *Republic* and the *Laws*; there is the famous and profoundly influential theory of exchange and of interest in the first book of the *Politics*, which affected so deeply the canonists of the Middle Ages. Such economic theory, subordinated as it is to political theory, which in turn is subordinated to (or, perhaps one should rather say, is the crown of) ethics, admits of no isolation of the economic motive, and of no abstraction of economic facts as a separate branch of enquiry and subject of science. It is a study of the ways in which households and cities can properly use the means at their disposal for the better living of a good life. Wealth, on this basis, is a means to a moral end; as such a means, it is necessarily limited by the end, and must be neither more (nor less) than what the end requires. This is not socialism; but it is a line of thought inimical to capitalism (which involves the unlimited accumulation of wealth), and through the influence of Ruskin it has, in its measure, tended to foster modern socialism.

There was, however, a certain amount of what we may call quasi-socialistic opinion in Greece in the fourth century. Plato, indeed, was not a socialist: the scheme of his *Republic* is a scheme for the divorce of political power from economic possession, under which the governing class (but not the governed) surrenders private property for the sake of a pure devotion to public concerns. He may have been misinterpreted (as he is by Aristotle in the second book of the *Politics*), and have thus come to be regarded as the advocate of a larger and more drastic policy. Some of the later plays of Aristophanes (the *Ecclesiazusae* and the *Plutus*, produced about 390 B.C.) contain a satire upon plans for the general socialization of private property, which must have been current before the *Republic* appeared (possibly about 387 B.C.), and with which its scheme may have been confused. But socialist schemes remained matters of airy speculation, which never penetrated to the people. The citizen of Athens was more often his own employer than an employee: there was little of a wage-system: if there were rich men, they were relieved by 'liturgies' of part of their wealth: if there were poor, there was the Theoric Fund and the system of payment for attending Assembly and law-court. The system of private property which Aristotle defends, on the ground that virtue needs its 'equipment' and personality its medium of expression, was never in any real danger. It was protected, as it perhaps will always be, by the conservatism of small farmers and small artisans working on their own account. The utmost extremity of the radical politician was a demand for redistribution of land (which is not the same as its socialization) and for cancellation of debts.

Slavery was more of a moot question. It was the enslavement of Greeks by Greeks which first began to raise questionings. What was to be thought of the enslavement of the defeated Athenians at Syracuse in 413 B.C.? Was not Callicratidas right when at the storming of Methymna in 406 B.C. he vowed that no Greek should be enslaved if he could prevent it? An echo of such doubts may be traced in Plato's protest against the enslavement of Greeks in the fifth book of the *Republic*. The question became acute when the Thebans liberated the Messenian serfs of the Spartans at the end of 370 B.C. Was this a theft of the private property of Sparta? Was it the restoration to the Messenians of the liberty which was their due? Isocrates defended the Spartan case: a certain Alcidamas spoke on the other side, and protested that 'God has sent all men into the world free, and nature has made no man a slave.' This was perhaps rhetorical exaggeration: Alcidamas may really have meant Greeks rather than men in general. Certainly neither Plato nor Aristotle protests against any and every form of slavery. If Plato objects in the *Republic* to the enslavement of Greeks, in the *Laws* he recognizes slavery and legislates for slaves, whom he couples with children as having imperfectly developed minds. Aristotle, recognizing that there has been much debate, makes no very clear pronouncement on the enslavement of defeated Greeks (Philip of Macedon had enslaved many Greeks since the days when the Thebans liberated the Messenian serfs, and the old rule of war might well seem to have been re-established), but he obviously inclines to regard slavery as only proper for barbarians who are 'by nature' slaves. The natural slave, as Aristotle conceives him, is a man whose chief use is his body, but who possesses mind enough, not indeed to control himself, but to understand and to profit by the control of a superior mind. He is a family slave, who is caught up into and elevated by the life of the family: if he serves its purposes, which after all are moral purposes, he enjoys its benefits, which are also moral benefits. There is no great harshness in Aristotle's view of slavery. From the *Ethics* we learn that the slave—not indeed as a slave, but as a man—may be his master's friend; at the end of the *Politics* we are promised (but not given) an explanation of the reason why 'it is better that all slaves should have freedom set before their eyes as a reward.' We may not be convinced by his argument for 'natural' slavery; but we must admit that, by treating slavery as a moral institution, he lent it the best sanction which it could receive. To defend slavery on the ground of its potential moral benefits is better than defence (or even attack) based merely on an economic calculus.

Another problem of family life debated in the fourth century was the position of women. The tragedies of Euripides show a certain feminism: the *Ecclesiazusae* of Aristophanes is a satire upon women's suffrage: Plato would have women emancipated from household drudgery for political service in his ideal State. In speculation of this order the emancipation of women was connected with community of wives, and it was assumed that women could only be free if the institution of marriage and the monogamous family were abolished. It was the negative assumption, rather than the positive proposal, which attracted attention and criticism; and Aristotle, for example, in his criticism of Plato's proposal, discusses only the question whether wives and children should be common to all citizens. Upon this line of argument he defends the private family as vigorously as he defends private property, and on the same ground: the family is justified by the moral development which it makes possible. This is very true; but the problem of the position of women is not solved by the justification of the family.

To discuss the theories of education advanced by Plato in the *Republic* and the *Laws*, and by Aristotle at the end of the *Politics*, would require a separate chapter. All that can be said in this place is that the city-state, conceived as an educational institution for the training of character and the fulfilment of human capacity, was regarded by both as finding its primary function in education; that education was therefore to be conducted by the state (and not by individuals or voluntary associations), and to be directed to the making of character; and that consequently—the consequence was readily apparent to Greeks living in a great age of art, and sensitive to its influence—the curriculum of education (apart from its higher and scientific ranges) was to be in the domain of noble poetry and noble music, such as might insensibly infect the mind and mould the character by its own nobility. No actual system of education in Greece was after this pattern. If Spartan education was conducted by the state, it was merely a military training: if Athenian education had its artistic side, it was neither conducted nor controlled by the state. Here, as in so many respects, the theory of Plato and Aristotle departs from contemporary facts. This is a consideration we have always to bear in mind. We must be very cautious in using the writings of Plato and Aristotle to illustrate or to explain contemporary political conditions, or the actual political thought of their time. Their philosophy is mainly ideal, because it is ethical, and because an ethical philosophy must deal with the ideal. Even when they deal with the actual, and criticize the actual—when, for instance, they are concerned with democracy—they deal with the actual as they saw it rather than as it actually was. The actual as they see it has already been brought into contact with the ideal: it has been, as it were, singed and blackened by the fire of the ideal. This is not to deny that they both started from the ground of the actual to attain their ideals. Nor is it to deny—least of all to Aristotle, who has a large capacity for analysis and appreciation of the given—that they understood the actual which they saw. It is only to say that they understood it in the light of their own philosophy, and condemned it because it was dark in that light.

But we must not do injustice to the sober inductive method of Aristotle, or to the width of the knowledge of facts which underlies his political theory. He made a collection of 158 polities, 'democratic, oligarchic, aristocratic and tyrannical': one of these, the *Constitution of Athens*, discovered some thirty-five years ago, remains to indicate their character. He also made a collection of 'customs' (the customs, it would seem, of the 'barbarians') in

four books: he wrote a treatise on the 'cases of constitutional law'
submitted by Greek cities to Philip of Macedon at Corinth: he
wrote a work 'On Kingship' for the benefit of Alexander, in
which he seems to have advised his pupil to distinguish between
Greeks and barbarians, dealing with the former as 'leader'
(ἡγεμών) and the latter as 'master' (δεσπότης): he wrote an
'Alexander or On Colonies,' in which he may have dealt with
Alexander's policy of planting Greek cities in Asia. The last two
treatises bring to the mind the curious question of the relation of
Aristotle to his pupil. The imagination of later ages seized on the
theme: a medieval *fabliau*, 'Le Lai d'Aristote,' makes the tutor
accompany his pupil to India as a sort of chaplain and confessor.
The actual facts are scanty enough. In the *Politics* there is a complete silence about Alexander, and an absorption in the city-state
as complete as if Alexander had never existed: it is only from
later bibliographies that we learn of the two treatises supposed to
have been written by Aristotle for the benefit of his pupil. The
connection between Aristotle at Athens and Alexander in Asia
would seem to have been confined in the main to the realm of
natural science. Alexander is said to have sent an expedition up
the Nile, to investigate its sources, at the suggestion of Aristotle:
he sent to Athens, for the use of the Peripatetic school, the observations on the fauna and flora of Asia made by the scientific staff
which accompanied his expedition. That is perhaps all. Certainly
Alexander's policy in dealing with the relations between Greeks
and 'barbarians' in Asia was not the policy supposed to have been
advocated by Aristotle. It was more in accord with that afterwards enunciated by Eratosthenes, who, 'refusing to agree with
those who divided all mankind into Greeks and barbarians and
advised Alexander to treat the former as friends and the latter as
foes, declared that it was better to divide men simply into the
good and the bad.'

V. THE END OF THE *POLIS* AND ITS
POLITICAL THEORY

The policy which Alexander developed during his conquest of
Asia was a policy essentially different from that which he had
entertained at the beginning of his conquest. In 336 he was the
generalissimo of the Greeks in a war against 'barbarians' who
were the natural enemies and the natural slaves of the Greeks: by
330 he had come to value Persian monarchy and to be attracted
by Persian nobility; and he was planning an Empire in which he

should be equally lord of Greek and Persian, and both should be knit together as equals by intermarriage and common military service. This meant a great revolution. It was much that men should rise from the idea of civic autonomy to that of Greek unity: it was more that they should rise from the idea of Greek unity to that of the unity of mankind—so far, at any rate, as mankind was yet known. If we analyse this last idea, we shall see that it really implies two conceptions—the conception of a single cosmopolis, and the conception of all men (Greek or barbarian, Jew or Gentile) as equal in that cosmopolis. These are two fundamental conceptions that inaugurate a new epoch—an epoch which succeeds that of the *Polis* and precedes that of the national state—an epoch which covers the centuries that lie between Aristotle and Alexander at one end, and Machiavelli and Luther at the other, and embraces in its scope the three Empires of Macedon and Rome and Charlemagne. They are the conceptions which dominate the theory of the Cynics and Stoics. They are again the conceptions which we find in the teaching of St Paul, who believed in one Church of all Christians which should cover the world, and held that in that Church there was 'neither Greek nor Jew... barbarian, Scythian, bond nor free[1].'

The city-state seems already to belong to a remote past, when we reflect on Alexander's sweeping plans and the revolution of thought which they helped to produce. But it still survived under tutelage. Alexander and his successors recognized a double citizenship in all the members of the Greek cities in their Empire —a citizenship of the city, and a citizenship of the Empire which took the form of adoration (or *proskynesis*) due to the divinity of the ruler who was 'God Manifest' and 'Saviour' of his people. In the sphere of their own citizenship the cities retained a certain measure of autonomy; and theorists might still debate about the proper constitution of the city. Such theories were somewhat academic, in days when an Antipater might (as in 322 B.C.) descend upon Athens, leave a garrison in Munychia, and abolish the democratic constitution in favour of the 'ancestral constitution' of Solon's day (p. 459 *sq*.). So long, however, as it ran in favour of a mixed constitution, with a moderate suffrage (like that instituted by Antipater at Athens, which left 9000 citizens with the franchise out of a previous 21,000), the politicians of the day were willing to tolerate political theory. Accordingly, the mixed constitution, propounded by Plato in the *Laws*, where he sought to blend

---

[1] See further, above, p. 436 *sq*.

Persian monarchy with Athenian democracy, and expounded by Aristotle in the *Politics*, under the form of a union of the better elements of democracy with the best of oligarchy, attained a general vogue in the new guise of a combination of the three elements of monarchy, aristocracy, and democracy. Dicaearchus of Méssana, a pupil of Aristotle, identified his name with this scheme: his *Tripoliticus*, in which Sparta, with its kings, ephors and apella, served as an example and a type, set a fashion; and the 'tripolity' became known as γένος Δικαιαρχικόν ('the species of Dicaearchus'). The same theory of the mixed constitution, with Sparta still as model, was adopted by the Stoics; and with Rome in place of Sparta, it was in turn accepted and expounded by Polybius and Cicero.

The last word in the political theory of the fourth century was but a barren formula. The 'tripolity' is only mechanism, and doctrinaire mechanism at that. The *Republic* of Plato had contained a genuine and profound philosophy of society and human order—its purposes as well as its methods: its life as well as its form. The γένος Δικαιαρχικόν is a form for which there is no matter—the skeleton of something which has never existed. The one feature of historic interest which it possessed was its cult of Sparta. Once it had been the Spartan system of moral training which had attracted political theorists. There are imitations of this system in the ideal state of Plato's *Republic*, though we have to remember that on the whole Plato regards the Spartan constitution, which really supplies the model for his 'timocracy,' as a corruption of the ideal. In the *Laws* Plato is the critic of Spartan training, on the ground that it is merely directed to the one virtue of courage, and neglects the greater things which belong to peace; but none the less he admires the mixed character of the Spartan constitution, so curiously and so subtly blended that it is difficult to decide whether it is tyranny, monarchy, aristocracy or democracy. In the *Politics* Aristotle is entirely inimical: he repeats the criticism of Plato, and adds a number of criticisms of his own; he has no praise for the mixed constitution of Sparta, and his own conception of such a constitution is something entirely different. It was left for his disciples, such as Dicaearchus, to renew and develop the admiration of Plato for the Spartan constitution. So Sparta, discredited in one part, entered the stage again, amid new applause, in another. She was more fortunate than deserving. If any state deserved ill of fourth-century Greece, it was Sparta. She was in league with the Persian king in the East and the tyrant of Syracuse in the West.

She suppressed federations, and sought to ensure the disunity of
Greece, which she thought to be the condition of her own power,
and which proved to be the cause of the victory of Macedonia.
If she had not broken the Chalcidian confederacy in 379, the
power of Philip might never have been established. It is idle to
speculate about the consequences which might have ensued.
Sparta perhaps served a purpose. The Greek cities might never
have achieved their own unification by their own efforts; and a
larger instrument was perhaps needed for the large end of a
general diffusion of Greek culture. But those who have been
touched by the tradition, and educated by the philosophy, of the
Greek city-state may be permitted to stand by its grave and remember its life: to wonder what, under happier auspices, it might
have achieved, and to lament that it was not given to a Greece
inspired by Athens to lead the Mediterranean world to a unity
deeper and more pervading, because more surely rooted in a
common culture—larger and more permanent, because more
firmly planted in a general freedom—than Rome was ever destined
to achieve.

CHAPTER XVII

GREEK ART AND ARCHITECTURE

I. CLASSICAL SCULPTURE: (ii) THE FOURTH CENTURY[1]

THE sculpture of the fifth century could be divided into three periods or four. In the fourth century also, one may speak of three periods: the early years; the time of Praxiteles and Scopas; and the time of Lysippus. But the bounding-lines are more indeterminate: the first phase is partly reaction from the art of the late fifth century, partly preparation for the second phase; and the second phase is not really superseded by the third, but passes into it, subsists side by side with it, and helps it to engender Hellenistic art. The ancients made the break at Lysippus, and so shall we: the first two phases will be considered together, the third by itself.

We begin as before with the naked male; and with what is for us the most important monument of fourth-century art, the Hermes of Praxiteles[2]. That carries us at once to the middle of the century or even a little past it: but standing there we can look back and see what changes have taken place; and we shall have an opportunity of retracing our steps. The motive, a young god playing with a child, is a light-hearted one. The attitude is one of those easy leaning postures which first appeared in sculpture about the thirties of the fifth century and which are great favourites in the fourth. The build of the figure is lighter than in the fifth century, but there is no touch of effeminate softness in the body, which is beautifully developed. In the head the features are smaller and finer, the bones of the skull, one would say, thinner. Body and face are not mapped out into big clearly-demarcated areas, as they still are even in the late fifth century: the areas are somewhat smaller, though not unduly small, and they slip and play into each other. With this difference goes another difference. Compare the Hermes with a fifth-century original: the fifth-century flesh seems made of some neutral substance, the flesh of the Hermes of muscle and fat: it has not only the surface bloom and sheen of life, but the warm lifted swell of a living organism. If body and face are less patternized than before, drapery and hair are still less.

[1] See vol. v, p. 435.   [2] See Volume of Plates ii, 82, *a*, *b*.

The Hermes is an original from the chisel of the great Athenian; there are no copies of it, and how much of its high-bred grace, subtle modelling, and gentle turns of head and body would survive in an ordinary copy? Speaking generally, fourth-century works suffer more than fifth-century at the copyist's hands. The strong and simpler wine of the fifth century travels: the fourth reaches us now dulcified now fortified, and nearly always robbed of its quintessence.

Other Praxitelean males have come down to us in copies. The boy satyr pouring wine, part of a group, is an early work and comparatively insignificant. The boy Apollo, like the Hermes, leans, and the median line of the figure is a pronounced double curve. A third leaner, the resting satyr, has survived in more copies than any other statue, because to the Roman it represented the spirit of the sweet half-wild. Praxiteles was famous for his satyrs and Erotes; of his female figures we shall speak presently. The athlete as such plays no part in his work: athletic youths, like the Hermes, do: but Praxiteles is always turning with special affection to adolescence and late childhood, away from the world to a realm of unshaken hours:

$$\tau\grave{o}\ \gamma\grave{a}\rho\ \nu\acute{e}a\zeta o\nu\ \acute{e}\nu\ \tau o\iota o\hat{\iota}\sigma\delta\epsilon\ \beta\acute{o}\sigma\kappa\epsilon\tau a\iota$$
$$\chi\acute{\omega}\rho o\iota\sigma\iota\nu\ a\mathring{v}\tau o\hat{v},\ \kappa a\acute{\iota}\ \nu\iota\nu\ o\mathring{v}\ \theta\acute{a}\lambda\pi o\varsigma\ \theta\epsilon o\hat{v},$$
$$o\mathring{v}\delta'\ \mathring{o}\mu\beta\rho o\varsigma,\ o\mathring{v}\delta\grave{e}\ \pi\nu\epsilon\upsilon\mu\acute{a}\tau\omega\nu\ o\mathring{v}\delta\grave{e}\nu\ \delta o\nu\epsilon\hat{\iota},$$
$$\mathring{a}\lambda\lambda'\ \mathring{\eta}\delta o\nu a\hat{\iota}\varsigma\ \mathring{a}\mu o\chi\theta o\nu\ \acute{e}\xi a\acute{\iota}\rho\epsilon\iota\ \beta\acute{\iota}o\nu.$$

The art of Praxiteles mirrors the life of Athens in his time, or at least the life of many Athenians: an intelligent life, quiet-tempered, fond of pleasure and tasteful in its pleasures, taking things lightly, or as lightly as one can. There are only glimpses of this frame of mind in Plato, for he was too passionate, and too full of hatred; but there is something like it in the poets, comic and other, of the fourth century, as we know them from the pages of Athenaeus.

In the temple of Aphrodite at Megara, Pausanias says, there were statues of Persuasion and another divinity whom they call Consolation, both by Praxiteles; and of Love, Yearning, and Desire, by Scopas. Eros might have been done by either: but the Megarians showed judgment in allocating the other statues —unless indeed it was the sculptors themselves who chose. For passion, which is excluded from the art of Praxiteles, is all in all to his Parian contemporary. We hear of no satyrs by Scopas: but his raging maenad, even in our small and fragmentary copy[1],

---

[1] See Volume of Plates ii, 84, b.

takes us back to the stormiest creatures of late archaic painting, and its strong twist on its axis is something new in the sculptural rendering of violent movement. Another of his masterpieces was a great many-figured group of Poseidon and the demi-gods and monsters of the deep: if the tritoness from Ostia is a copy of one of those figures, or even if it is only an imitation, Scopas was the first to embody in human form that eternal hunger and unrest[1]. A battle-scene and a hunting-scene decorated the pediments of the temple of Athena at Tegea: Scopas was the architect, and the sculpture, of which fragments remain, must be of his school and from his designs[2]. The massive heads with their thickish features and the fury in their deepset eyes are the opposite of everything Praxitelean, and remind us that there was another kind of Greek left besides the cultivated Athenian—especially in Arcadia. Such were not all but most of the men who fought against the Macedonian and for him, who swarmed over the east and north, and who brought not only Greek culture, but Greek valour and resolution, wherever they went.

The Christ Church Van der Goes used to bear the label 'Rembrandt or Mantegna': and Pliny says of the group of Niobe's children that authorities differed whether it were by Praxiteles or Scopas. It was doubtless by neither; and the same may be said of several works which have been attributed now to the one and now to the other in modern times. One of these is the Hypnos. The chief copy, in Madrid, lacks the arms[3]: small bronzes show that he held poppies in one hand and poured something from a horn—poppy-juice—over the eyes of the world. Another boy god; not however an adaptation of a boy Apollo, or a boy Dionysus, or a boy satyr, but a new and great imaginative creation: not made into sleep by his head-wings, or by what he scatters or pours, but through and through sleep, with his soft, sleek, well-liking body and his strong and noiseless onward tread.

Turning to female figures we are able to glance at two sculptors who although they overlapped with Praxiteles and Scopas were older men. The drapery-style of the late fifth century—or one of the drapery-styles—garments now clinging and transparent now tossing in the wind—is continued by an artist of great charm, the Athenian Timotheus. Timotheus, an inscription informs us, made the acroteria for the east front of the temple of Asclepius at Epidaurus, and furnished models for the pedimental sculpture. Fragments of both acroteria and pediments remain, and

---

[1] See Volume of Plates ii, 84, *a*.
[2] *Ib.* ii. 86, *a, b*.   [3] *Ib.* ii. 88, *a*.

enable us to connect with Timotheus two works which survive in copies only, the Leda of the Capitol, and the Rospigliosi Athena in Florence[1]. Both statues have much of the late fifth century in drapery, in big features, in strong-waved hair, but the fourth century shows itself in the emotion of the far-away upward gaze; and the early fourth century, rather than the later, in a certain delicacy and even frailty of form. Cephisodotus, another Athenian, also looks both backwards and forwards. His Eirene—Peace with the infant Wealth in her arms—was set up at Athens shortly after 375, and symbolizes the revival of Athenian prosperity after the great disaster and the generation of despair and half-hopes which succeeded it[2]. The Eirene harks back, in the simpler fall of its drapery, not to the grandiose goddesses of the late fifth century, but to those of the Parthenonian period and before. On the other hand, the tender intimate feeling is of the fourth century; and has the face not something ethereal which belongs to the spring of the period and not to the full bloom? Wealth is nothing without Health: and another famous Attic statue of the same time as the Eirene was the original of the Deepdene Hygieia; she also not one of the great deities, but a strong and kindly presence with a solid boon to bestow.

External evidence as well as internal points to a connection between Cephisodotus and Praxiteles: Cephisodotus was perhaps an elder brother, certainly the forerunner. The note of simplicity which he strikes persists in the draped figures that go back to Praxiteles and his circle: a different simplicity, of course, from that of the Hestia Giustiniani[3] or Amelung's goddess[4]; for it bears the imprint of a more conscious art. One of the chief ingredients in it is the toning-down of the two contrasts which had dominated the drapery of the later fifth century: the contrast between clinging parts and parts flying free; and the contrast between parts which reveal and parts which conceal. The garments now tend to wind equably round the body or hang equably over it, neither cleaving to it nor masking it, but swathing —or clothing it. This principle is not confined to Praxiteles, but appears for instance in the Hygieia, and in one of the noblest originals which have reached us from the fourth century, the seated figure of Demeter, from Cnidus, in the British Museum[5]. The deep impression which the Demeter leaves, as of the mother acquainted with grief, and enduring under it, is not due to the

---

[1] See Volume of Plates ii, 80, *b*. [2] *Ib.* ii, 80, *a*.
[3] *Ib.* ii, 40, *a*.   [4] *Ib.* ii, 40, *c*.   [5] *Ib.* ii, 88, *b*.

head alone, but in part also to the draped body—the garments drawn about it, and the legs turned with a suggestion of self-constraint.

Praxitelean drapery is not to be reduced to a formula: and one of the most charming of Praxitelean statues, the Artemis from Gabii in the Louvre, stands somewhat aside, for the motive of the girlish figure is the actual adjustment of the drapery. The most celebrated of the statues by Praxiteles was not a draped figure, but a naked one, the Aphrodite at Cnidus. Naked or half-naked female statues, rare in the fifth century, begin to be common in the fourth: but it has been suggested that the nakedness of the Cnidian, and her gesture as well, had a special authorization—were borrowed from some hallowed and primitive image preserved in the sanctuary from the dim past. The gesture of the hand, and the shrinking of the whole body which accompanies it, are reported to be instinctive expressions of modesty. In themselves they are mean; but from trivial or even disgusting motives, provided they beautifully unfurled the body, the sculptor of the Lizard-slayer was hardly the man to recoil. Such copies as we have of the Cnidian make it difficult to understand the reputation of the statue in antiquity. Here, if anywhere, we miss the sculptor's hand: judging from the Hermes, we must suppose that in the original these dull heavy forms were fused into a figure instinct with glowing life.

Let us not end this section on this note, but with a glance at three modest originals which belong to Praxiteles or to his school. The first two take us back to our starting-point the Hermes: the exquisite statuette of Artemis, from Cyprus, in Vienna, by its attitude[1]; the head of a girl goddess, from Chios, in Boston, by the large architecture which keeps its surface-delicacy from cloying[2]. The third, another head in Boston, this time from Athens[3], makes one think of the sons of Praxiteles, of whose style, a continuation of their father's, we now know a little from fragments found at Cos.

Aegina, Olympia, Parthenon: they summed the achievements of their epochs. There is no fourth-century monument corresponding to these. The Mausoleum comes nearest: but the difference is immense. Even if the Mausoleum were completely extant, how could the super-sepulchre of a hellenized Carian, even though the work of the most eminent Greek artists, be more than a 'wild enormity of ancient magnanimity' compared with the great civic

[1] See Volume of Plates ii, 100, a.   [2] Ib. ii, 86, c.
[3] Ib. ii, 86, d.

and national monuments of Greece? Its importance is nevertheless considerable, especially as its date is known, for Mausolus
died in 353 and his widow, who ordered the tomb, two years
later. Four great sculptors are said to have worked on the
building, Timotheus and Scopas, Bryaxis and Leochares, each
taking one side: but the apportionment of the fragments is not yet
beyond doubt. The most significant slabs of the amazonomachy,
though not the best-preserved, are those which by a curious
coincidence have been skied into the fancy restoration of the
order and replaced on the level of the eye by casts. These slabs
with their lean and terrifying figures and their novel whirl of
movement already speak the language of the later fourth century,
and are presumably Leocharean[1].

Another work done by a Greek for a foreigner is the so-called
Alexander sarcophagus in Constantinople, made for a Sidonian
prince[2]; remarkable for its marvellous preservation, colour and all,
for the admirable portraits of Alexander and his war-marked
marshal Parmenion, and for the intense animation of its hunting
and fighting scenes. There is nothing Lysippean in it, although
the date must be well on in the second half of the century; but
something of the spirit of Scopas and his Tegean pediments.

The greatest figure in the sculpture of the second half of the
fourth century is Lysippus of Sicyon: our literary sources represent him as a great realist, and the inventor of a new system of
proportions. The athlete scraping himself, in the Vatican, is in
all probability a copy of his bronze Apoxyomenus, and it is something new in sculpture[3]. The head is smaller, the legs longer than
before, so that the whole figure looks slenderer and taller: this
agrees with the description of Lysippean proportions in Pliny.
In the treatment of flesh it goes along with the Hermes of
Praxiteles as against the fifth century: but waist and joints are
more compressed than in the Hermes, and the muscles harder
and more prominent: in a word there is less fat: this is the siccity
or dryness of which Pliny speaks. The attitude of the body has
something momentary about it: it is not planted solidly with the
weight on one leg as in the fifth century: one leg is the supporting
leg and one is the free; but the contrast between the two is no
longer the dominant motive: the weight seems almost to be in
process of transference from the one to the other. Again, the
figure as a whole is not so much in one plane as earlier figures;
which are more or less flattened out before us, relief-like, so that

[1] See Volume of Plates ii, 90, *a*, *b*.
[2] *Ib.* ii, 90, *c*; 92, *a*, *b*.   [3] *Ib.* ii, 94, *a*.

we can enjoy, in a select view, the clarity and harmony of the contour which contains the figure. The position of the scraper in space is more like that of an actual person discovered in the dressing-room. The plane is constantly shifting as the eye passes from one part to the other; and the right arm stretches out straight towards us in strong foreshortening. This tridimensionalism is one of the last words in realism: and has been described as 'the final step taken by sculpture in the achievement of its specific perfection.' It opens up a fresh world of possibilities: but there is seldom gain without loss; and the new age produces too many statues which have many quite good views, but no perfect view; like the Lysippean Lansdowne Hermes[1], or the later Eros bending his bow.

From all these causes the Apoxyomenus is the very antithesis of the Doryphorus in aspect and tone. In tone, for although he is not facing an opponent but simply scraping himself, yet there is excitement not only in his face but in every limb. This is one form of the pathos of the fourth century, as contrasted with the ethos of the fifth. There is the same excitement in the Lansdowne Hermes, and the same in the athlete Agias from Delphi[2]. The Agias has been compared with the Lansdowne Heracles, which is a copy of a Scopaic work. There is a superficial resemblance in pose, and the Agias is not yet tridimensional like the Apoxyomenus. But there the resemblance ends: the Agias has the new proportions, the new balance on the legs, and the new emotion running through the figure from top to toe. The Agias is a fourth-century work, and has been thought with good reason to be a free copy of a bronze, though an early bronze, by Lysippus. Whether it is or not, it belongs to the new age, and the Scopaic Heracles—even if we replace the head by the better copy, in bronze, from Herculaneum—to the old.

Lysippus was an extraordinarily prolific artist, and there are a good many other statues which seem to be copies of works by him. The silen with the infant Dionysus[3], from the subject, and because it is a leaning figure, makes one think of the Hermes of Praxiteles, of his resting satyr: but there is as strong a contrast between these and the Lysippean silen, with his oldened and coarsened forms, his not graceful attitude, and the deeper and more sombre tone of the whole work, as between the smiling figures of late archaic art and the gravity of early classical sculpture.

Apoxyomenus and Agias are athlete statues, and the Lansdowne

[1] See Volume of Plates ii, 98, *a*.   [2] *Ib.* ii, 92, *c*; 94, *b*; 96, *a*.
[3] *Ib.* ii, 96, *b*.

Hermes is perhaps an athlete rather than Hermes. Athlete statues were made throughout the fourth century, but it is not surprising that they should be more significant in the time of Lysippus than in the earlier part of the period. Nor is it to be wondered at that Lysippus was famous for his portraits. Portraiture flourished throughout the century, and a realistic element, unfamiliar to earlier portraiture, was introduced by Demetrius of Alopece in the first decades. Many copies of fourth-century portraits have reached us, but usually only the head was copied, and that with the individuality exaggerated to caricature. Of the full-length portraits that have survived entire or nearly—and it is only in these that we can appreciate the achievements of the fourth century in portraiture—neither the Aeschines nor the Sophocles can have been a masterpiece of characterization: the Socrates, now known from the London statuette, must have been[1]. The greatest of all is the Demosthenes: its date is 280, so that it lies outside our period; but without Lysippus it would have been impossible.

In the treatment of drapery, the fourth century, as it advances, turns once more to contrast for its effects: to the old contrast of clinging and flying, as in the Florence Niobids, poor copies of a somewhat theatrical group of statues made in the late part of our period; and to the new contrasts set up, either by a heavy swag of massed drapery across the middle of the body, as in the Artemisia from the Mausoleum, or by the taut bands, made by the hand holding and pulling part of the garment, which dominate the drapery of the women from Herculaneum in Dresden. A realism in drapery, corresponding to Lysippean realism in the rendering of the body, it is difficult to find in the fourth century itself: for the maid of Antium, with her wonderful realistic drapery, seems to belong to the beginning of the next period.

We may conclude with a glance at the reliefs on the Attic tombstones of the fourth century. The series ends, owing to the sumptuary law of Demetrius of Phalerum, in 317. In the early part of the period fifth-century tradition persists: low relief with strong perpendiculars and horizontals; and a subdued tone. But the emotion of the fourth century soon makes its way in, and the right angles give place to curves and diagonals as mother yearns to son or daughter to mother. The relief becomes higher, and sheers backwards into depth, until in the late fourth century the figures are almost in the round, and the background, at first neutral, becomes a sort of dark shed-like room in which the figures

---

[1] See Volume of Plates ii, 100, *b*.

have their being. In the last stage, the new realism deepens the pathos. The survival of the fifth-century tradition, with only the beginning of change, may be illustrated by the wonderful stele of Sostrate in New York[1]: she looking at her father, who sits in the middle like a god, while her mother stands behind him holding her granddaughter, Sostrate's child, by the hand. Athens 870 shows the full fourth-century style[2]: the two quiet figures of the earlier tombstones, the seated and the standing woman, have become all gesture, action, and emotion: so that the meeting of older woman and younger, mother and daughter, takes one's mind to the great Visitations of Christian art. The feeling is enhanced by a third figure, the third age, the girl, not much more than a child, who watches and understands. In the stele from the Ilissus the pathos is of a different kind[3]: the young man, who has died, and the old man gazing at him and trying to fathom why such things happen: corresponding to the child in the last piece, a twofold foil—the dog alive and distressed, the little servant sleeping. The vigil for the dead, marvellously transfigured. Finally, the stele Athens 731[4]. The motive resembles that of the stele from the Ilissus, but is very differently treated. A young man, this time a soldier, and his father. No care for the old beauty of harmonious line or attitude, but all the beauty and force of the new realism.

II. CLASSICAL PAINTING: (ii) THE FOURTH CENTURY[5]

Greek painting was thought by the ancients to have reached its highest point in the fourth century, and Apelles was acclaimed the greatest of Greek painters. Apelles was an Ionian from Colophon, but the two great centres were those districts which had always been the eyes of artistic Greece: Athens and Sicyon. The topic was still figurework, narrative or representational; there was also portraiture, especially of the heroic kind: still-life, that is still-life for its own sake, was hardly beginning; there were landscape elements in pictures, but no landscape-painting. By the perfection of the encaustic process, painters could obtain subtler effects than before.

The works of Apelles and his peers have all perished; and our monumental sources of information are scanty and unsatisfactory. The vases tell us the story of vases, and something about contemporary painting as a whole: but the art of vase-painting is in full decline, and besides, it remains linear, whereas the great

---

[1] See Volume of Plates ii, 102, *a*.   [2] *Ib.* ii, 102, *b*.
[3] *Ib.* ii, 104, *a*.   [4] *Ib.* ii, 104, *b*.   [5] See vol. v, p. 443.

painters were now masters of light and colour, and thought in those as well as in line. One masterpiece survives in a copy, the Battle of Alexander and Darius. Roman decorative painting preserves something of others, but almost inextricably overgrown.

Attic vase-painting touches bottom in the early part of the fourth century. It subsists on the Meidian tradition diluted; and is so insipid and vulgar that it is not always recognized as Attic. In the second quarter of the century a revival begins. In the Kerch vases—as these latest of Attic red-figure vases are often called—there are flickers of beauty[1]. The tall, dignified figures are a relief from the debased roly-polies of the sub-Meidian period; but they in their turn are often vacuous and mannered, and with its predilection for three-quartered faces and three-quartered and frontal figures, and its neglect of the speaking contour, the style is not really suitable to vase-painting. It is not confined to vases, but appears in drawings on ivory and bronze[2]: it is the manner of some great painter or school of painting.

In Italy the prospect is not much more pleasing. Some of the phlyax vases, with their scenes from farces, are delightful[3]. The Dolon in London is not a farce, but a burlesque of epic[4]: in its pattern of men and trees, it is worthy to set beside Pollaiuolo's Battle of the Nudes; in its mastery of the comic, beside the Heracles and Busiris of the old Ionian. When we turn to the big Apulian vases of the second half of the century, we note the slickness of hand, and we can put up with a square inch or so here and there: but it is really time that vase-painting ceased; and practically it ceases, in Italy as well as in Attica, at the end of the century.

Our copy of the Battle of Alexander and Darius[5]—doubtless the Issus, freely treated—must be fullsize, and it bears every token of being an accurate copy: but it is mutilated; and it is in mosaic, and how much of the rush and terror of the original must have been lost! Think of the Miracle of St Mark in mosaic, or Rubens's Battle of the Amazons. Of the sober colour-scheme we have spoken before, and of the technical devices—modelling in light and dark, use of cast-shadows, high-lights, reflected lights: in so serried a composition, aerial perspective can have little place; but these seem to be traces of it; and Plato's censure shows that the art of diminishing the figures according to the supposed distance from the eye was familiar to the painters of his time. The extraordinary complexity of the composition has

---

[1] See Volume of Plates ii, 106, b.   [2] Ib. ii, 108, a, b.
[3] Ib. ii, 106, c.   [4] Ib. ii, 106, a.   [5] Ib. ii, 110.

often been remarked; the wealth of graphic and pictorial interest in detail; and the devastating total effect. The beauty of the actual painting-work we can guess, and we know that fourth-century painters and critics paid the closest attention to material and texture. The great figure-pieces of Velasquez come to the mind—not only because of the lances: but because of the colour-scheme and the colours, because there are no stopgaps or dead filling in the picture, and because the grand and purposed contrast of West and East plays as essential a part in the Battle of Alexander, as that of South and North in the Surrender of Breda.

The wall-paintings from Pompeii, Herculaneum, and else-where are more treacherous ground. The problem is different from that of sculptural copies: for there is nothing in painting which is parallel to the cast, and the statue is not part of a decora-tion but a work by itself. The Achilles and Briseis must go back to a painting by a fourth-century artist: but how much of the colouring and values is his? and what corresponded in the original to the vapid Briseis, or to the bores with trick helmets in the back-ground? Elsewhere we have more than one imitation of a single original, but the imitations agree in only the broadest outlines: so in the Paris and Helen, so in the Odysseus and Penelope. The patient study of Campanian wall-painting has taught us something about the painting of the classical period and will teach us more: but of the works inspired by fourth-century painting, there is not one which does not contain a disturbing number of elements that cannot be fourth-century.

Analogies from sculpture help, but must not be laboured. No one who reads about Apelles can help thinking of Praxiteles. But Apelles cannot have been a Praxiteles in painting: for the greater the artist the more he differs from all other artists. In the Greek paintings of the fourth century we have lost a world.

III. FOURTH-CENTURY DORIC ARCHITECTURE

In considering the architecture of the fifth century, our atten-tion was chiefly centred upon Athens, but it will be otherwise when we turn to the fourth. It is not surprising that after the amazing activity of the half century before Aegospotami the impoverished city was content, for the most part, to enjoy the legacy of her golden age. Nor can much work of importance now be traced in Sicily or Italy. For Doric we must look chiefly to Delphi and to the Peloponnese, for Ionic to Asia Minor. Corinthian was creeping into importance, but in this period it never ventured beyond interiors, except in such small and barely architectural works as the Choragic Monument of Lysi-crates.

At Delphi the chief work of the fourth century was the sixth temple of Apollo, which replaced the Alcmaeonid building, ruined, it would seem, by rain and subsidence, between 360 and 330 B.C.: but, though we know from inscriptions a great deal about its history, its remains are scanty and difficult to under-stand. As a type of fourth-century Doric on the grand scale it will be better to take the temple of Athena Alea at Tegea†[1] the largest and noblest in the Peloponnese, after that of Zeus at Olympia. Closely connected with Tegea is the temple of Zeus at Nemea, and since at Nemea three columns still stand, bearing part of the architrave, while Tegea is wholly ruined, it might seem wiser to choose the better preserved building as our text. The Tegean temple, however, has been better explored and published; moreover it was far more famous in antiquity, and probably served as Nemea's model. At Tegea certainly, and possibly at Nemea, the architect was the sculptor Scopas.

In one respect only the Tegean temple was old-fashioned, for it was narrower in proportion than any other temple of the fourth century. In fineness of workmanship it is almost unrivalled, except by the Erechtheum. The material was local marble. There were refinements in the setting of walls and columns, and the stylobate had horizontal curvature, which began in the foun-dations. Externally the chief definite sign of lateness was the slenderness of the columns, which can hardly be paralleled except at Nemea, long famous as the best example of this Ionic tendency in fourth-century Doric. The Nemean columns, indeed, are even slighter than the Tegean, but the resemblance between the two sets is very close, not only in slenderness, but in the lowness and straightness of the echinus, which has lost almost the last trace of that strong archaic curve, whose influence was still subtly perceptible in the Parthenon.

At Tegea the plan of the cella was simple, with pronaos and opisthodomos each distyle *in antis*. As at Bassae, and in the temple of Zeus at Olympia, no metopes were decorated with sculpture except those inside the colonnade, at each end of the cella: a notable severity in a sculptor's building, where seemingly no expense was spared. In the interior the whole decoration was purely Ionic in character, if Corinthian capitals may be treated

[1] In this and the following sections † with numeral refers to plan on the sheet facing p. 558. For the temple of Tegea see also Volume of Plates ii, 112.

as a development of Ionic. This decoration was used with austerity and restraint, though in detail its richness and complexity rival even the Erechtheum and the sixth-century Ionic treasuries of Delphi. The general disposition of the interior was a further development of the arrangements of Bassae (vol. v, p. 456 *sq.*). Here again half-columns were used, but they did not stand, as at Bassae, at the ends of projecting cross-walls, being engaged in the cella wall. There were fourteen Corinthian half-columns— seven on each side—and pilasters with elaborately moulded capitals in the four inner angles. All alike rested upon a beautiful base moulding, which ran round the wall and the feet of the half-columns and pilasters, as did the exterior base moulding of the Olympieum of Acragas. A side-door led into the cella from the middle of the northern peripteral colonnade. The bases of the Corinthian half-columns somewhat resembled those of the Ionic half-columns of Bassae: it will be convenient to discuss their capitals at a later point (p. 550 *sq.*). The exact date of the Tegean temple is uncertain, but we know that its predecessor was burnt in 395 B.C. It may perhaps be placed in the second third of the fourth century.

Two more mainland Doric buildings of the early fourth century deserve more than a passing reference, the circular peripteral *tholoi* of Delphi and Epidaurus, both externally Doric but internally Corinthian. This was an old type of ground-plan though it never became common. The fourth-century Delphian *tholos* was close to the 'Massaliote' Treasury in the small sanctuary of Athena Pronaia, and would seem to have been famous in antiquity, for Vitruvius (VII. *praef.* 12) records that Theodorus of Phocaea wrote a book 'de tholo qui est Delphis': it is far more likely that Theodorus wrote of this later work, than of the less remarkable sixth-century Doric *tholos*, probably peripteral, with old-fashioned columns, which stood in the sanctuary proper. The later *tholos* is one of the most carefully designed and perfectly executed works of antiquity. The single door faces exactly south. The visible parts of the building were all of marble or timber, except for a sparing use of black Eleusinian limestone. On a stylobate of three steps it had twenty exterior Doric columns, each with twenty flutes, and this outer colonnade carried a coffered marble ceiling, of simple and beautiful design. The restoration of the upper parts is doubtful in detail. There are remains of larger and smaller sets of triglyphs, sculptured metopes, and *simae*. The smaller triglyphs were at the top of the cella wall, inside the peripteral colonnade. It has been suggested that the cella walls rose above the roof of the outer colonnade and carried a separate cornice. This solution, however, raises technical difficulties, and no satisfactory place has been found for the smaller *sima*. Inside was a podium, moulded above and below, and faced with Eleusinian stone. It carried a series of Corinthian columns, slightly engaged. They were probably ten in number. Their capitals, which are important, will be discussed at a later point. The ceiling and roof were of timber, the tiles of marble: there is evidence that the architrave carried by the engaged columns was itself wooden. The date of this *tholos* is disputed. It is usually assigned to the early fourth century, but some authorities would place it in the last quarter of the fifth.

The date of the more famous Epidaurian *tholos* is fairly certain from the evidence of inscriptions: it was probably built between 360 and 330 B.C. The architect, according to Pausanias (II, 27, 5), was Polyclitus; clearly the younger artist of that name, a sculptor-architect like Scopas. It was probably inspired by the Delphian building, but surpassed it in size and in elaboration, though not in beauty and restraint. At Delphi the diameter of the stylobate was about 45 feet, but at Epidaurus it was about 107, and the other dimensions were, of course, proportionately greater. Unlike the Delphian *tholos*, which stands on a solid limestone foundation, the Epidaurian building rested on concentric rings of masonry, whose maze-like design has provoked much speculation of religious rather than architectural interest. In general plan it closely resembled the Delphian *tholos*, except that the exterior Doric columns, which were of limestone, numbered twenty-six, and the interior Corinthian columns, which were of marble, numbered fourteen, and were not engaged but free. The cella wall was mostly of limestone, but marble and Eleusinian stone were used at its crown and foot: its outer face did not, as at Delphi, carry a triglyph frieze. The ceiling was partly of marble and partly of wood. The nature of the roof is uncertain.

The metopes of the outer colonnade were decorated not with figured sculpture but with rosettes. The marble cofferings of the pteron ceiling were very elaborate, and the innermost pavement was composed of a diamond pattern of white marble and black Eleusinian stone. The most interesting things in the building are the Corinthian capitals, one of which, unused, was found buried, for unknown reasons, a yard under the ancient surface: but these also must be discussed at a later point.

That these two *tholoi* have much in common is obvious: but

there is something less obvious that links them both with Tegea
with Nemea, and with many other Doric works of the late fift
or fourth century of which there is here no space to speak: th
Metroum at Olympia, for instance, and the temples of Asclepiu
and Artemis at Epidaurus. In all we feel that Doric has becom
a new thing. In some way not easily defined—it is deeper thar
slenderness of proportion or richness of detail—Doric has drunl
the spirit of Ionic, and a new style has been born. Yet thes(
exquisite masterpieces were almost the last incarnation of monu
mental Doric. The great temples of the next generation wer(
pure Ionic, in the Asiatic tradition.

In truth Doric was dying. It was still to produce a few delightful temples, like that of Cori in Latium, but its spirit lived chiefly
in less ambitious works—in market porticoes for instance, and
in the charming colonnades of domestic peristyles. Yet the
sculptor-architects of this late Doric bequeathed to their Ionic
successors one momentous gift. The Corinthian capital, Ionic in
origin, but evolved by Doric artists as a subtle refinement of
interior decoration, was destined to drive both its rivals from the
field, and to remain for all time the most characteristic feature of
classical architecture.

IV. THE CORINTHIAN CAPITAL

It will be fitting here to say something of the development of
the Corinthian capital in the fourth century. This can be traced
chiefly in the buildings at Delphi, Tegea, and Epidaurus already
described, in the Choragic Monument of Lysicrates at Athens
and in the Philippeum of Olympia. Of these the Delphian
capitals are perhaps the earliest. Only fragments survive, but
they closely resemble in many respects the pioneer capital of
Bassae described in the last volume (vol. v, p. 457 *sq.*). Much of
the bell was bare and there were large pairs of inner spirals
placed low, with a big palmette between them entirely below the
abacus. It would seem however that these spirals did not spring
from the double ring of acanthus leaves which surrounded the
base of the capital but were continuous with the angle spirals
under the abacus. This scheme is not found in any other Greek
Corinthian capital, but recalls that of a unique archaic pilla
capital from Megara Hyblaea in Sicily.

The striking and attractive Tegean capitals[1] are hardly le
curious, and show how little the type was yet fixed. They are
unusually low and squat in proportion. At the base of the bell is

[1] See Volume of Plates ii, 114, *a.*

a double row of shaggy acanthus leaves: the angle spirals each spring from a fluted sheath or *cauliculus* crowned with an acanthus leaf, of the type which became orthodox, but appears here for the first time. There were, however, no inner spirals, and the central palmette was replaced by a single acanthus leaf, reaching to the bottom of the abacus.

The capitals[1] of the Epidaurian *tholos* are extraordinarily pleasing in a quite new way. The chief impression of the earliest capitals—at Bassae, Delphi, Tegea—is an impression of strength: the members are large and relatively simple, and the whole treatment is broad and forcible. At Epidaurus Polyclitus aimed above all at delicacy and grace. The capitals look almost like beautiful flowers; it is no accident that the central ornament, which has climbed one stage further towards its destined seat on the side of the abacus, is not here a palmette or an acanthus leaf, but a blossom. The spirals are slender and tall, and their slightness is enhanced by the fact that their stems are quite bare and separate, and do not spring from a *cauliculus*. Yet there is much that links these capitals with their predecessors, especially the bareness of the bell, and the solidity of the abacus. The acanthus leaves at the base, alternately short and tall, are orthodox in character.

Next in date come two sets of capitals carved in the third quarter of the fourth century, those of the Choragic Monument of Lysicrates, and those of the Philippeum at Olympia. The Choragic Monument (erected in 334 B.C.) is one of the best known works of antiquity. It is a small circular structure of Pentelic marble, standing on a quadrangular basement. The circular part is of marble, and consists of a sort of cella, hollow but not accessible, with six engaged Corinthian columns. These have Attic-Ionic bases, and an Ionic entablature, which shows the perhaps unprecedented combination of a continuous frieze, sculptured in relief, with dentils under the cornice. The roof is a single block of marble, carved to suggest a sort of tiling of laurel leaves. It was crowned with a magnificent finial of acanthus ornament, which originally carried the tripod of victory. The diameter of the circular structure is about seven feet. The capitals, which here chiefly concern us, are much mutilated, but their forms are fairly certain. In spirit they resemble those of Epidaurus, for they aim chiefly at richness and delicacy, but in certain important details they are nearer to the orthodox type of later times. Not only do the inner and outer volutes spring, as

[1] See Volume of Plates ii, 114, *b*.

at Tegea, from a single sheath, but the central ornament, a palmette, is almost on the abacus, which is elaborately moulded. The treatment of the leaves at the base is individual. The charm of these capitals, as of the whole structure, springs largely from the pleasant irresponsibility of an artist playing at architecture. The monument is a delightful toy.

The circular Philippeum at Olympia, probably erected by Alexander the Great, more nearly resembled the *tholos* of Delphi. It was a peripteral limestone structure, on a base of three marble steps, with marble cornice and tiles: the diameter on the top step was about fifty feet. The outer colonnade was of eighteen limestone Ionic columns, while inside were twelve engaged Corinthian columns, which seem to have supported a second row, similar but smaller. The inner columns had no bases. Their capitals[1] have many features which later became orthodox, such as large acanthus leaves in two rows, and angle spirals springing from fluted *cauliculi*; but the inner spirals and the central ornament were entirely omitted, this part of the bell being covered with upright leaves in relief.

This is not the place to discuss in detail the later development of the Corinthian capital. The second-century capitals of the Olympieum of Athens, with their fluted *cauliculi*, became the great models of Roman orthodoxy, but the Epidaurian type, with independent spirals, was popular in the Hellenistic age, and many other forms were employed, especially in Sicily and Italy. In the Roman Imperial period, however, abnormal capitals were usually conscious and often fantastic variations from the orthodox type.

In Asia, temple architecture was almost exclusively Ionic. Of the few exceptions one only, the temple of Athena Polias Nikephoros at Pergamum, has been assigned to the fourth century B.C. This dating rests chiefly upon the lettering of certain dedicatory inscriptions. It is likely from its position in the city, and from points of material and technique, that the temple is earlier than the bulk of Pergamene work, but the general style would scarcely point to a date earlier than 300 B.C. Moreover, the temple had double the traditional number of triglyphs, usually a late Hellenistic feature. It was a simple hexastyle peripteros, having six columns by ten, a late type of proportion. The columns were unfluted, except for a strip below the echinus.

[1] See Volume of Plates ii, 116, *a*.

V. IONIC ARCHITECTURE IN ASIA

The chief sites of fourth-century Ionic architecture in Asia are Ephesus, Priene, Halicarnassus, Miletus, and Sardes.

The old Artemisium of Ephesus was burnt in the fourth century B.C. The best-known tradition, derived from Theopompus, assigns this disaster to the night of Alexander's birth, in 356 B.C., but the new temple seems to have inspired so much of the architecture of the second half of the fourth century that it is not impossible that Eusebius is right in giving 395 B.C. as the date of the fire. In general plan this temple was almost identical with its gigantic sixth-century predecessor, being dipteral (eight columns by twenty in the outer row), and measuring about 167 by about 359 feet on the stylobate: but the raising of the floor level by some seven feet necessitated a great extension of the surrounding steps. There are no remains of a continuous frieze, and probably there was none: but the ruins are scanty, and fragments of dentils are likewise lacking. The height of the columns is unknown, but there are remains of bases, shafts and capitals, as well as of various mouldings, and of architrave, sima, roof-tiles and acroteria. The bases are of Asiatic-Ionic type, and probably rested on rectangular plinths. The capitals show a slightly later stage of development than those from Sardes which are assigned to the fifth century (see vol. v, p. 458). The most characteristic features of these Ephesian capitals are the strong projection of the echinus, the deep cutting round its eggs, the curved hollow of the volute-band, and the position of the eye, at once well outside the perpendicular of the upper diameter of the shaft and well above the horizontal of the bottom of the echinus. The general tendency in later work was for the capital to shrink both in height and width, so that the eye approached or touched the point where these lines intersect.

The most striking peculiarity of the Ephesian columns was the presence in many, but not in all, of tall drums carved with figures in relief: there were also some quadrangular pedestals of the same height and similarly carved, which evidently replaced the lowest portion of some of the columns. Both these features were inherited from the older temple. The exact arrangement of the carved pedestals and drums has been much disputed: the elder Pliny states that the total number of columns in the temple was 127, of which 36 had carving.

It is exceedingly difficult to judge of the original appearance

of this temple, or of those that are now to be described, especially
as some of them were not finished till Roman days: but, despite
their careful planning and magnificent decoration, it is impossible
not to suspect that they were uninteresting. The old freshness
has vanished, and the splendour that has replaced it is barren
and empty. The vulgarity so obvious in later Ionic is already
perceptible before the close of the fourth century.

The temple of Athena Polias at Priene†[2] (see Volume of
Plates ii, 116, *b*) was comparatively small, measuring about 64 feet
by about 122 feet on the stylobate: but it was very famous, and
its architect Pythios wrote a book about it, as Vitruvius twice
remarks. It was most carefully planned: the cella, for instance,
was 100 Greek feet long, the plinths below the column bases
1 foot high, 6 feet square, and 6 feet apart. It was a simple
peripteros, six by eleven, like several fourth century Doric temples
in Greece. The architectural forms seem to be indebted to those
of the later Ephesian temple. There were dentils but almost
certainly no continuous frieze. The temple was dedicated by
Alexander the Great, as an extant inscription from the south
anta of the pronaos states.

An even more famous work, built and described (in a lost
treatise) by the same architect, was the Mausoleum of Halicarnassus, the tomb begun by Mausolus of Caria, and finished by
his wife Artemisia, after his death in 353 B.C. The greatest
sculptors of the day are said to have competed in its decoration;
but its construction was no less renowned than its adornment.
Abundant remains have been recovered and the elder Pliny professes to give many of its measurements, but the problem of its
restoration is still hotly debated, and fresh schemes appear almost
every year. The language of ancient descriptions has led some
critics, even in recent times, to postulate a miracle of construction,
which suspended a heavy marble pyramid upon an open colonnade. It seems, however, almost certain that the monument
consisted of a huge rectangular basis, carrying a rectangular
cella surrounded by thirty-six Ionic columns, nine by eleven.
The cella and colonnade carried a rather low stepped pyramid,
which was crowned by a chariot-group. The stylobate seems to
have measured about 100 feet by 80 feet: the height of the
various parts is uncertain, for Pliny's figures are both doubtful
and obscure, and modern discussions have not been conclusive.
The architectural style closely resembles that of the Priene
temple, and there was certainly no frieze between architrave and
dentils. There were, however, three sculptured friezes, of which

notable remains survive: two were perhaps on the basis, one on the cella wall.

The oracular temple of Apollo at Didyma near Miletus†³ was one of the largest and most magnificent structures of the ancient world: it measured about 168 by 359 feet on the stylobate. An earlier temple on the site was burnt by the Persians in 494 B.C. and abandoned till the conquests of Alexander the Great. The oracle was reopened by 331 B.C., and some parts of the building seem to belong to the second half of the fourth century: Seleucus Nicator and his son Antiochus Soter were certainly active in its construction before 294 B.C., but the work dragged on till the time of Hadrian. The temple was dipteral, having ten columns by twenty in the outer row: it had a deep pronaos, containing twelve columns, but no opisthodomos. The greater part of the cella hardly deserves that name, for it was a court open to the sky; it was nearly fifteen feet lower in level than the peripteral colonnade and the pronaos, and contained the famous oracular spring. There was an intermediate room between pronaos and cella, at a still higher level than the pronaos; it was directly accessible only from the cella floor, by a great flight of steps. The pronaos was connected with the cella only by two descending passages with arched ceilings, on each side of the intermediate room: for though there was a huge door between the pronaos and the intermediate room, its threshold was nearly five feet high, and it must have served for the proclamation of oracles to visitors in the pronaos. The inner wall of the cella was adorned with pilasters standing on a dado at the level of the floor of the inter-mediate room. Little or none of this work, however, can confi-dently be assigned to the earliest period of construction, and the only part which calls for a detailed description in this chapter is the *naiskos*, or inner shrine, a little isolated temple within the cella, which seems definitely to belong to the fourth century B.C. It was a tetrastyle amphiprostyle structure, measuring about 28 by 48 feet. There was a pronaos but no opisthodomos. The en-tablature had a very low frieze, with formal ornament, between architrave and dentils. This shrine housed the famous statue by Canachus, which Seleucus Nicator sent back from Ecbatana, whither the Persians had carried it in the fifth century.

One more Asiatic temple calls for a few words here, the well-preserved temple of Artemis at Sardes. Its fifth-century form has already been briefly described (vol. v, p. 458). In its sur-viving state, like the Didymaeum, it is of many dates, difficult to disentangle, but its general scheme appears to belong to the last quarter of the fourth century. Externally it had eight columns by twenty. It was pseudo-dipteral at the sides, but not at the ends, where very deep prostyle porches projected from the cella to within one inter-columniation of the peripteral colonnade. The peripteral columns on the façades were so spaced as to produce inter-columniations widening gradually towards the centre, from about 17 feet to about 23 feet: the flank inter-columniations were a little narrower than the narrowest of those on the façades. Such unequal spacing on the façades was probably usual in Asiatic Ionic till Hellenistic times. At Ephesus it is thought that the central inter-columniations measured roughly twenty-eight feet.

The cella contained twelve columns in two rows, and behind it lay an inner chamber, containing two columns. The building had several curious features. The space, at each end, between the front columns of the porch and its back wall, measured more than 44 feet, and the clear width of the porch was more than 57 feet. Unlike the cella, these huge rectangles had no interior supports, and it is doubtful if they can have been roofed. Again, at the east end a simple flight of low steps, between balustrades, gave access to the stylobate, as in most of these colossal temples, whose principal steps were far too high for practical use: but at the back the remains of steps round the porch and outside the pteron suggest that here some of the columns at the angles of the pteron stood upon pedestals, a most unusual scheme. In any case four of the porch columns certainly stood upon square pedestals, namely the two at each end in the middle of the front row. These columns were smaller than any of the rest, and were probably reused relics of the fifth-century temple. The pedestals have a rough band, intended for relief-sculpture, but this was never carried out.

VI. CIVIL BUILDINGS: THERSILION
AND PHILON'S ARSENAL

It remains to speak of buildings other than temples. For private houses there is little to add to what was said of fifth-century practice in the last volume (p. 462 *sq.*). There is, however, at Olympia one large official residence, which deserves a word, the Leonidaeum. This was remodelled in Roman times, but its original plan can be traced. It was a huge rectangle, 263 by 243 feet, consisting of an open court surrounded by rooms. There was an inner peristyle of 44 Doric columns and a low outer colonnade of 138 Ionic ones.

Of purely public buildings the most interesting are the Thersilion at Megalopolis and Philon's arsenal at the Piraeus. The Thersilion†[4] was the assembly hall of that Arcadian league which sprang from the Theban victory at Leuctra (p. 91 *sq*.): Pausanias saw it already in ruins. Like Pericles' Odeum and the Telesterion at Eleusis (see above, vol. v, p. 461 *sq*.) it was a large rectangular building, with a forest of columns to carry its roof, but these were cleverly arranged in radiating lines, to minimize interference with sight and hearing. The columns were of stone, and probably Doric. The ground sloped downwards and inwards from north, east, and west, towards the space from which the lines of columns radiated, which lay south of the true centre of the building: the whole was perhaps floored with wood. The arrangements south of the central space are obscure. A large prostyle Doric porch, with fourteen columns in the front row, occupied the centre of the south front, facing the theatre, which was part of the same architectural scheme. Four columns originally divided the porch from the hall, but these were later replaced by a wall with doors. This change, with others designed to strengthen the fabric, was perhaps made in the third century B.C. In the original design some of the wooden architraves had a span of 34 feet. The Thersilion measured 218 by 172 feet. The influence of the theatre type upon its general plan is unmistakable.

The Piraeus arsenal, for the storage of naval tackle, was built soon after the middle of the fourth century by the same Philon who added the great porch to the Telesterion at Eleusis. The building was destroyed by Sulla, but a surviving inscription gives such full details of its construction and dimensions that few existing works are so completely intelligible. It was a long narrow structure, measuring externally 400 by 55 Attic feet, a little less than the corresponding English measures. There were no porches, and the external decoration was confined to plain pediments at the ends, and a triglyph frieze all round. Seventy stone columns thirty feet high, divided the interior into nave and aisles, and each aisle contained a wooden gallery. There was a plain window, 2 feet by 3, in the outer wall, behind each inter-columniation, and three more at each end. The roof was of a heavy and wasteful type: thick timber architraves connected the columns longitudinally, and beams of the same size joined each pair of opposite columns across the nave. Wooden blocks on the centres of the cross-beams supported a ridge-beam, and the framework of the roof, tiled with terra cotta, clay-bedded, rested upon outer walls, architrave, and ridge-beam. The principle of the trussed roof was wholly absent.

Of fourth-century theatres little need here be said, for re-modelling, in almost every case, has obscured or destroyed their most interesting features, and a general account of the subject was given in the last volume (pp. 459 *sqq.*). At Athens the surviving auditorium is fundamentally the work of Lycurgus, towards the close of the fourth century; it replaced an unfinished Periclean scheme. Lycurgus also built the first stone *skēnē*, but we know little of this, except that it had wings (*paraskēnia*), probably colonnaded, projecting forwards at each end. The *skēnē* of the fourth-century theatre at Eretria seems to have been of the same general type. The beautiful theatre at Epidaurus also dates from this period, but of its original stone *skēnē* we know practically nothing, and at Megalopolis the *skēnē* was of wood. Some theatres in Asia Minor, such as those of Priene and Magnesia, may date from the very close of the fourth century, but they belong essentially to the Hellenistic period: while the fourth-century theatre at Syracuse in Sicily preserves no clear remains of its original scenic arrangements.

In general, the architecture of this period was stationary and unenterprising. There was little use of new materials or methods. Alexander's conquests familiarized the Greeks with the burnt brick of Mesopotamia, but this material hardly appeared in Greece till Roman times; nor was concrete adopted, though Theophrastus knew and appreciated the strength of the gypsum mortar employed especially in Cyprus and Phoenicia. The arch alone, immemorial in Egypt and Mesopotamia, was creeping into prominence at the end of the fourth century. It had been used long before for town-gates in Acarnania and for minor purposes elsewhere, but the architects of Priene, about 300 B.C., were seemingly the first to employ it in important positions in a great city with high artistic standards. One of their town-gates had an arch with a span of thirteen feet.

Yet the systematic development and combination of these new materials and methods, destined in the hands of Roman engineers to revolutionize architectural construction, still lay far in the future. The prestige of the past was overwhelming. The fourth-century architects offered their successors no vision of new worlds to conquer. They bequeathed them nothing but a tradition, noble, indeed, and dignified, but stiffening into academic rigour, and already fatally touched with pretentiousness and vulgarity.

APPENDIX

THE ELEPHANTINE PAPYRI (p. 172)

Of the appeal of the Jews of Elephantine to their brethren in Judah and Samaria two drafts were found (Cowley, *Aramaic Papyri of the Vth Cent. B.C.*, nos. 30, 31). They are from the same papyrus roll and contain slight variants, some of which are indicated in the following translation, where references are made to various interesting terms which recur in the Old Testament. Like the other papyri, they are in an Aramaic dialect philologically earlier than the Aramaic of the book of Ezra (including the permits and documents quoted therein), and still more so than the Aramaic of the book of Daniel (dated on internal grounds to the second century B.C.).

To our lord Bagohi, the governor (*peḥah*) of Judah, thy servants Yedoniah and his colleagues (Ezra iv, 23), the priests who are in Yeb, the fortress (Neh. ii, 8 'castle'). The peace of our lord may the God of Heaven grant (cf. vol. II, p. 337) greatly at all times, and give thee favour before Darius the king and the members of the house—a thousandfold more than now, and long life may he grant thee, and be thou happy and prosperous at all times. Now thy servant Yedoniah and his colleagues thus say: In the month of Tammuz, the fourteenth year of Darius the king, when Arsames went forth and departed to the king, the *Kĕmārīm* (2 Kings xxiii, 5, R.V. mg.) of the god Knub in the fortress of Yeb gave money and property to (*var.* were in league with) Waidrang who was governor here (saying), 'let them take away thence the temple of Yahu the god which is in the fortress of Yeb.' Then this accursed (?) Waidrang sent a letter to Nephayan his son who was commander in the fortress of Syene, saying 'let them destroy the temple of the god Yahu which is in the fortress of Yeb.' Then Nephayan led the Egyptians together with other forces; they came to the fortress of Yeb with their weapons, they went up into this temple, they destroyed it to the ground, and the stone pillars there they broke. Also it came to pass that the five great gates of stone built of hewn blocks that were in this temple they destroyed and their doors they   (?), and the hinges of these doors were of bronze and the roof of cedar wood, the whole, with the rest of the detail[1], and the other things which were there they burnt with fire, and the bowls of gold and silver and whatsoever was in this temple they entirely took and made it their own. And from the days of the king (*var.* kings) of Egypt our fathers had built this temple in the fortress of Yeb, and when Cambyses came to Egypt he found this temple already built, and the temples of the gods of Egypt they wholly destroyed and no one did aught

[1] See Cowley on no. 26, l. 5. The word, which is of doubtful meaning, is that translated 'wall' in Ezr. v, 3 (but 'roof' in 1 Esd. vi, 4, see Charles' *Apoc. and Pseudepig.* I, p. 42).

of harm in this temple. And when they had done this, we together with our wives and sons were putting on sackcloth and fasting and praying to Yahu the Lord of Heaven who showed us our desire on (cf. Ps. lix, 10) this hound (?) Waidrang. They (? the hounds) removed the chain from his feet (*i.e.* they degraded him), and all the wealth which he had acquired they destroyed, and all the men who had sought evil against this temple were all of them killed; and we saw our desire on them. Also before this, at the time when this evil was done to us, we sent a letter to our lord and to Yeho-ḥanan the high priest, and his colleagues the priests that were in Jerusalem, and to Ostanes the brother of Anani, and the nobles (Neh. vi, 17) of Judaea (*var.* the Jews)—no letter did they send unto us. Also, from the month of Tammuz, the fourteenth year of king Darius even unto this day we have been wearing sackcloth and fasting, our wives are made as widows, with oil we do not anoint ourselves, and wine we do not drink. Also from that time even to this day of the seventeenth year of Darius the king, meal-offering, and incense and burnt offering are not offered up in this temple. Now, thy servants, Yedoniah and his colleagues, all citizens (*baals*) of Yeb, say thus: If it seems well to our lord, take thought concerning this temple to build it, inasmuch as they do not allow us to build it. See thy well-wishers and friends that are here in Egypt, let a letter be sent from thee unto them concerning the temple of the God Yahu to build it in the fortress of Yeb according as it was built aforetime; and meal-offerings and incense offerings and burnt offerings shall they (*var.* we) offer upon the altar of the God Yahu in thy name, and we will pray on thy behalf (cf. Ezra vi, 10) at all times, we, and our wives and our sons, and the Jews all that are here. If thou wilt so do (*var.* if they so do) that this temple shall be built, there shall be merit (right-eousness, Deut. xxiv, 13) to thee before Yahu the God of Heaven more than a man who should offer him burnt offering and sacrifices worth as much as a thousand talents of silver. And concerning the gold, in reference to this we have sent and made known[1]. Also all the words in a letter in our name did we send unto Delaiah and Shelemaiah the sons of Sanaballaṭ the governor of Samaria. Moreover, concerning this that was done to us Arsames knew nothing at all. On the 20th of Marheshwan, the seventeenth year of Darius the king.

The answer was a favourable one, and the messenger's formal document, corresponding to the tablet of earlier days (see vol. II, p. 335), ran as follows:

Memorandum (record, Ezra vi, 2) of Bagohi and Delaiah. They said to me[2], Memorandum, It shall be for thee in Egypt to say to Arsames concerning the altar-house of the God of Heaven which had been built in Yeb the fortress from of old before Cambyses, which that accursed (?) Waidrang destroyed in the fourteenth year of Darius the king, to build it in its place as it was afore-time, and meal-offerings and incense-offerings may they offer upon that altar according as it formerly used to be done.

[1] Possibly a reference to another papyrus (C. 33) where Yedoniah and others undertake, if the temple be rebuilt 'as before,' to pay 'our lord' (*i.e.* Bagohi or some other official) a quantity of barley.

[2] C. 32. The opening words could be translated: Memorandum, which B. and D. said to me.

LIST OF ABBREVIATIONS

Abh.	Abhandlungen.
Abh. Arch.-epig.	Abhandlungen d. archäol.-epigraph. Seminars d. Univ. Wien.
A.J.A.	American Journal of Archaeology.
A.J. Num.	American Journal of Numismatics.
A.J. Ph.	American Journal of Philology.
Ann. Serv.	Annales du Service des antiquités de l'Égypte.
Arch. Anz.	Archäologischer Anzeiger (in J.D.A.I.).
Arch. Phil.	Archiv für Geschichte d. Philosophie.
Ath. Mitt.	Mitteilungen des deutschen arch. Inst. Athenische Abteilung.
Bay. Abh.	Abhandlungen d. bayerischen Akad. d. Wissenschaften.
Bay. S.B.	Sitzungsberichte d. bayerischen Akad. d. Wissenschaften.
B.C.H.	Bulletin de Correspondance hellénique.
Beloch	K. J. Beloch's Griechische Geschichte. 2nd Ed.
Berl. Abh.	Abhandlungen d. preuss. Akad. d. Wissenschaften zu Berlin.
Berl. S.B.	Sitzungsberichte d. preuss. Akad. d. Wissenschaften zu Berlin.
Berl. Stud.	Berliner Studien.
B.I.C.	Bulletin de l'Institut français d'archéologie orientale au Caire.
B.P.W.	Berliner Philologische Wochenschrift.
B.S.A.	Annual of the British School at Athens.
B.S.R.	Papers of the British School at Rome.
Bull. d. I.	Bullettino dell' Istituto.
Bursian	Bursian's Jahresbericht.
Bury	J. B. Bury's History of Greece. 2nd Ed. 1922.
Busolt	G. Busolt's Griechische Geschichte.
C.A.H.	Cambridge Ancient History.
Cavaignac	E. Cavaignac's Histoire de l'antiquité.
C.I.S.	Corpus Inscriptionum Semiticarum.
C.J.	Classical Journal.
C.P.	Classical Philology.
C.Q.	Classical Quarterly.
C.R.	Classical Review.
C.R. Ac. Inscr.	Comptes rendus de l'Académie des Inscriptions et Belles-Lettres.
Diss.	Dissertation.
Ditt.[3]	Dittenberger, Sylloge Inscriptionum Graecarum. Ed. 3.
D.S.	Daremberg et Saglio, Dictionnaire des antiquités grecques et romaines.
E. Brit.	Encyclopaedia Britannica. 11th Ed.
E. Meyer	E. Meyer's Geschichte des Altertums.
Ἐφ. Ἀρχ.	Ἐφημερὶς Ἀρχαιολογική.
F.H.G.	C. Müller's Fragmenta Historicorum Graecorum.
G.G.A.	Göttingische Gelehrte Anzeigen.
Gött. Nach.	Nachrichten von der Königlichen Gesellschaft der Wissenschaften zu Göttingen. Phil.-hist. Klasse.
Harv. St.	Harvard Studies in Classical Philology.
Head H.N.[2]	Head's Historia Numorum. 2nd Ed. 1912.
Hicks and Hill	E. L. Hicks and G. F. Hill, Manual of Greek Historical Inscriptions. Oxford, 1901.
H.Z.	Historische Zeitschrift.

I.G.	Inscriptiones Graecae.
I.G.²	Inscriptiones Graecae. Editio minor.
Jahreshefte	Jahreshefte d. österr. archäol. Instituts in Wien.
J.D.A.I.	Jahrbuch des deutschen archäologischen Instituts.
J.E.A.	Journal of Egyptian Archaeology.
J.H.S.	Journal of Hellenic Studies.
J.I.d'A.N.	Journal International d'Archéologie Numismatique.
J.P.	Journal of Philology.
J.R.A.S.	Journal of the Royal Asiatic Society.
Klio	Klio (Beiträge zur alten Geschichte).
Liv. A.A.	Liverpool Annals of Archaeology.
M.B.B.A.	Monatsbericht der Berliner Akademie.
Mél. Arch.	Mélanges d'archéologie et d'histoire.
Mém. Ac. Inscr.	Mémoires de l'Académie des Inscriptions et Belles-Lettres.
Michel	Michel, Recueil d'Inscriptions Grecques, 1900.
Mon. Linc.	Monumenti antichi pubblicati per cura della R. Accademia dei Lincei.
Mon. d. I.	Monumenti Antichi dell' Instituto.
Mus. B.	Musée belge.
N.F.	Neue Folge.
N.J. Kl. Alt.	Neue Jahrbücher für das klassische Altertum.
N.J.P.	Neue Jahrbücher für Philologie.
N.S.	New Series.
Num. Chr.	Numismatic Chronicle.
Num. Z.	Numismatische Zeitschrift.
O.G.I.S.	Orientis Graeci Inscriptiones selectae.
O.L.Z.	Orientalistische Literaturzeitung.
Phil.	Philologus.
Proc.	Proceedings.
P.W.	Pauly-Wissowa's Real-Encyclopädie der classischen Altertumswissenschaft.
Rend. Linc.	Rendiconti della R. Accademia dei Lincei.
Rev. Arch.	Revue Archéologique.
Rev. E.G.	Revue des études grecques.
Rev. Eg.	Revue égyptologique.
Rev. H.	Revue historique.
Rev. N.	Revue numismatique.
Rev. Phil.	Revue de philologie, de littérature et d'histoire anciennes.
Rh. Mus.	Rheinisches Museum für Philologie.
Riv. Fil.	Rivista di Filologia.
Riv. Stor. ant.	Rivista di Storia antica.
Röm. Mitt.	Mitteilungen des deutschen arch. Inst. Römische Abteilung.
S.B.	Sitzungsberichte.
S.E.G.	Supplementum epigraphicum Graecum.
S.G.D.I.	Sammlung der griechischen Dialektinschriften.
St. Fil.	Studi italiani di filologia classica.
Wien Anz.	Anzeiger d. Akad. d. Wissenschaften in Wien.
Wien S.B.	Sitzungsberichte d. Akad. d. Wissenschaften in Wien.
Wien St.	Wiener Studien.
Z.A.	Zeitschrift für Assyriologie.
Z. Aeg.	Zeitschrift für aegyptische Sprache und Altertumskunde.
Z.D.M.G.	Zeitschrift der deutschen Morgenländischen Gesellschaft.
Z.N.	Zeitschrift für Numismatik.

BIBLIOGRAPHIES

These bibliographies do not aim at completeness. They include modern and standard works and, in particular, books utilized in the writing of the chapters. Many technical monographs, especially in journals, are omitted, but the works that are registered below will put the reader on their track.

The works given in the General Bibliography for Greek History are, as a rule, not repeated in the bibliographies to the separate chapters.

The first page only of articles in learned journals is given.

N.B. Books in English and French are, unless otherwise specified, published at London and Paris respectively.

GENERAL BIBLIOGRAPHY

I. GENERAL HISTORIES

Beloch, K. J. *Griechische Geschichte.* Ed. 2. Strassburg, 1912–.
Bury, J. B. *History of Greece.* Ed. 2. 1922.
Cavaignac, E. *Histoire de l'Antiquité.* 1913–.
Cicotti, E. *Griechische Geschichte.* (Hartmann's Weltgeschichte.) Gotha, 1920.
Droysen, J. G. *Geschichte des Hellenismus.* Ed. 2. Gotha, 1876–. See Bibl. to chaps. XII and XIII, II. B. 1.
Freeman, E. A. *History of Sicily.* Oxford, 1891–.
Glotz, G. *Histoire Grecque* = *L'Histoire Générale*, I; Histoire Ancienne, II. 1925–.
Grote, G. *A History of Greece.* New ed. 1888.
Holm, A. *Geschichte Griechenlands.* Berlin, 1886–. Engl. trans. 1894–.
—— *Geschichte Siciliens im Altertum.* Leipzig, 1870–.
Kaerst, J. *Geschichte des Hellenismus.* Ed. 2. 1917–.
Lehmann-Haupt, C. F. *Griechische Geschichte* in Gercke and Norden (below), vol. III.
Meyer, Eduard. *Geschichte des Altertums.* Stuttgart, 1893–.
—— *Forschungen zur alten Geschichte.* Halle, 1892–9.
Niese, B. *Geschichte der Griechischen und Makedonischen Staaten.* Gotha, 1893–1903.
v. Pöhlmann, R. *Griechische Geschichte und Quellenkunde.* Ed. 5. Munich, 1914. (In Iwan Müller's *Handbuch*, III, 4.)
Rostoftzeff, M. *A History of the Ancient World.* Trans. J. D. Duff. Vol. I. *The Orient and Greece.* Oxford, 1926.

II. WORKS ON CONSTITUTIONAL HISTORY, ETC.

Busolt, G. *Griechische Staatskunde.* (In Iwan Müller's *Handbuch*, IV, 1. 1.) Munich, 1920–6. (Very fully documentated.)
Gilbert, G. *Handbuch der Griechischen Staatsaltertümer.* Leipzig, 1881–5. Eng. trans. of vol. I, 1895.
Greenidge, A. H. J. *A Handbook of Greek Constitutional History.* 1902.
Halliday, W. R. *The Growth of the City State.* Liverpool, 1923.
Keil, B. *Griechische Staatsaltertümer* in Gercke and Norden (below), vol. III.
Swoboda, H. *Griechische Staatsaltertümer* (Hermann's *Lehrbuch*, I, iii). Tübingen, 1913.

Wilamowitz-Moellendorff, U. von. *Aristoteles und Athen.* 2 vols. Berlin, 1893.
—— *Staat und Gesellschaft der Griechen* (Kultur der Gegenwart, ii, iv, 1). Ed. 2. Leipzig and Berlin, 1923.
Zimmern, A. E. *The Greek Commonwealth.* Ed. 4. Oxford, 1924.

III. WORKS OF REFERENCE, DICTIONARIES, ETC.

Clinton, H. Fynes. *Fasti Hellenici.* 3 vols. Oxford, 1834. (F.H.)
Daremberg et Saglio. *Dictionnaire des antiquités grecques et romaines.* 1877–1919. (D.S.)
Encyclopaedia Britannica. Ed. xi. Articles on Greek History. (E. Brit.)
Gercke, A. and Norden, E. *Einleitung in die Altertumswissenschaft.* Ed. 2. Leipzig and Berlin, 1914. Ed. 3, part appeared.
Hermann, K. F. *Lehrbuch der griechischen Antiquitäten.* New ed. Tübingen, various dates. (Lehrbuch.)
Iwan Müller. *Handbuch der klassischen Altertumswissenschaft.* Munich, various dates. (Handbuch.)
Lübkers Reallexikon des klassischen Altertums. Ed. 8. Edited by J. Geffcken and E. Ziebarth. Berlin, 1914.
Pauly-Wissowa-Kroll. *Real-Encyclopädie der classischen Altertumswissenschaft.* Stuttgart, 1893– (in progress). (P.W.)
Roscher, W. *Ausführliches Lexikon der griechischen und römischen Mythologie.* Leipzig, 1884– (in progress). (Roscher.)
Whibley, L. *A Companion to Greek Studies.* Ed. 3. Cambridge, 1916.

CHAPTER I

PERSIA, FROM XERXES TO ALEXANDER

See the bibliography to chapters II–IV and VIII–IX, for matters dealing primarily with Greek affairs, the bibliography to chapter VI for matters dealing primarily with Egypt.

I. ANCIENT SOURCES

A. *Contemporary inscriptions*

Greek: To the Greek inscriptions cited in the bibliographies to chapters II–IV and VIII–IX, add:

Kalinka, E. *Tituli Lyciae* (Vienna, 1901), nos. 44 (in Lycian) and 45.

Wilhelm, A. *Ein Vertrag des Maussollus mit den Phaseliten.* Jahreshefte, I, 1898, p. 149.

For the Cypriote Greek Inscriptions see *S.G.D.I.* vol. I.

Persian: Oppert, J. *Inscriptions of the Persian Monarchs.* Records of the Past, IX, 1877, p. 65.

Weissbach, F. H. *Die Keilinschriften der Achaemeniden.* Leipzig, 1910.

Phoenician and Cyprian-Phoenician. *C.I.S.* Paris, 1881–.

Cooke, G. A. *A textbook of North Semitic Inscriptions.* Oxford, 1903. See also vol. IV, p. 615.

For coins see II (A, 2) below.

B. *Writers contemporary with some part of the period*

Herodotus, IX.

Ctesias. Ed. Gilmore, 1888.

Xenophon, *Anabasis*; *Hellenica*, III–VII; *Agesilaus*.

[Xenophon], *Cyropaedeia*, VIII, 8.

Hellenica Oxyrhynchia.

Plato, Ep. VI.

Isocrates, *Panathenaicus, Panegyricus, Philippus, Evagoras, Nicocles.*

Demosthenes, Or. XIV, XV, and scattered notices.

Aristotle: Epigram and Ode on Hermeias: Anth. Lyr. (Diehl), I, xxxxvi, 3, 5.

Fragments of Theopompus, *F.H.G.* I, p. 297, and Deinon (uncertain if contemporary), *ib.* II, pp. 93 *sqq.*

Scattered notices in Aristotle's *Politics*, Lysias, Aeschines and Aeneas Tacticus.

C. *Later writers*

[Aristotle], *Oeconomica*, II, 2.

Didymus, *Commentary on Demosthenes.*

Diodorus, XI–XVII (XI–XV are mainly derived from Ephorus).

Nicolaus Damasc. *F.H.G.* III, p. 461.

Plutarch, *Agesilaus*; *Artaxerxes*, II (the latter mainly derived from Deinon, Ctesias and Xenophon); *Moralia*, 173 C–174 B.

Justin, V, X, with Trogus' *Prologues* (the Persian part is derived from Deinon).

Cornelius Nepos, *Conon* and *Datames* (derived from Deinon), *Agesilaus, Chabrias, Iphicrates.*

Strabo, XIII, 610, 656 *sq.*

Polyaenus, VII, 14, 16, 17, 18, 20, 21, 23, 26, 27, 29, 33.

The so-called *Demotic Chronicle.* Ed. W. Spiegelberg. Leipzig, 1914.

Papyrus fragment dealing with 355–4 B.C. in *O. Hirschfeld's Festschrift*, 1903, p. 100.

Scattered references (mainly repetitions) in Polybius, Diogenes Laertius, Pausanias, Aelian, Suidas, Scholia to Demosthenes, Frontinus.

D. *Chronography*

Manetho. Many Babylonian contracts. See further bibliography to chapters XII–XIII, I. 2 (*c*).

II. MODERN LITERATURE

A. *On the Sources*

1. Literary

Jacoby, F. Art. *Ktesias* in P.W. 1922.

Krumbholz, P. *De Ctesia aliisque auctoribus in Plutarchi Artaxerxis vita adhibitis.* Eisenach, 1889.

Mess, A. v. *Untersuchungen über Ephoros.* Rh. Mus. LXI, 1906, p. 360.

Neuhaus, O. *Die Quellen des Trogus Pompeius in der persischen Geschichte* (7 parts). Königsberg, 1882 to 1900.

Richter, E. *Bericht über die Literatur zu Xenophon*, in Bursian, vol. 100, 1899, p. 33; vol. 117, 1903, p. 47; vol. 142, 1909, p. 341; vol. 178, 1919, p. 1. (Covers the years 1898 to 1918.) Add vol. 203, 1925, p. 1, by J. Mesk, for the years 1919 to 1924.

Theil, J. H. *De Dinone Colophonio Nepotis in vita Datamis auctore.* Mnemosyne, LI, 1923, p. 412.

2. Coins

Babelon, E. *Les Perses Achéménides, les satrapes et les dynastes tributaires de leur empire, Cypre et Phénicie.* Catalogue des monnaies grecques de la bibliothèque nationale, vol. XXIII. 1893.

—— *Traité des monnaies grecques et romaines.* Part 2, i and ii. 1907 and 1910.

Gardner, P. *A history of ancient coinage*, 700–300 B.C. Oxford, 1918.

Head, B. V. *Catalogue of the Greek coins in the British Museum: Caria, &c.* 1897.

—— *H.N.*

Hill, G. F. *Catalogue of the Greek coins in the British Museum: Lycaonia, Isauria, and Cilicia*, 1900; *Cyprus*, 1904; *Phoenicia*, 1910; *Arabia, Mesopotamia, and Persia*, 1922.

—— *Notes on the Imperial Persian coinage.* J.H.S. XXXIX, 1919, p. 116.

Howorth, Sir H. *A note on some coins generally attributed to Mazaeus.* Num. Chr. 1902, p. 81.

—— *The history and coinage of Artaxerxes III, his satraps and dependents.* Num. Chr. 1903, p. 1.

Newell, E. T. *Some rare or unpublished Greek coins.* A.J. Num. XLVIII, 1914, pp. 61, 70.

—— *Myriandros-Alexandria Kat' Isson.* Ib. LIII, 1919, part 2, p. 1.

Rouvier, J. *Répartition chronologique du monnayage des rois Phéniciens d'Arvad avant Alexandre le Grand.* J.I.d'A.N. I, 1898, p. 263.

—— *Numismatique des villes de Phénicie.* Ib. III, 1900, p. 125 (Arados); IV, 1901, p. 35 (Byblos) and p. 193 (Ake); V, 1902, p. 99 (Sidon, and Mazaeus); VI, 1903, p. 269 (Tyre).

—— *Les rois phéniciens de Sidon d'après leurs monnaies, sous la dynastie des Achéménides.* Rev. N. 1902, pp. 242, 317, 421.

Six, J. P. *Du classement des séries cypriotes.* Rev. N. 1883, p. 249.
—— *Le satrape Mazaios.* Num. Chr. 1884, p. 97.
—— *Monnaies grecques, inédites et incertaines.* Num. Chr. 1888, p. 97 and 1894, p. 334.

B. *Historical*

1. General

See also General Bibliography

Justi, F. *Geschichte Irans,* in Geiger and Kuhn's *Grundriss der iranischen Philologie,* vol. ii. Strassburg, 1896–1904.
Maspero, Sir G. *Histoire ancienne des peuples de l'Orient.* Ed. 7. 1905.
Nöldeke, Th. *Aufsätze zur persischen Geschichte.* Leipzig, 1887.
Prášek, J. von. *Geschichte der Meder und Perser bis zur makedonischen Eroberung.* Vol. ii. Gotha, 1910.
Rawlinson, G. *The five great monarchies of the ancient world.* Vol. iii. 1879.
Sykes, Sir P. M. *A history of Persia.* Vol. i. Ed. 2. 1921.

2. Special studies

(*a*) *Persia.*

Beloch, K. J. *Artabazos.* Janus (Festschrift für C. F. Lehmann-Haupt), i, 1921, p. 8. Vienna and Leipzig.
Buchholz, A. *Quaestiones de Persarum satrapis satrapiisque.* Leipzig, 1894.
Eiselen, F. C. *Sidon.* Columbia University Oriental Studies. Vol. iv. New York, 1907.
Foucart, P. *Étude sur Didymos.* Mém. Ac. Inscr. xxxviii, Part i, 1909.
Gutschmid, A. von. *Die Phönicier.* Kleine Schriften, ii, p. 36. Leipzig, 1890.
Hoffmann-Kutschke, A. *Iranisches bei den Griechen.* Phil. lxvi, 1907, p. 173.
Judeich, W. *Kleinasiatische Studien.* Marburg, 1892.
Krumbholz, P. *De Asiae Minoris satrapis Persicis.* Leipzig, 1883.
Kugler, F. X. *Sternkunde und Sterndienst in Babel,* ii, Teil ii, Heft 2. Münster i. W. 1924. (Chronology.)
Lehmann-Haupt, C. F. Art. *Satrap* in P.W.
Marquart, J. *Untersuchungen zur Geschichte von Eran.* Phil. liv, 1895, p. 489.
Meyer, E. *Forschungen zur alten Geschichte.* Vol. ii, § vi: Chronologische Untersuchungen. Halle, 1899.
—— Arts. *Persia* and *Artaxerxes* in E. Brit.
Pareti, L. *Per la storia di alcune dinastie greche nell' Asia Minore.* Atti Accad. Torino, xlvi, 1911, p. 615.
Weissbach, F. H. *Zur neubabylonischen und achämenidischen Chronologie.* Z.D.M.G. lxii, 1908, p. 629.
—— *Zur neubabylonischen Chronologie.* Studia Orientalia, I (Festschrift für K. Tallqvist), p. 359. Helsingfors, 1925.

(*b*) *Cyrus' expedition and the Ten Thousand.*

Bonner, R. J. *Desertions from the Ten Thousand.* C.P. 1920, p. 85.
Boucher, A. *L'anabase de Xénophon (Retraite des dix mille) avec un commentaire historique et militaire.* Paris-Nancy, 1913.
Bruhn, E. *De Menone Larisaeo.* Χάριτες Friedrich Leo dargebracht. Berlin, 1911. p. 1.
Cousin, G. *Kyros le Jeune en Asie Mineure.* Paris-Nancy, 1905.
Dürrbach, F. *L'Apologie de Xénophon dans l''Anabase.'* Rev.E.G. vi, 1893, p. 343.
Glover, T. R. *From Pericles to Philip.* Ed. 3. 1919.

Halliday, W. R. *Mossynos and Mossynoikoi.* C.R. xxxvii, 1923, p. 105.

Hoffmeister, E. von. *Durch Armenien, eine Wanderung und der Zug Xenophons bis zum Schwarzen Meere.* Leipzig-Berlin, 1911.

Kiepert, R. *Formae Orbis antiquae,* Map V and explanatory text. Berlin, 1909.

Kiessling, A., review of Hoffmeister (above). B.P.W. 1914, p. 144.

—— Art. *Gymnias* in P.W.

Körte, A. *Die Tendenz von Xenophon's Anabasis.* N.J. Kl. Alt. xlix, 1922, p. 15.

Kromayer, J. and Veith, G. *Schlachten-Atlas zur antiken Kriegsgeschichte.* 4th Lieferung. Marathon-Chaeroneia. Leipzig, 1926. (This work was published after this chapter was in type.)

Lane, W. H. *Babylonian Problems.* 1923.

Lehmann-Haupt, C. F. *Armenien einst und jetzt.* Berlin, 1910.

Mason, K. *Notes on the Canal System and Ancient Sites of Babylonia in the time of Xenophon.* Journ. Geog. Soc. lvi, 1920, p. 468.

Mesk, J. *Die Tendenz der Xenophontischen Anabasis.* Wien St. xliii, 1922–3, p. 136.

Meyer, E. *Die Lage von Opis und Kiš.* Berl. S.B. 1912, p. 1096.

Munscher, K. *Menon's Zug nach Kilikien.* Phil. lxvi, 1907, p. 491.

Pancritius, M. *Studien über die Schlacht bei Kunaxa.* Berlin, 1906.

Schaffer, F. *Die kilikischen Hochpässe und Menon's Zug über den Taurus.* Jahreshefte, iv, 1901, p. 204.

Segl, Fr. *Vom Kentrites bis Trapezus.* Erlangen [1925].

Siehe, W. *Der Marsch des Cyrus durch Kappadozien und Zilizien.* Petermann's Mitt. lix, ii, 1913, p. 233.

Streck, M. Art. *Seleukeia am Tigris* in P.W.

Weissbach, F. H. Art. Κούναξα and *Kyros* (no. 7) in P.W.

CHAPTERS II–IV

THE ASCENDANCY OF SPARTA, THE SECOND ATHENIAN LEAGUE, THEBES

A. SOURCES

1. Literary

(a) *Contemporary writers.*

Xenophon, *Hellenica*, III–VII; *Agesilaus*; *Respublica Lacedaemoniensium.*
Hellenica Oxyrhynchia.
Ctesias, *Persica*, ch. 63.
Lysias, *Orationes*, esp. XVI, XIX, XXII, XXVI *sqq.*, XXXI.
Andocides, *De Pace.*
Isocrates, *Orationes*, esp. IV (*Panegyricus*), V (*Philippus*), VI (*Archidamus*), VIII (*De Pace*), IX (*Evagoras*), XIV (*Plataicus*), XVIII (*c. Callimachum*).
[Demosthenes], XLIX (*c. Timotheum*), L (*c. Polyclem*).

(b) *Secondary writers.*

Aristotle, *Constitution of Athens*, XLII *sqq.*
Diodorus, XIV–XV.
Cornelius Nepos, *Agesilaus, Chabrias, Conon, Epaminondas, Iphicrates, Lysander, Pelopidas, Timotheus.*
Plutarch, *Agesilaus, Artaxerxes, Lysander, Pelopidas.*
Pausanias, III, 8 *sqq.*; VIII, 27; IX, 14 *sq.*
[Herodes], Περὶ Πολιτείας.

2. Archaeological

Dittenberger. *S.I.G.*³ I, nos. 116–86.
Head. *Historia Numorum.* Ed. 2. Oxford, 1911.
Hicks and Hill. *Greek Historical Inscriptions.* Oxford, 1901. Nos. 82–123.

B. MODERN WORKS ON ANCIENT SOURCES

1. Xenophon

Banderet, A. *Untersuchungen zu Xenophon's Hellenika.* Leipzig, 1919.
Schwartz, E. *Quellenuntersuchungen zur griechischen Geschichte.* Rh. Mus. XLIV, 1889, p. 161.
Underhill, E. *A Commentary on the Hellenica of Xenophon.* Oxford, 1900.

2. The Oxyrhynchus Historian

Benedetto, L. F. *Lo storico Cratippo.* Atti Torino, XLIV, 1908–9, p. 377.
Busolt, G. *Der neue Historiker und Xenophon.* Hermes, XLIII, 1908, p. 255.
—— *Zur Glaubwürdigkeit Theopomps.* Hermes, XLV, 1910, p. 220.
Costanzi, V. *Il frammento di prosa storica testè trovato a Oxyrhynchos.* Studi storici per l' antichità classica, I, 1908, p. 253.
Goligher, W. *The new Greek historical fragment attributed to Theopompus or Cratippus.* English Historical Review, XXIII, 1908, p. 277.
Grenfell, B. P. and Hunt, A. S. *Theopompus (or Cratippus).* The Oxyrhynchus Papyri, V, p. 110. Egypt Exploration Fund, 1908.
Judeich, W. *Theopomp's Hellenika.* Rh. Mus. LXVI, 1911, p. 94.
Lipsius, J. H. *Der Historiker von Oxyrhynchos.* S.B. der sächsischen Akademie, phil.-hist. Kl. LXVII, 1915, p. 1.

Meyer, E. *Theopomp's Hellenika*. Halle, 1909. pp. 120–56.
Pareti, L. *Cratippo e le 'elleniche' di Oxyrhynchos*. Studi italiani di Filologia, xix, 1912, p. 398.
De Sanctis, G. *L'Attide di Androzione e un papiro di Oxyrhynchos*. Atti della reale Accademia di Torino, xliii, 1907–8, p. 331.
Underhill, E. *Theopompus (or Cratippus), Hellenica*. J.H.S. xxviii, 1908, p. 277.
Walker, E. M. *Cratippus or Theopompus?* Klio, viii, 1908, p. 356.
—— *Hellenica Oxyrhynchia*. Oxford, 1913.

3. *Isocrates*

Kessler, G. *Isokrates und die panhellenische Idee*. Paderborn, 1910.
Wendland, P. *König Philippos und Isokrates*. Gött. Nach. phil.-hist. Kl. 1910, p. 123.

4. *Aristotle*

Colin, G. *Les sept derniers chapitres de l'*Ἀθηναίων Πολιτεία. Rev. E.G. xxx, 1917, p. 20.
Mathieu, G. *Aristote, Constitution d'Athènes*. 1915.
Sandys, Sir J. E. *Aristotle's Constitution of Athens*. Ed. 2. 1912.

5. [Ἡρώδης] περὶ Πολιτείας.

Adcock, F. E. and Knox, A. D. Ἡρώδης περὶ Πολιτείας. Klio, xiii, 1913, p. 249.
Drerup, E. [Ἡρώδου] περὶ Πολιτείας. Paderborn, 1908.
Meyer, E. *Theopomp's Hellenika*. pp. 259–83.
Schmid, W. Ἡρώδης περὶ Πολιτείας. Rh. Mus. lix, 1904, p. 512.

6. *Coins*

Gardner, P. *History of Ancient Coinage*. Oxford, 1918. Chapters 14–16, 18.

C. Modern Works

1. *General Histories*

See also General Bibliography.

Glover, T. R. *From Pericles to Philip*. 1917. Chapters 7–12.
Kaerst, J. *Geschichte des Hellenismus*. Ed. 2. Berlin, 1917. Vol. i, pp. 110–53.
v. Stern, E. *Geschichte der spartanischen und thebanischen Hegemonie*. Dorpat, 1884.

2. *Special Districts*

i (*a*) *Athens*.
Beloch, K. J. *Die attische Politik seit Perikles*. Leipzig, 1884. pp. 131–62, 344–61.
Cavaignac, E. *Les classes soloniennes et la répartition de la richesse à Athènes*. Vierteljahrsschrift für Social- und Wirtschaftsgeschichte, ix, 1911, p. 1.
Cloché, P. *La restauration démocratique à Athènes*. 1915.
—— *Le décret de 401/0 en l'honneur des métèques revenus de Philé*. Rev. E.G. xxx, 1917, p. 384.
—— *La politique de l'athénien Callistratos*. Rev. des Études Anciennes, xxv, 1923, p. 5.
Foucart, P. *Un décret athénien relatif aux combattants de Phylé*. Mém. Ac. Inscr. xlii, 1922, p. 323.
Frickenhaus, A. *Athens Mauern im vierten Jahrhundert v. Chr.* Bonn, 1905.
Gernet, L. *L'approvisionnement d'Athènes en blé*. 1909.
Hasebroek, J. *Zum griechischen Bankwesen der klassischen Zeit*. Hermes, lv, 1920, p. 113.

Johnson, A. C. *An Athenian Treasure List.* A.J.A. xviii, 1914, p. 1.

Kahrstedt, U. *Forschungen zur Geschichte des ausgehenden fünften und des vierten Jahrhunderts.* Berlin, 1910. pp. 207–33.

Perrot, G. *Le commerce des céréales en Attique au quatrième siècle avant notre ère.* Rev. H. iv, 1877, p. 1.

Robbins, F. *The cost to Athens of her Second Empire.* C.P. xiii, 1918, p. 361.

Stahl, J. M. *Die εἰσφορά und ihre Reform.* Rh. Mus. lxvii, 1912, p. 391.

i (*b*) *The Second Athenian Confederacy.*

Busolt, G. *Der zweite athenische Bund.* Jahrbücher für klassische Philologie, supplementary vol. vii, 1875, p. 641.

Gilbert, G. *The Constitutional Antiquities of Athens and Sparta.* Eng. trans. 1895. pp. 435–45.

Lipsius, J. H. *Beiträge zur Geschichte griechischer Bundesverfassungen.* S.B. der sächsischen Akademie, phil.-hist. Kl. l, 1898, p. 145.

Marshall, F. H. *The Second Athenian Confederacy.* Cambridge, 1905.

Swoboda, H. *Der hellenische Bund des Jahres 371 v. Chr.* Rh. Mus. xlix, 1894, p. 321.

ii. *Sparta.*

Bauer, A. *Die spartanischen Nauarchen der Jahre 397–5.* Wien St. xxxiv, 1910, p. 296.

Busolt, G. *Spartas Heer und Leuktra.* Hermes, xl, 1905, p. 387.

Kahrstedt, U. *Die spartanische Nauarchie.* Op. cit. pp. 179–204.

Pareti, L. *Ricerche sulla potenza marittima degli Spartani.* Memorie della reale Accademia di Torino, lix, 1909, p. 71.

Solari, A. *Ricerche spartane.* Leghorn, 1905. pp. 1–58, 231–65.

iii. *The Peloponnese.*

Bury, J. B. *The Double City of Megalopolis.* J.H.S. xviii, 1898, p. 15.

Cavaignac, E. *La population du Péloponnèse aux 5ème et 4ème siècles.* Klio, xii, 1912, p. 261.

Fougères, G. *Mantinée et l'Arcadie orientale.* 1898. pp. 130–61, 408–69.

Freeman, E. A. *History of Federal Government.* 1893. pp. 154–62.

Gardner, E. A., etc. *Excavations at Megalopolis.* J.H.S., Supplementary Papers 1. 1892.

Niese, B. *Beiträge zur Geschichte des arkadischen Bundes.* Hermes, xxxiv, 1899, p. 520.

—— *Drei Kapitel eleischer Geschichte.* Genethliakon C. Robert. Berlin, 1910. pp. 1–47.

Swoboda, H. *Griechische Staatsaltertümer.* Tübingen, 1913. pp. 219–27.

Weil, H. *Nochmals das altarkadische Gemeinwesen.* Z.N. xxix, 1912, p. 139

iv. *Central Greece.*

Bonner, R. J. *The Boeotian Federal Constitution.* C.P. v, 1910, p. 405.

—— *The Four Senates of the Boeotians.* C.P. x, 1915, p. 381.

Botsford, W. *The Constitution and Politics of the Boeotian League.* Political Science Quarterly, xxv, 1910, p. 284.

Bourguet, E. *L'administration financière du sanctuaire pythique au 4ème siècle av. J. C.* 1905. Chs. 3 and 4.

Cloché, P. *La politique thébaine de 404 à 395 av. J. Chr.* Rev. E.G. xxxi, 1918, p. 315.

Courby, F., in Homolle, Th. *Fouilles de Delphes.* 1915. Vol. ii, pp. 1–91, 112–15.

Glotz, G. *Le conseil fédéral des Béotiens.* B.C.H. xxxii, 1908, p. 271.

Meyer, E. *Theopomp's Hellenika.* Halle, 1909. pp. 81–102.
Pomtow, H. *Eine delphische Stasis im Jahre 363 v. Chr.* Klio, VI, 1906, pp. 89, 400.
—— *Ein arkadisches Weihgeschenk zu Delphi.* Ath. Mitt. XIV, 1889, p. 15.
—— *Studien zu den Weihgeschenken und der Topographie von Delphi.* Ath. Mitt. XXXI, 1906, p. 492.
Swoboda, H. *Griechische Staatsaltertümer.* pp. 256–70.
—— *Studien zur Verfassung Böotiens.* Klio, X, 1910, p. 314.
Walker, E. M. *Hellenica Oxyrhynchia.* Oxford, 1913. pp. 134–41.

v. *Northern Greece.*
Costanzi, V. *Saggio di Storia Tessalica.* Annali delle Università Toscane, XXVII, 1907, chs. 8, 10, 11.
—— *Studi di Storia Macedonica sino a Philippo.* Annali delle Università Toscane, XXXIII, 1915, p. 55.
—— *Le vicende di Aminta III nel primo decennio del suo regno.* Klio, VI, 1906, p. 297.
Foucart, P. *Les athéniens dans la Chersonèse de Thrace au 4ème siècle.* Mém. Inscr. XXXVIII, 1911, p. 83.
Gaebler, H. *Zur Münzkunde Makedoniens.* Z.N. 1925, p. 193.
Höck, A. *Das Odrysenreich in Thrakien im fünften und vierten Jahrhundert v. Chr.* Hermes, 1891, p. 83.
Köhler, V. *Makedonien unter König Archelaos.* Berl. S.B. 1893, p. 489.
Meyer, E. *Theopomp's Hellenika.* pp. 218–59. (On Thessaly.)
Niese, B. *Chronologie und historische Beiträge zur griechischen Geschichte der Jahre 370–64 v. Chr.* Hermes, XXXIX, 1904, p. 108.
Solari, A. *Sui dinasti dei Odrisi.* Pisa, 1912.
Swoboda, H. *Griechische Staatsaltertümer.* pp. 212–18. (On the Chalcidian League.)
Tropea, G. *Giasone il tago della Tessaglia.* Riv. Stor. ant. III, 1898, p. 5.
West, A. B. *The Formation of the Chalcidian League.* C.P. IX, 1914, p. 24.

vi. *Other Districts.*
Pistorius, H. *Beiträge zur Geschichte von Lesbos im vierten Jahrhundert v. Chr.* Bonn, 1913.
Prašek, J. *Geschichte der Meder und Perser.* Gotha, 1910. Vol. II, chs. 16, 17.
v. Stern, E. *Die politische und soziale Struktur der Griechencolonien am Nordufer der Schwarzmeergebiete.* Hermes, L, 1915, p. 161.

3. *Special Topics*

i. *The campaigns in Asia and Egypt.*
Dugas, Ch. *La campagne d'Agésilas en Asie Mineure.* B.C.H. XXXIV, 1910, p. 58.
Judeich, W. *Kleinasiatische Studien.* Marburg, 1892. pp. 1–281.
—— *Theopomp's Hellenika.* Rh. Mus. LXVI, 1911, p. 119.
Kromayer, J. and Veith, G. *Antike Schlachtfelder in Griechenland.* Berlin, 1926. Vol. IV, pt. 2, pp. 261–89. (On the battle of Sardes.)
Meyer, E. *Theopomp's Hellenika.* pp. 3–80.
Munro, J. A. R. *Dascylium.* J.H.S. XXXII, 1912, p. 57.
Pareti, L. *L' impresa di Tibrone in Asia nel 400/399 e nel 391 av. Cr.* Entaphia Pozzi, p. 48. Turin, 1913.
Rühl, F. *Randglossen zu den Hellenika von Oxyrhynchos.* Rh. Mus. LXVIII, 1913, p. 161.

ii. *Warfare in Greece Proper.*

Bauer, A. *Der zweimalige Angriff des Epaminondas auf Sparta.* H.Z. LXV, 1890, p. 240.

Cavaignac, E. *A propos de la bataille du torrent ae Némée.* Revue des études anciennes, 1925, p. 273.

Fabricius, E. *Die Befreiung Thebens.* Rh. Mus. XLVIII, 1893, p. 448.

Funk, E. *De Thebanorum ab anno 378 usque ad annum 362 gestis.* Berlin, 1890.

Grundy, G. B. *The Battle of Plataea.* 1894. Appendix on Leuctra.

Judeich, W. *Die Zeit der Friedensrede des Andokides.* Phil. LXXXI, 1926, p. 141.

Kromayer, J. *Antike Schlachtfelder.* Berlin, 1903. Vol. I, pp. 1–123; Vol. IV, pt. 2, pp. 317–23 (on the battle of Mantinea).

——— *Zu den griechischen Schlachtfelderstudien.—Mantinea.* Wien St. XXVII, 1905, p. 1.

Kromayer, J. and Veith, G. *Antike Schlachtfelder.* Vol. IV, pt. 2, pp. 290–316. (On the battle of Leuctra.)

Lammert, W. *Die neuesten Forschungen auf antiken Schlachtfeldern in Griechenland.* N.J. Kl. Alt. XIII, 1904, p. 112.

Loring, W. *Some Ancient Routes in the Peloponnese.* J.H.S. XV, 1895, p. 25.

Swoboda, H. *Zur Geschichte des Epaminondas.* Rh. Mus. LV, 1900, p. 460.

Zunkel, G. *Untersuchungen zur Geschichte der Jahre 395–386 v. Chr.* Weimar, 1911.

iii. *Greek armies in the fourth century.*

Beloch, K. J. *Aufgebote der griechischen Staaten, vornehmlich im vierten Jahrhundert v. Chr.* Klio, V, 1905, p. 341; VI, 1906, p. 34.

Busolt, G. See C. 2. ii above.

Cavaignac, E. See C. 2. iii above.

Delbrück, H. *Geschichte der Kriegskunst.* Berlin, 1900. Vol. I, pp. 109–35.

Kromayer, J. *Studien über Wehrkraft und Wehrverfassung in Griechenland.* Klio, III, 1903, pp. 47, 173.

Lammert, W. *Die geschichtliche Entwickelung der griechischen Taktik.* N.J. Kl. Alt. III, 1899, p. 1.

iv. *Chronology.*

Cloché, P. *La Grèce et l'Égypte de 405/4 à 342/1 av. J. C.* Rev. Ég. (N.S.), I, 1919, p. 210.

Kahrstedt, U. *Forschungen zur Geschichte des ausgehenden fünften und des vierten Jahrhunderts.* Berlin, 1910. Ch. 1 (on the kings of Egypt).

Lohse, E. H. *Quaestiones chronologicae ad Xenophontis Hellenica pertinentes.* Leipzig, 1905.

Niese, B. *Chronologie und historische Beiträge zur griechischen Geschichte der Jahre 370–64 v. Chr.* Hermes, XXXIX, 1904, p. 84.

v. *Biography.*

Lins, H. *Kritische Beiträge zur Geschichte des Agesilaos.* Halle, 1914.

Pauly-Wissowa. *Real-encyclopädie.* Articles by Niese, B., on *Agesilaus,* by Swoboda, H., on *Epaminondas* and *Euagoras.*

CHAPTER V

DIONYSIUS OF SYRACUSE

I. ANCIENT SOURCES

Aelian, *V.H.* I, 20; XII, 61.
[Aristotle], *Oeconomica*, II, 20, 41.
Aristotle, *Pol.* VIII (v), 1305 *sq.*; 1313 *b.*
Diodorus Siculus, XIII–XV.
Dion Hal., XX, 7.
Ephorus, *F.H.G.* I, pp. 268 *sqq.*
Frontinus, I, 1, 2, 4, 12; III, 4, 3–4, 12, 3.
Isocrates, *Panegyricus* (Or. IV); *ad Philippum* (Or. V).
[Inscriptions.] Dittenberger, W. *Sylloge inscriptionum graecarum.* Ed. 3. Vol. I.
    Berlin, 1915; no. 141; *I.G.* II, 1, 18, 101, 103, 105.
Justin, XX–XXI.
Livy, XXIV, c. 22.
Lysias, Or. XXXIII (fragment).
Nepos, *Dion.*
Philistus, *F.H.G.* I, pp. 190 *sqq.*
Plato, *Epistles*, III, VII, VIII.
Plutarch, *Dion.*
Polyaenus, II, 11; v, 2, 3, 8, 9, 10; VI, 16.
Polybius, I, 6; II, 39; XII, 4*a*, 10, 24; XV, 35.
Strabo, V, 212, 226, 241; VI, 258, 261.
Timaeus, frags. 108–126, *F.H.G.* I, pp. 220 *sqq.*
Xenophon, *Hellenica*, passim.

2. MODERN WORKS. (See also General Bibliography.)

See also articles in P.W. on separate states, *e.g.*, *Akragas, Karthago*, and on
Hannibal (2), *Himilkon* (1), Leptines (2).

Beloch, K. J. *Griechische Geschichte*, esp. II², 2, pp. 254 *sqq.*; III², 2, pp. 102 *sqq.*,
    107 *sqq.*, 185 *sqq.* (important).
Casson, S. *Macedonia, Thrace, and Illyria.* Oxford, 1926.
Costanzi, V. *Sulla cronologia del I trattato tra Roma e Cartagine.* Riv. Fil. LIII,
    1925, p. 381.
—— '*sguardo sulla politica di Siracusa.* Riv. di Storia Antica, II, 1896, p. 50.
Evans, Sir A. J. *Some New Lights on the Monetary Frauds of Dionysius.* Num.
    Chr. 1894, p. 216.
—— Supplements and Appendices to Freeman's *History of Sicily.* Vol. IV.
Freeman, E. A. *Sicily, Phoenician, Greek, and Roman.* Ed. 2. 1894.
Giesecke, W. *Sicilia numismatica.* Leipzig, 1923.
Graefe, F. *Karthagenische Seestrategie im Jahre* 406 *v. Chr.* Hermes, LII, 1917,
    p. 317.
Gsell, S. *Histoire de l'Afrique du Nord*, 1920. Vol. III. pp. 1–12.
Hill, G. F. *Coins of Ancient Sicily.* Westminster, 1903.
Kahrstedt, U. *Forschungen zur Geschichte des angehenden fünften und des vierten
    Jahrhunderts.* Berlin, 1910. p. 157.

Lloyd, A. H. The legend *ZIZ* on Siculo-Punic coins. Num. Chr. 1925, p. 129.

Meltzer, O. *Geschichte der Karthager.* Vol. 1. Berlin, 1879.

Niese, B. Art. *Dionysius* in P.W.

Pais, E. *Storia della Magna Grecia e Sicilia.* (Storia d' Italia, Parte I.) Turin, 1894.

Tudeer, L. *Die Tetradrachmenprägung von Syrakus in der Periode der signierenden Künstler.* Z.N. xxx, 1913, p. 1. [Survey of Syracusan coinage.]

Whitaker, J. L. S. *Motya, a Phoenician Colony in Sicily.* 1921.

Wilamowitz-Moellendorff, U. von. *Platon.* Berlin, 1920.

CHAPTER VI

EGYPT TO THE COMING OF ALEXANDER

1. GENERAL

v. Bissing, F. W. *Geschichte Aegyptens in Umriss.* Berlin, 1904.
Breasted, J. H. *A History of the Ancient Egyptians.* New York, 1908, 1920.
Budge, Sir E. A. W. *History of Egypt.* 1902.
—— *History of the Egyptian People.* 1914.
Griffith, F. Ll. Art. *Egypt* in E. Brit.
Krall, J. *Grundriss der altorientalischen Geschichte.* Vienna, 1899.
Maspero, Sir Gaston. *The Passing of the Empires:* 850 B.C.–330 B.C. 1900.
Meyer, E. *Geschichte des Altertums.* III–V.
Petrie, Sir W. M. F. *History of Egypt.* 2nd Ed. 1918.
Wiedemann, A. *Aegyptische Geschichte.* Gotha, 1884 (to be used with caution).

For general Greek authorities see bibliographies to chapters II–IV and VIII–IX, and for the fifth century the bibliography to volume V, chapters II–IV.

2. SOURCES

(a) Egyptian

Budge, Sir E. A. W. *The Book of the Kings.* 1908.
—— *Annals of Nubian Kings.* 1912.
Burchardt, M. *Datierte Denkmäler aus der Achämenidenzeit.* Z. Aeg. XLIX, 1911, p. 69.
Cowley, A. E. *Aramaic Papyri of the Vth cent. B.C.* Oxford, 1923.
Daressy, G. *La Chapelle de Psimaut à Karnak.* Ann. Serv. XVIII, 1919, p. 37.
—— *Statue de Zedher le Sauveur.* Ibid. p. 113; XIX, 66.
Gauthier, H. *Le Livre des Rois,* IV. Mémoires de l'Institut français d'Arch. orientale au Caire, XX. Cairo, 1916.
Griffith, F. Ll. *Catalogue of the Rylands Papyri.* Manchester, 1909.
—— *Stories of the High-Priests of Memphis.* Oxford, 1900.
—— *Meroitic Inscriptions.* 1911–12.
Hartmann, M. *Jamanijat: zu Halévy* 535. Z.A. 1895, 25. (Cf. Budge, *History of Egypt,* VI, Pref.)
Lefebvre, G. *Textes du Tombeau de Petosiris.* Ann. Serv. XX, 1920, pp. 207 *sqq.*
Maspero, Sir G. *Contes Populaires de l'Égypte ancienne.* 1882, 1889.
Reisner, G. *Outline of the Ancient History of the Sudan.* Sudan Notes and Records, II, 1919, p. 35.
—— *The Meroitic Kingdom of Ethiopia.* J.E.A. IX, 1923, pp. 34, 157.
Sachau, E. *Aramäische Papyrus und Ostraka aus einer jüdischen Militär-Kolonie zu Elephantine.* Leipzig, 1911.
Schäfer, H. *Die äthiopische Königsinschrift des Berliner Museums.* Leipzig, 1901.
Spiegelberg, W. *Correspondances du Temps des Rois-Prêtres.* 1895.
—— *Der Sagenkreis des Königs Petubastis.* Leipzig, 1910.
—— *Die sogenannte Demotische Chronik von Paris.* Leipzig, 1914.
—— *Demotische Texte auf Krügen.* Leipzig, 1912.
Staerk, W. *Anfänge der jüdischen Diaspora in Aegypten.* O.L.Z. 1908. Beiheft.

(b) Greek

The Greek sources for the history of Egypt where it affects Greek affairs in the fourth century will be found cited in the bibliographies to chapters II–IV and VIII–IX. Add to these, for the fifth century:

Ctesias. Ed. Gilmore. XIV–XVII = sections 61–74.
Diodorus, XI, 74, 77.
Herodotus, II; III, 12, 15; VII, 1, 4, 7, 89; VIII, 17, 32.
I.G. I², 929.
Philochorus, frag. 90 (*F.H.G.* I, 398).
Plutarch, *Pericles*, 37.
Thucydides, I, 104, 109 *sq.*, 112.

3. ARCHAEOLOGY

Griffith, F. Ll. *Oxford Excavations in Nubia.* Liv. A.A.
Lefebvre, G. *Le Tombeau de Petosiris.* Ann. Serv. xx, 1920, p. 41.
Maspero, Sir G. *Art in Egypt.* (Ars Una series.) 1921.
—— *Studies in Egyptian Art.* 1913.
Naville, E. *Goshen and the Shrine of Saft el-Henneh.* 1887.
Petrie, Sir W. M. F. and others. *Tanis.* 1885, 1888.
Reisner, G. *Reports, etc. on excavations in the Sudan.* (As cited in vol. III, p. 724.)
—— *Notes on the Harvard-Boston expedition at el-Kurruw and Barkal.* J.E.A. vi, 1920, pp. 61, 247.

4. MISCELLANEOUS

Ehrenberg, V. *Alexander und Aegypten.* Leipzig, 1926.
How, W. W. and Wells, J. *Commentary on Herodotus, I–III.* Oxford, 1912.
Jacoby, F. Art. *Herodot* in P.W.
Jéquier, G. *Le Livre de ce qu'il y a dans l'Hadès.* 1894.
Möller, G. *König Bocchoris.* Z. Aeg. LVI, 1920, p. 7.
—— *Noch einmal* Ἑρμοτύβιες. *Ib.* 78.
Schäfer, H. *Die Stele 'de l'excommunication.'* Klio, vi, 1906, p. 287.
Wells, J. See How.
—— *The Persian Friends of Herodotus.* J.H.S. xxvii, p. 37.
Werner Schur. *Zur Vorgeschichte der Ptolemäer.* Klio, xx, 1926, p. 270. (To be corrected from Egyptian sources.)
Wiedemann, A. *Herodots zweites Buch.* Leipzig, 1890.

For other miscellaneous works on the Greek side, see bibliographies cited under 1.

CHAPTER VII

THE INAUGURATION OF JUDAISM

Most of the general literature (commentaries, histories, etc.) has
already been specified in vol. III, pp. 729–740.

1. OLD TESTAMENT SOURCES

See the commentaries, etc., on the *books* Ezra and Nehemiah (and Kent's
annotated translation, 1905), also on Esther; on Isaiah xl–lxvi (more especially
lvi *sqq.*) and Malachi; on Job and Leviticus; and on other books or portions of books
now generally ascribed (in their present form) to the post-exilic age. A convenient
edition of select texts is that by M. Haller, *Das Judentum*, ed. 2, Göttingen, 1925.
For discussions of the critical questions see vol. III, 735 (*e*). A. van Hoonacker (*Rev.
Bibl.* Jan. 1924, pp. 33 *sqq.*, 44) upholds the sequence of the *figures* Nehemiah-
Ezra against Kugler.

For 1 Esdras in particular, see Cook and Hölscher in the editions of the Apocrypha
by R. H. Charles (Oxford, 1913), and Kautzsch (Freiburg i. B., 1900) respectively.

2. EXTERNAL SOURCES

Elephantine Papyri.

Cowley, A. *Aramaic Papyri of the Fifth Century B.C.* Oxford, 1923. (With full
bibliography, historical introduction and commentary.) See *O.L.Z.* xxvii, 272;
Journ. Theol. Stud. 1924, p. 293; *Aegyptus*, v, 90.
Sachau, Ed. *Aramäische Papyrus und Ostraka aus einer jüdischen Militär-Kolonie zu
Elephantine.* Leipzig, 1911. (Editio princeps, with plates.)
Babylonian tablets.
Daiches, S. *The Jews in Babylonia in the time of Ezra and Nehemiah according to
Bab. inscriptions.* London, 1910. (On p. 184 above, see pp. 8, 28, 35.)
Hilprecht, H. V. and Clay, A. T. *Business documents of Murashu sons of Nippur.*
Philadelphia, 1898. Also A. T. Clay. Philadelphia, 1912.
Miscellaneous.
Hölscher, G. *Palästina in d. persischen u. hellenist. Zeit.* Berlin, 1903.
Judeich, W. *Kleinasiatische Studien.* Marburg, 1892.

3. HISTORIES

See the works of Guthe, H. P. Smith, Stade, Wellhausen (cited in vol. III,
p. 734).
Cheyne, T. K. *Jewish Religious Life after the Exile.* New York, 1898.
Hunter, P. Hay. *After the Exile.* Edinburgh, 1890. (Popular.)
Kennett, R. H. *From Nebuchadnezzar to Alexander* in Cambridge Biblical Essays.
(Ed. Swete, 1909.)
Meyer, E. *Gesch. d. Alt.* Vol. III. Stuttgart and Berlin, 1901. Reprinted, 1912.

4. GENERAL STUDIES

Bennett, W. H. *Post-exilic prophets.* Edinburgh, 1907.
Bertholet, A. *Biblische Theologie des Alten Testaments.* Tübingen, 1911.
Browne, L. E. *Early Judaism.* Cambridge, 1920.
Carter, G. W. Zoroastrianism and Judaism. Boston, 1918.
Cheyne, T. K. *Job and Solomon.* 1887.
Gray, G. B. Art. *Law Literature* in Ency. Biblica.

Gressmann, H. In *Zeit. f. Alttest. Wissens.* 1924. p. 272. (On the teaching of Amen-em-ope.)

Hölscher, G. *Geschichte d. israelit. u. jüd. Religion.* Giessen, 1922.

Hoschander, J. *The Book of Esther in the Light of History.* Philadelphia, 1923.

Maynard, J. A. In *Journal of Bibl. Literature,* XLIV (1925), p. 163. (On the dissimilarities between Judaism and Mazdaism.)

Meyer, E. *Entstehung des Judenthums.* Halle, 1896.

—— *Ursprung und Anfänge des Christentums,* II, 1–120. Stuttgart and Berlin. 1921.

Montefiore, C. G. *The Hibbert Lectures.* 1892. (Chapters vi *sqq.*) Ed. 3, 1897.

Moore, G. F. Art. *Historical Literature* in Ency. Biblica.

—— *The rise of normative Judaism.* Harvard Theolog. Rev. XVII (1924), p. 307; XVIII (1925), p. 1.

Mowinckel, S. *Statholderen Nehemia.* Christiania, 1916.

—— *Ezra den Skriftlærde.* Christiania, 1916.

Naish, J. P. In *Expositor,* 1925, I, 34, 94. (On Job.)

Pfeiffer, R. H. *Edomitic Wisdom.* Zeit. f. Alttest. Wissens. 1926. p. 13.

Rothstein, J. W. *Juden und Samaritaner.* Leipzig, 1908.

Scheftelowitz, I. *Die altpersische Religion u. das Judentum.* Giessen, 1920.

Simpson, D. C. *The Hebrew Book of Proverbs and the Teaching of Amenophis.* J.E.A. XII, 232.

Smith, Sir G. A. *Jerusalem.* 2 vols. 1907.

Touzard, J. *L'âme juive au temps des Perses.* Revue Biblique, 1916 *sqq.* See also his reviews, *ib.* 1913, p. 283; 1915, pp. 59–133.

Wellhausen, J. *Prolegomena.* Ed. 6. Berlin, 1905. (English transl. Edinburgh, 1885.)

CHAPTERS VIII AND IX

THE RISE OF MACEDONIA, AND MACEDONIAN SUPREMACY IN GREECE

A. ANCIENT SOURCES

1. *Literary*

(*a*) *Contemporary writers.*
Isocrates, *Archidamus, de Pace, Areopagiticus, Philippus, Panathenaicus, de Antidosi*; and Letters 2, 3, 9.
Demosthenes, Orations 1–24; 34; 35; 39 § 16; 50; 51; 58 § 37; 59 §§ 3, 4; Prooem. 21; Letters.
Aeschines, Orations.
Hypereides, *pro Euxenippo, in Demosthenem*, and Fragments 28, 29, 31, 76.
Dinarchus, Orations.
Lycurgus, *in Leocratem.*
Xenophon, *Hellenica*, VI, iv §§ 35–7; *de Vectigalibus*, chapter V.
Aristotle, *Rhetoric*, III, X, 1411 a; *Politics*, V (VIII), V, 9, 1304 b, 18 *sqq.*
Theopompus, Fragments.
Ephorus, Fragments 151–7 (Müller).
Callisthenes, Fragment *ap.* Stobaeum, *Flor.* VI, 65.

(*b*) *Secondary writers.*
Diodorus, XIV, cxvii §§ 7, 8; XVI; XVII, ii, iii; XVIII, lvi.
Justin, VII–IX.
Philochorus, Fragments 126–35 (*F.H.G.* I, pp. 404–7).
Duris, Fragments 4–6 (*F.H.G.* I, pp. 470 *sq.*).
Nepos, Lives of Iphicrates, Chabrias, Timotheus, Phocion.
Plutarch, Lives of Demosthenes and Phocion; of Pelopidas, chapters 18, 26, 35; of Alexander, chapters 9, 10; *Quaest. Platon.* p. 1011 b; *Reip. ger. praecepta*, pp. 812 *sq.*; and Pseudo-Plut. *Vitae X Oratorum.*
Arrian, *Anabasis*, I, xxv § 1; II, xiv § 2; III, vi § 5.
Dionysius of Halicarnassus, *Ep. ad Ammaeum*, I; *de Dinarcho*, p. 664.
Polyaenus, II, xxxviii; III, ix, 29; IV; V, xvi, 2; VII, xiv, xxxiii; VIII, xl.
Didymus, *Commentary on Demosthenes* (Diels and Schubart, Berliner Klassikertexte, 1904).
Scholia to Demosthenes and Aeschines.
Polybius, V, X; IX, xxviii, xxxiii; XVII, xiv, xv; XVIII, xiv.
Strabo, VII, p. 307; VIII, p. 361; IX, p. 414; XIII, p. 610.
Pausanias, I, ix, 4; xxv, 3; xxix, 10; xxxiv, 1; II, xx, 1; III, X, 2, 4; xxiv, 6; IV, xxvii, 10; xxviii, 2, 4; V, iv, 9; VI, xviii, 2; VII, vi, 5; X, 3, 5; xv, 6; VIII, vi, 2; vii, 4–6; xxvii, 10; xxx, 6; xxxi, 9; IX, i, 8; vi, 5; xxxvii, 8; X, ii, iii, viii, xxxv, 3, 6; xxxvi, 3, 6.
Appian, IV, cii, cv.
Tacitus, *Annals*, IV, xliii.
Frontinus, I, iii § 4; iv §§ 6, 13; II, i § 9; iii §§ 2, 3; viii § 14; III, iii § 5, viii § 1, ix § 8; IV, i § 6; V § 12.
Harpocration, *sub vbb.* Δάτον, Δεκαδαρχία, Θεωρικά, Σιμός, Ἕμμηνοι, Ἰσοτέλης.
Suidas, *s.v.* Κάρανος.
Stephanus-Byzantinus, *s.v.* Ὠρεός.

2. *Archaeological*

(a)

Dittenberger³, *Sylloge Inscriptionum Graecarum*, Ed. 3. Vol. I, nos. 167–260; with C.I.A. II, 70.

Hicks, E. L. and Hill, G. F. *Greek Historical Inscriptions*, Ed. 2 (1901), nos. 123–53.

(Cf. Wilhelm, A. in *Wien S. B.*, *Phil.-hist. Klasse*, 1911, Abh. 6; and works mentioned under B, 3 *(a)*, *(e)* below.)

(b)

Gardner, P. *History of Ancient Coinage.* 1918. Chapters xv–xxi.

Head, B. V. *H.N. passim.*

Hill, G. F. *Historical Greek Coins.* 1908. pp. 80–97.

Strack, L. *Die Antiken Münzen von Thrakien.* Berlin, 1912.

West, A. B. *The Early Diplomacy of Philip II of Macedon, as illustrated by his Coins.* Num. Chr. 1923, p. 169.

B. Modern Authorities¹

See General Bibliography

1. *Modern Works on Ancient Authorities*²

(a)

Haake, A. *De Duride Samio Diodori auctore.* Bonn, 1874.

Pack, H. *Die Quelle des Berichtes über den heiligen Krieg im 16. Buche Diodors.* Hermes, XI, 1876, p. 179.

Schubert, R. *Untersuchungen über die Quellen zur Geschichte Philipps II von Makedonien.* Königsberg, 1904.

Schwartz, E. Art. *Diodorus* in P.W.

Uhlemann, K. *Untersuchungen über die Quellen der Geschichte Philipps von Makedonien und des heiligen Krieges im 16. Buche Diodors.* Strassburg, 1913.

Volquardsen, C. A. *Untersuchungen über die Quellen der griechischen und sikilischen Geschichte bei Diodor, Buch XI–XVI.* Kiel, 1868.

(b)

Meyer, E. *Theopomps Hellenika.* Halle, 1909.

(c)

Holzapfel, L. *Über die Abfassungszeit von Xenophon's* Πόροί. Phil. XLI, 1882, p. 242.

Pintschovius, Æm. *Xenophon de Vectigalibus V.* 9 *und die Überlieferung vom Anfang des phokischen Krieges.* Hadersleben, 1900.

(d)

Blass, F. *Die attische Beredsamkeit.* Vols. II and III. Ed. 2. Leipzig, 1892–8. (On Isocrates and other orators.)

Meyer, E. *Isokrates zweiter Brief an Philipp u.s.w.* See below, 5 *(c)*.

Miltner, F. J. *Die Datierung des Areopagitikos des Isocrates.* Mitt. des Vereins klassischer Philologen in Wien, I (1924). See *Phil. Woch.* 1925, col. 928.

v. Scala, R. *Isokrates und die Geschichts-schreibung.* Verhandl. der Münch. Philologen-Versammlung, 1891, pp. 102 *sqq.*

Wilamowitz-Moellendorff, U. von. *Aristoteles und Athen.* Berlin, 1893. Vol. II. pp. 380–99. (On Isocrates.)

¹ The headings in this classification inevitably overlap one another.

² The writer of these chapters would express his particular gratitude to Francotte's *Études sur Démosthène* and to the chronological and other writings of M. Cloché.

(*e*)

Foucart, P. *La Sixième Lettre attribuée à Démosthène.* Journ. des Savants, 1912, pp. 49–54.
Nitsche, W. *Demosthenes und Anaximenes.* Berlin, 1906.
Wendland, P. *Anaximenes von Lampsakos.* Berlin, 1905.

(*f*)

Florian, W. *Studia Didymea historica ad Saeculum IV. pertinentia.* Leipzig, 1908.
Foucart, P. *Étude sur Didyme.* Mém. Ac. Inscr. xxxviii, 1906.
Körte, A. *Zu Demosthenes' Didymos-Kommentar.* Rh. Mus. lxiii, 1905, p. 389.
Macher, E. *Die Hermias-episode im Demosthenes-Kommentar des Didymos.* Lundenburg, 1914.

2. *Special Treatises on the Athenian or General Greek History of the Period*

(*a*)

Beloch, K. J. *Die attische Politik seit Perikles.* Leipzig, 1884. Chapters ix–xiv.
Ferguson, W. S. *Hellenistic Athens.* 1911. Chapter i.
Kaerst, J. *Geschichte des Hellenismus.* Ed. 2. Berlin, 1917. Vol. i, Bks i, ii.
Lenschau, T. *Bericht über griechische Geschichte, 431–338.* Bursian, 1919.
Marshall, F. H. *The Second Athenian Confederacy.* Cambridge, 1905.
Sundwall, J. *Epigraphische Beiträge zur sozialpolitischen Geschichte Athens im Zeitalter des Demosthenes.* Klio, Beiheft iv, 1906.
Wendland, P. *Beiträge zur athenischen Politik und Publicistik des vierten Jahrhunderts.* Gött. Nach. 1910.

(*b*)

Böhnecke, K. *Forschungen auf dem Gebiete der attischen Redner und der Geschichte ihrer Zeit.* Berlin, 1843.
Drerup, E. *Aus einer Advokatenrepublik.* Paderborn, 1916. (See also review of this by P. Cauer in *Wochenschr. für Klass. Philologie*, xxxv, 1918, pp. 73–9.)
Hogarth, D. G. *Philip and Alexander of Macedon.* 1897.
Pickard-Cambridge, A. W. *Demosthenes and the last days of Greek freedom.* New York and London, 1914.
Schäfer, A. *Demosthenes und seine Zeit.* Ed. 2. Leipzig, 1885.
Valeton, M. *De nonnullis Demosthenis et Aeschinis controversiis.* Mnemosyne, xxxvi, 1908, p. 75.
Vorndran, L. *Die Aristocratea des Demosthenes als Advokatenrede und ihre politische Tendenz.* Paderborn, 1922.

(*c*)

Kahrstedt, U. *Forschungen zur Geschichte des ausgehenden fünften und des vierten Jahrhunderts.* Berlin, 1910.
Pokorny, E. *Studien zur griechischen Geschichte im sechsten und fünften Jahrzehnt des vierten Jahrhunderts v. Chr.* Greifswald, 1913.

(*d*)

Cloché, P. *La Grèce en 346–339.* B.C.H. xliv, 1920, p. 108.
Flathe, L. *Der phokische Krieg.* Plauen, 1854.
Glotz, G. *Philippe et la prise d'Elatée.* B.C.H. xxxiii, 1909, pp. 528–45.
Reichenbächer, W. *Die Geschichte der athenischen und makedonischen Politik vom Frieden des Philokrates bis zum korinthischen Bund.* Halle, 1897.
Rohrmoser, J. *Über den philokrateischen Frieden.* Zeitschr. für die österr. Gymn. 1874.
Weil, H. *La guerre d'Olynthe et la guerre d'Eubée.* Rev. Phil. iii, 1879, p. 1.
Weise, R. *Der athenische Bundesgenossenkrieg.* Berlin, 1895.

3. Special Treatises on Particular Departments of History, Countries and Districts

(a) Athenian Finance, etc.

Francotte, H. *Les Finances des cités Grecques.* Liège and Paris, 1909.

—— *Démosthène et le théorique.* Mus. B. 1913, p. 69.

Gernet, L. *L'approvisionnement d'Athènes en blé au Ve et IVe siècles.* Paris, 1909.

Kahrstedt, U. *Op. cit.* pp. 205–33.

Lipsius, J. H. *Die attische Steuerverfassung und das attische Staatsvermögen.* Rh. Mus. LXXI, 1913, p. 161, p. 584.

Motzki, A. *Eubulos von Probalinthos und seine Finanzpolitik.* Königsberg, 1903.

(b) Military History.

Cloché, P. *Les procès des Stratèges Athéniens.* Revue des Études Anciennes, 1924, p. 97.

Delbrück, H. *Geschichte der Kriegskunst.* Ed. 2. Berlin, 1908. Vol. I, pp. 173 *sqq.*

Hogarth, D. G. *Op. cit.* pp. 50–64.

Kaerst, J. Art. *Alexander* in P.W. and references there given.

Kromayer, J. *Antike Schlachtfelder.* Berlin, 1903. Vol. I, chapter ii (on Chaeronea).

Kromayer, J. and Veith, G. *Schlachten-Atlas zur antiken Kriegsgeschichte mit begleitendem Text.* Lief. I=Griech. Abt. I. Leipzig, 1926. See Blatt 5 and Text.

Roloff, G. *Probleme aus der griechischen Kriegsgeschichte.* Berlin, 1903. pp. 62–9 (on Chaeronea).

Soteriades, G. *Das Schlachtfeld von Chäronea.* Ath. Mitt. XXVIII, 1903, p. 301.

(c) Macedonia.

Abel, O. *Makedonien vor König Philipp.* Leipzig, 1847.

Casson, S. *Macedonia, Thrace and Illyria.* Oxford, 1926.

Costanzi, V. *Studi di Storia Macedonica fino a Filippo.* Pisa, 1914.

Flathe, L. *Geschichte Makedoniens und der Reiche, welche von Makedonischen Königen beherrscht wurden.* Leipzig, 1832.

Hatzidakis, G. N. *Zur Abstammung der alten Makedonien.* Athens, 1897.

Hoffmann, O. *Die Makedonen, ihre Sprache und ihr Volkstum.* Göttingen, 1906.

Hogarth, D. G. *Op. cit.*

Kazarow, G. *Observations sur la nationalité des anciens Macedoniens.* Rev. E.G. XXIII, 1910, p. 243.

Kretschmer, P. *Einleitung in die Geschichte der griechischen Sprache.* Göttingen, 1896. pp. 282 *sqq.*

(d) Thrace, etc.

Bürchner. Art. *Chersonesos* in P.W.

Casson, S. *The Sacred Mount of Pangaeum.* Discovery, III, 1922, p. 257.

Cloché, P. *Le Traité Athéno-Thrace de* 357. Rev. Phil. XLVI, 1922, p. 1.

Foucart, P. *Les Athéniens dans la Chersonèse de Thrace au IVe siècle.* Paris, 1909.

Höck, A. *Das Odrysenreich in Thrakien im* 5. *und* 4. *Jahrhundert.* Hermes, XXVI, 1891, p. 76.

—— *Die Söhne des Kersobleptes von Thrakien.* Hermes, XXXIII, 1897, p. 626.

Schwartz, E. *Demosthenes Erste Philippika.* Festschrift für Mommsen. 1893.

(e) Delphi.

Bourguet, E. *L'administration financière du sanctuaire pythien au IVe siècle.* Paris, 1905.

Cloché, P. *Les Naopes de Delphes et la politique Hellénique.* B.C.H. XL, 1916, p. 78; and XLIV, 1920, p. 312.

Homolle, Th. *Remarques Épigraphiques sur l'administration financière et la chrono-logie de la ville de Delphes au IVe siècle*. B.C.H. xxii, 1898, p. 602.

Pomtow, H. Art. *Delphoi* in P.W.

—— *Eine delphische Stasis im Jahre 363 v. Chr.* Klio, vi, 1906, p. 89.

(*f*) *North Greece* (excluding Delphi).

Hohmann, W. *Aitolien und die Aitoler bis zum lamischen Kriege*. Halle, 1908.

Klotzsch, C. *Epeirotische Geschichte bis zum Jahre 280 v. Chr.* Berlin, 1911.

Reuss, F. *König Arybbas von Epirus*. Rh. Mus. xxxvi, 1881, p. 161.

Swoboda, H. *Zur griechischen Kunstler-Geschichte*. Jahreshefte, vi, 1903, p. 203. (For Thessalian history.)

(*g*) *Asia-Minor, Persia, etc.*

Cloché, P. *La Grèce et l'Égypte de 405 à 342/1 av. J. C.* Rev. Ég. 1919, p. 210.

—— *Les Rapports des Grecs avec Égypte*. Revue des Études Anciennes, xxvii, 1925, p. 230.

Judeich, W. *Kleinasiatische Studien*. Marburg, 1892.

Kahrstedt, U. *Op. cit.* pp. 1–26 and *passim.*

Mallet, D. *Les Rapports des Grecs avec Égypte*. Mémoires de l'Institut français d'Archéologie orientale du Caire, xlviii (1922).

Smith, Sidney. *Babylonian Historical Texts*. 1924, p. 149.

4. *Chronology, etc.*

Baran, A. *Zur Chronologie des Euboischen Krieges und der Olynthischen Reden des Demosthenes*. Wien. St. vii, 1885, p. 190.

Cloché, P. *Étude chronologique sur la troisième Guerre Sacrée*. Paris, 1915.

—— *La Grèce et l'Égypte de 405 à 342/1 av. J. C.* Rev. Ég. 1919, p. 210.

Foucart, P. *Démosthène et les hieromnemons Thessaliens*. Rev. Phil. xxiii, 1899, p. 106.

Francotte, H. *Études sur Démosthène*. Mus. B. 1913, pp. 237–78; and 1914, p. 157.

Heimer, J. *De Demosthenis Oratione XIII*. Münster, 1912.

Kahle, F. *De Demosthenis Orationum Androtioneae, Timocrateae, Aristocrateae temporibus*. Göttingen, 1909.

Kahrstedt, U. *Op. cit.*

Pokorny, E. *Op. cit.*

Pomtow, H. *Neue Gleichungen attischer und delphischer Archonten*. Phil. liv, 1895, p. 211.

Radüge, E. *Zur Zeitbestimmung des Euboischen und Olynthischen Krieges*. Giessen, 1908.

Reuss, F. *Die Chronologie Diodors*. Jahrb. für Kl. Phil. xlii, 1896, p. 641.

Schwartz, E. *Demosthenes' Erste Philippika*. Festschrift für Mommsen. 1893.

—— *Die Zeit des Ephoros*. Hermes, xliv, 1909, p. 481.

Stavenhagen, C. *Quaestiones Demosthenicae*. Göttingen, 1907.

Wendland, P. Review of Kahrstedt, *op. cit.* G.G.A. 1912, p. 617.

See also above, under 1 (*a*), (*f*).

5. *Biography, etc.*

(*a*) *Philip.*

Hogarth. *Op. cit.*

Willrich, H. *Wer liess König Philipp von Makedonien ermorden?* Hermes xxxiv, 1889, p. 174.

(b) Demosthenes.

Drerup, E. *Demosthenes im Urteile des Altertums.* Würzburg, 1923.

Schäfer. *Op. cit.* Pickard-Cambridge. *Op. cit.* Drerup. *Op. cit.* Pokorny. *Op. cit.* pp. 77–115, 125–67. Kahrstedt. *Op. cit.* pp. 1–154.

Thalheim, Th. Art. *Demosthenes* in P.W.

(c) Isocrates.

Adams, C. D. *Recent views of the political influence of Isocrates.* C.P. VII, 1912, p. 343.

Kessler, J. *Isokrates und die panhellenische Idee.* Paderborn, 1910.

Koepp, F. *Isokrates als politiker.* Preussische Jahrb. LXX, 1892.

Meyer, E. *Isokrates zweiter Brief an Philipp und Demosthenes zweite Philippika.* Berl. S.B. 1909, p. 758.

v. Pöhlmann, R. *Isokrates und das Problem der Demokratie.* Bay. S.B. 1913.

Rostagni, A. *Isocrate e Filippo.* Turin, 1913.

(d) Others.

Buffenoir, H. *Phokion, un grand aristocrate Athénien.* Rev. crit. des idées et des livres, XXI, p. 415.

Rehdantz, C. *Vitae Iphicratis, Chabriae et Timothei.* Berlin, 1845.

Rüger, C. *Zur Charakteristik Phokions.* Zeitschr. für die österr. Gymn. 1908, pp. 679–91.

CHAPTER X

SICILY 367 TO 330 B.C.

I. ANCIENT AUTHORITIES

Plato, *Epistles* III, VII, VIII, XIII.
Anaximenes, *Rhetorica ad Alexandrum*, VIII, 3, p. 1420.
Aristotle, *Politics*, 1312 A–B.
Theopompus, frags. 179, 187, 188, 225 (Grenfell and Hunt).
Cicero, *Actio Secunda in Verrem*, II, 51.
Livy, VIII, 3, 17, 24.
Diodorus Siculus, XVI.
Cornelius Nepos, *Dion, Timoleon*.
Strabo, VI, pp. 253, 259, 280.
Plutarch, *Dion, Timoleon, Moralia*, 176–7, 523.
Aelian, *V.H.* IV, 8, 18; IX, 8.
Polyaenus, V, 4.
Justin, VIII, 6; XII, 2; XVII, 3; XXI, 1–5; XXIII, 1.
Athenaeus, X, 435 D–436 B (= Clearchus in *F.H.G.* II, 307); XII, 541 C.

II. GENERAL HISTORIES

See General Bibliography.

Gsell, S. *Histoire ancienne de l'Afrique du Nord.* Vols. II–III. 1913.
Meltzer, O. *Geschichte der Karthager.* Vol. I. Berlin, 1879.
Niese, B. *Geschichte der griechischen und makedonischen Staaten.* Gotha, 1893.
Pais, E. *Storia della Sicilia e della Magna Grecia.* (Storia d' Italia, Parte I.) Turin, 1894.

III. CHRONOLOGY AND SPECIAL HISTORY

See articles in *P.W.* on Dion (2), Dionysius (2), Hanno (3), Heraklides (24), Hiketas (2); also on separate states, *e.g.* Akragas, Karthago, Selinus.

Costanzi, V. *De bello Lucanico.* Riv. Fil. XXVI, 1898, p. 450.
Evans, A. J. *The Horsemen of Tarentum.* 1889.
Grote, George. *Plato and the Companions of Socrates.* 1875. Chapter III.
Holden, H. A. *Plutarchi Timoleon.* Cambridge, 1889.
Howald, E. *Die Briefe Platons.* Zürich, 1923.
Krug, O. *Quellenuntersuchung zur Geschichte des jüngeren Dionysios.* Diss. Kattowitz, 1891.
Pais, E. *Ricerche storiche e geografiche.* Turin, 1908. pp. 135 *sqq.*
Pomtow, H. *Ein sicilisches Anathem in Delphi.* Ath. Mitt. XX, 1895, pp. 484 *sqq.*
Post, L. A. *Thirteen Epistles of Plato.* Oxford, 1925.
Ritter, C. *Platon.* Munich, 1914. Vol. I, chapters I–V.
De Sanctis, G. *Storia dei Romani.* Turin, 1907. Vol. II, pp. 292 *sqq.*
Taylor, A. E. *Plato.* 1926. Chapter I.
Wilamowitz-Moellendorff, U. von. *Platon.* Berlin, 1920.
Zeller, E. *Die Philosophie der Griechen.* Ed. 4. II, 1, pp. 423 *sqq.*

CHAPTER XI

THE ATHENIAN PHILOSOPHICAL SCHOOLS

NOTE. This list contains only a small selection of works, to which the writer acknowledges obligations.

I. SOCRATES

Adam, A. M. *Socrates quantum mutatus ab illo.* C.Q. XII, 1918, p. 121.
Bruns, I. *Das literarische Porträt der griechen.* Berlin, 1896.
Burnet, J. *The Socratic doctrine of the Soul.* Proc. Brit. Acad. VII, 1916.
Bury, J. B. *The trial of Socrates.* R.P.A. Annual, 1926, p. 17.
Dittmar, H. *Aischines von Sphettos.* Berlin, 1912.
Dümmler, F. *Akademika.* Giessen, 1889.
Joel, K. *Der echte und der Xenophontische Sokrates.* Berlin, 1893.
Krauss, H. *Aeschines Socraticus.* Lipsiae, 1911.
Maier, H. *Sokrates.* Tübingen, 1913.
Pfleiderer, E. *Sokrates und Plato.* Tübingen, 1896.
Taylor, A. E. *Varia Socratica.* I. Oxford, 1911.
—— *Plato's Biography of Socrates.* Proc. Brit. Acad. VIII, 1917–18.
Zeller, E. *Philosophie der Griechen.* Vol. II. 4. Ed. Leipzig, 1889

II. PLATO

(a) Texts and Editions

Adam, J. *The Republic of Plato.* Cambridge, 1902.
—— *Platonis Euthyphro.* Cambridge, 1910.
Adam, J. and A. M. *Platonis Protagoras.* Cambridge, 1905.
Archer-Hind, R. D. *The Phaedo of Plato.* 1894.
—— *The Timaeus of Plato.* 1888.
Burnet, J. *Platonis Opera.* Oxonii, 1899–1907.
—— *Plato's Euthyphro, Apology, and Crito.* Oxford, 1924.
—— *Plato's Phaedo.* Oxford, 1911.
Bury, R. G. *The Philebus of Plato.* Cambridge, 1897.
—— *The Symposium of Plato.* Cambridge, 1909.
Campbell, L. *The Sophistes and Politicus of Plato.* Oxford, 1867.
—— *The Theaetetus of Plato.* Oxford, 1883.
Croiset, A. *Hippias Majeur. Charmide. Lachès. Lysis.* 1921.
—— *Protagoras.* 1923.
—— *Gorgias. Ménon.* 1923.
Croiset, M. *Hippias Mineur. Alcibiade. Apologie. Euthyphron. Criton.* 1920.
Diès, A. *Le Sophiste.* 1925.
—— *Parménide.* 1923.
—— *Théétète.* 1924.
England, E. B. *The Laws of Plato.* Manchester, 1921.
Gifford, E. H. *The Euthydemus of Plato.* Oxford, 1905.
Hackforth, R. *The authorship of the Platonic Epistles.* New York, 1913.
Howald, E. *Die Briefe Platons.* Zürich, 1923.
Rivaud, A. *Timée, Critias.* 1925.
Robin, L. *Phédon.* 1926.
Stallbaum, G. *Platonis Dialogi Selecti.* Gothae, 1827–60.
Thompson, E. S. *The Meno of Plato.* 1901.

Thompson, W. H. *The Phaedrus of Plato*. 1868.
—— *The Gorgias of Plato*. 1871.
Wyttenbach, D. *Platonis Phaedon*. Lugduni Batavorum, 1830.

(b) *Modern Works*

Arnim, H. von. *Platos Jugenddialoge*. Leipzig, 1914.
Bonitz, H. *Platonische Studien*. 3. Ed. Berlin, 1886.
Burnet, J. *Greek Philosophy*. Vol. 1. Thales to Plato. 1914.
Field, G. C. *Socrates and Plato*. Oxford, 1913.
Jackson, H. *Plato's Later Theory of Ideas*. J.P. x, p. 253; xi, p. 287; xiii, p. 1,
    p. 242; xiv, p. 173; xv, p. 280.
Lutoslawski, W. *Origin and Growth of Plato's Logic*. 1897.
Martin, H. *Études sur le Timée de Platon*. 1841.
Nettleship, R. L. *Lectures on the Republic of Plato*. 1898.
Peipers, D. *Erkenntnisstheorie Platos*. Leipzig, 1874.
Pohlenz, M. *Aus Platos Werdezeit*. Berlin, 1913.
Raeder, H. *Platons philosophische Entwickelung*. Leipzig, 1905.
Ritter, C. *Platon*. Munich, 1910.
Robin, L. *La Théorie platonicienne des Idées et des Nombres*. 1908.
Ross, W. D. *Aristotle's Metaphysics*. Oxford, 1924. Introduction, pp. xxxiii *sqq*.
Shorey, P. *The Unity of Plato's Thought*. Chicago, 1903.
Stenzel, J. *Zahl und Gestalt bei Platon und Aristoteles*. Leipzig, 1924.
—— *Studien zur Entwicklung der platonischen Dialektik*. Breslau, 1917.
Stewart, J. A. *The Myths of Plato*. 1905.
—— *Plato's Doctrine of Ideas*. Oxford, 1909.
Taylor, A. E. *Plato*. 1908.
Wilamowitz-Moellendorff, U. von. *Platon*. Berlin, 1920.
Zeller, E. *Philosophie der Griechen*. Vol. ii. 4. Ed. Leipzig, 1889.

III. ARISTOTLE

(a) *Texts, Editions, Translations*

Bekker, I. *Aristotelis Opera*. Berolini, 1831.
Bonitz, H. *Index Aristotelicus*. Berolini, 1870.
—— *Metaphysica*. Bonnae, 1848.
Burnet, J. *The Ethics of Aristotle*. 1900.
Butcher, S. H. *Aristotle's Theory of Poetry*. 1898.
Bywater, I. *Aristotle on the Art of Poetry*. Oxford, 1909.
Cope, E. M. and Sandys, J. E. *The Rhetoric of Aristotle*. Cambridge, 1877.
Grant, A. *The Ethics of Aristotle*. 1885.
Hicks, R. D. *De anima*. Cambridge, 1907.
Ideler, I. L. *Meteorologica*. Lipsiae, 1834.
Joachim, H. H. *De Generatione et Corruptione*. Oxford, 1922.
Newman, W. L. *The Politics of Aristotle*. Oxford, 1887.
Rose, V. *Aristotelis qui ferebantur librorum fragmenta*. Berolini, 1870.
Ross, G. R. T. *De Sensu and De Memoria*. Cambridge, 1906.
Ross, W. D. *Aristotle's Metaphysics*. Oxford, 1924.
Smith, J. A. and Ross, W. D. *The Works of Aristotle translated into English*. Oxford
    1908–.
Spengel, L. *Eudemi Rhodii Fragmenta*. Londini, 1866.
Stewart, J. A. *Notes on the Nicomachean Ethics*. Oxford, 1892.
Susemihl, F. and Hicks, R. D. *The Politics of Aristotle I–V*. 1894.
Waitz, T. *Organon*. Lipsiae, 1844.

(b) *Modern Works*

Bernays, J. *Die Dialoge des Aristoteles*. Berlin, 1863.

Bywater, I. *On a lost dialogue of Aristotle*. J.P. ii, 55. 1869.

Gercke, A. Art. *Aristoteles* in P.W.

Gohlke, P. *Die Entstehungsgeschichte der naturwissenschaftlichen Schriften des Aristoteles*. Hermes, lix, 1924, p. 274.

—— *Aus der Entstehungsgeschichte der Aristotelischen Metaphysik*. Satura Berolinensis. Berlin, 1924.

Gomperz, T. *Greek Thinkers*. Vol. iv. 1912.

Grote, G. *Aristotle*. 1880.

Jaeger, W. *Aristoteles*. Berlin, 1923.

—— *Studien zur Entstehungsgeschichte der Metaphysik*. Berlin, 1912.

Maier, H. *Die Syllogistik des Aristoteles*. Tübingen, 1896–1900.

Mansion, A. *Introduction à la Physique aristotélicienne*. Louvain, 1913.

Ross, W. D. *Aristotle*. 1923.

Taylor, A. E. *Aristotle*. n.d.

Windelband, W. *Geschichte der alten Philosophie*. 2nd Ed. Iwan Müller's Handbuch. Munich, 1894.

Zeller, E. *Philosophie der Griechen*. Vol. iii. 3. Ed. Leipzig, 1879.

CHAPTERS XII AND XIII

ALEXANDER; THE CONQUEST OF PERSIA AND ALEXANDER; THE CONQUEST OF THE FAR EAST

I. *Ancient Sources.* (On the stratification and interrelation of the literary sources see p. 352 *n.*)

1. Contemporary

(*a*) *Official.*

The Journal (Ephemerides)†[1].

Records of the bematists Diognetus†, Baeton†, and Amyntas†.

Alexander's official rescripts. Ditt.[3] 283, *O.G.I.S.* 1, 1: add text given by Th. Lenschau, *Leipziger Studien*, 1890, p. 186, and dedication Ditt.[3] 277, and cf. *S.E.G.* 1, 211.

Decrees of Greek cities, temple-lists, etc. Ditt.[3] 266–309, *I.G.*[2] 11, 328–368, 435, 457, *O.G.I.S.* 1, 2, 3, 8 (1, 11, 111), Michel's *Recueil* under the various states. For coinage see II A, 2, below.

(*b*) *Correspondence.*

Of Alexander, Olympias and others in Plutarch and other writers (many of these letters are not genuine).

(*c*) *Historians, etc.*

Fragments of Callisthenes†, Onesicritus†, Chares†, Anaximenes†, Ephippus†, Medius†, Nearchus†, Ptolemy I of Egypt†, Aristobulus†, Marsyas† (probably); Androsthenes† and Polyclitus† (geography). See footnote below.

The gazetteer of 324–3 B.C. represented by Diodorus, xviii, 5–6. (See *J.H.S.* xliii, 1923, p. 93.)

(*d*) *Orators.*

[Demosthenes], xvii. Scattered allusions in Demosthenes, Aeschines, Deinarchus, Hypereides. (See the bibliographies to chapters viii–ix and xiv.)

(*e*) *Philosophers.*

Material in Aristotle, especially *Meteorologica* and περὶ τῆς τοῦ Νείλου ἀναβάσεως =frags. 246–8, Rose[3], 248 being the *Liber de inundacione Nili*. Theophrastus, *ap.* Athen. x, 435 A and *Hist. Plant.* ix, 4.

2. Secondary

(*a*) *Historians, etc.* (not extant).

Clitarchus†, Duris, *F.H.G.* 11, pp. 472–7, Hegesias†, Agatharcides, *ib.* 111, p. 196, Dicaearchus, *ib.* 11, pp. 240 *sq.*, Timaeus, *ib.* 1, pp. 227–9, Phylarchus, *ib.* 1, pp. 336, 345 *sq.*, 354 *sq.*, Hegesander, *ib.* iv, pp. 414, 416, Carystius, *ib.* iv, p. 357, Hermippus, *ib.* 111, p. 47, Satyrus, *ib.* 111, pp. 161, 164. Eratosthenes, *ap.* Strab. 1, 66 *sq.*

(*b*) *Historians, etc.* (extant).

Arrian, *Anabasis,* Ἰνδική.

Diodorus, xvii–xviii, 6.

Q. Curtius Rufus.

---

[1] The fragments of the writers marked †, with those of several lesser authors, are collected by C. Müller, in Dübner's Arrian (Paris, 1846), as *Scriptores rerum Alexandri Magni.*

Justin, xi–xii, with Trogus, *Prologues.*

Plutarch, *Alexander, de Alexandri fortuna an virtute.*

—— *Moralia,* 179 D–181 F, 219 E, 221 A 9, 522 A, 557 B, 781 A, 804 B, 970 D, 1043 D.

The Lindian Chronicle, ed. Blinkenberg, Bonn, 1915.

[Aristotle], *Oeconomica,* ii, 2.

Strabo: chiefly bks xiv, 666 *sq.* and xv–xvii. (See A. Miller, *Die Alexander-geschichte nach Strabo,* Würzburg, 1882.)

Aelian, *V.H.* ii, 19; iii, 23; v, 6, 12; vii, 8; viii, 7; ix, 3; xii, 54; xiii, 7, 11.

Athenaeus, περὶ μηχανημάτων.

Polyaenus, iv, 3, 5 and 13; v, 44.

Pausanias, vi, xviii, 2–4; vii, v, 2–3.

Appian, *Mith.* 8.

Josephus, *Antiq.* xi, 8.

Oxyrh. Pap. iv, no. 679 and xv, no. 1798 (fragments of anonymous chronicles).

Scattered references in Pliny, *N.H.*, Macrobius, Pollux, Suidas, Stephanus, Zosimus, Frontinus, Daniel, Jerome's commentary on Daniel (Migne, *Patrologia Latina,* vol. xxv).

The material in many writers of the Roman period, *e.g.* Cicero, Livy, Seneca, Lucan, Lucian, Ps.-Diogenes, Dio Chrysostom, Orosius, belongs, as does the *Macedonian Dialogue* (Pap. Freiburg 2 in Gött. Nach. 1922, p. 32), not to sources but only to the history of opinion.

A very complete collection of references to literary sources will be found in H. Berve, *Das Alexanderreich auf prosopographischer Grundlage,* Munich, 1926.

(c) Chronography.

Marmor Parium, ed. Jacoby. *The Babylonian* 18-*year list,* and the list Spiegelberg, ii, p. 71 (given in E. Meyer, *Forsch.* ii). The Canon of Reigns. *Oxyrhynchus Chronicle* (Oxyrh. Pap. i, 25). Apollodorus, ed. Jacoby, Porphyrius, Eusebius, Jerome, Syncellus.

(d) Works showing affinity with the Romance.

Epitome rerum gestarum Alexandri (Metz Epitome). N.J.P., Supp. Band xxvi, 1900.

Fragment of a Jerusalem codex, Granicus to Gaugamela. Rev. E.G. v, 1892, p. 306. *Itinerarium Alexandri.*

Berlin papyrus 13044 (Alexander and the Indian gymnosophists). Berl. S.B. 1923, p. 150.

(e) The Romance (Pseudo-Callisthenes).

The most important versions are the three Greek, A, B, C of Müller; the Syriac, Ethiopian and Armenian; Julius Valerius; and Leo, *Nativitas et victoriae Alexandri Magni Regis,* commonly called *historia de preliis.* Fragments of many other versions are known.

(f) The Alexander-sarcophagus of Sidon; statues and works of art (see below II, H.)

II. Modern Literature

A. *The Sources*

1. Literary

(See generally for the older literature F. Susemihl, *Geschichte der griechischen Literatur in der Alexandrinerzeit*, Leipzig, 1891; and W. v. Christ, *Geschichte der griechischen Literatur*, ed. 6 by Schmid, in Iwan Müller's *Handbuch*, vols. 7, 1 and 7, ii, 1, 1912 and 1920).

(a) The Official Tradition.

Endres, H. *Die officiellen Grundlagen der Alexander-überlieferung und das Werk des Ptolemäus.* Würzburg, 1913.

Kaerst, J. *Ptolemaios und die Ephemeriden Alexanders des Grossen.* Phil. LVI, 1897, p. 334.

—— Art. *Ephemerides* in P.W.

Lehmann-Haupt, C. F. *Zu den Ephemeriden Alexanders des Grossen.* Hermes XXXVI, 1901, p. 319.

Meyer, E. *Arrian's Geschichte Alexanders des Grossen.* Hermes XXXIII, 1898, p. 648.

Reuss, F. *Arrian und Appian.* Rh. Mus. LIV, 1899, p. 446.

Wachsmuth, C. *Alexander's Ephemeriden und Ptolemaios.* Rh. Mus. LVI, 1901, p. 220.

Wilcken, U. Ὑπομνηματισμοί. Phil. LIII, 1894, p. 80.

(b) Alexander's Correspondence.

Adler, M. *De Alexandri Magni epistularum commercio.* Leipzig, 1891.

Hoffmann, O. *Die Makedonen, ihre Sprache und ihr Volkstum.* Göttingen, 1906. Chap. I, § 3.

Kaerst, J. *Der Briefwechsel Alexanders des Grossen.* Phil. L, 1891, p. 602 (see *ib.* LVI, 1897, p. 406).

Pridik, E. *De Alexandri Magni epistularum commercio.* Dorpat, 1893.

Zumetikos, A. M. *De Alexandri Olympiadisque epistularum fontibus et reliquiis.* Berlin, 1894.

(c) The Vulgate and Aristobulus.

Corssen, P. (See D (2, *b*) below.)

Jacoby, F. Art. *Kallisthenes* (part 1) and *Kleitarchos* in P.W.

Keller, E. *Alexander der Grosse nach der Schlacht von Issos.* Historische Studien, vol. XLVIII. Berlin, 1904.

Radet, G. *La valeur historique de Quinte Curce.* C.R. Ac. Inscr. 1924, p. 356.

Reuss, F. *Aristobul und Kleitarch.* Rh. Mus. LVII, 1902, p. 581.

—— *Hellenistische Beiträge: Kleitarchos.* Rh. Mus. LXIII, 1908, p. 58.

Ruegg, A. *Beiträge zur Erforschung der Quellenverhältnisse in der Alexandergeschichte des Curtius.* Basle, 1906.

Schnabel, P. *Berossos und Kleitarchos.* 1912 (= ch. III of Berossos und die babylonisch-hellenistische Literatur, Leipzig, 1923).

Schwartz, E. *Aristoboulos, Curtius* (no. 31), and *Diodorus* (no. 38) in P.W.

Steele, R. B. A number of articles in *A.J. Ph.* and *C.P.* from 1915 onwards.

Wachsmuth, C. *Das Alexander-buch des Kallisthenes.* Rh. Mus. LVI, 1901, p. 233.

Wenger, F. *Die Alexandergeschichte des Aristobul von Kassandreia.* Würzburg, 1914.

(*d*) *Anti-Alexander traditions.*

Eiche, L. *Veterum philosophorum qualia fuerint de Alexandro Magno judicia.* Rostock, 1909.

Hoffmann, W. *Das literärische Porträt Alexanders des Grossen in griechischen und römischen Altertum.* Leipzig, 1907.

Weber, F. *Alexander der Grosse im Urteil der Griechen und Römer bis in die konstantinische Zeit.* Borna-Leipzig, 1909.

(*e*) *Other Writers.*

Körte, A. *Anaximenes von Lampsakos als Alexanderhistoriker.* Rh. Mus. LXI, 1906, p. 476.

Nachstadt, W. *De Plutarchi declamationibus quae sunt de Alexandri fortuna.* Berlin, 1895.

Reuss, F. *Eratosthenes und die Alexanderüberlieferung.* Rh. Mus. LVII, 1902, p. 568.

(*f*) *The Romance.*

(The following versions and works may suffice for its relation to history.)

Ausfeld, A. *Der griechische Alexanderroman.* Leipzig, 1907.

Budge, Sir E. A. W. *History of Alexander the Great.* Cambridge, 1889. (The Syriac version.)

—— *Life and Exploits of Alexander the Great.* Cambridge, 1896. (The Ethiopian version.)

Kroll, W. Art. *Kallisthenes* (part 2) in P.W.

—— *Historia Alexandri Magni (Pseudo-Callisthenes).* Vol. I. Berlin, 1926.

Meusel, H. *Pseudo-Callisthenes nach der Leidener Handschrift herausgegeben.* Leipzig, 1871.

Müller, C. *Pseudo-Callisthenes.* 1846. (In the Paris Arrian.)

Nöldeke, Th. *Beiträge zur Geschichte des Alexanderromans.* Vienna, 1890.

Raabe, R. ἱστορία Ἀλεξάνδρου. Leipzig, 1896. (The Armenian version, in Greek.)

Rohde, E. *Der griechische Roman und seine Vorläufer.* Ed. 3. Leipzig, 1914.

Spiegel, E. *Die Alexandersage bei den Eraniern,* in Eranische Altertumskunde. Vol. II. Leipzig, 1873.

Zacher, J. *Pseudo-Callisthenes.* Halle, 1867.

2. Coins

(See generally Head, H. N. and Gardner, P., *A history of ancient coinage* 700–300 B.C. Oxford, 1918.)

(*a*) *The Alexander coinage.*

Dussaud, R. *L'ère d'Alexandre le Grand en Phénicie.* Rev. N. 1908, p. 445.

Hill, G. F. *Notes on the Alexandrine coinage of Phoenicia.* Nomisma 4, 1909, p. 1.

—— *Alexander the Great and the Persian Lion-Gryphon.* J.H.S. XLIII, 1923, p. 156.

Lederer, Ph. *Ein Goldstater Alexanders des Grossen.* Z.N. XXXIII, 1922, p. 185.

Müller, L. *Numismatique d'Alexandre le Grand.* Copenhagen, 1855.

Newell, E. T. *Reattribution of certain tetradrachms of Alexander the Great.* A.J. Num. XLV, 1911, pp. 1, 37, 113, 194; XLVI, 1912, pp. 22, 37, 110.

—— *Some Cypriote 'Alexanders.'* Num. Chr. 1915, p. 294.

—— *The dated Alexander coinage of Sidon and Ake.* Yale Oriental Researches. Vol. II. New Haven and London, 1916.

—— *Tarsos under Alexander.* A.J. Num. LII, 1918, p. 69.

—— *The Alexandrine coinage of Sinope.* Ib. p. 117.

Newell, E. T. *Myriandros-Alexandria Kat' Isson.* A. J. Num. LIII, 1919, part 2, p. 1.
—— *Alexander Hoards* in Numismatic Notes and Monographs. New York. (1) Introduction and Kyparissia Hoard, in no. 3, 1922. (2) Demanhur, in no. 19, 1923. (3) Andritsaena, in no. 21, 1923.
Rouvier, J. *L'ère d'Alexandre le Grand en Phénicie.* Rev. E.G. 1899, p. 362.
—— *Numismatique des villes de la Phénicie.* (See Bibliography to chapter 1.)
—— *Nouvelles recherches sur l'ère d'Alexandre le Grand.* Rev. N. 1909, p. 321.

(*b*) *Satrapal and other coins.*

Hill, G. F. *Catalogue of the Greek coins in the British Museum: Arabia, Mesopotamia, Persia.* 1922.
Howorth, Sir H. *Some coins attributed to Babylon by Dr Imhoof-Blumer.* Num. Chr. 1904, p. 1.
Imhoof-Blumer, F. *Die Münzstätte Babylon.* Num. Z. 1895, p. 1 and 1905, p. 1.
—— *The mint at Babylon: a rejoinder.* Num. Chr. 1906, p. 17.
Rapson, E. J. *Ancient silver coins from Baluchistan.* Num. Chr. 1904, p. 311. (Sophytes.)
Reinach, Th. *Trois royaumes de l'Asie Mineure.* 1888. (Ariarathes.)
Robinson, E. S. G. *A find of coins of Sinope.* Num. Chr. 1920, p. 1. (Ariarathes.)

(For Mazaeus see bibliography to chapter 1, and for the Andragoras and Vakshuvar coins bibliography to chapter xv.)

B. *Historical*

1. Histories and Biographies. (See also General Bibliography.)

Berve, H. *Das Alexanderreich auf prosopographischer Grundlage.* Munich, 1926. (Appeared after these chapters were in type.)
Bevan, E. R. Art. *Alexander* in E. Brit. 1910.
Birt, Th. *Alexander der Grosse und das Weltgriechentum.* Leipzig, 1924.
Droysen, J. G. *Geschichte des Hellenismus.* Vol. 1. Ed. 2. Gotha, 1877. French translation under the direction of A. Bouché-Leclercq, revised by Droysen, sub tit. *Histoire de l'Hellénisme.* Vol. 1. Paris, 1883. Latest German reprint sub tit. *Geschichte Alexanders des Grossen,* with Droysen's latest notes and introduction by A. Rosenberg. Berlin, 1917.
Freeman, E. A. *Alexander the Great: Historical Essays.* Vol. II. p. 161. 1873.
Hogarth, D. G. *Philip and Alexander of Macedon.* 1897.
Jäger, O. *Alexander der Grosse als Regent.* Preussische Jahrbücher LXX, 1892, p. 68.
Köpp, F. *Alexander der Grosse.* Bielefeld-Leipzig, 1899.
Otto, W. *Alexander der Grosse.* Marburg, 1916.
Reinach, A. J. and others. *L'hellénisation du monde antique.* 1914.
Sykes, Sir P. M. *A history of Persia.* Vol. 1. Ed. 2. 1921.
Wheeler, B. I. *Alexander the Great.* London and New York, 1900.
Wilamowitz-Moellendorff, U. von. *Alexander der Grosse.* (In Reden aus der Kriegszeit, v, xi.) Berlin, 1916.

2. Miscellaneous

Bauer, A. *Der Todestag Alexanders des Grossen.* Zeitschr. für die österr. Gymn. 1891, p. 1.
Bretzl, H. *Botanische Forschungen des Alexanderzugs.* Leipzig, 1903.
Budge, Sir E. A. W. *A history of Egypt.* Vol. VII. 1902. (Ammon.)
Cauer, F. *Philotas, Kleitos, Kallisthenes.* N.J.P. Supp. Band xx, 1893, p. 1.
Cook, A. B. *Zeus.* Vol. 1. Cambridge, 1914. (Ammon.)
Deonna, W. *Le nœud Gordien.* Rev. E.G. xxxi, 1918, pp. 39 and 141.
Ehrenberg, V. *Alexander und Ägypten.* Leipzig, 1926.

Gomperz, Th. *Anaxarch und Kallisthenes.* Commentationes phil. in honorem Th. Mommseni, p. 471. Berlin, 1877.

Hagen, B. von. *Isokrates und Alexander.* Phil. LXVII, 1908, p. 113.

Köhler, U. *Über das Verhältniss Alexanders des Grossen zu seinem Vater Philipp.* Berl. S.B. 1892, p. 497.

Lenschau, Th., in *Bursian,* 1904, p. 26, 1907, p. 135, and 1919, p. 188.

Pfister, F. *Eine jüdische Gründungsgeschichte Alexandrias.* Mit einem Anhang über Alexander's Besuch in Jerusalem. Heidelberg, 1914.

Radet, G. *Notes critiques sur l'histoire d'Alexandre.* Bordeaux-Paris, 1925.

Schubert, R. *Der Tod des Kleitos.* Rh. Mus. LIII, 1898, p. 98.

Spak, J. *Der Bericht des Josephus über Alexander den Grossen.* Königsberg, 1911.

Strack, M. L. Review of Kaerst in *G.G.A.* 1903, p. 856.

Tarn, W. W. *Heracles son of Barsine.* J.H.S. XLI, 1921, p. 18.

—— *The massacre of the Branchidae.* C.R. XXXVI, 1922, p. 63.

Willrich, H. *Wer liess König Philipp von Makedonien ermorden?* Hermes XXXIV, 1899, p. 174.

C. *Military*

1. The Army and generally

Bauer, A. *Kriegsaltertümer* in Handbuch, IV, 1, ii², 1893, with very full bibliography of earlier works.

Beloch, K. J. Das Heer Alexanders, in vol. III, ii² of his *Griechische Geschichte,* 1923.

Delbrück, H. *Geschichte der Kriegskunst.* Vol. I. Ed. 3. Berlin, 1920.

v. Domaszewski, A. *Die Phalangen Alexanders und Caesar's Legionen.* Heidelberger S.B. 1925–6, Abh. 1. (Appeared after these chapters were in type.)

Hoffmann, O. *Die Makedonen, ihre Sprache und ihr Volkstum.* Göttingen, 1906.

Hogarth, D. G. *The army of Alexander.* J.P. XVII, 1888, p. 1.

Schneider, R. *Griechische Poliorketiker.* III. Göttingen Abh. XII, no. 5. Berlin, 1912. (Diades' machines.)

Wartenburg, Graf Yorck von. *Kurze Übersicht der Feldzüge Alexanders des Grossen.* Berlin, 1897.

Articles in *P.W. s.v.* ἑταῖροι (G. Plaumann); Reiterei and Sarisse (E. Lammert); Schlachtordnung (Makedonen) and Kriegskunst (E. and F. Lammert).

2. The Battles

Bauer, A. *Der Brief Alexanders des Grossen über die Schlacht gegen Porus.* Festgaben für Max Büdinger, p. 71. Innsbruck, 1898.

—— *Die Schlacht bei Issos.* Jahreshefte II, 1899, p. 105.

Dieulafoy, M. *La bataille d'Issus.* Mém. Ac. Inscr. 1914, p. 41.

Dittberner, W. O. C. *Issos.* Berlin, 1908.

Gruhn, A. *Das Schlachtfeld von Issos.* Jena, 1905.

Hackmann, F. *Die Schlacht bei Gaugamela.* Halle, 1902.

Janke, A. *Auf Alexanders des Grossen Pfaden.* Diss. Berlin, 1904.

—— *Die Schlacht bei Issos.* Klio, X, 1910, p. 137.

Judeich, W. *Die Schlacht am Granikos.* Klio, VIII, 1908, p. 372.

Kaerst, J. *Zum Briefwechsel Alexanders des Grossen.* Phil. LVI, 1897, p. 406 (deals with the battle with Porus).

Keil, J. *Der Kampf um den Granikosübergang und das strategische Problem der Issosschlacht.* Mitt. d. Vereins klass. Phil. in Wien, I, 1924, p. 13.

Lammert, E. Review of Gruhn, *B.P.W.* 1905, col. 1596 and 1906, col. 254.

Lehmann, K. *Die Schlacht am Granikos.* Klio, XI, 1911, p. 230.
Schier, T. *Zur Lage des Schlachtfeldes von Issos und des Pinarus.* Wien St. XXXI, 1909, p. 153.
Schubert, R. *Die Porus-Schlacht.* Rh. Mus. LVI, 1901, p. 543.
Veith, G. *Der Kavalleriekampf in der Schlacht am Hydaspes.* Klio, VIII, 1908, p. 131.

D. *Topography and Routes* (except India)

1. Europe (the Danube Campaign)

Bovis, R. de. *Alexandre le Grand sur le Danube.* Reims, 1908.
Jacobs, W. O. *Militärisch-philologische Untersuchungen zum Feldzug Alexanders gegen die Triballer.* Münster, 1920.
Vulič, N. *Alexander's Zug gegen die Triballer.* Klio, IX, 1909, p. 490.
—— *Alexandre-le-Grand sur le Danube.* Ξένια, Hommage International à l'Université Nationale de Grèce, p. 181. Athens, 1912.

2. Asia (with Egypt)

(*a*) *Current ideas of the geography of Asia and Africa.*
Bolchert, P. *Aristoteles' Erdkunde von Asien und Libyen.* Berlin, 1904.
Endres, H. *Geographischer Horizont und Politik bei Alexander den Grossen.* Würzburg, 1924.
Ruge, W. Review of Bolchert, *N.J. Kl. Alt.* XXV, 1910, p. 380.
See also (*b*) below.

(*b*) *The supposed exploration of the Nile.*
Bolchert, P. *Liber Aristotelis de inundacione Nili.* N.J. Kl. Alt. XXVII, 1911, p. 150.
Capelle, W. *Die Nilschwelle.* Ib. XXXIII, 1914, pp. 317, 347.
Corssen, P. *Das angebliche Werk des Olynthiers Callisthenes über Alexander den Grossen.* Phil. LXXIV, 1917, p. 1.
Partsch, J. *Das Aristoteles Buch 'Über das Steigen des Nil.'* Leipzig. Abh. XXVII, 1909, p. 551.

(*c*) *The itinerary.*
Bunbury, Sir E. H. *A history of ancient geography.* Ed. 2. 1883.
Herzfeld, E. *Pasargadae.* Klio, VIII, 1908, p. 1.
Holdich, Sir H. T. *Notes on the antiquities, history, and ethnography of Las Bela and Makran.* Gov. of India publication, 1894.
—— *The gates of India.* 1910. (Gedrosia and Nearchus; good maps.)
Marquart, J. *Untersuchungen zur Geschichte von Eran II*; § 2, Alexander's Marsch von Persepolis nach Herāt. Phil. Supp.-Band X, 1907, p. 1.
Reuss, F. *Baktra und Zariaspa.* Rh. Mus. LXII, 1907, p. 591.
v. Schwartz, F. *Alexanders des Grossen Feldzug in Turkestan.* Ed. 2. Stuttgart, 1906.
Stahl, A. F. von. *Notes on the march of Alexander the Great from Ecbatana to Hyrcania.* Journ. Geog. Soc. LXIV, 1924, p. 312.
Sykes, Sir P. M. *Ten thousand miles in Persia.* 1902. (Good map.)
Tomaschek, W. *Zur historischen Topographie von Persien.* Wien S.B. CII, 1883, p. 145.
—— *Topographische Erläuterung der Küstenfahrt Nearchs vom Indus bis zum Euphrat.* Wien S.B. CXXI, 1890, Abh. VIII.

E. *India*

1. Conditions before Alexander

Barnett, L. D. *An Aramaic inscription from Taxila.* J.R.A.S. 1915, p. 340.

Cambridge History of India. Vol. 1, chap. XIV, by A. V. Williams Jackson (with bibliography). Cambridge, 1922.

Cowley, A. *The first Aramaic inscription from India.* J.R.A.S. 1915, p. 342.

Decourdemanche, J. A. *Notes sur les anciennes monnaies de l'Inde dites 'punch-marked.'* Journal Asiatique, 1912, p. 117.

Kennedy, J. *The early commerce of Babylon with India, 700–300 B.C.* J.R.A.S. 1898, p. 241.

Milne, J. G. *A hoard of Persian sigloi.* Num. Chr. 1906, p. 1.

Rapson, E. J. *Indian coins.* G. Bühler's Grundriss der Indo-Arische Philologie und Altertumskunde, Band 2, Heft 3. Strassburg, 1897.

Rawlinson, H. G. *Intercourse of India and the western world.* Cambridge, 1916.

2. Alexander's expedition: general

Anspach, A. E. *De Alexandri Magni expeditione Indica.* Leipzig, 1903.

Cambridge History of India. Vol. 1, chaps. XV–XVI, by E. R. Bevan (with bibliography). Cambridge, 1922.

Cunningham, General A. *The ancient geography of India.* 1871.

McCrindle, J. *Ancient India, its invasion by Alexander the Great.* Ed. 2. Westminster, 1896.

Rapson, E. J. *Ancient India.* Cambridge, 1914.

Smith, V. A. *Early History of India.* Oxford. 2nd ed. 1908; 3rd, 1914. (The third edition omits certain discussions.)

3. Alexander's expedition: special studies

Foucher, A. *Notes sur la géographie ancienne du Gandhāra.* Hanoi, 1902. Translation by H. Hargreaves, *Notes on the Ancient Geography of Gandhāra.* Gov. of India publication, 1915. (Good map.)

Haig, General M. R. *The Indus Delta Country.* 1894.

Holdich, Sir T. H. *Report of the Proceedings of the Pamir Boundary Commission: Historical Notes.* 1896.

—— *The Indian Borderland.* 1901.

—— *The Gates of India.* 1910. (Good maps.)

Marshall, Sir J. *Archaeological Survey of India, Annual Reports from 1912–13 onwards.* (Excavation of Taxila.)

—— *A guide to Taxila.* Calcutta, 1918.

Raverty, Major H. G. *The Mihrān of Sind and its tributaries.* Journ. Asiatic Soc. Bengal, 1892, part 1, p. 155.

Sivewright, R. *Cutch and the Ran.* Journ. Geog. Soc. XXIX, 1907, p. 518.

Smith, V. A. *The position of the autonomous tribes of the Punjab conquered by Alexander the Great.* J.R.A.S. 1903, p. 685.

Stein, Sir M. A. *Report of archaeological survey work in the N.W. frontier provinces and Baluchistan for the year Jan. 2, 1904–Mar. 31, 1905.* Gov. of India publication, 1905. (Ascent of Mahaban.)

—— *Serindia.* Vol. 1, chap. 1. Oxford, 1921.

—— *Alexander the Great.* The Times, Oct. 25 and 26, 1926. (Aornos.)

Tarn, W. W. *Alexander and the Ganges.* J.H.S. XLIII, 1923, p. 93.

F. *Policy and Administration*

1. The Greek cities

Dareste, R. and others. *Recueil des Inscriptions juridiques grecques*, II, 1898–, no. 35. (Recall of the exiles.)

Kasten, H. *Das Amnestiegesetz der Tegeaten vom Jahre* 324. Hamburg, 1922.

Köhler, U. *Die Eroberung Asiens durch Alexander den Grossen und der korinthische Bund.* Berl. S.B. 1898, p. 120.

Plassart, A. *Règlement Tégéate concernant le retour des bannis à Tégée en* 324 B.C. B.C.H. XXXVIII, 1914, p. 101.

Wilcken, U. *Beiträge zur Geschichte des korinthischen Bundes.* Bay. S.B. 1917, Abh. 10.

Wilhelm, A. *Attische Urkunden*, 1. Vienna, 1911.

2. Asia (including the land system) and Egypt

Baumbach, A. *Kleinasien unter Alexander den Grossen.* Jena, 1911.

Buckler, W. H. and Robinson, D. M. *Greek Inscriptions from Sardis.* A.J.A. XVI, 1912, p. 11.

Droysen, J. G. *Die Städtegründungen Alexanders und seiner Nachfolger.* (Geschichte des Hellenismus, III. Ed. 2. Beilage 1.)

—— *Beiträge zu der Frage über die innere Gestaltung des Reiches Alexanders des Grossen,* reprinted in Kleine Schriften, II, p. 232. Leipzig, 1894.

Groningen, B. A. van. *De Cleomene Naucratita.* Mnemosyne, LIII, 1925, p. 101.

Haussoullier, B. *Études sur l'histoire de Milet et du Didymeion.* 1902.

—— *Une loi grecque inédite sur les successions ' ab intestato.'* Rev. hist. du droit français et étranger, 1923, p. 515. (Doura-Europos.)

Julien, P. *Zur Verwaltung der Satrapien unter Alexander den Grossen.* Weida i. T. 1914.

Köhler, A. *Reichsverwaltung und Politik Alexanders des Grossen.* Klio, V, 1905, p. 303.

Lehmann-Haupt, C. F. Art. *Satrap* in P.W.

Lenschau, Th. *De rebus Prienensium.* Leipziger Studien, XII, 1890, p. 111.

Meyer, E. *Blüte und Niedergang des Hellenismus in Asien.* Berlin, 1925.

Rostowzew, M. *Studien zur Geschichte des römischen Kolonates.* Leipzig-Berlin, 1910.

Scholz, G. *Die militärischen und politischen Folgen der Schlacht am Granikos.* Klio, XV, 1917, p. 199.

Wilcken, U. *Alexander der Grosse und die hellenistische Wirtschaft.* Schmoller's Jahrbuch, XLV, 1921, p. 349.

List of the Alexandrias in *P.W.*, especially No. 13. (Charax-Mohammerah.)

G. *Deification and World Rule*

Berve, H. *Die angebliche Begründung des hellenistischen Königskultes durch Alexander.* Klio, XX, 1926, p. 179.

Beurlier, E. *De divinis honoribus quos acceperunt Alexander et successores ejus.* Paris, 1890.

Bevan, E. R. *The deification of kings in Greek cities.* Eng. Hist. Review, XVI, 1901, p. 625.

—— Art. *Deification,* in Enc. of Rel. and Ethics.

Endres, H. *Krateros, Perdikkas, und die letzten Pläne Alexanders.* Rh. Mus. LXXII, 1917–18, p. 437.

Ferguson, W. S. *Legalised absolutism en route from Greece to Rome.* Amer. Hist. Rev. 1912, p. 29.
—— *Greek Imperialism.* London, Boston and New York, 1913.
Hogarth, D. G. *The deification of Alexander the Great.* Eng. Hist. Review, II, 1887, p. 317.
—— *Alexander in Egypt and some consequences.* J.E.A. II, 1915, p. 53.
Kaerst, J. *Alexander der Grosse und der Hellenismus.* H.Z. LXXIV, 1895, pp. 1 and 193.
—— *Studien zur Entwicklung und theoretischen Begründung der Monarchie in Altertum.* Historische Bibliothek, VI, p. 1. Munich-Leipzig, 1898.
—— *Die antike Idee der Oikumene in ihrer politischen und kulturellen Bedeutung.* Leipzig, 1903.
Kampers, J. *Alexander der Grosse und die Idee des Weltimperiums in Prophetie und Sage.* Freiburg i. B. 1901.
Kolbe, W. *Das Weltreich Alexanders des Grossen.* Rostock, 1916.
Kornemann, E. *Zur Geschichte der antiken Herrscherkulte.* Klio, I, 1901, p. 51.
—— *Die letzten Ziele der Politik Alexanders des Grossen.* Klio, XVI, 1920, p. 209.
Maspero, Sir G. *Comment Alexandre devint dieu en Égypte.* 1897: republished in *Études de mythologie et d'archéologie égyptiennes,* VI, p. 263. 1912.
Meyer, E. *Alexander der Grosse und die absolute Monarchie.* Kleine Schriften, I, p. 283. Halle, 1910.
Niese, B. *Zur Würdigung Alexanders des Grossen.* H.Z. LXXIX, 1897, p. 1.
Radet, G. *La déification d'Alexandre.* Revue des Universités du Midi, 1895, p. 129.
Schnabel, P. *Die Begründung des hellenistischen Königskultes durch Alexander.* Klio, XIX, 1923–4, p. 113.
—— *Zur Frage der Selbstvergötterung.* Klio, XX, 1926, p. 398.
Tarn, W. W. *Alexander's ὑπομνήματα and the 'World-kingdom.'* J.H.S. XLI, 1921, p. 1.
Wilcken, U. *Über Werden und Vergehen der Universalreiche.* Bonn, 1915.

H. *Art and Portraiture*

Bagnani, G. *Hellenistic sculpture from Cyrene.* J.H.S. XLI, 1921, p. 232.
Bernouilli, J. J. *Die erhaltenen Darstellungen Alexanders des Grossen.* Munich, 1905.
Bieber, M. *Ein idealisiertes Porträt Alexanders des Grossen.* J.A.I. XL, 1925, p. 167.
Blum, G. *Contribution à l'imagerie d'Alexandre.* Rev. Arch. 1911, 2, p. 290.
Bruckmann, F. and Arndt, P. *Griechische und römische Porträts.* Lieferungen 19, 48, 49, 58. Munich, 1891–. (In progress.)
Furtwängler, A. *Ancient sculptures at Chatsworth House.* J.H.S. XXI, 1901, p. 209.
Ghislanzone, E. *Statua colossale di Alessandro il Grande.* Notiziario archeologico del Ministero della Colonie II, fasc. 1, 2, p. 105. Rome, 1916.
Hamdy Bey, O. and Reinach, Th. *Une nécropole royale à Sidon.* 1892. (The Alexander-Sarcophagus.)
Hekler, A. *Greek and Roman portraits.* 1912.
Köpp, F. *Über das Bildniss Alexanders des Grossen.* Zweiundfünfzigstes Program zum Winckelmannsfeste d. arch. Gesell. z. Berlin. 1892.
Michon, E. *L'Hermès d'Alexandre dit Hermès Azara.* Rev. Arch. 1906, 1, p. 79.
Perdrizet, P. *Venatio Alexandri.* J.H.S. XIX, 1899, p. 273.
—— *Un type inédit de la plastique grecque: Alexandre à l'égide.* Monuments Piot, XXI, 1913, p. 59.
Pomtow, H. *Delphica III: Die Krateroshalle (Alexanderjagd).* B.P.W. 1912, col. 1010.

Poulsen, Fr. *Greek and Roman portraits in English country houses*. Oxford, 1923.

Reinach, S. *Deux nouvelles images d'Alexandre*. Rev. Arch. 1906, 2, p. 1.

Schreiber, Th. *Ueber neue Alexandrinische Alexanderbildnisse*. Strena Helbigiana, p. 277. Leipzig, 1900.

—— *Studien über das Bildniss Alexanders des Grossen*. Leipzig, 1903.

Six, J. *Ikonographische Studien*. Röm. Mitt. xiv, 1899, p 83; xviii, 1903, p. 207.

Thiersch, H. *Lysipp's Alexander mit der Lanze*. J.D.A.I. xxiii, 1909, p. 162.

Ujfalvy, K. J. *Le type physique d'Alexandre le Grand*. 1902.

A new statue of Alexander Aegis in the British Museum. J.H.S. xliii, 1923, xvii.

CHAPTER XIV

GREECE: 335 TO 321 B.C.

I. *Sources*

1. Contemporary

(*a*) *Inscriptions.*

Ditt.[3] 275–310, 317, 326, 327, 329, 341, 346. *O.G.I.S.* 2. *I.G.*[2] II, 328–377, 407, 408, 435, 448, 457, 467, 493, 505, 554, 1156, 1191 (decrees), together with accounts and dedications given for these years in *I.G.* II, 2 and 3 with supplements in *I.G.* II, 5. *S.E.G.* I, 211. Michel, *Recueil*, under the various states.

To these may be added: Ἐφημερὶς Ἀρχαιολογική, 1918, p. 73, no. 95. Ἀρχαιολογικὸν Δελτίον, I, 1915, p. 195. Ferri, S., *Alcune Iscrizioni di Cirene*, No. 3; Berlin, 1926.

(*b*) *Orators.*

Demosthenes, XVIII, XXXIV, LVI.

[Demosthenes], XVII.

Aeschines, *in Ctesiphontem.*

Lycurgus, *in Leocratem*; a fragment of the speech *in Menesaechmum* (Berlin Pap. 11748, in Gött. Nach. 1922, p. 45, no. VIII).

Deinarchus, *in Demosthenem, in Aristogeitonem, in Philoclem.*

Hypereides, *in Demosthenem, Epitaphios.*

(*c*) *Other writers.*

Aristotle, *Constitution of Athens.*

Diyllus, *F.H.G.* II, p. 361, Theopompus, *ib.* I, p. 325, Dicaearchus, *ib.* II, p. 266 *sq.*

Fragment of the Satyr-play *Agen* (Nauck, *Tragicorum Graecorum fragmenta*, ed. 2, Leipzig, 1889, p. 810).

2. Secondary writers

Arrian, *Anabasis*, and τὰ μετ' Ἀλέξανδρον.

Diodorus, XVII–XVIII.

Justin, XII–XIII, with Trogus' *Prologues.*

Plutarch, *Demosthenes* and *Phocion.*

—— *Moralia*, 187 F–189 A, 235 B 54, 472 E, 525 C.

[Plutarch], *Vitae X Oratorum.*

Cornelius Nepos, *Phocion.*

Dionysius of Halicarnassus, *de Dinarcho.*

Diogenes Laertius, *Lives of Aristotle, Xenocrates and Theophrastus.*

Polyaenus, IV, 4.

Polybius, IX, 29. 1–4; XVIII, 14.

Pausanias, I, xxxvii, 5; II, xxxiii, 4–5.

Aelian, *V.H.* II, 19; V, 12.

Fragments of Duris (*F.H.G.* II, pp. 471 *sq.*, 474), Philochorus (*ib.* I, p. 407), Demochares (*ib.* II, p. 448 *sq.*), Craterus (*ib.* II, p. 622), Hermippus (*ib.* III, p. 50), Phylarchus (*ib.* I, p. 354), Poseidonius (*ib.* III, p. 259).

Scattered references in Plutarch's *Lives of Alexander, Agis* and *Camillus*, Suidas.

The late Lives of Demosthenes by Photius, Zosimus, Libanius, Suidas, Tzetzes, and an anonymous writer, are of little value.

II. *Modern Literature*

A. Sources: the Orators

For the historians see bibliography to chapters XII–XIII

Blass, F. *Die attische Beredsamkeit*, vol. III, i, Ed. 2 (Demosthenes), and III, ii, Ed. 2 (Demosthenes' Genossen und Gegner). Leipzig, 1893 and 1898.

Drerup, E. *Demosthenes im Urteile des Altertums*. Studien zur Geschichte und Kultur des Altertums. Vol. XII. Würzburg, 1923.

Emminger, K. *Bericht über die Literatur zu den attischen Rednern*: part 3 (1886–1912), Lycurgus, Hypereides, Aeschines, Deinarchus; part 4 (1887–1914), Demosthenes. In Bursian, vols. CLXI (1913) and CLXVI (1914).

Poulsen, F. *Un portrait de l'orateur Hypéride*. Monuments Piot, XXI, 1913, p. 47.

—— *Ikonographische Miscellen*. Copenhagen, 1921. (Hypereides.)

Radermacher, L. *Dinarchus*. Phil. LVIII, 1899, p. 161.

Schiller, S. *Über den Verfasser der Rede περὶ τῶν πρὸς Ἀλέξανδρον συνθηκῶν*. Wien. St. XIX, 1897, p. 211.

Thalheim, Th. Art. in P.W.; *Demades, Deinarchos, Demosthenes* (with bibliography of the speeches), *Hypereides*.

Wilamowitz-Moellendorff, U. von. *Lesefrüchte*. Hermes, LVIII, 1903, p. 61 (Hypereides.)

B. Historical (see also the General Bibliography)

1. *General.*

Beloch, K. J. *Die attische Politik seit Perikles*. Leipzig, 1884.

Drerup, E. *Aus einer Advokatenrepublik*. (Demosthenes und seine Zeit.) Studien zur Geschichte und Kultur des Altertums, vol. VIII. Paderborn, 1916.

Dürrbach, F. *L'Orateur Lycurgue*. 1889.

Ferguson, W. S. *Hellenistic Athens*. 1911.

Pickard-Cambridge, A. W. *Demosthenes*. London and New York, 1914.

Schäfer, A. *Demosthenes und seine Zeit*. Vol. III. Ed. 2. Leipzig, 1887.

2. *Special.*

Adams, C. D. *The Harpalos case*. Trans. of the American Phil. Ass. XXXII, 1901, p. 121.

Bauer, K. J. *Demosthenes und der harpalische Prozess*. Freiburg i. B. 1900.

Cloché, P. *Les naopes de Delphes et la politique hellénique de 356 à 327 av. J.C.* B.C.H. XL, 1916, p. 78.

Francotte, H. *Le pain à bon marché et le pain gratuit dans les cités grecques*. Mélanges Nicole, p. 135. Geneva, 1905.

Gernet, L. *L'approvisionnement d'Athènes en blé au Ve et IVe siècles*. Mélanges d'histoire ancienne: Bibliothèque de la Faculté des Lettres à Paris, vol. XXV, 1909.

Jardé, A. *Les céréales dans l'antiquité grecque*. 1925.

Johnson, A. C. *A new inscription from the Acropolis at Athens*. A.J.A. XVII, 1913, p. 506.

Kirchner, J. *Prosopographia Attica*. (3263 Demades, 3597 Demosthenes, 9142 Leosthenes, 9251 Lycurgus, 13912 Hypereides.) Berlin, 1901 and 1903.

Köhler, U. *Attische Psephismen aus den Jahren der Teuerung*. Ath. Mitt. VIII, 1883, p. 211.

Körte, A. *Der harpalische Prozess*. N.J. Kl. Alt. XXVII, 1924, p. 217.

Schubert, R. *Die Quellen zur Geschichte der Diadochenzeit.* Leipzig, 1914.
(Lamian war.)

Walek, T. *Les opérations navales pendant la guerre lamiaque.* Rev. Phil. XLVIII,
1924, p. 23.

For the recall of the exiles see bibliography to chapters XII–XIII.

C. Athens: constitution and organization

Boeckh, A. *Seeurkunden über das Seewesen des attischen Staates.* Berlin, 1840.
(Vol. III of the Staatshaushaltung, 1st ed.; never re-edited.)

Brandis. Art. διοίκησις in P.W.

Brenot, A. *Recherches sur l'éphébie attique et en particulier sur la date de l'institution.*
1920.

Caillemer, E. Art. *Dermatikon* in D.S.

Dröge, C. *De Lycurgo Atheniensi pecuniarum publicarum administratore.* Minden,
1890.

Francotte, H. *Les finances des cités grecques.* 1909.

Frickenhaus, A. *Athens Mauern im IV Jahrhundert v. Chr.* Bonn, 1905.

Glotz, G. *La date des comptes relatifs au portique d'Eleusis.* Rev. E.G. XXXI, 1918,
p. 207.

Johnson, A. C. *Studies in the financial administration of Athens.* A.J. Ph. XXXVI,
1915, p. 424.

Kolbe, W. *Zur athenischen Marineverwaltung.* Ath. Mitt. XXVI, 1901, p. 377.

Lofberg, J. O. *The date of the Athenian 'Ephebeia.'* C.P. XX, 1925, p. 330.

Noack, F. *Die Mauern Athens.* Ath. Mitt. XXXII, 1907, pp. 123 and 474.

Panske, P. *De magistratibus atticis qui saeculo quarto pecunias publicas curabant.*
Leipzig, 1890.

Sundwall, J. *Epigraphische Beiträge zur sozial-politische Geschichte Athens im
Zeitalter des Demosthenes.* Leipzig, 1906.

Wilamowitz-Moellendorff, U. von. *Aristoteles und Athen.* Vol. I. Berlin, 1893.

CHAPTER XV

THE HERITAGE OF ALEXANDER

I. Ancient Sources

1. *Contemporary*

(*a*) *Official.*

Rescripts of Philip III (*O.G.I.S.* 8, v). Polyperchon (Diodorus, xviii, 56). Antigonus (*O.G.I.S.* 5 and 8, vi, and Ditt.³ 344).

Greek inscriptions. Besides those in Ditt.³ 311–53, 361, 374, 409. *O.G.I.S.* 4–9. *I.G.*² ii, 378–402, 448–639, 657, 682, 1129, 1191, 1193, 1201, 1222, 1260 (decrees), together with accounts and dedications given for these years in *I.G.* ii, 2 and 3 with supplements to these in *I.G.* ii, 5, *I.G.* xi, iv, 566, 1036. *S.E.G.* i, 75 and 349–62. Michel's *Recueil* and *S.G.D.I.* under the various states, the following may be noted:

Blinkenberg, C. *Die lindische Tempelchronik.* Bonn, 1915.

Buckler, W. H. and Robinson, D. M. *Greek Inscriptions from Sardis.* A.J.A. xvi, 1912, p. 11. (On the date see H. C. Butler, *Sardis*, i, part i, p. 52, n. 2.)

Gardner, E. A. and others. *Excavations in Cyprus*, 1887–8. J.H.S. ix, 1889, p. 186 *sq.*

Keil, J. *Ephesische Bürgerrechts- und Proxenie-dekrete.* Jahreshefte, xvi, 1913, p. 231.

Pomtow, H. *Delphica* II and III. B.P.W. 1909, col. 286, 1912, col. 480.

Wiegand, Th. *Milet*, III. The Delphinion inscriptions, by A. Rehm. Berlin, 1914.

Oriental inscriptions. Cyprian-Phoenician in *C.I.S.* Vol. i, part i, Paris, 1881.

The satrap-stele of Ptolemy I and other Egyptian material in Sir E. A. W. Budge, *History of Egypt*, and A. Bouché-Leclercq, *Histoire des Lagides.*

(*b*) *Greek Historians, etc.*

Hieronymus (*F.H.G.* ii, pp. 452 *sqq.*), Diyllus (*ib.* ii, p. 361), Demetrius of Phalerum (*ib.* ii, pp. 361 *sqq.*), Duris (*ib.* ii, pp. 471, 475 *sq.*), Demochares (*ib.* ii, pp. 448 *sq.*).

'Alexander's Testament' (in the Metz Epitome and Ps.-Callisthenes) does not belong to history.

(*c*) *Babylonian documents.*

A chronicle concerning the Diadochi, in S. Smith, *Babylonian Historical Texts*, 1924.

An astronomical table bearing on the Ipsus campaign (see above, p. 494, n. 2).

2. *Secondary*

Diodorus, xviii–xx.

Arrian, extracts from τὰ μετ' Ἀλέξανδρον. (The Photius extracts are given by C. Müller in Dübner's Arrian, Paris, 1846, the extracts from the Vatican palimpsest by R. Reitzenstein, *Breslauer Phil. Abh.* iii, part iii, 1888, the lexicographical fragments by U. Köhler in *Berl. S.B.* 1890, p. 557, and by A. G. Roos, *Studia Arrianea*, Leipzig, 1912. The whole will be collected in Roos' edition of Arrian.)

Plutarch, *Eumenes, Demetrius* and *Phocion. Moralia*, 182 a–183 b.

Justin, xiii–xv, with Trogus, *Prologues.*

Q. Curtius Rufus, x, 6–end.

Appian, *Syriaca*, 53–8.

Strabo, VII, 330, nos. 21, 24, 25; IX, 398; XI, 533; XIII, 597; XVI, 794.

Aelian, *V.H.* XII, 49, 64.

Pausanias, I, vi, 2–8; ix, 5–8; xvi, 1; xxv, 3–6; iv, xxvii, 10; v, xxiii, 3; ix, vii, 1–4.

Polyaenus, IV, 6, 7, 8, 9, 11, 12, 14, 19.

Cornelius Nepos, *Eumenes, Phocion.*

Suidas, s.v. Δημήτριος, ᾽Αντίπατρος and other scattered references.

Heidelberg Epitome. Ed. G. Bauer. Leipzig, 1912.

A papyrus fragment on the siege of Rhodes. *Berl. S.B.* 1918, p. 752.

Fragments of Memnon (Nymphis), *F.H.G.* III, pp. 529 *sq.* Philochorus, *ib.* I, pp. 408 *sq.* Craterus, *ib.* II, p. 622. Agatharchides, *ib.* III, p. 196. Dexippus, *ib.* III, pp. 667 *sqq.* Nicolaus Dam. *ib.* III, p. 414. Ctesicles, *ib.* IV, p. 375. Carystius, *ib.* IV, p. 358. Hegesander, *ib.* IV, p. 419. Heracleides Lembos, *ib.* III, p. 169. Hermippus, *ib.* III, p. 47. Phylarchus, *ib.* I, p. 341.

Scattered allusions, etc. in Lycophron's *Alexandra*, Ps.-Hecataeus, Josephus, Frontinus, and the lexicographers.

Chronographers: Marmor Parium, ed. Jacoby. Apollodorus, ed. Jacoby. The Canon of Reigns. Porphyrius, Eusebius, Jerome, Syncellus.

The Demades Papyrus (*Berlin. Klass. Text,* VII, p. 13) does not belong to history.

3. *Coins* (see generally B. V. Head, *H.N.*)

(*a*) Antigonus and Cassander

Newell, E. T. *Tyrus Rediviva.* New York, 1923.

Oikonomos, G. P. Νομίσματα τοῦ βασιλέως Κασσάνδρου: τὸ χαλκοῦν κόμμα. ᾽Αρχαιολογικὸν Δελτίον, IV, 1918, p. 1.

Seltman, C. T. *A synopsis of the coins of Antigonus I and Demetrius Poliorcetes.* Num. Chr. 1909, p. 264.

Six, J. P. *Antigone, roi de Babylone.* Num. Chr. 1898, p. 219.

Lysimachus' coinage belongs to the next period.

(*b*) Dynasts and Satraps

De la Fuye, A. *Monnaies incertaines de la Sogdiane.* Rev. N. 1910, p. 281. (The Vakshuvar coins.)

Hill, G. F. *Catalogue of the Greek coins in the British Museum*: Cyprus, 1904, and Arabia, Mesopotamia, Persia, 1922.

—— *Andragora.* Atti e memorie dell' Inst. Italiano di num. III, 2, 1919, p. 23.

Newell, E. T. *Some Cypriote Alexanders.* Num. Chr. 1905, p. 294.

—— *Nicocles king of Paphos. Ib.* 1919, p. 64.

Robinson, E. S. G. *Quaestiones Cyrenaicae* II. Num. Chr. 1915, pp. 137, 168. (Ophellas.)

—— *Aspeisas, satrap of Susiana. Ib.* 1921, p. 37.

II. MODERN LITERATURE

A. *On the Sources*

Ausfeld, A. *Das angebliche Testament Alexanders des Grossen.* Rh. Mus. LVI, 1901, p. 57.

Bauer, G. *Die Heidelberger Epitome.* Leipzig, 1912.

Bury, J. B. *Ancient Greek Historians.* 1909.

Grimmig, F. *Arrian's Diadochengeschichte.* Halle, 1914.

Jacoby, F. Art. *Hieronymus* in P.W.

Nietzold, W. *Die Ueberlieferung der Diadochengeschichte bis zur Schlacht von Ipsos.* Dresden, 1905. (Gives full bibliography.)

Reuss, F. *Hieronymus von Kardia*. Berlin, 1876.
Rohde, A. *De Diyllo Atheniensi Diodori auctore*. Weimar, 1909.
Schubert, R. *Die Quellen zur Geschichte der Diadochenzeit*. Leipzig, 1914.

B. *Historical*

1. General or Comprehensive works

Besides the works cited in the General Bibliography, see also:
Ferguson, W. S. *Hellenistic Athens*. 1911.
—— *Greek Imperialism*. London, Boston, and New York, 1913.
Lenschau, Th. *Jahresbericht über griechische Geschichte*. Bursian for 1907 (years 1903–6) and 1919 (years 1907–14).
Mahaffy, J. P. *Greek life and thought from the death of Alexander to the Roman conquest*. Ed. 2. London, 1896.

2. Special subjects

(a) The Successors

Bevan, E. R. *The House of Seleucus*. Vol. I. 1902.
Bouché-Leclerq, A. *Histoire des Lagides*. Vols. I and IV. 1903–.
—— *Histoire des Séleucides*. 1913.
Budge, Sir E. A. W. *A history of Egypt*. Vols. VII–VIII. 1902.
Costanzi, V. *La pace fra Antigono e i dinasti coalizzati contro di lui nel* 311. Annali delle Università Toscane, XXXV, 1916, p. 1.
—— *L' eredità politica d'Alessandro Magno*. Pisa, 1918.
Denicolai, M. *La pace del* 311 *av. Cr.* Atti Acc. Torino, LII, 1916–17, p. 691.
Endres, H. *Krateros, Perdikkas, und die letzten Pläne Alexanders*. Rh. Mus. LXXII, 1917–18, p. 437.
Ghione, P. *Note sul regno di Lisimaco*. Atti Acc. Torino, XXXIX, 1903–4, p. 619.
Hünerwadel, W. *Forschungen zur Geschichte des Königs Lysimachos von Thrakien*. Zürich, 1900.
Köhler, U. *Ueber einige Fragmente zur Diadochengeschichte*. Berl. S.B. 1891, p. 207.
—— *Das Asiatische Reich des Antigonus*. Ib. 1898, p. 824.
—— *Korrespondenz zwischen Antigonos und der Stadtgemeinde der Skepsier*. Ib. 1903, p. 1057.
Kromayer, J. *Alexander der Grosse und die hellenische Entwicklung in dem Jahrhundert nach seinem Tode*. H.Z. c, 1908, p. 11.
Kugler, F. X. *Von Moses bis Paulus*. Münster i. W. 1922.
—— *Sternkunde und Sterndienst in Babel*. II, Teil II, Heft 2. Münster i. W. 1924.
Laqueur, R. *Zur Geschichte des Krateros*. Hermes, LIV, 1919, p. 205.
Munro, J. A. R. *A Letter from Antigonus to Scepsis*, 311 B.C. J.H.S. XIX, 1899, p. 330.
Oppert, J. *Une complainte des villes chaldéennes sur la suprématie de Babylon*. C.R. Ac. Inscr. 1901, pp. 822, 830.
Otto, W. in *Bay. S.B.* 7 Nov. 1925.
Possenti, G. B. *Il re Lisimaco di Tracia*. Turin, 1901.
Ramsay, Sir W. M. *Military Operations on the North Front of Mount Taurus*. IV. The campaigns of 319 and 320 B.C. J.H.S. XLIII, 1923, p. 1.
Schachermeyr, Fr. *Zu Geschichte und Staatsrecht der frühen Diadochenzeit*. Klio, XIX, 1925, p. 435.
Smith, S. *Babylonian Historical Texts*. 1924.
—— *The chronology of Philip Arrhidaeus, Antigonus, and Alexander IV*. Revue d'Assyriologie, XXII, 1925, p. 179.

Tarn, W. W. *Alexander's ὑπομνήματα and the 'World-kingdom.'* J.H.S. xli, 1921, p. 1.
—— *Heracles son of Barsine. Ib.* xli, 1921, p. 18.
—— *The proposed new date for Ipsus.* C.R. xl, 1926, p. 13.
Vezin, A. *Eumenes von Kardia.* Münster i. W. 1907.
Wilamowitz-Moellendorff, U. von. *Hellenistische Dichtung in der Zeit des Kallimachos,* 1. Berlin, 1924.

(*b*) *The burial of Alexander.*
Jacoby, F. *Die Beisetzungen Alexanders des Grossen.* Rh. Mus. lviii, 1903, p. 461.
Müller, C. F. *Der Leichenwagen Alexanders des Grossen.* Leipzig, 1905. (Discussed by Wilamowitz, J.D.A.I. 1905, p. 103; Petersen, N.J. Kl. Alt. 1905, p. 698; Bulle, J.D.A.I. 1906, p. 52; and Reuss, Rh. Mus. 1906, pp. 408 and 635.)
Rubensohn, O. *Das Grab Alexanders des Grossen in Memphis.* Bull. Soc. Arch. d'Alexandrie, 1910, p. 83.
Thiersch, H. *Die Alexandrinische Königsnekropole.* J.D.A.I. xxv, 1911, p. 55.

(*c*) *The revived League of Corinth.*
Cary, M. *A constitution of the United States of Greece.* C.Q. xvii, 1923, p. 137.
Kougeas, S. B. Τὸ Κοινὸν τῶν Ἑλλήνων κατ᾽ ἐπιγραφὴν Ἐπιδαύρου. Ἐφ. Ἀρχ. 1921, p. 1.
Larsen, J. A. O. *Representative Government in the Panhellenic Leagues.* C.P. xx, 1925, p. 313; xxi, 1926, p. 52.
Levi, M. A. *L' ordinamento d' una federazione ellenica* (303–2). Atti Acc. Torino, lix, 1924, p. 215.
Roussel, P. *Le renouvellement de la Ligue de Corinthe en 302.* Rev. Arch. xvii, 1923, p. 117.
Tarn, W. W. *The constitutive act of Demetrius' League of 303.* J.H.S. xlii, 1922, p. 198.
Wilcken, U. *Ueber eine Inschrift aus dem Asklepieion von Epidaurus.* Berl. S.B. 1922, p. 122.
Wilhelm, A. *Zu griechischen Inschriften und Papyri.* Anzeiger Ak., Wien, 1922, nos. xv–xviii.

(*d*) *The League of the Islanders.*
Delamarre, J. *Les deux premiers Ptolémées et la confédération des Cyclades.* Rev. Phil. xx, 1896, p. 103.
Dürrbach, F. *Décrets de la Confédération des Nésiotes.* B.C.H. xxviii, 1904, p. 93.
—— Ἀντιγόνεια-Δημητρίεια: *les origines de la confédération des Insulaires.* B.C.H. xxxi, 1907, p. 208.
Homolle, Th. *Les Archives de l'intendance sacrée à Délos.* 1887.
König, W. *Der Bund der Nesioten.* Halle, 1910.
Roussel, P. *La confédération des Nesiotes.* B.C.H. xxxv, 1911, p. 441.
Swoboda, H. *Der Nesioten-Bund,* in his *Staatsaltertümer.* Freiburg i. B. **1913**.
Tarn, W. W. *The political standing of Delos.* J.H.S. xliv, 1924, p. 1.

(*e*) *Athens.*
Bates, F. O. *The five post-Cleisthenean tribes.* Cornell Studies in Classical Philology, 8. New York, 1894.
Cloché, P. *Les dernières années de l'Athénien Phocion.* Rev. H. cxliv, 1923, p. 161 and cxlv, 1924, p. 1.
Cohen, D. *De Demetrio Phalereo.* Mnemosyne, liv, 1926, p. 88.

De Sanctis, G. *Contributi alla storia Ateniense della guerra Lamiaca alla guerra Cremonidea*. Studi di storia antica, 2. Rome, 1893. p. 1.

—— *I nomophylakes d'Atene*. Entaphia in memoria d'E. Pozzi. Turin, 1913. p. 1.

Ferguson, W. S. *The Laws of Demetrius of Phalerum and their Guardians*. Klio, XI, 1911, p. 265.

Francotte, H. *Les finances des cités grecques*. Liége and Paris, 1909.

Johnson, A. C. *Studies in the financial administration of Athens*. A.J. Ph. XXXVI, 1915, p. 424.

Kirchner, J. *Die Zusammensetzung der Phylen Antigonis und Demetrias*. Rh. Mus. XLVII, 1892, p. 550 and LIX, 1904, p. 294.

Sundwall, J. *De institutis reipublicae Atheniensium post Aristotelis aetatem commutatis*. Acta soc. scient. Fennicae, XXXIV, No. 4, 1907.

Wilhelm, A. *Bürgerrechtsverleihungen der Athener*. Ath. Mitt. XXXIX, 1914, p. 257.

—— *Beschlüsse der Athener aus dem Jahre des Archon Apollodoros 319–18 v. Chr.* Jahreshefte XI, 1908, p. 82.

(*f*) *Miscellaneous.*

Heberdey, R. Νικάνωρ Ἀριστοτέλους Σταγειρίτης. In Festschrift für Th. Gomperz. Vienna, 1902.

Klotzsch, C. *Epeirotische Geschichte bis zum Jahre 280 v. Chr.* Berlin, 1911.

Nilsson, M. P. *Studien zur Geschichte des alten Epeiros*. Lunds Universitets Årsskrift, N.F. Afd. 1, Bd. 6, nr. 4, 1909.

Spendel, A. *Zum Heerwesen der Diadochen*. Breslau, 1915.

CHAPTER XVI

GREEK POLITICAL THOUGHT AND THEORY IN THE FOURTH CENTURY

I. ANCIENT AUTHORITIES

Aristophanes. *Ecclesiazusae*. Latin introd. and notes by J. van Leeuwen. Leyden, 1905. English trans. and notes by B. B. Rogers. 1902.
—— *Plutus*. Latin introd. and notes by J. van Leeuwen. Leyden, 1904. English trans. and notes by B. B. Rogers. 1907.
Aristotle. *Politics*. Ed. by W. L. Newman. Oxford, 1887–1902. Trans. by B. Jowett in the Works of Aristotle translated into English. Oxford, 1921.
—— *Atheniensium Respublica*. Text by F. G. Kenyon. Oxford, 1920. Trans. by F. G. Kenyon in the Works of Aristotle translated into English. Oxford, 1920.
—— *Ethics*. Ed. by J. Burnet. London, 1900. Trans. by W. D. Ross in the Works of Aristotle translated into English. Oxford, 1925.
—— *Rhetoric*. Ed. by E. M. Cope, revised by J. E. Sandys. Cambridge, 1877. Trans. by R. C. Jebb, revised by J. E. Sandys. Cambridge, 1909.
—— *Oeconomica*. Trans. by E. S. Forster in the Works of Aristotle translated into English. Oxford, 1920.
—— *On Education*. Being extracts from the Ethics and Politics, translated and edited by J. Burnet. Cambridge, 1903.
Demosthenes. *Orationes*. Text by S. H. Butcher and W. Rennie. Oxford, 1903, etc.
—— *Public Orations*. Trans. by A. W. Pickard-Cambridge. Oxford, 1912.
[Herodes Atticus.] Περὶ Πολιτείας. Ed. by E. Drerup (Studien zur Geschichte und Kultur des Altertums, Bd. 2, Heft 1). Paderborn, 1908.
Isocrates. *De Antidosi, de Pace, Panathenaicus*, and *Panegyricus*. Text by F. Blass. Leipzig, 1889–98. See also R. C. Jebb, *The Attic Orators*, 1876–93.
Plato. *Republic*. Ed. by J. Adam. Cambridge, 1905, etc.
—— *Laws*. Ed. by E. B. England. Manchester, 1921. See also C. Ritter, *Platos Gesetze*. Leipzig, 1896.
—— *Politicus*. Text by J. Burnet. Oxford, 1905.
—— *Gorgias*. Text by J. Burnet. Oxford, 1903.
—— *Protagoras*. Ed. by J. and A. M. Adam. Cambridge, 1893.
—— *Dialogues*. Trans. by B. Jowett. Oxford, 1892.
Xenophon. *Cyropaedia*. Text and trans. by W. Miller (Loeb series). 1914.
—— *Hiero*. Ed. by H. A. Holden. 1888.
—— *Oeconomicus*. Ed. by H. A. Holden. 1895.
Complete text of Xenophon's works by E. C. Marchant, Oxford, 1900, etc.

II. MODERN WRITERS

Abbott, E. *Hellenica*. (Essays by A. C. Bradley and R. L. Nettleship.) Ed. 2. 1898.
v. Arnim, Hans. *Die politischen Theorien des Altertums*. Vienna, 1910.
—— *Zur Entstehungsgeschichte der aristotelischen Politik*. Leipzig. 1924.
Barker, E. *Greek Political Theory: Plato and his Predecessors*. 1918.
Burnet, J. *Greek Philosophy*. 1914.
Busolt, G. *Griechische Staatskunde*. Munich, 1920–26.
Gomperz, Th. *Greek Thinkers*. Translated by L. Magnus. 1901–2.
Henkel, H. *Studien zur Geschichte der griechischen Lehre vom Staat*. Leipzig, 1872.

Hildenbrand, K. *Geschichte und System der Rechts- und Staatsphilosophie.* I. Die Griechen. Leipzig, 1860.

Jaeger, W. *Aristoteles.* Berlin, 1923.

Natorp, P. *Plato's Staat und die Idee der Sozialpädagogik.* Berlin, 1895.

Nettleship, R. L. *Lectures on the Republic of Plato.* 1910.

Newman, W. L. Edition of Aristotle's *Politics,* vol. 1. Oxford, 1887.

Nohle, K. *Die Staatslehre Platos.* Jena, 1880.

Oncken, W. *Die Staatslehre des Aristoteles.* Leipzig, 1870, 1875.

Pöhlmann, R. von. *Geschichte des antiken Kommunismus und Sozialismus.* Munich, 1893. (Ed. 2, entitled Geschichte der Socialen Frage und des Sozialismus in der antiken Welt. Munich, 1912.)

Pohlenz, M. *Staatsgedanke und Staatslehre der Griechen.* Leipzig, 1923.

Ross, W. D. *Aristotle. London,* 1923.

Swoboda, H. Edition of Hermann's *Lehrbuch der Griechischen Antiquitäten,* 1, Abt. 3. Tübingen, 1913.

Taylor, A. E. *Plato, the man and his work.* 1926.

Vinogradoff, P. *Historical Jurisprudence.* Vol. 11 (The Jurisprudence of the Greek City). Oxford, 1922.

Wilamowitz-Moellendorff, U. von. *Staat und Gesellschaft der Griechen.* Berlin (Ed. 2), 1923.

—— *Platon.* Berlin, 1919.

—— *Aristoteles und Athen.* Berlin, 1893.

Zeller, E. *Outlines of the History of Greek Philosophy.* English trans. 1901.

Zimmern, A. E. *The Greek Commonwealth.* Ed. 4. Oxford, 1911.

CHAPTER XVII

GREEK ART AND ARCHITECTURE

A. ART. (Sections I–II)

Greek art, especially in the fourth century. N.B. The bibliography to these sections is supplementary to the bibliography to Vol. IV, chap. XVI and Vol. V, chap. XV.

Amelung, W. *Neue Beiträge zur Kenntnis des älteren Kephisodot.* Röm. Mitt. XXXVIII–XXXIX, 1923–4, p. 41.

—— *Saggio sull' Arte del IV Secolo av. Cristo.* Ausonia, III, 1908, p. 91.

—— *Die Basis des Praxiteles aus Mantinea.* Munich, 1895.

Ashmole, B. *Hygieia on Acropolis and Palatine* in B.S.R. x (1927).

Neugebauer, K. *Studien über Skopas.* Leipzig, 1913.

—— *Timotheos in Epidauros* in J.D.A.I. XLI, 1926, p. 82.

Dugas, Ch. and Berchmans, J. *Le sanctuaire d'Aléa Athéna à Tégée.* 1924.

Blinkenberg, Chr. *Den knidiske Afrodite.* Copenhagen, 1920.

Marshall, J. *Of a head of a youthful goddess, found in Chios.* J.D.A.I. XXIV, 1909, p. 73.

Bieber, M. *Die Söhne des Praxiteles* in J.D.A.I. XXXVIII–IX, 1923–4, p. 242.

Studniczka, F. *Artemis und Iphigenie.* Abh. der Sächs. Akademie, XXXVII, 1926.

Lippold, G. *Sarapis und Bryaxis.* Festschrift Paul Arndt. Munich, 1925.

Wolters, P. and Sieveking, J. *Der Amazonenfries des Maussoleums.* J.D.A.I. XXIV, 1909, p. 171. See also works of Neugebauer cited above.

Brueckner, A. *Form und Ornament der attischen Grabstelen.* Strassburg, 1886.

—— *Der Friedhof am Eridanos.* Berlin, 1909.

von Salis, A. *Das Grabmal des Aristonautes.* 84th Berlin Winckelmannsprogramm, 1926.

Arndt, P. and Lippold, G. *Griechische und römische Porträts.* Munich, 1908–.

Delbrück, R. *Antike Porträts.* Bonn, 1912.

Hekler, A. *Greek and Roman Portraits.* 1912.

Lippold, G. *Griechische Porträtstatuen.* Munich, 1912.

Hamdy Bey, O. and Reinach, Th. *Une nécropole royale à Sidon.* 1892. See also Winter, *Das Alexander-Mosaik*, pll. 2–3.

Ducati, P. *Saggio di studio sulla ceramica attica figurata del secolo IV av. Cr.* Rome, 1916.

Tillyard, E. M. W. *The Hope Vases.* Cambridge, 1923. (For Italiote vases.)

Winter. *Das Alexander-Mosaik aus Pompeji.* Strassburg, 1909.

B. ARCHITECTURE. (Sections III–VI)

1. *General*

See the lists in the bibliographies to vol. IV, chapter XVI, p. 656, and vol. V, chapter XV, pp. 526 *sqq.* For theatres the general works named in vol. V, p. 529 will provide detailed references.

2. *Doric.* (Sites in alphabetical order)

Delphi.
Temple of Apollo. See vol. IV, p. 657.
Tholos in sanctuary of Athena Pronaia.

Homolle, T. and others. *Les Fouilles de Delphes,* vol. II, fasc. 4. *Le Sanctuaire d'Athéna Pronaia*: Charbonneaux, J., *La Tholos,* 1925 (plates separate). The capital from Megara Hyblaea is illustrated in Durm, J., *Die Baukunst der Griechen.* Ed. 3, 1910, fig. 310.

Epidaurus (Tholos and temples of Asclepius and Artemis).
Defrasse, A. and Lechat, H. *Épidaure*. 1895.
Kavvadias, P. *Fouilles d'Épidaure*. I. Athens, 1893.
—— Τὸ ἱερὸν τοῦ Ἀσκληπιοῦ ἐν Ἐπιδαύρῳ. Athens, 1900.
—— In Πρ. 1905, p. 44 (Temple of Asclepius).
—— In Πρ. 1906, p. 91 (Temple of Artemis).
—— In *Berl. S.B.* 1909, p. 536 (Tholos).

Megalopolis (Thersilion).
Bather, A. G. In *J.H.S.* xiii, 1892–3, p. 328.
Benson, E. F. In *J.H.S.* xiii, 1892–3, p. 319.
Gardner, E. A. and others. *Excavations at Megalopolis*. 1892.

Nemea (Temple of Zeus).
Clemmensen, M. and Vallois, R. In *B.C.H.* xlix, 1925, p. 1.

Olympia (Leonidaeum and Metroum). See general references in vol. iv, p. 658, and vol. v, p. 528.

Pergamum (Temple of Athena Polias).
Bohn, R. and others. *Altertümer von Pergamon*. Vol. ii. Berlin, 1885.

Piraeus (Philon's Arsenal).
Choisy, A. *Études sur l'architecture grecque*. I. 1883.
Dörpfeld, W. In *Ath. Mitt.* viii, 1883, p. 147.
Fabricius, E. In *Hermes*, xvii, 1882, p. 551.
Marstrand, V. *Arsenalet i Piraeus*. Copenhagen, 1922.
The inscription is *I.G.* ii, 2, 1054; Dittenberger, *Sylloge³*, no. 969; Roberts, E. S. and Gardner, E. A., *Introduction to Greek Epigraphy*, ii, 1905, p. 360.

Tegea (Temple of Athena Alea).
Dugas, C. and others. *Le Sanctuaire d'Aléa Athéna à Tégée au IVᵉ siècle*. 1924.

3. *Ionic*

(*a*) General (especially Ephesus, Mausoleum, and Priene).
Lethaby, W. R. *Greek buildings represented by fragments in the British Museum*. 1908.
Smith, A. H. *Catalogue of Sculpture in the British Museum*. Vol. ii. 1900.

(*b*) Sites in alphabetical order.
Ephesus (Temple of Artemis). To references in vol. iv, p. 659, add
Picard, C. *Éphèse et Claros*. Bibl. des écoles franç. d'Athènes et de Rome, Fasc. 123, 1922.
Wood, J. T. *Discoveries at Ephesus*. 1877.

Halicarnassus (Mausoleum).
Krischen, F. In *Bonner Jahrbücher*, cxxviii, 1923, p. 1.
Krüger, E. In *Bonner Jahrbücher*, cxxvii, 1922, p. 84.
Newton, C. *A History of Discoveries at Halicarnassus, etc.* Text. 2 parts. 1862, 1863. Plates. 1862.

Lesbos.
Temple at Messa (pseudodipteral, 8 × 14: Koldewey, who dated it early fourth century, thought it combined frieze with dentils).
Koldewey, R. *Die antiken Baureste der Insel Lesbos*. Berlin, 1890.
Lattermann, H. *Griechische Bauinschriften*. Strassburg, 1908. p. 96.
For criticism of Koldewey's views, see
Krischen, F. In *Ath. Mitt.* xlviii, 1923, p. 89.
Schede, M. *Antikes Traufleisten-Ornament*. Strassburg, 1909. p. 73.

Miletus (Didymaeum).

Pontremoli, E. and Haussoullier, B. *Didymes.* 1904.

Rayet, O. and Thomas, A. *Milet et le golfe latmique.* 2 vols. and atlas. 1877.

Wiegand, T. *Siebenter vorläufiger Bericht* and *Achter vorläufiger Bericht.* Berl. Abh. v, 1911 and 1, 1924.

Olympia (Philippeum). See under Doric above.

Priene (Temple of Athena).

Wiegand, T. and Schrader, H. *Priene.* Berlin, 1904.
  On the frieze question, see
von Gerkan, A. In *Ath. Mitt.* XLIII, 1918, p. 165.

Wilberg, W. In *Ath. Mitt.* XXXIX, 1914, p. 72.

Sardes (Temple of Artemis).

Butler, H. C. *Sardis.* Vol. II, part 1. Leyden, 1925. Contains valuable discussion of evolution of Ionic capital.

4. *Corinthian*

See references under Delphi, Epidaurus, Olympia, and Tegea above, and under Bassae in vol. v, p. 527 *sqq.*; also

Athens (Monument of Lysikrates).

Philadelpheus, A. In Ἐφ. Ἀρχ. 1921, p. 83.

Smith, A. H. *Catalogue of Sculpture in the British Museum.* Vol. I. 1892.

Stuart, J. and Revett, N. *The Antiquities of Athens.* Vol. I, 1762, p. 27.

GENERAL INDEX

493, 495, 501; and Sparta, 88, 225; and
the Lamian War, 455 *sqq.*, 459; and
Thebes, 91, 95, 100; art of, 544
Side, 364, 373
Sidon, 156, 181; Alexander and, 374 *sqq.*,
421, 428; and Persia, 22, 152 *sq.*, 249
Sidus, 48, 51
Siege-warfare, of Alexander, 359, 374 *sq.*;
of Demetrius, 500; of Dionysius I, 114,
120 *sq.*; of Philip, 254 *sqq.*
Sigeum, 211
Silistria, 355
Silk Route from China, 393, 435
Silver Shields, *see* 'Argyraspids'
Simaethus, 119 *n.*
Simmias, 381 *sq.*
Simon, 202
Simus, 219
Sinai, 193
Sind, 402, 409 *sq.*, 414
Sinkashid, 143 *n.*
Sinope, 11, 14 *sq.*, 20, 373, 387
Sinopion, 166
Si-Osirei, 163 *sq.*
Siphnos, 444
Sipontum, 300
Sippara, 10
Siris, 300
Sistovo, 355
Sitalces, 390, 416
Sittace, 10
Siva, 405
Siwah, 154, 165, 377
Slavery, in Egypt, 162; in Greek politics,
443, 522, 529 *sq.*; in Palestine, 177
Smicythion, 202
Smyrna, 41, 429, 491
Sochi, 366
Socialism and Greek political theory,
528 *sq.*
Socrates of Achaea, 5, 10
— the philosopher, 133; philosophy of,
302–324, 332, 345, 347, 349; political
theory of, 515; statue of, 543
Sogdiana, 380, 392, 394 *sq.*, 397, 426, 432
Sogdianus, 3
Soli, 373, 391
Solomon, 176, 187, 435
Solon, constitution of, 116, 460; *see* Vol. IV,
Index
Solus, 126
Sookaytur, 408
Sopd, 149
Sophaenetus of Stymphalus, 5, 8, 15
Sophanes, 234
Sophist of Plato, 325–329
Sophists, 302 *sq.*, 305, 309, 313, 327, 519 *sq.*
Sophocles (the poet), 443; statue of, 543; *see*
Vol. v, Index
— 498
Sophronistai, 442

Sostrate, stele of, 544
Soteriades, 262 *n.*
Spain, mercenaries from, 93, 109 *sq.*, 295
Sparta, 16, 18, 105, 127, 200, 221, 223 *sqq.*,
369, 507; and Alexander, 355 *sq.*, 363,
373, 377, 379, 383, 388; and Egypt, 21,
150 *sq.*; and Persia, 5 *sq.*, 17, 19 *sq.*, 37–
54, 78, 94, 108, 139, 142–146, 250, 374,
444, 534; and Philip, 238, 245, 266 *sq.*;
and Second Athenian Confederacy, 70–
79; and Syracuse, 124, 131 *sq.*, 135, 275,
283, 285, 534; and Tarentum, 300 *sq.*;
and the 'King's Peace,' 54 *sqq.*, 59 *sq.*;
and the Sacred War, 213 *sq.*, 225 *sq.*,
234 *sq.*, 238, 241; and Thebes, 63–70,
74 *sq.*, 80–84, 87, 89–92, 100 *sq.*, 275,
507, 529; ascendancy of, Ch. II; attacks
Chalcidian League, 61–64, 508; attacks
Mantinea, 60 *sq.*; attacks Phlius, 61;
constitution of, 516, 518, 534 *sq.*; loses
hold on the Peloponnese, 87–102; under
Macedonian supremacy, Ch. XIV *passim*,
501
'Spartocidae,' 71
Spercheus, 84
Speusippus, 275 *sqq.*, 334, 350
Sphodrias, 66 *sqq.*, 96
Spitamenes, 391–396
Spithridates, 361 *sq.*
Squillace (= Scylletium), 130
Stagirus, 230, 332
Stasander, 470, 483
Stasanor, 359, 391 *sq.*, 394, 470, 503
Statesman (= *Politicus*) of Plato, 325 *sq.*, 328,
525
Statira, 3, 9
Stein, Sir A., discovery by (Aornos), 405 *n.*
Stele, from the Ilissus, 544; Metternich-,
164; Minaean, 138; of Hor, 138; of
Naucratis, 149; of Sostrate, 544
Stoics, 310 *n.*, 437, 497, 533 *sq.*
Strategos autocrator, 112, 116
Stratocles (Athenian demagogue), 452 *sq.*,
496 *sq.*, 501
— (Athenian general), 262 *sq.*
— of Amphipolis, 207
Stratus, 486
Struthas, 50, 52
Strymon, 355
Suez, Gulf of, 421
— Isthmus of, 153
Sunium, 450
'Superintendent of the Administration,' at
Athens, 441, 497
Susa, 2, 5, 7, 10, 21, 45, 50, 53, 94, 137,
146, 150 *sqq.*, 156, 169, 470; Alexander
at, 383, 416 *sq.*, 428; occupied by
Antigonus, 478
Susiana, 416 *sq.*, 463, 470, 477 *sq.*, 483,
488
Sutlej, 410

INDEX TO MAPS

Maps containing more than a few names have each their own index and reference is made here only to the number of the map. The alphabetical arrangement ignores the usual prefixes (lake, etc.).

INDEX OF PASSAGES REFERRED TO